P9-BZD-256

ADULT DEVELOPMENT AND AGING

BIOPSYCHOSOCIAL PERSPECTIVES

Fourth Edition

Susan Krauss Whitbourne, Ph.D.
University of Massachusetts Amherst

Stacey B. Whitbourne, Ph.D.
VA Boston Healthcare System

WILEY

John Wiley & Sons, Inc.

VP AND EXECUTIVE PUBLISHER	Jay O'Callaghan
ACQUISITIONS EDITOR	Robert Johnston
ASSOCIATE EDITOR	Eileen McKeever
EDITORIAL ASSISTANT	Mariah Maguire-Fong
SENIOR MARKETING MANAGER	Danielle Torio
SENIOR MEDIA EDITOR	Lynn Pearlman
PHOTO MANAGER	Hilary Newman
PHOTO RESEARCHER	Teri Stratford
PRODUCTION MANAGER	Janis Soo
ASSISTANT PRODUCTION EDITOR	Yee Lyn Song
COVER DESIGNER	Seng Ping Ngieng
COVER PHOTO CREDIT	Claude Monet, Water Lilies/Peter Willi/SuperStock

This book was set in 10.5/12.5 Berkley-Book by Laserwords Private Limited, and printed and bound by R.R. Donnelley–Von Hoffman. The cover was printed by R.R. Donnelley–Von Hoffman.

Founded in 1807, John Wiley & Sons, Inc. has been a valued source of knowledge and understanding for more than 200 years, helping people around the world meet their needs and fulfill their aspirations. Our company is built on a foundation of principles that include responsibility to the communities we serve and where we live and work. In 2008, we launched a Corporate Citizenship Initiative, a global effort to address the environmental, social, economic, and ethical challenges we face in our business. Among the issues we are addressing are carbon impact, paper specifications and procurement, ethical conduct within our business and among our vendors, and community and charitable support. For more information, please visit our website: www.wiley.com/go/citizenship.

This book is printed on acid free paper. ∞

Copyright © 2011, 2008, 2005, 2001 John Wiley & Sons, Inc. All rights reserved. No part of this publication may be reproduced, stored in a retrieval system or transmitted in any form or by any means, electronic, mechanical, photocopying, recording, scanning or otherwise, except as permitted under Sections 107 or 108 of the 1976 United States Copyright Act, without either the prior written permission of the Publisher, or authorization through payment of the appropriate per-copy fee to the Copyright Clearance Center, Inc. 222 Rosewood Drive, Danvers, MA 01923, website www.copyright.com. Requests to the Publisher for permission should be addressed to the Permissions Department, John Wiley & Sons, Inc., 111 River Street, Hoboken, NJ 07030-5774, (201)748-6011, fax (201)748-6008, website http://www.wiley.com/go/permissions.

Evaluation copies are provided to qualified academics and professionals for review purposes only, for use in their courses during the next academic year. These copies are licensed and may not be sold or transferred to a third party. Upon completion of the review period, please return the evaluation copy to Wiley. Return instructions and a free of charge return shipping label are available at www.wiley.com/go/returnlabel. Outside of the United States, please contact your local representative.

Library of Congress Cataloging-in-Publication Data

Whitbourne, Susan Krauss.
   Adult development and aging: biopsychosocial perspectives / Susan Krauss Whitbourne, Stacey B. Whitbourne. — 4th ed.
      p. cm.
   Includes bibliographical references and index.
   ISBN 978-0-470-64697-7 (hardback)
1. Gerontology. 2. Older people—Psychology. 3. Older people—Health and hygiene. 4. Older people—Social conditions. I. Whitbourne, Stacey B. II. Whitbourne, Susan Krauss. Adult development & aging. III. Title. IV. Title: Adult development & aging.
   HQ1061.W48 2011
   305.26—dc22

                                                2010037952

Printed in the United States of America

10 9 8 7 6 5 4

Everyone ages. This very fact should be enough to draw you into the subject matter of this course, whether you are the student or the instructor. Yet, for many people, it is difficult to imagine the future in 50, 40, or even 10 years from now. The goal of our book is to help you imagine your future and the future of your family, your friends, and your society. We have brought together the latest scientific findings about aging with a more personal approach to encourage you to take this imaginative journey into your future.

The fourth edition of *Adult Development and Aging: Biopsychosocial Perspectives* is significantly different from the previous editions in that there are now two authors. Susan invited a co-author, Stacey, who happens to be her daughter and a professional in the field of aging. Much of the material remains based on the course that Susan teaches at the University of Massachusetts Amherst on the Psychology of Aging. She continues to incorporate her day-to-day teaching of the course into the text. What you will read follows very closely with the way she approaches the course and engages her students in the learning process. Examples, figures, and tables, as well as the words in the text, reflect what she has found to be of most interest to her students.

Stacey was inspired to pursue the field of aging after taking her mother's course in 1999. She continued her graduate work in social and developmental psychology focusing on cognitive functioning in later adulthood. Stacey's contributions to the fourth edition are based on her current research projects on genetic epidemiology and aging. The addition of Stacey as a co-author brings a third generation begun by Susan's father, who specialized in geriatric medicine. Susan became interested in the scholarly field of aging as an undergraduate when she decided to write a paper on personality and adaptation in a developmental psychology course. At the same time, her father's professional activities had a profound influence and made the choice of gerontology (the scientific study of aging) a natural one.

It is our hope and belief that you will find that the study of aging has many fascinating aspects. Not only is everyone around you aging, but also the issues that are raised within this field extend from the philosophical to the practical. Why do living things age? Is there a way to slow down the aging process? How will society deal with the aging of the Baby Boomers? How will job markets be affected by an aging society? Will you age differently than your parents and grandparents? All of these, and more, are questions that you will find yourself asking as you explore the many complexities of the process that causes people to change and grow throughout life. At the same time, you will gain many advantages from learning the material in this course. You will learn the keys to healthy development in the years of adulthood. As a result, you will learn not only how people grow older but also how to grow older in a way that is healthy and satisfying.

THEMES OF THE BOOK

The biopsychosocial model emphasized in our text is intended to encourage you to think about the multiple interactions among the domains of biology, psychology, and sociology. According to this model, changes in one area of life have effects on changes in other areas. The centerpiece of this model is identity, your self-definition. You interpret the experiences you have through the framework provided by your identity. In turn, your experiences often stimulate you to change your self-definition.

This is an exciting time to be studying adult development and aging. The topic is gaining increasing media attention and tremendous momentum as an academic discipline within life-span development. The biopsychosocial model fits within the framework of contemporary approaches that emphasize the impact of social context on individuals throughout all periods of life. Entirely new concepts, sets of data, and practical applications of these models are resulting in a realization of the dreams of many of the classic developmental psychologists whose work shaped the field in the early 20th century.

ORGANIZATION

There is a logical organization to the progression of chapters in this book, essentially from the "bio" to the "psycho" to the "social." However, this is not a strict progression. Instructors may find that they would prefer to switch the order of certain chapters or sections within chapters, and that will be fairly easy to do. We have stuck to the integrative theme of the biopsychosocial model in that many of the topics, regardless of where they appear in the book, bring together this multifaceted approach.

We feel strongly that the final chapter should not be not about death and dying, as is often the case in other books in the field, but about successful aging. This point is reflected in our choice of a cover, a painting of water lilies by Monet in his later years. The painting was also a very personal choice for us; after seeing it at an exhibit we were struck by its beauty and relevance to our book. You will read more about Monet in Chapter 14, where we discuss creativity and aging. The painting is a remarkably vivid expression of the vitality that characterizes successful aging.

FEATURES

Up-to-Date Research

The topics and features in this text are intended to involve you in the field of aging from a scholarly and a personal perspective. You will find that the most current research is presented throughout the text, with careful and detailed explanations of the studies that highlight the most important scholarly advances.

Aging in the News

Each chapter includes one news story featuring the accomplishments of noted older adults ranging from Betty White (who famously hosted *Saturday Night Live* at the age of 88) to Jack LaLanne, who at age 95 (in 2010) remains the most famous fitness guru in the world.

Engaging Figures and Tables

We have given the text a new look by significantly updating figures and tables that contain review points and clearly show important research findings. Our selection of these materials connects to the PowerPoint slides that instructors can download from the Wiley Web site.

Contemporary Approach

Wording from the previous edition was revised to incorporate the perspective of the second author in order to appeal to the college-aged student. We use references to current trends (such as Facebook and iPods) to illustrate our points. The first author now writes a *Psychology Today* blog on aging, which picks up on many of the themes of our book.

STUDENT LEARNING AIDS

Numbered Summaries

Each chapter contains a numbered summary that will assist students in reviewing the important material from the chapter.

Glossary Terms

Bold items in each chapter indicate glossary terms. Because students may encounter a term more than once after it is introduced in a particular chapter, all the glossary items appear at the end of the book, as do the references.

Ample Illustrations

Tables and figures pick up on major points in the text. There are also photographs intended to highlight particularly interesting or relevant issues.

CHANGES IN THE FOURTH EDITION

The first edition of *Adult Development and Aging: Biopsychosocial Perspectives* was intended to provide a fresh and engaging approach to the field of the psychology of adult development and aging by focusing on three themes: a multidisciplinary approach, positive images of aging, and the newest and most relevant research. The fourth edition maintains the experience for students of participating in a live classroom. We also have simplified a number of the research presentations. This makes it possible for students to gain a fuller appreciation of the main points they need to know in order to master the subject matter. We hope this approach makes the instructor's job easier. Students will be more motivated to complete their readings if they like the text and feel that they can relate to it.

We did not change the organization of chapters. Instructors who have developed their course based on earlier editions will not need to change the basic structure of their lectures and assignments. However, we condensed some sections, deleted others, and introduced new sections to reflect changes in the field. We also deleted the boxed features that, in our experience, students were not reading. Instead, we integrated such features as critical thinking, biopsychosocial perspectives, and self-focused exercises into the writing of the text itself.

Throughout the fourth edition, references have been substantially updated. Approximately half of the references are from 2008 or later, and one third are from 2009 and 2010. To maintain the same length of the text, outdated references were deleted and sections were updated to reflect the newest research. New U.S. Census data were completely integrated into demographic material presented throughout the text, as have special reports on older adults published by the Administration on Aging, the U.S. Department of Health and Human Services, and the Centers for Disease Control and Prevention. In addition to presenting updated information on the United States,

substantial information was added from international statistics, particularly in the area of health.

We revamped our approach to presenting biological, physiological, and cognitive approaches to aging. The incorporation of new figures and tables will appeal visually to students and guide them through their reading of the text. As in previous editions, we aimed to provide studies that were as interesting as possible to illustrate major points. We continued to expand the treatment of brain imaging studies, an area that has grown tremendously in the past three to four years. New data on genetics and aging were included in relevant sections. We have also drawn heavily from studies such as Whitehall II that show the importance of social class as an influence on health and aging. These exciting changes in the field continue to illustrate the importance of a biopsychosocial perspective.

Supplements

Wiley is pleased to offer an online resource containing a wealth of teaching and learning material at http://www.wiley.com/college/whitbourne.

Web Site Links

References in this edition show the Web sites that students and instructors can consult to gather updated information on changes in the field.

INSTRUCTOR RESOURCES

Instructor's Manual

The content in the Instructor's Manual reflects over 30 years of experience in teaching this course. You will find chapter outlines, key terms, learning objectives, and lecture suggestions. Video suggestions are also provided as well as resources for finding documentaries, movies, and even pop music.

PowerPoint Slides

Prepared for use in lectures, a complete set of PowerPoint slides tailored to the book are available for download. Contained on the slides are highlights of chapters and extensive visual illustrations of chapter concepts and key terms.

Test Bank

A complete downloadable test bank includes 50 to 70 questions in each chapter that follow along with the order that the concepts are presented in the text. Each multiple-choice question is labeled according to which concept it tests, along with its difficulty level. Included are short answer and essay questions corresponding to each section of the chapter.

ACKNOWLEDGMENTS

Our first set of acknowledgments go to our families. Husbands Richard O'Brien and Erik Gleason have graciously provided important support that allowed us to spend the many hours required over the period of a year in revising the book. Jennifer O'Brien, daughter and sister, is a wonderful sounding board for our ideas and as she continues her career in

clinical psychology, we look forward to continued "collaboration" with her.

Throughout the writing of this book, students in the Psychology of Aging class at the University of Massachusetts Amherst provided valuable insights and observations. As we were revising the book and preparing the lectures, they continued to provide us with fresh perspectives. Their good humor, patience, and willingness to experiment with some new ideas makes it possible to add the all-important student viewpoint to the finished product.

We feel extremely fortunate to have had the guidance of the editor at John Wiley & Sons, Chris Johnson, who helped us prepare this and the previous edition. His insights, support, and friendly advice have been central to our ability to maintain the book's strength while widening its appeal. We would also like to give special thanks to our associate editor, Eileen McKeever. She maintains the tradition of Wiley's efficiency and helpful attention that we have had the good fortune to receive throughout the revision process. Hilary Newman, Photo Manager, and Teri Stratford, Photo Researcher, have helped

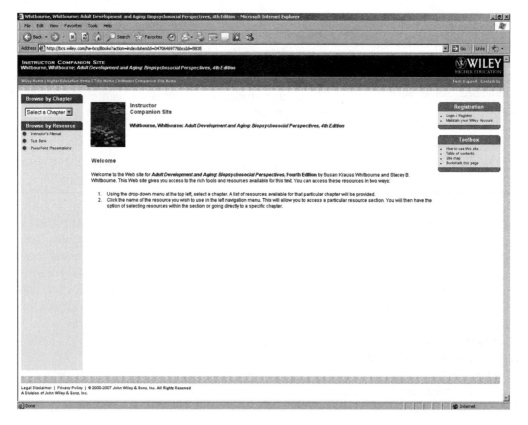

us tremendously in meeting our requests for great illustrative material. Yee Lyn Song, the production editor, provided helpful and friendly feedback. The marketing team, Danielle Torio and Melissa Kleckner, ensure that you and your colleagues know all about the book. Finally, the work of Seng Ping Ngieng, the designer, has ensured that the book is attractively presented. These individuals provide behind-the-scenes help that every author knows is invaluable to the creation of an excellent text.

Our final thanks go to the reviewers who provided helpful comments and suggestions throughout the revision process. Their insightful observations and thoughtful proposals for changes helped us tighten and focus the manuscript and enhance the discussion of several key areas of interest in the field. Thank you to Gary Creasey (Illinois State University), Carrie Andreoletti, (Central Connecticut State University), Richard Tucker (University of Central Florida), Renee Babcock (Central Michigan University), Susan Bell (Georgetown College), Susan H. Mcfadden (University of Wisconsin, Oshkosh), Katie E. Cherry (Louisiana State University), Joseph E. Gaugler (University of Minnesota), and Victoria Hilkevitch Bedford (University of Indianapolis). We have also benefited from informal reviews provided by our colleagues who use the book in their teaching and we greatly appreciate their helpful suggestions.

In conclusion, we hope that we have given you something to look forward to as you venture into the fascinating field of adult development and aging, and that the subsequent pages of this book will fulfill these expectations. We have tried to present a comprehensive but clear picture of the area and hope that you will be able to apply this knowledge to improving your own life and the lives of the older adults with whom you may be preparing to work. We hope you will come away from the course with a positive feeling about what you can do to "age better" and with a positive feeling about the potentialities of later life. And maybe, just maybe, as has happened on many past occasions with people who have read this book, you will decide to pursue this field and we can welcome you as colleagues in the coming years.

Finally, we would like to comment on the process of working together as a mother–daughter team. The first author was pregnant with the second author when she embarked on her first textbook in the field, the precursor to the present volume. Little did she know that the child she was about to have would become a psychologist, much less a specialist in aging. We have had an enjoyable time working on the revision and are proud and happy to be able to share our perspectives with you, the reader.

Susan Krauss Whitbourne, Ph.D.
Stacey B. Whitbourne, Ph.D.
June 2010

ABOUT THE AUTHORS

Susan Krauss Whitbourne, Ph.D., Professor of Psychology at the University of Massachusetts Amherst, received her Ph.D. in Developmental Psychology from Columbia University in 1974 and completed a post-doctoral training program in Clinical Psychology at the University of Massachusetts at Amherst, having joined the faculty there in 1984. Her previous positions were as Associate Professor of Education and Psychology at the University of Rochester (1975–84) and Assistant Professor of Psychology at SUNY College at Geneseo. Formerly the Psychology Departmental Honors Coordinator at the University of Massachusetts Amherst, she is Director of the Office of National Scholarship Advisement. In addition, she is Faculty Advisor to the University of Massachusetts Chapter of Psi Chi, a position for which she was recognized as the Eastern Regional Outstanding Advisor for the year 2001 and as the Florence Denmark National Faculty Advisor in 2002. She served as Eastern Region Vice President of Psi Chi in 2006–07 and as Chair of the Program Committee for the National Leadership Conference in 2009. Her teaching has been recognized with the College Outstanding Teacher Award in 1995 and the University Distinguished Teaching Award in 2001. Her work as an advisor was recognized with the Outstanding Academic Advisor Award in 2006. In 2003, she received the American Psychological Association (APA) Division 20 (Adult Development and Aging) Master Mentor Award and the Gerontological Society of America (GSA) Behavioral and Social Sciences Distinguished Mentorship award.

Over the past 20 years, Dr. Whitbourne has held a variety of elected and appointed positions in APA Division 20 including President (1995–96), Treasurer (1986–89), Secretary (1981–84), Program Chair (1997–98), Education Committee Chair (1979–80), Student Awards Committee Chair (1993–94), Continuing Education Committee Chair (1981–82), and Elections Committee Chair (1992–93). She has chaired the Fellowship Committee and serves as the Division 20 Representative to the APA Council (2000–2006 and 2009–present). She is a Fellow of Divisions 1 (General Psychology), 2 (Teaching of Psychology), 12 (Clinical Psychology), and 20. She has served on the APA Committee on Structure and Function of Council and chaired the Policy and Planning Board in 2007. She currently serves on the APA Membership Board.

Dr. Whitbourne is also a Fellow of the American Psychological Society and the Eastern Psychological Association, for which she serves on the Executive Board. She is a Fellow of the Gerontological Society of America, and currently serves on the Behavioral and Social Sciences Executive Board. She is Chair-Elect of the Council of Professional Geropsychology Training Programs. A founding member of the Society for the Study of Human Development, she was its President from 2005 to 2007. She also serves on the Board of Directors of the National Association of Fellowship Advisors. In her home of Amherst, Massachusetts, she has served on the Council on Aging (2004–07) and was the President of the Friends of the Amherst Senior Center (2007–09).

Her publications include 15 published books, many in multiple editions, and more than 140 journal articles and chapters, including articles in *Psychology and Aging, Psychotherapy, Developmental Psychology, Journal of Gerontology, Journal of Personality and Social Psychology*, and *Teaching of Psychology*, and chapters in the *Handbook of the Psychology of Aging, Clinical Geropsychology, Comprehensive Clinical Psychology (Geropsychology)*, the *Encyclopedia of Psychology*, and the *International Encyclopedia of the Social and Behavioral Sciences*. She has been a Consulting Editor for *Psychology and Aging* and serves on the Editorial Board of the *Journal of Gerontology* and is a Consulting Editor for *Developmental Psychology*. Her presentations at professional conferences number over 200, and include several invited addresses, among them the APA G. Stanley Hall Lecture in 1995, the EPA Psi Chi Distinguished Lecture in 2001, and the SEPA Invited Lecture in 2002.

Stacey B. Whitbourne, Ph.D., received her Ph.D. in Social and Developmental Psychology from Brandeis University in 2005 where she was funded by a National Institute on Aging Training Fellowship. She completed her post-doctoral fellowship at the Boston University School of Public Health, Department of Epidemiology, funded by a National Institute on Aging Grant and a Department of Veterans Affairs Rehabilitation Research and Development Service Grant. Currently, she is a Research Health Scientist at the Massachusetts Veterans Epidemiology and Research Information Center (MAVERIC), an independent research center housed within the V.A. Boston Healthcare System. The author of several published articles, she is also a co-author on a chapter for the Sage Series on Aging in America. She is a member of the American Psychological Association Division 20 and the Gerontological Society of America. A member of the Membership Committee of Division 20, she has also given more than 30 presentations at national conferences. As an undergraduate, she received the Psi Chi National Student Research Award. In graduate school, she was awarded the Verna Regan Teaching Award and an APA Student Travel Award. She has taught courses on adult development and aging at Brandeis University and the University of Massachusetts Boston.

CONTENTS

1

Themes and Issues in Adult

Aging affects every individual. From the second you are born, your aging process begins. If you are reading this book, you are most likely of traditional college age, a time of transition from adolescence to adulthood. The concept of being an adult may be new to you and the idea of growing older may seem far into the future. Our purpose in writing this book is to help you think about your own aging as well as the aging of others. You may have chosen to take this course to help understand your aging relatives or trends in society, but before long, you will find that you start to think about what will happen to you with age.

Let us start by asking you whether you think of yourself as an "adult." How do you define yourself in terms of your age? Questions involving self-definition based on age will be relevant to the scope and coverage of this book. We will examine definitions of adulthood, including the meaning and definition of "age," as well as the various approaches researchers have taken to understanding the biological, psychological, and social changes that occur between adolescence and old age.

Our goal is to engage you by presenting you with information that is of both personal and professional interest. We will explore the variety of ways individuals can affect their own aging process, such as through incorporating behaviors and activities designed to maintain high levels of functioning well into the later decades of life. For our traditional college-age students embarking into younger adulthood, we hope to help you appreciate that it is never too early to start incorporating these changes into your lifestyle. And for our readers of nontraditional college age, we hope to help you see that it is never too late to initiate behaviors that can maintain if not enhance your everyday functioning.

Apart from the personal exploration we hope to encourage you to undertake, we will draw on current events relevant to the field of adult development and aging. In presenting these, we will ask you to evaluate their meaning based on the knowledge you gain from both this book and your course. A key goal that we had in writing this book was to involve you in the progression of your aging process and show you ways to be an active part of your own development.

Development and Aging

THE BIOPSYCHOSOCIAL PERSPECTIVE

The **biopsychosocial perspective**, a view of development as a complex interaction of biological, psychosocial, and social processes, will be a recurring theme throughout this book. As shown in Figure 1.1, biological processes include how the body's functions and structures change throughout the aging process. The psychological processes examine the thoughts, feelings, and behaviors involved with development, through exploring topics such as cognition, personality, and emotions. The social processes of aging reflect the environment or context, and include indicators of your position within various social structures in the family, community, culture, country, and the world. The theories and models of life-span development, which we discuss in Chapter 2, attempt to examine how biological, psychological, and social processes intersect and interact throughout each person's lifetime. Thus, drawing on an assortment of disciplines, we will examine aging from many different vantage points.

The biopsychosocial model implies that fields such as biology, medicine, nursing, sociology, history, and even the arts and literature provide crucial **perspectives** to enhance the understanding of the psychology of adulthood and aging. Knowledge, theories, and perspectives from all disciplines contribute importantly to the study of the individual over time.

FIGURE 1.1

The Biopsychosocial Model

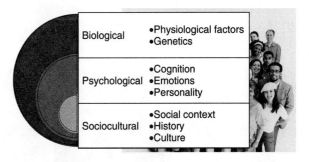

Biological	•Physiological factors •Genetics
Psychological	•Cognition •Emotions •Personality
Sociocultural	•Social context •History •Culture

TABLE 1.1
The Four Principles of Adult Development and Aging

Principle	Meaning
1. Changes are continuous over the life span	Individuals remain the "same" even though they change
2. Only the survivors grow old	Aging individuals are increasingly self-selected
3. Individuality matters	People vary within and between age groups
4. "Normal" aging is different from disease	Intrinsic aging processes are different from those associated with illness

Within the biopsychosocial model, the concept of **identity** plays a central role. Identity is defined as a composite of how people view themselves in the biological, psychological, and social domains of life. The interaction of these domains forms an overall view of the "self."

FOUR PRINCIPLES OF ADULT DEVELOPMENT AND AGING

The field of adult development and aging is built on a set of four principles that form the foundation of the following chapters (see Table 1.1). Despite theoretical differences within the discipline, a general consensus exists about these underlying premises. Below we capture the four principles that will guide this book.

1. Changes Are Continuous Over the Life Span

The first principle of adult development and aging is that changes over the **life span** happen in a continuous fashion. In other words, changes that occur in later adulthood build on what has occurred during one's past. This concept, referred to as the "continuity principle," has theoretical as well as practical implications.

From a theoretical approach, changes in old age occur against the backdrop of an individual's prior developmental history. For example, biologically, changes that may occur in the cardiovascular system with age depend in many ways on the prior functioning of that system throughout life.

Practical implications of the continuity principle can encompass the way in which people feel about themselves, and how they are viewed by others. People do not feel that they have somehow transformed into a different person just because they reach a certain birthday. Although everyone's appearance has and will continue to change throughout life, people still tend to feel that they are the "same" inside.

However, outward appearance plays a large role in the way people are perceived by others. Consequently, when looking at a middle-aged or older adult, it is common to focus on that person's age rather than on a characteristic of personality or ability. It is important to keep in mind that as people develop through adulthood they think of themselves as the "same," only older. Just as you may resent being lumped together with other college students on the basis of your age and stage in life rather than who you are as an individual, older adults often resent being treated in a certain way because of their age and the way they appear.

2. Only the Survivors Grow Old

The second principle of adult development and aging is one that is perhaps obvious (and contrary to the Billy Joel song "Only the Good Die Young"), but it is important to highlight nonetheless. Simply put, in order for people to become old, they have to

Over the progression of time, as shown in these photos of the same man from ages 3 through 82, people may feel the same inside even though their outer appearance changes.

not die. In essence this may seem like an obvious (and perhaps ridiculous) tidbit of information, but consider its importance as we study aging. People who live to an old age have survived the many threats to life that can cause others to fall by the wayside. They were not involved in fatal vehicular accidents, issues of conflict, natural or human-made disasters, and they did not engage in risky behaviors such as excessive drug and alcohol use that could lead to an early death. The very fact that these people have managed to avoid death suggests they may have inherited good genes (biological factors), are emotionally healthy (psychological factors), or have surrounded themselves with a good support system (social factors), or a combination of the above plus a dose of good luck. Table 1.2 shows the five most common behaviors that prevent people from living a longer life; the survivors most likely did not engage in these behaviors (Kamimoto, Easton, Maurice, Husten, & Macera, 1999).

When you consider what it takes to become an older adult, it is hard not to appreciate that the people who survive to later adulthood have some incredibly special characteristics. This notion has implications for the way that we make sense out of scientific data on human aging. All older adults are survivors of the conditions that others did not endure. With increasing age into later life, they become more select in such characteristics as physical functioning, health, and intelligence. Consequently, when we examine differences between younger and older people, we must keep in mind that the older people alive today are a more restricted (and perhaps superior) group

than the younger ones. The younger adults have not yet been subjected to the same conditions that could threaten their lives.

A concrete example helps illustrate this principle. Consider data on the psychological characteristic of cautiousness. One of the tried and true findings in the psychology of aging contends that older people are less likely to take risks than younger people. Older adults are also less likely to engage in criminal behavior. What accounts for these findings? One possibility is that people become more skilled at moderating their behavior with age. They choose to refrain from engaging in actions that could bring them harm or get them arrested. Alternatively, people more likely to make risky decisions early on in life are most likely no longer in the population. Their choices may have led to an early death, or they have been imprisoned for their actions.

3. Individuality Matters

A long-held myth regarding development is that as people age, they all become alike. This view is refuted by the third principle of adult development and aging, which asserts that as people age, they become more different from each other rather than more alike. With increasing age, older adults become a more diverse segment of the population in terms of their physical functioning, psychological performance, and conditions of living. In one often-cited study, researchers examined a large number of studies of aging to compare the amount of variability in older versus younger adults (Nelson & Dannefer, 1992). This research established that the variability, or how differently people responded to the measures, was far greater among older adults. Research continues to underscore the notion that individuals continue to become less alike with age. Such findings suggest that diversity becomes an increasingly prominent theme during the adult years, a point we will continue to focus on throughout this book.

The fact that there are increasing differences among adults as they grow older also ties into the importance of experiences in shaping development. As people go through life, their experiences cause them to diverge from others of the same age in more and more ways. You have made the decision to go to college, while others in your age group may have

TABLE 1.2
Five Ways to Shorten Your Life

Ways to Shorten Your Life
1. Being overweight
2. Drinking and driving
3. Eating inadequate fruits and vegetables
4. Being physically inactive
5. Smoking

Source: Kamimoto, L. A., Easton, A. N., Maurice, E., Husten, C. G., & Macera, C. A. (1999). Surveillance for five health risks among older adults—United States, 1993–1997. *Morbidity and Mortality Weekly Reports*, 48(SSO*), 89–130.

enlisted for military service. You may meet your future spouse in college, while your best friend remains on the dating scene for years. Upon graduation, some may choose to pursue graduate studies as others enter into the workforce. You may or may not choose to start a family, or have already begun the process. With the passage of time, your differing experiences build upon each other to help mold the person you become. The many possibilities that can stem from the choices you make help to illustrate that the permutations of events in people's lives are virtually endless. Personal histories move in increasingly idiosyncratic directions with each passing day, year, and decade of life.

The principle that people become more different from each other with age relates to the notion of **inter-individual differences**, or differences between people. As demonstrated in Figure 1.2, people of the same age may vary so dramatically from one another that they may more closely resemble people from different age groups, even on measures typically thought to decline with age.

The contrasting notion of **intra-individual differences** describes the differences within an individual, also referred to as the multidirectionality of development (Baltes & Graf, 1996). According to this principle, not all systems develop at the same rate within the person—while some functions may increase over time, others decrease. Even within a construct such as intelligence, an individual may show gains in one area, losses in another, and stability in yet another domain.

Important to the study of individual differences are findings that demonstrate cases in which some older adults outperform younger adults on tasks typically shown to decline with age. Although traditionally younger adults have faster reaction times than older adults, exceptions to the norm are common. While you may think of average-age college students as being able to run faster, lift heavier weights, or solve crossword puzzles in a shorter time than people three times their age, consider the differences between a sedentary 21-year-old and a 72-year-old triathlete. Chances are, the triathlete will outperform the sedentary adult in all categories. We will continue to explore the notion that functioning does not necessarily need to "go downhill" as people get older.

4. "Normal" Aging Is Different From Disease

The fourth principle of adult development differentiates between normal, impaired, and optimal aging (see Figure 1.3). **Normal aging** or **primary aging** refers to a set of changes built into the hard wiring of the organism, which progress at different rates among individuals but nevertheless are universal, intrinsic, and progressive. Changes due to disease, referred to as **impaired aging** or **secondary aging**, are a function of an abnormal set of changes afflicting a segment rather than the entirety of the older population (Aldwin & Gilmer, 1999). Skin wrinkling is an example of primary aging; the development of cancer in later life is an example of secondary aging.

Optimal aging, also called "successful aging," refers to the way the aging process is slowed or altered because the individual has engaged in

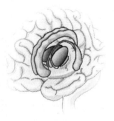

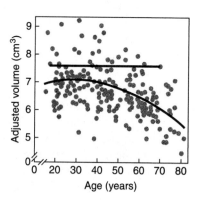

FIGURE 1.2

Inter-individual Differences in Development

This figure shows age differences in the volume of cells in the hippocampus, a part of the brain involved in memory. The straight line shows that people in their 70s may have the same brain volumes as people in their 20s.

Source: Hedden, T., & Gabrieli, J. D. (2004). Insights into the ageing mind: A view from cognitive neuroscience. *Nature Review Neuroscience, 5,* 87–96.

This highly fit triathlete has physical skills that would rival those of a sedentary young adult, further illustrating the principle of individual differences. He also provides an example of optimal aging.

preventative and compensatory strategies to avoid negative changes that would otherwise occur with normal or impaired aging. Returning to the example of changes in the skin, optimal aging would occur in a person who has minimal wrinkling and discoloration due to having taken precautions to avoid or slow down primary and prevent secondary aging.

It is important for both practical and scientific reasons to distinguish between normal aging and disease. Health care specialists who work with middle-aged and older adults need to recognize and treat the onset of a disease rather than dismiss it simply as "getting older." For example, an 80-year-old man exhibiting symptoms of depression can be successfully treated, assuming that the clinician does not write his symptoms off as a feature of normal aging. Personality development in adulthood does not inevitably lead to the depressive symptoms of lowered self-esteem, excessive guilt, changes in appetite, or lack of interest in activities. If the clinician mistakenly thinks that these symptoms are part of the normal aging process, the proper course of treatment may not be able to ultimately alleviate the depressed person's suffering.

THE MEANING OF AGE

The study of aging implies that age is the major variable of interest. As we describe in more detail below, there is utility in categorizing individuals in later life based on their age. At the same time, though, there is a certain arbitrariness to the numerical value that is attached to people on the basis of the continuous underlying processes that occur over the span of time. The crossing over from an age that ends in "9" to an age that ends in "0" (such as going from 39 to 40) often provokes intense self-scrutiny if not somewhat disturbing birthday cards from friends invoking the "over the hill" metaphor. In truth, however, the body does not change in such discrete fits and starts.

FIGURE 1.3

Three Types of Aging

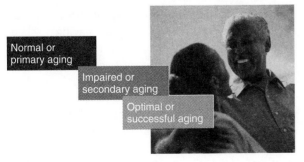

Normal or primary aging

Impaired or secondary aging

Optimal or successful aging

Chronological age has some value in describing a person, but like other descriptive features of a person such as **gender**, hair color, or eye color, it is the social meaning attached to chronological age that often outweighs any intrinsic usefulness. As we have already shown, people of the same age can vary wildly from one another, and people of different ages can be more similar than different. Chronological age is a number based on events in the universe that occur and its units are not necessarily inherently tied to the aging process. The body does keep time in a cycle that approximates a 24-hour period, but there is no evidence at the moment to suggest that this time pacemaker is related to aging. To say that chronological age (or time) "means" anything with regard to the status of the body's functioning is, based on current evidence, questionable. The popularity of such phrases as "30 becoming the new 20" and "60 the new 50" have captured the difficulty of defining age based solely on a number.

Using Age to Define "Adult"

Now that we have you thinking about the meaning of this very basic fact that so many people take for granted, we will move on to the next challenge—the meaning of the world "adult." As we have discussed, this term may mean different things to you as a reader. Adult may be synonymous with "mature," which in turn conjures up images of a person reaching a certain level of accomplishment or growth. Consider, for example, the term "mature" in reference to an apple. A mature apple is one that is ready to be eaten, and you can judge that by examining the apple's color, size, and texture. An apple's maturity level is relatively easy to measure compared to judging the maturity of humans, but the complexity of the biopsychosocial processes are far more difficult to quantify.

You might think that the most logical definition of maturity is based on physical development. Yet you also know that a 13-year-old male who has essentially reached his full physical development would, in contemporary Western society, be regarded as anything but an adult. Although his physical attributes define him as an adult, the psychological and social standards would not. Perhaps a standard based on ability is a better option? Consider 16 years, the age when most people can legally drive. Or,

alternatively, consider the age of 18, when U.S. society ordains the person with the right to vote. Using the age of 21 presents another possible demarcation point. As it is the age when American adults can legally drink alcohol, for many, the turning of 21 represents a defining mark of the beginning of adulthood. However, the United States is in a small minority of nations that set the drinking age at 21. Some Canadian provinces set the drinking age at 19 (though it is 18 in most); countries such as Germany, Barbados, and Portugal use the age of 16. These conflicting age demarcations for even such a seemingly concrete behavior as drinking alcohol show that deciding when a person is an adult on this basis has very limited utility. Parenthetically, the variation around the legal drinking age shown from country to country (and even within a country) shows the interaction of biological and sociocultural factors in setting age-based parameters around human behavior.

Many students comment that 25 has secured an important place in adulthood, as it is the age in the United States when you can rent a car (without having to pay a tremendous surcharge), reflecting the demarcation between the age of highest accident risk and the next age decade. The age of 25 has no intrinsic relationship to the ability to drive safely, but on a statistical basis it does relate to the tendency to engage in risky behaviors such as drinking and driving.

Another set of criteria related to the age of adulthood pertains to the crossing of the boundary between when a person can marry with or without parental consent. There again, we find huge variation. Just within the United States alone, the so-called age of consent varies from state to state (in South Carolina it is 14, while other states deem 16 or 18 the appropriate age).

Given these contradictory definitions of "adult," it might be wise to recommend that the threshold into adulthood depends on the individual having reached the chronological age associated with the expectations and privileges of a given society or subculture. For example, in the United States, individuals may be considered to have reached adulthood at the age when they are eligible to vote, drink, drive, and get married. For the majority of U.S. states, the age of 21 is therefore considered the threshold to adulthood. In other countries, these criteria may be reached at the age of 18. Regardless of the varying definitions, the first three or four years of adulthood represent the period of "emerging adulthood," or the transition prior to assuming the full responsibilities associated with adulthood (Arnett, 2000). These responsibilities may occur during the years that follow college graduation or, for those individuals who do not attend college, when the need to find full employment or make family commitments is faced.

Divisions by Age of the Over-65 Population

Traditionally, 65 years of age has been viewed as the entry point for "old age." However, for a variety of reasons, individuals who are 65 face different issues than those who are 85. Such challenges pertain mainly to the quality of physical functioning and health, but there are also different economic constraints and social opportunities that each age group within the older-65 population faces. To reflect these considerations, gerontologists make the distinction among **young-old** (ages 65 to 74); **old-old** (ages 75 to 84); and **oldest-old** (ages 85 and older). Aware of the dangers of placing too much credence in a number, gerontologists find these rough age groupings, on average, to have some value. Bernice Neugarten, one of the early pioneers in psychological gerontology, proposed these distinctions in the mid-1960s, and they have remained in use because using the age of 65 to differentiate middle age from old age is truly not very informative—a fact that is even more true today than it was 50 years ago.

With more and more people living to the oldest-old category, the divisions of the 65+ age group are undergoing further revision. Those over the age of 100, known as **centenarians**, are becoming more and more common in the population, as we will show later in the chapter. It will not be long before the very highest age category becomes more prominent—the **supercentenarians,** who are the age of 110 and older. Typically, the oldest person in the world at any given time is between the ages of 114 and 116. Jeanne Louise Calment, the oldest documented living human, was 122 at the time of her death. Supercentenarian will probably retain its definition as 110 and over, though, at least for the foreseeable future.

Discontented with the entire concept of chronological age, a number of gerontologists are devising a new classification system that is based not on what the calendar says but on how people function (see Figure 1.4). A coherent system based on **functional age** could potentially have much clearer meaning both as an indicator of a person's true characteristics and abilities and as a way to understand aging trends in a society. Currently, three types of functional age have been proposed, and each has certain distinct advantages.

Biological age is based on the quality of an individual's bodily systems. Standards of performance on various biological measures for an individual can be compared with the age norms for those measures. For example, a 50-year-old may have the blood pressure readings of the 25–30 age segment of the population, and be considered youthful on that particular measure of biological age. Popular culture has certainly caught on to the notion of biological rather than chronological age. There are a multitude of online "biological age tests," in which various values are entered to estimate life expectancy or to determine how well one will age. Though the validity of such tests may be questionable, their very existence highlights the interest of the general public in assessing age as "not just a number."

FIGURE 1.4

Alternative Indices of Aging

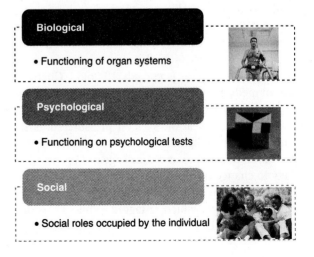

Biological
• Functioning of organ systems

Psychological
• Functioning on psychological tests

Social
• Social roles occupied by the individual

The calculation of **psychological age** follows a similar logic, whereby the quality of an individual's functioning on psychological measures such as intelligence, memory, and learning ability is measured. For example, people can be classified based on their ability to perform cognitive tasks, considered to be important aspects of functioning in everyday life. Because cognitive performance changes over the course of adulthood, an index of psychological age would accurately characterize a person's ability to meet the cognitive demands of the environment.

The third type of functional index is **social age**, the characterization of a person's age based on occupying certain social roles. Social age takes into account the person's family, work, and role within the community. For example, a grandparent would have an older social age than would a parent, although the grandparent might easily be chronologically younger than the parent. Occasionally the media reports on seemingly impossible cases of grandparents in their late 20s and, conversely, women who become mothers in their late 60s (in 2010, a TV series aired an episode entitled "Pregnant at 70"). Accordingly, a retiree would have an older social age than would a person still working, although again their chronological ages might be in reverse order. Athletes typically retire in their 30s or earlier, depending on their sport; and politicians or religious figures may not retire until their late 80s, if at all.

As stated earlier, an advantage of using functional indices of aging is that they have greater accuracy in many ways than does chronological age. Of course, they are not quite so convenient. In addition, they require continuing calibration and re-calibration to ensure that they retain their value. For example, a biological index based in part on blood pressure may require adjustments as health practitioners change the definition of what is considered "old." Changes both in medical knowledge and in population norms for particular age groups may mean that the definition of an average 60-year-old's blood pressure shifts so that it would now be more typical of a person in the 70s. Psychological age and social age indices are also likely to change over time. Consequently, functional age must continuously be re-established compared to chronological age, which is tagged explicitly to the passing of time. Despite its faults, then, chronological age may be the most expedient index for many areas of functioning, as long as we keep in mind that it does not tell the whole story.

Personal Versus Social Aging

It is clear that age is more than a number. Researchers in the field of human development use age as a shorthand way to describe processes that occur within the individual along with the passage of time such as, for example, alterations in the skin, lungs, nervous system, and heart. Yet these changes within the individual do not occur in a vacuum but in a social context that reflects events in the ever changing world. In order to get a handle on the distinction between changes within the person and those within the world, developmental researchers speak of changes within the individual as **personal aging.** By this, they mean ontogenetic change (with "onto" referring to "being," and "genesis" to "development"). To capture the fact that aging occurs in the context of the social world, the process of **social aging** is considered to represent the fact that people change along with or perhaps as the result of changes that occur in their environments.

There are three major categories of influences on the process of social aging (see Figure 1.5). These influences, identified by psychologist Paul Baltes (1979), include normative age-graded influences, normative history-graded influences, and nonnormative influences. They represent three interacting systems of influence that regulate the nature of life-span development.

The normative influences stem from the term "norm" and mean that the lives of the majority of individuals within a given culture or society are affected by them.

Normative age-graded influences lead people to choose experiences that their culture and historical period attach to certain ages or points in the life span. In Western society, individuals are affected by normative age-graded influences that lead them to graduate from college when they are in the early 20s, get married and begin a family in the 20s or 30s, retire in their 60s, and become grandparents in their middle to later years, usually in the decades of the 50s, 60s, and beyond. You expect that people will

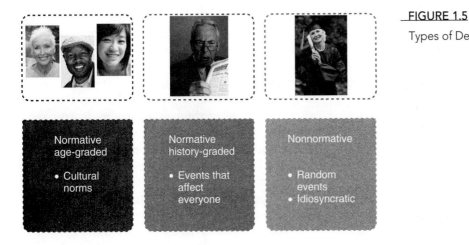

FIGURE 1.5

Types of Developmental Influences

undergo these experiences at these ages because it is what is most typical ("normative").

Events that occur in response to normative age-graded influences occur in part because a given society has developed expectations about what is assumed for people of certain ages. The decision to retire at the age of 65 years can be seen as a response to the norm regarding when it is appropriate (and for many desirable) to leave the labor market. Graduation from high school generally occurs at the age of 18 years because in most industrialized societies, children start school at the age of 5 or 6 and the educational system is based on 12 or 13 grades. It is entirely possible that a 40-year-old may consider retiring but feel reluctant to do so because it is not what is expected for a person of that age unless he or she were in an employment field in which early retirement is expected. Similarly, a young person may prefer not to marry or to have children, but feel pressured into doing so by other family members, friends, or the society at large.

It is true that though partly determined by social context, biology plays a role in the optimal timing of certain events. Take for example parenthood, which traditionally occurs between the ages of 20 and 40, at the peak of a woman's reproductive cycle. Normative age-graded events can set the pattern for later events to occur as a result, so that if an adult becomes a parent at the age of 30, a lower limit is set on the age at which the adult can become a grandparent. If the child also follows a normative age-graded influence, the parent will become a grandparent for the first time somewhere between the ages of 55 and 65 years.

Normative age-graded influences are associated with the life span of the individual although they may reflect environmental or social factors. By contrast, influences associated with changes in society as a whole are referred to as **normative history-graded influences**. These are events that occur to everyone within a certain culture or geopolitical unit (regardless of age) and include large-scale occurrences such as world wars, economic trends, or sociocultural changes in attitudes and values. The impact of these events on people's lives may be felt immediately, but they can have continuing impact for many years on subsequent patterns of work, family, and quality of life. For example, World War II veterans who entered the military after their families were already established were more likely upon their return to get divorced or separated, to suffer career setbacks, and even experience poorer physical health after they turned 50 (Elder, Shanahan, & Clipp, 1994).

Historical events may not directly affect the individual, but may have an indirect influence by virtue of the changes they stimulate in social awareness, as was true for the current generation of people in their mid 50s and early 60s. In high school and college during the Vietnam War years, this generation underwent tremendous turmoil and unrest. Many in the world today are currently being impacted by historical events such as the wars in Iraq and Afghanistan, global warming, and the aftermath of natural disasters such as Hurricane Katrina in

In the summer of 2010, a massive oil spill in the Gulf of Mexico affected the lives and livelihood of millions of individuals living on the Gulf Coast and beyond. Normative history-graded events such as this one can have long-lasting effects on development.

2005 and the Haitian earthquake in 2010, and the worldwide economic downturn that began in late 2008 and the Gulf of Mexico oil spill in the summer of 2010.

If the life course was influenced only by normative age- and history-graded influences, predicting the course of development of people of the same age living in the same culture would be relatively easy. However, people's lives are also affected by idiosyncratic factors. These factors occur due to a combination of coincidence, the impact of earlier decisions made on later events, and relationships with other people. Little is written about these **nonnormative influences** in the developmental literature because there is virtually no way of predicting their occurrence. Developmentalists can only observe these phenomena as they occur and then generalize what the impact of certain unpredictable life events on individuals may be.

There are almost an infinite number of examples of nonnormative influences. Some are due to good luck, such as winning the lottery or making a smart investment. Nonnormative influences can also be negative, such as a car accident, fire, or the untimely death of a relative. One moment your life is perfectly normal, and in an instant, your life course can be permanently altered. Other nonnormative influences may unfold over a gradual period, such as being fired from a job (due to personal, not large-scale economic reasons), developing a chronic illness not related to aging, or going through a divorce. In everyday language, you talk about someone benefiting from the "right place, right time" effect or suffering a negative fate from being in the "wrong place at the wrong time."

As you have read about the various types of influences on life, it may have crossed your mind that the way in which they interact with each other is also important. Consider the example of divorce. Although society's norms have changed considerably regarding this life event, many would still consider this a nonnormative occurrence because the norm (and certainly the hope) of married couples is to remain married. And although a divorce is a personal occurrence, it may be seen in part as a response to larger social forces. For example, a couple who is exposed to financial hardship because one or both partners lost a job due to living in harsh economic times (normative historical influence) is now faced with severe emotional stress. If they are in their middle years, when couples are expected to have reached a degree of financial comfort (age-graded normative influence), their problems may be exacerbated. Yet some couples may feel closer to each other when exposed to such adversity, and this is where the idiosyncratic nonnormative factors come into play.

This example illustrates the dilemmas faced by researchers in human development who attempt to separate out not only personal from social aging, but also the impact of particular influences that fall into the category of social aging. Though challenging, the very complexity of the equation fascinates those of us who try to understand what makes humans "tick" and what causes that ticking to change over the decades of the human lifespan.

SOCIAL FACTORS IN ADULT DEVELOPMENT AND AGING

The study of adult development and aging involves an understanding of concepts that describe the characteristics of individuals according to certain social factors or indicators. Along with age, these social factors help to shape the structures of opportunities available to people throughout their lives.

Sex and Gender

The term gender refers to the individual's identification as being male or female. It is generally considered distinct from a person's biological sex, which refers to an individual's anatomy. Both sex and gender are important in the study of adult development and aging. Physiological factors relevant to sex influence the timing and nature of physical aging processes, primarily through the operation of sex hormones. For example, the sex hormone estrogen is thought to play at least some role in affecting a woman's risks of heart disease, bone loss, and possibly cognitive changes.

Social and cultural factors relevant to gender are important to the extent that the individual assumes a certain role in society based on being viewed as a male or female. Opportunities in education and employment are two main areas in which gender influences the course of adult development and becomes a limiting factor for women. Although progress has certainly occurred in both domains over the past several decades, women continue to face a more restricted range of choices and the prospects of lower earnings than do men. Furthermore, these

differences are important to consider when studying the current generation of older adults, as they were raised in an era with more traditional gender expectations.

Race

A person's **race** is defined in biological terms as the classification within the species based on physical and structural characteristics. However, the concept of race in common usage is broader than these biological features. Race has come to be used in a broader fashion to refer to the cultural background associated with being born within a particular biologically defined segment of the population. The "race" that people use to identify themselves is more likely to be socially than biologically determined. In addition, because few people are solely of one race in the biological sense, social and cultural background factors assume even greater prominence.

The U.S. Census, a count of those living in the United States conducted every 10 years, attempts to provide an accurate depiction of the size and makeup of the country. The 2010 U.S. Census (conducted in April 2010) defined race on the basis of a person's self-identification. In addition, the census also included categories based on national origin and allowed individuals to select more than one racial category. To the extent that race is

AGING IN THE NEWS

www.wiley.com/college/whitbourne   OLDER ADULTS WHO MADE THE HEADLINES   -VOL. 4, CHAPTER 1-

OLDEST DOG WINS TOP TROPHY

At the ripe old dog age of 10, Stump, a Sussex spaniel, became the oldest Best in Show Winner ever at the Westminster Kennel Club, coming out of retirement only a week before walking off with the top prize. Stump won the Sporting Group in 2004; the following year he almost died following a serious medical condition that required 19 days under the care of veterinarians. What was the secret to Stump's win? According to his owner, Scott Sommer, nothing more than a walk around the neighborhood!

biologically determined, however, racial differences in functioning in adulthood and aging may reflect differences in genetic inheritance. People who have inherited a risk factor that has been found to be higher within a certain race are more likely to be at risk for developing that illness during their adult years.

Racial differences in risk factors may also interact with different cultural backgrounds associated with a particular race. For example, people at risk for a disease with a metabolic basis (such as inability to metabolize fats) will be more likely to develop that disease depending on whether cooking foods high in fat content is a part of their culture.

Social and cultural aspects of race may also alter an individual's development in adulthood through the structure of a society and whether there are systematic biases against people who identify with that race. As we will demonstrate throughout this book, health problems are higher among the African American population than among the White population. Part of the differences in health may be attributed to lack of opportunities for education and well-paying jobs, but systematic discrimination is also believed to take a toll on health by increasing the levels of stress experienced by African Americans (Green & Darity, 2010). Throughout the book, we will also examine a large national study known as Whitehall II conducted in the United Kingdom, which provides important data on the interrelationships among health, social class, and occupation.

Ethnicity

The concept of **ethnicity** captures the cultural background of an individual, reflecting the predominant values, attitudes, and expectations in which the individual has been raised. Along with race, ethnicity is often studied in adult development and aging as an influence on a person's family attitudes and experiences. For example, people of certain ethnic backgrounds are thought to show greater respect for older adults and feel a stronger sense of obligation to care for their aging parents. Ethnicity also may play a role in influencing the aging of various physiological functions, in part through genetic inheritance and in part through exposure to cultural habits and traditions. Finally, discrimination against people of certain ethnic backgrounds may serve the same function as race in limiting the opportunities for educational and occupational achievements.

The term ethnicity is gradually replacing the term race as a categorical variable in social research. We will follow that tradition in this book unless there is a clear-cut reason to refer specifically to race (i.e., if we are describing research that also uses this term). However, there are occasional points of confusion in that the U.S. Census occasionally combines race (White or Black) and ethnicity (Hispanic or non-Hispanic).

Socioeconomic Status

An individual's **socioeconomic status (SES)**, or "social class," is defined according to the values assigned to level of education and prestige level of occupation. Various researchers have developed scales of socioeconomic status that give differing weights to these values in coming up with a total score. People with higher levels of education tend to have occupations that are higher in prestige, and so some researchers use level of education alone as the index of SES.

Income levels are not necessarily associated with socioeconomic status. High-prestige jobs (such as teachers) are often associated with mid- or even low-level salaries. However, as a proxy for or in addition to SES, some researchers use income as the basis for analyzing social class differences in health and opportunities.

Religion

Religion, or an individual's identification with an organized belief system, has received increased attention as a factor influencing development in adulthood. Organized religions form an alternative set of social structures that are partly connected with race and ethnicity. More important, religion provides many people with a source of coping strategies, social support in times of crisis, and a systematic basis for interpreting life experiences (Klemmack et al., 2007).

Unfortunately there is relatively little research on the role of organized religion in the lives of aging adults, and even less on spirituality and its role in middle and later adulthood. There are some researchers who are now beginning to examine this area but there is much that remains to be learned.

THE BABY BOOMERS GROW UP: CHANGES IN THE MIDDLE-AGED AND OLDER POPULATIONS IN THE UNITED STATES AND THE WORLD

A quick snapshot of the U.S. population according to age and sex appears in Figure 1.6 (U.S. Bureau of the Census, 2010a). The age–sex structure provides a useful way of looking at the population. A "young" population is shaped like a pyramid, an "old" population is depicted by an upside-down pyramid, and a population considered stable is shaped like a rectangle. From the figure, the "bulge" in the middle of the population is clear, reflecting the Baby Boom generation of people born between 1945 and 1964. As this bulge continues to move upward throughout the 21st century, this generation will have a continued impact on the nature of society, particularly in the way everyone views aging, as indeed it already has (Whitbourne & Willis, 2006).

United States

In 1900, the number of Americans over the age of 65 years made up about 4% of the population (constituting 3.1 million people). By 2008, this number increased more than 12 times to 36.7 million. People 65 and older now represent 12.3% of the total U.S. population (U.S. Bureau of the Census, 2009a). As shown in Figure 1.7 (Federal Interagency Forum on Age-Related Statistics, 2009), beginning in 2010 with an estimated 40.2 million adults 65 and older, this number will more than double to 88.5 million by the year 2050, or 20.2% of the total U.S. population (U.S. Bureau of the Census, 2010a). A disproportionate rise in the population 85 years and older will also occur. Perhaps most impressive is the estimate in the growth in the number of centenarians. In 1990, an estimated 37,306 people over the age of 100 lived in the United States. By 2004 this number increased 73% to 64,658, and by 2050 there will be over 1.1 million of these exceptionally aged individuals.

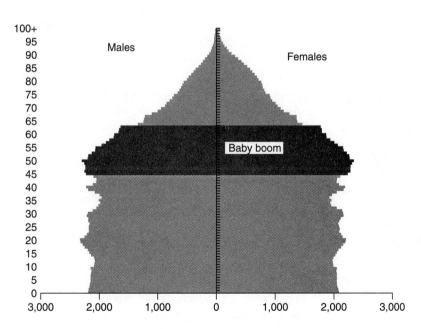

FIGURE 1.6

U.S. Population by Age and Sex, 2010

Source: U.S. Bureau of the Census. (2010a). Projected U.S. population by age and sex: 2010. Retrieved from http://www.census.gov/population/www/projections/tablesandcharts/chart_1.pdf.

FIGURE 1.7

Number of People Age 65 and Over by Age Group, for Selected Years 1900–2006 and Projected 2010–2050

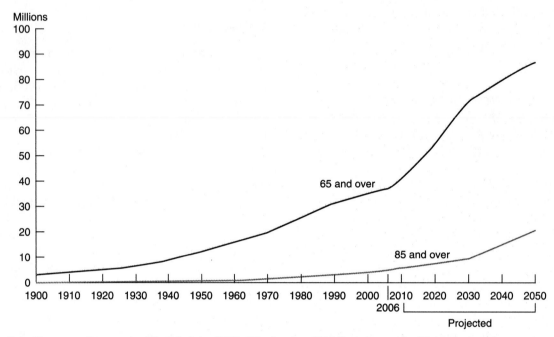

Source: Federal Interagency Forum on Age-Related Statistics. (2009). Older Americans 2008: Key indicators of well-being. Retrieved from http://www.agingstats.gov/Agingstatsdotnet/Main_Site/default.aspx.

The major explanation for these large increases in the 65 and older population can be accounted for by the movement of the **Baby Boomers** through the years of middle and later adulthood. Important to consider is not just that these individuals were born during a period of high birth rates, but that they are expected to live into their 80s, 90s, and 100s, increasing the numbers of very-old individuals society will experience throughout the century.

Increases in the aging population reflect the vast advances that have taken place in the average length of life. **Life expectancy** constitutes the average number of years of life remaining to the people born within a similar period of time. To calculate life expectancy, statisticians take into account death rates for a particular group within the population, and use these figures to project how long it will take for that entire group to die out completely.

Life expectancy from birth rose overall from 62.9 years in 1940 to 77.9 years in 2007 (Xu, Kochanek, Murphy, & Tejeda-Vera, 2010). Many factors have contributed to increases in life expectancy, including reduced death rates for children and young adults. People are also living longer once they reach the age of 65, at which point the life expectancy becomes 83.5 years of age (Centers for Disease Control and Prevention, 2010c).

Geographic Variations Within the United States. There are important variations within the United States in where people 65 and older are living (see Figure 1.8). As of 2008, slightly over one half of persons 65 and over lived in nine states. With 4.1 million people 65 and older, California has the largest number of older adults, but because the state's population is so large, this age group constitutes a relatively small proportion (11%) of the population. As you may have guessed, Florida has the highest percent of people 65 and older (17.4%). The greatest percentage increases in the aging population between the years 1998 and 2008 occurred in the states of Alaska, Nevada, Arizona, Utah, New Mexico, and Idaho with increases ranging from 31% (Idaho) to Alaska (50%) (Administration on Aging, 2009).

Gender and Racial Variations in the Over-65 Population. Women over the age of 65 currently outnumber men, amounting to approximately 58% of the total over-65 population. This gender disparity is expected to diminish somewhat by the year 2050, as the last of the Baby Boomers reach advanced old age. At that time, 56% of the 65 and older population in the United States will be female and 44% will be male (U.S. Bureau of the Census, 2010c).

Changes are also evident in the distribution of White and minority segments of the population. As shown in Figure 1.9, in 2006, whereas 20% of the over-65 population was made up of members of racial and ethnic minorities, this number will rise to between 39 and 42% by the year 2050 (U.S. Bureau of the Census, 2010c). The Hispanic population of older adults is expected to grow at the fastest rate, increasing from what was approximately 6 million in 2003 to over 18 million by 2050 (He, Sangupta, Velkoff, & DeBarros, 2005).

Aging Around the World

Data from around the world confirm the picture of an increasingly older population throughout the 21st century. In 2010, there were 531 million people worldwide over the age of 65. Predictions suggest that this number will triple to 1.53 billion by the year 2050 (U.S. Bureau of the Census, 2010c). China currently has the largest number of older adults (106 million), but Japan has the highest percentage of people 65 and older (20%) (Kinsella & He, 2009).

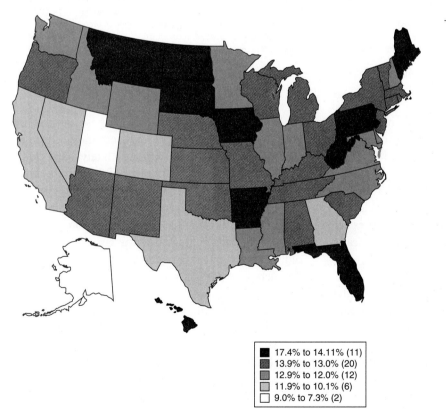

FIGURE 1.8

Percent of Persons 65 and Over in 2008 by State

17.4% to 14.11% (11)
13.9% to 13.0% (20)
12.9% to 12.0% (12)
11.9% to 10.1% (6)
9.0% to 7.3% (2)

Source: Administration on Aging. (2009). A profile of older Americans: 2009. Retrieved from http://www.aoa.gov/AoARoot/Aging_Statistics/Profile/2009/8.aspx.

FIGURE 1.9

U.S. Population Age 65 and Over by Race and Hispanic Origin, 2006 and Projected 2050

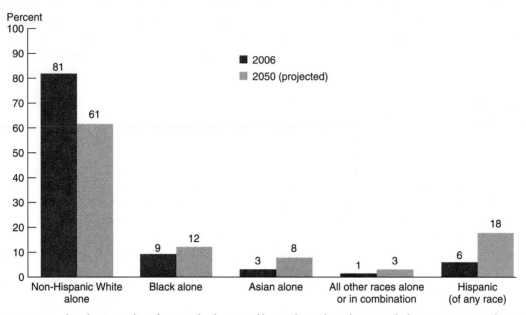

The term "non-Hispanic White alone" is used to refer to people who reported being White and no other race and who are not Hispanic. The term "Black alone" is used to refer to people who reported being Black or African American and no other race, and the term "Asian alone" is used to refer to people who reported only Asian as their race. The use of single-race populations in this report does not imply that this is the preferred method of presenting or analyzing data. The U.S. Census Bureau uses a variety of approaches. The race group "All other races alone or in combination" includes American Indian and Alaska Native, alone; Native Hawaiian and Other Pacific Islander, alone and all people who reported two or more races.
Reference population: These data refer to the resident population.
Source: Federal Interagency Forum on Age-Related Statistics. (2009). Older Americans 2008: Key indicators of well-being. Retrieved from http://www.agingstats.gov/Agingstatsdotnet/Main_Site/default.aspx.

World population statistics are often reported in terms of "developed" and "developing" countries. Developed countries include all those in Europe, North America, Japan, Australia and New Zealand plus some nations formerly in the Soviet Union. All other nations of the world are classified as developing (Kinsella & He, 2009). The developing countries are those that have an agrarian-based economy, typically with lower levels of health care, education, and income.

As shown in Figure 1.10, the proportion of the population 65 years and over living in developing countries will show a precipitous rise in the next decade and will continue to exceed the rate of growth in developed countries. The larger proportion of the aging population in the world will place a strain on the economies and health care systems of all nations, but particularly developing nations (Kinsella & He, 2009).

What are the implications of these figures for your future as you enter into and move through your adult years? First, you will likely have more friends and associates than is true of the current older population, simply because there will be more peers of your age group to socialize with. If you are male, the news is encouraging; you will be more likely to live into old age compared to the current cohorts of older adults. For those of you younger than the Baby Boomers, the statistics are also encouraging if you are considering a career related to the field of aging, given the higher number of older clientele. Changes in various aspects of lifestyle can also be expected in the next decades, as adjustments to the aging population in the entertainment world and media are made. Just as society is getting used to the idea of an aging Paul McCartney, many others will follow in his footsteps to change views about prominent celebrities in Western society and, indeed, around the world.

FIGURE 1.10

Average Annual Percent Growth of Older Population in Developed and Developing Countries, 1950–2050

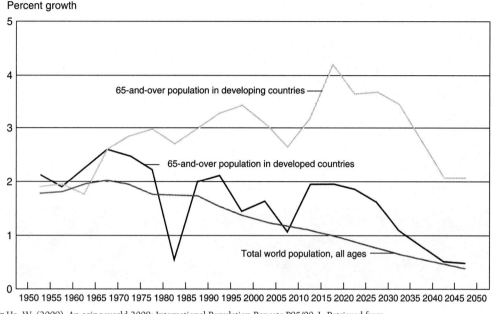

Percent growth

65-and-over population in developing countries

65-and-over population in developed countries

Total world population, all ages

Kinsella, K., & He, W. (2009). An aging world 2008: International Population Reports P95/09-1. Retrieved from http://www.census.gov/prod/2009pubs/p95-09-1.pdf.

SUMMARY

1. This book is based on the biopsychosocial model, which regards development as a complex interaction of biological, psychological, and social processes. The four principles of adult development and aging include the assumptions that: changes are continuous over the life span; only the survivors grow old; individual differences are important to recognize; and "normal" aging is different from disease. Distinctions must be drawn between primary aging (changes that are intrinsic to the aging process) and secondary aging (changes due to disease).

2. It is difficult to define the term "adult" given the range of possible criteria. For purposes of this book, we will consider the ages of 18–22 to serve as a rough guideline. The over-65 population is generally divided into the subcategories of young-old (65–74), old-old (75–84), and oldest-old (85 and over). These divisions have important policy implications, as well as to highlight the need to make distinctions among individuals over 65. Biological, psychological, and social age all provide alternative perspectives to describe an individual. Whereas personal aging refers to changes within the individual over time, social aging reflects normative age-graded influences, normative history-graded influences, and nonnormative influences.

3. Social factors important to the study of adult development and aging include gender, race, ethnicity, socioeconomic status, and religion.

4. The "graying" of the world and the United States is reflected in the sheer numbers of older adults. 36.7 million Americans are over the age of 65, constituting 12.3% of the total U.S. population. Countries around the world will show increases in the over-65 population as well, particularly among developing countries. Implications of these changes will impact the way in which we view later adulthood, as well as prepare for what will happen in your later years.

2

Models of Development: Nature

The study of adult development and aging has evolved from the field of developmental psychology to incorporate the years beyond childhood and adolescence into a unified view of the life span. For many years, the field of developmental psychology was synonymous with the field of child development. Starting in the 1960s, several influential theorists decided that emphasis should be more inclusive of changes within the individual throughout life. They argued that designating a point when people stopped developing did not make sense because people do not stop growing and changing once they become adults. Although within groups of developmental psychologists the focus continues to emphasize the early years of development, the middle and later years have solidified their importance within the field. If for no other reason than the shifting demographics of the world, this expanded view of development is reflected particularly in a higher number of programs that train future developmentalists.

The **life span perspective** views development as continuous from childhood through old age (see Figure 2.1). This expanded view of the life span also includes a focus on the social or **contextual influences on development.** At one time, developmental psychologists debated whether changes in life occurred due to nature or nurture. However, researchers are showing convincingly that both nature and nurture must be considered as influences on life span change. Reflecting these changes in approaching life span change, the term **developmental science** is gradually replacing the term developmental psychology, as the focus on life span development continues to encompass a broader variety of domains than a focus on the psychology of the individual (Magnusson, 1996). The use of the term science conveys this shift toward understanding the systematic effects of multiple influences on the growing individual over time.

Developmental scientists no longer look solely at psychological domains such as cognition and personality, but instead apply their analytic methods to areas of functioning more traditionally in other fields such as biology, health, and sociology. The inclusion of social context implies that it is no longer sufficient to look only within the individual's immediate environment in order to understand change over time (Ford & Lerner, 1992). Particularly important to the field of

and Nurture in Adulthood

developmental science is a desire to understand the dynamic interactions among and within each level of analysis of change, from the biological to the social (Lerner, 1996).

With the refocus toward developmental science, researchers now attempt to explain the underlying processes of development rather than simply to describe changes over time that occur as people get older. The descriptive approach to development

FIGURE 2.1

Expanded Views of Development

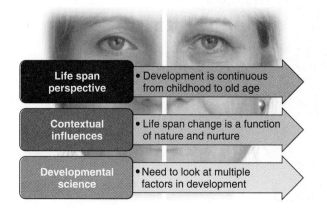

was practiced for many decades as researchers attempted to establish the ages at which different events occur within the individual. This approach characterized the work of such early child psychologists as Arnold Gesell, who wrote books on "the child at two," "the child at three," and so on. Developmental scientists are clearly attempting to discover orderly principles underlying growth through life: the "whys" and not just the "whats."

In summary, the emerging role of developmental science implies the view that individuals continue to grow and change over the entire course of their lives. Additionally, multiple influences are important to consider, and understanding the social context plays an integral role in understanding change over time.

MODELS OF INDIVIDUAL–ENVIRONMENT INTERACTIONS

Classic developmental psychology evolved around the notion that growth in childhood occurred primarily as a result of "nature." This was the assumption of early 20th-century writers who, like Gesell, believed in chronicling the changes that occurred from birth to adolescence. These changes, it was thought, would reflect the influence of ontogenesis, or maturational processes, as they unfolded within the child. The role of the environment was minimal in this approach, restricted to that of parents providing the right growing conditions, much as you would provide water and light to a plant seedling. However, it was not long until the "nurture" position emerged among child psychologists. The founder of American behaviorism, John B. Watson, writing some 20 years after Gesell, claimed that a child's future could be molded entirely by the environment provided by the parents.

The nature–nurture debate stimulated many of the classic studies in child development, conducted at a time when researchers attempted to prove their position on the basis of findings such as the differences between identical twins reared together and apart. Perhaps the most hotly debated of these discussions revolved around whether intelligence is inherited or acquired. Gradually data began to accumulate showing that neither influence alone could account for individual differences in performance on intelligence tests—in children or adults.

One contribution that changed the tone of the nature–nurture debate occurred when the concept of **niche-picking** (Scarr & McCartney, 1983) was introduced. According to this concept, genetic and environmental factors work together to influence the direction that children's lives take. Children are born with certain abilities and predispositions that lead them to explore certain types of activities. Once started down a particular pathway, further changes occur that influence the later development of those particular abilities.

Consider the example of a child whose genetic potential predisposes her to be a talented dancer. She has a great deal of flexibility, poise, and a good sense of rhythm; all characteristics that reflect strong "dance" genes. At the age of 4, her parents take her to a ballet performance. She sits glued to her seat, fascinated by the twirling and jumping that she sees taking place on stage. This event triggers her to beg her parents to enroll her in ballet lessons, and soon they do. The child has chosen dancing as her "niche," having been exposed to the ballet performance, and once allowed to pursue her talent, she continues to thrive. Thus, her "dance genes" lead her to develop an interest in exactly the activity that will allow her talents to flourish.

At the same time the notion of a gene–environment interaction was proposed by child development researchers and theorists, other experts expanded the focus of child development to include the years of adulthood. The middle years of adulthood (primarily studied by educators in the field of adult learning) were swept up in the movement to

These young children are expressing an interest in dance, which will become their "niche" as they continue to develop further their interests and abilities.

TABLE 2.1

Models of Individual–Environmental Interactions

	Organismic	*Mechanistic*	*Interactionist*
Nature of change	Qualitative	Quantitative	Multidirectional Multidimensional
Contribution of organism	Active	Passive	Active
Main force in development	Biological (intrinsic)	External (environmental)	Reciprocal

Source: Adapted from Lerner, R., M. (1995). Developing individuals within changing contexts: Implications of developmental contextualism for human development, research, policy, and programs. In T. J. Kindermann & J. Valsiner (Eds.), *Development of person-context relations* (pp. 13–37). Hillsdale NJ: Lawrence Erlbaum.

integrate studies of development previously kept distinct. People in the field of **gerontology**, the study of the aging process, began to examine development prior to old age. Out of these converging interests, a unified view of the life span began to evolve.

The general philosophical and theoretical discussions revolving around the expansion of child psychology to life span development produced very clear but divergent statements of the models underlying the nature–nurture debate (Lerner, 1995). Table 2.1 presents the essential elements of these models.

As you look through this table, think about which approach best fits your own philosophy about why people change over time. Are you on the side of "nature" and do you therefore assume that people go through life stages as a result of their genetic blueprint? Alternatively, do you think that people change because the environment shapes and molds the course their lives take? Or, perhaps you fall in the middle, and believe that life changes reflect the interaction of both inheritance (nature) and life circumstances (nurture)? You may also feel that it is too simplistic to take an either/or position or even conclude that both factors are important without saying how much each contributes. Perhaps some aspects of behavior reflect a greater proportion of genetic inheritance and others reflect a greater influence of the environment. Thinking further about the idea of niche-picking, you may also find it helpful to consider the ways in which life choices influenced the environments to which you were exposed, which in turn influenced further choices you made, and so on.

The **organismic model** (taken from the term "organism") is based on the notion that "nature" drives development. According to this model, growth in childhood and beyond is the manifestation of

genetic predisposition as expressed in the physical and mental development of the individual. Those who believe in this model propose that qualitative or structural alterations in the individual's psychological qualities such as intelligence and personality are the cause of change. This model is the basis for stage theories of development, which postulate that change over the life span occurs in "leaps" or steps rather than in a continuous fashion.

The **mechanistic model** of development (taken from the word "machine") is based on the premise that "nurture" is the primary force in development. People who believe in the mechanistic model propose that growth throughout life occurs through the individual's exposure to experiences that present new learning opportunities. Because this exposure is gradual, the model assumes that there are no clear-cut or identifiable stages. Instead, development is a smooth, continuous set of gradations as the individual acquires new experiences.

On the column in the extreme right of Table 2.1 is the **interactionist model**, the perspective that the evolving field of developmental science most closely represents. According to the interactionist model, not only do genetics and environment interact in complex ways (as suggested by the niche-picking concept), but the individual also actively participates in his or her development through reciprocal relations with the environment. Another important aspect of this model is the proposition of **multidirectionality**, a term we first introduced in Chapter 1. According to this principle, there are multiple paths in development; development does not proceed according to a series of linear stages operating along a single pathway. Researchers who ascribe to the interactionist model assume that there is **plasticity** in development, meaning that the course of development may be altered (is "plastic"), depending on the nature of the individual's specific interactions in the environment.

Each theory of development can be classified within one of these three models. Theories proposing that development is the result of ontogenetic changes fall within the organismic model. Learning theory, which proposes that development proceeds according to environmental influences, is categorized into the mechanistic model. Theories that regard development as the product of joint influences fit within the interactionist model. Clearly, the biopsychosocial perspective falls within the interactionist model of development because it considers multiple influences on development and views the individual as an active contributor to change throughout life.

As we explore the processes of development in adulthood and old age, the usefulness of the concepts of **multidimensionality**, multidirectionality, and plasticity will become apparent. We have already discussed the need to examine the aging process from a multidimensional point of view, and along with this notion is the idea that development can proceed in multiple dimensions across life. The concept of plasticity fits very well with the notion of compensation and modifiability of the aging process through actions taken by the individual, a concept that we will continue to explore throughout this book. From our point of view, the interactionist model provides an excellent backdrop for the biopsychosocial perspective and a basis for viewing the processes of development in later life on a continuum with developmental processes in the early years.

Reciprocity in Development

You can see that an important assumption of the interactionist model is that adults are products of their experiences. However, adults also shape their own experiences, both through active interpretation of the events that happen to them and through the actions they take. These observations emphasize the **reciprocal nature of development**, the explicit recognition that people both influence and are influenced by the events in their lives (Bronfenbrenner & Ceci, 1994).

Consider the reciprocal process as it has affected your own life. You were influenced by earlier events to choose a particular course that has brought you to where you are right now. Perhaps you and your best friend from high school decided to apply to the same college and as a result you are here now. Perhaps you chose this college because you knew you wanted to major in psychology and you were impressed by the reputation of the faculty in your department. Or perhaps your choice was made randomly, and you are unsure of what exactly led to your being in this place at this time. In any case you are where you are, having been influenced one way or another by your prior life events. That is one piece of the reciprocal process.

The second piece relates to the effect you have on your environment, and this in turn will affect subsequent events in your life. For example, by virtue of your existence you affect the people who know you, your "life footprint," as it were. It is not only very possible but very likely that their lives may have already been altered by their relationship with you. Your impact as a student at your college may have lasting effect on both you and your institution.

Everyone knows of great student athletes, scholars, or musicians who bring renown to their institutions. Even if you don't become a famous alum, your contributions to the school may alter it nevertheless. Have you ever asked a question in class that may have taken your professor by surprise? Perhaps, as a result, you may have permanently altered the way that professor approaches the problem in the future. It is not improbable to imagine that your question stimulates your professor to investigate a new research question, and the investigation may ultimately produce new knowledge in the field, drawing attention to your school's contributions to the area. This is what happened to a colleague at the University of Massachusetts whose fascinating research on the World War II political cartoons drawn by Dr. Seuss (who hailed from nearby Springfield) was stimulated by a student's question during class. The professor went on to conduct research on the early political cartoon career of this well-known children's writer.

Though you may not become the source of groundbreaking research by a well-known academic writer, you may influence the people around you in much smaller ways that would nevertheless lead to important changes. Some of these influences may be good ones, as when you express kindness to a stranger who in turn has reason to smile, and for that instant, feels a bit better about the world. Others may be less positive, as when a single wrong turn while you are behind the wheel has the unfortunate effect of causing an accident. In a split second, any person can influence others for better or worse, and the same is true of the way that others affect each individual.

The reciprocal process takes as a basic assumption the idea that people are not passive recipients of environmental effects. Instead, choices and behaviors made by each person leave a mark on the environment. Subsequently, the changes in that environment may further alter people in significant ways, which leads to further impacts on society. Reciprocal views of development regard these continuing processes as both ongoing and, to some extent, unpredictable.

SOCIOCULTURAL MODELS OF DEVELOPMENT

The models of development we have just examined set the stage for looking in more depth at particular theoretical approaches to adult development and aging. We begin by focusing on those approaches that give relatively more emphasis to the environment as an influence on development.

Ecological Perspective

The **ecological perspective** (Bronfenbrenner, 1995) identifies multiple levels of the environment that interact with individual processes of change (see Figure 2.2). The inner biological level represents the physiological changes that take place over time that affect the functioning of the body. The next level of individual functioning includes cognition, personality, and other processes of adaptation. The third level is the **proximal social relational level**, which involves the individual's relationships with significant others, peers, and members of the nuclear family. At the **sociocultural level** are relations with the larger social institutions of educational, public policy, governmental, and economic systems. Although interactions at both social levels occur throughout development, the interactions regarded as having the greatest impact on an individual's life occur at the proximal level in the immediate environment.

FIGURE 2.2

Bronfenbrenner's Ecological Perspective

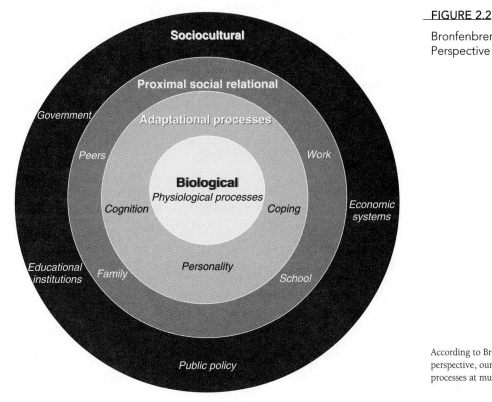

According to Bronfenbrenner's ecological perspective, our development is affected by processes at multiple levels.

In thinking about this model, it is important to keep in mind the fact that development in one sphere interacts with development in other spheres. The concentric circles are not just static in that sense. Events that take place in the outer perimeter of the circle, such as changes in your country's economy or political systems or changes in the world as a whole, also have an impact on your life, even at the inner biological level. For example, when the economy suffers, as it has in the late 2000s and early 2010s, people experience deprivation in ways that affect their physical functioning and overall health, not to mention their mental health as well.

Research from the Whitehall II Study (Marmot & Brunner, 2005), a large-scale prospective cohort study conducted in the United Kingdom on Civil Service employees, provides compelling evidence to support the importance that social factors play in determining health status. Although you may typically think of your overall health as functioning within your inner biological level, researchers working within the Whitehall II Study are continuing to demonstrate the significance of relations with others and social roles on health. In Figure 2.3, we have illustrated one of the key findings that men and women working at lower employment levels had lower overall physical functioning.

A later study provided evidence of an association between psychosocial factors at work (such as social support in the workplace) and coronary heart disease (Hintsa et al., 2009), even after controlling for factors such as family history of the disease and education. Given that a key objective of Whitehall II is to examine

health from a biological, psychological, and social context, we will continue to describe findings from this landmark study throughout the book to illustrate the biopsychosocial perspective.

The Life Course Perspective

The **life course perspective** emphasizes the importance of age-based norms, roles, and attitudes as influences that shape events throughout development. Through the life course perspective, sociologists and social gerontologists attempt to form links between these broad social factors and individual adjustment. These social scientists distinguish the term life "course" from life "span" in emphasizing the non-biological factors that influence changes over time.

Falling broadly within the life course perspective are theories that attempt to link social factors with individual adaptation. **Disengagement theory** (Cumming & Henry, 1961) was one of the first theories in the field of social gerontology to propose a set of specific linkages between social roles and well-being among older adults. It was given the name "disengagement" because it proposed that the normal and natural evolution of life causes older adults to wish to loosen their social ties. This natural loosening, it was argued, is not only inevitable but desirable. Aging is accompanied, so the theory says, by a mutual process of withdrawal of the individual and society. Within this approach, retirement and isolation from family members are circumstances that older adults wish for and benefit from in terms of having higher levels of well-being.

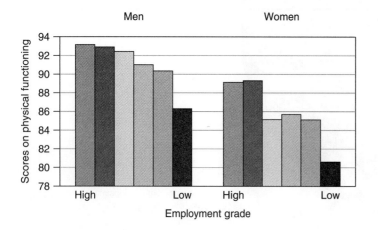

FIGURE 2.3

Results from the Whitehall II Study

As can be seen from this figure, scores on physical functioning were lower among men and women in Whitehall II from lower employment grades.

Source: Marmot, M., & Brunner, E. (2005). Cohort profile: The Whitehall II Study. *International Journal of Epidemiology, 34*, 251–260.

AGING IN THE NEWS

www.wiley.com/college/whitbourne   OLDER ADULTS WHO MADE THE HEADLINES   -VOL. 4, CHAPTER 2-

HOLLYWOOD TO ACTRESSES: LESS BOTOX PLEASE

April 23, 2010. Casting director Sande Alessi speaks for a growing list of Hollywood moviemakers issuing their preference for more natural-looking leading ladies. Although it will be difficult to convince most actresses to follow the lead of women who accept their aging with grace such as Meryl Streep and Helen Mirren, the backlash against overuse of plastic surgery is likely to have an impact. Lisa Kudrow, in a recent interview with *New York* magazine, seemed happy to own up to the fact that the face viewers saw on an episode of "Cougar Town" was hers, age lines and all. "Look, time marches on," she said. "You still want to look good, but there's a line between looking like yourself and looking like a character from a Batman movie."

When it was first proposed in the early 1960s, gerontologists were shocked and outraged by the propositions of disengagement theory. The idea that older adults wanted to be put "on the shelf" and even benefited from social isolation was considered reinforcement of the negative treatment of older adults by society. Rather than describing a desirable end product of a mutual withdrawal process, disengagement theory was seen by its critics as disrespectful of older adults and justification for what is already harsh treatment by society of its older adult members.

The prevailing views in social gerontology in the late 1950s were based on **activity theory,** the view that older adults would rather be involved and not forced out of productive social roles (Cavan, Burgess, Havighurst, & Goldhamer, 1949). According to activity theory, older adults do not seek disengagement from society but instead prefer to remain active and involved. Older adults should be given as many opportunities as possible, according to activity theory, to be engaged in their work, families, and community.

Eventually a resolution of sorts was forged between the countervailing views of disengagement and activity theory. **Continuity theory** (Atchley, 1989) proposes that whether disengagement or activity is beneficial to the older adult depends on the individual's personality. Some older adults prefer to withdraw from active involvement with their families

and communities; others are miserable unless they are in the thick of the action.

According to continuity theory, older adults will be negatively affected and suffer a loss of well-being by being excluded from social roles—if this exclusion goes against their will. One implication is that forced retirement or forced activity will lead to lower adjustment and self-esteem in middle-aged and older adults than would finding their own "just right" amount of involvement.

Ageism as a Social Factor in the Aging Process

The social context in which aging occurs is, unfortunately, one that is not necessarily favorable to the overall well-being of older adults, many of whom are affected by **ageism,** a set of beliefs, attitudes, social institutions, and acts that denigrate individuals or groups based on their chronological age. Similar to other "isms" such as racism and sexism, the components of ageism represent stereotyped views of different age groups. Theoretically the term could also apply to teenagers, who are often stereotyped as lazy, impulsive, rebellious, or self-centered. However, for all practical purposes, ageism is used to refer to stereotyped views of the older adult population. Disengagement theory was thought of by its critics as a justification for ageism, as a way to conveniently move older people to the backdrop of society. Moreover, by implying that all older adults have the same drive to withdraw, the theory perpetuates the stereotype that all older adults have similar personalities.

The primarily negative feature of ageism is that, like other stereotypes, it is founded on overgeneralizations about individuals based on a set of characteristics that have negative social meaning. Oddly enough, that negative social meaning may have a positive spin (Kite & Wagner, 2002). Ageism applies to any view of older adults as having a set of characteristics, good or bad, that are the same for everyone. Calling an older adult "cute" or "with it" is as much an expression of ageism as is referring to that person as "cranky" or "senile."

One effect of ageism is to cause younger people to avoid close proximity to an older person. In fact, ageism may also take the form of not being overtly hostile but of making older adults "invisible"; that is, not worthy of any attention at all. Ageism is often experienced in the workplace, and although prohibited by law (a topic explored in Chapter 10), older workers are penalized for making mistakes that would not incur the same consequence if made by younger workers (Rupp, Vodanovich, & Crede, 2006). Ironically, aging is the one stereotype that, if you are fortunate enough to survive to old age, you will most likely experience. Unlike the other "isms," people who hold aging stereotypes will eventually become the target of their negative beliefs as they grow old.

Those young people most likely to experience ageist attitudes are actually the ones who identify most strongly with their own age group. Young adults who have less of an identification with their own age group seem to have more favorable attitudes toward older adults (Packer & Chasteen, 2006).

Ageism has many possible causes. One plausible notion is that negative attitudes toward aging represent fear of death and dying. By their very presence, older adults remind younger people of the inevitability of their own mortality (Martens, Greenberg, Schimel, & Landau, 2004).

A second view is that the status of older adults is negatively related to the degree of industrial development in a given society. According to the **modernization hypothesis**, the increasing urbanization and industrialization of Western society have led to lower social value for older persons

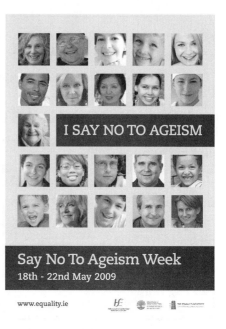

Each year the Republic of Ireland sponsors a "Say No to Ageism Week" intended to promote awareness and understanding of ageism and how ageist attitudes can exclude older people from participating in, and contributing to, society.

(Cowgill & Holmes, 1972). Critics, however, argue that this hypothesis is overly simplistic (Luborsky & McMullen, 1999). For example, in the United States, even when life expectancy was lower and there were fewer older adults in the population, attitudes toward age were not consistently positive (Achenbaum, 1978). Evidence for negative attitudes toward elders is found in current preindustrialized societies. Conversely, in some highly developed countries older adults are treated with reverence and respect and are well provided for through health care and economic security programs. The status of older adults in a given society is determined by many complex factors.

Related to the concept of ageism is the **multiple jeopardy hypothesis** (Ferraro & Farmer, 1996) which states that older individuals who fit more than one discriminated-against category are affected by biases against each of these categorizations. Thus women are subject to ageism and sexism, and minority-status women are subject to racism, ageism, and sexism. Heterosexism and classism (biases against people of working class backgrounds) further add to multiple jeopardy. These systematic biases interact with age to produce greater risk for discrimination in attitudes and the provision of services to specific subgroups of older adults.

One alternative to the multiple jeopardy hypothesis is the age-as-leveler view, which proposes that as people become older, age overrides all other "isms." Older adults, regardless of what characteristics have been applied to them, become victims of the same stereotypes. In this view, minorities and women are no more disadvantaged than other persons of their age. A second alternative is the inoculation hypothesis, which proposes that older minorities and women become immune to the effects of ageism through years of exposure to discrimination and stereotyping. These years help them to develop a tolerance, so that they are better able to withstand the negative attitudes applied to older adults than their counterparts.

The process known as the **social clock**, the normative expectations for the ages at which major life events should occur (Hagestad & Neugarten, 1985), may account for some of the preoccupation that people have with age. Events such as parenthood have a biological component; other life events are based on calendars that are set by society, such as the need to establish one's career by the early 30s. Such events are evaluated according to whether they are "on-time" or "off-time" with regard to the social clock. When a person's life is off-time, the individual may feel a great deal of personal distress and perhaps criticism from others who expect people to follow the normative prescriptions for their age group. Nonevents, which are the failure to experience an expected life change, may have as much of an influence on an individual's life as actual events.

Increasingly, however, individuals are setting their own unique social clocks, as exemplified by people like former astronaut and Ohio senator John Glenn. At the age of 77, Glenn joined the space shuttle *Discovery* crew on a 9-day orbital mission. His ability to meet the arduous physical requirements of the voyage was aptly captured in his statement: "Too many people, when they get old, think that they have to live by the calendar."

These views of ageism become important in examining the health and well-being of older adults. Interestingly enough, neither ageism nor multiple jeopardy appears to have deleterious effects on feelings of happiness and well-being, a topic we explore in Chapter 14. However, the effects of less access to health care and exposure to negative views of aging on those who are subjected to the "isms" may take their toll on physical health and therefore are a matter of vital concern.

For many people, the social clock provides a measure of evaluating their life's successes.

PSYCHOLOGICAL MODELS OF DEVELOPMENT IN ADULTHOOD

In the broadest sense, psychological models attempt to explain the development of the "person" in the person–environment equation from the standpoint of how adaptive abilities unfold over the course of life. It is taken as a given that the body undergoes significant changes, but of interest within the psychological approaches are the changes that occur in the individual's self-understanding, ability to adjust to life's challenges, and perspective on the world.

Erikson's Psychosocial Theory

Perhaps the best known life span psychological theory is Erik Erikson's (1963), which focuses on the development of the self or **ego** through a series of eight stages. In this theory, each stage of development is defined as a crisis in which particular stage-specific issues present themselves as challenges to the individual's ego. The theory is called **psychosocial**, but could easily be characterized by the term biopsychosocial. Figure 2.4 illustrates the eight-stage matrix.

Erikson proposed that individuals pass through a series of transitions in which they are particularly vulnerable to a complex interaction of biological, psychological, and social forces characteristic of their period of life. For example, during the intimacy versus isolation stage, the young adult is biologically capable of engaging in sexual relationships, psychologically capable of serious emotional involvement with another adult, and socially expected to "settle down" and find a partner. The "crisis" is not truly a crisis in the sense of being a catastrophe or disaster. Instead, each psychosocial stage is a time during which the individual may move closer to either a positive or negative resolution of a particular psychosocial issue. The success of this resolution is measured by favorable or unfavorable attributes. These attributes are qualities of the ego that will develop based on how the crisis is resolved. Depending on the outcome of the stage, you will be more or less able to adapt to the changing demands that life presents to you.

Another aspect crucial to Erikson's theory is the **epigenetic principle**, which asserts that each stage unfolds from the previous stage according to a predestined order. These stages are set in much the same manner as the programming for the biological development of the individual throughout life. They are built, according to Erikson, into the hard-wiring of the human being.

Erikson's theory has fascinated researchers and developmental theorists, in part because of his compelling writing and in part because it presents an organized, cohesive view of development from birth to death. The matrix of ages by stages, which forms the heart of the theory, is elegant but deceptively simple. At first glance, it might appear that development proceeds in a series of steps moving steadily from childhood to old age. However, a more careful inspection shows that the diagonal line is not the

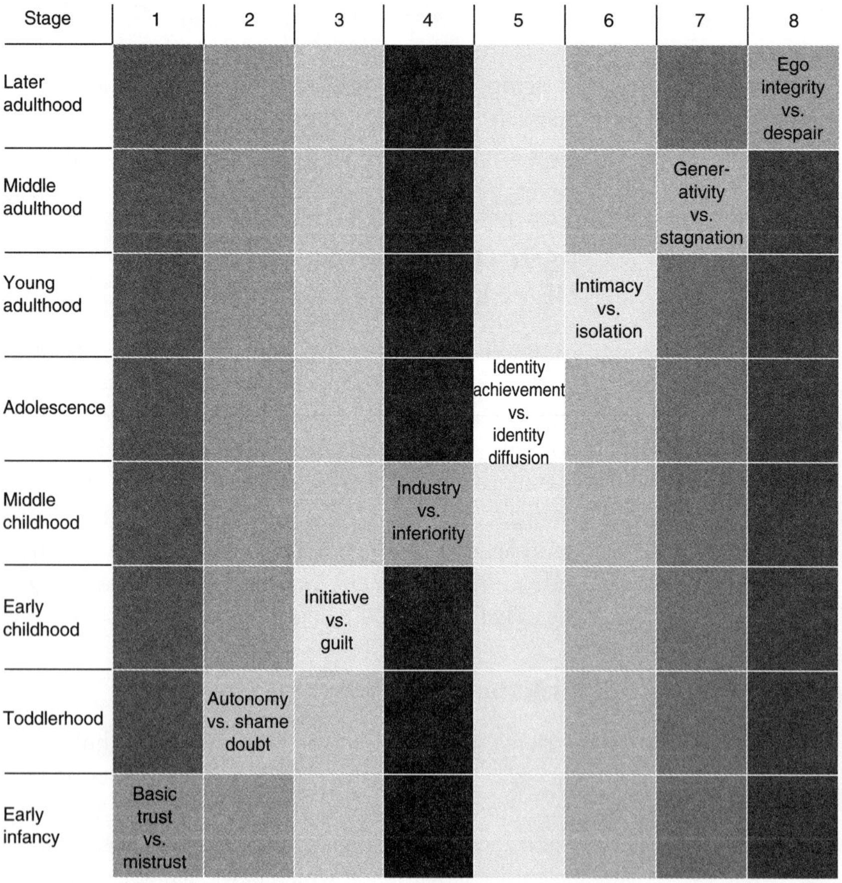

Stage	1	2	3	4	5	6	7	8
Later adulthood								Ego integrity vs. despair
Middle adulthood							Generativity vs. stagnation	
Young adulthood						Intimacy vs. isolation		
Adolescence					Identity achievement vs. identity diffusion			
Middle childhood				Industry vs. inferiority				
Early childhood			Initiative vs. guilt					
Toddlerhood		Autonomy vs. shame doubt						
Early infancy	Basic trust vs. mistrust							

FIGURE 2.4

Stages in Erikson's Psychosocial Theory

Source: Adapted from Erikson, E. H. (1963). *Childhood and society* (2nd ed.). New York: Norton.

only possibility for development of the ego, although it may be the most evident. The matrix format implies that developments may occur in boxes outside of the diagonal line. Thus, the issues characterizing each stage (such as Trust versus Mistrust for infancy) may coexist as relevant concerns throughout adulthood. Any stage may reach ascendancy in response to events that stimulate its reappearance.

Consider the example of an 80-year-old woman who is mugged while walking on a city sidewalk, robbed of her purse, and left emotionally shaken and in pain. This incident may traumatize her for some time and in the process, she becomes fearful of leaving her home. In Eriksonian terms, she is reliving the issues of "trust" experienced in infancy, and must regain the feeling of safety in her environment. The woman may also be left feeling vulnerable that with her increasing years, declines in her physical functioning have made her a target. Autonomy may be revisited as an issue in later adulthood when the individual begins to experience limitations in mobility associated with the physical aging process (Erikson, Erikson, & Kivnick, 1986).

Another implication of the epigenetic matrix is that a crisis may be experienced before its "time." A 35-year-old woman diagnosed with breast cancer may be faced with issues relevant to mortality, precipitating her to contemplate the psychosocial issues that normally confront much older people. The crisis stages can be considered "critical periods" during which certain issues are most likely to be prominent, but they are not meant to be discrete steps that proceed from youth to old age.

Given these qualifications regarding the correspondence of the stages with chronological age, let us move on to look at the stages that most typically are associated with the adult years. The first of the eight stages directly relevant to adulthood is **Identity Achievement versus Identity Diffusion**. This stage first emerges in adolescence, yet continues to hold importance throughout adulthood and forms a cornerstone of subsequent adult psychosocial crises (Erikson, Erikson, & Kivnick 1986; Whitbourne & Connolly, 1999). An individual who achieves a clear identity has a coherent sense of purpose regarding the future and a sense of continuity with the past. By contrast, identity diffusion involves a lack of direction, vagueness about life's purposes, and an unclear sense of self.

Mentoring is one activity associated with generativity; as shown here, this older worker is trying to give helpful advice to his younger colleague.

Intimacy versus Isolation is the next stage to emerge in early adulthood. The attainment of intimacy involves establishing a mutually satisfying close relationship with another person to whom a lifelong commitment is made. We can think of the perfect intimate relationship as the intersection of two identities but not a total overlap because each partner preserves a sense of separateness. The state of isolation represents the other end of the spectrum, in which a person never achieves true mutuality with a life partner. Theoretically, isolation is more likely to develop in individuals who lack a strong identity because establishing close relationships with others depends to some extent on how securely formed the individual's sense of self is.

The motive for caring for the next generation emerges from the resolution of the intimacy psychosocial crisis. The stage of **Generativity versus Stagnation** focuses on the psychosocial issues of procreation, productivity, and creativity. The most common pathway to generativity is through parenthood, an endeavor that involves direct care of the next generation. However, individuals who do not have children can nevertheless develop generativity through such activities as teaching, mentoring, or supervising younger people. A career that involves producing something of value that future generations can enjoy is another form of generativity. The main feature of generativity is a feeling of concern over what happens to the younger generation, along with a desire to make the world a better place for them. Stagnation, by contrast, occurs when the individual turns concern and energy inward or solely to others of one's own age group rather than to the next generation. A person who is high on the quality of stagnation lacks interest or may even go so far as to reject the younger generation. Of course, being a parent is no guarantee of achieving generativity; the crucial component of generativity is concern and care for the people who will follow one's own generation.

Toward the end of adulthood, individuals face psychosocial issues related to aging and facing their mortality, and enter into the stage of **Ego Integrity versus Despair**. Older individuals who establish a strong sense of ego integrity can look back at their experiences with acceptance. Ego integrity also involves an ability to look at and accept the positive and negative attributes of one's life and self, even if it may be painful to acknowledge past mistakes or personal flaws. This sense of acceptance of the past and present self allows the individual to also view mortality with the acceptance that life inevitably must end. It may be difficult for a young person to imagine how a person who is happy with life could also be happy with or at least not devastated by the thought of death. According to Erikson, acceptance of the past and present helps people attain acceptance of the end of life. In contrast, despair is the outcome of the individual's realization that death is unavoidable and that it will come too soon to make possible a righting of previous wrongs. The individual in a state of despair feels discontent with life and is melancholic, perhaps to the point of despondency, at the thought of death. Although this person's daily life is filled with unhappiness, the thought of life ending before past mistakes can be corrected is more frightening.

Erikson's views about development were a radical departure from the personality theories prevalent at the time of his work. His theory was proposed as a reaction to other psychologists who felt that human development was completely shaped, if not by childhood, then no later than adolescence. Erikson's radical re-envisioning of the life span challenged these notions by contending that development is a lifelong process, with struggles that help to mold and shape and reshape the individual. Identity, intimacy, generativity, and ego integrity are now considered central themes of adult development and inform much of what we cover in this book.

Piaget's Cognitive-Developmental Theory

Jean Piaget, a Swiss psychologist, became fascinated with the development of intelligence after watching his own young children at play as they explored their environment. Based on watching them gain mastery over their toys and surroundings, he theorized development as the reciprocal relationship between the child and the physical-social environment. Although the focus of Piaget's theory was cognitive development in childhood, the terms and concepts central to his theory can be applied more generally to a life span model of psychological functioning.

A major feature of Piaget's cognitive-development theory is the description of a series of stages occurring in childhood cognition. More generally, Piaget identified two basic ways in which people interact with their experiences. The process of **assimilation** is engaged when individuals interpret new experiences in terms of their existing mental structures, what he referred to as **schemas**. The term assimilation, in this context, does not have its common meaning, as when you say that a person has become assimilated to a new culture. In Piaget's model, assimilation has the opposite meaning, referring to the situation in which individuals try to fit their experiences into their schemas or current ways of viewing the world.

As an example, let's say that you have a very limited understanding of different varieties of birds. You may call all little birds "sparrows" and all large birds "crows." You are forcing into two categories what actually may be eight or ten different varieties of birds in your neighborhood. According to Piaget, people engage in this assimilative process until they are able to gain experiences that allow them to refine their concepts or schemas. If you go for a walk with an avid bird watcher who points out the differences among sparrows, finches, and chickadees (all small birds), you will emerge with a refinement to your previous categorization system. In Piaget's terms, you have changed your existing schema, a process he referred to as **accommodation**. Such processes occur throughout early development, as young children learn to differentiate and categorize objects in their world.

In Piaget's theory, children become better able to adapt to the world through alternating between assimilation and accommodation. The ideal state is one in which people are able to interpret experiences through a consistent framework (assimilation) but are able to change this framework when it no longer is helpful in organizing experiences (accommodation). Such an ideal state is referred to as **equilibrium**, and the process of achieving this balance is called equilibration.

Identity Process Theory

Integrating Erikson's and Piaget's theories provides an excellent vantage point for making predictions about psychosocial development in adulthood and, in particular, the way that people adapt to the aging process. According to **identity process theory** (Whitbourne, Sneed, & Skultety, 2002), the processes of assimilation and accommodation can account for interactions between the individual and experiences through the schema or framework provided by identity.

In identity process theory, we assume that people approach their experiences from the vantage point provided by their personal identities, namely, their ideas or concepts about the self. Everyone has a certain bias to view oneself in a favorable light. Most people prefer a self-view that includes being physically and mentally competent, being liked by others, and adhering to such principles as honesty and concern for the welfare of others.

Using Piaget's terminology, **identity assimilation** refers to a tendency to interpret new experiences relevant to a person's self-view as competent, well liked, and ethical. A positive feature of identity assimilation is that people are able to feel happy and effective, despite being less than perfect. The downside of identity assimilation is when it leads to a distorted interpretation of experiences that challenge the rosy view people have of themselves. For example, receiving a bad grade on an exam could lead you to question your intelligence, which could ultimately compromise your self-esteem. Using identity assimilation, you might protect your self-esteem by blaming your score on the poorly written test or the ineptitude of the professor rather than questioning your own abilities.

Although identity assimilation preserves a positive view of the self, continual failure that people refuse to incorporate into their self-appraisals can ultimately have negative consequences. As with the example of the bird classification, it may be necessary to resolve a discrepancy between the self-view and reality of experiences that challenge these views in order for development to continue successfully. If you continue to blame the professor or the test for your poor grades, you will never find yourself at fault for your failures. Eventually, these limitations need to be confronted. Whether this signifies that

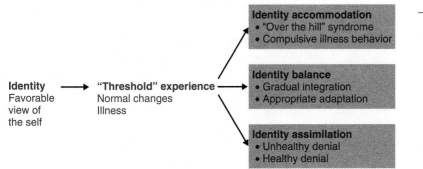

FIGURE 2.5

Identity Process Theory

People interpret "threshold" experiences in one of three ways: identity accommodation (changing your view of yourself), identity balance (maintaining a stable sense of yourself but making some changes), or identity assimilation (not changing your sense of self).

you are in the wrong major, are not studying hard enough, or may not be as smart as you once thought, learning to accept your imperfections is vital to your own growth. Ideally the realization of your flaws will trigger the process of **identity accommodation**, through which people change their identity to incorporate a view of the self that is not perfect.

Identity accommodation may seem like a negative process, but changing your self-view to include shortcomings can be advantageous. For example, people who successfully cope with a tragedy may find an inner strength they did not know existed. Turning one's life around after overcoming a battle with alcoholism represents the positive aspect to identity accommodation. As with identity assimilation, however, relying too heavily on identity accommodation can have destructive consequences. Individuals who define themselves entirely on the basis of their experiences, such as being viewed negatively by others, may be devastated by an event when they feel rejected. Imagine if every criticism ever leveled at you throughout your life caused you to question your personal qualities and think that you are a deeply flawed person. You would become extremely insecure and your identity would fail to include the central compass that would ultimately allow you to have confidence in your abilities.

Ideally, as in Piaget's theory, a balance between identity assimilation and identity accommodation can be achieved in adulthood. Piaget proposed that the natural tendency is to use assimilation when confronted with a new situation. People use what has worked in the past to help understand what is happening in the present. However, in order to adapt and be as well adjusted as possible, accommodation is necessary when the situation warrants changes. Though it would hardly be ideal to change your self-view completely when someone criticizes you, if the criticism is consistent enough and comes from enough different quarters, you may be well advised to look honestly at yourself and see whether something should be changed.

Throughout adulthood, identity processes are constantly brought to bear as changes to physical and cognitive functioning occur. These changes can be thought of as occurring through a sequence of phases over time, or a set of "multiple thresholds"

(Whitbourne & Collins, 1998). The **multiple threshold model** of change in adulthood proposes that individuals realize the fact that they are getting older through a stepwise process as aging-related changes occur. Each age-related change (such as wrinkling of the skin or a decreased reaction time) brings with it the potential for another threshold to be crossed. Areas of the greatest significance to identity are likely to be monitored with great care or vigilance, while thresholds not of great importance may be crossed with little thought. Your hair turning gray may be an area of particular concern and provide a threshold for you, but experiencing diminished weakness in your muscles is not. Someone else may feel oppositely, and disregard gray hair but fixate on the loss of muscle strength.

Whatever the area of greatest relevance, at the point of crossing a threshold, people are prompted to recognize the reality of the aging process in that particular area of functioning. It is during the process of moving from identity assimilation to identity accommodation through the occurrence of these thresholds that a new state of balance is reached. Ultimately, people will only be able to adapt to age-related changes once they have examined the meaning of the change and incorporated it into their existing view of the self.

Figure 2.5 illustrates how a person's identity can influence the reactions to age-related changes. Experiences are interpreted in terms of existing identity, which, for most people, has a positive value. Then a "threshold" experience occurs, such as noticing an age-related change, experiencing a health problem, or feeling a loss of a valued cognitive skill. At that point, people use one of the three identity processes to navigate.

In **identity accommodation**, the threshold experience is taken very seriously, to the point that the person completely redefines his or her identity. You might know someone who complains about feeling out of breath or in pain after an arduous workout, who then decides to quit engaging in that activity due to being "over the hill." It is also possible that such an experience leads the person to become preoccupied with this change, worrying incessantly about the consequences of this change, and doing everything possible to avoid or stop the change.

For many people, age-related changes in appearance serve to stimulate changes in identity.

The term "senior moment" is one that has unfortunately (in our opinion) gained popularity among Baby Boomers, and provides an interesting example of how overuse of identity accommodation can lead to problems. Generally used as a humorous explanation for forgetting a well-known piece of information such as someone's name or telephone number, the phrase "having a senior moment" is often applied to any instance of memory lapse. The use of this term represents, from an identity perspective, crossing the memory threshold. Despite the joking tone of the phrase, for people with serious concerns about age-related memory loss, it may take on a more ominous tone. We will revisit this topic later in Chapter 6 when we cover the dynamic relationship between a self-fulfilling prophecy and memory loss; we explore the idea that memories worsen with age because people expect them to do so.

Overuse of identity accommodation is a maladaptive way to react to age-related changes, as it can lead people to feel a total loss of control over their fate. Similarly, overuse of identity assimilation also presents problems. One scenario takes the form of unhealthy denial in which people fail to take advantage of preventative measures designed to maintain optimal functioning. For instance, individuals exhibiting unhealthy denial may continue to eat foods high in fat and sugar, refuse to exercise, or carry on harmful behaviors such as smoking. They mistakenly fail to see that they are aging and that these behaviors, especially when carried out to excess, will take their toll on their physical functioning if not cause them to develop a terminal illness. Though unhealthy denial can be detrimental to an individual, there can also be a form of denial that is healthy in which people do not become overly preoccupied with the deeper implications of age-related changes. Healthy deniers continue or begin engaging in preventive behaviors, without overthinking their actions and reflecting at length about their own mortality.

Identity balance is the most positive way to react to age-related changes. People who use identity balance accept that they are aging without adopting a defeatist attitude. Individuals engaging in identity balance take steps to ensure that they will remain healthy, but do not become preoccupied with conditions or limitations they may already have developed. Additionally, they are not deluded by thinking that they will be young forever.

The advantages of identity balance (and to an extent healthy denial) are that the older adult adopts an active "use it or lose it" approach to the aging process. By remaining active, people can delay or prevent many if not most age-related negative changes. On the other hand, there are many "bad habits" or ways in which a person's behavior can accelerate the aging process. Some of the most common negative behaviors, described in Chapter 1, include overexposure to the sun and smoking. Ideally, people adapt to the aging process by taking advantage of the use-it-or-lose-it approach and avoiding the bad habits. Less of a strain will be placed on both identity assimilation and accommodation if people can maintain functioning designed to promote good health for as long as possible.

BIOLOGICAL APPROACHES TO AGING IN ADULTHOOD

Biological changes throughout later life, as is true in the years of infancy, childhood, and adolescence, are based on genetically determined events or changes in physiological functioning brought about by intrinsic changes within the organism. As we discussed at the beginning of this chapter, the interactionist model of development predicts that environmental factors influence the expression of biological or genetic predispositions. According to the principle of reciprocity, the individual's activities interact with preset biological programs based on genetic inheritance. The result is that relatively large individual differences occur in the nature and timing of age-related changes in physical and cognitive functioning. Ultimately, the aging of the body sets the limit of the **life span**, but compensation through behavioral measures for many of the changes associated with the aging process alters the timing of these events. Inevitably, the body's biological clock continues to record the years.

Having acknowledged this "fact of life" about the biological aging process, the next step is to question why aging happens. Why do living organisms grow old and die? If you are a fan of science fiction, you have surely read stories of a world in which biological aging does not occur, or develops at a different rate so that people live for hundreds of years. While these fictional accounts may be engrossing and even tempting to imagine, there are some obvious problems associated with prolonged or eternal life. Outcomes such as overpopulation, a lack of adequate resources, and intergenerational strife are just some of the possibilities. Birth rates would be reduced to a virtual standstill to account for the overpopulation.

The problems of a static society highlight the fact that while the process of death may be unpleasant, it also keeps the cycle of life moving along. Perhaps it is far more "efficient" to have a world in which the older generation is continually turned over, making room for new generations whose entry into the population assures its vitality.

The idea that aging is the result of a correctable defect in living organisms underlies concepts of some of the major biological theories that we will turn to shortly. Also reflected is the theory that organisms are programmed to survive until they reach sexual maturity. Having guaranteed the survival of their species, organisms are programmed to deteriorate or diminish once the genes programmed to keep them alive past that point are no longer of use to the species. Biologically speaking, reproduction is the primary purpose of life, and once this criterion has been met, there are no longer guidelines for what happens next.

Genes and DNA

Inherited characteristics are found in the **genome**, the complete set of instructions for "building" all the cells that make up an organism (see Figure 2.6). The human genome is found in each nucleus of a person's many trillions of cells. The genome for each living creature consists of tightly coiled threads of the molecule **deoxyribonucleic acid** (**DNA**). DNA resides in the nucleus of the body's cells as two long, paired strands spiraled into a double helix, a shape that resembles a twisted ladder. The components of DNA encode the information needed to manufacture proteins, which are large, complex molecules made up of long chains of subunits called amino acids. Protein is the primary component of all living things. There are many kinds of proteins, each with different functions. Some proteins provide structure to the cells of the body, whereas other proteins called enzymes

FIGURE 2.6

From Genome to Protein

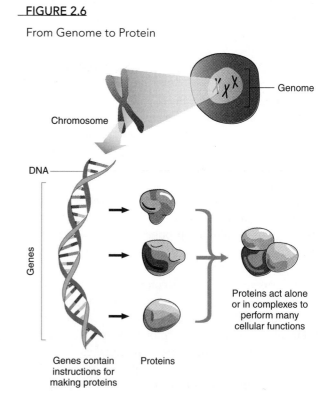

assist biochemical reactions that take place within the cells. Antibodies are proteins that function in the immune system to identify foreign invaders that need to be removed from the body. The entire process of protein manufacture is orchestrated by the genetic code contained in DNA.

A **gene** is a functional unit of a DNA molecule carrying a particular set of instructions for producing a specific protein. Human genes vary widely in length, but only about 10% of the genome actually contains sequences of genes used to code proteins. The rest of the genome contains sequences of bases that have no apparent coding or any other function. Some of the proteins that the genes encode provide basic housekeeping functions in the cell. These genes constantly stay active in many types of cells; more typically, a cell activates just the genes needed at the moment and suppresses the rest. Through this process of selective activation of genes, the cell becomes a skin cell, for example, rather than a bone cell.

The genome is organized into **chromosomes**, which are distinct, physically separate units of coiled threads of DNA and associated protein molecules. In humans, there are two sets of 23 chromosomes, one set contributed by each parent. Each set has 23 single chromosomes: 22 are called "autosomes" and contain nonsex-linked information, and the 23rd is the X or Y sex chromosome. The presence of the Y chromosome determines maleness, so that a normal female has a pair of X chromosomes and a male has an X and Y pair. Although each chromosome contains the same genes, there is no rhyme or reason to the distribution of genes on chromosomes. A gene that produces a protein that influences eye color may be next to a gene that is involved in cellular energy production.

Genes may undergo alterations, called **mutations**, when DNA reproduces itself. When a gene contains a mutation, the protein encoded by that gene will most likely be abnormal. Sometimes the protein can function despite the damage, but in other cases, it becomes completely disabled. If a protein vital to survival becomes severely damaged, the results of the mutation can be serious. Genetic mutations are either inherited from a parent or acquired over the course of one's life. Inherited mutations originate from the DNA of the cells involved in reproduction (sperm and egg). When reproductive cells containing mutations are combined in one's offspring, the mutation is in all the bodily cells of that offspring. Inherited mutations are responsible for diseases such as cystic fibrosis and sickle cell anemia. They also may predispose an individual to developing cancer, major psychiatric illnesses, and other complex diseases.

Acquired mutations are changes in DNA that develop throughout a person's lifetime. Remarkably, cells possess the ability to repair many of these mutations. If these repair mechanisms fail, however, the mutation can be passed along to future copies of the altered cell. Mutations can also occur in the mitochondrial DNA, which is the DNA found in the tiny structures within the cell called mitochondria. These structures are crucial to the functioning of the cell because they are involved in producing cellular energy.

Biologists have provided many fascinating perspectives on the aging process. The completion of the Human Genome Project in 2003 and progress by the International HapMap project (Frazer et al., 2007) paved the way for researchers to identify successful analytic techniques to map complete sets of DNA. Genome-wide association studies, in which the entire genome is searched for genetic variations related to complex diseases, offer a promising avenue for aging research. Hundreds of studies have successfully identified novel genes involved in aging-related diseases such as heart failure (Velagaleti & O'Donnell, 2010), Alzheimer's disease (Harold et al., 2009), and osteoarthritis (Richards et al., 2009). For around $1,000, you can have your entire genome scanned, and receive a personal genetic profile that calculates your risk of developing certain diseases. As exciting as this research is, it is important to keep in mind that genetic variations do not account solely for the likelihood of disease progression; environmental variables (and their interaction with genetic variables) play an important role in disease development.

Programmed Aging Theories

The biological theories of aging are divided into two categories (Hayflick, 1994): programmed aging and random error. Programmed aging theories are based on the assumption that aging and death are built into the hard-wiring of all organisms. Following from this assumption is the notion that there are "aging genes" that count off the years past maturity, just as "development genes" lead to the point of maturity in youth. One argument long used to support this assumption is based on the fact that the life span varies according to species, suggesting that life span is part of an organism's genetic makeup. For example, butterflies have life spans of 12 weeks, and giant tortoises have life spans of 180 years. Humans, the mammals with the longest life spans, have life spans of 120 years.

The relationship between the age span of a species and the age of its death (or life span), is expressed in the **Gompertz equation**, a mathematical function showing the relationship between age and probability of death. The originator, Benjamin Gompertz, was an 18th-century British mathematician who worked as an actuary, a profession where the financial impact of risk is calculated. In 1825 he applied calculus to

mortality data and showed that the mortality rate increases in a geometric progression with age. When plotted as a logarithmic function, it takes the form of a straight line. Figure 2.7 compares the Gompertz functions of several species of field and deer mice (Sacher, 1977). The horizontal axis of this graph shows the age of the organism in days with the longest-living species reaching about 9 years and the shortest-living for about one year. The vertical axis shows the death rate per day and the plot points show the number that die per day with increasing age of the species. There is a different Gompertz function for each species, supporting the idea that longevity is an inherited, species-specific trait.

Findings in support of genetic theories are particularly intriguing in view of the considerable progress being made in the field of genetics. The

FIGURE 2.7

Gompertz Curve

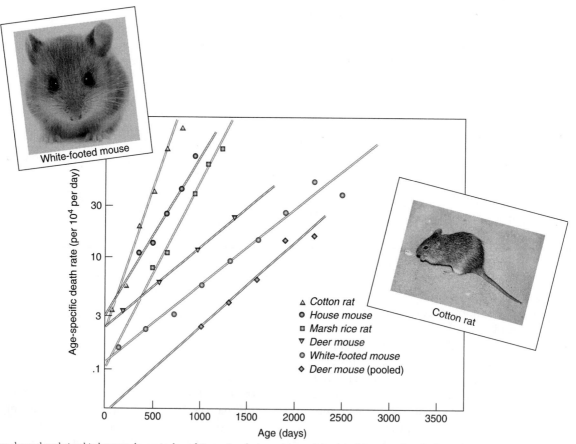

This figure shows the relationship between the age in days of six species of mice and rats and the rate of dying per day. The fact that different species have different functions supports the notion of genetic contributions to longevity.

Source: Sacher, G. A. (1977). Life table modification and life prolongation. In C. E. Finch & L. Hayflick (Eds.), *Handbook of the biology of aging* (pp. 582–638). New York: Van Nostrand Reinhold.

FIGURE 2.8

FIGURE 2.8

The Telomere Theory of Aging

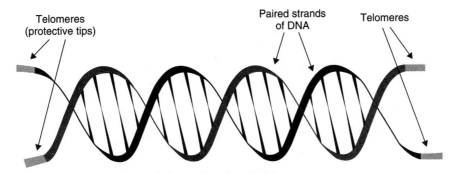

According to the telomere theory, aging is caused by loss of telomeres from the ends of chromosomes.

ability to identify and then control the "aging" gene or genes would go a long way toward changing the very nature of aging. However, despite the appeal of a genetic theory based on the concept that one or multiple genes control the aging process from birth to death, there are limitations in this approach. We cannot say for sure that evolution has selected for the aging process so that old generations die in order to make room for new ones. Historically, few species survived long enough to be exposed to the evolutionary selection process.

A more defensible alterative to genetic theory is that evolution has selected for species that are vigorous up to the point that sexual maturity has passed. In the postreproductive years, "good genes gone bad" (Hayflick, 1994) take over and lead to the ultimate destruction of the organism. Researchers continue to investigate the notion that the very genes that have a positive effect on development during early life create susceptibility to a variety of diseases in later life (Caruso et al., 2000). For example, senescent cells may act as a protective device against the replication of cancerous cells. The senescent cells, in turn, are eliminated by the immune system. However, the immune system does not destroy all of the senescent cells, and so they continue to remain present in the body's tissues (Hornsby, 2009).

The most compelling attempts to explain aging through genetics are based on the principle of **replicative senescence**, or the loss of the ability of cells to reproduce. Scientists have long known that there are a finite number of times (about 50) that normal human cells can proliferate in culture before they become terminally incapable of further division (Hayflick, 1994).

Until relatively recently, scientists did not know why cells had a limited number of divisions. It was only when the technology needed to look closely at the chromosome developed that researchers uncovered some of the mystery behind this process.

As we saw in Figure 2.6, the chromosome is made up largely of DNA. However, at either end of the chromosomes are **telomeres**, repeating sequences of proteins that contain no genetic information (see Figure 2.8). The primary function of the telomere is to protect the chromosome from damage. With each cell division, the telomeres become shorter, ultimately altering patterns of gene expression affecting the functioning of the cell and the organ system in which it operates. Once telomeres shorten to the point of no longer being able to protect the chromosome, adjacent chromosomes fuse, the cell cycle is halted, and ultimately the cell dies (Shin, Hong, Solomon, & Lee, 2006). Evidence linking telomere length to mortality in humans suggests that the telomeres may ultimately hold the key to understanding the aging process (Cluett & Melzer, 2009).

However, biology does not completely explain the loss of telomeres over the course of life. Supporting the idea of biopsychosocial interactions in development, researchers have linked telomere length to social factors. Analyzing blood samples from more than 1,500 female twins, researchers in the United Kingdom determined that telomere length was shorter in women from lower socioeconomic classes (Cherkas et al., 2006). There was a difference of seven "biological years" (measured in terms of telomeres) between twins with manual jobs and their co-twins in higher-ranking occupations. The researchers attributed this difference to the stress of being in a lower-level occupation in which people have less control over their day-to-day activities. Body mass index, smoking, and lack of exercise were additional factors influencing telomere length. A subsequent study on this sample provided further research of the important role of lifestyle factors. Even after the researchers adjusted for such factors as age, socioeconomic status, smoking, and body mass index, people who engaged in higher levels of physical activity had longer telomeres than those who did not (Cherkas et al., 2008).

Although many cells in the body are thought to be affected by the shortening of the telomeres, not all experience this effect of the aging process. For example, when tumor cells are added to normal cells, they replicate indefinitely. Because of the danger posed by these multiplying tumor cells, senescence may be thought of as a form of protection against cancer. The key to extending the life span based on the telomere theory would be for scientists to find a way to keep cells replicating longer without increasing the risk of cancer cell proliferation (Ohtani, Mann, & Hara, 2009).

Random Error Theories

Random error theories are based on the assumption that aging reflects unplanned changes in an organism over time. The wear and tear theory of aging is one that many people implicitly refer to when they say they feel that they are "falling apart" as they get older. According to this view, the body, like a car, acquires more and more damage as it is exposed to daily wear and tear from weather, use, accidents, and mechanical insults. Programmed aging theories, in contrast, would suggest that the car was not "built to last," but rather was meant to deteriorate over time in a systematic fashion. (See Table 2.2.)

Cross-linking theory proposes that aging causes deleterious changes in **collagen**, the fibrous protein that makes up about one quarter of all bodily proteins (see Figure 2.9). Collagen provides structure to many of the body's tissues, such as the skin, tendons, muscle, and cartilage. The collagen molecule is composed of three chains of amino acids wound together in a tight helix. Strands of collagen molecules are attached through horizontal strands of cross-linking proteins,

TABLE 2.2
Random Error Theories of Aging

	Brief Summary	*Supporting Evidence*
Cross-linking	• Collagen molecules form cross-links	• Cross-links do increase in older organisms
Free radical	• Free radicals cause destructive changes in cells	• Mixed data on anti-oxidants, caloric restriction and resveretrol
Error catastrophe	• Mutations lead to deleterious changes	• Errors in mitochondrial DNA may be a source of harmful changes

similar to rungs on a ladder. Increasingly with age, the rungs of one ladder start to connect to the rungs of another ladder, causing the molecules to become increasingly rigid and shrink in size. The process of cross-linking occurs because exposure to certain types of sugars leads to a process known as glycation, which in turn leads to the formation of what are called advanced glycation end-products (appropriately named "AGE"). The AGEs induce cross-linking of collagen, which in turn increases, for example, stiffness of skeletal muscle and cartilage (Semba, Bandinelli, Sun, Guralnik, & Ferrucci, 2010).

An issue yet to be determined is whether cross-linking theory adequately explains the cause of aging or whether it describes a process that occurs due to the passage of time and cumulative damage caused by a lifetime of exposure to sugar in the diet. The **free radical** theory, or oxidative stress theory (Sohal, 2002), focuses on a set of unstable compounds known as free radicals, produced when certain molecules in cells react with oxygen. The primary goal of a free radical is to seek out and bind to other molecules. When this occurs, the molecule attacked by the free radical loses functioning. Although oxidation caused by free radicals is a process associated with increasing age, researchers have questioned the utility of this approach as a general theory of aging (Perez et al., 2009). Antioxidants, chemicals that prevent the formation of free radicals and contain superoxide dimutase (SOD), are advertised widely as an antidote to aging since they destroy free radicals. No doubt you have seen advertisements that promote the intake of foods high in vitamins E

FIGURE 2.9

Diagram of a Collagen Molecule

Collagen is a long fibrous protein whose strands form a triple helix. It makes up much of the connective tissue in the body (skin, cartilage, tendons, bone, lens of the eye) so when it forms cross-links, these tissues become less flexible.

and C, including grapes, blueberries, strawberries, and walnuts. However, other than perhaps having slight beneficial effects on cognitive functioning (Joseph, Shukitt-Hale, & Willis, 2009), there is no evidence that intake of these foods will slow down the aging process (Lapointe & Hekimi, 2010; Park, Tedesco, & Johnson, 2009).

One implication of the free radical theory relates to caloric restriction. Biologist Roy Walford devoted his career to proving the **caloric restriction hypothesis**, the view that restriction of caloric intake is the key to prolonging life (Walford, Mock, Verdery, & MacCallum, 2002). Caloric restriction is thought to have a beneficial impact in part because it reduces the formation of free radicals. After many years of experimental research involving nonhuman species, particularly rodents, evidence is beginning to emerge to support the value of caloric restriction in humans, with or without exercise (Lefevre et al., 2009).

Promising findings regarding free radical theory suggest that resveratrol, a natural compound found in grapes and consequently wine, is a highly potent antioxidant. Levels of resveratrol are highest among varieties of red wine. Laboratory mice fed on a high-calorie diet plus resveratrol had a survival rate approximating that of mice on a normal diet, both of whom had higher survival rates (but not longevity rates) than animals on a high-calorie diet (Pearson et al., 2008). Exercise further increases the life-enhancing effect of resveratrol (Murase, Haramizu,

Ota, & Hase, 2009). Although it has now become fairly well established that red wine is related to reduced effects of aging, researchers debate the cause of these positive effects. Rather than having its effects through mechanisms involving free radicals, other researchers propose that red wine's benefits are the result of procyanidins, tannins present in red wine, which have beneficial effects on the arteries.

The autoimmune theory proposes that aging is due to faulty immune system functioning. In addition to a loss of the immune system's ability to do its job in fighting off the invasion of bacteria and viruses into the body, the immune system mistakenly recognizes cells of invading organisms rather than the cells of the body. When autoimmunity occurs, the body attacks its own cells, causing damage to bodily tissues. Autoimmunity is at the heart of certain diseases prevalent in older adults, such as some forms of arthritis, systemic lupus erythematosus, and cancer (Larbi, Fulop, & Pawelec, 2008).

Error theories propose that mutations acquired over the organism's lifetime lead to malfunctioning of the body's cells. According to one variant of this theory, the error catastrophe theory, random errors are not solely responsible for changes associated with aging, but rather errors in the manufacturing of proteins, a process that plays a key role in the maintenance of the body's cells. Similar to a bridge that suddenly collapses after unrepaired damage is allowed to accumulate over the years, the impairment in the cell would lead to widespread tissue and organ malfunction. Although researchers have not established error catastrophe as a generalized process leading to aging, evidence of its applicability to certain age-related diseases (as well as more widespread changes throughout the bodily tissues) has emerged along with new techniques to analyze these processes (Amara et al., 2008). The source of the errors is thought to be in the mitochondrial DNA (Kukat & Trifunovic, 2009).

As we can see, biologists have made significant advancements in trying to solve the puzzle of why humans and our counterparts across the animal kingdom experience the changes associated with aging that eventually lead to death. At the present time, genetic theories are considered more likely to hold the ultimate answer, but other approaches cannot yet be ruled out. Furthermore, though it is likely that aging ultimately will be accounted for by a combination of these theories, it is also likely that some theories provide better ways to understand age-related changes in the body than others. Rather than exploring one overarching theory, many researchers take the approach of applying specific theories to specific alterations with age in particular organ systems or tissues, such as using cross-linking theory to explain changes in the body's connective tissues.

In looking at perspectives on the aging process that derive from the social sciences, it is important to keep in mind the central role of biological factors. These factors form the "nature" component to the complex "nature–nurture" interactions assumed to characterize development in the adult years. Clearly all three models must be brought to bear in attempting to understand the complexities of nature and nurture.

SUMMARY

1. The life span perspective is increasingly replacing the view of development as ending in adolescence. Current life span models emphasize contextual influences on development, and the term "developmental science" is emerging to reflect the need to take a broad, interdisciplinary approach to the study of change over time.

2. Interactionist models of development emphasize processes such as niche-picking in which there is a reciprocal interaction between the individual and the environment. Organismic models regard development as an unfolding of genetic processes, and mechanistic models emphasize the role of the environment in shaping development. Interactionist models include the concepts of multidimensionality and multidirectionality, and they regard plasticity as an important element of development. Reciprocal processes in which individuals affect and are affected by their environment are a focus of interactionist models. The biopsychosocial perspective fits within the interactionist model.

3. Sociocultural models of development emphasize the effects of the environment on individuals, focusing on variables such as age and sex structures within the population, income, and social class. The life course perspective highlights age-related norms, roles, and attitudes as influences on individuals. Ecological perspectives examine multiple levels of organization within the environment, such as the proximal social relational level and the sociocultural level.

4. Ageism is a set of stereotyped views about older adults, reflected in negative as well as positive images. Some historians believe that older adults were more highly regarded in preindustrial societies, a view known as the modernization hypothesis. However, it appears that mixed views of aging have existed throughout history and across cultures. Theories that relate the well-being of the older individual to the level of social involvement include disengagement theory, activity theory, and continuity theory. These propose different relationships between individuals and society. According to the multiple jeopardy hypothesis of aging, older adults who are of minority status and are female face more discrimination than White male individuals.

5. Erikson's psychosocial development theory is an important psychological model of development in adulthood. It proposes a series of eight psychosocial crisis stages that correspond roughly to age periods in life in the growth of psychological functions. The eight stages follow the epigenetic principle, which means that each stage builds on the ones that come before it. However, later stages can appear at earlier ages, and early stages can reappear later in life. According to Piaget's theory of development, individuals gain in the ability to adapt to the environment through the processes of assimilation and accommodation. The ideal state of development is one of equilibration or balance. According to the identity process theory, identity assimilation and identity accommodation operate throughout development in adulthood as the individual interacts with experiences. The multiple threshold model was proposed as an explanation of how identity processes influence the interpretation of age-related events such as changes in physical or cognitive functioning.

6. There are two major categories of biological theories, all of which regard aging as the result of

changes in the biological makeup of the organism. Programmed aging theories are based on the observation that species differ in life spans (represented by the Gompertz equation) and propose that aging is genetically determined. The telomere theory, which emerged in part from observations of replicative senescence, proposes that cells are limited in the number of times they can reproduce by the fact that each replication involves a loss of the protective ends of chromosomes known as telomeres. Random error theories view aging as an accident resulting from cellular processes that have gone awry. Studies on caloric restriction provide support for the free radical theory, which also proposes that antioxidants can slow down the aging process.

3

The Study of Adult Development

Aging is inherently linked with the passage of time. The relationship between age and time presents a dilemma that researchers in adult development and aging must confront when designing and implementing research. As difficult as it is to understand the nature of change over time, the importance of such research is crucial to the scientific understanding of the aging process. Without empirical data, there would be little basis for establishing an understanding of how the aging process affects people. In this chapter, we examine the methodologies designed by researchers to capture information that can gain an accurate view of development in adulthood and later life.

VARIABLES IN DEVELOPMENTAL RESEARCH

A variable is a characteristic that "varies" from individual to individual. Behavioral scientists attempt to understand why some people are higher on a particular variable while others may be lower on the same variable. The variable on which people

are observed to differ is the **dependent variable** in research designs, and is often referred to as the outcome variable. The **independent variable** explains or "causes" the range of scores on the dependent variable. Although developmental psychologists classify age as an independent variable, age is truly not "independent" because its value cannot be controlled or manipulated, as you will read more about shortly. To overcome this challenge, methodologists have devised a range of statistical techniques designed to handle the complex nature of age.

An **experimental design**, often considered the gold standard of research, involves the manipulation of an independent variable followed by the measurement of scores on the dependent variable. Respondents are randomly assigned to treatment and control groups and then measured on the dependent variable. It is assumed that people vary on the dependent measure because they were exposed to different levels of the independent variable. Clinical trials typically compare the effectiveness of a drug on one group compared to another, and can provide compelling experimental evidence regarding cause and effect.

and Aging: Research Methods

The use of experimental designs in the study of adult development presents a problem given that age is not a true independent variable. People cannot be randomly assigned to an age group. This means that you can never state with certainty that aging "caused" people to receive certain scores on a dependent variable of interest. What you can establish is whether different age groups varied in their responses to different levels of the independent variable. If a manipulation produces a different effect in a younger age group than in an older one, you may infer that the treatment has some relationship to age.

For example, consider an experiment in which special instructions are given for a memory test to a younger and an older age group. If the performance significantly improved across both age groups but to a greater degree for the older adults, you could deduce that age is related to sensitivity to the type of manipulation involved in these instructions. This is an example of an interaction between variables—the manipulation affects both groups, but the effect is stronger for one group than for the other. Important to remember in this situation is that random assignment to age group is impossible. The study of

aging therefore presents a methodological challenge. Even in the above example, you are not able to determine that age "caused" differences in responses to the treatment groups.

Instead, studies of aging use the **quasi-experimental design**, the term used to describe the process of comparing groups on predetermined characteristics. You cannot conclude that the predetermined characteristic caused the variations in the dependent variable, but are able to use the results to describe the differences between groups. Consider a study involving comparisons in levels of happiness between older adults living in the community and older adults in assisted living facilities. Since random assignment did not occur, you cannot conclude which living situation caused higher levels of happiness in one group over the other. Other factors may account for the differences in happiness rather than living situation. What you can do is attempt to rule out other alternatives, such as levels of physical functioning, which may account for differences in happiness. Once you feel that other explanations have been ruled out, and if the differences are repeatedly demonstrated, you can make the cautious inference that living situation had something to do with variations in people's happiness scores.

Similarly, when comparing age groups on performance on a variable of interest, such as on memory performance for lists of numbers, you cannot conclude that age caused older adults to perform differently than the comparison age groups. As you will see later, ruling out alternative explanations is of tremendous importance not only when diverse age groups are compared, but also on other characteristics associated with age.

DESCRIPTIVE RESEARCH DESIGNS

As you just learned, studies of aging are by definition quasi-experimental and thus do not allow cause and effect conclusions. A secondary issue is that age is entangled with other associated variables. For example, the period of history in which people were born can influence their performance. Designs attempting to rule out these possible influences have been developed, as we will discuss shortly. First, however, we will cover the traditional research designs used to study aging that do not account for these differences.

We use the term "descriptive" to refer to studies in which age alone is the variable of interest. For instance, if you hear a news story stating that older adults are more likely to have a certain health problem than younger adults, you may jump to the conclusion that age "causes" this particular health problem. However, chances are that the study compared older and younger adults at one point in time. It is possible that the older people had the health problem because of something that happened to them in their youth. Perhaps the older people were exposed to poorer nutritional practices than their younger counterparts; therefore the findings reflect disparities in early life experiences rather than age.

This example highlights the types of issues facing developmental researchers. Many studies in the psychology of adult development and aging involve the use of simple designs in which people of different ages are compared on the variable of age. Researchers are able to do little except state that age differences exist. Although descriptive research designs lack the ability to determine cause and effect, understanding differences between age groups still serves a useful purpose. More complex designs are then needed to examine factors other than age.

Age, Cohort, and Time of Measurement

Three factors jointly influence the individual's performance on a given psychological measure at any point in life: age, cohort, and time of measurement (see Table 3.1). As you will see, these variables are highly related to each other, and untangling them presents many challenges requiring both creativity and scientific rigor.

Age is measured chronologically, and is most generally quantified in years. As we discussed in Chapter 1, age is an objectively determined measure based on number of years and it is not necessarily a good measure of an individual's internal characteristics. The older a person is, the more calendar years that person has experienced. There may or may not be a direct connection between these calendar years and the changes going on within the person. Developmental psychologists use it as convenient shorthand but understand that age is an imperfect index.

Social aging refers to exposure to changes over time in the society of which the individual is a part and is indexed by two measures: the year of a person's birth and the time at which measurements are taken. The year (or period) of birth is referred to as **cohort**. Conceptually, the term "cohort" represents the more familiar term "generation" in that it refers to the group of people who were born during (and hence lived through) some of the same social influences. For example, Americans in the cohort who were in college during the Vietnam War–era shared certain experiences (such as serving in the armed forces, taking part in protests, and/or living at the height of the Cold War). The particular nature of these experiences were specific to this period of history

TABLE 3.1
Age, Cohort, and Time of Measurement

Term	*Definition*	*Measurement of*
Age	• Chronological age measured in years	• Change within the individual
Cohort	• Period of birth measured in interval of time	• Influences relative to history at time of birth
Time of measurement	• Date at which testing occurs	• Current influences on individuals being tested

and although wars and protests have gone on during different eras, the experiences in the 1960s had their own distinct features.

Time of measurement is the year or period in which testing occurs. Like cohort, its meaning goes beyond the calendar in that it indicates the social and historical influences on the individual at the point when data are collected. For instance, adults tested now are more proficient at using computers than were adults tested in the 1980s, when personal computers were far less available or accessible. A measure of development that depends on being able to use a computer is influenced by the year in which the study is conducted.

The connection between time of measurement and cohort creates difficulties when investigators attempt to separate these indices of social and historical context. Time of measurement is inherently linked to cohort; people of the same age are also part of the same cohort, because time of measurement minus cohort year equals age. This fundamental problem means that unless other controls are imposed, researchers

never know whether results are due to aging or to the exposure of participants to historical change.

Descriptive research designs fall into two categories based on whether people are followed up over time or whether two or more differing age groups are compared. A summary of these two designs, including their advantages and disadvantages, is shown in Table 3.2.

Longitudinal Designs

In a **longitudinal** study, people are followed repeatedly over time. By observing and studying people as they age, researchers aim to determine whether participants have changed over time as the result of the aging process. You have very likely experienced the equivalent of a longitudinal study in watching what happens to you and the people you know as they get older. Consider your own experience from the start of kindergarten to high school graduation. Many of you may have attended school with the same set of students throughout your early educational experiences, and watched your friends and peers grow and

TABLE 3.2
Characteristics of Descriptive Research

	Advantages	Disadvantages	Corrective Step
Longitudinal	• Measures age changes and therefore "development"	• Effects of aging cannot be separated from historical change. • Takes many years to complete. • Expensive. • Researcher will not have publishable results. • Selective attrition of respondents. • Practice effects on tests may lead to improved performance. • Original test may become outdated.	• Devote administrative resources to maintaining the respondents in the study. • Use alternate forms of the test to avoid practice effects. • Rescore outdated measures using newer theoretical frameworks. • Examine data from multiple studies conducted at different time periods.
Cross-sectional	• Quick and inexpensive. Latest theories can be tested	• Measures differences between age groups and not changes over time. • Results may reflect cohort differences and not differences due to aging. • Tasks may not be equivalent for different cohorts. • Survivor problems exist because the older adults are a select group. • Appropriate age ranges are difficult to determine.	• Control for cohort differences by careful attention to selection of samples. • Validate test procedures on different age groups before comparing them. • Regard results as tentative rather than conclusive. • Replicate studies, preferably with more sophisticated methods.

There are advantages and disadvantages to each of the descriptive research designs. Investigators must weigh the pros and cons of each method before embarking on a particular study.

A longitudinal study in action. The Class of 1966 High School reunion 40th anniversary pose in front of Webster Groves High School in Webster Groves St. Louis.

develop along with you. Perhaps you marveled at how some friends remained the same over the years while others were not at all like they were when they were younger. Your best friend in first grade became your enemy in high school. Peers you thought you would never associate with in 7th grade became close friends and confidantes in 11th grade.

Now that you are in college, your relationships with your childhood friends will change even more with the passage of time. You may be attendants at their weddings or even find romance with past loves. Fast forward to your 10-year reunion (or if you have already attended yours, reflect back), when you are reminded of the person you were during your adolescent development. Many of your former classmates will look and act the same, and you may remark that the years have done little to change these people. However, other classmates may be difficult or impossible to recognize. The head cheerleader, considered flighty and vain during high school, may have entered the Peace Corps in an attempt to make the world a better place. As you catch up with her, you are struck by how sincere and down to earth she has become—quite a different person from her teenage self. The characteristic nerd has evolved into a shrewd and successful businessman, who no longer resembles the awkward and shy teenager you remembered.

As you interact with your former classmates, you develop your own hypotheses regarding reasons for the changes you have witnessed. One possibility is that they have not changed so much as has your understanding of who they are. Maybe you were too harsh to judge the cheerleader or nerd and it is only now that you can see them as the complex and multifaceted people they were all along. Of course, you may not have to wait until your 10-year reunion, as social networking sites such as MySpace and Facebook make following (or "Facestalking") the development of past classmates as easy as turning on your computer.

Fascination with the forces that drive people to change over time is often what attracts most researchers to the field of adult development and aging. When researchers are lucky enough to have longitudinal data, they often feel that they have gained true insight into the very essence of change over time in human behavior. However, similar to descriptive research designs, longitudinal studies are not without their limitations.

Theoretically, researchers are unable to state with certainty that the changes observed over time are a result of the person's own aging or the result of the changing environment in which the person functions. The individual cannot be removed from the environment to see what would happen if he or she had lived in a different time or place. It is simply not possible to know if people are inherently changing or whether they alter due to the circumstances in which they are aging. This is the key limitation to longitudinal studies: the inability to differentiate between personal and historical time.

In addition to the theoretical problems, practical problems also plague longitudinal research. The most prominent concern is the length of time longitudinal research takes to conduct. In order to be of greatest value to the study of adult development and aging, longitudinal studies should generally span at least a decade or more. As a result, they can be quite costly to conduct. Furthermore, the results are often not available for many years, creating problems for researchers who do not have the luxury or patience to see the outcomes. In the many scenarios, the original investigator may not even live long enough to see the results come to fruition.

Participants in a longitudinal study are also likely to be lost over time, a problem referred to as **selective attrition**. The loss of participants from the original sample creates a host of practical and theoretical problems. Practically, as the number of participants diminishes, it becomes increasingly difficult to complete statistical analyses on the data. Power calculations are performed to determine how large a sample should be to detect differences between groups (such as sex, social class, or race). If the sample size is too small, the study may lack the potential to answer the original research questions.

The loss of participants also hampers the investigator's ability to draw inferences from the sample to the population as a whole. The people who

disappear from the sample do so for a variety of reasons such as poor health or death, lack of motivation, or an inability to continue in the study because they have moved from the area or are otherwise unreachable. The study "survivors" may be higher on all or some of these factors. Conclusions made about the survivors may therefore not apply to the general population.

Consequently, longitudinal data may be skewed given that different types of people are present in the samples across succeeding test occasions. Researchers studying the phenomenon of attrition worry that the survivors still present for testing many years into the study were healthier, more motivated, or in other ways different from the people who are no longer in the study. The researcher may erroneously conclude that participants in the sample "improved" when in reality, the sicker and less motivated are simply gone from the sample (see Figure 3.1).

To address the problem of attrition, longitudinal researchers typically conduct analyses to determine whether the pattern of participant dropout was random, or whether it reflected a systematic bias that kept the healthier and more motivated participants in the sample. Such a technique is referred to as non-random sampling, and means that successive samples are increasingly unlike the populations they were intended to represent. Various statistical techniques are employed to determine whether non-random sampling has occurred, and if so, whether

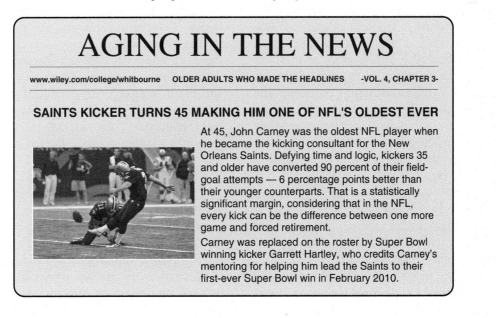

AGING IN THE NEWS

www.wiley.com/college/whitbourne   OLDER ADULTS WHO MADE THE HEADLINES   -VOL. 4, CHAPTER 3-

SAINTS KICKER TURNS 45 MAKING HIM ONE OF NFL'S OLDEST EVER

At 45, John Carney was the oldest NFL player when he became the kicking consultant for the New Orleans Saints. Defying time and logic, kickers 35 and older have converted 90 percent of their field-goal attempts — 6 percentage points better than their younger counterparts. That is a statistically significant margin, considering that in the NFL, every kick can be the difference between one more game and forced retirement.

Carney was replaced on the roster by Super Bowl winning kicker Garrett Hartley, who credits Carney's mentoring for helping him lead the Saints to their first-ever Super Bowl win in February 2010.

FIGURE 3.1

The Problem of Selective Attrition in Longitudinal Studies

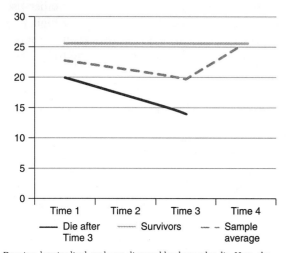

Data in a longitudinal study are distorted by those who die. Here, the average appears to increase between Times 3 and 4 even though the survivors never changed.

relationships between the variables are affected. Without such procedures, the study's results become difficult to interpret.

A variety of methods can also address the practical problems encountered in longitudinal research. Researchers are motivated to retain their samples for as long as possible. A vigilant monitoring and maintenance of databases containing contact information is critical. Large-scale longitudinal studies are often housed in established institutions or agencies that have clerical assistance available to the investigator. Administrative personnel whose job it is to retain study participants can maintain the "care and feeding" of the sample in between testing occasions. The research staff may send out greeting cards for holidays and birthdays, or update participants on study progress via newsletters and e-mails. Many longitudinal studies use Web sites to allow participants to engage interactively.

Creating a personal touch encourages respondents to continue participation, and also enables investigators to keep better track of moves, deaths, or other issues. Other approaches to tackling attrition include the use of a simulated longitudinal design, in which several cohorts are followed up over a 5- or 10-year period. For example, a study could include people in

their 30s, 40s, and 50s who are followed up over a 10-year period. A second study may recruit people in their 50s, 60s, and 70s and follow them up 10 years later as well. Results from both studies can be combined to produce a simulated longitudinal design that includes participants from the ages of 30 to 70 and took 20 instead of 40 years to complete. Sophisticated statistical methods are used to analyze and interpret results from these designs so that they simulate the effect of a much longer-term study.

Practice effects are another complication in longitudinal studies. Participants who complete tests on multiple testing occasions may become better at answering the questions. If, for example, the particular test measures intelligence, participants may purposely learn the answers in between testing occasions. Similarly, in studies examining personality, a participant may suspect or find out the meaning of a response that implies something unfavorable. On the next test occasion, the respondent may be less likely to endorse that statement. Researchers often use alternate forms of tests on different testing occasions to avoid such problems.

From the investigator's point of view, a far more serious dilemma is posed by the nature of the tests themselves which, over time, may become outdated. The cutting edge theory developed in the 1980s may have since been refuted, but the researcher is still left with measures based on that theory and not the newer one. One way to address this problem is to reanalyze or rescale the test scores to correspond to the newer theory, if possible. This was the strategy used in studies of personality development by researchers at the Institute for Human Development in Berkeley, who began a study of child development in the late 1920s, a project that continued far longer than initially planned. By the time participants were in their adult years, the original measures were no longer theoretically relevant. The researchers rescored the data using newer theoretical and empirical frameworks that were also more age-appropriate.

Despite their flaws, longitudinal studies have the potential to add invaluable data on psychological changes in adulthood and old age. Furthermore, as data accumulate from multiple investigations concerning related variables, it is possible to overcome the limitations of any one particular study to gain as accurate a depiction of change across adulthood as possible. Even though one study may have its problems, convergence across several investigations allows researchers to feel greater confidence when findings are similar from one study to the next.

Cross-Sectional Designs

The alternative to following people over time is to compare groups of different ages at one point in time. The **cross-sectional** design is by far the more frequently used research method in the field of developmental science in general, but particularly in research on aging.

The goal of cross-sectional research on adult development and aging is to describe age differences. However, a key aim is being able to draw conclusions about changes associated with the aging process that cause these differences. To ensure that they are correct in their assumption, researchers attempt to control for cohort differences that could potentially obscure or exaggerate the effects of age. They can best achieve this control by selecting samples comparable in important factors such as amount of education and social class. Even if they cannot achieve this level of control, they can ensure that differences relevant to the main purpose of the study are kept to a minimum. For instance, in a study of aging and verbal memory, it would be important for researchers to ensure that the age groups being compared have similar vocabulary or verbal comprehension skills.

Like the longitudinal design, the cross-sectional design is only applicable to one historical period.

Age differences obtained in a cross-sectional study are specific to the cohorts of people compared. For example, people born in the 1950s and tested in the 2000s at the age of 50 may be higher on an attribute than people born in the 1970s and tested in the 1990s at the age of 20 because of social factors specific to each of these cohorts. A similar difference between 20- and 40-year-olds may not be encountered among people compared in a study conducted in the 1980s, when the samples were born 10 years earlier. For example, although commonsense wisdom regards young adults as less conservative than middle-aged adults, it is possible that middle-agers who lived through the 1960s are less conservative than young people growing up in the 1980s. The same difference between age groups may not reveal itself if the study is conducted in a different historical era.

One case illustrating the problem of cohort differences in cross-sectional studies is shown in Figure 3.2. The graph is from an investigation comparing the relative amounts of white matter in the brains of young, middle-aged, and older adult samples (Brickman et al., 2006). The higher the amount of white matter, the better the individual's brain functions. From the figure, it would seem that because the younger age groups have more white matter, their brains are functioning better compared to the older adult brains. However, the story is not so simple. The age groups were not comparable in education, with the older adults having the fewest years of formal schooling. The cohort difference in education makes it impossible to know whether it

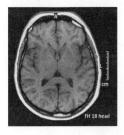

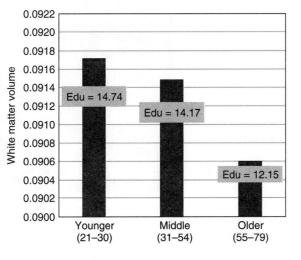

FIGURE 3.2

The Problem of Cohort Differences in Cross-Sectional Research

This cross-sectional study, showing apparent decreases in white matter volume with age (see photo), fails to take into account cohort differences in years of education.

Source: Brickman, A. M., Zimmerman, M. E., Paul, R. H., Grieve, S. M., Tate, D. F., Cohen, R. A., . . . Gordon, E. (2006). Regional white matter and neuropsychological functioning across the adult lifespan. *Biological Psychiatry, 60*, 444–453.

was age or education that most strongly influenced the white matter of these three age groups.

Selective survival, the bane of longitudinal investigators, also serves to challenge cross-sectional researchers. Study participants, by definition, are survivors of their respective age groups. Thus, they may represent a healthier or luckier group of people than those in their cohort who did not live as long. Perhaps they are the ones who are more cautious, smarter, and genetically hardier and so were able to avoid the many diseases that could have caused their death prior to old age. As a result, older adults in a cross-sectional study may look different from the younger ones because the two groups are drawn from two different populations—those who die young (but are still represented in the young adult group) and those who survive to be old. The sampling of young adults drawn exclusively from a college population, a common technique in psychological research, may not be representative of the younger cohort either. Any time you read about a study comparing younger and older adult samples, keep in mind the demographic makeup of the younger sample and not just the comparison between samples of different ages.

The problem of assigning participants to specific age groups presents additional difficulties with cross-sectional research. If researchers wish to compare "young adults" with older adults, should they restrict themselves to the sort of typical 18–22 year range or should they allow the age range to expand to the mid- or even late 20s? As it turns out, the age range of older adult samples is rarely defined as narrowly as is the range of those in college. Often, researchers have to settle for an age range for the older group that is larger than is desirable. In some studies, the range is as large as 20 to 30 years (or more). Some studies define the "older" sample as all respondents over the age of 50 or 60 and, having done so, fail to look for any possible age differences within the older sample. By the time all is said and done, age differences in the older sample may be as great, if not greater than, differences between the older and younger samples.

A related problem to determining acceptable age ranges is the question of how to divide the adult age range when selecting samples. Is it better to divide samples of people in cross-sectional studies into decades and then examine age differences continuously across the adult years? Or perhaps is it better to compare people at the two extremes of the adult span? Researchers increasingly include middle-aged samples along with the younger and older adults rather than compare only those at the two extremes of the age distribution. The inclusion of three age groups creates a more justifiable basis for "connecting the dots" between their scores on measures of psychological functioning across the adult years.

We raise these problems not necessarily because we have all the perfect answers but to sensitize you to the need to look closely at study samples when you are examining research on aging. After this course, when you come across an article in the newspaper about a study that claims to have discovered an important truth about the aging process, be sure to read between the lines to determine how carefully the samples were selected.

Another area of concern to researchers conducting cross-sectional studies is the need to be sensitive to how different age groups will react to the test materials administered in research settings. In studies of memory, for example, there is a risk that the older adults will find some of the measures challenging and perhaps intimidating because they are not used to having their abilities evaluated in a formal setting such as the psychology lab. Young adults are far more comfortable with test situations either because they are currently or were recently in school where they were frequently tested. To an older adult, particularly

Older adults may be less familiar with test-taking, a factor that may lead their abilities to be underestimated in a laboratory setting.

one who is sensitive to memory loss, anxiety about the situation rather than actual performance can result in decreased scores, a topic we address further below.

Task equivalence also applies to the way different cohorts react to measures of personality and social attitudes. The same item may have very different meanings to people of different generations or people of different educational or cultural backgrounds. A common problem in personality and mental health research is that a measure of, for example, depression, may have been tested on a young adult sample but not on an older sample. Items on such a scale concerning physical changes, such as alterations in sleep patterns presumably related to depression, may in fact reflect normal age-related differences and not differences in depression. Older adults will therefore receive a higher score on the depression scale by virtue of changes in their sleep patterns alone, not because they are actually suffering from depression.

These problems aside, cross-sectional studies are relatively quick and inexpensive compared to longitudinal studies. Another advantage of cross-sectional studies is that the latest and most up-to-date technology can be implemented, whether in the biomedical area or in the psychological and social domains. If a new tool or technique comes out one year, it can be tested cross-sectionally the next. Researchers are not tied to obsolete methods that were in use some 30 or 40 years ago.

The best cross-sectional studies, though never able to permit causal inferences about aging, employ a variety of controls to ensure that differences other than age are kept to a minimum and that the ages selected for study span across the adult years. Most researchers regard their cross-sectional findings as tentative descriptions of the effects of aging on the function of interest. They are aware of the importance of having their findings replicated and verified through studies employing a longitudinal element.

SEQUENTIAL RESEARCH DESIGNS

We have probably convinced you by now that the perfect study on aging is virtually impossible to conduct. Age can never be a true independent variable because it cannot be manipulated. Furthermore, age is inherently linked with time, and so personal aging can

never be separated from social aging. However, considerable progress in some areas of research has been made through the application of **sequential designs**. These designs consist of different combinations of the variables age, cohort, and time of measurement. Simply put, a sequential design involves a "sequence" of studies, such as a cross-sectional study carried out twice (two sequences) over a span of 10 years. The sequential nature of these designs is what makes them superior to the truly descriptive designs conducted on one sample, followed over time (longitudinal design) or on different-aged samples, tested on one occasion (cross-sectional design). Not only do sequential studies automatically provide an element of replication, but when they are carried out as intended, statistical analyses can permit remarkably strong inferences to be drawn about the effect of age as distinct from cohort or time of measurement.

The Most Efficient Design

One of the most influential articles to be published in the field of adult development and aging was the landmark work by psychologist K. Warner Schaie (1965) in which he outlined what would later be called the **Most Efficient Design**, a set of three designs manipulating the variables of age, cohort, and time of measurement. It is "most efficient" because it enables the most amount of information to be condensed into the most inclusive data framework.

The general layout for the Most Efficient Design is shown in Table 3.3. Researchers organize their data by constructing a table that combines year of birth (cohort) with year of testing (time of measurement). The three designs that make up the Most Efficient Design and the respective factors they include are the time-sequential design (age by time of measurement), the cohort-sequential design (cohort by age), and the cross-sequential design (cohort by time of measurement). When all three designs are analyzed, they make it theoretically possible for the researcher to obtain separate statistical estimates of the effects of each of the three factors. Schaie and his collaborators have employed such techniques to the Seattle Longitudinal Study, a large-scale study of intelligence.

Thus, depending on the pattern of significant effects, the researcher may be able to draw conclusions about the relative influences of personal and

TABLE 3.3
The Most Efficient Design

Year of Birth (Cohort)	Year of Testing (Time of Measurement)			
	1980	*1990*	*2000*	*2010*
1940	40 yrs	50 yrs	60 yrs	70 yrs
1930	50 yrs	60 yrs	70 yrs	80 yrs
1920	60 yrs	70 yrs	80 yrs	90 yrs

Longitudinal

Cross-sectional

historical aging on test performance. For example, if age effects are significant in the time-sequential and cohort-sequential designs and there are no cohort or time effects in the cross-sequential design, then "true" aging effects may exist. Another scenario involves significant effects of time of measurement in both the time-sequential and cross-sequential designs, patterns that suggest it was the time in history rather than the age of the participants that most influenced the pattern of scores. Similarly, if the cohort factor is significant in the two designs in which it is used and significant age or time of measurement effects are not observed, then the researcher may look at early childhood environmental factors in these samples.

Figure 3.3 provides an example of the advantage of conducting sequential analyses. The data come from a study conducted by the first author, which began as a follow-up to a study of college students (the 1946 cohort) conducted in the mid-1960s (Constantinople, 1969). In the late 1970s, the 1946 cohort was retested and a new group of college students (the 1957 cohort) was added (Whitbourne & Waterman, 1979). The next follow-up occurred in 1988–89, when both cohorts were again retested and a new group of college students were included (Whitbourne, Zuschlag, Elliot, & Waterman, 1992). By 2000–02, as shown in the figure, the 1946 and 1957 cohorts showed different patterns of change in the measure of intimacy over time (Whitbourne,

FIGURE 3.3

Results from a Sequential Study of Psychosocial Development

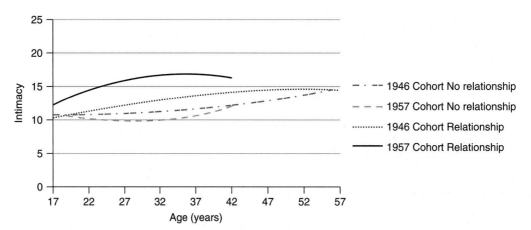

Source: Whitbourne, S. K., Sneed, J. R., & Sayer, A. (2009). Psychosocial development from college through midlife: A 34-year sequential study. *Developmental Psychology, 45*, 1328–1340.

Sneed, & Sayer, 2009). Had only the 1946 cohort been tested over this age span, the results would have looked very different than if the 1957 cohort was tested as well. The data are superior to what would have been obtained through traditional longitudinal methods because they were based on the study of more than one cohort over more than one test occasion. In addition, the scores shown in the figure illustrate the relevance of a relationship status on intimacy. Take a look at the 1946 cohort scores. Those who were not in a long-term relationship by their early 30s had lower intimacy scores in college but at subsequent testings, their intimacy scores rose. Most of them were in long-term relationships by their 50s, at which point the scores on intimacy in both groups converge. The 1957 cohort seems to be on the same track as judged by the direction of their curves.

CORRELATIONAL DESIGNS

An alternative approach to describing group differences using the quasi-experimental design is the **correlational design**, in which relationships are observed among variables as they exist in the world. The researcher makes no attempt to divide participants into groups or to manipulate variables.

Simple Correlational Designs

Comparisons of age groups or groups based on divisions such as year of birth or time of measurement are useful for many research questions in the field of gerontology. However, often this approach is neither the most efficient nor the most informative. By grouping people into categories, researchers lose a great deal of information that could be preserved if they used actual age in years. The variable of age is a continuous variable, meaning that it does not have natural cutoff points as does a categorical variable such as gender. There may be a difference between people of 42 and people of 45 years of age, but when they are all grouped in the "40-year-old" category, this distinction is obscured.

In the correlational design, age can be treated as a continuous variable and it is therefore unnecessary or even desirable to put people into arbitrarily defined groups. The relationship between age and another

variable is expressed through the statistic known as the correlation (represented by the letter r) whose value can range from $+1.0$ to -1.0. A significant positive correlation indicates that the two variables are positively related so that when the value of one variable increases, the other one does as well. A significant negative correlation indicates that the two variables are negatively related so that when one increases in value the other one decreases. A correlation of zero indicates no relationship between the variables.

In a correlational study, the researcher makes no assumptions about what caused what—there are no "independent" or "dependent" variables. A correlation between two variables means simply that the two variables are related, but like the proverbial chicken and egg, the researcher cannot say which came first.

Let's consider as an example the relationship between age and response speed. The correlation between these two variables is most often positive; that is, when age increases, response speed does as well (keep in mind that a higher response speed indicates slower performance). When interpreting this relationship, the researcher may be tempted to conclude that age "caused" the increase in response speed. However, this conclusion is not justified because age was not experimentally manipulated. In a correlational study, there are no independent or dependent variables. Therefore, the possibility that variable A accounts for variable B is equal to the possibility that B accounts for A. It may be tempting to assume that response speed does not cause increasing age; rather, age causes increasing response times. However, since an experiment was not conducted, the possibility that increased response speed caused aging cannot be ruled out.

Here is another example to clarify this point. There is a correlation between certain Type A personality characteristics and cardiovascular disease. People with Type A personality, who are hard-driving, competitive, often hostile, and impatient, are more likely to have heart disease. Does the personality type cause heart disease (which might seem most logical), or does heart disease cause people to have personality problems? Because the design is correlational, neither possibility can be excluded.

Figure 3.4 shows the results of a study in which men with cardiovascular disease were tested on a measure of hostility, one of the Type A characteristics

FIGURE 3.4

Correlation Between Hostility and Blood Pressure

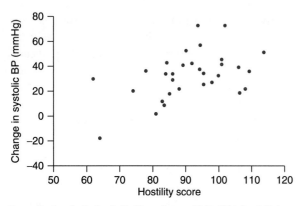

Source: Brydon, L., Strike, P. C., Bhattacharyya, M. R., Whitehead, D. L., McEwan, J., Zachary, I., . . . Steptoe, A. (2010). Hostility and physiological responses to laboratory stress in acute coronary syndrome patients. *Journal of Psychosomatic Research, 68,* 109–116.

(Brydon et al., 2010). The rise in their blood pressure was measured after being subjected to laboratory tasks designed to induce stress (defending themselves publicly against a fabricated shoplifting charge). As you can see in this figure, hostility was positively correlated with increases in blood pressure.

If you are a psychology student, you have probably incorporated the mantra "correlation does not equal causation" into your everyday language. This phrase refers in part to the fact that correlations do not allow researchers to state that one variable was the direct cause of another. However, the other implication of this phrase refers to the possibility that a third but unmeasured variable accounts for the apparent relationship between the two observed variables. In the case of the relationship between age and response speed, this third variable might be "number of functioning brain cells." Age may be related to number of brain cells, and number of brain cells may be related to response speed. The apparent correlation between age and response speed might disappear entirely when number of brain cells is measured and factored into the relationship.

Returning to the example in Figure 3.4, the correlation between hostility and blood pressure might be accounted for entirely by an unmeasured third variable such as cigarette smoking. Perhaps people with certain personality types are more likely to smoke

cigarettes, and cigarette smoking is related to heart disease. This unmeasured variable could be responsible for the apparent relationship between the other two. To control for this possibility, the investigators took smoking status into account before calculating the hostility–blood pressure increase correlation.

When examining data from a typical correlational study, it is important to keep in mind that causation cannot be inferred from correlation and to be on the lookout for competing hypotheses related to unmeasured variables. While this is no less true of gerontology than of other disciplines, because arguments related to age are often so compelling, it is particularly easy to fall into the trap.

Correlational studies contain a wealth of information despite their inability to determine cause and effect. The value of the correlation itself provides a useful basis for calculating the strength of the relationship. Furthermore, it is possible to manipulate a larger number of variables at one time than is generally true in studies involving group comparisons. Advanced correlational methods have become increasingly available in the past 20 years that allow researchers to navigate the difficulties involved in causality with traditional correlational methods, and we will turn to those next.

Multivariate Correlational Designs

In contrast to simple correlational designs, which involve determining the statistical relationship between two variables (called a bivariate relationship), a **multivariate correlational design** involves the analysis of relationships among more than two variables (see Table 3.4). The researcher using a multivariate design can simultaneously evaluate the effects of many potentially important factors, rather than being restricted to the study of two variables, which can lead to overlooking an important third (or fourth) variable.

Multivariate correlational methods also enable researchers to test models in which a set of variables is used to "predict" scores on another variable. In **multiple regression analysis**, the predictor variables are regarded as equivalent to the independent variables, and the variable that is predicted is regarded as equivalent to a dependent variable. Although the design is still correlational in that the experimenter does not manipulate an independent variable, the statistics involved enable investigators to suggest and test inferences about cause–effect relationships.

A variant of multiple regression is **logistic regression**, in which researchers test the likelihood of an individual receiving a score on a discrete yes-no variable. For example, a group of investigators may want to test the probability that a person will receive a diagnosis of cardiovascular disease or not, depending on whether the person has one of several risk factors. Logistic regression is often used to determine whether non-random sampling has occurred, as discussed earlier with subject attrition in longitudinal studies. Using the yes-no variables of "survivor" and "dropout," researchers can attest to whether differences between survivors and dropouts are due to chance or to other factors.

Multivariate correlational designs have the potential to test complex models and so are increasingly being used in research on adult development and aging in which there are so many problems with age as a variable. In **structural equation modeling (SEM)**, researchers develop hypotheses regarding the relations among observed (measures) and latent (underlying) variables or factors (Hoyle, 1995). SEM serves purposes similar to multiple regression, in a more powerful way, taking into account the possibilities that there are complex relationships among the variables and factors of interest. This method, illustrated in Figure 3.4, helped to identify religious participation as a predictor of mortality above and beyond the effects of physical functioning.

A multivariate method recently introduced to developmental research is **hierarchical linear modeling** (HLM) (Raudenbush & Bryk, 2002). In this method, also referred to as multilevel modeling, individual patterns of change are examined over time rather than simply comparing mean scores of people at different ages. Such a technique is particularly important in longitudinal research, because not every participant exhibits the same patterns of change over time. While some individuals may increase, others may decrease, and some may not change at all. Solely looking at overall mean scores fails to capture this individual variation. In HLM, individual patterns can be explored statistically in addition to examining whether particular variables affect some individuals more than others. This method produces the type of graph shown in Figure 3.3 in which intimacy growth was tracked over time.

TYPES OF RESEARCH METHODS

Data on adult development and aging can be captured using a variety of data collection strategies, or research methods. Each method has advantages and disadvantages that are important to consider according to the particular field of study, the nature of the sample, available resources, and desired applications.

Laboratory Studies

The majority of information about physical and cognitive changes associated with the aging process comes from **laboratory studies**, in which participants

TABLE 3.4
Advantages of Multivariate Correlational Design

- Control for confounds related to age
    - ✓ Can add in other variables

- Allow investigations of "causality"
    - ✓ Significance of paths can be tested

- Provide ways to examine change over time
    - ✓ Can model individual variations in growth

are tested in a systematic fashion using standardized procedures. The laboratory method is considered the most objective way of collecting data because each participant is exposed to the same treatment, using the same equipment and the same data recording procedures. For example, in a study of memory, participants may be asked to recall a set of items presented on a computer. At a later point, they may be asked at to recall as many of those items as possible using some type of automated response system.

There are obvious advantages to the **laboratory study**. The objective and systematic way in which data are recorded provides the investigator assurance that the results are due to the variables being studied rather than to extraneous factors. For instance, in the memory study, all participants would be presented with the recall items systematically, in a way that does not depend on the voice inflections of the researcher, the quality of the visual stimuli, or the amount of time used to present the items.

A limitation of the laboratory study is the inability to apply the stimuli presented to real-life experiences of most adults. It is possible that the older person feels uncomfortable when tested in an impersonal and possibly intimidating manner using unfamiliar equipment. Consequently, the findings may underestimate the individual's abilities in everyday life, and may not generalize to real-world scenarios.

Qualitative Studies

There are often instances in which researchers wish to explore a phenomenon of interest in an open-ended fashion. The investigation of social influences on adult development such as, for example, personal relationships, may demand the researcher use a method that captures potentially relevant factors within a broad spectrum of possible influences (Allen & Walker, 2000). Qualitative methods allow for the exploration of such complex relationships outside the narrow restrictions and assumptions of quantitative methods. In other cases, researchers may be working in an area in which conventional methods are neither practical nor appropriate for the problem under investigation. Qualitative methods are also used in the analysis of life history information, which is likely to be highly varied from person to person and not easily translated into numbers. The main advantage for using qualitative methods is that they

provide researchers with alternative ways to test their hypotheses. The qualitative method can be adapted in a flexible manner to the nature of the problem at hand.

Archival Research

In **archival research**, investigators use existing resources that contain data relevant to a question about aging. The archives might consist of a governmental data bank, or the records kept by an institution, school, or employer. Another source of archival data is newspaper or magazine reports.

An advantage of archival research is that the information is readily accessible, especially given the growth of Web-based data sets including those of the U.S Census. Data files can be downloaded directly from the Internet, or publications can be accessed using portable document files (PDFs) that are easily read and searched. Disadvantages are that the researcher does not necessarily have control over the form of the data. For instance, a governmental agency may keep records of employment by age that do not include information on specific occupations of interest to the researcher. Another disadvantage is that the material may not be systematically collected or recorded. Newspaper or school records, for example, may have information that is biased or incomplete.

Surveys

Researchers rely on the **survey** method to gain information about a sample that can then be generalized to a larger population. Surveys are typically short and easily administered with simple rating scales to use for answers. For instance, surveys are given to poll voters on who they will be casting their ballots for in upcoming elections. Occasionally, more intensive surveys may be given to gain in-depth knowledge about aging and its relationship to health behaviors, health risks, and symptoms. The U.S. Census was collected through survey methodology. However, it is considered archival in that it has extensive historical records going back to the year 1750 when the first U.S. Census was conducted.

Surveys have the advantage of providing data that allow the researcher to gain insight into the behavior of more people than it would be possible to study

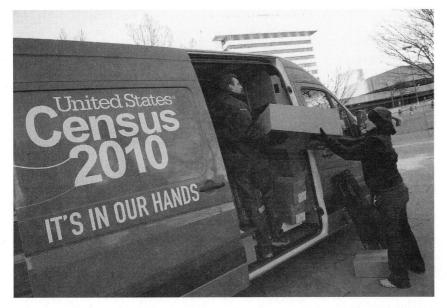

Data from the 2010 U.S. Census are collected through survey methodology; the results become archived and available for historical analyses.

in the laboratory or other testing site. They can be administered over the telephone or, increasingly, via the Web. Interview-based surveys given by trained administrators provide knowledge that is easily coded and analyzed while still providing comprehensive information about the behavior in question. Typically, however, surveys tend to be short with questions that are subject to bias by respondents, who may attempt to provide a favorable impression to the researcher. Consequently, although the data may be generalizable to a large population, the quality of the data itself may be limited.

Case Reports

When researchers want to provide an in-depth analysis of particular individuals, they use the **case report**, which summarizes the findings from multiple sources for those individuals. Data may be integrated from interviews, psychological tests, observations, archival records, or even journal and diary entries. The focus of the case report is on the characteristics of the individual and what has influenced his or her development and life experiences. Personal narratives may also be obtained with this method, in which individuals describe their lives as they have experienced them along with their ideas about why their lives have evolved in a given manner.

Although the case report has the benefit of providing insights into the lives of individuals as

they change over time, it relies heavily on clinical judgments by the researcher. Therefore, for a case report to provide valuable information, a high level of expertise is required so that the findings are presented in a manner that balances the objective facts with the subjective analysis of the researcher.

Focus Groups

A less formal research method is a **focus group**, which is a meeting of a group of respondents oriented around a particular topic of interest. In a focus group, an investigator attempts to identify important themes in the discussion and keep the conversation oriented to these themes. The goal is to develop concrete research questions to pursue in subsequent studies. For example, attitudes toward mental health providers by older adults may be assessed by a focus group in which participants 65 and older share their concerns and experiences with counselors and therapists.

An advantage of the focus group is that issues can be identified through a focus group prior to conducting a more systematic investigation. This approach, often considered a pilot study, is particularly useful when little preexisting research on the topic is available. An obvious disadvantage is that the method is not particularly systematic, and the data cannot readily be analyzed or systematically interpreted.

Observational Methods

In the **observational method**, researchers draw conclusions about behavior through careful and systematic examination in particular settings. Recordings may be made using videotapes or behavioral records. In one type of observational method known as participant-observation, the researcher participates in the activities of the respondents. For example, a researcher may wish to find out about the behavior of staff in a nursing home. The researcher may spend several days living with people in the nursing home. The researcher's subjective experiences would become part of the "data."

There are elaborate procedures available for creating behavioral records in which the researcher precisely defines the behavior to be observed (the number of particular acts) and specifies the times during which records will be made. This procedure may be used to determine whether an intervention is having its intended effects. If an investigator is testing a method to reduce aggressive behavior in people with Alzheimer's disease, behavioral records could be made before and after the intervention is introduced. After observing the effects of the intervention, the method's effectiveness could be determined by a return to baseline condition to assess whether the aggressive behavior increases without the intervention.

MEASUREMENT ISSUES IN ADULT DEVELOPMENT AND AGING

Research designs, no matter how cleverly engineered, are unable to yield worthwhile results if the methods used to collect the data are flawed. Researchers in adult development and aging, like all other scientists, must concern themselves with the quality of the instruments they use to capture data. The task is made more difficult because the instruments must be usable with people who are likely to vary in ability, educational background, and sophistication with research instruments. Earlier we pointed out the problems involved in comparing older and younger adults on measures used in cross-sectional studies. Here we will look specifically at some of the ways developmental researchers can ensure that their measures are equivalent across age groups.

The first measurement issue to consider is that of **reliability**. A measure is reliable if it yields consistent results every time it is used. The importance of reliability is highlighted by considering the analogy of measurements used in cooking. If your tablespoon were unreliable (say, it was made of floppy plastic), the amount of ingredients added would vary with every use. Your cookies may be hard and crunchy one time and soft and gooey the next. A psychological test must also provide similar scores upon repeated administration. This principle is one of the first qualities psychologists look for in a measure—its ability to provide consistent scores. Reliability can be assessed by test-retest reliability, which is determined by giving the test on two occasions to assess whether respondents receive similar scores across both administrations. Another form of reliability relates to internal consistency, which indicates whether respondents answer similarly on comparable items.

The second criterion used to evaluate a test is **validity**, meaning that the test measures what it is supposed to measure. A test of intelligence should measure intelligence, not how good your vision is. Returning to the example in the kitchen, if a tablespoon were marked "teaspoon," it would not be measuring what it is supposed to measure, and your baked products would be ruined. Tablespoons are fairly easy to assess for validity, but unfortunately psychological tests present a far greater challenge. For this reason, validity is a much more difficult quality to capture than reliability.

The concept of validity varies depending on the intended use of the measure. Content validity provides an indication of whether a test designed to assess factual material accurately measures that material. Your next exam may very well include questions testing how well you have understood the topics covered in this chapter. Criterion validity indicates whether a test score accurately predicts performance on an indicator measure, as would be used in a test of vocational ability that claims to predict success on the job. Finally, construct validity is used to assess the extent to which a measure intended to assess a psychological construct is able to do so.

Construct validity is difficult to establish and requires two types of evidence: convergent and divergent validity. Convergent validity is needed to determine that the measure relates to other measures

In a behavioral observation, researchers collect data by counting the frequency of specific behaviors.

that are of theoretical similarity. A test of intelligence should have a positive relationship to another test of intelligence that has been well-validated. Divergent validity demonstrates that the measure does not relate to other measures that have no theoretical relationship to it. A test of intelligence should not be correlated with a test of personality, unless the personality test assesses some aspect of intelligence.

Although psychologists are generally aware of the need to establish the reliability and validity of measures used in both research and practical settings, less attention is focused on psychometric properties when used in gerontological research. Measures whose reliability and validity were established on young adult samples are often used inappropriately without testing their applicability to samples of adults of varying ages. The process can become quite complicated. If Form A of a measure is found to be psychometrically sound with college students but only Form B has adequate reliability and validity for older adults, the researcher is faced with the prospect of having to use different forms of a test within the same study. Nevertheless, sensitivity to measurement issues is crucial if conclusions drawn from the research are to have value.

ETHICAL ISSUES IN RESEARCH

All scientists who engage in research with humans or other animals must take precautions to protect the rights of their participants. In extreme cases, such as in medical research, the life of an individual may be at stake if the individual is subjected to risky procedures. Research in which respondents are tested or put through stressful experimental manipulations also requires that standard protocols are followed. Recognizing the importance of these considerations, the American Psychological Association developed a comprehensive set of guidelines for psychologists that includes the appropriate treatment of human participants in research (American Psychological Association, 2003). We have summarized the main features of these guidelines in Table 3.5.

Researchers must present a potential respondent as full a disclosure as possible of the risks and benefits of becoming involved in any research project. When the individual is a minor child or an adult who is not able to make independent decisions, the researcher is obligated to inform the individual's legal guardian about the nature of the study. Having provided information about the study, the researcher must then obtain a legal signature indicating that the participant understands the risks and benefits involved in the study. At this point the researcher is able to obtain the full **informed consent** of the respondent or the respondent's legal representative. When the individual is an animal, the researcher is similarly bound to ensure that the animal is not mishandled or subjected to unnecessary harm, although different protective procedures are followed.

TABLE 3.5

Summary of APA Ethical Guidelines for Research on Human Participants

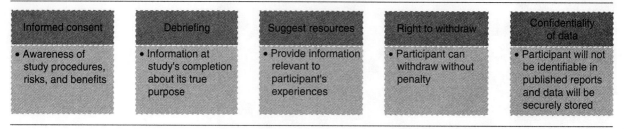

Informed consent	Debriefing	Suggest resources	Right to withdraw	Confidentiality of data
• Awareness of study procedures, risks, and benefits	• Information at study's completion about its true purpose	• Provide information relevant to participant's experiences	• Participant can withdraw without penalty	• Participant will not be identifiable in published reports and data will be securely stored

Source: Adapted from American Psychological Association. (2003). Ethical Principles of Psychologists and Code of Conduct. Retrieved from http://www.apa.org/ethics/code2002.html&8_02.

Research participants are also entitled to know what the study was about after completion in a process called **debriefing**. If you have ever participated in research, you may have been curious during the course of the study to know what was being tested. In some cases you might have been surprised to find out about the "real" purpose of the study. Perhaps you were told that you were going to be asked to fill out a series of questionnaires in a quiet laboratory room. In the middle of the questionnaire, you hear a loud noise in the hallway, followed by a man screaming. Although you may think the point of the study is to gather information about you, the goal of the research was to assess your response to the sudden commotion. After the experiment is over, the researcher is obligated to tell you the truth about the purpose of the study. You may be embarrassed if in fact you did not get up to help, but you at least had a right to know that you were being tested on this attribute. The debriefing might make you feel better because you would realize that your response of not helping reflected the experimental manipulation rather than a malevolent personality attribute you possess.

As this example illustrates, research participants may learn information about themselves that is potentially upsetting or damaging. In fact, ethical guidelines for research in psychology dictate that the researcher not only provides feedback but also must be ready to suggest support or counseling for people who become distressed while involved in the experiment. Respondents are also entitled to withdraw from a study without risk of penalty should they choose to do so. The experimenter should not coerce them into completing the study, and even if they decide to discontinue participation, they should

still receive whatever reimbursement was initially promised. If they are students in a class or clients receiving services (such as hospital patients), they should not fear having their grades lowered or services withheld from them.

Finally, research participants are entitled to know what will happen to their data. In all cases, the data must be kept confidential, meaning that only the research team will have access to the information provided by the participants. The other condition usually attached to the data is that of anonymity. Participants are guaranteed that their names will not be associated with their responses. The condition of anonymity obviously cannot be kept if the study is a longitudinal one because the researchers must maintain access to names for follow-up purposes. In this case, the condition of confidentiality applies, and the researchers are obligated to ensure that all records are kept private and secure.

These ethical standards are enforced in all institutions receiving federal or local funding for research through Institutional Review Boards (IRBs), which review all proposed studies to be carried out at that institution or by anyone employed by that institution. These reviews ensure that the rights of research participants are adequately protected according to the criteria discussed above. In addition, the American Psychological Association's ethical guidelines ensure that studies conducted specifically in the field of psychology meet predetermined criteria for protection of human and animal subjects. An important development in the area of protection of human participants was the implementation in April 2003 of national standards within the United States to protect the privacy of personal health information.

The Health Insurance Portability and Accountability Act, referred to as HIPAA, is the first-ever federal privacy standards to protect patients' medical records and other health information provided to health plans, doctors, hospitals and other health care providers. HIPAA protects research participants by ensuring that a researcher must meet standards to maintain the privacy of health-related information. With these guidelines in place, there is assurance that respondents in research will be appropriately treated.

SUMMARY

1. The study of aging is intimately tied up with the passage of time, and researchers on aging have attempted to develop innovative methods to increase the reliability of their findings. The variables in developmental research are age, cohort, and time of measurement. Age represents processes going on within the individual, and cohort and time of measurement are regarded as measures of social aging. These three variables are interdependent because as soon as two are known, the third is determined.

2. Descriptive research designs include longitudinal and cross-sectional. Both of these designs are quasi-experimental because they do not involve the manipulation of age as an independent variable. Each has advantages and disadvantages, but the main problem is that they do not allow for generalizations to be made beyond a single cohort or period of history. Sequential designs are necessary to attempt to control for the effects of social aging because they allow researchers to make estimates of the influence of factors other than age on performance. The Most Efficient Design was developed by Schaie to provide a framework for three types of sequential studies.

3. Correlational designs involve studying the relationship between age (or another variable) and other measures of interest. A simple correlational design involves two variables, and a multivariate correlational design involves analyzing relationships among multiple variables. Structural equation modeling is a form of multivariate correlational analysis in which complex models involving age can be statistically evaluated. In hierarchical linear modeling, patterns of change over time are analyzed, taking into account individual differences in change.

4. There are several methods of research available to investigators who study aging. In the laboratory study, conditions are controlled, and data are collected in an objective manner. Archival research uses existing records, such as census data or newspaper records. Surveys involve asking people to provide answers to structured questions, with the intention of generalizing to larger populations. Case reports are used to provide in-depth analyses of an individual or small group of individuals. Focus groups gather information about people's views on particular topics. Observational methods provide objective data on people in specific settings and under specific conditions.

5. Researchers in adult development and aging must concern themselves with finding the most appropriate measurement tools available. The science of studying measurement instruments is known as psychometrics. Of particular concern is the need to establish the appropriateness of the same measurement instrument for adults of different ages. Reliability refers to the consistency of a measurement instrument, and validity assesses whether the instrument measures what it is intended to measure.

6. Ethical issues in research address the proper treatment of participants by researchers. Informed consent is the requirement that respondents be given adequate knowledge about a study's procedures before they participate. Debriefing refers to notification of participants about the study's real purpose. Respondents also have the right to withdraw at any time without penalty. Finally, respondents must be told what will happen to their data, but at all times the data must be kept confidential. All research institutions in the United States are required by federal law to guarantee the rights of human and animal subjects.

4

Physical

According to the biopsychosocial perspective, changes in physical functioning interact with both psychological processes and social context. Biologically based changes have an effect on behavior, which in turn can modify the manifestation of these changes in the individual. Furthermore, changes that occur in the body are a reflection of social factors such as class, race, and gender. These social factors affect how people interpret changes in their physical functioning. Identity plays an important role in this process. The way that people feel about themselves is affected in part by physical appearance and competence.

In this chapter, we examine changes in the body, brain, and sensory systems throughout middle and later adulthood, with an emphasis on their interactions with identity processes. We will pay special attention to preventive measures that if adopted now, can help you grow older more successfully regardless of your current age. You will see that the most commonly referred to measure we suggest is physical activity. While we may have a bias toward the adoption and maintenance of activity given that we are both avid exercisers, it may surprise

you to see just how beneficial it can be to develop a physically active lifestyle.

APPEARANCE

Have you ever tried to guess the age of one of your parents' friends, a professor, or someone you work with? Chances are you gather the most information about age from that person's face and hair. Certainly, body build and posture can also provide clues; however, the face is ultimately most informative. You might find that often your guesses are wrong, sometimes by 5 years, 10 years, or more. Some people happen to look older or younger than their actual age. People who look younger than they are may have worked hard to maintain their youthful appearance. People who appear older, in contrast, may have inherited genes that cause their appearance to age prematurely, or may have engaged in lifestyle choices that eventually took their toll on their visible facial and bodily features. A person who has spent life sitting by the pool with a cigarette in one hand and drink in the other may certainly fit this description.

Changes

When you think about which physical changes associated with the aging process are the most telling about age, wrinkles and gray hair are generally at the top of the list. Even though these outward signs are not necessarily good indices of what is happening inside the body, many adults regard these as some of the most important aspects of the changes that occur as they get older.

Skin

Skin, the largest organ in the body, is most vulnerable to a series of age-related changes that become visible as early as the 20s, although they are rarely noticeable until the mid- or late 30s. At that time, the skin starts to show small wrinkles, slight drooping or loss of resilience, and some changes in color. With increasing age, the skin also becomes more translucent, making it easier to see the underlying bones and veins, particularly in the hands. Skin discolorations and small outgrowths accumulate so that by the 50s, the skin (particularly in the face) shows distinctive marks of the passage of time. What you see on the surface is an expression of changes occurring within the skin's three layers. The outermost layer (epidermis) is a thin covering of skin cells that protects the deeper two layers. Over time, the epidermal skin cells lose their regular patterning, although this change is not visible to the naked eye. Changes in the middle layer, the dermis, are considerably more noticeable, as the cells responsible for the skin's flexibility and elasticity decrease their functioning (see Figure 4.1).

Collagen, the protein molecule that makes up a large percentage of the body's connective tissue, undergoes the cross-links discussed below. As a result, the skin becomes less flexible. Elastin, a second important protein in the dermis, becomes less able to return to its original shape after it is stretched, similar to a rubber band. As years of constant movement take their toll, the skin eventually can no longer return to its original state of tension after it has been stretched through so many repeated movements.

At the same time, the sebaceous glands, which normally provide oils that lubricate the skin, become less active. Consequently, the skin surface becomes drier and more vulnerable to damage from being rubbed or chafed.

Lying under the top two layers of the skin is the subcutaneous fat layer that provides the cushioning,

FIGURE 4.1

Cross-section of the Skin

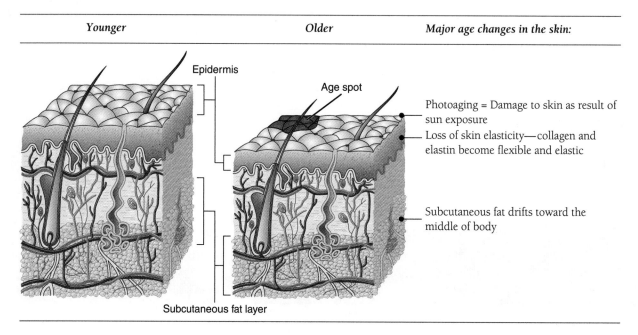

| *Younger* | *Older* | *Major age changes in the skin:* |

Epidermis

Age spot

Photoaging = Damage to skin as result of sun exposure

Loss of skin elasticity—collagen and elastin become flexible and elastic

Subcutaneous fat drifts toward the middle of body

Subcutaneous fat layer

giving the skin its opacity and smoothing the curves of the arms, legs, and face. Starting in middle adulthood, this layer starts to thin, which might seem to be a plus but in actuality accentuates the other changes. As the fatty layer thins, there is less support for the layers above it, which then exacerbates the wrinkling and sagging caused by changes in the dermis.

The skin's coloration also changes over the course of adulthood, most visibly in fair-skinned people. Discolored areas, typically referred to as "age spots" (officially called *lentigo senilus*) start to develop. These areas of brown pigmentation that show up on the skin of fair-skinned people are more likely to occur in the sun-exposed areas of the face, hands, and arms. Pigmented outgrowths (moles) and elevations of small blood vessels on the skin surface (angiomas) can also develop, further causing skin discolorations. Capillaries and arteries in the skin may dilate and generally are more visible due to the loss of subcutaneous fat. Large irregularities in the blood vessels, known as varicose veins, may develop and appear on the skin of the legs. As a result, the skin's appearance can change quite drastically with increasing age in adulthood.

The nails are a part of the skin and are also subject to age-related changes. The toenails in particular grow more slowly and may become yellowed, thicker, and ridged. Adding to these normal age-related changes in the nails is the fact that many older adults develop fungal infections in their toenails, causing them to thicken and separate from the nail bed. Older adults experience more difficulty caring for their own feet given that they often have limited joint movement and flexibility (Mitty, 2009).

The general changes that occur in the skin contribute to the aging of the face but the face's underlying structure also changes as a result of bone loss in the skull, particularly in the jaw. Changes in the cartilage of the nose and ears cause them to become longer, further altering the face's shape. Changes in the muscles of the face also reduce the relative difference between the face at rest and while smiling (Desai, Upadhyay, & Nanda, 2009).

The teeth become somewhat discolored due to loss of their enamel surface and staining from lifetime intake of substances such as coffee, tea, certain types of food, and tobacco. With increasing age, many people lose their teeth, a process which affects not only their appearance, but is also related to aspects of their health in general. In the United States about 26% of adults 65 and older have lost all their natural teeth (Schoenborn & Heyman, 2009). The rates are double for people in lower income brackets and those who lack private insurance. Current generations of middle-aged adults may suffer less from problems related to tooth loss than their previous counterparts, thanks to improvements in dental hygiene in the past several decades, particularly increased rates of flossing. Nevertheless, some changes in the teeth are bound to occur; if not in the teeth, then in the gums (Deng, Miao, Liu, Meng, & Wu, 2010).

Changes in the skin also affect the appearance of the eyes, which develop bags, small lines at the creases ("crows feet"), areas of dark pigmentation, and puffiness. In addition, the need for eyeglasses, which increases in middle adulthood, means further changes in the appearance around the eyes.

Genetic background plays an important role in the rate of skin aging. Fair-skinned people tend to display more rapid effects of aging than those with darker skin. Above and beyond genetic

inheritance, lifestyle habits are perhaps the next greatest influence on the aging of the skin. The most significant lifestyle habit is exposure to the sun, which causes **photoaging**, or age changes caused by radiation (Coelho et al., 2009). The sun's ultraviolet rays accelerate the process of cross-linking, cause mutations that alter protein synthesis by the cells, and increase the production of free radicals.

Although it is impossible to completely avoid exposure to the sun (and small doses of vitamin D from the sun's rays are good for you), there are many protective measures that you can take; the most significant one is proper use of sunscreen. Not only should sunscreen be applied and be reapplied within a certain time period, it should also meet certain requirements. The sun protection factor (SPF) measures how long you can stay in the sun before burning and provides protection from UV rays. Ideally, a sunscreen should contain at least 15 SPF and be broad enough to block both UVA and UVB light. Though by now most health-conscious people are aware of the importance of sunscreen, there is still considerably limited knowledge about its proper

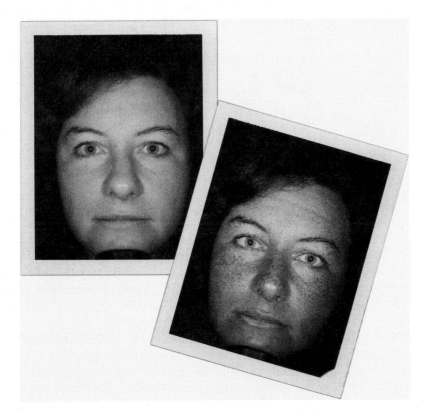

These photos demonstrate how sun damaged skin looks under UV light (right). The sun damage occurred after 20 years of beach exposure without sunblock.

use (Wang & Dusza, 2009). Additionally, despite the health risks posed by overexposure to the sun, many people (particularly younger adults), in an effort to get a "healthy glow," continue to tan excessively. Using sunscreen is not enough, however, to protect the skin from environmental factors. Other harmful habits can interact with exposure to the sun, most notably cigarette smoke (Burke & Wei, 2009).

The cosmetics industry, taking advantage of many people's desire to remain youthful in appearance, is flooding the marketplace with new anti-aging products. Although many of the early formulations were nothing other than glorified moisturizers, newer entries are using technology developed from advances in the biology of aging combined with improved delivery systems for such ingredients as collagen and tretinoin (the active ingredient in retinol). This is not to say that all of the newer products are in fact anything other than moisturizers, which in fact does have some value, but they do vary in their effectiveness and their price. Paying more for such a product does not guarantee that it will bring results, though, and it is important to know what to look for, particularly as the number of formulations multiplies. Moisturizer with SPF-15 and UVA/UVB protection can be obtained relatively inexpensively and, if used on a daily basis, can help to counteract the fragility, sensitivity, and dryness of the exposed areas of skin. The addition of alpha-hydroxy acid agents to a basic moisturizer can help stimulate cell growth and renewal to offset sun damage (Yamamoto et al., 2006). As mentioned above, tretinoin (vitamin A) is an anti-wrinkle agent that helps to preserve the collagen matrix of the skin, and when combined with moisturizer can treat changes in pigmentation as well as other consequences of photoaging (Tucker-Samaras et al., 2009).

Other anti-aging treatments for the face can only be provided by a plastic surgeon or dermatologist. The most popular is the injection of botulinum toxin (Botox®). In a Botox® treatment, a syringe containing a small amount of a nerve poison is injected into the area of concern such as around the eyes or in the middle of the forehead muscle. This procedure paralyzes the muscle, hence relaxing the skin around it and causing a temporary reduction in the appearance of the wrinkle. Although cosmetics companies have invested heavily in finding over-the-counter alternatives, at present there are no substitutes for this procedure (Beer, 2006). While the use of Botox® has come under fire citing studies of adverse reactions, the procedure remains the most popular cosmetic operation. Celebrities such as Vanessa Williams, Kim Cattrall, and even Simon Cowell have touted its benefits.

There are a host of other interventions performed by dermatologists and plastic surgeons such as injections of artificial fillers, laser resurfacing treatments, and microdermabrasion. Increasingly, products that simulate these procedures are being introduced into the market so that in coming years, people who seek to reverse or alter the course of their face's aging will have a wider variety of affordable and convenient options.

Hair

There is undoubtedly no need to point out one of the most obvious changes to occur with the aging of the body—namely, the graying of the hair. But what might not be quite so obvious is the fact that the hair does not, literally, turn gray. Instead, the number of pigmented (colored hairs) diminishes over time while the number of hairs that no longer are pigmented increases. The reason that hair loses its pigment is that the production of melanin, which gives hair its color, slows and eventually ceases. It is very likely that by the time a person reaches the age of 75 or 80 there are virtually no naturally colored hairs left on the scalp or other hair-covered areas of the body, but there are variations in the rate at which these changes take place. You may have an older relative or friend whose hair is only slightly gray or, conversely, know people in their 20s who have a significant amount of gray hair already.

The thinning of the hair, though more visible in men, actually occurs in both sexes. In general, hair loss results from the destruction of the germination centers that produce the hair in the hair follicles (see Figure 4.2). The most common form of hair loss with increased age is male and female pattern hair loss, technically known as **androgenetic alopecia**. This is a condition that affects, to some degree, 95% of adult men and 20% of adult women. Androgenetic alopecia causes the hair follicles to stop producing the long, thick, pigmented hairs known as terminal hair and instead, produce short, fine, unpigmented and largely invisible hair known as vellus hair. Eventually, even the vellus hair is not visible, because it no longer protrudes from the follicle, which itself has shrunk.

FIGURE 4.2

Forms of Male and Female Pattern Baldness

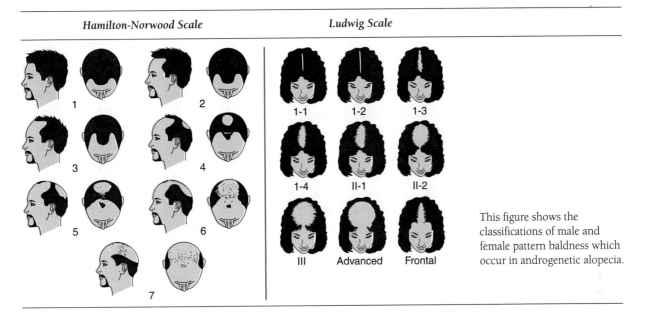

This figure shows the classifications of male and female pattern baldness which occur in androgenetic alopecia.

Although hair stops growing on the top of the head where it is desired, it may appear in larger amounts in places where it is not welcome, such as the chin on women, the ears, and in thicker clumps around the eyebrows in men.

Pharmaceutical companies are actively working to find a solution for baldness. The multitude of products designed to stop or mask the balding process range from chemicals applied directly to the scalp, most notably topical minoxidil (Rogaine), to herbal remedies and surgically implanted hair plugs. Available by prescription only, oral finasteride (Propecia) is another more radical alternative. Although there is no "cure" for gray hair or baldness, improvements in products that stimulate hair growth and the production of melanin are probably not far off in the future. Researchers are currently investigating the efficacy of a steroid used in treating a condition in which the prostate gland becomes enlarged (discussed later in the chapter) as a way to reverse hair loss in men (Alsantali & Shapiro, 2009).

BODY BUILD

The concept of being "grown up" implies that growing has ceased and the body has reached its final, mature form. However, throughout adulthood, the body is a dynamic entity, continuously changing in size and shape. By the time people reach their 50s and 60s, their bodies may have only a passing resemblance to what they looked like when they first reached physical maturity.

The first set of changes in body build involves height. Cross-sectional and longitudinal studies convincingly show that people get shorter as they get older, a process that is more pronounced for women. So although you may think of yourself as being 5 foot 9 now and therefore will be 5 foot 9 for the rest of your life, the chances are good that you will lose as much as an inch of height over the coming decades. The reason for this loss of height is the loss of bone material in the vertebrae. With the weakening of the vertebrae, the spine collapses and shortens in length (Pfirrmann, Metzdorf, Elfering, Hodler, & Boos, 2006).

The body's shape also changes significantly for most people in the adult years. The lean tissue, or fat-free mass (FFM), decreases. Countering this decrease is an increase in the **Body Mass Index (BMI)**, an index of body fat. The BMI is calculated by dividing weight in kilograms by (height in meters) squared (see Table 4.1). According to the Centers for Disease Control, an ideal BMI is in the range of 18.5 to less than 25. Adults with BMIs of 25 to 29.9 are considered "overweight" and those who have BMIs

TABLE 4.1
Calculate and interpret your BMI

Measurement Units	Formula and Calculation
Kilograms and meters (or centimeters)	Formula: weight (kg) / [height (m)].^{2} With the metric system, the formula for BMI is weight in kilograms divided by height in meters squared.
	Since height is commonly measured in centimeters, divide height in centimeters by 100 to obtain height in meters.
	Example: Weight = 68 kg, Height = 165 cm (1.65 m) Calculation: $68 \div (1.65)^2 = 24.98$
Pounds and inches	Formula: weight (lb) / [height (in)]^2 × 703. Calculate BMI by dividing weight in pounds (lbs) by height in inches (in) squared and multiplying by a conversion factor of 703.
	Example: Weight = 150 lbs, Height = 5′5″ (65″) Calculation: $[150 \div (65)^2] \times 703 = 24.96$

BMI	Weight Status
Below 18.5	Underweight
18.5–24.9	Normal
25.0–29.9	Overweight
30.0 and above	Obese

Source: Centers for Disease Control and Prevention. (2010). About BMI for adults. Retrieved from http://www.cdc.gov/healthyweight/assessing/bmi/adult_bmi/index.html#Interpreted.

of 30 and above are "obese" (Centers for Disease Control and Prevention, 2010a).

The overall pattern of body weight in adulthood shows an upside-down U-shaped trend reflecting the fact that most people increase in their weight from the 20s until the mid-50s, after which their weight decreases. Most of the weight gain that occurs through the years of middle adulthood is due to an increase in BMI (Ding, Cicuttini, Blizzard, Scott, & Jones, 2007), which is manifested mainly as the accumulation of body fat around the waist and hips (commonly referred to as the "middle-aged spread"). The loss of body weight in the later years of adulthood is not, however, due to a loss of this accumulated fat and so does not mean that older adults necessarily become healthier or more fit. Instead, older adults lose pounds because they suffer a reduction of FFM due to loss of muscle mass, even if they maintain high levels of activity (Manini et al., 2009).

At the other end of the spectrum, some older adults continue to gain weight to the point of developing a BMI that places them in the overweight or obese categories. Between the mid-1990s and mid-2000s, the percent of older adults classified as overweight increased from 60 to 69% and as obese from 22 to 31% (Houston, Nicklas, & Zizza, 2009).

Fortunately, much of the impact of aging on body build and composition can be offset by exercise. For example, one short-term study lasting only 20 weeks showed that women with mild to moderate cases of bone loss gained bone and muscle strength as a result of this training (Tolomio, Ermolao, Travain, & Zaccaria, 2008).

On the basis of extensive research on both short- and long-term exercise benefits, the American College of Sports Medicine (Chodzko-Zajko et al., 2009) summarized the most efficacious amounts and forms of exercise recommended for older adults (see Table 4.2). Exercise can have beneficial effects not only on physiological status but also on feelings of psychological well-being. Recall our discussion at the beginning of the chapter on the interactions of aging and identity. One intriguing study provided dramatic support for this relationship. Researchers tested older adults on a measure of "social physique anxiety," the extent to which one is afraid of what other people think of one's body. Over the course of a 6-month exercise training study, older adults decreased

TABLE 4.2
Recommendations for exercise from the American College of Sports Medicine

The current consensus recommendations of the ACSM and AHA with respect to the frequency, intensity, and duration of exercise and physical activity for older adults are summarized below. The ACSM/AHA Physical Activity Recommendations are generally consistent with the *2008 DHHS Physical Activity Guidelines for Americans*, which also recommend 150 min · wk^{-1} of physical activity for health benefits. However, the DHHS Guidelines note that additional benefits occur as the amount of physical activity increases through higher intensity, greater frequency, and/or longer duration. The DHHS Physical Activity Guidelines stress that if older adults cannot do 150 min of moderate-intensity aerobic activity · wk^{-1} because of chronic conditions, they should be as physically active as their abilities and conditions allow.

Endurance exercise for older adults:

Frequency: For moderate-intensity activities, accumulate at least 30 or up to 60 (for greater benefit) min · d^{-1} in bouts of at least 10 min each to total 150–300 min · wk^{-1}, at least 20–30 min · d^{-1} or more of vigorous-intensity activities to total 75–150 min · wk^{-1}, an equivalent combination of moderate and vigorous activity.

Intensity: On a scale of 0 to 10 for level of physical exertion, 5 to 6 for moderate-intensity and 7 to 8 for vigorous intensity.

Duration: For moderate-intensity activities, accumulate at least 30 min · d^{-1} in bouts of at least 10 min each or at least 20 min · d^{-1} of continuous activity for vigorous-intensity activities.

Type: Any modality that does not impose excessive orthopedic stress; walking is the most common type of activity. Aquatic exercise and stationary cycle exercise may be advantageous for those with limited tolerance for weight bearing activity.

Resistance exercise for older adults:

Frequency: At least 2 d · wk^{-1}

Intensity: Between moderate- (5–6) and vigorous- (7–8) intensity on a scale of 0 to 10.

Type: Progressive weight training program or weight bearing calisthenics (8–10 exercises involving the major muscle groups of 8–12 repetitions each), stair climbing, and other strengthening activities that use the major muscle groups.

Flexibility exercise for older adults:

Frequency: At least 2 d · wk^{-1}.

Intensity: Moderate (5–6) intensity on a scale of 0 to 10.

Type: Any activities that maintain or increase flexibility using sustained stretches for each major muscle group and static rather than ballistic movements.

Balance exercise for frequent fallers or individuals with mobility problems:

ACSM/AHA Guidelines currently recommend balance exercise for individuals who are frequent fallers or for individuals with mobility problems. Because of a lack of adequate research evidence, there are currently no specific recommendations regarding specific frequency, intensity, or type of balance exercises for older adults. However, the ACSM Exercise Prescription Guidelines recommend using activities that include the following: (1) progressively difficult postures that gradually reduce the base of support (e.g., two-legged stand, semitandem stand, tandem stand, one-legged stand), (2) dynamic movements that perturb the center of gravity (e.g., tandem walk, circle turns), (3) stressing postural muscle groups (e.g., heel stands, toe stands), or (4) reducing sensory input (e.g., standing with eyes closed).

The ACSM/AHA Guidelines recommend the following special considerations when prescribing exercise and physical activity for older adults. The intensity and duration of physical activity should be low at the outset for older adults who are highly deconditioned, functionally limited, or have chronic conditions that affect their ability to perform physical tasks. The progression of activities should be individual and tailored to tolerance and preference; a conservative approach may be necessary for the most deconditioned and physically limited older adults. Muscle strengthening activities and/or balance training may need to precede aerobic training activities among very frail individuals. Older adults should exceed the recommended minimum amounts of physical activity if they desire to improve their fitness. If chronic conditions preclude activity at the recommended minimum amount, older adults should perform physical activities as tolerated so as to avoid being sedentary.

Source: Chodzko-Zajko, W. J., Proctor, D. N., Fiatarone Singh, M. A., Minson, C. T., Nigg, C. R., Salem, G. J.,. . . Skinner, J. S. (2009). American College of Sports Medicine position stand. Exercise and physical activity for older adults. *Medicine and Science in Sports and Exercise, 41*, 1510–1530.

their social physique anxiety and felt more fit. They also gained on a measure of self-efficacy, or the feeling of confidence in being able to complete physically demanding tasks (McAuley, Marquez, Jerome, Blissmer, & Katula, 2002). In subsequent studies, social physique anxiety in middle-aged obese women in turn predicted their level of involvement in physical activity (Ekkekakis, Lind, & Vazou, 2009).

MOBILITY

You are able to move around in your environment due to the actions of the structures that support this movement, including the bones, joints, tendons, and ligaments that connect the muscles to the bones, and the muscles that control flexion and extension. In the average person, all these structures undergo age-related changes that compromise their ability to function effectively. Beginning in the 40s (or earlier in the case of injury), each component of mobility undergoes significant age-related losses. Consequently, a gradual reduction of walking speed occurs (Shumway-Cook et al., 2007). You have probably observed these changes when interacting with older relatives or friends, who tend to take longer than you to reach the same destination. Unfortunately, older adults may find it hard to adapt to their slower walking speed, leading them to be more likely than the young to make mistakes when predicting how long it will take them to cross the street (Lobjois & Cavallo, 2009). Thus, there are practical implications of these changes in mobility that can have far-reaching consequences on the older adult's life and health (see Figure 4.3).

Muscles

The adult years are characterized by a progressive age-related loss of muscle tissue, a process known as **sarcopenia**. There is a reduction in the number and size of muscle fibers, especially the fast-twitch fibers involved in speed and strength. As indicated by research from cross-sectional studies, muscle strength (as measured by maximum force) reaches a peak in the 20s and 30s, remains at a plateau until the 40s to 50s, and then declines at a faster rate of 12 to 15% per decade (Kostka, 2005), with more pronounced decreases, at least cross-sectionally,

for men. Muscular endurance (as measured by isometric strength) is, however, generally maintained throughout adulthood (Lavender & Nosaka, 2007). There are also relatively minor effects of age on eccentric strength, the action involved in such activities as lowering arm weights (such as the downward motion of a bicep curl), or going down the stairs. Eccentric strength is preserved through the 70s and 80s in men and women (Roig et al., 2010).

Muscle-mass changes predict age-related reductions in strength in adulthood (Raj, Bird, & Shield, 2010) but not entirely. One other contributor comes from disruptions in the signals the nervous system sends to the muscles telling them to contract (Klass, Baudry, & Duchateau, 2007). A second contributor is increased tendon stiffness, which makes it more difficult to move the joint and hence exert muscular strength (Carroll et al., 2008).

The loss of muscle mass brings with it a set of negative consequences including increased risk of falling, limitations in mobility, and reduced quality of everyday life. Unfortunately, sarcopenia can become part of a vicious cycle because the greater the loss of muscle mass, the greater the difficulty in undertaking exercise, causing an exacerbation of muscle loss and further weakening (Lang et al., 2009). If sarcopenia occurs in the presence of gains in fat, a condition known as sarcopenic obesity may develop (Zamboni, Mazzali, Fantin, Rossi, & Di Francesco, 2008).

Strength training with free weights or resistance machines is known to be the top preventative measure that can counteract the process of sarcopenia in adulthood (Jones et al., 2009). Although older adults do not achieve as high a degree of improvement as do younger adults, even a program as short as 16 weeks of resistance training can improve fast-twitch muscle fiber numbers to the size of those found in the young (Kosek, Kim, Petrella, Cross, & Bamman, 2006). Even older adults in their 90s can benefit from muscle strength training (Kryger & Andersen, 2007). Effective training typically involves 8 to 12 weeks, three to four times per week, at 70 to 90% of the one-repetition maximum. In order for these benefits to be maintained, the exercise has to be continued, so it is not enough to exercise for a year or two and then stop. Aerobic exercise is also a beneficial approach to maintaining muscle strength in older adults (Harber et al., 2009).

FIGURE 4.3

Age-related Changes in Muscles, Bones, and Joints

Type of tissue	Young	Old	Age change
Muscle	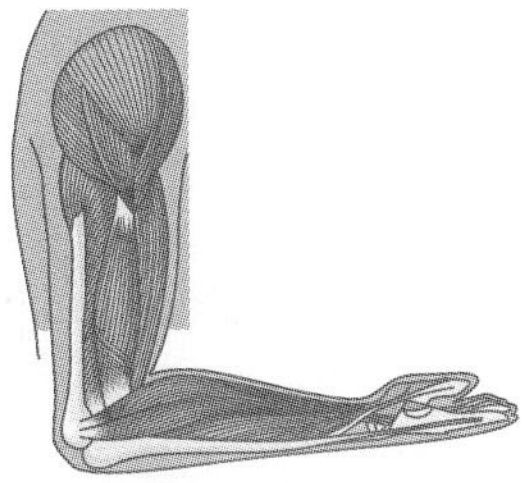	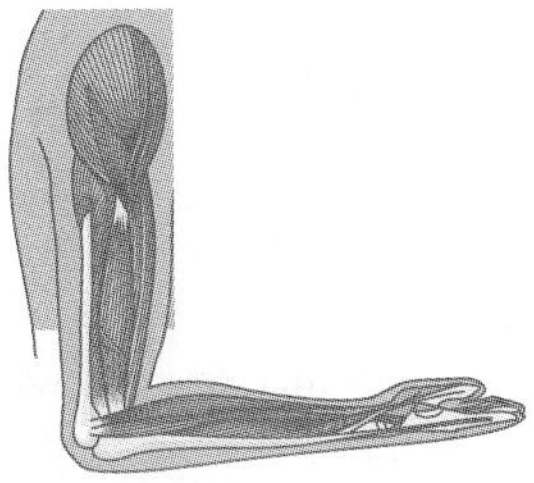	Sarcopenia
Bones	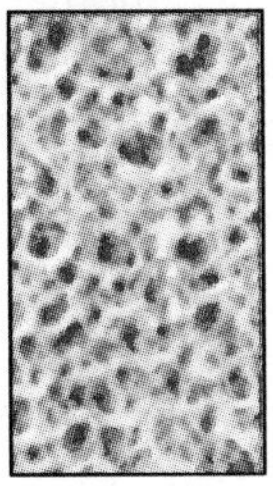	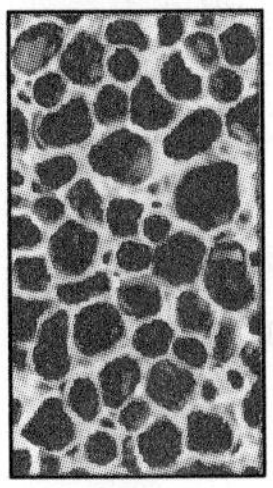	Loss of bone mineral content
Joints	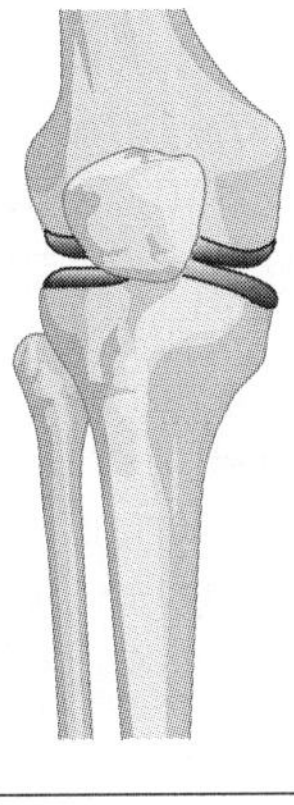	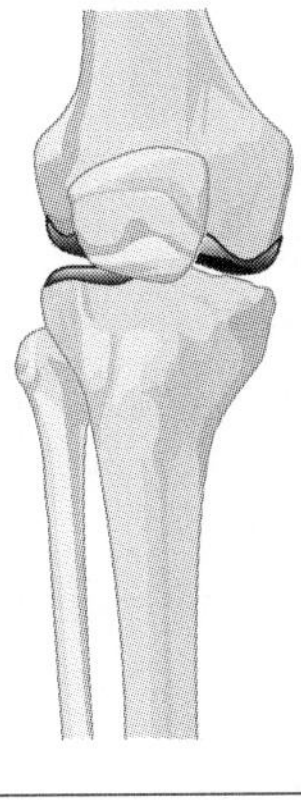	Loss of articular cartilage

One of the major benefits of muscle training is that the stronger the muscles become, the more pull they exert on the bones. As we will see next, loss of bone strength is as, if not more, significant a limitation on the health and well-being of older adults than is loss of muscle mass.

Bones

Bone is living tissue that constantly reconstructs itself through a process of bone remodeling in which old cells are destroyed and replaced by new cells. The general pattern of bone development in adulthood involves an increase in the rate of bone destruction compared to renewal and greater porosity of the calcium matrix, leading to loss of bone mineral content. The remodeling process that leads to these changes is controlled in part by a set of protein-like substances that act on the bone cells (Cao et al., 2005). These substances are, in turn, under the influence of the sex hormones estrogen for women (Maltais, Desroches, & Dionne, 2009) and testosterone for men (Travison et al., 2009). Therefore, as people experience decreases in sex hormones, they also lose bone mineral content (Sigurdsson et al., 2006).

Estimates of the decrease in bone mineral content over adulthood are about .5% per year for men and 1% per year for women (Emaus, Berntsen, Joakimsen, & Fonnebo, 2006). Further weakening occurs due to microcracks that develop in response to stress placed on the bones (Diab, Condon, Burr, & Vashishth, 2006). Part of the older bone's increased susceptibility to fracture can be accounted for by a loss of collagen, which reduces the bone's flexibility when pressure is put upon it (Saito & Marumo, 2009). The problem is particularly severe for the upper part of the thigh bone right below the hip, which does not receive much mechanical pressure during walking and therefore tends to thin disproportionately (Mayhew et al., 2005).

People lose bone at varying rates as the result of a number of other causes. Genetic factors are estimated to account for as much as 70% of bone mineral content in adulthood (Ferrari & Rizzoli, 2005). Consequently, not all older adults experience loss of bone mineral; in one longitudinal study of aging and bone mineral density, a subset of older adult women showed no significant bone loss (Cauley et al., 2009).

Heavier people in general have higher bone mineral content, so that they lose less in adulthood, particularly in the weight-bearing limbs involved in mobility. However, the amount of muscle mass rather than the weight is important since greater fat mass is related to higher loss of bone mineral content (Hsu et al., 2006). Perhaps a reflection of greater mobility, people living in rural areas have higher bone density than people living in urban environments (Pongchaiyakul et al., 2005). Bone loss is greater in women, especially White women, who lose bone at a higher rate than do African American women (Cauley et al., 2008). Conversely, African American men seem to lose bone mineral density at a higher rate than do White men (Sheu et al., 2009).

The process of bone loss does not generally pose a significant problem until people reach their 50s or 60s. However, well before these ages there are ways in which to slow down the rate of bone loss. The key lifestyle factors appear to be maintaining high levels of physical activity, not smoking, and maintaining a BMI of approximately 25 (Wilsgaard et al., 2009). Resistance training with weights can help slow down the rate of bone loss (Tolomio et al., 2008). Other ways to slow bone loss include ingesting high amounts of dietary protein (Devine, Dick, Islam, Dhaliwal, & Prince, 2005), increasing calcium intake prior to menopause, and using vitamin D (Dawson-Hughes & Bischoff-Ferrari, 2007). Adequate intake of magnesium (found in foods such as bananas, certain types of nuts, and potatoes) also seems to reduce the risk of bone loss (Ryder et al., 2005) as does a diet high in caretenoids (Sahni et al., 2009).

Environmental factors play a role as well. People who live in climates with sharp demarcations between the seasons appear to be more likely to suffer from earlier onset of bone loss; for example, people living in Norway have among the highest rates of bone fracture of anyone in the world (Forsmo, Langhammer, Forsen, & Schei, 2005).

Joints

Although most adults do not feel that they are getting "creaky" until their 40s, deleterious processes are at work even before people reach the age of skeletal maturity. These changes continue steadily throughout the adult years and appear to affect women more than men (Ding et al., 2007). By the 20s and 30s, the articular cartilage that protects the joints has already begun to degenerate, and as it does so, the bone underneath wears away. Over the course of adulthood, joint problems are exacerbated by outgrowths of cartilage that begin to develop, further interfering with the smooth movement of the bones against each other. The fibers in the joint capsule become less pliable, reducing flexibility even more.

Unlike muscles, joints do not benefit from constant use. On the contrary, the joints lose flexibility and become more painful the more stress they endure. In fact, over half of the adults in the United States report that they experience chronic joint pain or movement restriction (Leveille, 2004).

Exercise can ameliorate some effects of aging on the joints if practiced with caution (Hunter & Eckstein, 2009). Strength training that focuses on the muscles that support the joints can be beneficial in helping the individual to use those joints while placing less stress upon impaired tendons, ligaments figments, and arterial surfaces (Boling,

Bolgla, Mattacola, Uhl, & Hosey, 2006). In addition to increasing muscle strength, resistance training in which people use weight machines can also increase the flexibility of the tendons, allowing the muscle to operate more effectively (Reeves, Narici, & Maganaris, 2006). Particularly important is flexibility training that increases the range of motion of the joint (Oken et al., 2006). Because the increased weight associated with obesity contributes to joint pain and stiffness, and loss of cartilage volume (Teichtahl et al., 2009), an exercise program should also focus on lowering body fat.

Precautions taken during your younger years can reduce the chance of losses in middle age and beyond (see Table 4.3). Most important to minimizing joint pain is proper footwear (Dufour et al., 2009). Although it might not always be practical, people who engage in occupational activities that involve repetitive motions of the wrist should try as much as possible to minimize damage by the use of ergonomically designed accessories. For example, if you are a frequent computer user (and research suggests 98.4% of college students are) (EDUCAUSE Center for Applied Research, 2008),

ergonomic corrections such as adjusting the height of your chair and distance from the computer screen can help reduce the likelihood of developing carpal tunnel syndrome (see Table 4.3). Middle-aged individuals already experiencing joint damage can benefit from flexibility exercises that expand a stiff joint's range of motion. Exercise that strengthens the muscles supporting the joint also helps to improve its functioning. Both kinds of exercise have the additional benefit of stimulating circulation to the joints, thereby enhancing the blood supply that promotes repair processes in the tendons, ligaments, and surfaces of the exercising areas.

VITAL BODILY FUNCTIONS

Survival is ultimately determined by the quality of the bodily systems that support life such as the heart, lungs, and kidneys. As a very general estimate, we can say that the age-related change across all bodily systems is in the neighborhood of 1% per year (Bortz, 2005) (see Figure 4.4). Despite the impressive nature of this figure, there is much that you can do to reduce

TABLE 4.3
Evaluation checklist from the U.S. Occupational Safety and Health Administration for a safe workstation

WORKING POSTURES–The workstation is designed or arranged for doing computer tasks so it allows your	Y	N
1. **Head** and **neck** to be upright, or in-line with the torso (not bent down/back). If "no" refer to Monitors, Chairs and Work Surfaces.	☐	☐
2. **Head, neck**, and **trunk** to face forward (not twisted). If "no" refer to Monitors or Chairs.	☐	☐
3. **Trunk** to be perpendicular to floor (may lean back into backrest but not forward). If "no" refer to Chairs or Monitors.	☐	☐
4. **Shoulders** and **upper arms** to be in-line with the torso, generally about perpendicular to the floor and relaxed (not elevated or stretched forward). If "no" refer to Chairs.	☐	☐
5. **Upper arms** and **elbows** to be close to the body (not extended outward). If "no" refer to Chairs, Work Surfaces, Keyboards, and Pointers.	☐	☐
6. **Forearms, wrists**, and **hands** to be straight and in-line (forearm at about 90 degrees to the upper arm). If "no" refer to Chairs, Keyboards, Pointers.	☐	☐
7. **Wrists** and **hands** to be straight (not bent up/down or sideways toward the little finger). If "no" refer to Keyboards, or Pointers.	☐	☐
8. **Thighs** to be parallel to the floor and the **lower legs** to be perpendicular to floor (thighs may be slightly elevated above knees). If "no" refer to Chairs or Work Surfaces.	☐	☐
9. **Feet** rest flat on the floor or are supported by a stable footrest. If "no" refer to Chairs, Work Surfaces.	☐	☐

Source: U.S. Department of Labor. (2009). Good working positions: Computer workstations. Retrieved from http://www.osha.gov/SLTC/etools/computerworkstations/.

FIGURE 4.4

Age-related Changes in Vital Organ Systems

Bodily system	Young	Old	Age change
Cardiovascular			Decrease in aerobic capacity of 1% per year
Respiratory			Decrease in expiratory volume
Urinary			Slower excretion rates

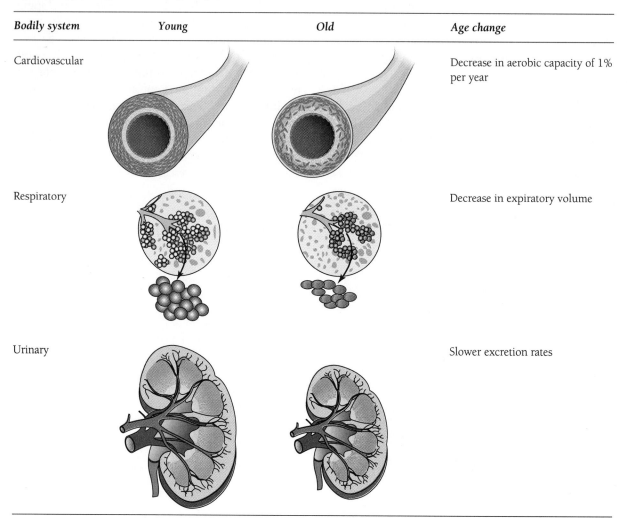

or offset the impact on aging on the majority of these functions. Not surprisingly, we will refer repeatedly to physical activity as a major form of intervention.

Cardiovascular System

Aging of the cardiovascular system involves changes that begin in middle age in both the heart itself and the arteries that circulate blood throughout the body. Of greatest relevance to aging is the left ventricle of the heart, the chamber that pumps oxygenated blood out to the arteries. It is this important structure whose loss of efficiency over time contributes the most to the deleterious changes in the cardiovascular system as a whole. The left ventricle wall becomes thicker and less able to contract, causing a reduction of diastolic functioning. This has the effect of ejecting less blood into the aorta with each of the heart's contractions (Nikitin et al., 2006). This problem is compounded by the fact that the arteries become less able to accommodate the flow of blood that the left ventricle ejects (Otsuki et al., 2006). In part, the changes in the arteries occur because deposits of plaque accumulate along the arterial walls. These deposits consist of cholesterol, cellular waste products, calcium, and fibrin (a clotting material in the blood). There are also sex differences in diastolic blood pressure, with women more likely to experience greater deterioration with age than men (Okura et al., 2009).

Cardiovascular efficiency is indexed by **aerobic capacity**, the maximum amount of oxygen that can be delivered through the blood, and **cardiac output**, the amount of blood that the heart pumps per minute. Both indices decline consistently at a rate of about 10% per decade from age 25 and up so that the average 65-year-old has 40% lower cardiovascular efficiency than the young adult (Betik & Hepple, 2008). The decline is more pronounced in males than females (Goldspink et al., 2009). Maximum heart rate, the heart rate achieved at the point of maximum oxygen consumption, also shows a linear decrease across the years of adulthood.

Declines in aerobic capacity occur even in highly trained athletes, but those who continue to exercise at a high level of intensity maintain their aerobic capacity longer than non-athletes (Tanaka & Seals, 2003). One study of former football players followed into middle age showed that they had favorable body composition and reduced risks of cardiovascular disease and osteoporosis (Lynch, Ryan, Evans, Katzel, & Goldberg, 2007). The major factor determining whether an athlete remains fit appears to be the difficulty of maintaining an active training program in the late 70s. Complications other than those involving the cardiovascular system, such as joint pain, interfere with the ability of even the most motivated person to participate in high-intensity exercise (Katzel, Sorkin, & Fleg, 2001).

Continued involvement in exercise throughout adulthood therefore does not appear to result in stopping the biological clock. However, exercise can slow down the clock by benefiting functional capacity, lifestyle, and control over body mass. Add to this the benefits of avoiding cigarette smoking, and the impact on cardiovascular functioning (and hence the quality of daily life) of these positive health habits can be significant (Heckman & McKelvie, 2008).

Short-term training studies provide more consistent findings about the value of exercise for middle-aged and older adults (Chodzko-Zajko et al., 2009). To be maximally effective, exercise must stimulate the heart rate to rise to 60 to 75% of maximum capacity, and this training must take place three to four times a week. Some recommended aerobic activities are walking, hiking, jogging, bicycling, swimming, and jumping rope. However, even moderate or low-intensity exercise can have positive effects on previously sedentary older people. The increasing popularity of incorporating heart rate monitors (such as a chest strap that connects wirelessly to a watch) into an exercise program has made it relatively simple to track the intensity of how hard the heart is working during a workout. In addition to incorporating aerobic exercise into one's workout routine, resistance training is also recommended to give an optimal boost to the functioning of the heart (Karavirta et al., 2009). Not only does exercise help maximize the heart's functioning, but it also can counteract the increased stiffness of the arteries. In one training study, a simple program of daily walking for 12 weeks was sufficient to have beneficial effects (Teichtahl et al., 2009).

Improvements in blood pressure associated with short-term training may in part reflect the favorable effect that exercise has on enhancing lipid metabolism. Exercise increases the fraction of **high-density lipoproteins (HDLs)**, the plasma lipid transport mechanism responsible for carrying lipids from the peripheral tissues to the liver where they are excreted or synthesized into bile acids. It is highly beneficial to have a high level of HDLs and a low level of low-density lipoproteins (LDLs) (Cooney et al., 2009). As is true for the effects of exercise on aerobic power and muscle strength, even moderate levels of exercise can have a beneficial impact on cholesterol metabolism (Walker, Eskurza, Pierce, Gates, & Seals, 2009). Conversely, smoking has deleterious effects on cholesterol, leading to decreased HDLs and increased LDLs, as well as the accumulation of other harmful forms of fat in the blood (Kuzuya, Ando, Iguchi, & Shimokata, 2006).

In summary, although there are a number of deleterious cardiovascular changes associated with aging, they are by no means uniformly negative. More important, there are many ways that you can both prevent and compensate for these changes. With regard to aerobic functioning, exercise is one of the best ways you can slow down the rate of your body's aging process.

Healthy exercise habits can keep adults functioning at optimal levels throughout their later years.

Respiratory System

The function of the respiratory system is to bring oxygen into the body and move carbon dioxide out. The respiratory system accomplishes these goals through the mechanical process of breathing, the exchange of gases in the innermost reaches of tiny airways in the lungs, and the transport of gases to and from the body's cells that occur in these airways. Aging affects all of these components of the respiratory system. The respiratory muscles lose the ability to expand and contract the chest wall, and the lung tissue itself is less able to expand and contract during inspiration (Britto, Zampa, de Oliveira, Prado, & Parreira, 2009). Consequently, measures of lung functioning in adulthood tend to show age-related losses from about age 40 and on. These losses are more severe in women (Harms, 2006) and particularly pronounced when stress is placed on the respiratory system during exercise (Zeleznik, 2003).

Despite these perhaps discouraging findings, exercise has positive effects on the respiratory system, strengthening the chest wall thereby compensating for the loss of pumping capacity of the respiratory muscles. People who do not engage in exercise show significantly poorer respiratory functioning than those who do (Jakes et al., 2002). However, even aerobic exercise is not enough to overcome the changes in the lung tissue itself (Womack et al., 2000). The best approach is to minimize the effects of aging on the lungs, a tactic that can be accomplished in one of two ways. The first may be the most obvious—to stay away from or quit smoking cigarettes. People who smoke show a greater loss of forced expiratory volume in later adulthood than those who do not, leading them to have an older "lung age" (Mitsumune, Senoh, Nishikawa, Adachi, & Kajii, 2009). Although it is better to quit smoking than continue smoking, there are unfortunately deleterious change in the body's cells that remain for at least several decades after a person has quit smoking (Masayesva et al., 2006). Maintaining a low BMI is the second way to preserve the functioning of the respiratory system. Researchers have determined that obesity is related to poorer respiratory functioning (Harrington & Lee-Chiong, 2009).

Urinary System

The urinary system is made up of the kidneys, bladder, ureters, and urethra. The kidneys are composed of nephron cells that serve as millions of tiny filters that cleanse the blood of metabolic waste. These waste products combine in the bladder with excess water from the blood to be eliminated as urine through the urethra.

At one time it was thought that the fate of the kidneys in older adults was to decline steadily due to loss of nephrons over time. However, the jury is still out on this question in part because although age differences are still documented in the kidney (Lerma, 2009), many factors other than age can compromise the nephrons. One of these factors is cigarette smoking, which can lead to serious kidney disease in older adults with other risk factors (Stengel, Couchoud, Cenee, & Hemon, 2000) perhaps through its effect on changes within the nephron's ability to filter wastes (Elliot et al., 2006). Studies conducted on samples in the past may have yielded exaggerated estimates of the effects of normal aging on the kidneys, reflecting instead the unhealthy effects of the once widespread habit of smoking. However, when the kidneys of older adults are placed under stress, such as through illness, extreme exertion, or extreme heat, they are less able to function normally (Fuiano et al., 2001).

Regardless of the cause of changes in the kidney with age, there are important implications to consider. Glomerular filtration rate (GFR) is the volume of fluid filtered through the kidneys, and is most typically measured by creatinine clearance. Older adults are likely to have slower excretion rates of chemicals from the body, as evidenced by lower GFR even in healthy older adults (Sun et al., 2009). Given these changes, levels of medications must be carefully monitored in middle-aged and older adults to avoid inadvertent overdoses (Wyatt, Kim, & Winston, 2006).

Changes with aging may also occur in the elastic tissue of the bladder such that it can no longer efficiently retain or expel urine. Older adults also experience slight changes in the perception that they need to urinate, although the bladder itself does not shrink in size in normal aging (Pfisterer, Griffiths, Schaefer, & Resnick, 2006). Adding to intrinsic changes in the bladder that lower the rate of urinary flow in men is the fact that many men experience hypertrophy (enlargement) of the prostate, a gland located on top of the bladder. This puts pressure on the bladder and can lead men to feel frequent urges to urinate.

Approximately 30% of all adults 65 and older suffer from urge incontinence, a form of urinary incontinence in which the individual experiences a sudden need to urinate, and often results in urine leakage. Stress incontinence involves loss of urine experienced during exertion. The prevalence of daily incontinence ranges from 12% in women 60 to 64 years old to 21% in women 85 years old or older; for about 14% of all women reporting incontinence,

about 14% reported daily occurrences with an additional 10% reporting weekly incontinence (Anger, Saigal, & Litwin, 2006).

Among the risk factors for urge incontinence in women are White race, diabetes treated with insulin, symptoms of depression, and current use of estrogen (Jackson et al., 2004). Related to urge incontinence is overactive bladder, which includes additional symptoms of frequent urination. Overactive bladder affects 25% of the population 65 and older (Wagg, Wyndaele, & Sieber, 2006). Although these conditions associated with bladder functioning can be particularly distressing, the large majority of older adults are symptom-free. Consequently, it is important to remember that urinary incontinence is not a part of normal aging.

However, older adults with overactive bladder and incontinence often experience associated psychological problems, including symptoms of depression, difficulty sleeping, and sexual dysfunction (Coyne et al., 2007). They are also likely to experience embarrassment and concern over having an accident. A greater prevalence of falls and fractures can also occur because of the greater risk of falling when an individual who has incontinence tries to rush to the bathroom.

A variety of treatments are available to counteract incontinence, but because people often mistakenly assume that bladder dysfunction is a normal part of aging, they are less likely to seek active treatment. In one study of more than 7.2 million patients diagnosed with overactive bladder, 76% went untreated (Helfand, Evans, & McVary, 2009). Medications such as tolderodine (Detrol LA) are becoming increasingly available to help control bladder problems. A number of behavioral controls alone (Burgio, 2009) or combined with medication (Tran, Levin, & Mousa, 2009), can also help to reduce the symptoms of overactive bladder and incontinence. Pelvic muscle training can be particularly effective for this purpose (Felicissimo et al., 2010). In this exercise, the urinary sphincters are contracted and relaxed for a short period of time (both men and women can engage in this exercise). Behavioral therapies, such as setting regular schedules for bathroom use, can help to improve incontinence. Such methods not only reduce incontinence but also help to alleviate the depression often associated with this condition (Tadic et al., 2007).

Kegel exercises, or pelvic muscle training, can help compensate for or even prevent urinary incontinence.

Digestive System

You no doubt hear a great deal in the media about middle-aged and older people requiring aids to their digestive system, such as treatments for heartburn (acid reflux), gas, bloating, and bowel irregularity. Surprisingly, the reality is that the majority of older people do not experience significant losses in their ability to digest food. For example, physiological changes in the esophagus are relatively minor (Achem & Devault, 2005), as are changes (for people in good health) in the remaining organs of the stomach and lower digestive tract (Bharucha & Camilleri, 2001). Decreases in saliva production occur (Eliasson, Birkhed, Osterberg, & Carlen, 2006), fewer gastric juices are secreted, and the stomach empties more slowly in older adults (O'Donovan et al., 2005). There is also a decrease in liver volume and blood flow through the liver (Serste & Bourgeois, 2006). However, these changes vary tremendously from person to person, as well as considerably according to overall health status (Drozdowski & Thomson, 2006). Smoking status and medications also affect digestive system functioning in older adults (Greenwald, 2004).

Despite the images depicted in the media of all older adults suffering from changes in their bowels, problems such as fecal incontinence affect only 4% of the over-65 population (Alameel, Andrew, & Macknight, 2010). As is true with urinary incontinence, training in behavioral controls can help to manage the condition (Byrne, Solomon, Young, Rex, & Merlino, 2007). Increasing the amount of fiber in the diet can also be of value in older adults (Markland et al., 2009).

Physiology is not the only determinant that regulates how well the digestive system functions in later life. Many lifestyle factors that change in middle and later adulthood contribute to overall digestive health. For example, families typically become smaller as children move out of the home, financial resources may decrease with retirement, and age-related mobility and cognitive problems can make cooking harder for the older adult. Such factors can detract from the motivation to eat. However, the constant advertising of the need for dietary supplements, digestive aids, and laxatives beginning in middle age can lead people to expect and then ultimately see changes in their digestion.

BODILY CONTROL SYSTEMS

Each of the organ systems we have discussed so far plays a crucial role in a person's daily physical and mental well-being. Overseeing how these systems operate is the job of the endocrine and immune systems. Researchers continue to learn about their important roles in a variety of processes ranging from the way the body utilizes energy, to sleep habits, and even to sexuality.

Endocrine System

The endocrine system is a large and diverse set of glands that regulate the actions of the body's other organ systems (referred to as "target" organs). **Hormones** are the chemical messengers produced by the endocrine systems.

Changes with age in the endocrine system can occur at many levels. The endocrine glands themselves may release more or less of a particular hormone. The target organs may also respond differently to stimulation from the hormones. Complicating matters are findings demonstrating that the endocrine system is highly sensitive to levels of stress and physical illness. Alterations that appear to be due to normal aging in the endocrine system may instead reflect other factors such as the effects of disease.

The hypothalamus and anterior (front) section of the pituitary gland, located deep within the base of the brain, are the main control centers of the endocrine system. Hypothalamus-releasing factors (HRFs), hormones produced by the hypothalamus, regulate the secretion of hormones in turn produced by the anterior pituitary gland. HRFs are not the only source of stimulation for pituitary hormones—signals from target organs carried through the blood, indicating that more pituitary hormones are needed, can also lead to greater hormone production. HRFs may also be stimulated by information sent from other parts of the nervous system.

Six hormones are produced by the anterior pituitary: growth hormone (GH, also called somatotropin), thyroid-stimulating hormone (TSH), adrenocorticotropic hormone (ACTH), follicle-stimulating hormone (FSH), luteinizing hormone (LH), and prolactin. Each of these hormones acts on specific target cells within the body and some (such as TSH) stimulate the production of other hormones. Below, we focus on the growth and thyroid-stimulating hormones as they relate to the aging process.

Growth Hormone (GH). In youth, GH stimulates the growth of bones and muscles and regulates the growth of most internal organs. Throughout life, GH affects the metabolism of proteins, lipids, and carbohydrates. A related hormone produced by the liver, IGF-1 (insulin-like growth factor-1), stimulates muscle cells to increase in size and number.

Together, GH and IGF-1 are called the somatotrophic axis. A decline in their activity, called **somatopause of aging**, is thought to account for a number of age-related changes in body composition across adulthood, including loss of bone mineral content, increases in fat, and decrease in muscle mass as well as losses in strength, exercise tolerance, and quality of life in general (Lombardi et al., 2005). There are also age differences in the activity of GH. In young people, GH production shows regularly timed peaks during nighttime sleep; in older adults, this peak is smaller, possibly contributing to sleep changes (Espiritu, 2008); a topic we will discuss shortly. GH also rises during exercise, but in adults age 60 and older this response is attenuated (Weltman et al., 2006).

Given the importance of GH to so many basic processes affected by aging, GH replacement therapy has been increasingly viewed by some as an antidote to stop the aging process. Low doses, administered in conjunction with testosterone to men, have demonstrated positive effects in increasing lean body mass and reducing fat mass, and improving overall aerobic capacity (Giannoulis et al., 2006). However, many questions remain about the practicality of this approach as well as its safety. In addition to being extremely expensive (US$10,000 to $30,000 per year), researchers maintain that the side effects include substantial negative results that outweigh any of its possible advantages (Hersch & Merriam, 2008). GH is linked to joint pain, enlargement of the heart, enlargement of the bones, diabetes, high blood pressure, and heart failure. As a result, human growth hormones (HGH) are banned from most competitive sports, although mounting evidence suggests that the use of HGH does not improve athletic performance (Liu et al., 2008).

Cortisol. We turn next to cortisol, the hormone produced by the adrenal gland. Given that cortisol provides energy to the muscles during times of stress, researchers regard it as the "stress hormone." With increases in cortisol, the body becomes energized and ready to react to the stressful encounter. Unfortunately the increase in cortisol negatively affects memory and other forms of cognitive functioning in older adults (Comijs et al., 2010). The idea that aging causes dangerous increases in cortisol levels is known as the **glucocorticoid cascade hypothesis** (Angelucci, 2000). According to this view, increased cortisol levels accelerate neuronal loss in the hippocampus. Repeated (cascading) increases in cortisol over the lifetime lead to further degeneration.

Not all studies support the glucocorticoid cascade hypothesis. Some researchers find that age changes are not demonstrated under normal conditions (Feldman et al., 2002). Most significant is that when the data are collected longitudinally rather than cross-sectionally (which is true for all of the above studies), individual variations exist in the pattern of changes over time (Lupien et al., 1996). Another factor that may relate to cortisol levels is obesity; at one time researchers believed that obesity presented a risk for higher cortisol, but in a large-scale longitudinal study it was weight loss rather than gain that was associated with higher cortisol levels in men (Travison, O'Donnell, Araujo, Matsumoto, & McKinlay, 2007).

Thyroid Hormones.   Controlling the rate of metabolism (also known as the basal metabolic rate; BMR) are hormones produced by the thyroid gland, located in the neck. The BMR begins to slow in middle age and is responsible for the weight gain that occurs even when a person's caloric intake remains stable. Changes in BMR are at least in part related to age-related decreases in thyroid hormones over adulthood (Meunier et al., 2005). Subclinical hypothyroidism can affect as many as 15 to 18% of adults over the age of 60 (Diez & Iglesias, 2004) and is associated with cognitive impairment (Hogervorst, Huppert, Matthews, & Brayne, 2008).

Melatonin.   Sleep–wake cycles are controlled in part by melatonin, the hormone manufactured by the pineal gland, located deep within the brainstem. **Circadian rhythm**, the daily variations in various bodily functions, is therefore affected by this hormone. As we will discuss later, significant changes in circadian rhythm throughout middle and later adulthood occur that some researchers believe correspond to declines in melatonin production across adulthood (Mahlberg, Tilmann, Salewski, & Kunz, 2006).

A segment of researchers believe that melatonin supplements can reduce the effects of aging and

AGING IN THE NEWS

www.wiley.com/college/whitbourne   OLDER ADULTS WHO MADE THE HEADLINES   -VOL. 4, CHAPTER 4-

JACK LALANNE CELEBRATES 95TH BIRTHDAY

Shown here on his 95th birthday, LaLanne seems as vigorous as ever. LaLanne personifies the "use it or lose it" mentality, an attitude to which he credits his excellent health. A lifelong fitness buff, LaLanne has written books and videos on the values of exercise and careful diet. He continues to work out at home for a minimum of two hours per day. On previous birthdays he has been known to haul a series of boats equaling the number of his age. Not only is he an avid exerciser, but he controls his food intake, avoiding all dairy products. Taking the advice of the CDC, he also consumes large amounts of fruits and vegetables each day. In 2005, he was inducted into the National Fitness Hall of Fame and by 2010 showed no signs of slowing down.

age-associated diseases, especially in the brain and immune system. Melatonin supplements for women can lead to improved pituitary and thyroid functions (Bellipanni, Bianchi, Pierpaoli, Bulian, & Ilyia, 2001) and reduce the incidence of sleep problems (Gubin, Gubin, Waterhouse, & Weinert, 2006). Although supplements may offer a solution to decreases in melatonin, the side effects are yet to be fully identified, and the safety, effectiveness, and purity of available supplements has not been approved by the FDA. Additionally, melatonin supplements can interfere with sleep cycles if taken at the wrong time. Significant side effects, including confusion, drowsiness, headaches, and constriction of blood vessels also occur, posing danger to people with high blood pressure. Finally, the dosages usually sold in over-the-counter medications may be as high as 40 times the amount normally found in the body, and the effect of such large doses taken long term has not been determined (National Library of Medicine, 2010).

DHEA. The most abundant steroid in the human body, dehydroepiandrosterone (DHEA), is a weak male steroid (androgen) produced by the adrenal glands located adjacent to the kidneys. DHEA is a precursor to the sex hormones testosterone and estrogen, and is believed to have a variety of functions such as increasing production of other sex steroids and availability of IGF-1 as well as positively influencing some central nervous system functions.

DHEA, which is higher in males than females, shows a pronounced decrease over the adult years, reducing by 60% between the ages of 20 and 80 (Feldman et al., 2002). This phenomenon, termed **adrenopause**, is greater in men, although men continue to have higher levels than women throughout later life because they start at a higher baseline. Extremely low levels of DHEA have been linked to cardiovascular disease, some forms of cancer, immune system dysfunction, and obesity (von Muhlen, Laughlin, Kritz-Silverstein, & Barrett-Connor, 2007).

Although there are no definitive answers about DHEA's role in aging other than the decline in DHEA is likely, DHEA replacement therapy rivals GH and melatonin in the anti-aging industry. However, like GH therapy, health risks are notable, mainly liver problems and an increase in risk of prostate cancer (Arnold et al., 2007). A natural substitute for some of the positive effects of DHEA replacement therapy is exercise, which can help to compensate for its loss in the later adult years (Igwebuike et al., 2008).

Female Sexual Changes. Technically speaking, **menopause** is the point in a woman's life when menstruation stops permanently. As used in common speech, however, menopause has come to mean a phase in middle adulthood covering the years in which a woman's reproductive capacity diminishes. The more precise term for this gradual winding down of reproductive ability is **climacteric**, a term that applies to men as well. For women, the climacteric occurs over a 3- to 5-year span called the **perimenopause**, ending in the menopause when the woman has not had her menstrual period for 1 year. The average age of menopause is 50 years, but the timing varies among individuals. Menopause occurs earlier in women who are thin, malnourished, or who smoke.

Throughout the perimenopause, there is a diminution in the production by the ovarian follicles of estrogen, the primary female sex hormone. Since the other female hormone, progesterone, is produced in response to ovulation, progesterone levels also decline during this time. The process of estrogen decline begins about 10 to 15 years before menopause, at some point in the mid-30s. By the mid-40s, the ovaries have begun to function less effectively and produce fewer hormones. Eventually, menstrual cycles by the early to middle 50s have ended altogether. There is still some production of estrogen, however, as the ovaries continue to produce small amounts and the adrenal glands stimulate the production of estrogen in fat tissue. Follicle-stimulating hormone (FSH) and luteinizing hormone (LH) levels rise dramatically during the perimenopausal period as the anterior pituitary sends out signals to produce more ovarian hormones. In turn, the hypothalamus produces less gonadotropin-releasing factor (GnRH).

Although women vary considerably in their progression through the menopause (as they do during puberty), there are certain characteristic symptoms, many of which you have probably heard discussed by middle-aged and older women (there was even an off-Broadway musical called

Menopause). One of the most prominent symptoms is the occurrence of "hot flashes," which are sudden sensations of intense heat and sweating that can last from a few moments to half an hour. These are the result of decreases in estrogen levels, which cause the endocrine system to release higher amounts of other hormones that affect the temperature control centers in the brain. Fatigue, headaches, night sweats, and insomnia are other physiological symptoms thought to be the result of fluctuating estrogen levels. Menopausal women also report that they experience psychological symptoms such as irritability, mood swings, depression, memory loss, and difficulty concentrating, but the evidence regarding the connection between these symptoms and the physiological changes involved in menopause is far from conclusive.

Along with hormonal changes, menopause is associated with alterations in the reproductive tract. Because of lower estrogen levels, there is a reduction in the supply of blood to the vagina and surrounding nerves and glands. The tissues become thinner, drier, and less able to produce secretions to lubricate before and during intercourse. The result is the possibility of discomfort during intercourse (da Silva Lara et al., 2009). In addition, women may become more susceptible to urinary problems such as infections and stress incontinence in which urine leaks out of the urethra upon exertion.

More widespread throughout the body are other effects of menopause associated with the impact of decreasing estrogen levels on other bodily systems. Weaker bones, high blood pressure, and cardiovascular disease become more prevalent among postmenopausal women. Estrogen appears to provide protection against these diseases, which is lost at menopause. There are also changes in cholesterol levels in the blood associated with menopause, causing postmenopausal women to be at higher risk of atherosclerosis and associated conditions.

Estrogen-replacement therapy (ERT) was introduced in the 1940s to counteract the negative effects of estrogen loss on postmenopausal women. Later, estrogen was combined with the hormone, progestin, to reduce cancer risk. Administration of both hormones is referred to as **hormone replacement therapy (HRT)**.

Initial studies on HRT's effects on the body provided enthusiastic support, citing positive effects on skin tone and appearance, bone mineral density, immune functioning, thickness of the hair, sleep, accidental falls, memory, and mood. However, over the past decade, the pros and cons of HRT have become hotly debated by researchers and the jury is still out on whether the benefits outweigh the risks (Alexandersen, Karsdal, & Christiansen, 2009). There is also evidence that the specific chemical composition of the hormone replacement may have differing effects on cancer risk (Schneider, Jick, & Meier, 2009). At the same time, there may as yet be unidentified benefits of HRT such as reduced risk of colon cancer (Weige, Allred, & Allred, 2009).

For women not willing to experiment with HRT given the conflicting data, alternatives are available. Other recommended approaches to counteract the effect of hormonal changes include exercise, quitting smoking, lowering the cholesterol in the diet, and perhaps, more enjoyably, having one alcoholic drink a day.

Male Sexual Changes. Although men do not experience a loss of sexual function comparable to the menopause (despite what you might hear about the "male menopause"), men undergo **andropause**, which refers to age-related declines in the male sex hormone testosterone. The decline in testosterone is equal to 1% per year after the age of 40, a decrease observed in longitudinal as well as cross-sectional studies (Feldman et al., 2002). The term "late-onset hypogonadism" or "age-associated hypogonadism" has begun to replace the term andropause, although all three terms are currently in use.

Abnormally low levels of testosterone levels are found in 6 to 10% of men between the ages of 40 and 70, but these rates are far higher (15–30%) in men who are diabetic or obese (Tostain & Blanc, 2008). Testosterone supplements for aging men were long considered an unnecessary and potentially dangerous proposition. However, with greater empirical support and acceptance in the medical community, testosterone supplements are in greater use, with the condition that treatment is accompanied by regular medical screening (Theodoraki & Bouloux, 2009). The benefits associated with testosterone supplements include maintained or improved bone density, greater muscle strength, lowered ratio of fat to lean muscle mass, increased strength, libido, and sexual function (Seidman, 2007), and even lower rates of cognitive decline (Janowsky, 2006).

In contrast to findings of early studies, there is no evidence that prostate mass increases as long as the treatment maintains a man's testosterone within a normal range. Also contrasted with previous work, higher testosterone levels are associated with lowered cardiovascular risk, including more favorable cholesterol levels (Munzer, Harman, Sorkin, & Blackman, 2009).

Erectile dysfunction (ED), a condition in which a man is unable to achieve an erection sustainable for intercourse, is estimated to increase with age in adulthood, from a rate of 31% among men 57–65 to 44% of those 65 and older. ED is related to health problems in older men, including metabolic syndrome (Borges et al., 2009). Compared to younger men, however, premature climax is less common in the 65 and older population (Waite, Laumann, Das, & Schumm, 2009).

You are no doubt familiar with the "cure" for ED: the little blue pill known as Viagra. Phospho-diesterase type 5 inhibitors, including Viagra (the technical term is sildanefil), can be effective in treating ED, alleviating the difficulties experienced by men and their sexual partners (Morales, Mirone, Dean, & Costa, 2009). Researchers now believe that the combination of testosterone supplements with other ED medications can be particularly beneficial (Corona & Maggi, 2010). However, there are risks. You may recall the scene from the 2003 movie *Something's Gotta Give* in which Jack Nicholson's character, suffering from a heart attack, admits to taking Viagra only after learning that the combination with the nitro drip could be fatal.

Based on the relationship between ED and metabolic syndrome as well as hypertension, diabetes, and obesity (Chitaley, Kupelian, Subak, & Wessells, 2009), it would also be a worthwhile strategy to recommend exercise to an older man experiencing this condition (Lamina, Okoye, & Dagogo, 2009).

Immune System

Regulating the body's ability to fight off stress, infection, and other threats to well-being and health is the immune system. In addition to protecting the body, the immune system is closely linked to the nervous system and, consequently, to behaviors, thoughts, and emotions (Lupien, McEwen, Gunnar, & Heim, 2009).

Researchers believe that there are widespread age-related declines in immune system functioning, a process known as **immune senescence** (see Figure 4.5). The two primary types of immune lymphocytes include "T cells" and "B cells," both

FIGURE 4.5

Age-related Changes in the Immune System (above) and Possible Rejuvenation Strategies (below)

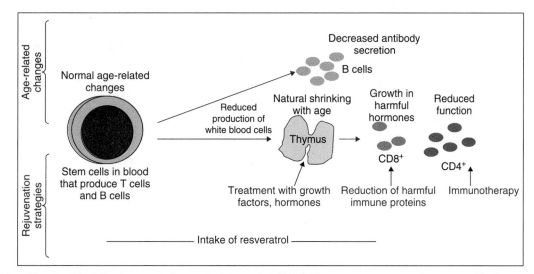

Source: Adapted from Dorshkind, K., Montecino-Rodriguez, E., & Signer, R. A. (2009). The ageing immune system: Is it ever too old to become young again? *Nature Reviews Immunology, 9,* 57–62.

of which are involved in destroying bodily invaders known as antigens. In immune senescence, these cells fail to develop properly and lose their ability to perform effectively, causing older adults to be less resistant to infections (Grubeck-Loebenstein, 2010). Thus, although children are more likely to develop influenza infection during seasonal flu season, the mortality is almost entirely among older adults. Exceptions occur during pandemic years, such as during the outbreak of the H1N1 virus in late 2009. According to the Centers for Disease Control, 13% of adults 50 and older were hospitalized with the flu compared to 37% of adults between the ages of 18 and 49. Flu experts theorized that adults over the age of 50 had immunity or protection from the H1N1 strain and were therefore not considered at high risk (Centers for Disease Control and Prevention, 2010b).

Interactions between the immune system and other physical and psychological processes are important to consider during the aging process. For example, cortisol and DHEA have opposing actions on the immune system and changes in their balance with age can alter the activity of immune system cells (Buford & Willoughby, 2008). Micronutrients, found in certain vitamins and minerals such as vitamin E and zinc, are believed to improve immune responsiveness and prevent infection (Mocchegiani et al., 2008). Protein intake is also crucial to maintaining adequate immune functioning of older adults (Aoi, 2009). Moderate exercise can play a role in enhancing immune functioning by offsetting declines that would otherwise occur in the system's adaptive ability (Senchina, 2009). Conversely, chronic stress can accelerate the rate of the immune system's aging (Gouin, Hantsoo, & Kiecolt-Glaser, 2008).

Previous research examining the effects of aging on the immune system may have failed to control (statistically) for variables measuring diet and exercise; such a lack of control might account for the fact that the effects of aging on the immune system are highly variable (Dorshkind, Montecino-Rodriguez, & Signer, 2009). There may also be some protective mechanisms not completely understood at present that help maintain the immune functioning of certain healthy agers. For example, studies of centenarians have revealed that some of the basic cells in the immune system were as healthy in this hardy group of older adults as in young adults (Alonso-Fernandez,

TABLE 4.4
Models of Aging and the Nervous System

Model	Proposed Effects of Aging	Relevant Research
Neuronal fallout	Losses occur in numbers of neurons and synapses	Decreases in prefrontal cortex, hippocampus. Increases in white matter hyperintensities.
Plasticity	Continued growth through dendritic elaboration	Diet and exercise preserve brain function and cognition.

Puerto, Mate, Ribera, & de la Fuente, 2008). Despite the emerging and potentially conflicting research, it is best to be aware of the potentially negative effect aging may have among people who do not maintain ideal levels of diet and exercise. An immune system compromised by a disease such as cancer is a major contributor to mortality in middle and later adulthood.

NERVOUS SYSTEM

The two components of the nervous system serve to regulate all behavior; consequently, researchers who study the aging process have focused heavily on changes in this system. The central nervous system makes it possible to monitor and then prepare responses to events in the environment, conceive and enact thoughts, and maintain connections with other bodily systems. The autonomic nervous system controls involuntary behaviors, the body's response to stress, and the actions of other organ systems that sustain life.

Central Nervous System

Early research on nervous system functioning in adulthood was based on the hypothesis that there is a progressive loss of brain tissue across the adult years that is noticeable by the age of 30 because neurons do not have the ability to replace themselves when they die (see Table 4.4). The model of aging based on this hypothesis was called the **neuronal fallout model**. However, in the years intervening since the development of this model, it has become clear that in the absence of disease, the aging brain maintains much of its structure and function. The first evidence in this direction was provided in the late 1970s by an innovative team of neuroanatomists who found that mental stimulation can compensate for loss of neurons.

According to the **plasticity model**, while neurons die, the remaining ones continue to develop, allowing older adults to compensate for neuronal losses (Goh & Park, 2009). For example, areas of the brain involved in complex language and word processing skills continue to develop and reach maturity in middle age (Bartzokis et al., 2001). Diet and physical exercise are important ways to maintain brain function (Pinilla, 2006) and, consequently, cognitive functioning (Dishman et al., 2006). Aerobic exercise in particular appears to be most beneficial in preserving and maximizing the functioning of the brain (Colcombe et al., 2006), particularly in areas involved in attentional control and verbal memory (Erickson & Kramer, 2009) (see Figure 4.6).

Over the past 20 years, the increasing availability and sophistication of brain imaging methods, such

as magnetic resonance imaging (MRI) brain scans, has produced a wealth of new data about the impact of aging on the central nervous system. Normal aging seems to have major effects on the prefrontal cortex, the area of the brain most involved in planning and the encoding of information into long-term memory, as well as in the temporal cortex, involved in auditory processing (Fjell et al., 2009). The hippocampus, the structure in the brain responsible for consolidating memories, becomes smaller with increasing age, although this decline is more pronounced in abnormal aging such as in Alzheimer's disease (Zhang et al., 2010). Nevertheless, evidence exists in support of the plasticity model within the cells of the hippocampus (Lister & Barnes, 2009).

Aging is also associated with changes in the frontal lobe in the form of abnormalities known as **white matter hyperintensities** (WMH). These abnormalities are thought to be made up of parts of deteriorating neurons. Their presence appears to interfere with long-term memory because they disrupt the integrity of the white matter (Charlton, Barrick, Markus, & Morris, 2009). There is great variability among the older adult population, however, reflecting the likely inclusion in research studies of participants

FIGURE 4.6

Impact of Aerobic Exercise on Brain Functioning

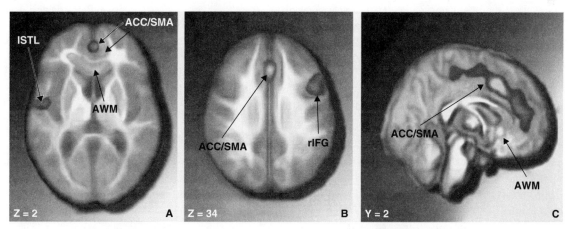

MRIs of the brains of older adults who engaged in an aerobic fitness training program compared with older adults who participated in a stretching and toning program. A and B show horizontal slices of the brain, and C shows a vertical slice. The dark areas indicate increased gray matter volume in aerobic vs. non-aerobic exercisers, and the lighter highlighted regions show increased white matter, all areas that help promote memory.
Source: Colcombe S. J., Erickson, K. I., Scalf, P. E., Kim, J. S., Prakash, R., McAuley, E.,... Kramer, A. F. (2006). Aerobic exercise training increases brain volume in aging humans. *Journal of Gerontology Series A: Biological Sciences and Medical Sciences, 61A,* 1166–1170.

with hypertension (Burgmans et al., 2010). Many puzzles remain in understanding WMH's role in the aging of the nervous system and the impact, in turn, on memory. For example, in individuals over 60 years of age, these abnormalities account for a significant amount of the variation in cognitive functioning (Vannorsdall, Waldstein, Kraut, Pearlson, & Schretlen, 2009).

Sleep

The literature on sleep in adulthood clearly refutes a common myth about aging, namely, that as people grow older they need less sleep. Regardless of age, everyone requires 7 to 9 hours of sleep a night (Ancoli-Israel & Cooke, 2005). In fact, sleeping 9 hours or more a night is associated with higher mortality risks and greater incidence of stroke in women (Chen et al., 2008). However, changes in various aspects of sleep-related behavior and sleep problems can affect the mental and physical well-being of the middle-aged and older adult, and it is estimated that up to half of all older adults have difficulty sleeping (Neikrug & Ancoli-Israel, 2009). These changes relate in part to lifestyle as well as physiology. You almost certainly know from your own experience that sleep patterns can be particularly

disrupted during periods of stress. For instance, middle-aged adults who live with high degrees of job-related stress suffer sleep disturbances. Other lifestyle factors also play an important role, including obesity, physical inactivity, and alcohol use (Janson, Lindberg, Gislason, Elmasry, & Boman, 2001).

Though the cause of sleep changes is not known, there are different patterns of behavior shown by older adults in sleep patterns. Older adults spend more time in bed relative to time spent asleep. They take longer to fall asleep, awaken more often during the night, lie in bed longer before rising, and have sleep that is shallower, more fragmented, and less efficient (Fetveit, 2009). EEG sleep patterns show some corresponding age alterations, including a rise in Stage 1 sleep and a large decrease in both Stage 4 and REM (rapid eye movement) sleep (Kamel & Gammack, 2006). These changes occur even for people who are in excellent health.

Perhaps related to changes in sleep is that people shift from a preference to working in the later hours of the day and night to a preference for the morning at some point during middle to late adulthood. Adults over 65 tend to classify themselves as "morning" people and the large majority of younger adults classify themselves as "evening" people (see Figure 4.7). The biological basis for this shift in preferences presumably occurs

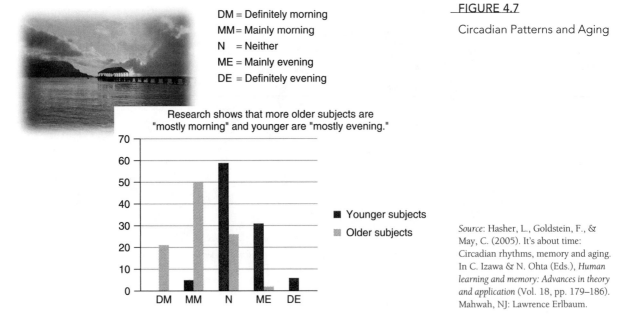

DM = Definitely morning
MM = Mainly morning
N = Neither
ME = Mainly evening
DE = Definitely evening

Research shows that more older subjects are "mostly morning" and younger are "mostly evening."

■ Younger subjects
▨ Older subjects

FIGURE 4.7

Circadian Patterns and Aging

Source: Hasher, L., Goldstein, F., & May, C. (2005). It's about time: Circadian rhythms, memory and aging. In C. Izawa & N. Ohta (Eds.), *Human learning and memory: Advances in theory and application* (Vol. 18, pp. 179–186). Mahwah, NJ: Lawrence Erlbaum.

gradually throughout adulthood, along with changes in hormonal contributors to sleep and arousal patterns (Benloucif et al., 2004).

One intriguing implication of changes in circadian rhythm with age is that when studies of cognitive functioning take place at nonoptimal times of the day, older adults perform poorer than young adults tested at their off-peak times (Rowe, Hasher, & Turcotte, 2009). To the extent that cognitive researchers fail to take this into account, there is a systematic bias against the older participants. Interestingly, the effect of time of day on memory performance is less pronounced among older adults who engage in regular patterns of physical activity compared with their sedentary peers (Bugg, DeLosh, & Clegg, 2006).

Changes in sleep patterns in middle and later adulthood may be prevented or corrected by one or more alterations in sleep habits. As a sedentary lifestyle is a major contributor to sleep problems, exercise can improve sleep at night. A variety of psychological disorders can also interfere with the sleep of middle-aged and older adults, including depression, anxiety, and bereavement (Kim et al., 2009). Medical conditions that disturb sleep include arthritis, osteoporosis, cancer, chronic lung disease, congestive heart failure, and digestive disturbances (Bloom et al., 2009; Spira, Stone, Beaudreau, Ancoli-Israel, & Yaffe, 2009). People with Parkinson's disease or Alzheimer's disease also suffer serious sleep problems (Gabelle & Dauvilliers, 2010). Finally, the normal age-related changes that occur in the bladder lead to a more frequent urge to urinate during the night and thereby cause sleep interruptions. Menopausal symptoms can lead to frequent awakenings during the night, although exercise seems to help minimize the impact of menopause on aging (Chedraui et al., 2010). Periodic leg movements during sleep (also called nocturnal myoclonus) are another source of nighttime awakenings (Ferri, Gschliesser, Frauscher, Poewe, & Hogl, 2009).

All of these conditions, when they interrupt sleep, can lead to daytime sleepiness and fatigue, creating in turn a higher risk of falling, difficulty concentrating, and negative changes in quality of life (Ancoli-Israel & Cooke, 2005). A vicious cycle begins when the individual starts to establish a pattern of daytime napping, which increases the chances of sleep interruptions occurring at night (Foley et al., 2007).

One physical condition that particularly interferes with sleep is **sleep apnea**, also called sleep-related breathing disturbance. People with this condition, typically in middle and late adulthood, experience a particular form of snoring in which a partial obstruction in the back of the throat restricts airflow during inhalation. A loud snore is followed by a choking silence when breathing actually stops. When the airway closes, the lack of oxygen is registered by the respiratory control centers in the brain, and the sleeper awakens. There may be 100 such episodes a night, and to make up for the lack of oxygen that occurs during each one, the heart is forced to pump harder to circulate more blood. As a result, there are large spikes in blood pressure during the night as well as elevated blood pressure during the day. Over time, the person's risk of heart attack and stroke is increased. In addition, the individual experiences numerous periods of daytime sleepiness that interfere with everyday activities. Sleep apnea is more common in older adults with cardiovascular or cerebrovascular disease (Fetveit, 2009). The condition can be treated with a continuous positive airway pressure (CPAP) device, which keeps airways open during sleep, although users often complain that the burdensome equipment inhibits sleep patterns (Wolkove, Elkholy, Baltzan, & Palayew, 2007).

Although changes in sleep occur as a normal feature of the aging process, severe sleep disturbances do not. Exercise can be helpful in resetting disturbed circadian rhythms (Benloucif et al., 2004). Sleep specialists can offer innovative approaches such as light therapy, which "resets" an out-of-phase circadian rhythm, and encouragement of improvements in sleep habits (Klerman, Duffy, Dijk, & Czeisler, 2001).

Temperature Control

Every summer or winter, when many regions of the world suffer extreme weather, older adults are among those reported to be at greatest risk of dying from hyper- or hypothermia, conditions known together as **dysthermia**. Between 1998 and 2006, 700 people per year in the United States died from hyperthermia, of whom 40% were 65 or older. Ten times as many deaths per year are attributed to the opposite condition, hypothermia (Centers for Disease Control and Prevention, 2006). Aging alone, however, does not seem to be the main cause of deaths due to hyperthermia, as the majority of those who die in conditions of extreme heat have heart disease (Luber & Sanchez, 2006). Nevertheless, in less extreme conditions there remain changes in the ability of older adults to adjust to high heat levels due to a decrease in sweat output, causing the body's core temperature to rise to a greater degree (Dufour & Candas, 2007). In addition, the reduction of the dermal layer of the skin further contributes to an impairment in skin cooling (Petrofsky et al., 2009).

Deaths due to hypothermia in older adults seem to be on the rise (Fallico, Siciliano, & Yip, 2005). The cause of the higher death rates under conditions of hypothermia may be an impaired ability of older adults to maintain their core body temperature during extremely cold outside temperatures (Thompson-Torgerson, Holowatz, & Kenney, 2008).

SENSATION AND PERCEPTION

A variety of changes occur in adulthood throughout the parts of the nervous system that affect sensation and perception. These changes reduce the quality of input that reaches the brain to be integrated in subsequent stages of information processing (see Table 4.5).

TABLE 4.5
Age-related Changes in Vision and Hearing

Sense	Changes	
Vision	Presbyopia Cataracts	
Hearing	Presbycusis	

Vision

Changes in vision take several forms. You may associate growing older with the need to wear reading glasses and in fact, this is what occurs. Most people require some form of corrective lenses by the time they reach their 50s or 60s. **Presbyopia,** or loss of the ability to focus vision on near objects, is the primary culprit for the need for reading glasses, and is the visual change that most affects people in midlife and beyond.

Presbyopia is caused by a thickening and hardening of the lens, the focusing mechanism of the eye (Sharma & Santhoshkumar, 2009). As a result, the lens cannot adapt its shape when needed to see objects up close to the face. By the age of 50, presbyopia affects the entire population. Treatment for the cause of presbyopia does not exist, and although bifocals were the only correction since the time of Benjamin Franklin (who invented them) newer multifocal contact lenses are increasingly becoming available on the market (Woods, Woods, & Fonn, 2009). Though you cannot cure presbyopia, you may be able to alter its onset because lifestyle habits seem to affect the rate at which the presbyopic aging process occurs. For example, smoking accelerates the aging of the lens (Kessel, Jorgensen, Glumer, & Larsen, 2006).

Older adults are also likely to experience the loss of visual acuity, or the ability to see details at a distance. The level of acuity in an 85-year-old individual is approximately 80% less than that of a person in their 40s. Increasing the level of illumination is an effective strategy to compensate, but at the same time, older adults are more sensitive to glare. As a result, making lights brighter may actually impair rather than improve an older person's visual acuity.

In addition to experiencing normal age-related changes in vision, older people become increasingly vulnerable to visual disorders. About one-half of adults over the age of 65 years report that they have experienced some form of visual impairment. The most common impairment is a **cataract**, a clouding that develops in the lens. This results in blurred or distorted vision because images cannot be focused clearly onto the retina. The term "cataract" reflects the previous view of this condition as a waterfall behind the eye that obscured vision.

Cataracts usually start as a gradual cloudiness that progressively grows more opaque. Although they are most often white, they may develop yellow or brownish coloring. Cataracts appear to develop as a normal part of the aging process, but other than the changes that occur in the lens fibers, their cause is not known. Factors such as heredity, prior injury, and diabetes may play roles in causing cataract formation. Cigarette smoking and nutritional deficits are additional risk factors for the development of cataracts (Rhone & Basu, 2008). Evidence suggests that a high intake of carbohydrates may increase the probability of developing cataracts (Chiu, Milton, Gensler, & Taylor, 2006). Conversely, taking vitamin C may reduce their formation (Yoshida et al., 2007).

The main form of eye disease, cataracts affect about 17% of the over-40 population (Congdon et al., 2004). The development of cataracts occurs gradually over a period of years during which the individual's vision becomes increasingly blurred and distorted. If the cataracts have a yellow or brown tone, colors will take on a yellow tinge similar to the effect of wearing colored sunglasses. A person's vision becomes increasingly impaired both under conditions of low light, as acuity is reduced, and under conditions of bright light, due to increased susceptibility to glare. Bright lights may seem to have a halo around them. These are significant limitations and can alter many aspects of the person's everyday life. It is more difficult to read, walk, watch television, recognize faces, and perform work, hobbies, and leisure activities. Consequently, people with cataracts may suffer a reduction in independence, as they find it more difficult to drive or even go out at night with others.

Despite the common nature of cataracts and their pervasive effect on vision, they can be successfully treated. Enormous strides have been made in the treatment of cataracts due to advances in surgical procedures. Currently, cataract surgery is completed in about an hour or less, under local anesthesia, and with no hospital stay. Visual recovery is achieved usually within 1 to 7 days, and many people's vision is so improved that they rely only minimally on corrective lenses.

A second significant form of blindness that becomes more prevalent in later adulthood is **age-related macular degeneration (ARMD)**. An estimated 15% of people 80 and older have this disease (Oneill, Jamison, McCulloch, & Smith, 2001), which is one of the leading causes of blindness in those over the age of 65 (Coleman, Chan, Ferris, & Chew, 2008).

ARMD involves destruction of the photoreceptors located in the central region of the retina known as the macula. This area of the retina is normally used in reading, driving, and other visually demanding activities so that the selective damage to the receptors in the macula that occurs is particularly incapacitating. Although there is no known treatment for ARMD, antioxidants and avoidance of cigarette smoking (once again) can serve to reduce a person's risk (Zanon-Moreno, Garcia-Medina, Zanon-Viguer, Moreno-Nadal, & Pinazo-Duran, 2009). Exposure to light is yet another risk factor, so wearing protective lenses may serve as prevention (de Jong, 2006). If you find yourself squinting outside in the sunlight, you might think about decreasing your risk of developing ARMD in the future by putting on a pair of sunglasses. Treatments for the "wet" form of ARMD, which is related to damage to the vascular supply to the retina, so far include only medications that can slow its progression by reducing the growth of new blood cells (Brucker, 2009).

Glaucoma is the term used for a group of conditions causing blindness related to changes in pressure within the eyeball. The most common type of glaucoma develops gradually and painlessly without symptoms. Therefore, it may not be detected until the disease reaches advanced stages. Eventually glaucoma causes a loss of peripheral vision and, over time, may cause the remaining vision to diminish altogether. More rarely the symptoms appear suddenly, including blurred vision, loss of side vision, perception of colored rings around lights, and experience of pain or redness in the eyes.

Glaucoma is the third most common cause of blindness in the United States, and the most common form of glaucoma is estimated to affect about 3 million Americans. It is diagnosed in 95,000 new patients each year. Blacks are at higher risk than Whites, as are people who are nearsighted, have diabetes, or have a family history of glaucoma. Arthritis (Perruccio, Badley, & Trope, 2007) and obesity (Imai et al., 2010) are additional risk factors. Some forms of glaucoma can be controlled but not cured, and others can be treated successfully through surgery.

Visual disturbances in older adults, whatever their cause, require attention of health care professionals. Not only might they be treatable, but even if not, their presence can relate to psychological symptoms including depression and isolation. Moreover, visual problems can create difficulties in other areas of functioning, such as increasing the likelihood of a person's falling or making medication errors that can have serious consequences in their own right (Pelletier, Thomas, & Shaw, 2009).

Hearing

Hearing loss is a common occurrence in later adulthood, as depicted in Table 4.5. The most common form of age-related hearing loss is **presbycusis,** in which degenerative changes occur in the cochlea or auditory nerve leading from the cochlea to the brain. Presbycusis is most often associated with loss of high-pitched sounds, because the cochlear cells that are triggered by high-frequency stimuli are located at the outside of the cochlea and therefore are more exposed to damage.

Hearing loss clearly has an effect on the older adult's ability to engage in conversation (Murphy, Daneman, & Schneider, 2006). In turn, older adults may be more likely to avoid potentially noisy situations, such as eating at a restaurant.

Fortunately, although hereditary factors play a role in presbycusis, there are important steps you

can take to protect yourself from environmental contributors. Various health problems such as diabetes, heart disease, and high blood pressure can also put a person at higher risk (Aimoni et al., 2010). However, exposure to loud noise is the most frequent cause of presbycusis (Mohammadi, Mazhari, Mehrparvar, & Attarchi, 2009). The next time you turn up your iPod or go to a loud concert, think about the long-term effects on your hearing, particularly if you wake up the following morning with your ears still ringing (see Figure 4.8).

Another hearing disturbance that is relatively common in older people is **tinnitus**, a symptom in which the individual perceives sounds in the head or ear (such as a ringing noise) when there is no external source. The condition can be temporarily associated with the use of aspirin, antibiotics, and anti-inflammatory agents. Changes in the bones of the skull due to trauma and the buildup of wax in the ears may also contribute to tinnitus. Although treatments are available for tinnitus (generally dependent on the cause of the symptom), there is no cure.

Using hearing aids can help adults with hearing loss overcome many hearing-related problems. With increasing improvements in the quality of hearing aids as well as reductions in size, the need to rely on outwardly detectable devices has been greatly reduced. These miniature devices, effectively invisible to the outside observer, considerably reduce the social stigma many associate with the need to wear a hearing

FIGURE 4.8

How Loud is Too Loud?

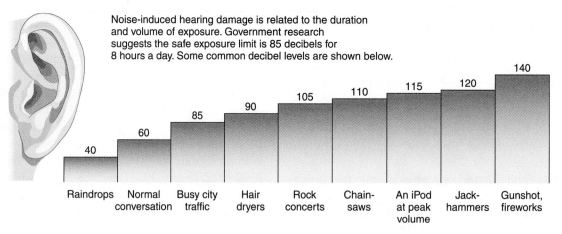

Noise-induced hearing damage is related to the duration and volume of exposure. Government research suggests the safe exposure limit is 85 decibels for 8 hours a day. Some common decibel levels are shown below.

aid. In addition, certain communication strategies can be used by others to ensure that they are heard, such as avoiding interference, speaking in low tones, and facing the person while speaking.

A variety of communication strategies can be employed to ensure that a person with presbycusis can hear what you are saying. One is to face the person directly in a well-lit situation so that he or she can see your face. It is also important to avoid background noise such as a television or a radio in the room so there will be minimal interference from competing sources of sound. In restaurants and social gatherings, it is better to find a place to talk that is as far as possible from crowded or noisy areas. Chewing food or gum makes understanding you more difficult. It is also important to speak at a pace that is not too fast (Janse, 2009).

Additionally, rather than increasing interference with the speech signal by shouting, use a low, clear voice and focus on careful enunciation. Avoid talking to the person as if he or she is a child, and refrain from referring to the individual in the third person or leaving the person out of the conversation altogether. Providing context is also useful because this provides additional cues to the listener about your topic of conversation. You can also gauge whether you are being understood by paying careful attention to how the other person is responding to you, both verbally and nonverbally. Finally, rather than becoming frustrated or upset with the listener, maintaining a positive and patient attitude will encourage the listener to remain engaged socially.

Balance

As important as the maintenance of visual and auditory functioning are with increasing age, the sense of balance can mean the difference between life and death. Loss of balance is one of the main factors responsible for falls in older adults (Dickin, Brown, & Doan, 2006). In 2007 alone, more than 15,800 people 65 and older were known to have died directly from injuries related to falls (Kung, Hoyert, Xu, & Murphy, 2008); 1.8 million were treated in emergency departments for fall-related nonfatal injuries, and about 460,000 of these people were hospitalized (Stevens, Ryan, & Kresnow, 2006).

In addition to changes in balance, fall risk is predicted by the experience of previous falls, strength, gait, and medication use (Tinetti & Kumar, 2010). Older individuals who have more difficulty detecting body position are more likely to lose their balance or fail to see a step or an obstacle in their path on a level surface.

It is natural that people who have a painful and perhaps frightening experience of a fall become anxious in a subsequent situation where they feel insecure; subsequently they become even more unsteady in their gait (Reelick, van Iersel, Kessels, & Rikkert, 2009). The "fear of falling" or what is also called low falling self-efficacy can create a vicious cycle in which older individuals increasingly restrict their movement. When they become less physically active, they further risk losing their strength, which in turn increases the risk of a fall.

The two symptoms most frequently associated with age-related vestibular dysfunction are dizziness and vertigo. Dizziness is accompanied by feelings of lightheadedness and the sensation of floating. **Vertigo** refers to the sensation of spinning when the body is at rest, comparable to being on a Tilt-A-Whirl at an amusement park. Because the vestibular system is so intimately connected to other parts of the nervous system, symptoms of vestibular disturbance may also be experienced as problems such as headache, muscular aches in the neck and back, and increased sensitivity to noise and bright lights. Other problems can include fatigue, inability to concentrate, unsteadiness while walking, and difficulty with speech. Increased sensitivity to motion sickness is another common symptom. Some of these changes may come about with diseases that are not part of normal aging, and others may occur as the result of normative alterations in the vestibular receptors.

Exercise can help older adults learn to compensate for factors that increase their chance of falling (Kim, Yoshida, & Suzuki, 2010). This can include receiving assisted practice in stepping (Hanke & Tiberio, 2006), strengthening the leg muscles (Takahashi, Takahashi, Nakadaira, & Yamamoto, 2006), and reducing medications taken for other conditions that can cause confusion or disorientation (Kannus, Uusi-Rasi, Palvanen, & Parkkari, 2005). Compensation for deficits or abnormalities of the vestibular system involves ensuring proper eyeglass prescriptions, use

Practicing Tai Chi can help older adults maintain their balance and flexibility to offset age changes that can increase their risk of falling.

of a prosthetic aid in walking, outfitting the home with balance aids such as handrails, and developing greater sensitivity to the need to take care while walking. Balance training, including Tai Chi, can also be an effective preventative method to lessen the likelihood of falling (Harmer & Li, 2008). Most recently, researchers have suggested martial arts training as an effective intervention (Groen, Smulders, de Kam, Duysens, & Weerdesteyn, 2010).

It is also important to correct for sensory losses in other areas that could contribute to faulty balance. Having an accurate eyeglass prescription is crucial given that vision provides important cues to navigating the environment. Accordingly, older adults with uncorrected visual problems are more vulnerable to falls (Vitale, Cotch, & Sperduto, 2006). An older individual suffering from vestibular problems can obtain a balance aid such as a walking stick. When at home, finding ways to adapt to situations in which standing poses a risk is of great importance. For example, a person can use a shower chair or bath bench in the tub, and install a handheld shower head. Learning to sit while performing ordinary grooming tasks, such as shaving further reduces the need to maintain balance while standing. Similar adaptations can be made in the kitchen, such as sitting rather than standing at the counter to cut

vegetables. Having multiple telephones in the home is another useful strategy so that the need to hurry to reach the phone (and possibly fall) is avoided.

In addition to practical strategies, older individuals can learn to develop greater sensitivity to the need to be careful when moving from one floor surface to another, such as stepping onto a tile floor from a carpet. They can also be given training to reduce their fear of falling by helping to recognize situations that realistically should be avoided, gaining a greater sense of personal control over the likelihood of falling, and learning to increase their levels of activity within safe limits (Zijlstra et al., 2009).

Smell and Taste

You are able to enjoy food thanks to your taste buds (responsible for the sense of gestation) and smell receptors (responsible for the sense of olfaction). Smell and taste belong to the chemical sensing system referred to as chemosensation. The sensory receptors in these systems are triggered when molecules released by certain substances stimulate special cells in the nose, mouth, or throat. Despite the fact that the olfactory receptors constantly replace themselves, the area of the olfactory epithelium shrinks with age, and ultimately the total number of receptors becomes reduced throughout the adult years. At birth, the olfactory epithelium covers a wide area of the upper nasal cavities, but by the 20s and 30s, its area has started to shrink noticeably.

Approximately one third of all older adults suffer some form of olfactory impairment (Shu et al., 2009) with almost half of those 80 years and older having virtually no ability to smell at all (Lafreniere & Mann, 2009). The loss of olfactory receptors reflects intrinsic changes associated with the aging process, as well as damage caused by disease, injury, and exposure to toxins. Research suggests that these environmental toxins may play a larger role in olfactory impairment than changes due to the aging process. Chronic diseases, medications, and sinus problems may be a more significant source of impairment than age per se over the life span (Rawson, 2006).

Tobacco smoke is a major source of interference with taste and smell. Although people who quit smoking eventually experience an improvement in their sense of smell, this can take many years (equal to the number of years spent smoking). Dentures are another cause of loss of taste sensitivity because these may block the receptor cells of the taste buds. Add to this the fact that certain medications also interfere with taste disorders (Schiffman, 2009), and it is difficult to determine whether aging brings with it inherent changes in taste or not.

Cognitive changes are also believed to be associated with loss of smell sensitivity. Older adults who have experienced the greatest impairment in cognitive functioning may be the most vulnerable to loss of odor identification abilities. In one longitudinal study researchers followed older adults over a 3-year period and observed that people with the most rapid decline in cognitive processes had the greatest rate of decline on the ability to label various odors (Wilson, Arnold, Tang, & Bennett, 2006).

Although nothing can be done to reverse age-related losses of smell and taste once they occur, people who suffer from severe losses may benefit from medical evaluations and treatments for underlying conditions (Welge-Lussen, 2009). Apart from such interventions, older people can also take advantage of strategies to enhance the enjoyment of food, such as expanding their food choices, planning meals in pleasant environments, and finding good dining companions.

Somatosensory System

You are able to move around in the environment through the operation of the somatosensory system, which translates information about touch, temperature, and position to the nervous system. Awareness of bodily position is made possible by proprioception, which provides information about where the limbs are placed when you are standing still. Kinesthesis applies to the knowledge that receptors in the limbs provide when the body is moving. Through proprioception, you would know that you are poised at the top of a staircase, ready to take your first step downward, and through kinesthesis you would know that you are actually moving down those stairs.

Touch.   A well-established body of evidence links loss of the ability to discriminate touch with the aging process throughout adulthood. Age differences have been documented in such areas as the ability to differentiate the separation of two points of pressure on the skin and the detection of the location of a stimulus applied to the skin. One estimate places the loss at 1% per year over the years from 20 to 80. However, the rate of loss varies according to body part. The hands and feet are particularly subject to the effects of aging compared with centrally located areas such as the lip and tongue. These losses can compromise the adult's ability to grasp, maintain balance, and perform delicate handwork, and can also interfere with speech (Wickremaratchi & Llewelyn, 2006).

Pain.   The question of whether older adults are more or less sensitive to pain is a topic of considerable concern for health practitioners. Changes in pain perception with age could make life either much harder or much easier for individuals with illnesses (such as arthritis) that cause chronic pain.

There is no evidence that older adults become somehow immune or at least protected from pain by virtue of age changes in this sensory system. Lower back pain for at least 30 days in the past year was reported among 12% of a large scale sample of Danish elders (Leboeuf-Yde, Nielsen, Kyvik, Fejer, & Hartvigsen, 2009). Although benign back pain shows a decrease across adulthood, back pain that is more severe and disabling increases in the later years (Dionne, Dunn, & Croft, 2006).

Most older adults are able to maintain their daily functioning despite the presence of chronic pain, but as one would expect, the pain makes it more difficult for them to carry out their everyday activities (Covinsky, Lindquist, Dunlop, & Yelin, 2009). The experience of pain can also interfere with cognitive performance in addition to being a limitation in an individual's everyday life. In one sample of more than 300 older adults, poorer performance on tests of memory and spatial abilities was observed among individuals who suffered from chronic lower back pain (Weiner, Rudy, Morrow, Slaboda, & Lieber, 2006). In a study of more than 11,000 elders in the United Kingdom, researchers found that regardless of the presence of other complicating conditions such as depression and anxiety, the experience of chronic pain had a direct relationship to the experience of cognitive symptoms (Westoby, Mallen, & Thomas, 2009). This finding should be kept in mind when evaluating studies of cognitive performance in older adults, because it is possible that many reports of age differences reflect the fact that they are distracted by pain.

Psychological factors may also interact with the experience of pain in older adults. Symptoms of benign pain may diminish during the aging process because older adults have become habituated to the daily aches and pains associated with changes in their bones, joints, and muscles. It is also possible that cohort factors interact with intrinsic age changes to alter the likelihood that complaints about pain will be expressed. The experience of pain is associated with the personality trait of stoicism (the tendency to suffer in silence) (Yong, 2006). Older adults may simply not wish to admit to others, or even themselves, that they are feeling some of those aches and pains.

The risk of pain in later adulthood can be minimized by controlling for factors related to greater pain prevalence. Obesity is highly associated with chronic pain even after controlling for education and related conditions such as diabetes, hypertension, arthritis, and depression (McCarthy, Bigal, Katz, Derby, & Lipton, 2009). Thus, controlling for weight would seem to be an important and effective intervention. At the same time, rather than relying on pain medications, all of which carry the risk of abuse or at least interactions with treatments for other conditions, helping older people manage their pain through holistic methods is also recommended (McCleane, 2007).

In summary, changes in physical functioning have important interactions with psychological and sociocultural factors, and can influence the individual's identity in the middle and later years of adulthood. Fortunately, there are many preventative and compensating steps that people can take to slow the rate of physical aging.

SUMMARY

1. Appearance is an important part of a person's identity, and throughout adulthood, changes in the components of appearance all undergo change. Many age changes in the skin are the result of photoaging. The hair thins and becomes gray, and in men in particular, baldness can develop. There are significant changes in body build, including loss of height, increase of body weight to the 50s followed by a decrease, and changes in fat distribution. However, adults of all ages can benefit from exercise, which can maintain muscle and lower body fat.

2. Mobility reflects the quality of the muscles, bones, and joints. The process of sarcopenia involves loss of muscle mass, and there is a corresponding decrease in muscle strength. Strength training is the key to maintaining maximum muscle functioning in adulthood. Bones lose mineral content throughout adulthood, particularly in women. Diet and exercise are important areas of prevention. The joints encounter many deleterious changes, and although exercise cannot prevent these, middle-aged and older adults can benefit from flexibility training, which maintains range of motion even in damaged joints.

3. The cardiovascular system undergoes changes due to alterations in the heart muscle and arteries that lower aerobic capacity, cardiac output, and maximum heart rate. It is crucial for adults to avoid harmful fats in the diet and to engage in a regular pattern of aerobic exercise to minimize changes in the cardiovascular system. The respiratory system loses functioning due to stiffening of lung tissue. The most important preventive action is to avoid (or quit) cigarette smoking. Changes in the urinary system make the kidney more vulnerable to stress and less able to metabolize toxins, including medications. The bladder of older adults becomes less able to retain and expel urine, but the majority of people do not become incontinent. Behavioral methods can correct normal age-related changes in urinary control. The digestive system becomes somewhat less efficient in older adults, but there is not a significant loss of functioning. Many older people are misinformed by the media and take unnecessary corrective medications to control their gastrointestinal functioning.

4. The endocrine system is the site of many changes in the amount and functioning of the body's hormones. The climacteric is the period of gradual loss of reproductive abilities. After menopause, women experience a reduction in estrogen. Decreases in testosterone level in older

men are not consistently observed. Changes in the immune system, referred to as immune senescence, are observed primarily in a decline in T-cell functioning. Diet and exercise can counteract loss of immune responsiveness in older adults.

5. Normal age-related changes in the nervous system were once thought of as neuronal fallout, but it is now recognized that there is much plasticity in the aging brain. Brain scans reveal considerable variation in age-related alterations in brain structure. There is a rise in Stage 1 and a decrease in Stage 4 and REM (dream-related) sleep. Changes in circadian rhythms lead older adults to awake earlier and prefer the morning for working. Poor sleep habits and the coexistence of psychological or physical disorders (such as sleep apnea) can interfere further with the sleep patterns of middle-aged and older adults. In many cases, dysthermia is related to the presence of disease.

6. Visual acuity decreases across adulthood, and presbyopia leads to a loss of the ability to focus the eye on near objects. Cataracts, age-related macular degeneration, and glaucoma are medical conditions that can lead to reduced vision or blindness. Presbycusis can interfere with the ability to communicate. Older adults are more vulnerable to loss of balance, particularly when they suffer from dizziness and vertigo. Balance training can compensate for these changes. There is loss of the perception of the position of the feet and legs, adding to other age-related changes in balance. Smell and taste show some losses with age, but both senses are extremely vulnerable to negative effects from disease and environmental damage. Findings on pain are inconclusive.

5

Health and

Chronic illnesses can significantly interfere with the quality of a person's daily life, causing effects such as limitations of activity, pain and anxiety, and difficulties in carrying out simple cognitive tasks. In addition, for older adults, physical illness can also present complicating factors in the diagnosis and treatment of psychological disorders. Although it is important to distinguish illness from normal aging, there are significant chronic diseases to which people become increasingly susceptible with age. You can see a summary of the prevalence of the major chronic illnesses from ages 45 and older in the United States in Table 5.1.

In this chapter, we will look at the major physical diseases that affect older adults. We also examine dementia, the set of conditions in which individuals suffer cognitive changes due to neurological damage and other diseases that can affect cognitive functioning in later life.

DISEASES OF THE CARDIOVASCULAR SYSTEM

We begin with cardiovascular diseases, a set of abnormal changes in the heart and arteries that not only can cause chronic disability but are also the number one cause of death. Because the distribution of blood throughout the body is essential for the normal functioning of all other organ systems, diseases of the cardiovascular system can have widespread effects on health and everyday life.

Cardiac and Cerebrovascular Conditions

As we described in Chapter 4, fat and other substances accumulate in the walls of the arteries throughout the body as a part of the normal aging process. In the disease **atherosclerosis** (from the Greek words *athero* meaning paste and *sclerosis* meaning hardness), these fatty deposits collect at an abnormally high rate, so much so that they substantially reduce the width of the arteries and limit the circulation of the blood (see Figure 5.1). **Arteriosclerosis** is a general term for the thickening and hardening of arteries, a condition that also occurs to some degree in normal aging. Many people live with atherosclerosis and do not encounter significant health problems. However, the progressive buildup of plaque that occurs with this disease may eventually lead to partial or total blockage of the blood's flow through an artery. The organs or tissues

Prevention

that are fed by that artery will then suffer serious damage due to the lack of blood supply. When this occurs in arteries leading to the heart muscle, the outcome is called **coronary heart disease**. The term **myocardial infarction** refers to the acute condition in which the blood supply to part of the heart muscle (the myocardium) is severely reduced or blocked.

Systolic and diastolic refer to blood pressure at the stages of the heart during contraction and at rest, respectively. **Hypertension** is the disease in which an individual chronically suffers from blood pressure that is greater than or equal to 140 mm Hg systolic pressure and 90 mm Hg diastolic pressure. Changes in the arteries associated with atherosclerosis are

thought to be due to the damaging effects of hypertension. If a person's blood pressure is virtually always elevated, the blood is constantly putting strain on the walls of the arteries. Eventually, the arterial walls develop areas of weakness and inflammation, particularly in the large arteries where the pressure is greatest. Damage to the walls of the arteries makes them vulnerable to the accumulation of substances that form plaque, causing further thickening and limitation of blood flow.

The increased resistance existing in the arteries also increases the workload on the heart, which is forced to pump harder than it otherwise would have to do. Consequently, people with hypertension are

TABLE 5.1
Percent Within Age Groups of Chronic Conditions

Age	Heart Disease	Coronary Heart Disease	Heart Attack	Stroke	Cancer, All	Arthritis	Diabetes
45–64 years	12.2	6.9	3.7	2.7	8.4	29.3	11.0
65–74 years	26.7	18.0	10.1	6.7	18.7	46.6	19.3
75–84 years	35.9	24.2	13.7	10.8	25.5	52.3	18.4
85 and over	41.2	28.6	15.3	14.0	27.1	54.7	14.1

Source: Centers for Disease Control and Prevention. (2010). Health data interactive. Retrieved from http://www.cdc.gov/nchs/hdi.htm.

FIGURE 5.1

Development of Atherosclerosis

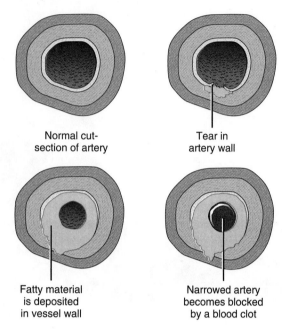

Normal cut-section of artery

Tear in artery wall

Fatty material is deposited in vessel wall

Narrowed artery becomes blocked by a blood clot

more likely to develop hypertrophy (overgrowth) of the left ventricle of the heart, which limits its ability to do its job of pumping the blood.

Congestive heart failure (or heart failure) is a condition in which the heart is unable to pump enough blood to meet the needs of the body's other organs. Blood flows out of the heart at an increasingly slower rate, causing the blood returning to the heart through the veins to back up. Eventually the tissues become congested with fluid. This condition can result from a variety of diseases including coronary heart disease, scar tissue from a past myocardial infarction, hypertension, disease of the heart valves, disease of the heart muscle, infection of the heart, or heart defects present at birth. People with congestive heart failure are unable to exert themselves without becoming exhausted and short of breath. Edema, a condition in which fluid builds up in their bodies, causes a swelling of the legs. They may also experience fluid buildup in their lungs along with kidney problems.

The term "cerebrovascular disease" refers to disorders of circulation to the brain. This condition may lead to the onset of a **cerebrovascular accident**, also known as a "stroke" or "brain attack," an acute condition in which an artery leading to the brain bursts or is clogged by a blood clot or other particle. The larger the area of the brain deprived of blood, the more severe the deterioration of the physical and mental functions controlled by that area. Another condition caused by the development of clots in the cerebral arteries is a **transient ischemic attack (TIA)**, also called a ministroke. The cause of a TIA is the same as that of a stroke, but in a TIA, the blockage of the artery is temporary. The tissues that were deprived of blood soon recover, but chances are that another TIA will follow. People who have had a TIA are also at higher risk of subsequently suffering from a stroke.

Incidence Rates

Heart disease is the number one killer in the United States, resulting in 25% of all deaths in the year 2007 (Xu et al., 2010). Together, heart and cerebrovascular disease accounted for 35% of all deaths in the United States of people 65 and older (Kung et al., 2008), a figure that is comparable to the rate observed in Canada (Tu et al., 2009). However, given that deaths occur disproportionately in the population, with over half of all deaths occurring in people 75 years and older, technically heart disease is the number one killer among the oldest segment of the population.

Worldwide, coronary heart disease was the leading cause of death in 2002, amounting to 7.2 million deaths or nearly one third of all deaths around the globe. Another 5.5 million people per year die from cerebrovascular disease. The countries with the highest death rates as of 2009 were Russia, Bulgaria, Hungary, and Romania; the United States ranked 13th and Canada ranked 26th in the world (Lloyd-Jones et al., 2009).

Behavioral Risk Factors

Understanding the contribution of lifestyle factors to heart disease is one of the most heavily researched topics in the biomedical sciences. As a result of this research, a great deal is being learned about the ways that even people who have a strong genetic predisposition to cardiovascular disease can reduce their risks. These behavioral risk factors fall into essentially four areas of lifestyle choices people can make to reduce their risk of developing heart disease (see Table 5.2). We discussed many of these choices in the context of the normal age-related changes covered in Chapter 4 so they may seem familiar, but they play out somewhat differently in the case of cardiovascular disease.

A sedentary lifestyle is the first major risk factor for heart disease. The relationship between leisure activity and heart disease is well established (Yung et al., 2009), with estimates ranging from a 24% reduction in the risk of myocardial infarction among non-strenuous exercisers to a 47% reduced risk among individuals engaging in a regular pattern of strenuous exercise (Lovasi et al., 2007). As it happens, the majority of adults at highest risk for heart disease (i.e., those 75 and older) are the least likely to exercise. Only about 36% of people 65 to 74 and 16% of those 75 and older engage in vigorous leisure activity (National Health Interview Survey, 2009).

The second risk factor for heart disease is smoking. Although it is not known exactly why smoking increases the risk of heart disease, most researchers believe that smoking damages the arteries, making them more vulnerable to plaque formation and ultimately leading to the deleterious changes we outlined earlier. Though having long-lived parents is related to lower level of cardiovascular risk factors,

among women who smoke, the advantages of heredity benefits are offset (Jaunin et al., 2009).

Approximately one fifth of all adults in the United States are current smokers. The rates of current smokers decrease across age groups of adults to 10% of those 65 and older (National Health Interview Survey, 2009). It is very possible that the smoking rates decrease not only because older adults are less likely to smoke but also because the nonsmokers are more likely to survive.

The third risk factor for cardiovascular disease is alcohol intake. Moderate alcohol consumption appears to have a protective effect on the risk of cardiovascular disease as well as on functional health declines in general (Chen & Hardy, 2009), at least for women (Djousse, Lee, Buring, & Gaziano, 2009). Moreover, there may be gender differences in the relationship between alcohol intake and metabolic syndrome, with men showing a stronger relationship than exists for women (Buja et al., 2009). Beyond that point, heavy alcohol intake (more than 60 grams of alcohol—2 beers or 2 glasses of wine a day) may be associated with increased stroke risk (Reynolds et al., 2003).

Body weight is the fourth risk factor for cardiovascular disease. An analysis of 57 longitudinal studies conducted in Western Europe and North America showed a causal relationship between high BMI and

TABLE 5.2
Behavioral Risk Factors for Cardiovascular Disease

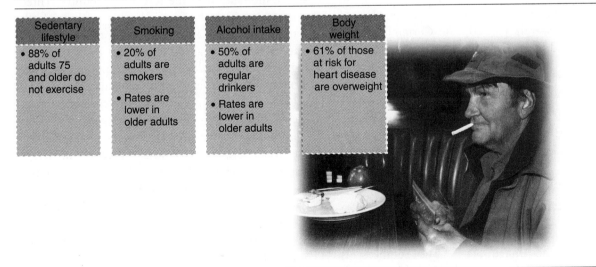

Sedentary lifestyle	Smoking	Alcohol intake	Body weight
• 88% of adults 75 and older do not exercise	• 20% of adults are smokers • Rates are lower in older adults	• 50% of adults are regular drinkers • Rates are lower in older adults	• 61% of those at risk for heart disease are overweight

FIGURE 5.2

Stroke Rates by State, United States, 2005

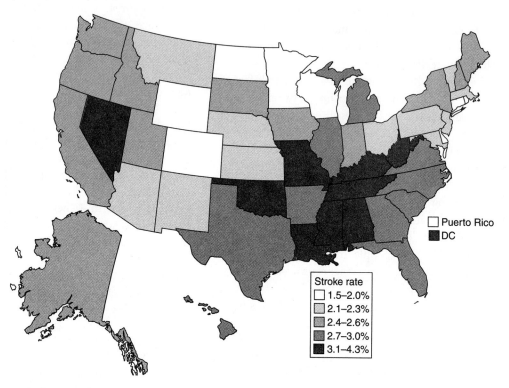

Stroke rate
☐ 1.5–2.0%
2.1–2.3%
2.4–2.6%
2.7–3.0%
■ 3.1–4.3%

☐ Puerto Rico
■ DC

The "stroke belt" can be seen in this map as the Southeastern portion of the United States where stroke rates are highest.
Source: Centers for Disease Control and Prevention. (2007). Prevalence of stroke—United States, 2005. *Morbidity and Mortality Weekly Report, 56, 469–474.*

mortality due to vascular disease (Whitlock et al., 2009). According to the CDC, dramatic increases in overweight and obesity have occurred among United States adults over the past 20 years. Currently, 30.3% of the United States population is considered obese by government standards. According to the Organisations for Economic Co-operation and Development (2007), this is the highest percent in the world. Intake of high-cholesterol foods in particular is the component of obesity that places individuals at greater risk for developing cardiovascular disease and stroke (Erqou et al., 2009). Conversely, high levels of the "good" cholesterol (HDL) are related to lower risk of cardiovascular disease (Cooney et al., 2009).

Variations in stroke rates by race/ethnicity, social class, and poverty have emerged as issues of national concern in the United States. The Southeast is considered the "stroke belt" of the United States, with 8 to 12 states in this region having substantially higher stroke mortality than the rest of the country. Three states comprising the "stroke buckle" include North Carolina, South Carolina, and Georgia. The high rates of stroke are attributed in part to diets in this region that are based on high consumption of sodium, monounsaturated fatty acids, polyunsaturated fatty acids and cholesterol, and the low consumption of dietary fiber (see Figure 5.2).

Although stroke rates are in general elevated for the stroke belt, there are racial differences in factors that contribute to stroke risk. In a study of more than 23,000 men and women 45 years and older, researchers found higher scores for Blacks than Whites on measures related to stroke risk including hypertension, systolic blood pressure, diabetes, smoking, and hypertrophy of the left ventricle of the heart (Cushman et al., 2008).

Other factors contributing to the high stroke rates are lower levels of education and access to health care in the states within this region of the United States. Regardless of the cause for the elevated incidence of stroke, the data suggest that a variety of interventions are urgently needed, particularly given the high costs incurred by this at-risk population for health care (more on this topic in Chapter 12).

The concept of **metabolic syndrome** has come into use within the past several years to draw attention to the cluster of symptoms associated with cardiovascular disease (see Table 5.3). The symptoms include high levels of abdominal obesity, abnormal levels of blood cholesterol (low "good" cholesterol or HDL and high "bad" cholesterol or LDL), hypertension, insulin resistance, high blood fats (known as triglycerides), high levels of C-reactive proteins in the blood (an indication of inflammation), and the presence of coronary plaques. Even possessing three of the risk factors involved in the metabolic syndrome increases a person's risk of mortality from cardiovascular disease (Clarke et al., 2009).

Prevention of Heart Disease and Stroke

Advances in the understanding of the causes of heart disease and stroke have resulted in safer and more effective medical and dietary supplements that have lowered cardiovascular death rates. The lowering of cholesterol through preventive medications is becoming the primary mode of intervention. Chief among these medications are statins, which work by lowering the levels of harmful cholesterol (LDL) in the blood. However, in addition to or instead of medication, anyone can benefit from the control of diet and participation in exercise as preventive strategies; the earlier you begin to follow these strategies, the better.

As we noted in Chapter 1, a diet high in fruits and vegetables significantly lowers mortality; the positive effect is mainly due to the reduction of cardiovascular disease (Bazzano, 2006). Research has continued to advocate the benefits of the "Mediterranean diet," or the consumption of meals that include minimally processed fruits, vegetables, nuts, seeds, grains, olive oil, and low amounts of red meat and dairy foods (Rumawas, Meigs, Dwyer, McKeown, & Jacques, 2009). Intake of the Mediterranean diet is also associated with a diminished risk of metabolic syndrome (Perez-Lopez, Chedraui, Haya, & Cuadros, 2009).

Another essential ingredient of the Mediterranean diet is low to moderate amounts of wine (Serra-Majem, Roman, & Estruch, 2006). Finally, exercise is a vital component of all preventive programs aimed at reducing the prevalence of heart disease (Haskell et al., 2007). In addition to exercise, older adults with hypertension can also benefit from relaxation training; even a 12-session audio relaxation training program was shown in one study to have beneficial effects (Tang, Harms, Speck, Vezeau, & Jesurum, 2009).

There are significant national differences in risk of heart disease, as well as other major illness. Eastern European countries, such as Russia, Bulgaria, Romania, and Poland, have the highest death rates from cardiovascular disease (Lloyd-Jones et al., 2009). An analysis of the dietary habits and food intake of almost 27,000 people living in the countries of

TABLE 5.3
Criteria for the Metabolic Syndrome

Risk Factor	Defining Level
Abdominal obesity (waist circumference)	Men: > 40 in Women: > 35 in
Triglycerides	> = 150 mg/dL
HDL cholesterol (the good kind)	Men: < 40 mg/dL Women: <50 mg/dL
Blood pressure	> = 130/> = 85
Fasting glucose	> = 100 mg/dL

Diagnosis requires three or more of the five characteristics.
dL = milligrams per deciliter.

Central and Eastern Europe suggested that poor dietary habits contribute significantly to the high rates of morbidity and mortality in these countries (Boylan et al., 2009). The United States has higher rates of the six major chronic diseases associated with mortality (Banks, Marmot, Oldfield, & Smith, 2006).

It is important to remember in our discussion of available preventive treatments that changing people's lifestyle habits is difficult, particularly when these changes are needed in adulthood. One failure can decrease a person's self-efficacy and confidence about the ability to enact these lifestyle changes. Therefore it is important to allow people to feel that even small steps toward improved health habits represent progress (Resnick et al., 2009).

CANCER

Cancer is a generic term for a group of more than 100 diseases. Each type of cancer has its own symptoms, characteristics, treatment options, and overall effect on a person's life and health. In 2009, it was estimated that nearly 1.5 million Americans received a diagnosis of cancer (not including skin cancer or noninvasive cancers) and that about 10.5 million are living with the disease. The lifetime risk of developing cancer is about 1 in 2 for men and 1 in 3 for women (American Cancer Society, 2009). Skin cancer is the most prevalent type of cancer in the United States, with an estimated 1 million new

cases occurring each year. Lung cancer accounts for 30% of the deaths in men and 26% in women.

Risk Factors and Preventions

All cancer is genetically caused in the sense that it reflects damage to the genes that control cell replication. Some damage is associated with genetic mutations linked to an inherited tendency for developing cancer, most often involving breast and colon cancer. About 5% of women with breast cancer have a hereditary form of this disease. Similarly, close relatives of a person with colorectal cancer are themselves at greater risk, particularly if it has affected many people within the extended family. However, most cancer is not of the inherited variety. Instead, cancer develops when random mutations occur that cause the body's cells to malfunction. The mutations develop either as a mistake in cell division or in response to injuries from environmental agents such as radiation or chemicals.

Most cancers become more prevalent with increasing age in adulthood because age is associated with greater cumulative exposure to harmful toxins (carcinogens) in the environment (see Table 5.4). Lifestyle also plays a vital part. The three greatest lifestyle risk factors for the development of cancer during adulthood are exposure to the sun, cigarette smoking, and lack of control over diet.

Skin cancer, the most common form of cancer in adults, is directly linked to exposure to ultraviolet

TABLE 5.4
Risk Factors for Cancer

Risk Factor	Relevant Data
Exposure to sun	Increased risk in higher UV exposed cities
Cigarette smoking	80–90% of lung cancer deaths are due to smoking
Diet	Intake of red meat related to colon cancer
Environmental toxins	Work-related toxins associated with increased cancer risk

(UV) radiation from the sun. In the United States, for example, melanoma is more common in Texas than it is in Minnesota, given that the levels of UV radiation from the sun are stronger in the South. Around the world, the highest rates of skin cancer are found in South Africa and Australia, areas that receive substantial amounts of UV radiation. Artificial sources of UV radiation, such as sunlamps and tanning booths, can cause skin cancer despite the claims that the manufacturers make about their safety. In fact, researchers have determined that women in developed countries who use tanning beds before the age of 30 increase their risk of developing skin cancer by 75%. Cancer of the eye is also more likely to develop in people who use artificial tanning devices (El Ghissassi et al., 2009).

Cigarette smoking is the next greatest health risk, and is in many ways more dangerous than UV exposure given that the forms of cancer related to cigarettes are generally more lethal than skin cancer. Most lung cancer is caused by cigarette smoking, and exposure to cigarette smoke is a risk factor for developing cancers of the mouth, throat, esophagus, larynx, bladder, kidney, cervix, pancreas, and stomach. The risk of lung cancer begins to diminish as soon as a person quits smoking. People who have had lung cancer and stop smoking are less likely to get a second occurrence of lung cancer than are people who continue to smoke. Exposure to cigarette smoke ("secondhand smoke") can be just as great a risk, if not greater, for lung cancer. Though you are probably aware of the risks of cigarette smoke in developed countries such as the United States, Canada, and Europe, you may not realize that carcinogens are present in substances such as betel quid, which includes the toxic substance areca nut. Approximately 600 million people in India and parts of Southeast Asia, or perhaps as many as 80% of adults in parts of India, chew betel quid. Even if there is no tobacco in the betel quid, this habit greatly increases the risk of liver and esophageal cancer (Secretan et al., 2009).

Diet is the third risk factor for cancer. A nationwide study of over 900,000 adults in the United States who were studied prospectively (before they had cancer) from 1982 to 1998 played an important role in identifying the role of diet. During this period of time, there were more than 57,000 deaths within the sample from cancer. The people with the highest BMIs had death rates from cancer that were 52% higher for men and 62% higher for women compared with men and women of normal BMI. The types of cancer associated with higher BMIs included cancer of the esophagus, colon and rectum, liver, gallbladder, pancreas, and kidney. Significant trends of increasing risk with higher BMIs were observed for death from cancers of the stomach and prostate in men and for death from cancers of the breast, uterus, cervix, and ovary in women (Calle, Rodriguez, Walker-Thurmond, & Thun, 2003). We can conclude from this research that maintaining a low BMI is a critical preventive step in lowering your risk of cancer.

In addition to BMI, eating specific foods seems to play a role in cancer prevention. Stomach cancer is more common in parts of the world—such as Japan, Korea, parts of Eastern Europe, and Latin America—in which people eat foods that are preserved by drying, smoking, salting, or pickling. By contrast, fresh foods, especially fresh fruits and vegetables, may help protect against stomach cancer. Similarly, the risk of developing colon cancer is thought to be higher in people whose diet is high in fat, low in fruits and vegetables, and low in high-fiber foods such as whole-grain breads and cereals. For instance, New Zealand and the United States have the higher rates of colon cancer and also consume the largest amount of meat (National Cancer Institute, 2010).

There are several additional specific types of experiences that seem to make certain people more vulnerable to cancer. Environmental toxins include chemical compounds found in the air, food, and water. Such compounds include asbestos, arsenic, beryllium, cadmium, chromium, and nickel. Exposure to these compounds significantly increases the risk of cancer in various sites in the respiratory system including the lung and nasal cavity. Increased risk of bladder cancer is associated with exposure to arsenic, and ovarian cancer with asbestos exposure. In addition, leather, silica, and wood dust increase the risk of several forms of respiratory cancers (Straif et al., 2009). Certain occupations are more at risk of exposure to these carcinogenic substances, including iron and steel founding, manufacture of isopropyl alcohol, painting, and rubber manufacturing (Baan et al., 2009).

A host of other lifestyle habits and choices that people make can further contribute to the risk of developing cancer. In the intensive efforts to find the causes of breast cancer, a variety of lifestyle factors

AGING IN THE NEWS

www.wiley.com/college/whitbourne   OLDER ADULTS WHO MADE THE HEADLINES   -VOL. 4, CHAPTER 5-

80-YEAR-OLD FORMER ASTRONAUT DANCES WITH THE STARS

April 2010. Looking debonair in his tux and medals, former astronaut Buzz Aldrin danced the cha-cha with partner Ashly Costa until eliminated after the third week.

"I did this show for the fighter pilots out there, the military people and the elder geezers like me, who would just like to see an elder come back week after week," Aldrin said in his sign-off.

have been suggested, such as amount of alcohol consumed and having an abortion or a miscarriage. The evidence is somewhat stronger for the effect of personal history in the case of cervical cancer, which has a higher risk among women who began having sexual intercourse before age 18 and/or have had many sexual partners. For men, efforts are under way to determine whether having had a vasectomy increases the risk of prostate cancer.

In addition to a person's lifestyle and history of disease, variations due to race and ethnicity are observed among certain types of cancers. Skin cancer is more likely to develop in people with fair skin that freckles easily, while Black people are less likely to develop any form of skin cancer. Other cancers varying according to race include uterine cancer (more prevalent among Whites), and prostate cancer (more prevalent among Blacks). Stomach cancer is twice as prevalent in men and is more common in Black people, as is colon cancer. Rectal cancer is more prevalent among Whites.

Finally, hormonal factors are thought to play an important role in the risk of certain forms of cancer. Although the cause of prostate cancer is not known, the growth of cancer cells in the prostate, like that of normal cells, is stimulated by male hormones, especially testosterone. Along similar lines, estrogen is thought to increase the likelihood of a woman's developing uterine cancer, though combined intake of progesterone and estrogen may reduce the risk associated with its use (Grosse et al., 2009). Therefore, the link found between higher weight and uterine cancer in women may be due to increased production of estrogen among heavier women, so that the estrogen rather than fat increases the risk of uterine cancer. Likewise, findings that diabetes and high blood pressure increase the risk of uterine cancer may be related to the fact that these conditions are more likely to occur in overweight women who have higher levels of estrogen (Wedisinghe & Perera, 2009).

Treatments

The best way to treat cancer is to prevent it. Cancer detection with frequent screenings is the primary step in treatment. Public interest organizations such as the American Cancer Society and the Canadian Cancer Society publicize the need for tests such as breast self-examination and mammograms for women, prostate examinations for men, and colon cancer screenings for both men and women. There is mixed evidence for the effectiveness of this publicity and within recent years, considerable debate over the value of screenings.

In November 2009, the U.S. Preventive Services Task Force (USPSTF) released a controversial update to the 2002 recommendation statement for breast cancer screening. The 2002 recommendation advocated breast mammography every 1–2 years for women over 40. The 2009 statement, citing insufficient evidence to assess the benefits and harms of screening, recommends against routine mammography screening in women between the ages of 40 and 49. Biennial screening mammography is recommended for women between the ages of 50 and 74. For women over the age of 75, the USPSTF determined insufficient evidence to assess the additional benefits and harms of mammography. Uncertainties pertaining to the harm of screening (including misdiagnosis) were cited as a basis for the recommendations. When the report was made public, countless groups and organizations were quick to criticize harshly the recommendations, sparking debate in the medical field and media outlets (Woolf, 2010).

Time will tell whether the USPSTF recommendations will result in a decrease in mammography screening among women. The percentage of women in the United States who have had mammograms in the past 2 years rose from 29 to 70% between 1987 and 2003 but then dropped again slightly to 68% by 2008. However, the distribution of women who take this preventative step varies by race, education, and poverty status, with lower rates among low-income, uninsured, and Hispanic women (National Center for Health Statistics, 2009).

Depending on the stage of cancer progression at diagnosis, various treatment options are available. Surgery is the most common treatment for most types of cancer when it is probable that all of the tumor can be removed. Radiation therapy involves the use of high-energy X-rays to damage cancer cells and stop their growth, while chemotherapy uses drugs to kill cancer cells. Patients are most likely to receive chemotherapy when the cancer has metastasized to other parts of the body. Biological therapy is treatment involving substances called biological response modifiers that improve the way the body's immune system fights disease and may be used in combination with chemotherapy to treat cancer that has metastasized. As more information is gathered through the rapidly evolving program of research on cancer and its causes, new methods of treatment and prevention can be expected to emerge over the next few decades. Furthermore, as efforts grow to target populations at risk for the development of preventable cancers (such as lung cancer), it may

be expected that cancer deaths will be reduced even further in the decades ahead.

DISORDERS OF THE MUSCULOSKELETAL SYSTEM

Although not generally fatal, musculoskeletal diseases can be crippling and may even lead to injury or bodily damage that can eventually end the afflicted individual's life. Two primary disorders of the musculoskeletal system affecting middle-aged and older adults are arthritis and osteoporosis (see Table 5.5). These relatively common disorders range in their effects on the individual, and can be classified from minor to severe.

Osteoarthritis

Arthritis is a general term for conditions that affect the joints and surrounding tissues. It refers to any one of several diseases that can cause pain, stiffness, and swelling in joints and other connective tissues. The most common form of arthritis is known as **osteoarthritis**, a painful, degenerative joint disease that often involves the hips, knees, neck, lower back, or the small joints of the hands. Osteoarthritis typically develops in joints injured by repeated overuse in the performance of a particular job or a favorite sport. Obesity, associated with the carrying of excess body weight, is another risk factor. There may also be causes common to both obesity and osteoarthritis that further increase the risk for osteoarthritis (Gabay, Hall, Berenbaum, Henrotin, & Sanchez, 2008).

Eventually, injury or repeated impact thins or wears away the cartilage that cushions the ends of the bones in the joint so that the bones rub together. The articular cartilage that protects the surfaces of the bones where they intersect at the joints wears down, and the synovial fluid that fills the joint loses its shock-absorbing properties. Joint flexibility is reduced, bony spurs develop, and the joint swells. These changes in the joint structures and tissues cause the individual to experience pain and loss of movement.

Pain management is an important feature of the treatment for osteoarthritis and typically involves medication such as aspirin, acetaminophen, ibuprofen, and nonsteroidal anti-inflammatory drugs (NSAIDs). Unfortunately, the use of NSAIDs can lead to the development of gastrointestinal problems, including ulcers. Corticosteroids can also be injected directly into joints to reduce swelling and inflammation. These drugs are used sparingly, however, because chronic use can have destructive effects on bones and cartilage. Pain medications only alleviate symptoms; they do not provide a cure for the disease. More active forms of treatment are becoming available to people who have osteoarthritis, including injection of a synthetic material into an arthritic joint to replace the loss of synovial fluid. A second option is injection of sodium hyaluronate into the joint, an injectable version of a chemical normally present in high amounts in joints and fluids. Increasingly common is the total replacement of an affected joint, such as a hip or a knee. While replacement surgery may seem like a drastic measure, it is one that typically proves highly satisfactory.

Short of control through medication or surgery, exercise can have beneficial effects on reducing the pain of arthritis (Kujala, 2009). Clearly the type of exercise must be carefully monitored as is true for normal age-related changes in the joints. Exercise can also be beneficial in weight reduction, further improving the arthritic patient's prognosis. Finally, although mechanical strain increases the risk of osteoarthritis, maintaining high muscle strength may compensate for the strain placed on the joints (Verweij, van Schoor, Deeg, Dekker, & Visser, 2009).

Osteoporosis

As we saw in Chapter 4, normal aging is associated with loss of bone mineral content due to an imbalance between bone resorption and bone growth. The technical term for the loss of bone mineral content is **osteoporosis** (literally, "porous bone"), and occurs when the bone mineral density is more than 2.5 standard deviations below the mean of young, White, non-Hispanic women.

It is estimated that 8 million women and 2 million men in the United States suffer from osteoporosis (Sweet, Sweet, Jeremiah, & Galazka, 2009). Women are at higher risk than men because they have lower bone mass in general but nevertheless, osteoporosis is a significant health problem in men. Rates of osteoporosis-related bone fracture are equivalent to the rates of myocardial infarction (Binkley, 2009). Women vary by race and ethnicity in their risk of developing osteoporosis; White and Asian women have the highest risk, whereas Blacks and Hispanics the lowest. In addition, women who have small bone structures and are underweight have a higher risk for osteoporosis than heavier women.

Alcohol and cigarette smoking increase the risk of developing osteoporosis. Conversely, risk is reduced by an adequate intake of calcium through dairy products, dark green leafy vegetables, tofu, salmon, and foods fortified with calcium such as orange juice, bread, and cereal (a regimen similar to that recommended to prevent heart disease). A diet high in protein and a variety of other nutrients such as magnesium, potassium, vitamin K, several B vitamins, and carotenoids can also be of value in preventing osteoporosis (Tucker, 2009). Vitamin D, obtained through exposure to sunlight (while wearing sunblock of course!), or as a dietary supplement, is another

TABLE 5.5
Osteoarthritis and Osteoporosis

Disease	Risk Factors	Treatment
Osteoarthritis: *Painful, degenerative joint disease*	Overuse Obesity Injury	Pain management Flexibility Replacement
Osteoporosis: *Abnormal loss of bone mineral content*	Race Ethnicity Hormonal changes Lack of vitamin D	Exercise (resistance) Nutritional supplements Medications

important preventative agent (Bischoff-Ferrari et al., 2009). Exercise and physical activity are also significant factors in reducing the risk of osteoporosis.

Prevention and treatment of osteoporosis involve an attempt to restore bone strength through nutritional supplements and a regular program of weight-bearing exercise (Guadalupe-Grau, Fuentes, Guerra, & Calbet, 2009). Medication may also be prescribed to slow or stop bone loss, increase bone density, and reduce fracture risk. Alendronate is a bisphosphonate used to increase bone density, and calcitonin is a naturally occurring hormone involved in the regulation of calcium and bone metabolism. Each of these has advantages but also can have serious side effects that make them more or less useful for particular individuals. For example, they may increase bone loss in the jaw among patients with dental problems.

For both men and women, a deficiency of sex hormones may play a causative role in osteoporosis; as discussed above, the risks of hormone replacement therapy need to be weighed against the gains in preserving bone health (Pietschmann, Rauner, Sipos, & Kerschan-Schindl, 2009). Calcitrol, though linked to risks involving buildup of calcium byproducts in the body, may also prove to be effective when combined with other treatments (Peppone et al., 2009). Interestingly, certain types of alcohol may be preventive for women. In a study of beer drinkers compared to women who drank no alcohol or other forms of alcohol, it was the women who consumed beer who had the lowest rates of osteoporosis, perhaps due to the fact that beer contains a form of estrogen (Pedrera-Zamorano et al., 2009).

DIABETES

A large fraction of the over-65 population suffers from Type 2 diabetes, a disease that begins in adulthood. This form of diabetes is associated with long-term complications that affect almost every organ system, contributing to blindness, heart disease, strokes, kidney failure, the necessity for limb amputations, and damage to the nervous system.

Characteristics of Diabetes

Diabetes is caused by a defect in the process of metabolizing glucose, a simple sugar that is a major source of energy for the body's cells. Normally, the digestive process breaks food down into components that can be transported through the blood to the cells of the body. The presence of glucose in the blood stimulates the beta cells of the pancreas to release insulin, a hormone that acts as a key at the cell receptors within the body to "open the cell doors" to let in the glucose. Excess glucose is stored in the liver or throughout the body in muscle and fat. After it is disposed of, its level in the blood returns to normal. In Type 2 diabetes, the pancreas produces some insulin, but the body's tissues fail to respond to the insulin signal, a condition known as insulin resistance. Because the insulin cannot bind to the cell's insulin receptor, glucose cannot be transported into the body's cells to be used. Eventually the excess glucose overflows into the urine and is excreted. The body therefore loses a main source of energy, although large amounts of glucose are potentially available in the blood.

The symptoms of diabetes include fatigue, frequent urination (especially at night), unusual thirst, weight loss, blurred vision, frequent infections, and slow healing of sores. These symptoms develop more gradually and are less noticeable in Type 2, compared with Type 1 (child-onset), diabetes. If blood sugar levels become too low (hypoglycemia), the individual can become nervous, jittery, faint, and confused. When hypoglycemia develops, the individual must eat or drink a sugary substance as quickly as possible. Alternatively, the person can also become seriously ill if blood sugar levels rise too high (hyperglycemia). Women who develop diabetes while pregnant (a condition known as gestational diabetes) are more likely to experience complications, and their infants are more likely to develop birth defects.

Incidence and Risk Factors

It is estimated that 10 million Americans have been diagnosed with diabetes, and there may be as many as 5 million people who have the disease but have not received a diagnosis. Diabetes is estimated to afflict 10.3 million people 60 years of age and older: approximately 21% of adults in this age category. The CDC estimates that having diabetes doubles the risk of death compared with other people in one's own age group (Centers for Disease Control and Prevention, 2010d). Though Type 1 diabetes was once considered a children's disease, higher rates of Type 2 diabetes in children have increased at an alarming rate. Such findings will have important health implications for future generations of older adults.

According to the World Health Organization, the number of people suffering from diabetes worldwide is approximately 171 million in 2010, a number that will double by 2030. Approximately 3.2 million deaths per year are due to complications of diabetes. The United States is third following India and China in the number of people who suffer from diabetes, but the rise in cases is greater in the developing countries (World Health Organization, 2010).

Diabetes can be understood in terms of the biopsychosocial perspective in that it involves physical, behavioral, and sociocultural risk factors (see Figure 5.3). The main risk factors for diabetes are obesity and a sedentary lifestyle. Epidemiologists attribute the rise in diabetes to the increase in BMI, noted earlier in the chapter as a risk factor for heart disease. Researchers in this area warn that older adults are becoming increasingly likely to experience metabolic syndrome, insulin resistance, high lipid levels, and hypertension, leading to greater risk of cardiovascular and kidney disease (Bechtold, Palmer, Valtos, Iasiello, & Sowers, 2006). Echoing the findings of other research on the benefits of moderate consumption of alcohol, research on diabetes risk also indicates a protective effect of between 20 and 50–60 grams of alcohol per day or between 1 and 2 ounces (Baliunas et al., 2009).

Other risk factors contributing to diabetes risk are race and ethnicity. The incidence of diabetes is about 60% higher in African Americans and 110 to 120% higher in Mexican Americans and Puerto Ricans compared with Whites. The highest rates of diabetes in the world are found among Native Americans. Half of all Pima Indians living in the United States, for example, have adult-onset diabetes.

Prevention and Treatment

Given the clear relationship between obesity and diabetes, the most important means of preventing Type 2 diabetes are control of glucose intake, control of blood pressure, and control of blood lipids. Moderate alcohol consumption also seems to offer a protective effect (Paulson, Hong, Holcomb, & Nunez, 2010).

Once an individual has Type 2 diabetes, diet and exercise continue to be important. Frequent blood testing is also necessary to monitor glucose levels, although saliva testing advancements are under way. Much of this treatment involves trying to keep blood sugar at acceptable levels. Many individuals with Type 2 diabetes must take oral drugs or insulin to lower their blood glucose levels. In addition to medication and monitoring of diet, people with diabetes are advised to develop an exercise plan to manage their weight and to lower blood pressure and blood fats, important steps that can lead to reductions in blood sugar levels.

RESPIRATORY DISEASES

The main form of respiratory disease affecting adults in middle and late life is **chronic obstructive pulmonary disease (COPD)**, a group of diseases that involve obstruction of the airflow into the respiratory system. Two related diseases—chronic bronchitis and chronic emphysema—often occur together in this disease (see Figure 5.4). People with COPD experience coughing, excess sputum, and difficulty breathing even when performing relatively easy tasks, such as putting on their clothes or walking on level ground. According to the internationally-based Global Initiative for COPD (2009), the disease is the fourth leading cause of chronic illness and death and

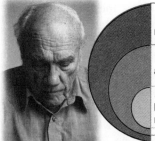

Biological = Changes in glucose metabolism, obesity

Psychological = Sedentary lifestyle; also associated with depression and stress

Sociocultural = Habitual eating patterns, lack of education, low economic resources

FIGURE 5.3

Biopsychosocial Model of Diabetes

FIGURE 5.4

Components of COPD

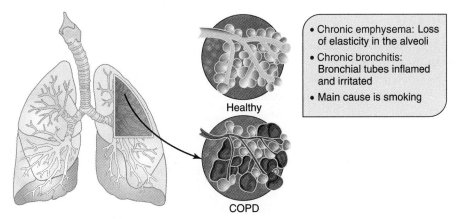

Healthy

COPD

- Chronic emphysema: Loss of elasticity in the alveoli
- Chronic bronchitis: Bronchial tubes inflamed and irritated
- Main cause is smoking

the fifth in the world in terms of the burden of disease. COPD's prevalence increases with age, such that the disease is estimated to affect about 25% of those 75 and older (Iyer Parameswaran & Murphy, 2009).

Chronic bronchitis is a long-standing inflammation of the bronchi, the airways that lead into the lungs. The inflammation of the bronchi leads to increased production of mucus and other changes, which in turn leads to coughing and expectoration of sputum. People with this disorder are more likely to develop frequent and severe respiratory infections, narrowing and plugging of the bronchi, difficulty breathing, and disability. Chronic emphysema is a lung disease that causes permanent destruction of the alveoli. Elastin within the terminal bronchioles is destroyed, leading to collapse of the airway walls and an inability to exhale. The airways lose their ability to become enlarged during inspiration and to empty completely during expiration, leading to a lowering of the quality of gas exchange. For people with COPD, the symptom they are most aware of is shortness of breath. They also suffer from restrictions in their ability to enjoy daily life, including limitations in mobility (Reardon, Lareau, & ZuWallack, 2006).

Although the cause of COPD is not known, it is generally agreed that cigarette smoking is a prime suspect. Exposure to environmental toxins such as air pollution and harmful substances in the occupational setting also may play a role, particularly for people who smoke. The specific mechanism involved in the link between smoking and emphysema is thought to involve the release of an enzyme known as **elastase**,

which breaks down the elastin found in lung tissue. Cigarette smoke stimulates the release of this enzyme and results in other changes that make the cells of the lung less resistant to elastase. Normally there is an inhibitant of elastase found in the lung, known as alpha-1 antitrypsin (AAT). However, cigarette smoke inactivates AAT and allows the elastase to destroy more lung tissue. Of course, not all smokers develop COPD, and not all people with COPD are or have been smokers. Heredity may also play a role. There is a rare genetic defect in the production of AAT in about 2 to 3% of the population that is responsible for about 5% of all cases of COPD.

Apart from quitting smoking, a necessary first step in prevention and treatment, individuals with COPD can benefit from medications and treatments. These include inhalers that open the airways to bring more oxygen into the lungs or reduce inflammation, machines that provide oxygen, or, in extreme cases, lung surgery to remove damaged tissue.

DEMENTIA AND RELATED NEUROLOGICAL DISORDERS

Dementia is a clinical condition in which the individual experiences a loss of cognitive function severe enough to interfere with normal daily activities and social relationships. Dementia can be caused by a number of diseases that affect the nervous system, including cardiovascular disorders, a variety of neurologically based disorders, and abnormalities in other bodily systems. Alzheimer's disease receives the most attention, most likely since it is the most common cause of dementia.

Alzheimer's Disease

The disorder now known as **Alzheimer's disease** has been given many names over the years, including senile dementia, presenile dementia, senile dementia of the Alzheimer's type, and organic brain disorder. The current terminology reflects the identification of the condition as a disease by Alois Alzheimer (1864–1915), a German neurologist who was the first to link changes in brain tissue with observable symptoms. Alzheimer treated Auguste D., a woman in her 50s who suffered from progressive mental deterioration marked by increasing confusion and memory loss. Taking advantage of what was then a new staining technique, he noticed an odd disorganization of the nerve cells in her cerebral cortex. In a medical journal article published in 1907, Alzheimer speculated that these microscopic changes were responsible for Auguste D.'s dementia. The discovery of brain slides from this patient confirmed that these changes were similar to those seen in the disease (Enserink, 1998). In 1910, as a resulting number of autopsies from severely demented individuals showed the same abnormalities, a foremost psychiatrist of the era, Emil Kraepelin (1856–1926), gave the name described by his friend Alzheimer to the disease.

Prevalence

The World Health Organization estimates the prevalence of Alzheimer's disease worldwide of people over 60 as 5% of men and 6% of women (World Health Organization, 2001). The incidence rates of new cases is less than 1% a year for those aged 60 to 65 or possibly as high as 6.5% in those 85 and older (Kawas, Gray, Brookmeyer, Fozard, & Zonderman, 2000). A commonly quoted figure regarding the number of people in the United States with Alzheimer's disease is 5–5.5 million people, representing a rate of over 12% of the over-65 age groups and 50% or higher of those over 85 years of age. The media and other sources have projected this number to soar into the mid-21st century, reaching a staggering 14 million individuals who will suffer from the disease by 2050 unless a cure is found (Alzheimer's Association, 2010).

However, it is necessary to look more carefully at these statistics, which, according to other estimates, are overly high. In the first place, the estimates originate from a non-peer-reviewed publication of the privately funded Alzheimer's Association. The number they project in this report is based on a study of 856 U.S. residents living in 42 states ranging in age from 71 and older. U.S. prevalence statistics were extrapolated from the figures in this sample (Plassman et al., 2007). This approach of generalizing from a relatively small sample has characterized much of the Alzheimer's prevalence research and thus has led to disputes among researchers about the validity of this estimate. Others have arrived at an estimated prevalence of about half the media number at 2.3 million (Brookmeyer, Corrada, Curriero, & Kawas, 2002; Hy & Keller, 2000). Furthermore, norms for diagnostic tests for the disorder vary by education and age, so estimates of its prevalence in the oldest-old and the less well educated might result in inflated figures (Beeri et al., 2006). Although the numbers presented by the media draw attention to an important problem, they can also reinforce the notion that "senility" is an inevitable feature of aging.

Particularly important when evaluating statistics on the prevalence of Alzheimer's disease is whether the data refer specifically to dementia due to Alzheimer's disease only or whether they include vascular dementia. Approximately 20% of cases of dementia are due to cerebrovascular disease (Knopman, 2007). This is an important distinction because, as you will learn later, other forms of dementia are different in their cause, prognosis, and treatment.

Psychological Symptoms

The psychological symptoms of Alzheimer's disease evolve gradually over time (see Table 5.6). The earliest signs are occasional loss of memory for recent events or familiar tasks. Although changes in cognitive functioning are at the core of this disease's symptoms, changes in personality and behavior eventually become evident as well. By the time the disease has entered the final stage, the individual has lost the ability to perform even the simplest and most basic of everyday functions. The rate of progression in Alzheimer's disease varies from person to person, but there is a fairly regular pattern of loss over the stages of the disease. The survival time following the diagnosis is 7 to 10 years for people diagnosed in

TABLE 5.6
Stages of Alzheimer's Disease

Not Alzheimer's	Early-stage	Middle-stage	Late-stage
• Forgetting things occasionally • Misplacing items, like keys, eye glasses, bills, paper work • Forgetting the names or titles of some things, like movies, books, people's names • Some reduction in ability to recall words when speaking • Being "absent-minded" or sometimes hazy on details • "Spacing things out," such as appointments	• Short-term memory loss, usually minor • Being unaware of the memory lapses • Some loss, usually minor, in ability to retain recently learned information • Forgetting things and unable to dredge them up, such as the name of a good friend or even family member • Function at home normally with minimal mental confusion, but may have problems at work or in social situations • Symptoms may not be noticeable to all but spouse or close relatives/friends	• Short-term memory loss deepens, may begin to forget conversations completely or name of street where you live, names of loved ones or how to drive a car • Mental confusion deepens, trouble thinking logically • Some loss of self-awareness • Friends and family notice memory lapses • May become disoriented, not know where you are • Impaired ability to perform even simple arithmetic • May become more aggressive or passive • Difficulty sleeping • Depression	• Severe cognitive impairment and short-term memory loss • Speech impairment • May repeat conversations over and over • May not know names of spouse, children, or caregivers, or what day or month it is • Very poor reasoning ability and judgment • Neglect of personal hygiene • Personality changes; may become abusive, highly anxious, agitated, delusional, or even paranoid • May need extensive assistance with activities of daily living

Source: ConsumerReports.org. (2010). Alzheimer's drugs: Summary of recommendations. Retrieved from http://www.consumerreports.org/health/best-buy-drugs/alzheimers.htm.

their 60s and 70s, and drops to 3 years for people diagnosed in their 90s (Brookmeyer et al., 2002).

Biological Changes

One set of changes that Alzheimer discovered in the brain of Auguste D. consisted of what looked like the accumulated waste products of collections of dead neurons. Now known as **amyloid plaques**, they can develop 10 to 20 years before behavioral symptoms become noticeable and are thought to be one of the first events in the pathology of the disease. **Amyloid** is a generic name for protein fragments that collect together in a specific way to form insoluble deposits (meaning that they do not dissolve). The form of amyloid most closely linked with Alzheimer's disease consists of a string of 42 amino acids and is therefore referred to as beta-amyloid 42.

Beta-amyloid is formed from a larger protein found in the normal brain, referred to as **amyloid precursor protein (APP)**. As APP is manufactured, it embeds itself in the neuron's membrane. A small piece of APP is lodged inside the neuron and a larger part of it remains outside. In healthy aging, the part of APP remaining outside the neuron is trimmed by enzymes called **secretases** so that it is flushed with the neuron's outer membrane. In Alzheimer's disease, something goes wrong with this process so that the APP is snipped at the wrong place, causing beta-amyloid 42 to form. The cutoff fragments eventually clump together into beta-amyloid plaques, the abnormal deposits that the body cannot dispose of or recycle (see Figure 5.5).

Apart from its tendency to form insoluble plaques, beta-amyloid seems to have the potential to kill neurons. **Caspase** theory proposes that beta-amyloid stimulates the production of substances called caspases, enzymes that are lethal to neurons. This destruction of neurons, referred to as **apoptosis**, ultimately leads to the loss of cognitive functioning that occurs in Alzheimer's disease (Galvan et al., 2006).

The second mysterious change observed in Auguste D.'s brain was a profusion of abnormally twisted fibers within the neurons themselves, known

FIGURE 5.5

Steps in the Formation of a Beta-amyloid Plaque

(a)

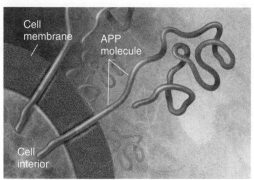

Cell membrane

APP molecule

Cell interior

(b)

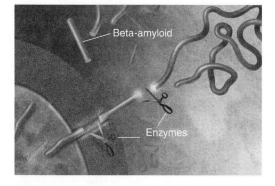

Beta-amyloid

Enzymes

(c)

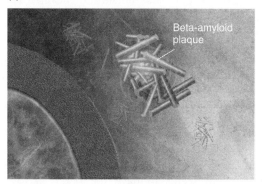

Beta-amyloid plaque

Proposed steps in the formation of beta-amyloid plaque. (a) As it is being made, APP sticks through the neuron's membrane. (b) Enzymes cleave beta-amyloid protein, releasing it into the space outside the neuron. (c) Clumps of beta-amyloid collect and begin to form a plaque.

as **neurofibrillary tangles** (literally, tangled nerve fibers). It is now known that the neurofibrillary tangles are made up of a protein called **tau** (see Figure 5.6), which seems to play a role in maintaining the stability of the microtubules that form the internal support structure of the axons. The microtubules are like train tracks that guide nutrients from the cell body down to the ends of the axon. The tau proteins are like the railroad ties or crosspieces of the microtubule train tracks. In Alzheimer's disease, the tau is changed chemically and loses its ability to separate and support the microtubules. With their support gone, the tubules begin to wind around each other and they can no longer perform their function. This collapse of the transport system within the neuron may first result in malfunctions in communication between neurons and may eventually lead to the death of the neuron.

Like the formation of plaques, the development of neurofibrillary tangles appears to occur early in the disease process and may progress quite substantially before the individual shows any behavioral symptoms. The earliest changes in the disease appear to occur in the hippocampus and the entorhinal region of the cortex, the area near the hippocampus, and are critical in memory and retention of learned information (Reitz, Honig, Vonsattel, Tang, & Mayeux, 2009).

Proposed Causes of Alzheimer's Disease

One certainty about Alzheimer's disease is that it is associated with the formation of plaques and tangles, particularly in areas of the brain controlling memory and other vital cognitive functions. Great uncertainty remains as to what causes these changes. It is also not clear whether the development of plaques and tangles is the cause of neuron death, or whether these changes are the result of other underlying processes that cause neurons to die and produce these abnormalities in neural tissue as a side product. Moreover, the existence of these changes in the brain is not a sure sign that an individual will have cognitive symptoms, highlighting the fact that this is a disorder affected by environmental as well as biological factors (Styczynska et al., 2008). Although the progression of Alzheimer's tends to lead to an inevitable loss of functioning, there is variability in its physical and cognitive symptoms (Burton, Strauss, Hultsch, Moll, & Hunter, 2006).

The theory guiding most researchers is that genetic abnormalities are somehow responsible for the neuronal death that is the hallmark of Alzheimer's

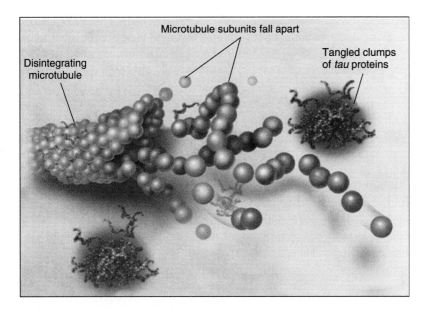

_FIGURE 5.6

Formation of a Neurofibrillary Tangle in Alzheimer's Disease

disease, with new "suspects" regularly being introduced into the literature (Tanzi & Bertram, 2008). The genetic theory began to emerge as an explanation after the discovery that certain families seemed more prone to a form of the disease that struck at the relatively young age of 40 to 50 years. These cases are now referred to as **early-onset familial Alzheimer's disease**, and though it is tragic, scientists have been able to learn a tremendous amount from studying the DNA of afflicted individuals. The four genes discovered so far, thought to account for about half of all early-onset familial Alzheimer's disease, are linked to excess amounts of beta-amyloid protein. Since the discovery of the early-onset form of the disease, genetic analyses have also provided evidence of another gene involved in familial Alzheimer's disease that starts at a more conventional age of 60 or 65 years. This form of the disease is called **late-onset familial Alzheimer's disease**. However, only 5% of all cases of Alzheimer's disease are familial, and the rest show no inherited pattern.

Clearly, even though genetic theories have considerable appeal, they do not tell the whole story. One of the prime genes thought to be involved in the late-onset familial pattern is the **apolipoprotein E (ApoE) gene**, located on chromosome 19. ApoE is a protein that carries cholesterol throughout the body, but it also binds to beta-amyloid, possibly playing a

role in plaque formation. Although the ApoE gene has received more attention, the first genetic defects found to be associated with familial Alzheimer's disease were on the **APP gene** on chromosome 21. The APP gene appears to control the production of APP, the protein that generates beta-amyloid. Most early-onset familial Alzheimer's disease cases are associated with defects in the so-called **presenilin genes (PS1 and PS2)**. Researchers speculate that these genes somehow lead APP to increase its production of beta-amyloid, which in turn causes neurofibrillary tangles and amyloid plaques (Zhang et al., 2009).

Higher education and continued mental activity throughout life are environmental factors that can protect the individual from development of Alzheimer's. In a unique longitudinal study of aging among Sisters of Notre Dame, nuns who agreed to donate their brains upon their death were studied while alive and their cognitive performance related to the studies of their brain upon autopsy. One of the original findings of the study was that despite the appearance of plaques and tangles in autopsy, many of the sisters did not show symptomatic deficits in cognitive performance. More recently, researchers found that higher mental activity in early adulthood seemed to protect the sisters from showing signs of cognitive decline in later life despite the presence of these changes in the brain (Iacono et al., 2009).

Extensive social networks can also be a protective factor, reducing the risk even among people who have high levels of brain pathology (Bennett, Schneider, Tang, Arnold, & Wilson, 2006). Physical exercise also seems to serve a protective function against the type of cognitive changes that may precede the development of Alzheimer's disease, particularly if it is performed at least at a moderate level of intensity (Geda et al., 2010).

Limited alcohol intake in earlier adult life may be protective against dementia later in adulthood (Peters, Peters, Warner, Beckett, & Bulpitt, 2008). Also related to lower risk is higher thyroxine levels (de Jong et al., 2009). The extent to which the individual participates in exercise may be another lifestyle contributor to the development of or progression of Alzheimer's disease. Both physical exercise and exercise in the form of stimulation along multiple sensory channels aid in slowing cognitive decline, and could potentially provide success to individuals with dementia (Briones, 2006). Finally, one of the most intriguing prospects in the search for causes of Alzheimer's disease relates to diet. People who follow the Mediterranean diet have a lower risk of developing the disease, even after controlling for factors such as ApoE4 genotype, BMI, age, sex, and smoking (Lopez-Miranda et al., 2009).

Diagnosis

The diagnosis of dementia is made by psychiatrists and clinical psychologists when the individual in question meets the criteria for clinical signs of dementia. These signs include progressively worsening memory loss, aphasia (loss of language ability), apraxia (loss of ability to carry out coordinated movement), agnosia (loss of ability to recognize familiar objects), and disturbance in executive functioning (loss of the ability to plan and organize) (American Psychiatric Association, 2000).

The diagnosis of Alzheimer's disease through clinical methods is traditionally done using the process of exclusion, as no one specific test or clinical indicator can definitively identify the disorder. Though methods of diagnosis are improving considerably, only an autopsy will reveal the presence of neurofibrillary tangles and beta-amyloid plaques that are the sure signs of the presence of Alzheimer's disease

rather than another form of dementia. In 2009, UCLA researchers reported a way to measure the amount of beta-amyloid in the blood absorbed by immune cells in the blood. A risk of Alzheimer's may be indicated if the immune system is not properly clearing the beta-amyloid (Avagyan et al., 2009). Early diagnosis of Alzheimer's also made significant advancements in 2009. The use of a simple skin test detects defective enzymes involved with memory functioning, and can detect Alzheimer's with 98% accuracy. Byrostatin, a drug used for chemotherapy, acts to reactivate the defective enzymes, possibly helping to restore memory (Sun, Hongpaisan, & Alkon, 2009). The FDA has approved further clinical trials to determine the effectiveness of the treatment.

In the mid-1980s, spurred by the desire to categorize a comprehensive set of diagnostic guidelines, a joint commission of the National Institute of Neurological and Communicative Disorders and Stroke and the Alzheimer's Disease and Related Diseases Association was formed (McKhann et al., 1984). The committee developed a set of medical and neuropsychological screening tests, behavioral ratings, and mental status measures based on observations of large numbers of cases. At the time, these recommendations significantly improved the chances of a correct diagnosis with 85 to 90% accuracy in the disease's later stages. Through the continued improvement of brain scanning, the ability to provide a reliable diagnosis in the early to moderate stages of the disorder is becoming ever more likely (Xiong, Yang, Gong, & Zhang, 2010). Ultimately, as treatments improve, early diagnosis would make it possible for clinicians to intervene and either slow or stop the degeneration of the patient's brain.

Of particular interest and importance is the need to differentiate the type of moderate memory loss that may reflect the early form of the disease from what is known as **mild cognitive impairment (MCI)**, a subtle loss of memory and learning abilities (Levey, Lah, Goldstein, Steenland, & Bliwise, 2006). MCI is a controversial diagnosis. In part this is because it is not clear whether this is a separate entity from Alzheimer's disease (Allegri, Glaser, Taragano, & Buschke, 2008). However, it is also not clear whether it is more directly related to Alzheimer's disease or to dementia caused by vascular disease, a topic we will turn to shortly (Zhou & Jia, 2009).

Medical Treatments

As researchers continue to make advances in identifying the cause or causes of Alzheimer's disease, the hope is that medications will be found that can reverse its course. Current medications temporarily alleviate symptoms but do not slow the progression of the disease (Salloway, 2008) (see Figure 5.7).

Two drugs approved by the Food and Drug Administration (FDA) for the treatment of memory loss in Alzheimer's disease target acetylcholine, a neurotransmitter involved in memory. These drugs are the **anticholinesterase treatments** given the names THA or tetrahydroaminoacridine (also called tacrine and given the brand name Cognex) and donepezil hydrochloride (Aricept). They are labeled anticholinesterase because they work by inhibiting the action of acetylcholinesterase (also called cholinesterase), the enzyme that normally destroys acetylcholine after its release into the synaptic cleft. Declines in the levels of acetylcholine, particularly in the hippocampus, are thought to be a factor in the memory loss that accompanies Alzheimer's disease. By inhibiting the action of acetylcholinesterase, these drugs slow the breakdown of acetylcholine, maintaining it at normal levels in the brain.

Initial excitement accompanying the approval of tacrine in 1993 was followed by disappointing reports that it could produce toxic effects in the liver if taken in required doses. Aricept was approved three years later, although it also has gastrointestinal side effects

FIGURE 5.7

Medications Used to Treat Symptoms of Alzheimer's Disease

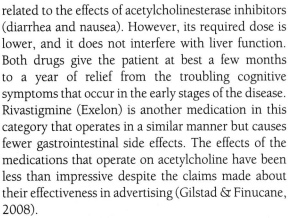

- Anticholinesterases: Decreases action of cholinesterases, allowing more acetylcholine to remain in the brain
- Memantine: Block glutamate receptors, which reduces neuronal death
- Antioxidants: Make oxygen more available to neurons

related to the effects of acetylcholinesterase inhibitors (diarrhea and nausea). However, its required dose is lower, and it does not interfere with liver function. Both drugs give the patient at best a few months to a year of relief from the troubling cognitive symptoms that occur in the early stages of the disease. Rivastigmine (Exelon) is another medication in this category that operates in a similar manner but causes fewer gastrointestinal side effects. The effects of the medications that operate on acetylcholine have been less than impressive despite the claims made about their effectiveness in advertising (Gilstad & Finucane, 2008).

The second category of medications is **memantine** (Namenda), which operates on the glumatate system. Glutamate is an excitatory neurotransmitter found widely throughout the brain. The theory is that glutamate essentially overexcites the neurons and leads to deleterious chemical changes that cause neuron death. By targeting glutamate, memantine is thought to exert a protective effect against this damage (Lipton, 2006). However, memantine's effectiveness is also at this point very limited (Clerici et al., 2009).

Current research is aimed at identifying medications that will interfere with the disease progression rather than at treating its symptoms (Gauthier & Scheltens, 2009). One approach targets beta-amyloids, and the second focuses on neuroprotective agents that will protect neurons from cell death. These agents would be most effective if used in the early stages of the disease when it is possible to intervene most effectively (Salloway, 2008). Researchers believe that a medical cure for Alzheimer's disease will eventually be found, and may occur in your lifetime. However, it is unlikely that one "magic bullet" will serve this function. Instead, treatments will need to be targeted for specific at-risk individuals based on their genetic vulnerability, medical history, and exposure to environmental toxins (Roberson & Mucke, 2006).

Psychosocial Treatments

As intensively as research is progressing on treatments for Alzheimer's disease with the hope of someday soon finding a cure, the reality is no cure presently exists. Meanwhile, people with this disease and their families must find ways to deal on a daily basis with the incapacitating cognitive and sometimes physical symptoms that accompany the deterioration of brain tissue. Clearly, until a cure can be found, mental health workers will be needed to provide assistance in this difficult process, so that the individual's functioning can be preserved for as long as possible.

A critical step in providing this kind of management of symptoms is for health care professionals to recognize that Alzheimer's disease involves families as much as it does the patients. Family members are most likely to be the ones providing care for the patient, particularly when the patient is no longer able to function independently. This responsibility most likely falls to wives and daughters. These individuals, called **caregivers**, have been the focus of considerable research efforts over the past two decades. Results from such research have demonstrated that people in the role of caregivers are very likely to suffer adverse effects from the constant demands placed on them. The term **caregiver burden** is used to describe the stress that these people experience in the daily management of their afflicted relative. As the disease progresses, caregivers must provide physical assistance in basic life functions, such as eating, dressing, and toileting. As time goes by, the caregiver may experience health problems that make it harder and harder to provide the kind of care needed to keep the Alzheimer's patient at home.

Given the strain placed on caregivers, it should come as no surprise that health problems and rates of depression, stress, and isolation are higher among these individuals than among the population at large. Research suggests that daughters caring for parents with dementia suffer significantly more cardiovascular stress compared to wives caring for their spouse (King, Atienza, Castro, & Collins, 2002). Fortunately, support for caregivers of people with Alzheimer's disease has become widely available. Local chapters of national organizations in the United States, such as the Alzheimer's Association, provide a variety of community support services for families in general and caregivers in particular. Caregivers can be taught ways to promote independence and reduce distressing behaviors in the patient, as well as to learn ways to handle the emotional stress associated with their role. We summarize suggestions from the National Institute of Aging (2009) for caregivers to care for themselves in Figure 5.8.

FIGURE 5.8

Suggestions for Caregivers

Caring for yourself

Taking care of yourself is one of the most important things you can do as a caregiver. This could mean asking family members and friends to help out, doing things you enjoy, using adult day care services, or getting help from a local home health care agency. Taking these actions can bring you some relief. It also may help keep you from getting ill or depressed.

How to take care of yourself

Here are some ways you can take care of yourself:

- Ask for help when you need it.
- Join a caregiver's support group.
- Take breaks each day.
- Spend time with friends.
- Keep up with your hobbies and interests.
- Eat healthy foods.
- Get exercise as often as you can.
- See your doctor on a regular basis.
- Keep your health, legal and financial information up-to-date.

Source: National Institute of Aging. (2009). Caring for a person with Alzheimer's Disease. NIH Publication Number: 09-6173. Retrieved from http://www.nia.nih.gov/NR/rdonlyres/6A0E9F3C-E429-4F03-818E-D1B60235D5F8/0/100711_LoRes2.pdf.

An important goal in managing the symptoms of Alzheimer's disease is to teach caregivers behavioral methods to maintain functional independence in the patient. The idea behind this approach is that, by maintaining the patient's functioning for as long as possible, the caregiver's burden is somewhat reduced. For example, the patient can be given prompts, cues, and guidance in the steps involved in getting dressed and then be positively rewarded with praise and attention for having completed those steps. Modeling is another behavioral strategy, in which the caregiver performs the desired action (such as pouring a glass of water) so that the patient can see this action and imitate it. Again, positive reinforcement helps to maintain this behavior once it is learned (or more properly, relearned). The caregiver then has less work to do, and the patients are given the cognitive stimulation involved in actively performing these tasks rather than having others take over their care completely.

Another strategy that caregivers can use to maintain independence is to operate according to a strict daily schedule for the patient to follow. The structure provided by a regular routine of everyday activities can give the patient additional cues to use as guides. In addition to increasing the extent to which people with Alzheimer's disease engage in independent activities, caregivers can also use behavioral strategies to reduce or eliminate the frequency of actions such as wandering or being aggressive. In some cases this strategy may require ignoring problematic behaviors, with the idea that by eliminating the reinforcement for those behaviors in the form of attention, the patient will be less likely to engage in them. However, it is more likely that a more active approach will be needed, especially for a behavior such as wandering. In this case the patient can be provided with positive reinforcement for not wandering. Even this may not be enough, however, and the caregiver may need to take such precautions as installing a protective device in doors and hallways.

It may also be possible for the caregiver to identify certain situations in which the patient becomes particularly disruptive, such as during bathing or riding in the car. In these cases the caregiver can be given help in targeting those aspects of the situation that cause the patient to become upset and then modify it accordingly. For example, if the problem occurs while bathing, it may be that a simple alteration such as providing a terry cloth robe rather than a towel helps reduce the patient's feeling of alarm at being undressed in front of others.

It is also important for caregivers to understand what to expect as the disease progresses. In a study of more than 300 nursing home patients with advanced dementia, fewer interventions considered burdensome, such as tube feeding, were used when those responsible for the patient's treatment were aware of the prognosis and typical course of the disease (Mitchell et al., 2009).

FIGURE 5.9

Components of a Multidisciplinary Approach to Interventions with Alzheimer's Caregivers

- Support groups
- Coping
- Exercise
- Legal aid
- Financial advice

Creative approaches to managing the recurrent stresses involved in the caregiver's role may help to reduce the feelings of burden and frustration that are so much a part of daily life (Figure 5.9). Along with the provision of community and institutional support services, such interventions can go a long way toward helping the caregiver and ultimately the patient (Callahan et al., 2006).

Other Neurological Diseases That Can Cause Dementia

The condition known as dementia is frequently caused by Alzheimer's disease in later life, but many other conditions can affect the status of the brain and cause loss of memory, language, and motor functions.

Vascular Dementia. In **vascular dementia**, progressive loss of cognitive functioning occurs as the result of damage to the arteries supplying the brain. Dementia can follow a stroke, in which case it is called acute onset vascular dementia, but the most common form of vascular dementia is **multi-infarct dementia** or **MID**, caused by transient ischemic attacks. In this case, a number of minor strokes ("infarcts") occur in which blood flow to the brain is interrupted by a clogged or burst artery. Each infarct is too small to be noticed, but over time, the progressive damage caused by the infarcts leads the individual to lose cognitive abilities. There are important differences between MID and Alzheimer's disease. The development of MID tends to be more rapid than Alzheimer's disease, and personality changes are less pronounced. The higher the number of infarcts, the greater the decline in cognitive functioning (Saczynski et al., 2009).

Vascular dementia seems to be related to risk factors that are similar to those for cardiovascular disease. Diabetes mellitus is associated with moderate cognitive deficits and changes in the physiology and structure of the brain, increasing the risk of dementia (Baquer et al., 2009). These cognitive deficits are particularly likely to develop early in the course of the disease (van den Berg et al., 2008). Metabolic syndrome also is associated with a higher risk of vascular dementia (Solfrizzi et al., 2009). Excess fat (adiposity) in the midsection further increases the risk of dementia in late life (Whitmer et al., 2008).

Frontotemporal Dementia. **Frontotemporal Dementia (FTD)** characterizes a group of rare disorders affecting the frontal and temporal lobes of the brain. Currently, FTD encompasses primary progressive aphasia, and semantic dementia. Symptoms emerge as changes in behavior or language problems. Behavioral symptoms may reflect personality changes such as apathy, lack of inhibition, obsessiveness, addictive behaviors, and loss of judgment, and neglect of personal hygiene (Caycedo, Miller, Kramer, & Rascovsky, 2009). FTD also includes **Pick's disease**, which involves an accumulation of unusual protein deposits called Pick's bodies.

People with FTD are more likely to suffer behavioral problems rather than language disturbances although they may have difficulty speaking or correctly naming objects. As the disease progresses, people with FTD have more difficulty with reading and writing. Eventually the individual with FTD may discontinue using language altogether. Although there is no treatment for FTD, medications ranging from antidepressants to anti-phychotics can be prescribed to alleviate symptoms.

Parkinson's Disease. People who develop **Parkinson's disease** show a variety of motor disturbances, including tremors (shaking at rest), speech impediments, slowing of movement, muscular rigidity, shuffling gait, and postural instability or the inability to maintain balance. Dementia can develop during the later stages of the disease, and some people with Alzheimer's disease develop symptoms of Parkinson's disease. Patients typically survive 10 to 15 years after symptoms appear.

There is no cure for Parkinson's disease, but medications have been developed that have proved relatively successful in treating its symptoms. The primary drug used is Levadopa (L-dopa), but over the years this medication loses its effect and may even be toxic. Major advances have also been made in neurological treatments, including high-frequency deep brain stimulation of subcortical movement areas of the brain that in the past were excised surgically (Espay, Mandybur, & Revilla, 2006). Research examining the activation of brain cells with flashes of light offers promising treatment for Parkinson's disease (Gradinaru, Mogri, Thompson, Henderson, & Deisseroth, 2009).

Lewy Body Dementia. **Lewy bodies** are tiny spherical structures consisting of deposits of protein found in dying nerve cells in damaged regions deep within the brains of people with Parkinson's disease. Lewy body dementia, first identified in 1961, is very similar to Alzheimer's disease with progressive loss of memory, language, calculation, and reasoning, as well as other higher mental functions. Estimates are that this form of dementia accounts for 10 to 15% of all cases of dementia (McKeith, 2006).

The dementia associated with the accumulation of Lewy bodies fluctuates in severity, at least early in the disease. The disease also includes episodes of confusion and hallucinations, which are not typically found in Alzheimer's disease. Individuals with pure Lewy body dementia also show impairments in motor skills and in specific skills, including tasks demanding concentrated attention, problem solving, and spatial abilities.

Reversible Dementias. **Reversible dementias** are due to the presence of a medical condition that affects but does not destroy brain tissue. If the medical condition is left untreated, permanent damage may be done to the central nervous system, and the opportunity for intervention will be lost. Furthermore, if the condition is misdiagnosed as Alzheimer's disease, the patient will be regarded as untreatable and not be given the appropriate care at the appropriate time.

A neurological disorder known as **normal pressure hydrocephalus**, though rare, can cause cognitive impairment, dementia, urinary incontinence, and difficulty in walking. The disorder involves an obstruction in the flow of cerebrospinal fluid, which causes the fluid to accumulate in the brain. Early treatment can divert the fluid away from the brain before significant damage has occurred. Head injury can cause a **subdural hematoma**, which is a blood clot that creates pressure on brain tissue. Again, surgical intervention can relieve the symptoms and prevent further brain damage. The presence of a brain tumor can also cause cognitive deficits, which can be prevented from developing into a more severe condition through appropriate diagnosis and intervention.

Delirium is another cognitive disorder that is characterized by temporary but acute confusion that can be caused by diseases of the heart and lung, infection, or malnutrition. Unlike dementia, however, delirium has a sudden onset. Because this condition reflects a serious disturbance elsewhere in the body, such as infection, it requires immediate medical attention.

Prescribed medications given in too strong a dose or in harmful combinations are included as other potentially toxic substances that can cause dementia-like symptoms. The condition called **polypharmacy,** in which the individual takes multiple drugs, sometimes without the knowledge of the physician, can be particularly lethal. Recall that the excretion of medications is slower in older adults because of changes in the kidneys, so that older adults are more vulnerable to such toxic effects of medications.

Wernicke's disease is an acute condition caused by chronic alcohol abuse involving delirium, eye movement disturbances, difficulties maintaining balance and movement, and deterioration of the nerves to the hands and feet. Providing the individual with vitamin B1 (thiamine) can reverse this condition. Unfortunately, if it is not treated, Wernicke's disease progresses to the chronic form of dementia known as **Korsakoff syndrome**.

Older adults who suffer from clinical depression may show cognitive changes that mimic those involved in Alzheimer's disease. The symptoms of depression in older adults may include confusion, distraction, and irritable outbursts, and these symptoms may be mistaken for Alzheimer's disease. When these symptoms appear, causing impairment similar to dementia, the disorder is referred to as **pseudo-dementia**. Depression may also occur in conjunction with dementia, particularly in older adults who are in the early stages of a dementing disorder. In either case, the depression is treatable, and when appropriate interventions are made, the individual's cognitive functioning can show considerable improvement.

The many possible causes of dementia, and the difficulty in distinguishing dementia due to Alzheimer's disease from other forms of cognitive decline, supports the notion that the prevalence of Alzheimer's disease may be overestimated, particularly with the rise in obesity in the United States, which presents a significant risk factor for certain forms of dementia.

Clearly, Alzheimer's disease and the variety of dementias described here are major potential limitations on the lives of older adults. Contrary to the impression given by the media, they afflict a minority of older people. Nevertheless, breakthroughs in their treatment, along with contributions to understanding other major diseases, will be among the most significant achievements of science in the 21st century.

SUMMARY

1. Diseases in middle and later adulthood can be highly disabling. However, many are preventable, starting with actions taken in early adulthood. Cardiovascular diseases in which there are pathological changes in the arteries are arteriosclerosis and atherosclerosis. Heart disease includes coronary artery disease, myocardial infarction, and congestive heart failure. Cerebrovascular accidents involve a cutting off of blood to the brain and may be acute or transient. Cardiovascular diseases are the leading cause of death in the over-75 population, with men having a higher risk, particularly Black men. Behavioral risk factors include sedentary lifestyle, smoking, high BMI, and excessive alcohol intake. Heart disease can be largely prevented by careful monitoring of diet and exercise.

2. Cancer is a group of diseases in which there is abnormal cell growth. Skin cancer is the most prevalent form in the United States in the adult population overall. Breast cancer is the most frequent cancer in women, but lung cancer is the deadliest for men and women. There are many behavioral risk factors for cancer, including smoking, sun exposure, and lack of control over diet. Environmental toxins can increase cancer risk. Cancer treatment includes surgery, radiation therapy, chemotherapy, and biological therapy.

3. Several musculoskeletal disorders are more common in older adults than in the younger population. Osteoarthritis is a degenerative joint disease in which the cartilage deteriorates. Osteoporosis is an extreme loss of bone mineral content that primarily affects women. Preventative steps include

calcium intake, vitamin D, exercise, dietary control, and estrogen-replacement therapy.

4. Type 2 diabetes is an increasingly common chronic disease in older adults caused by a defect in metabolizing glucose. Prevention and treatment involves weight control and exercise.

5. Chronic respiratory diseases, including chronic emphysema and chronic bronchitis, are thought to be caused primarily by cigarette smoking. They have no cure at present. Dementia is a clinical condition involving loss of memory and other cognitive functions.

6. Alzheimer's disease is the most common form of dementia, affecting an estimated 7% of the over-65 population. Biological changes include development of amyloid plaques and neurofibrillary tangles. Alzheimer's disease is thought to have genetic causes, possibly involving abnormalities on the ApoE, APP, and presenilin genes that lead to formation of plaques and tangles. The caspase theory focuses on the neurotoxic role of amyloid. Diagnosis of Alzheimer's disease can be made only from autopsy, but there are improved methods such as those involving brain scans. Medical treatments being tested include anticholinesterases and memantines. Psychosocial treatments attempt to control behaviors and to provide support to caregivers. Other forms of dementia are vascular dementia, fronterotemporal dementia, Parkinson's disease, Lewy body dementia, and Pick's disease. There are also reversible dementias, including pseudodementia, which, if treated, can lead to a return to normal cognitive functioning.

6

Basic Cognitive Functions: Information

Your abilities to learn, remember, solve problems, and gain knowledge are basic to your sense of self and adaptation to everyday life. As these abilities change during adulthood, they also have the potential to alter your fundamental understanding of yourself and the world.

The field of **cognition** is central to the field of adult development and aging. In addition to being of theoretical and scientific interest, there are practical ramifications of changes in the ability to apply cognitive skills to situations in everyday life. Consider, for example, the effect that changes in cognitive functioning with age have on the ability to drive or process information quickly.

The concept of the "senior moment" discussed in Chapter 2 relates to more deep-seated anxiety that middle-aged individuals have about losing their memories. In this chapter, we will see whether such anxiety is warranted. As a preview, it is safe to say that although losses in speed and memory occur with age, normal age-related changes are not entirely negative. Furthermore, from the perspective of identity, there are many ways that people can compensate for memory changes. The key is to adopt

a balanced approach rather than become convinced that everything is going downhill or, conversely, that there are no changes at all. Recognizing that you are undergoing cognitive changes and then trying to maximize your performance will help preserve your abilities and maintain them to their fullest potential.

INFORMATION PROCESSING

Researchers working within the **information processing** perspective regard the cognitive functioning of humans as comparable to the functioning of a computer. The "data" from experiences enter into the brain through various sensory routes, where they progress through a series of stages of analysis. Like a computer, the brain can discard the information, store it for future purposes, or use it instantly. Studies of information processing in adulthood focus on whether and how the aging process alters the efficiency and effectiveness of these analytical phases. Findings from laboratory studies on information processing can have significant importance to daily life.

Processing, Attention, and Memory

Psychomotor Speed

Theories about changes in the overall quality of information processing in adulthood are based on studies of **psychomotor speed**, the amount of time it takes to process a signal, prepare a response, and then execute that response. Researchers believe that psychomotor speed reflects the integrity of the central nervous system (Madden, 2001).

The basic framework of a study on psychomotor speed is fairly straightforward. You enter a laboratory equipped with a computer set up to record your responses. The screen flashes a stimulus array (or a number of items organized in a specific way) that you are asked to examine. Your instructions typically tell you how to respond when a particular stimulus, known as a target, appears in that array. The time taken to respond (called **reaction time**) is recorded. Building on this basic procedure, experimenters then manipulate conditions to determine what factors influence the speed of performance. Simple reaction time involves viewing one stimulus at a time; in choice reaction time tasks, respondents must select from an array. Some procedures use cuing, in which participants are given a prompt to direct their attention to a particular region of the screen. In some studies, misleading or irrelevant cues are presented to determine whether older adults are more distracted by such information. The measurement of the effects of these manipulations (compared to simple or cued reaction time) forms the basis for research on age differences in psychomotor speed.

Researchers know with certainty that your reaction time as a young adult will be lower (i.e., you will be quicker) than it will be as you get older. The question is, how much lower and under what circumstances will it increase as you get older? The documented increases in reaction time with age in adulthood are typically a matter of several hundreds of milliseconds, not enough to be particularly noticeable in everyday life, but enough to be significant under the scrutiny of the laboratory researcher.

The rate at which reaction time changes occur may vary considerably from person to person. Despite this increasing variability in reaction times with age, overall, the net effect of the changes are negative across adulthood, particularly for choice reaction time tasks (Der & Deary, 2006).

Why do reaction times slow as people age? According to the **general slowing hypothesis** (Salthouse, 1996), the increase in reaction time reflects a general decline of information processing speed within the nervous system of the aging individual. Related to this idea is the **age-complexity hypothesis**, which proposes that through slowing of central processes in the nervous system, age differences increase as tasks become more complex and processing resources are stretched more and more to their limit.

The general slowing hypothesis was derived through examinations of cross-sectional studies on reaction times. The reaction times of older groups of adults were plotted against the times of younger adults on a graph called a **Brinley plot**. As you can see from Figure 6.1, older adults perform at similar speeds on tasks completed relatively quickly by a young adult (500 ms). On tasks that take longer for young adults (1,000 ms), older adults take proportionately longer (1,500–2,000 ms) than they do on the 500 ms tasks.

The general slowing hypothesis is consistent with a large body of data on reaction time performance in adulthood. This hypothesis does not identify any particular stage or component of information processing as the culprit causing age differences in reaction time,

though there is the assumption that slowing reflects lack of efficiency in the nervous system. As we will see later, the general slowing hypothesis is also used to explain age differences in memory. Loss of speed leads to memory impairments, as a backlog develops in cognitive processes when multiple operations must be completed simultaneously or within a limited time.

Attention

The slowing of reaction time with age may be attributed to many factors. One that has intrigued researchers is the hypothesis that older adults are particularly disadvantaged in the attentional stage of information processing. **Attention** involves the ability to focus or concentrate on a portion of experience while ignoring other features of that experience, to be able to shift that focus as demanded by the situation, and to be able to coordinate information from multiple sources. Once your attention is focused on a piece of information, you are then able to perform further cognitive operations, such as those involving memory or problem solving.

If you are someone who has difficulty concentrating or focusing your attention for long periods of time, you are certainly aware of how frustrating it can be to

FIGURE 6.1

Brinley Plot

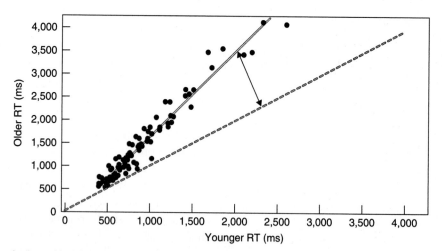

Deviation of dots from the diagonal line shows the extent to which older adults are disproportionately slower as the task becomes more challenging for young adults.

Source: Sliwinski, M. J., & Hall, C. B. (1998). Constraints on general slowing: A meta-analysis using hierarchical linear models with random coefficients. *Psychology and Aging, 13,* 169. American Psychological Association. Reprinted with permission.

Reaction time tasks typically present information on a screen. Manipulations of the array allow researchers to infer the effects of aging on attention.

miss important information or details. Persistent and serious attentional problems characterize people with attention deficit disorder who, as a result, may have difficulty learning new information or performing more than one task at a time. The attentional deficits associated with the normal aging process can involve deficits of a similar nature, particularly when complex decisions must be made quickly.

Types of Attentional Tasks.   Studies of attention are important for understanding the cognitive functions of adults of varying ages and their abilities to function in various real-life situations in which cognitive resources must be focused on some target or goal. Researchers approach these issues by breaking down the attentional tasks involved in everyday life into components to examine in the laboratory. For the most part, these studies suggest that people become less efficient in the use of attentional processes as they get older.

One particularly important area of attentional performance involves dividing the focus of attention between multiple inputs. Commonly known as "multitasking," you most likely engage in dividing your attention on a regular basis throughout your day. You may be reading this book while listening to your iPod, watching television, or intermittently updating your Facebook status. Experiments that attempt to replicate this real-life situation use a **dual task** paradigm (also called a **divided attention** task),

in which the individual is given information from two input sources and must attend to both sources at once to identify a target.

Most people are disadvantaged when it comes to multitasking. Accident data showing the risks of texting or talking on a cell phone while driving are now on the books in several U.S. states and are being proposed in others. Disadvantages of multitasking increase progressively with age (Kramer & Madden, 2008). To a certain extent, older adults appear to compensate for attentional deficits under multitasking conditions by shifting activation of regions of the brain involved in attentional processing. For example, it appears that they reduce the activity of frontal regions of their brains (responsible for planning) while increasing activity in brain regions involved in the storage of visual and spatial information (Fernandes, Pacurar, Moscovitch, & Grady, 2006). The ability of older adults to compensate for attentional losses in later life by shifting brain activation is a phenomenon observed over a number of other areas of performance, as we will see throughout this chapter.

A number of investigations of attention and aging use an inhibitory task in which the individual must deliberately suppress one response in order to perform another. The purpose of this type of task is to determine whether older adults are able to ignore aspects of a stimulus that are irrelevant. One of the best known inhibitory attention tasks is the Stroop

FIGURE 6.2

Theories of Attention and Aging

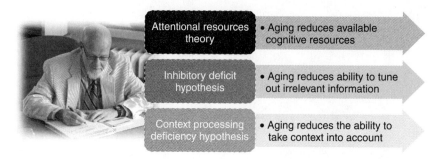

test, in which you are told to name the color of ink in which a word is printed. Critical trials on the Stroop test involve comparing your performance when the color and the word match (e.g., the word "red" printed in red) with your performance when the color and the word do not match ("red" is printed in green). The inhibitory part of this test is surprisingly difficult because you have to dissociate your reading of the word from your naming of the color.

The third type of attentional task involves the ability known as **sustained attention**. This type of task requires the participant to be on guard for a change in a stimulus array; many video games require a similar process of monitoring the screen for moving objects that demand a response of some sort. Laboratory tasks of sustained attention are similar in principle though not as elaborate. For example, a typical experiment requires participants to watch a computer screen as a series of stimuli are presented and told to respond only when the target stimulus appears (such as the letter "X" moving onto a screen containing all "Y"s). The experimenter manipulates the cuing conditions that determine how long it will take you to detect the target. Older adults typically have more difficulty on sustained attention tasks than do younger adults (Dennis, Daselaar, & Cabeza, 2007).

Studies on aging and attentional performance suggest that not all abilities decline. For example, although older adults are typically slower when processing information from visual displays, they can remember the location of an item presented in a visual display and may even be more efficient at this task than younger adults (Kramer et al., 2006).

Theories of Attention and Aging. There are three approaches to understanding age differences in attentional tasks (see Figure 6.2). The **attentional resources** theory regards attention as a process reflecting the allocation of cognitive resources. When you must focus on a particular object, you must dedicate a certain proportion of your mental operations to that object. According to this theory, older adults have greater difficulty on attentional tasks because they have less energy available for cognitive operations than do their younger counterparts (Blanchet, Belleville, & Peretz, 2006).

The second theory of attention and aging, the **inhibitory deficit hypothesis**, suggests that aging reduces the individual's ability to inhibit or tune out irrelevant information (Butler & Zacks, 2006). As we discussed earlier, one important feature of attention is the ability to focus on one element of a stimulus array while ignoring others. If older adults cannot ignore irrelevant information, their attentional performance will suffer.

The inhibitory deficit hypothesis is widely supported by a variety of studies based on psychological and electrophysiological methods. For example, studies of event-related potentials (ERPs), which measure the brain's electrical activity in response to stimuli, show that older adults are less able to block out distracting stimuli when completing a task. Their pattern of response suggests that there are deficits in the prefrontal cortex, the area of the brain involved in the control of inhibiting irrelevant information (West & Schwarb, 2006). These deficits add to those that occur early in processing, at least for information that is presented visually (Gazzaley et al., 2008).

The inhibitory deficit hypothesis implies that middle-aged and older adults focus most effectively when distractions are kept to a minimum. One source of such distraction may be their own concern over how they are performing which therefore may cause them to perform even more poorly than they otherwise would. Imagine that you are a computer programmer anxious about the possibility of being laid off or reassigned because you are not as quick as you once were in your job of inspecting arrays of new data. The more you worry about how you are performing, the less able you are to concentrate on your task. Your performance deficits might ultimately lead you to lose your job or be reassigned to other duties. Thus, people who are worried about the aging of their cognitive abilities may be more likely to engage in identity accommodation—the "over the hill" mentality—a process that will ultimately contribute to poorer performance.

However, older adults are not entirely disadvantaged in inhibitory attentional tasks. They can benefit from practice with the Stroop test in ways similar to younger adults (Davidson, Zacks, & Williams, 2003), suggesting that performance on certain types of attention can be improved regardless of age. Additionally, changes related to color perception with age may account for some of the age differences in the Stroop task (Ben-David & Schneider, 2009).

The **context processing deficiency** hypothesis of aging and information processing proposes that the ability to judge the context of information during situations such as the sustained attention task becomes less efficient in later adulthood. The reasoning behind this theory is as follows. Anytime you are asked to perform a sustained attention task, you need to remain conscious of the fact that your responses are supposed to be made only to certain targets. For instance, you might be told to push a key when you see an "X" that follows an "A" but not when you see an "X" that follows a "B." This situation is comparable to a video game in which you get points only when, for example, you are supposed to shoot at a flying asteroid if it follows an exploding star but not an exploding spaceship.

Context processing deficiency theory proposes that older adults are particularly affected when they must remember the task instructions because they have fewer resources to devote to a task when they must constantly remind themselves of when they are supposed to make their response (Braver & Barch, 2002). Even if the cue remains in front of them during the trial, older adults are less able to use the context provided by the cue information (Paxton, Barch, Storandt, & Braver, 2006).

Age differences in continuous attention performance are not readily explained by the inhibitory

AGING IN THE NEWS

www.wiley.com/college/whitbourne   OLDER ADULTS WHO MADE THE HEADLINES   -VOL. 4, CHAPTER 6-

CHESLEY ("SULLY") SULLENBERGER, HERO OF CRASH

For the first time in 50 years of commercial jet flight, the pilots of US Airways Flight 1549 successfully executed one of the most technically challenging maneuvers—landing a jetliner on water without fatalities. Though he retired one year later, Chesley Sullenberger showed that experience is a key factor in maintaining successful performance even in a job with heavy reliance on reaction time.

deficit or general slowing hypothesis, but instead suggest a unique contribution of context processing difficulties (Rush, Barch, & Braver, 2006). Because they have greater difficulty keeping the task demands in mind while watching out for the target, older adults make more errors and are slower in these continuous performance tasks.

However, experience can compensate for age-related changes in sustained attention. In a simulated air-traffic control experiment, older adults who showed deficits on laboratory attentional tasks were able to perform well on the complex tasks required in the situations they encountered on the job on a daily basis (Nunes & Kramer, 2009).

DRIVING AND AGING

As we mentioned earlier, age-related changes in information processing have effects on many aspects of daily life. The ability to drive is probably one of the most important. This is a particularly sensitive topic for older adults and it is a topic that continues to receive attention in the media. Questions about whether older adults have lost the cognitive abilities to drive are often raised in the aftermath of an accident involving an older driver if there has been loss of life or significant property damage. As we examine the actual data on driving and aging, however, we will show that some of these media reports are exaggerated and that older drivers, though experiencing attentional deficits, have other abilities and resources that they use to compensate for these deficits.

As we saw in Chapter 4, there are also a number of changes in the visual system that can impair the performance of older drivers, including loss of visual acuity, increased sensitivity to glare, and difficulty seeing in the dark. In addition, many driving situations involve rapid cognitive judgments. Given that reaction time is greater for older adults, they may be particularly disadvantaged when they need to evaluate a complex situation in which they have to make a quick decision.

Yet the effects of age on vision and cognition do not necessarily translate into higher accident rates of older drivers compared to some of their younger counterparts. According to the National Highway Traffic Safety Administration, in the United States, the highest fatality rates (27 per 100,000) are for 16- to 25-year-olds; people 65 and older have a much lower fatality rate (18 per 100,000 population).

The lights and the signs at this intersection on the University of Massachusetts campus present a complex visual array and may create confusion in older drivers.

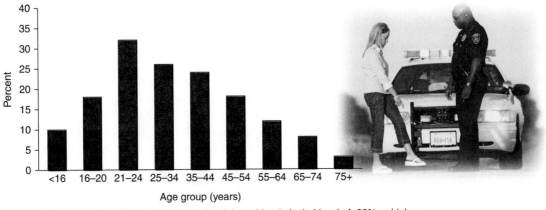

Percent of all fatalities within each age group involving a blood alcohol level of .08% or higher

Source: National Highway Traffic and Safety Administration. (2010). Fatality analysis reporting system encyclopedia. Retrieved from http://www-fars.nhtsa.dot.gov/QueryTool/QuerySection/Report.aspx.

Younger people are also involved in many more crashes than older drivers per mile driven; the rates of motor vehicle accidents among teen drivers 16 to 19 years old are four times the rates of accidents for drivers 65 and older. Some of the factors involved in the higher accident rates of younger drivers include driving at higher speeds, failing to wear seat belts, following too closely behind the vehicle in front of them, and tending to underestimate or not sufficiently recognizing hazardous situations (Centers for Disease Control and Prevention, 2010e). As we reported in Chapter 1, drivers under the age of 25 are also far more likely than older drivers to drink and drive (see Figure 6.3). Distractions incurred while driving (such as text messaging, eating, or searching for a dropped cell phone) also constitute a major concern for younger drivers, prompting a summit by the U.S. Department of Transportation in 2009 on the dangers of distracted driving. Research suggests that even hands-free devices (such as the use of a Bluetooth earpiece) do not improve driving performance (Ishigami & Klein, 2009). In other words, any type of talking on the phone while driving is unsafe.

By contrast, older adults are more likely to be involved in a crash at an intersection when making a left-hand turn, at least in the United States. The opposite is true in Australia, where people drive on the left, making a right-hand turn more complex and dangerous there (Braitman, Kirley, Chaudhary, & Ferguson, 2006). Tasks requiring a high demand of visual attention while driving (such as merging or yielding to oncoming traffic) are associated with greater problems navigating the environment (Richardson & Marottoli, 2003).

Therefore, we can conclude that older drivers have certain difficulties but do not pose the fatal threat that many in the media associate with this age group, particularly compared to teens who drive under the influence of substances. Yet, as we have discussed earlier, fear of loss of abilities can become a self-fulfilling prophecy, particularly for older adults who interpret their driving-related experiences through identity accommodation. Older adults who doubt themselves more frequently will hesitate before making a response due to worries about their abilities, or may suffer internal distractions because they are so preoccupied with their own concerns. Prejudice against them by younger people can exacerbate whatever fears and concerns older drivers already have about their changing abilities. They may hear derogatory phrases such as "driving while old" or "gray head" and become even more concerned and hence distracted.

Driving provides a perfect example of the importance of adopting a biopsychosocial perspective to understand the aging process. Biology (changes in vision and reaction time) and psychology (internal distractions causing anxiety) each play important roles. The sociocultural component of the equation provides further insight into this comprehensive model. Driving is virtually a requirement of the ability to live independently in many regions of the United States and other countries that lack comprehensive public transportation but require automobiles to get from place to place. Older adults who live in suburban or rural areas with limited or no public transportation lose an important connection to the outside world, and risk becoming housebound and socially isolated.

Yet, it is also important to recognize that many older drivers are able to self-regulate their behaviors to compensate for changes in cognitive and perceptual abilities. They avoid driving at night, on interstate highways, or situations in which they must make risky left-hand turns (Okonkwo, Crowe, Wadley, & Ball, 2008). Although younger people complain about the slower habits of older drivers, data show that older people have fewer accidents per person.

Interestingly, the data on aging and driving correspond closely to research about aging and crash prevalence among older airline pilots, who have fewer fatal and nonfatal accidents than younger pilots (Broach, Joseph, & Schroeder, 2003). Pilots who are older and more experienced also take better advantage of training sessions to improve their performance in flight simulators, tasks where decision time and judgment both play an important role (Taylor, Kennedy, Noda, & Yesavage, 2007). Older, experienced pilots are also more likely to identify and elaborate problems encountered in complex flight situations compared with younger, less experienced pilots (Morrow et al., 2009).

Chesley Sullenberger was 57 years old when in 2009, he avoided loss of life by landing U.S. Airways flight 1549, which lost its engines, in the Hudson River. His performance in this life and death situation is a testimony to the positive role that years of experience can play in compensating for attentional deficits. Up until 2007, when the federal government raised the mandatory retirement age for commercial airline pilots from 60 to 65, Sullenberger would have been forced to retire just 3 years later (though he did retire in 2010).

Consider Sullenberger's performance compared to the pilots of the ill-fated Colgan Air Flight 3497 that crashed just a few weeks later outside of Buffalo, New York; the cause was determined to be pilot

error. Neither the pilot (age 47) nor the co-pilot (age 24) had sufficient hours in the cockpit to enable them to overcome the relatively minor problems of icing that brought down the plane, resulting in the deaths of 50 people. There are likely countless other less well-publicized examples in the area of driving performance that attest to the value of greater experience as a factor that prevents accidents involving older adults.

Nevertheless, there is value to maintaining precautions to protect all drivers from accidents caused by distracted driving, visual losses, or slowing of response speed. Current licensing policies and procedures are not well equipped to handle the influx of older drivers. Recommendations to address this growing public safety concern include identifying older drivers who may be medically at-risk and impaired, rather than all older drivers (Dobbs, 2008) (see Table 6.1). As the number of older drivers continues to grow with the increased longevity of the Baby Boomer generation, appropriate safeguards for older drivers, such as driving tests and safety classes, are being considered by public officials. Highway safety experts are also exploring alternatives to the traditional intersection, such as substituting well-designed roundabouts for the type of complex junction that can cause so many accidents while turning.

As you sort through the pro–con arguments about age versus experience in driving, it might be worthwhile to consider that speed is not everything when it comes to navigating your way around the highways and byways of your community. Allowing more time for older drivers to get where they are going might not be such a bad idea and might even make the roads safer for everyone. It is also important to remember that prevention efforts should focus on the avoidable fatalities involving younger drivers who are under the influence of alcohol or other substances. The real "number one killer"—in the United States, at least—is not heart disease but fatal accidents involving driving under the influence because people die at much younger ages than biology would dictate.

MEMORY

One of the most feared changes to occur with aging is loss of memory. The data on the effects of aging on memory suggest that the aging process indeed

TABLE 6.1
Checklist for older drivers to rate their abilities

For the following questions use this scale:

1. Always or Almost Always	*2. Sometimes*	*3. Never or Almost Never*

- ☐ I signal and check to the rear when I change lanes
- ☐ I wear a seat belt
- ☐ I try to stay informed on changes in driving and highway regulations
- ☐ Intersections bother me because there is so much to watch from all directions
- ☐ I find it difficult to decide when to join traffic on a busy interstate highway
- ☐ I think I am slower than I used to be in reacting to dangerous driving situations
- ☐ When I am really upset, I show it in my driving
- ☐ My thoughts wander when I am driving
- ☐ Traffic situations make me angry
- ☐ I get regular eye checks to keep my vision at its sharpest
- ☐ I check with my doctor or pharmacist about the effects of my medications on driving ability (If you do not take any medication, skip this question)
- ☐ I try to stay abreast of current information on health practices and habits
- ☐ My children, other family members or friends are concerned about my driving ability

For the remaining questions use this scale:

1. None	*2. One or Two*	*3. Three or More*

- ☐ How many traffic tickets, warnings, or "discussions" with officers have you had in the past 2 years?
- ☐ How many accidents have you had during the past 2 years?

Source: American Automobile Association. (2010). Drivers 55 plus: Self-rating form. Retrieved from http://www.aaafoundation.org/quizzes/index.cfm?button = driver55.

has negative effects on many aspects of memory. However, as was true for attention, not all aspects of memory are affected in the same way by aging, nor is everyone affected the same way by the aging process.

Working Memory

The part of memory that keeps information temporarily available and active, called **working memory**, seems to be particularly vulnerable to the effects of aging. You use your working memory when you have information in "consciousness," whether it is new information you are trying to learn or previously learned information that you are recalling or "bringing to mind." Working memory and attention are closely linked, since controlled attention is required to juggle multiple thought processes.

Researchers assess working memory by assigning a task to participants that prevents them from consciously rehearsing the information they are supposed to remember. The "n-back" task, a commonly used working memory test, requires you to repeat the "nth" item back in a list of items presented to you in serial order. For example, a series of visual stimuli, such as a yellow triangle, a red square, a green circle, and a blue diamond appear on a computer screen. In each instance you are asked whether the stimulus is new or one previously seen. In the "1-back" task, you are shown the yellow triangle followed by the red square followed by the yellow triangle and asked to remember the stimulus shown prior to the red square (the yellow triangle). The further back in the series (for example, in the "2-back"), the harder the task because the more demands are placed on working memory.

According to Baddeley (2003), there are four components to working memory (see Figure 6.4). Auditory memory (memory for what you hear) is held within the phonological loop. This information can be rehearsed by repeating the material over and over again "in your head" such as when you try to remember a phone number and have no way to

FIGURE 6.4

Components of Working Memory

Phonological loop	• Auditory memory
Visuospatial scratch pad	• Visual memory
Episodic buffer	• Retrieving information from long-term memory
Central executive	• Allocates cognitive resources

write it down. Memory for information that you see is maintained within the visuospatial scratch pad such as when you are trying to remember the route home from a store you have visited once by imagining it in your mind. The third component of working memory, the episodic buffer, is responsible for recalling information you already have within long-term memory by bringing it temporarily into working memory. The term **episodic memory** refers, similarly, to memory for past events. We will talk more about episodic memory below. The central executive, the fourth component of working memory, integrates the other three components of working memory. The central executive is responsible for deciding how to allocate cognitive resources to a particular task.

The components of working memory are increasingly being understood as linked to particular cortical brain regions (Baddeley, 2003). Working memory also reflects activity of the hippocampus, a structure in the brain's limbic system, located beneath the cortex, that plays an important role in consolidating short-term memories into long-term memory and for years has been the focus of research on aging (Kadar, Silbermann, Weissman, & Levy, 1990). More

recent evidence continues to support the importance of the hippocampus to age-related changes in working memory (Ystad et al., 2009). However, researchers are also continuing to examine the prefrontal cortex, which, as the planning and control center of the brain, serves as the primary region for the central executive. In support of this proposal, white matter hyperintensities that accumulate in the prefrontal cortex are associated with working memory deficits in older adults (Vannorsdall et al., 2009).

There is now a substantial body of research supporting the view that in normal cognitive aging, structural changes in areas of the brain involved in working memory are compensated by heightened activation of the prefrontal cortex (Park & Reuter-Lorenz, 2009). According to this view named, appropriately enough, the "scaffolding theory," older adults are able to recruit alternate neural circuits as needed by task demands to make up for losses suffered elsewhere. Thus, there are age-related declines in working memory, but there are also compensatory mechanisms available that can circumvent these declines.

Effects of Aging on Long-Term Memory in Adulthood

We turn next to **long-term memory**, the repository of information that is held for a period of time ranging from several minutes to a lifetime. Long-term memory contains information that includes the recent past, such as remembering where you put your cell phone half an hour ago, to information from many years ago, such as what happened at your fourth birthday party. In Figure 6.5 we show the "Aging and Memory Scorecard" that summarizes effects of aging on the various types of long-term memory.

Research suggests that older adults experience impairments in episodic memory, both in encoding and retrieving information (Old & Naveh-Benjamin, 2008). Memory for word meanings and the storehouse of factual information is referred to as **semantic memory**. The third component of long-term memory involves nonverbal memories, which are stored in **procedural memory.** This is your knowledge of how to perform (without instructions) physical activities such as sewing on a button, playing the piano, and riding a bike.

Contemporary researchers believe procedural memory is a variant of **implicit memory**, the recall of information acquired unintentionally. In testing implicit memory, researchers present participants with a task that involves manipulating but not necessarily remembering information. For example, you might be presented with a list of words and asked to place them into categories, but not to recall them. Later, you would be asked to remember the words you had previously only been told to categorize. Another way to test implicit memory is through priming. Here you are shown information that leads you to think of a certain thing, topic, or situation. For instance, you may see a list of words containing the word "apple." Then the researcher shows you a word fragment such as "a–p– –" and asks you to fill in the remaining three blanks. Implicit memory is demonstrated when your response is "apple" rather than "ample." Cognitive researchers regard procedural memory, your memory for performing well-practiced tasks, as a variant or form of implicit memory. The majority of verbal memory tasks on aging and memory involve **explicit memory** but as we will see later, research on aging and implicit memory provides important insights as well.

In **source memory,** participants are asked to state where they saw or heard a piece of information. In everyday life, source memory is useful when you are trying to remember which of your friends said she would give you tickets to an upcoming concert or which professor hinted at an impending pop quiz.

Two other long-term memory phenomena relate to recall of information from the past. **Remote memory** involves, as the term implies, recall of information from the distant past in general, and **autobiographical memory** is recall of information from your own past. Finally, **prospective memory** encompasses the recall of events to be performed in the future. In prospective memory, you must remember your intention to perform an action, such as calling that friend who promised the tickets to decide where to meet.

Older adults who experience a reduction in working memory have difficulty acquiring and storing new information. Because working memory is central to other mental operations, it was one of the first cognitive processes studied with regard to aging. Early on, several surprising findings emerged. First, it was discovered that older adults had no difficulty remembering short strings of digits. Second, researchers found that older adults performed relatively well on recognition memory tasks in which they only needed to state whether a stimulus word was one they had seen before or not. Recall memory, in which test words have to be generated (rather than just recognized) did show consistent deficits across age groups. Such findings indicated that memory changes in later adulthood are not a simple story of straightforward decline.

Thus, although in general episodic memory shows significant age deficits, particularly for free recall tasks, there are areas of preserved functioning. Consider the case of "flashbulb" memories, which are important and distinctive events that stand out

FIGURE 6.5

The Aging and Long-term Memory Scorecard

Abilities that decline	Abilities that do not decline
Episodic memory	Flashbulb memory
Source memory	Semantic memory
False memory	Procedural memory
Tip-of-the-tongue (names)	Implicit memory
Prospective memory	Autobiographical memory ("reminiscence bump")

from other memories of past events. Undoubtedly you have heard older family members recall where and what they were doing the day John F. Kennedy was assassinated on November 22, 1963. You may recall what you were doing the morning of September 11, 2001 during the terrorist attacks on the World Trade Center in New York City. When older adults form such memories, they are as likely as younger adults to recall them correctly, as evidenced by research assessing recall of source memory for the news of the September 11 terrorist attacks (Davidson, Cook, & Glisky, 2006). One factor that preserves flashbulb memory in older adults is exposure to an event that is both personally relevant and frequently thought about (Tekcan & Peynircioglu, 2002).

Semantic memory is also spared from the negative effects of the aging process (Wiggs, Weisberg, & Martin, 2006). Older adults are able to remember word meanings and a broad array of factual information on a comparable level with younger adults. We will see in the next chapter that memory for this type of information forms an important component of the ability of older adults to retain high levels of performance on certain types of intelligence tests.

Procedural memory is yet another area that holds up well with age. In one particularly impressive study, a sample of approximately 500 adults ranging from 18 to 95 years were tested on their ability to learn a fine motor task in which they had to use their fingers to slide a small nut off a rod as quickly as possible. Not only did older adults show significant improvement in performance over a series of five learning trials, but they retained their memory for the task for as long as 2 years later with no drop-off in performance (Smith et al., 2005). The study, interestingly enough, was replicated in a sample of young and old rhesus monkeys given the same task and tested over a 2-year period with findings comparable to those for humans (Walton, Scheib, McLean, Zhang, & Grondin, 2008). So there is truth to the saying that "old monkeys," if not dogs, can learn new tricks.

A well-maintained procedural memory contributes to the ability of older adults to compensate for some of their loss of speed and working memory in diverse areas including bridge playing, chess, reading, cooking, gardening, and typing (Mireles & Charness, 2002). The experienced bridge player, for example, is able to examine a round of cards without giving each individual card a great deal of thought or study. Through years of playing, many of the choices about which card to play follow established conventions and rules, so that the older bridge player does not have to remember as much about each of the hand of 13 cards they are dealt for each round of play.

Findings on procedural memory are important because they highlight an area spared from the effects of aging. Because procedural memory is a form of implicit memory, the findings fit with other data, suggesting that when older adults do not intentionally sit down to learn and later remember information, they actually perform better than when they know they will be tested on their memory (Caggiano, Jiang, & Parasuraman, 2006).

An area not spared from aging's effects is source memory. Older adults seem to have greater difficulty on memory tasks when they must judge where they saw an item on a previous occasion (Thomas & Bulevich, 2006). Older adults also are more likely to have what researchers call "illusory memories" in which they say they remember something that never happened (Dodson, Bawa, & Slotnick, 2007). They may think that one person said something when in reality it was said by someone else or perhaps not said at all.

Along these lines, older adults are also more susceptible to the planting of false memories. An ingenious test of false memory was developed over 50 years ago and then updated in what is now called the Deese–Roediger–McDermott (DRM) paradigm. In the DRM paradigm, individuals are presented with a list of words (such as "cake," "honey," "candy," etc.) that are all from the same category ("sweet"). However, they are not given the category label. The critical trial occurs when participants are given a recognition test in which "sweet" is included among other distracters as well as words that were on the original list (e.g. "honey" and "point"). Most people think that they were presented with the word "sweet" because the other words in the category primed them to think of things that were sweet. Very few people are immune from this effect, but when warned, younger participants are better able to avoid the false memory implantation.

Problems in retrieval from long-term memory appear in research on the tip-of-the-tongue phenomenon in adulthood. You are most likely to have a tip-of-the-tongue experience when you are trying to remember a name such as the 1998 movie starring Drew Barrymore and Adam Sandler (answer: *The Wedding Singer*). The tip-of-the-tongue phenomenon is most likely the cause of the "senior moment" we discussed earlier. You know the information is there somewhere, but you are momentarily unable to retrieve it. Although the information eventually can be recalled (often when you have stopped trying to recall the information), the experience can certainly be inconvenient and embarrassing, such as failing to remember the name of your professor if you see her outside of the classroom.

In fact, the tip-of-the-tongue effect is observed more in older adults in both laboratory and everyday life situations. Young adults occasionally experience this effect when they are trying to retrieve an abstract word, but for older persons, retrieval failure is more likely to occur when trying to remember a person's name (Shafto, Burke, Stamatakis, Tam, & Tyler, 2007), particularly when the person has a name that sounds similar to someone else's (O'Hanlon, Kemper, & Wilcox, 2005). Evidence from imaging studies suggests that the area of the brain used for phonological production is subject to age-related neural declines, a fact that might explain retrieval failure (Shafto, Stamatakis, Tam, & Tyler, 2010).

In general, information stored and not accessed from remote memory becomes increasingly difficult to retrieve with passing years. A popular myth is that older people can remember information from many years in the past better than they can remember more recent information. However, this myth is not supported by data on remote memory (Piolino, Desgranges, Benali, & Eustache, 2002). In one study, older adults were asked to recall events from television shows. Their memory for recent programs was superior to their ability to remember programs from many years ago (Squire, 1989).

The exception to this research on remote memory occurs in the area of autobiographical memory, or recall of one's own past. Many people seem to experience a "reminiscence bump" of very clear memories for the ages of about 10 to 30 years (Rubin, Rahhal, & Poon, 1998), an effect that is particularly strong for happy memories (Gluck & Bluck, 2007). Researchers believe that these memories are preserved in part because they are central to identity (McLean, 2008). Remote memories that are not as personally relevant fade with the passage of time.

Prospective memory, or the ability to remember to "do" something, is particularly important in everyday life. Older adults commonly complain (and you may as well) that they cannot remember what they were supposed to get when they went into a room. Although a nuisance, this type of forgetting is not as detrimental as the type of forgetting involved in not taking a medication at a certain time. Older people do indeed appear to have more prospective memory slips than do younger adults. In one study involving a simulated shopping task, older adults forgot more items on their grocery list than did younger adults (Farrimond, Knight, & Titov, 2006). Fortunately, if they are aware of their prospective memory problems older adults can take advantage of reminders through notes, date books, and cell phones, all of which have so far been demonstrated to work effectively for adults in the young-old age category (Schnitzspahn & Kliegel, 2009).

Identity, Self-Efficacy, Stereotype Threat, and Control Beliefs

The empirical evidence we have just covered supports in part the commonly held belief that at least some forms of memory suffer as people get older—what varies is perhaps how much, exactly which type, and when. However, countervailing data suggests that how you think about your memory may play just as important a role as your actual age. The results of research on these important topics are summarized in Figure 6.6.

FIGURE 6.6

Relationships Among Identity Self-efficacy, Memory Control Beliefs, and Stereotype Threat

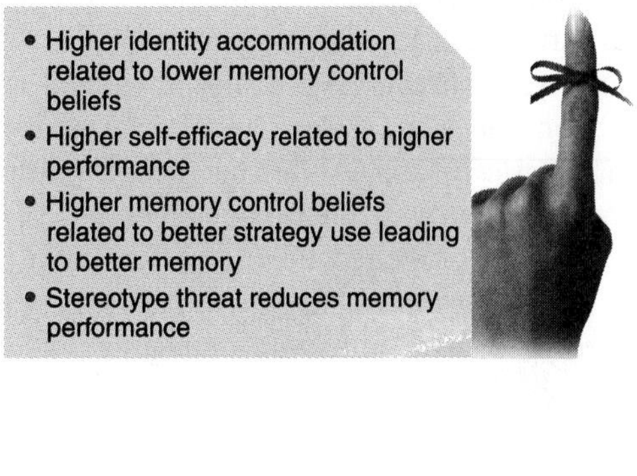

- Higher identity accommodation related to lower memory control beliefs
- Higher self-efficacy related to higher performance
- Higher memory control beliefs related to better strategy use leading to better memory
- Stereotype threat reduces memory performance

First we will look at the role of identity in memory performance and aging. People who fall prey to the "over-the-hill" form of identity accommodation are more likely to succumb to society's negative stereotypes about aging and suffer more severe age effects than people who are able to maintain a positive view of their abilities using identity assimilation. The "over-the-hill" believers start on a downward spiral that causes them to be painfully aware of each instance of forgetting and to become even more pessimistic about their memory performance in the future. We know that middle-aged adults are highly sensitive to age-related changes in memory (Whitbourne & Collins, 1998), and through self-efficacy this sensitivity may affect their actual performance.

Memory self-efficacy refers to the confidence you have in your memory; specifically, the degree to which you feel that you can successfully complete a memory task. The higher your memory self-efficacy, the greater the likelihood that you will perform to your maximum ability. With increasing age, people feel less and less confident about their memory and consequently, their self-efficacy suffers (West, Thorn, & Bagwell, 2003). They are affected by the so-called "implicit theory" about aging and memory: namely, that memory functioning suffers an inevitable decline in later life (McDonald-Miszczak, Hertzog, & Hultsch, 1995).

An impressive display of the power of memory self-efficacy comes from a 6-year longitudinal study conducted in the Netherlands of a healthy community sample of more than 1,800 individuals 55 and older (Valentijn et al., 2006). Individuals with a lower sense of memory self-efficacy, particularly with regard to the belief that their memory had declined, showed poorer memory performance over the course of the study. Whether their lower self-efficacy caused their poorer performance or whether it reflected actual negative changes was impossible to determine. However, other investigations suggest that lower memory self-efficacy may turn into a self-fulfilling prophecy.

Stereotype threat is a concept drawn from research on the standardized test performance of African Americans suggesting that people perform in ways consistent with negative stereotypes of the group to which they see themselves as belonging (Steele, Spencer, Aronson, & Zanna, 2002). Research on stereotype threat and aging suggests that the older person's self-identification as "old" contributes to lower memory test scores. Since older adults are stereotyped as having poorer memories, this belief causes poorer performance. Although through identity assimilation older adults can overcome stereotype threat (Whitbourne & Sneed, 2002), it is difficult to be impervious to society's negative views about aging and memory (Cuddy, Norton, & Fiske, 2005).

Researchers in the area of stereotype threat and aging propose that identification with negative images of aging interferes with memory performance in older adults by lowering their feelings of self-efficacy. Ultimately, they become less able to take advantage of mnemonic strategies (systematic procedures designed to enhance memory, such as ROY G. BIV to remember the colors in the rainbow) (Hess, Auman, Colcombe, & Rahhal, 2003). However, in keeping with the premise of identity process theory, people vary in the way they respond to stereotype threat; sometimes the oldest participants are the least rather than the most affected by stereotype threat. Supporting this view, one study of aging and stereotype threat showed that the oldest participants (those in their 80s) were least affected by these negative unconscious attitudes (Hess & Hinson, 2006). Although identity processes were not investigated in this particular study, the investigators proposed that individual differences in response to threat may mediate the way that older individuals react to negative information about aging and memory.

We might hypothesize that identity assimilation can protect older adults from the harmful effects of believing that aging is associated with inevitable memory loss. Conversely, identity accommodation about memory performance, known to be higher in midlife adults (Whitbourne & Collins, 1998), could also account for the finding that stereotype threat regarding memory performance on the basis of age is higher among middle-aged compared to older adults (O'Brien & Hummert, 2006).

We may even go so far as to say that there is no way of knowing just how much stereotype threat could account for many of the findings on aging and memory. The slightest hint of a memory test can be enough to activate stereotype threat, ultimately leading to poorer performance by older adults. In a study comparing traditional and nontraditional instructional conditions in relation to memory for trivia, age differences were observed in the traditional, but not nontraditional, instructional condition (Rahhal, Colcombe, & Hasher, 2001). A similar explanation could account for the age differences observed in explicit but not implicit memory tasks.

Memory controllability refers to beliefs about the effects of the aging process on memory, such as the extent to which the individual believes that memory decline is inevitable with age (Lachman, 2006). Older people who rely heavily on identity accommodation are more likely to hold negative beliefs about their ability to control their memory as they age (Jones, Whitbourne, Whitbourne, & Skultety, 2009). In turn, older people who believe they cannot exert control over loss of memory do perform more poorly on memory tests (Riggs, Lachman, & Wingfield, 1997). If people believe that they can control their memory, then they are more likely to take advantage of the strategies to ensure they actually do achieve higher performance (Lachman & Andreoletti, 2006).

Memory and Health-Related Behaviors

Given the relationship of various health-related behaviors to the functioning of the central nervous system, as we discussed in Chapter 4, it should be no surprise that memory in later adulthood is also related to health-related behaviors (see Figure 6.7). For example, cigarette smoking is known to cause deleterious changes in the brain. One longitudinal study conducted in Scotland provided impressive data showing that people tested as children who eventually became smokers had significantly lower memory and information processing scores when followed up at ages 64 and 66 years, controlling for early life intelligence (Starr, Deary, Fox, & Whalley, 2007).

FIGURE 6.7

Lifestyle Factors and Memory

- Avoid smoking
- Dietary control
- Maintain physical activity
- Avoid stress
- Practice using memory skills

A second health-related behavior relevant to memory involves diet and specifically the consumption of fish. You have probably heard the saying that fish is "brain food," and evidence suggests that it can be, particularly fish high in omega-3 fatty acids (such as salmon or tuna). Participants in the large-scale Chicago Health and Aging Study (with over 3,700 participants) were followed over a 6-year period during which they were asked to report their food consumption. Approximately 20% of the sample ate two or more meals containing fish per week. Controlling for a host of relevant factors, the rate of cognitive decline in individuals who consumed one or more fish meals a week was reduced by 10 to 13% per year (Morris, Evans, Tangney, Bienias, & Wilson, 2005). A subsequent study of nearly 900 older adults from England and Wales showed that socioeconomic status may also play a role in affecting the relationship between cognitive performance and fish consumption in that people with higher social status are more likely to include fish in their regular diets (Dangour et al., 2009).

Investigators have established a link between enhanced memory performance in older adults and other dietary components, including vitamin B12, vitamin B6, and folate (Smith & Refsum, 2009). Conversely, homocysteine, an amino acid found in the blood and acquired mainly from eating meat, is negatively related to memory performance (van den Kommer, Dik, Comijs, Jonker, & Deeg, 2008). Vitamin D is another dietary component thought to be linked to cognitive functioning (Wilkins, Sheline, Roe, Birge, & Morris, 2006). Flavonoids, found in certain foods ranging from fruits and vegetables to red wine and dark chocolate, can also have a beneficial influence on cognition. In a longitudinal study conducted in France over a 10-year period, high levels of flavonoid intake were associated with significantly lower memory declines (Letenneur, Proust-Lima, Le George, Dartigues, & Barberger-Gateau, 2007).

In contrast to the documented effects of these substances, one popular natural memory "cure" shows no beneficial effects. Findings from a large randomized, double-blind, placebo-controlled study of more than 3,000 adults ranging in age from the 70s to the 90s challenge the claims of gingko biloba's effectiveness. Over a period of approximately 6 years, twice-daily doses produced no significant improvements in cognitive functioning (Snitz et al., 2009).

In Chapter 4, we saw that aerobic exercise can contribute to increases in brain areas involved in cognition. Older people who are aerobically fit are not only physically but also mentally more fit (Newson & Kemps, 2006). Research on exercise and cognition repeatedly illustrates that attention, memory, accuracy, and information processing all improve with each heart-pumping activity session, although the mechanisms by which these improvements occur remain unclear (Erickson et al., 2009; Marks, Katz, & Smith, 2009). Moderate- to high-intensity strength training contributes to increased information processing (Chang & Etnier, 2009) and executive functioning (Liu-Ambrose et al., 2010). Accompanying these findings is research demonstrating that strength training through weight lifting can also improve memory performance of older adults (Lachman, Neupert, Bertrand, & Jette, 2006).

Additionally, research on exercise self-efficacy and control beliefs among a group of older adults engaged in a strength training intervention demonstrated that higher exercise beliefs during the intervention were related to higher levels of resistance and maintenance of exercise after the intervention (Neupert, Lachman, & Whitbourne, 2009).

Health may also play a role in cognition through the route of metabolic factors. As we saw in Chapter 5, people with metabolic syndrome are at increased risk for Alzheimer's disease. Impaired glucose tolerance, a component of metabolic syndrome, shows a clear relationship to cognitive functioning in normal aging individuals (Di Bonito et al., 2007). Older adults with Type 2 diabetes are more likely to experience slowing of psychomotor speed as well as declines in executive functioning (Yeung, Fischer, & Dixon, 2009). Even impaired glucose tolerance, a condition known as pre-diabetes, can be a risk factor for greater declines in cognition. High-fat diets appear to play an important role in this process (Devore et al., 2009).

One possible route through which metabolic factors can affect psychomotor slowing and memory involves insulin growth factor-1 (IGF-1). IGF-1 is one of three growth hormones involved in insulin regulation that also has a protective effect on neurons. As part of the Nurses' Health Study, a nationwide investigation involving more than 120,000 registered female nurses studied from midlife on, researchers obtained blood samples and then several years later conducted telephone interviews of cognitive functioning from a sample of 590 women 70 years of age and older. After adjusting for possible confounding factors (such as education, smoking history, alcohol use, and BMI), the women with low levels of IGF-1 showed slower decreases with age in cognitive functioning than women with high levels of this substance (Okereke et al., 2007).

As we also discussed in Chapter 5, health-related behaviors include those that are involved in the management of stress. Given that stress takes its toll on health and emotions, it makes sense that it would also affect cognitive functioning. You undoubtedly have had the experience of forgetting something important when you were preoccupied with other concerns such as financial strains, increased demands at school or work, or problems in your close relationships. Researchers investigating this issue have provided support for the notion that stress can interfere with memory performance among older adults. In one intriguing investigation, a sample of more than 300 older adults in the Veterans Affairs Normative Aging Study were asked to keep a daily diary of their interpersonal stressors and their memory failures. By tracking the relationship of stressful experiences to memory on a daily basis, researchers were able to establish the lagged effect showing that stressors on one day predicted memory failures on the next (Neupert, Almeida, Mroczek, & Spiro, 2006).

Interference of your emotions with your memory performance is another experience you have probably encountered. For example, if you are feeling particularly blue, you may feel as well that your mental powers are operating at less than 100% efficiency. A prospective longitudinal study of widows (begun before the widows lost their husbands), confirmed this idea among older women. Independent of the effect of losing a spouse on depressive symptoms, women in the Longitudinal Aging Study Amsterdam were found to have lower memory performance at the end of a 6-year period. Although the women who eventually lost their husbands started out with lower memory scores, even after controlling for this difference, the widows showed greater memory loss than did the non-widows over the course of the study (Aartsen, Van Tilburg, Smits, Comijs, & Knipscheer, 2005).

Looking directly at memory performance and its relationship to stress, another group of investigators provided impressive evidence to support the idea that the deficit shown by older adults on working memory tasks can be accounted for in part by the experience of daily stressors (Sliwinski et al., 2006). In this study, a group of more than 100 older community-living adults with intact mental status were compared to young adults on the n-back working memory task. The amount of daily stress in their lives was determined through an interview in which participants were asked questions such as, "Did you have an argument or disagreement with anyone?" and "Did anything happen to a close friend or relative that turned out to be stressful for you?" Testing occurred over six occasions, allowing the investigators to examine within-person variations in the relationship between stress and memory as well as between-person age group differences.

Interestingly, the young adults in the sample were more likely to say "yes" to these and the other four questions assessing interpersonal stress. For instance, young adults said they had an argument on 26% of the days on which a given stressor occurred compared to 5% for older adults. The study's main finding was that on days in which people experienced stress, the performance of people in both age groups was significantly poorer. Emotional strains can interfere with memory in anyone regardless of age. Why does stress have this impact on memory?

Sliwinski and his colleagues (2006) maintain that preoccupation with stress occupies attentional resources that could otherwise be devoted to the memory task. However, there is evidence that older adults are perhaps more anxious than younger adults about their memory performance and therefore their memories are more vulnerable to such emotional interference (Andreoletti, Veratti, & Lachman, 2006).

Memory Training Studies

One mission of aging and memory research is to find ways to help older adults offset deleterious changes in memory. Many researchers in this field are true "gerontological optimists" who believe that their work can help improve cognitive functioning in older adults. They have established, for example, the fact that even simple practice can produce significant improvements in memory task performance, offsetting the negative effects of mental inactivity. Interventions aimed at improving episodic memory can be beneficial even for individuals suffering from the clinical condition known as mild cognitive impairment (Belleville et al., 2006).

Although the simple task of practice can result in enhanced memory performance, there are advantages to encouraging strategy use among older adults. Providing training intended to improve the memories of older adults also has the benefit of increasing feelings of the individual's self-efficacy (West, Bagwell, & Dark-Freudeman, 2008). When this training is provided in a group setting, it can be particularly effective in boosting not only self-efficacy but also memory performance (Hastings & West, 2009).

One of the most ambitious cognitive training interventions is a multisite study known as Advanced Cognitive Training for Independent and Vital Elderly (ACTIVE) carried out over a 2-year period on more than 2,800 adults 65 to 94 years of age (Ball et al., 2002). Training consisted of 10 one-hour sessions over a 5- to 6-week period. The participants were trained in one of three types of cognitive skills—memory, reasoning, or speed of processing—while a control group received no training. These cognitive functions were selected because they show the most improvement in laboratory work and are related to everyday living tasks (e.g., telephone use, shopping, food preparation, housekeeping, laundry, transportation, medication use, and management of personal finances). For instance, those who received memory training were taught ways to remember word lists and sequences of items, text, and the main ideas and details of stories. Training in the area of reasoning involved learning how to solve problems that follow patterns, such as reading a bus schedule or filling out an order sheet. Training in speed of processing involved learning how to identify and locate visual information quickly for use in tasks such as looking up a phone number, finding information on medicine bottles, and responding to traffic signs.

Testing conducted at the end of the training period demonstrated that the majority of participants in the speed (87%) and reasoning (74%) groups showed improvement; about one quarter (26%) in the memory group showed improvement. Two years later, the gains were still evidenced, although these were larger for participants who participated in booster sessions. We will discuss more findings from this major study in the next chapter.

In conclusion, attentional and memory processes in adulthood are important in everyday life. Older adults appear to suffer deleterious changes, but these changes are neither universal nor irreversibly negative. Identity and other memory-related beliefs play an important role in determining whether individuals are able to take advantage of compensatory strategies. Future research will help uncover more of these personality–memory linkages as well as to identify which strategies can be most effective in maximizing cognitive performance throughout middle and later adulthood.

SUMMARY

1. Cognitive functions are an important component of an individual's identity, and in middle and later adulthood, individuals become concerned about the loss of these abilities. However, many cognitive abilities are maintained well into later life, and there are preventative strategies individuals can use. Psychomotor speed, measured by reaction time, is an important variable in research on cognitive aging. There is a consistent increase of reaction time throughout adulthood. The general slowing hypothesis explains this increase as a decline of information processing speed, and the related age-complexity hypothesis proposes that the loss is greater for more difficult tasks. Studies of attention and aging involve the tasks of priming, search, divided attention, and sustained attention. Patterns of age differences on these tasks are interpreted in terms of the theory of attentional resources and aging, which proposes that older adults have limited resources, and by the inhibitory deficit hypothesis, according to which older adults are less able to inhibit irrelevant information in attentional tasks. The context processing deficiency proposes that older adults are less able to take advantage of cues from the environment.

2. Memory is studied in terms of its components. The study of aging and memory involves attempts to determine how each component is affected by age-related changes in the processes of storing, encoding, and retrieving information. Working memory is significantly poorer in older adults.

3. In long-term memory, tasks of episodic memory are most sensitive to age effects, and older adults have more difficulty in everyday memory tasks as well as in standard laboratory experiments. Semantic memory, however, is not affected by the normal aging process. Procedural memory is also retained in older adults, as is implicit memory. However, older adults have more difficulty with tasks involving source memory, tip-of-the-tongue, and remote memory. Certain personal memories are well retained into later life, particularly those from adolescence and early adulthood. Prospective memory is retained when an individual can be prompted by the time rather than by an event. Researchers are attempting to establish connections between changes in the nervous system and age-related deficits in working memory.

4. Researchers are investigating the interaction of memory changes with changes in control beliefs, identity, and self-efficacy. The concept of stereotype threat implies that older adults may perform more poorly on memory tasks that activate negative stereotypes about aging and memory.

5. Memory in later adulthood is related to a variety of health-related behaviors, including cigarette smoking, consumption of fish high in omega-3 fatty acids, vitamin B12, vitamin B6, folate, and flavonoids. Aerobic exercise can contribute to increases in brain areas involved in cognition. Health may also play a role through the route of metabolic factors. Impaired glucose tolerance, a component of metabolic syndrome, shows a clear relationship to cognitive functioning in normal aging individuals. Stress can also interfere with memory performance.

6. Interventions aimed at improving episodic memory can be beneficial, particularly those that teach strategy use among older adults. One of the most ambitious cognitive training interventions was a multisite study known as Advanced Cognitive Training for Independent and Vital Elderly (ACTIVE), which found that training in memory and reasoning improved the performance of older adults on daily living tasks.

7

Language, Problem Solving,

Information processing and memory are basic cognitive operations that make it possible for you to perform a variety of critical adaptive functions in your everyday life. They also form the basis for your ability to analyze, reason, and communicate with others. These higher-order cognitive skills guide your use of judgment, knowledge, and decision making. Without these abilities, your potential to learn new information and integrate it with your existing body of knowledge would be very limited.

Researchers are interested in understanding higher-level cognitive functions in adulthood and later life. Given that cognition is a key ingredient of job performance, this knowledge has many practical implications. Furthermore, information on thinking and learning in later adulthood can provide a greater understanding of the potential for "lifelong learning." With many adults retooling in order to find new positions in the rapidly changing labor market, determining the factors that contribute to the most effective training strategies is crucial to helping people find and keep their jobs.

LANGUAGE

The use of language involves a wide range of cognitive functions, including comprehension, memory, and decision making. As we discussed in Chapter 6, many of these functions are negatively affected by the aging process. However, the majority of researchers believe that the average healthy older adult does not suffer significant losses in the ability to use language effectively under normal speaking conditions (Hoyte, Brownell, & Wingfield, 2009). The basic abilities to carry on a conversation, read, and write remain intact throughout later life. The "Language and Aging Scorecard" in Table 7.1 summarizes this research.

Cognitive Aspects of Language

Despite the lack of demonstrated age-related changes in language abilities, it is still possible that changes with age in cognitive processes may affect an older adult's ability to use and maximize language most effectively. For example, even older adults

and Intelligence

with normal age-related vision read at slower rates compared to younger adults (Nygaard, Echt, & Schuchard, 2008). As we saw in Chapter 4, changes in hearing and speech perception have the potential to influence the ability to comprehend spoken language. For example, older adults may find it more difficult to hear all the words spoken in a conversation so that they have to work harder to make sense out of what other people are saying (Janse, 2009).

In using written language, older adults may experience deficits in retrieval that can lead to spelling errors for words they once knew (Burke, 1997). You can most likely relate to this problem if you have ever looked at a word you have just written that has repeated letters (such as "recommendation") and wondered whether there are one or two "c's".

Their slower cognitive processes may also have an effect on the complexity of grammatical structures that older adults use. As you form sentences, you must keep one clause in mind while you compose the next one, a process that places demands on your working memory. As we saw in Chapter 6, working memory undergoes significant changes with age. Consequently, compared with young adults, older adults speak in simpler sentences (Kemper, Marquis, & Thompson, 2001). Their writing also becomes simpler, in both the expression of ideas and the use of grammatical complexity (Kemper, Greiner, Marquis, Prenovost, & Mitzner, 2001). Thus, although older adults retain their knowledge of grammatical rules (a form of semantic memory), declines in working memory can cause older adults to lose track of what they mean to say while they are saying it.

On the positive side, their greater experience with language gives older adults the potential to compensate for other cognitive changes that affect their ability to produce and understand speech. Most older adults retain the ability to understand individual words (James & MacKay, 2007). They can grasp and remember the descriptions provided in language relating to the thoughts and actions of a character in

TABLE 7.1
Language and Aging Scorecard

Factors that Contribute to Decline	Factors that Contribute to Preservation
Slower reading rate	Semantic memory is retained or greater
Changes in hearing and speech perception	Able to get the "gist" of a story
Slowing of cognitive functions	No problem with paralinguistic elements of speech
Retrieval deficits	Activate the right hemisphere more
Simpler grammatical structures	Greater experience with language
Working memory deficits	More cognitive complexity

a story (Stine-Morrow & Miller, 1999). Older adults are also able to use strategies effectively to maximize their comprehension of written text (Stine-Morrow, Milinder, Pullara, & Herman, 2001). They can also put together the structure of the sentence with the speaker's emphasis (Titone et al., 2006).

Neuroimaging evidence suggests that older adults compensate for deficits in one area of the brain by recruiting alternative brain regions in the processing of speech (Wong et al., 2009). Older adults activate the right hemisphere of the brain when processing speech, a reversal of the left hemispheric dominance seen in most younger adults (Tyler et al., 2010). They also increase activation in frontal regions of the brain typically not activated in younger adults (Peelle, Troiani, Wingfield, & Grossman, 2010).

Experience is another way that older adults compensate for changes in memory and speed. This is particularly true for highly educated older adults, whose extensive vocabularies allow them to take advantage of the context in language (Osorio, Ballesteros, Fay, & Pouthas, 2009). In general, though, older adults also have a rich backlog of experiences from which to draw when they listen or read. Even if they are unable to hear each word, they are often able to derive the meaning of words used in a straightforward conversation (Stewart & Wingfield, 2009). You have likely encountered this experience of filling in missing information in speech that is directed toward you. Someone approaches you at a loud party, and it is probably safe to assume, even if you are unable to hear, that he or she is saying "Hello" or "What's up?" You are pretty safe in returning the greeting. The advantage of greater experience also manifests itself in reading. Older adults are able to glean information more quickly, particularly if the material is of a relatively familiar nature. Consequently, they can skim for information rather than stop and examine every word or phrase.

Thus, older adults have well-developed structures of information that allow them to anticipate and organize information that may typically overwhelm a novice. Even in situations that do not involve expert knowledge of a skill, previous experience can make up for slower processing of new linguistic information. For example, an avid soap opera watcher can anticipate what the characters will say (and often do) rather than needing to hear every single spoken word in a particular interchange between characters. When reading magazines or newspapers, a knowledgeable older reader is able to make up for changes in working memory by relying on more effective structures for retrieving related information from written text (Stine-Morrow, Soederberg Miller, Gagne, & Hertzog, 2008).

Social Aspects of Language

Corresponding to changes in language use and comprehension throughout adulthood are changes in the way that older adults use language socially. Perhaps most striking is the tendency of older adults to reminisce with others about experiences from the past. As they do so, they often polish and refine their storytelling so that by the time their reminiscences have been practiced and rehearsed, the stories have considerable impact on the listener. In your own family you may have heard an older relative tell the same story over and over again so often that you can repeat it by heart. Watching the reaction of your friends when they first hear the same story may cause you to realize that it is a pretty good story after all. This is perhaps one reason why comedians in their 60s, 70s, and beyond have become such masters of the punch line.

Reminiscences about the past may also serve a function for older adults in solidifying relationships and building shared identities with others from their generation. As they do so, they can enhance and strengthen their relationships with their long-time friends and family members.

Younger adults may become annoyed with the older adults they know well, and feel that the older people's speech is too repetitive or focused on the past (Bieman-Copland & Ryan, 2001). At times older adults may also speak more off-topic, particularly when they are giving instructions about how to perform an action. Younger adults seem to be better able to focus their speech in such situations (Trunk & Abrams, 2009).

The problem of intergenerational communication is made worse if the older person tends to focus on his or her current disabilities or health limitations. Talking extensively about a topic in which the listener has no interest or that makes the listener uncomfortable can have an effect opposite to that intended and possibly isolate the older individual. Such examples highlight the downside to changes in these conversational patterns when they have the unintended effect of turning off the listener.

Intergenerational communication can take a decidedly nasty turn. **Elderspeak** is a speech pattern directed at older adults similar to the way people talk to babies. If you have ever heard an older adult referred to as "cute," or being called "honey," or "sweetie," you have heard one form of elderspeak. More generally, elderspeak involves simplifying your speech much as you would talk to a child by leaving out complex words or talking in a patronizing

AGING IN THE NEWS

www.wiley.com/college/whitbourne   OLDER ADULTS WHO MADE THE HEADLINES   -VOL. 4, CHAPTER 7-

OLDEST TWITTERER DIES AT 104

Ivy Bean, who was widely considered to be the oldest Twitter user, died in her care home in a small town in England at the age of 104.

The news was published on Bean's Twitter account, @IvyBean104, which regularly informed followers about Bean's deteriorating condition over the last couple of days.

"Ivy passed away peacefully at 12.08 this morning… Im sorry it took me so long to tell you but it was a very difficult thing to do," the tweets said.

Bean was a popular Twitter user with more than 56,000 followers at the time of her death, as well as a fairly active one, with more than 1,000 tweets. As one might expect, Bean was also an avid Facebook user; she joined at the age of 102.

Mrs. Bean's example showed that social media truly knows no boundaries, and that tools such as Twitter and Facebook are open to everyone who wants to participate. We'll miss you, Ivy.

or condescending tone of voice. Younger people who speak in this manner do so because, either consciously or unconsciously, they equate the older and perhaps frailer adult as being equal in status to a child. Offering unnecessary help, making personal comments about clothing or appearance, or talking in short, simple sentences are just some examples of this type of speech pattern.

Researchers investigating elderspeak have proposed that its use fits into the **communication predicament model** of aging. The predicament is that older adults are thought of as mentally incapacitated, leading younger people to speak to them in a simplified manner, which over time can have the effect of reducing the older adult's actual ability to use language. (See Figure 7.1.) In addition, failure to encourage independent behaviors in the older person, a part of the communication predicament, leads to a further spiraling downward of the older person's abilities (Ryan, Hummert, & Boich, 1995).

The communication predicament model is part of a larger phenomenon known as infantilization in which the older person loses the incentive to attempt to regain self-sufficiency in the basic activities of daily life (Whitbourne, Culgin, & Cassidy, 1995; Whitbourne & Wills, 1993). Moreover, when older adults in a residential facility are treated by younger staff in an infantilizing manner, they lose the desire to socialize with each other, potentially leading to social isolation (Salari & Rich, 2001). The self-fulfilling nature of infantilization can also increase the older person's awareness of age stereotypes, causing a self-fulfilling prophecy to spread across a wide domain of areas of functioning. If you think you are unable to carry out a task because you are too old, infirmed, or enfeebled, then the chances are you will eventually lose the ability to carry out that task. Research examining communication issues within assisted living facilities focuses on reducing infantilizing behaviors by staff (Williams & Warren, 2009).

EVERYDAY PROBLEM SOLVING

From figuring out why your computer is freezing up the night before a paper is due to managing your dwindling bank account, you must constantly deal with problems requiring solutions in your daily life. Researchers have increasingly moved these daily challenges into the laboratory to evaluate the ability of older adults to manage such everyday tasks as handling their personal finances, maintaining their medication schedules, and monitoring their diets (Allaire & Marsiske, 2002). Ultimately, it is performance on tasks such as these that helps to contribute to an older person's quality of life (Gilhooly et al., 2007) and may even predict mortality independently of basic cognitive abilities (Weatherbee & Allaire, 2008).

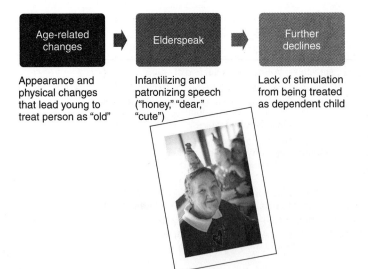

Age-related changes	➡	Elderspeak	➡	Further declines
Appearance and physical changes that lead young to treat person as "old"		Infantilizing and patronizing speech ("honey," "dear," "cute")		Lack of stimulation from being treated as dependent child

FIGURE 7.1

Social Elements of Language: The Communication Predicament Model

Source: Adapted from Ryan, E. B., Hummert, M. L., & Boich, L. H. (1995). Communication predicaments of aging: Patronizing behavior toward older adults. *Journal of Language and Social Psychology, 14,* 144–166.

Characteristics of Problem Solving

Psychologists approach the topic of problem solving by identifying types of problems and the stages involved in successfully approaching and resolving them. Essentially, problem solving involves assessing a current situation, deciding on a desired end-state, and finding ways of transforming the current into the desired state. The final step is evaluating the outcome of the solution to determine its efficacy. For example, when you are planning your budget for the month, you begin by assessing how much money is in your account (current state). You then decide how much money to allocate for food, entertainment, and transportation based on your desired end-state (having money left at the end of the month). At the end of the month, you assess whether your plan worked out and if not, revise your strategy and hope it works out better than the one you just used.

Problems vary tremendously in their structure and complexity. This example of a monthly budget is one that is fairly well structured in that there are specific constraints (there is only so much money in your account), and there is a clear set of steps that must be followed. With problems that lack clear goals or when the steps that must be followed are difficult to discern, an increased cognitive burden is placed on the individual. This is what happens to your monthly budget if you encounter an unexpected event, such as paying to get your car out of the impound lot after it was towed or having to lend your best friend some money.

As technology has continued to advance, so has the cognitive burden of figuring out how to use technology to a maximum advantage. In part, the cognitive burden is exacerbated by the relative vagueness of the instructions that manufacturers of technology provide for people to use. You have most likely become quite skilled in figuring out how to program your cell phone or iPod without relying too heavily on the instruction manuals. However, what happens when you come across a problem that you could not solve and are forced to consult an instruction manual? You can see what a challenge this might pose for the older adult not accustomed to high-tech gadgets. In fact, it is becoming typical for instruction manuals to require downloading from the Web. If you are trying to set up a printer that comes without a manual you might be forced to go online

where, ironically enough, you would be expected to print it. Making matters worse is the notoriously cryptic nature of such instructions. Even if a manual is provided with the product, it is printed in tiny print on thin paper and with as few words as possible.

Instructions are also ambiguous and conflicting. Consider this excerpt from a digital video camera: "During Easy Handycam operation, you can set basic options, such as changing the image size or deleting images, among the setting and adjustment items. . . . When Easy Handycam operation is started, nearly all menu settings are reset to the default settings automatically. (Some menu items retain the settings that were made before Easy Handycam operation.)" If you had no idea what all of this meant, you would understandably be confused by the last statement, and wonder which items retain the settings and which do not.

Complexity and vagueness in instructions is not limited to high-tech areas, though. Cooking recipes often are based on the assumption that you know whether or not to grease a pan before adding dough, what "simmer" means, and whether a piece of meat is truly "brown" or onions are "wilted."

Problem Solving in Adulthood

As we have just noted, everyday problems are multidimensional, and the steps in solving them are not always clear. Taking these factors into account, everyday problem solving is defined as involving problems that typically occur in people's everyday lives, that can be solved in more than one way, and that require the problem solver to decide which strategy will lead to the desired result (Thornton & Dumke, 2005). Table 7.2 summarizes the negative and positive effects of aging on problem-solving abilities.

As people get older, they gain in some problem-solving skills at the expense of others. They may become slower and have more memory lapses, but if they are very familiar with a problem or a type of problem, they can get to a solution more quickly and effectively than can a novice. If you have stood by in awe as your grandmother produced a perfectly formed pie crust in under 2 minutes while your own dough sticks hopelessly to the rolling pin, then you can relate to this observation. Indeed, researchers have found that the greater experience of older adults can enhance not only problem-solving performance

TABLE 7.2
Problem-solving Changes in Adulthood

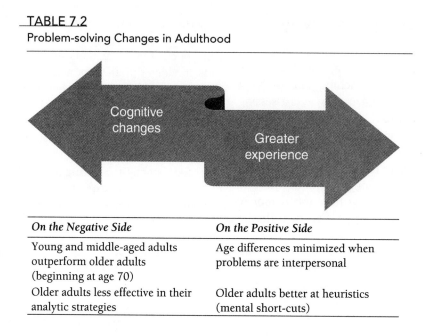

On the Negative Side	On the Positive Side
Young and middle-aged adults outperform older adults (beginning at age 70)	Age differences minimized when problems are interpersonal
Older adults less effective in their analytic strategies	Older adults better at heuristics (mental short-cuts)

(Crawford & Channon, 2002) but also feelings of self-efficacy (Artistico, Cervone, & Pezzuti, 2003).

Because middle-aged and older adults have acquired expertise through their years of exposure to certain kinds of problems associated with their jobs, hobbies, or daily routines, they have many advantages as they approach familiar everyday situations. They develop an ability to search for the relevant factors in a problem and learn to avoid irrelevant information. Consider your first year of college, when arriving to class on time meant learning the layout of your campus. Within a few times of taking the route you probably discovered a faster and more efficient course, and now you can get to your classes with time to spare. When you look back on how far experience has shaped your ability to solve complex problems up to now, imagine the growth you will continue to develop with each coming year.

Expert problem solvers are able to avoid information overload by honing in on specific areas that experience has taught them are important to consider. For example, in the area of medical decision making, older people are able to weigh a number of factors and make complex choices more quickly than can young adults (Meyer, Talbot, & Ranalli, 2007).

Older adults may also make choices that are better founded and less subject to extraneous factors. One study on decision making found that in general, older adults avoid what is known as the "attraction effect" (see Figure 7.2). In tests of the attraction effect, you are told to choose between two alternatives. A third alternative is then added to see whether that choice alters your preference. For example, if you say you would choose to eat a scoop of vanilla ice cream when given the choice between strawberry and vanilla, then logically, you should also prefer vanilla when presented with the choice of vanilla, strawberry, or chocolate. You have already made clear that you do not want the strawberry ice cream. If you are showing the attraction effect, the addition of chocolate as a choice makes you more likely to pick strawberry than you did before.

A comparison of older and younger adults on the attraction effect showed a greater susceptibility of younger adults in switching their choice when the third alternative is presented, meaning that they are less consistent in their decision-making (Tentori, Osherson, Hasher, & May, 2001). This study is particularly interesting because it relates to the concept of behavioral economics, an emerging field that investigates the illogical choices that consumers make in everyday situations. According to the results of the attraction effect study, then, older adults should be wiser consumers.

Increased experience enhances problem solving in the later years by allowing older adults to sift quickly through information, honing in on what is relevant and arriving at a solution. As we have just seen, this ability to mobilize a familiar strategy can have advantages, but it can create difficulties in some situations, particularly when it is important to look at possible alternative approaches. For example, an automobile mechanic who goes directly to the distributor as the source of a stalled engine may not notice a more serious wiring flaw elsewhere. Older problem solvers may think that they are doing a better job at solving the problem but, by objective criteria, they may not be considering alternative solutions as effectively as do younger adults and therefore can make a decision that is in error (Thornton & Dumke, 2005).

In addition to focusing on one solution rather than considering others, older adults may stick with one pattern of response when the solution calls for a range of ideas. Tests of verbal fluency ask respondents to produce as many items as possible to one stimulus, such as listing as many possible words that begin with the letter "K" in a set amount of time. Older adults are more likely to perseverate on such a task, meaning that they continue to produce the same words, such as "King," "Keel," "Kept," "King," "Kite," where "King" counts as a perseveration. Although perseveration is often taken in clinical settings as indicative of frontal lobe deficits (affecting problem solving, memory, and language), older adults show some difficulties on this type of task, though less so when intelligence is taken into account (Henry & Phillips, 2006). For older adults who do suffer deficiencies, however, it will be more difficult for them to generate novel solutions to problems, because they continue to repeat the ones they have already produced.

Further evidence of difficulties in problem solving comes from a study of the planning ability in Japanese monkeys (Kubo, Kato, & Nakamura, 2006). In this study, monkeys were given the task of finding food hidden behind nine small openings in a panel. In the experimental condition, the food was hidden behind white plastic circles. In the control condition, the food was visible through clear plastic plates. The highest score was awarded to the monkeys who found and retrieved all food items in nine consecutive attempts. Errors were counted if the monkey reached again through a hole from which it had already retrieved the food.

Differences between the age groups showed that the older monkeys made considerably more errors on the experimental trials—that is, trials in which the food was hidden behind the white plates. Additionally, they were inconsistent in their selection strategies and rather than using a deliberate strategy, seemed to make their choices more randomly.

Making up for losses in their strategic planning ability, older problem solvers have the advantage of more experience and improved access to relevant information. As we have already pointed out, people with experience have well-organized storehouses of knowledge that they can easily access and put to use. You may have an older relative who likes to travel abroad and can quickly tell you the pros and cons of a trip you are planning to a foreign country that you never visited. After years of traveling internationally, this sage advisor can give you knowledge about the country's hotels, places of interest, weather patterns, and the best travel deals. Sports trivia buffs have a similar mastery of large amounts of content matter because they have that knowledge organized into systematic units, such as which 16 teams are in the U.S. American Football Conference versus the 16 in the National Football Conference. These are good people to know if you are looking for information but not good people to challenge in a trivia contest because you will undoubtedly lose.

FIGURE 7.2

The Attraction Effect

Attraction effect:
A versus B—pick A
(e.g. strawberry versus vanilla)

Add choice C (chocolate)
More likely to pick B,
because B now looks more desirable

Research on adults' decision-making speed confirms that older people are able to reach an answer more quickly than younger people who either lack the knowledge or the ability to categorize that knowledge. However, older persons are also more apt to make quicker decisions in areas in which they may not have expertise. Furthermore, they are less likely to seek additional information once their decision has been made. It is possible that the rapid problem solving shown by older adults reflects the fact that their greater experience has given them an advantage in many areas of decision making. Therefore they are not as dependent on incoming information as younger adults. The other possibility is that older adults are less able to organize multiple sources of information, leading their decisions to be based on prior experience rather than on new data presented about the problem (Marsiske & Margrett, 2006).

The finding that older adults are faster at solving problems conflicts with the majority of research on adult development and cognition. The types of measures and outcomes used in studies of problem solving do not always capture timed responses, as is true for studies of psychomotor speed. Rather, studies of problem solving involve measures based on the amount of information that the participant gathers prior to making a decision, and these measures are not as sensitive to small changes in reaction time. Supporting the findings from studies of aging

and cognition are results from neuropsychological testing. For midlife adults, performance on the familiar problem-solving tasks used in this context such as sorting cards appears to be maintained (Garden, Phillips, & MacPherson, 2001) though age-related effects become apparent in older adults (Head, Kennedy, Rodrigue, & Raz, 2009).

Variations among the older population affect everyday problem solving. Education is related to scores on the Everyday Problems Test (EPT) (Burton, Strauss, Hultsch, & Hunter, 2006) (see Figure 7.3), a measure designed to replicate the steps used to solve problems encountered in daily life. For example, the EPT assesses the ability to read and comprehend instructions for thawing a turkey, or determine the best long-distance telephone plan. Poorer performance on the EPT is related to slower and inconsistent reaction times for older adults (Burton, Strauss, Hultsch, & Hunter, 2009). Among African Americans, in particular, health status plays a role in influencing the quality of decisions they make on this task (Whitfield, Allaire, & Wiggins, 2004).

In everyday situations involving practical decision making, middle-aged and older adults appear to have an advantage when confronted with familiar choices. Their greater experience and expertise in terms of content and process allow them to appraise the problem, come up with a strategy, and then enact that strategy. However, when a familiar dilemma appears

Indications: Temporarily Relieves Cough Due to Minor Throat and Bronchial Irritation as May Occur with a Cold.

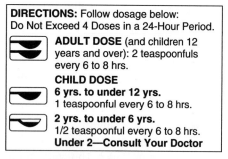

1. What is the maximum number of teaspoons an adult should take in 24 hours?

2. Mr. Jones smokes and has smoker's cough. What is the maximum number of doses he should take per day?

Warnings—A persistent cough may be a sign of a serious condition. If cough persists for more than 1 week, tends to recur, or is accompanied by fever, rash, or persistent headache, consult a doctor. Do not take this product for persistent or chronic cough such as occurs with smoking, asthma, emphysema, or if cough is accompanied by excessive phlegm (mucus) unless directed by a doctor.

FIGURE 7.3

Sample Item from the Everyday Problems Test

Source: Willis, S. L., & Marsiske, M. (1997). Everyday Problems Test. Retrieved from http://geron.psu.edu/sls/(101)EPT%20%20open%20ended%20I.pdf.

Working together to solve problems, these older adults seem to be enjoying both the opportunity for mental challenges and socializing. Perhaps they are updating a Facebook page.

with a new twist, or when a premature decision leads to avoiding important information, older adults are relatively disadvantaged. Young problem solvers may suffer from their lack of familiarity with many situations, but because they can process larger amounts of information in a shorter time, they may avoid some of the traps that befall their elders.

Adult Learners

The literature on problem solving in adulthood emphasizes the ability to come to a resolution when dealing with a dilemma. However, the ability to "find" problems seems to be an equally compelling aspect of adult cognition. Research and theory on this aspect of adult cognition was stimulated, in part, by Swiss psychologist Jean Piaget's concept of **formal operations**, the ability of adolescents and adults to use logic and abstract symbols in arriving at solutions to complex problems. Adult development researchers have proposed that there is a stage of **postformal operations**, referring to the way that adults structure their thinking over and beyond that of adolescents (Commons, Richards, & Armon, 1984; Sinnott, 1989). Thinking at the postformal operational level

incorporates the tendency of the mature individual to use logical processes specifically geared to the complex nature of adult life. The postformal thinker is also able to judge when to use formal logic and when, alternatively, to rely on other and simpler modes of representing problems. For example, you do not need to use the rules of formal logic to unplug a stopped drain. Hands-on methods are generally suitable for dealing with practical situations like this one involving actions in the physical world.

Related to the postformal stage of cognitive development is **dialectical thinking**, which is an interest in and appreciation for debate, arguments, and counterarguments (Basseches, 1984). Dialectical thinking involves the recognition that often the truth is not "necessarily a given," but that common understandings among people are a negotiated process of give and take. People may not be able to find the ideal solution for many of life's problems, but through the process of sharing their alternative views with each other, most reasonable adults can at least come to some satisfactory compromises. Although you may not agree with some of your friends who have vastly different political opinions than your own, you have learned to respect their viewpoints, no matter how difficult it may be for you to do so and remain on speaking terms.

The proposition that there is a postformal stage of thinking beyond that of formal operations has a great deal of intuitive appeal. Many questions have no right or wrong answer such as the appropriate punishment for a juvenile offender. On a daily basis, average adults face many ambiguities and uncertainties in dilemmas ranging from how to resolve conflicts with their friends to how to make the best choices for their children's education. Many people actively seek out the opportunity to engage others in dialogue and intellectual engagement. It would be boring to face a world in which all the gray areas were removed from life's "real" problems.

The possibility that adults operate according to postformal operations leads to a variety of interesting implications about adults as thinkers, problem solvers, and, particularly, learners. Adult learners are increasingly becoming part of the concerns of those who teach at the college level; as of 2005 more than half of the adult population ages 16 to 40 and large percentages of adults over 40 (48% of those 41 to 50 and 41% of those 51 to 65) were involved in adult education (U.S. Bureau of the Census, 2010f).

In the classroom, adult learners may rely more on attaining mastery of the material through using strategies such as taking more copious notes and relying on them more heavily as they are trying to acquire new information (Delgoulet & Marquie, 2002). The adult learner is also more likely to challenge the instructor to go beyond the information and explore alternative dimensions. Such tendencies, though fascinating in the classroom, can lead to problems when it comes to evaluation. For a person who can see all the alternate angles to a standard multiple-choice exam question, it can be very difficult to arrive at the correct answer because more than one has virtues that merit attention. The adult thinker and learner may find it equally fascinating to ponder ambiguities rather than settle on one choice even though only one choice is graded as correct.

Not all adult learners have these characteristics, of course, and variation from person to person may be related to personality factors, such as willingness to be open to new experiences (discussed in Chapter 8). However, the emergence of alternative modes of thought, and their continued evolution throughout adulthood, provide an important counterpoint to the findings on the tendencies of older adults to become potentially more closed minded with age and experience.

INTELLIGENCE

If you were asked to define the term "intelligence," you would probably guess that it represents the quality of a person's ability to think. Formal definitions of intelligence in psychology come very close to this simple idea of intelligence as an individual's mental ability. Psychologists have struggled for decades to agree on the specific meaning of the term intelligence beyond the notion that it represents the overall quality of the individual's mental abilities. For nearly as long, psychologists have grappled with the issue of determining the course of development in adulthood for this poorly understood quality of the human mind.

The existence of age effects on intelligence in adulthood has many practical and theoretical ramifications. For practical reasons, it is important to find out the relative strengths and weaknesses of younger versus older workers. As we noted earlier in our discussion of problem solving, there appear to be fairly distinct differences in the styles that adults of different ages use when making decisions. Employers in the public and private sectors can put to practical use the data that psychologists produce from studies using standard intelligence test scores. From a theoretical standpoint, research on intelligence in adulthood has provided new perspectives on the components of thought. This research has also provided insight into the perennial question of how mental processes are affected by "nature versus nurture" as researchers have continued to exploit and explore the application of complex research designs to data on intelligence test scores in adulthood.

Just as physical abilities partially define a person's identity, intelligence serves as an attribute of the person that forms part of the sense of self. People have a good idea of whether they are "smart" or "not as bright," a self-attribution that they can carry for years (Leonardelli, Hermann, Lynch, & Arkin, 2003). People who value the products of the mind, such as their ability to solve tough crossword puzzles and score well on board games, may be more vigilant for changes in intelligence associated with aging than people who take pride in their physical strength or dexterity. In some cases, these changes may be more imagined than real, particularly as people age and begin to believe the media images portraying older adults as losing their mental abilities. When the changes are not just imaginary, however, this may prove to be a tough change for some to acknowledge.

Adult Intelligence: Historical Background

Research on intelligence in adulthood emphasizes the description and analysis of individual differences in the years from the 20s and older. The individual differences approach is reflected in the use of standardized intelligence tests as basic data for these studies. Historically, it was the desire to develop age norms across adulthood for tests of intelligence that were originally developed on children that formed the impetus for the first studies on aging. The first intelligence test, the Stanford-Binet, was designed to evaluate the mental abilities of children. When it became evident that this was not a suitable tool for measuring adult intelligence (in part because it peaked out at age 16), the goal of developing appropriate tests and normative standards prompted investigations of the performance of adults across the entire age range.

The initial forays into the field of adult intelligence involved cross-sectional and longitudinal comparisons. For example, David Wechsler, who developed the widely used **Wechsler Adult Intelligence Scale (WAIS)** in 1955, administered the tests that comprise this instrument to representative samples of adults drawn from each succeeding decade ranging from early adulthood to old age. The scale is currently in its fourth revision. Standardization data were developed from these scores, but they were also used to describe age-related differences in performance on various facets of intelligence. Early findings proposed that age differences across adulthood followed the "classic aging pattern" (Botwinick, 1977) of an inverted U-shaped pattern, with a peak in early adulthood followed by steady decline. Results from the Wechsler scales, which supported the view that intelligence generally erodes over successive decades in adulthood, contrasted a smaller but uniform body of evidence from longitudinal studies. When samples of adults were followed through repeated testings using the Wechsler scales or other standardized tests, the finding was either no decline or a decline that did not become apparent until very late in life.

The previous versions of the WAIS tests were divided into Verbal and Performance scales; older samples were consistently found to maintain their scores on the Verbal scales, particularly vocabulary (Kaufman, Kaufman, McLean, & Reynolds, 1991). This differential age pattern for verbal and nonverbal abilities is the foundation for one of the major theoretical approaches to adult intelligence that is still in use today, the "fluid-crystallized" ability distinction, which we discuss shortly. Age-related declines with each revision of the Wechsler scales have become less distinct since the 1950s, particularly for processing speed (Miller, Myers, Prinzi, & Mittenberg, 2009). The WAIS-IV (Wechsler, 2008) restructures the subscales (see Table 7.3). Critics suggest that this revision does not consistently work for different age groups of adults and is not an improvement over the fluid-crystallized distinction (Benson, Hulac, & Kranzler, 2010).

Theoretical Perspectives on Adult Intelligence

Theories of intelligence differ in the number and nature of abilities proposed to exist. Fortunately, researchers working in the field of adult development and aging have come to a resolution, in theory if not practice, of how best to characterize the nature of adult intelligence. Most believe that there are two main categories of mental abilities corresponding roughly to verbal and nonverbal intelligence.

The Concept of "g". As background to the current approaches to adult intelligence, let us look back at the state of psychology in the early 1900s. British psychologist and statistician Charles Spearman set forth to formulate a comprehensive theory of intelligence (1904; 1927). He proposed the existence of a "general factor" of intelligence, that he called "g." Spearman intended that "g" would encompass the ability to infer and apply relationships on the basis of experience. According to Spearman, individuals with high levels of "g" should be able to receive high scores

TABLE 7.3
Scales on the WAIS-IV

Scale	Subtest	What is Tested
Verbal Comprehension	Similarities Vocabulary Information Comprehension	Abstract reasoning Vocabulary Cultural information (Supplemental)
Perceptual Reasoning	Block design Matrix reasoning Visual puzzles	Spatial perception Inductive reasoning Non-verbal reasoning
Working Memory	Digit span Arithmetic	Attention, concentration Concentration while manipulating mental information
Processing Speed	Symbol search Coding	Visual perception, speed Visual-motor coordination

Source: Adapted from Wechsler, D. (2008). Wechsler Adult Intelligence Scales–IV. Retrieved from http://www.pearsonassessments .com/HAIWEB/Cultures/en-us/Productdetail.htm?Pid=015-8980-808.

on various tests that tap into specific mental abilities (each of which is called "s" for specific). Such tests included the intelligence test devised by Binet, which is the one now known as the Stanford-Binet.

Although many theorists disputed Spearman's notion, the concept of a unitary factor in intelligence emerged more recently in a large statistical analysis of age–performance relationships among adults 18 to 84 years. Salthouse identified a broad "g-type" factor associated with age that was also related to age-related deficits in speed and memory (Salthouse, 2001; Salthouse & Ferrer-Caja, 2003).

Primary Mental Abilities

Despite the popularity of intelligence tests based on "g," the idea that intelligence is a unitary construct is often criticized for being overly simplistic. Contrasting theories propose that there are multiple abilities or dimensions of abilities that together comprise intelligence. The multidimensional approach proven to be the most productive for understanding adult intelligence is the **primary mental abilities** framework proposed by Thurstone (1938). According to Thurstone, seven primary mental abilities exist: verbal meaning, word fluency (the ability to generate words following a certain lexical rule), number (arithmetic), spatial relations, memory, perceptual speed, and general reasoning. These seven abilities are considered

separate and distinct from one another, and together they are thought to cover all possible abilities that characterize intelligence. As you will soon learn, the **Primary Mental Abilities (PMA)** test was used in one of the largest investigations of adult intelligence conducted to date.

Fluid-Crystallized Theory. Out of the primary mental ability theory emerged the proposal by theorist Raymond Cattell (1963) that the seven abilities actually group into two broad sets: one based on educational training and one set based on untutored thought processes. Cattell regarded these abilities as **secondary mental abilities**, a concept based on a statistical method of analysis that attempts to capture the broad constructs that underlie specific abilities.

In writing about the characteristics of these abilities, Cattell, in conjunction with psychologist John Horn (1966), defined them as "so pervasive relative to other ability structures and so obviously of an intellectual nature that each deserves the name intelligence" (p. 254). The first ability, **fluid intelligence** (also called **Gf**), is defined as the individual's innate abilities to carry out higher-level cognitive operations involving the integration, analysis, and synthesis of new information, "the sheer perception of complex relations" (Cattell, 1971). Fluid intelligence reflects the quality of biopsychological factors such as the functioning of the

FIGURE 7.4

Example of "Sudoku" Puzzle—a Good Test of Fluid Intelligence

FIGURE 7.4

Example of "Sudoku" Puzzle—a Good Test of Fluid Intelligence

3	7	1		4			6	
			7	1				4
		4			6	9	1	
	6		2	7		8		9
			6	9	4			
7		9		8	3		2	
	4	7	1			6		
6				5	7			
	5			6		7	8	2

nervous system and sensory structures and therefore cannot be trained or taught.

Tests of fluid intelligence measure the ability to develop and infer abstract relationships independently of culture-specific information. The items on these tests either are novel combinations of figures and shapes or are well within the inventory of any individual such as letters and common words. For instance, in a fluid intelligence test, you may be asked to predict the next letter in a series based on the pattern that is set in the question (e.g., what letter would follow "A-C-E-G"?). You probably recall items such as these from the SATs in which you had to imagine what an abstract shape or figure would look like when it was rotated 180 degrees. Another example that you might encounter on a more frequent basis is the game "Sudoku" (see Figure 7.4), which has you place numbers in matrices so that they do not repeat across rows and columns. You do not have to know anything about arithmetic in order to solve these visual puzzles.

The second broad set of abilities within the Cattell model is **crystallized intelligence** (also called **Gc**), which represents the acquisition of specific skills and information gained through familiarity with the language, knowledge, and conventions of one's culture. It involves the learned ability to infer relationships, make judgments, analyze problems, and use problem-solving strategies.

In contrast to fluid intelligence measures, tests of crystallized intelligence include items involving language, logic, and factual information. In keeping with the definition by Cattell and his colleagues of crystallized intelligence as culturally based ability,

some of the other tests used in their studies assessed such functions as the use of tools and the ability to solve everyday problems, such as computing gasoline mileage or balancing a checkbook.

Together, fluid and crystallized intelligence can be seen as forming a biopsychosocial definition of intelligence. They incorporate the biological factors related to the integrity of the nervous system (fluid), the psychological factors involved in cognitive processing (crystallized), and the social factors derived from education and experience in one's culture (also crystallized).

Fluid and crystallized intelligence were originally thought of as statistically and conceptually independent from each other. In reality, though, the two are intrinsically connected. Years after Cattell proposed his theory, this connection was experimentally tested. A longitudinal investigation of 111 participants originally tested through the ages of 4 to 64 showed that over time, fluid abilities helped to shape crystallized (McArdle & Hamagami, 2006). To acquire the skills and knowledge specific to your culture and system of education, it is necessary to have the fluid abilities to support the learning of new information.

The hypothesized life span course of crystallized and fluid intelligence reflects the combination of factors thought to affect each of the two secondary abilities (Horn, 1970). Age changes in these abilities are summarized in Figure 7.5.

The peak of fluid intelligence is thought to occur during adolescence, when the nervous system and sensory structures are (at least theoretically) at optimum levels. The changes associated with aging

FIGURE 7.5

The Structure of Fluid and Crystallized Intelligence

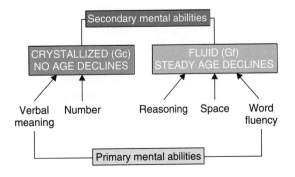

that reduce the efficiency of these systems lead to a downward trajectory in fluid intelligence after this point. Conversely, crystallized intelligence continues to develop throughout adulthood as the individual acquires experience and culture-specific knowledge. Day-to-day exposure to people, places, and things enhances such abilities as higher vocabulary and an increased knowledge of the world (Beier & Ackerman, 2001).

To understand why crystallized intelligence would increase for much of the course of life, consider your own experiences. Most people learn a new word or two (at least) in the process of solving a crossword puzzle. For example, the commonly used term "jai alai" in crosswords (referring to a sport dating back to Egyptian times) has a low frequency in everyday use, at least in the United States, but becomes ingrained in avid puzzle solvers. Assuming you are able to remember this seemingly useless information in the future, you would have increased your crystallized intelligence by coming across this word in the puzzle. As these experiences accumulate over a lifetime, this component of your intelligence will continue to grow. The challenge becomes how to best organize, catalogue, and recall new information as it is acquired.

Alternative Views of Intelligence

Despite the broad use of measures such as the WAIS and the PMA, many psychologists believe that the traditional views of intelligence are overly restrictive in their definition. Critics of traditional intelligence theories have proposed alternative views based on their belief that intelligence should be classified in terms of knowledge of the world and ability to adapt to it.

The **theory of multiple intelligences** proposed by Howard Gardner (1983; 1993) suggests that there are eight independent categories of intelligence, each of which can contribute to an individual's ability to adapt to the world. In addition to the conventional areas included in other theories of intelligence, such as knowledge of math and vocabulary, Gardner's theory goes beyond what people learn in school to include a variety of qualities that promote individual success, ranging from musical to naturalistic intelligence. For instance, you may be high in the ability to use your body effectively in sports or dance, but low in the ability to understand other people. According

to Gardner, each person has a range of strengths and weaknesses, not just one or two overall abilities.

Challenges to traditional views of intelligence were also raised by Robert Sternberg (1985), who based his **triarchic theory of intelligence** on analyses of the strategies used by expert problem solvers. The three aspects of intelligence that Sternberg proposed are componential (the ability to think and analyze), contextual (practical intelligence or "street smarts"), and experiential (the ability to think creatively). Most intelligence tests assess componential ability. Like Gardner's approach, Sternberg's emphasizes a variety of nonacademic skills people need in daily life.

Sternberg's theory stresses that doing well on an intelligence test does not necessarily give you the ability to do well in life. He defined **successful intelligence** as the ability to achieve success in life according to your personal standards and in the framework of your sociocultural context (Sternberg, 1999). Included in successful intelligence are the processing skills identified in the triarchic theory (which he renamed analytical, creative, and practical). People high in successful intelligence are able to apply these skills to adapt, shape, and select environments, and they are able to capitalize on their strengths and correct and compensate for their weaknesses.

Sternberg's theory has the potential to enhance and enrich current formulations of adult intelligence. For example, Sternberg's **balance theory of wisdom** (Sternberg, 1998) views wisdom as the ability to integrate the various components of triarchic intelligence and to apply them to problems involving the common good or welfare of others. Sternberg's approach complements the frameworks developed within the tradition of life span developmental psychology by Baltes and his colleagues (see below). Together, these formulations greatly expand the notion of intelligence as a quality that goes beyond the ability to receive good grades on a test.

Empirical Evidence on Adult Intelligence

K. Warner Schaie's study of intelligence on the Seattle sample has produced a compelling literature on the complex nature of adult intelligence and the factors affecting its development. The archives of the Seattle Longitudinal Study (SLS) are considered to be the major repository of data on intelligence in adulthood.

The SLS began in the 1950s, when Schaie, a doctoral student, compared 500 residents of Seattle, 50 from each of 10 five-year age intervals, sampled from participants in a prepaid medical plan. He used the PMA, based on Thurstone's theory, as the basis for the SLS data. This allowed him to analyze the components of crystallized and fluid intelligence within the PMA; six of these are shown in Figure 7.6.

The first set of findings the SLS produced were based on cross-sectional analyses and showed negative age differences beginning in the 50s. However, 7 years later, Schaie published a follow-up in which people's scores were compared within age groups between 1956 and 1963. Surprisingly, for most abilities, there was an increase or no change between the first and second testings, even among the oldest age group. The stage was set for what has now become a 45-year-plus exploration for the factors accounting for the aging (or nonaging) of intelligence. Schaie's foresight in planning a study that would make possible the sophisticated developmental research designs described in Chapter 3 has provided a wealth of information on intelligence in adulthood and the factors that affect its fluctuations.

Longitudinal estimates of changes in the PMA scale, shown in Figure 7.6, reveal that there is an overall picture of relatively stability until the 50s or 60s, followed by decline through the oldest age tested. However, caution is required in making conclusions from these findings (Schaie, 1996). For example, although some individuals may show declines in intelligence by the mid-50s, there are not significant losses until the decade of the 70s. Secondly, none of the participants showed general deterioration of functioning, even at the oldest age tested of 88 years. Thus the age changes in cognitive functioning, though in a negative direction, did not occur significantly across the board. Fortunately, most people are able to retain competent performance of familiar skills, particularly those that are of importance to the individual.

Other studies support the SLS findings. One large cross-sectional investigation (Schroeder & Salthouse, 2004) involved testing a sample of nearly 5,400 individuals seeking vocational aptitude testing on a variety of key intellectual variables. The findings support the proposal that crystallized intelligence (vocabulary) increases through middle adulthood, as can be seen in Figure 7.7. Longitudinal data on the fluid-crystallized theory analyzed with HLM show that the crystallized-fluid distinction helps to explain patterns of individual variations in intelligence test performance over time (McArdle, Ferrer-Caja, Hamagami, & Woodcock, 2002).

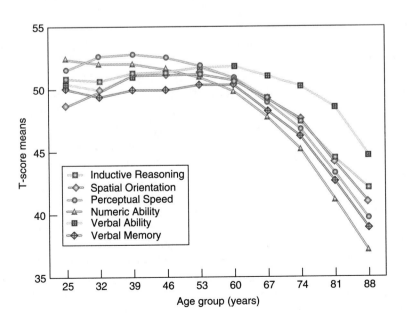

FIGURE 7.6

Findings from the Seattle Longitudinal Study

Source: Schaie, K. W., Willis, S. L., & Caskie, G. I. (2004). The Seattle Longitudinal Study: Relationship between personality and cognition. Aging, *Neuropsychology and Cognition, 11,* 304–324.

TABLE 7.4

Factors that Affect the Aging of Intelligence

Factor	Type of Effect
Smoking	Cigarette smokers show greater IQ declines
Obesity	Among men, obesity predicts lower IQ scores
Lifestyle	People with more active engagement show less of an intelligence decline

Even while attempting to document age effects on intelligence, researchers in this field have sought to identify individual health and personality factors that could have an impact on the rate of change (see Table 7.4). One factor thought to affect intelligence test scores is an individual's health status. As we saw in Chapter 3, retrospective studies show that people close to death show diminished intellectual functioning. Findings from the SLS suggest that health status is indeed related to intelligence test performance. Arthritis, cancer, and osteoporosis are health conditions associated with intelligence test scores (Schaie, 1996), as is metabolic syndrome (Akbaraly et al., 2009). These effects are not limited to Western countries; similar findings were reported among a study of more than 3,200 Chinese age 60 and older, even after controlling for age, smoking, hypertension, and diabetes (Liu et al., 2009).

Taking advantage of the types of healthy behaviors we discussed in Chapter 1 also seems to help preserve "executive function," or the ability to allocate cognitive resources. The Whitehall II Study showed greater declines in this type of intellectual ability among those in the sample who smoked, abstained entirely from alcohol, did not participate in exercise, and consumed low amounts of fruits and vegetables (Sabia et al., 2009). Not surprisingly, these were also the individuals who showed the largest increase in BMI over adulthood (Sabia, Kivimaki, Shipley, Marmot, & Singh-Manoux, 2009).

Though for the most part it would make sense that lifestyle choices would have an impact on intellectual functioning, it is also possible that the cause of poorer lifestyle choices is related to poorer intellectual functioning (Elovainio et al., 2009). As we noted earlier, metabolic syndrome is associated with fluid intelligence, but after controlling for education,

this relationship becomes much smaller (Akbaraly, Singh-Manoux, Marmot, & Brunner, 2009).

Whatever the contribution of lifestyle and diet to fluid intelligence, there is increasing evidence showing a relationship between measures of brain activation and test scores. Activation of the prefrontal cortex seems to play a role in fluid intelligence among both older and younger adults even when memory performance is controlled (Waiter et al., 2010). Variations in neurological abilities may also account for findings that older individuals with lower fluid intelligence also show greater fluctuations in scores over time (Ram, Rabbitt, Stollery, & Nesselroade, 2005). Perhaps these older individuals are more vulnerable to the physiological changes that can exacerbate the aging of the abilities that underlie fluid intelligence. In fact, researchers in the Canadian Study of Health and Aging have observed a predictive effect of low fluid intelligence test scores on a higher rate of mortality in older adults (Hall, Dubin, Crossley, Holmqvist, & D'Arcy, 2009).

Another important source of individual differences is gender, and differences between men and women are indeed observed in intelligence test performance in adulthood. Men outperform women on numerical skill, the crystallized ability of knowledge of general information, and spatial orientation. However, women receive higher scores on a fluid intelligence measure called Digit Symbol, involving the substitution of symbols for digits in a speeded coding task (Kaufman et al., 1991; Portin, Saari-jaervi, Joukamaa, & Salokangas, 1995). Women tend to decline earlier across the life span on fluid abilities, whereas men show earlier losses on crystallized abilities (Dixon & Hultsch, 1999). Risk factors for cognitive decline in both crystallized and fluid intelligence are related to gender, with obesity being more strongly related to deficits in men than in women (Elias, Elias, D'Agostino, Silbershatz, & Wolf, 1997).

Individual differences in intelligence test scores are related to social and cultural factors as well (Schaie & Zanjani, 2006). Higher socioeconomic status seems to provide protection from the negative effects of aging on intelligence (Aartsen, Smits, van Tilburg, Knipscheer, & Deeg, 2002). People with higher levels of education receive higher test scores on fluid intelligence measures and, in fact, when controlling for education, even cross-sectional differences in middle adulthood disappear (Ronnlund & Nilsson, 2006). Research also suggests that the more stimulating a person's environment after retirement, the greater the chances of maintaining his or her intellectual abilities (Schaie, Nguyen, Willis, Dutta, & Yue, 2001). As is true for cognitive functioning in general, participation in exercise training can also benefit intelligence by promoting brain plasticity (Eggermont, Milberg, Lipsitz, Scherder, & Leveille, 2009). Expertise may also play a role in preserving an individual's intellectual abilities. An intriguing study of players of the Chinese game "Go" revealed that among those with high levels of expertise, the expected decline in memory-based measures of fluid intelligence was not observed (Masunaga & Horn, 2001).

Personality may also play a role in the maintenance or decline of cognitive abilities. Feeling confident in your abilities, being liberal and autonomous in attitudes, and having an open-minded approach to new experiences, thoughts, and feelings are also related to higher PMA scores over time (Schaie, Willis, & Caskie, 2004). Adding to the complexity of understanding the relationship between lifestyle factors and intellectual changes in adulthood are findings on personality and intellectual functioning. People who are more anxious exhibit poorer performance on a variety of fluid and crystallized tasks (Wetherell, Reynolds, & Gatz, 2002).

It is important to mention the problem of cause and effect when examining research on lifestyle and intelligence. Do the intellectually more abled seek out more stimulating environments, or does involvement in a rich environment lead to greater preservation of mental abilities? Perhaps older people with high levels of intelligence purposefully search for ways to maximize their abilities. They may also seek out certain complex problems and situations because these fit with their abilities. Research suggests that crystallized intelligence exhibits a stronger relationship to activity than does fluid among older adults who engage in cognitively demanding activities (Dellenbach & Zimprich, 2008). Another possibility is that people with higher intellectual abilities and better problem-solving abilities are able to take advantage more fully of health maintenance and treatment strategies.

Crystallized intelligence can also facilitate learning among older individuals. In one study, researchers assessed the extent to which scores on fluid and crystallized intelligence predicted learning about health-related topics. Although prior knowledge about the topic was related to the amount of new learning that took place, people higher in crystallized intelligence were able to learn more independently of the amount of previous knowledge they had about the topic. Thus, focusing only on deficits in fluid intelligence can provide an unduly negative portrayal of the learning abilities of older adults (Beier & Ackerman, 2005).

Research on twin studies provides a classic example of the contrast between genetic and environmental effects even through the later years of life.

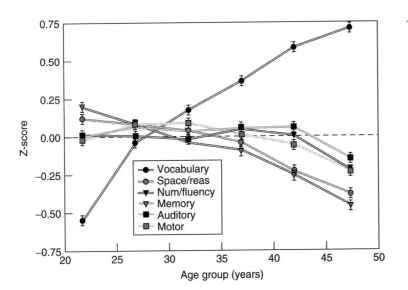

Source: Schroeder, D. H., & Salthouse, T. A. (2004). Age-related effects on cognition between 20 and 50 years of age. *Personality and Individual Differences, 36,* 393–404.

FIGURE 7.7

Intelligence Test Scores from Ages 20 to 50

A study of Swedish twin pairs from 41 to 91 years of age examined the relative influence of these effects on levels of ability and changes in ability over time. Although heredity seemed to influence individual variations in ability levels, environmental factors had effects on the rate of change over time (Reynolds, Finkel, Gatz, & Pedersen, 2002). Similar findings were obtained in a study of Danish twins, who were measured using a cohort-sequential design and were retested every 2 years for up to four testings. As with the Swedish study, overall intellectual ability appeared to be a function of genetics, but the rate of change over time was a function of environmental influences (McGue & Christensen, 2002).

Training Studies

Researchers have for decades tried to develop effective intervention strategies to examine ways to counteract the effects of age on intelligence. There is a long tradition within the developmental perspective advocated by Schaie, Baltes, and Willis of seeking ways to help preserve people's functioning as strongly and as for long as possible (Schaie, 2005).

The underlying theoretical and philosophical perspective for this approach evolved from some of the earliest work in this area by Baltes and Schaie (1976), who made the case that: "Our central argument is one for plasticity of intelligence in adulthood and old age as evidenced by large interindividual differences, multidirectionality, multidimensionality, the joint significance of ontogenetic and historical change components, and emerging evidence on modifiability via intervention research" (p. 724). To put it more simply, Baltes and Schaie argued for the need to see intelligence as "plastic" or modifiable rather than simply an attribute that declines with age. Much like the debate between the neuronal fallout and plasticity models of aging of the central nervous system, the view of intelligence as "plastic" assumes that declines are not inevitable even though some resources may be sensitive to the effects of aging. The basic assumption that adult intelligence is responsive to interventions was a driving force behind later research, particularly as part of the SLS (Willis et al., 2009).

According to Baltes and Schaie, if older adults could learn to improve intelligence as measured on various tests, the plasticity model would garner major support. In a handful of early studies conducted in

the early 1970s at Penn State University, Baltes, Willis, and their colleagues demonstrated that, given practice and training in test-taking strategies, older adults could improve their scores on tests of fluid intelligence (Hofland, Willis, & Baltes, 1980; Plemons, Willis, & Baltes, 1978; Willis, Blieszner, & Baltes, 1981). These studies pioneered the way for current studies on this important topic, which continue to confirm and expand these findings. For example, training older adults in the strategies used to solve inductive reasoning problems can lead to gains in scores, particularly for older adults with higher education (Saczynski, Willis, & Schaie, 2002).

Keeping in mind that fluid intelligence is theoretically intended to be a "pure" measure of ability; educational experiences should have little influence. However, the training studies challenged even this basic notion. The Penn State Adult Development and Enrichment Project (ADEPT) involved pretest–posttest designs, with the intervention consisting of 5 hours of group training in the requisite skills demanded by the fluid ability tests. Similar training methods with individuals were employed with members of the SLS sample. The longitudinal design of the study made it possible to examine additional factors relevant to the effects of training over time. Even after a 7-year period in between training and testing, older adults who were part of the intervention study were able to maintain their advantage

FIGURE 7.8

Conceptual Model of ACTIVE Trial

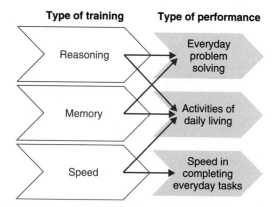

Source: Adapted from Willis, S. L., Tennstedt, S. L., Marsiske, M., Ball, K., Elias, J., Koepke, K. M., . . . Wright, E. (2006). Long-term effects of cognitive training on everyday functional outcomes in older adults. _Journal of the American Medical Association, 296,_ 2805–2814.

FIGURE 7.9

Model of Selective Optimization with Compensation

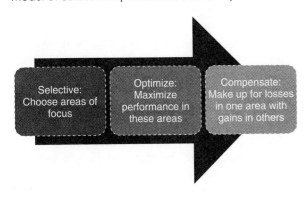

over their nontrained age peers (Schaie, 1994). Furthermore, these positive training effects were evident with people who had shown a previous decline in their intellectual functioning in the period prior to training. Booster sessions also proved helpful in maintaining gains in between training and testing. Impressively, the gains shown in training studies generalize from one test of a particular ability to another test of that same ability involving different sets of items.

Most recently, the ADEPT findings were expanded in ACTIVE, the large multisite intervention study we described in Chapter 6, which showed a positive impact of training on the cognitive functions of memory, reasoning, and speed of processing. In an innovative variant on the overall training paradigm, the ACTIVE researchers investigated the impact of training in these areas on actual abilities to maintain functional independence in everyday life. Training in the area of reasoning had a significantly positive impact on the ability of the older adults in the study to manage in daily activities, an effect that was maintained over a 5-year period (Willis et al., 2006). (See Figure 7.8.)

THE PSYCHOLOGY OF WISDOM

In moving from training studies to broader conceptualizations of intelligence in adulthood, Baltes suggested several principles that highlight and extend the notions of variability and modifiability. The principle of **reserve capacity** is that older adults possess abilities that are normally untapped and therefore unproven (Staudinger, Marsiske, & Baltes, 1995). Training studies allow adults the opportunity to express this reserve capacity by making it possible for them to reach their maximum potential. You can think of reserve capacity as your ability to perform to your highest level when you are positively motivated by a teacher, coach, competitor, or friend. You may not have even thought such a strong performance was possible until you completed it successfully.

Following on the principle of reserve capacity is that of **testing the limits**. This is the method developed by Baltes and Kliegl (1992) to determine to what extent the performance of older adults can be increased through training. Through this technique, the amount of reserve capacity available can be quantified and compared to that of younger people. One set of researchers used an ingenious procedure to demonstrate that even reaction time, a measure that declines in later adulthood, has a developmental reserve capacity that is normally untapped (Bherer et al., 2008). In this research, participants are given feedback on whether or not their responses are correct as well as guided instructions on their performance. This feedback makes it possible for them to improve their performance across successive practice trials and hence "test the limits" on their abilities. As a result, older adults are able to reach the accuracy levels of young adults.

The concept of reserve capacity also leads to another principle developed by Baltes, that of **selective optimization with compensation** (see Figure 7.9) (Baltes & Baltes, 1990). According to this principle, adults attempt to preserve and maximize the abilities that are of central importance and they put less effort into maintaining those that are not. Older people make conscious decisions regarding how to spend their time and effort in the face of losses in physical and cognitive resources. Through training, they may be given the incentive and necessary skills to bring an atrophied ability back up to a higher level, but if left to themselves, adults become increasingly likely to pick and choose their battles.

The principle of selective optimization with compensation implies that at some point in adulthood, people deliberately begin to reduce efforts in one area in order to focus more on achieving success in another. It is likely that the areas people choose to focus on are those that are of greater importance and in which the chances of success are higher. Time and health limitations may also be a factor. If someone who has enjoyed high-impact aerobics finds the activity too exerting or hard on the knees, this person may compensate by spending more time doing yoga. Similar processes may operate in the area of intellectual functioning. The older individual may exert more effort toward solving word games and puzzles and spend less time on pastimes that involve spatial and speed skills, such as fast-moving computer games. If reading becomes too much of a chore due to fading eyesight, the individual may compensate by switching to audio books.

Concepts from the multiple threshold model may accentuate the notion of selective optimization with compensation. People may make choices based on what aspects of functioning are central to their identities. Those who value the mind will compensate for changes in mental abilities by finding other intellectually demanding activities that they can still perform rather than switching their focus entirely. Those who are able to make accommodations to age-related changes without becoming overwhelmed or preoccupied will be able to reestablish a sense of well-being after what may be an initially difficult period.

Ultimately, adults may decide to put their efforts not into intellectual activities but into the successful completion of life tasks. Those of you still in school may find it both enjoyable and relevant to devote your energies to games and activities of the mind, but for many people, cognitive activities hold no compelling interest or attraction. No doubt you have acquaintances with no plans of continuing an academic lifestyle once they have graduated. Baltes referred to this switch from cognitive efforts to involvement in personal enjoyment and relationships as the movement toward the **pragmatics of intelligence**, in which people apply their abilities to the solution of real-life problems. Such problems may involve how to help a troubled granddaughter whose parents have divorced, how to rescue an unsuccessful business venture, or whether to move to a warmer climate after retirement. These abilities become more important to adults than the **mechanics of intelligence**, which involve the cognitive operations of speed, working memory, and fluid intelligence.

Baltes believed that adults become increasingly capable of dealing with higher-level conceptual issues that are not tested by conventional intelligence tests. Through his research on the pragmatics of intelligence, he showed that cognitive development in adulthood involves growth in the ability to provide insight into life's many dilemmas, particularly those that are psychosocial or interpersonal. This is where the quality of wisdom emerges.

According to Baltes and his colleagues, **wisdom** is a form of expert knowledge in the pragmatics of life (Baltes & Smith, 2008) and, although closely linked, is not equivalent to intelligence. With increasing age in adulthood, through the process of selective optimization with compensation, individuals develop an increasing interest in and capacity to exercise their judgment. The insights that people gain as wisdom develops include awareness of the finitude of life and the role of culture in shaping their lives and personalities ("life-span contextualism"). They become less likely to judge others, and have a greater appreciation for individual differences in values, life experiences, and beliefs ("value relativism"). People who are wise also possess a rich base of factual or declarative knowledge and an extensive background of procedural knowledge (Baltes, Staudinger, Maercker, & Smith, 1995). Finally, another quality, not always emphasized in the more cognitive approaches to wisdom, is the ability to recognize and manage uncertainty as a fact of life (Ardelt, 2004).

These conclusions about wisdom developed through studies identifying the characteristics of people nominated by others to be wise and by observing the types of decisions made by these people in real-life dilemmas. Through such research, Baltes and his coworkers observed that people considered "wise" are more likely to be found among the older adult population (Staudinger, Smith, & Baltes, 1993)

Theories and models about wisdom are increasing in the field of adult development and aging; however, empirical support for these constructs is often lacking. Accurately capturing and measuring wisdom remains a challenge, as many of the proposed instruments demonstrate poor internal reliability and validity. The Model of Wisdom Development, first introduced by Brown (2004), utilizes the Wisdom Development Scale (WDS) (Brown & Greene, 2006), a measure designed to tap into six components: Self-knowledge, Understanding of Others, Judgment, Life Knowledge, Life Skills, and Willingness to Learn. Research from both college-age and community samples demonstrates high reliability and construct validity of the WDS

(Greene & Brown, 2009), providing support for a theoretically effective measure to assess wisdom.

Recent research among college students in 26 countries supports this notion that aging is associated with increases in wisdom and knowledge. However, age alone does not foster wisdom. The development of this mature form of intelligence is brought about through a set of favorable life influences, including a willingness to learn from experience, interest in the welfare of others, training, and mentoring by others (Baltes & Smith, 2008). Simply clocking more hours on the planet is not sufficient; you must be able to take advantage of what life's lessons (and teachers) have to offer.

SUMMARY

1. The higher cognitive functions include language, problem-solving ability, and intelligence. Changes in memory contribute in part to age-related losses in language such as the ability to derive meaning from spoken or written passages, spell, and find words. As a result, older adults use simpler and less specific language. However, many language abilities are maintained, and older adults are able to use nonlanguage cues to help them derive meanings from language. The way that younger persons speak to older adults can also be problematic if this involves elderspeak, which is patronizing and infantilizing speech directed at an older person. The communication predicament describes the negative effects on cognition and language when older persons are communicated to in this manner.

2. Throughout the adult years, there is a trade-off in the factors affecting everyday problem solving between alterations in speed of processing and working memory, and gains in experience as individuals encounter a wider variety of problems as well as more depth in their own fields of expertise. However, because experienced problem solvers tend to seek answers to familiar problems by seeking familiar solutions, they may miss something important that is unique to a particular problem. In addition to focusing on one solution rather than considering others, older adults may also tend to stick with one pattern of responding when the situation calls for being able to call on a range of ideas.

3. There are a number of theories of intelligence, but the majority of research on adult intelligence is based on the fluid-crystallized theory. Studies on the primary mental abilities support the theory's proposal that fluid (unlearned, nonverbal) abilities decrease gradually throughout adulthood. By contrast, the crystallized abilities that are acquired through education and training steadily increase through the 60s and show a decrease only after that point. Other conceptions of intelligence, including the theory of multiple intelligences and triarchic theory, have not been tested yet on adults of varying ages but hold potential to offer a broader view of intelligence.

4. The most extensive study of adult intelligence is the Seattle Longitudinal Study, in which sequential methods have been applied to the Primary Mental Abilities test. In addition to providing data on age patterns in intelligence test scores, this study has highlighted relationships with intelligence among health, personality, lifestyle, and sociocultural factors.

5. Intervention studies in which older adults are given training in the abilities tapped by intelligence test scores have yielded support for the notion of plasticity. Even 5 hours of training can result in improved scores across tests for as long as a 7-year period. Following from these training studies, researchers have proposed establishing the reserve capacity of older adults not demonstrated in ordinary life by using a method known as testing the limits.

6. According to the principle of selective optimization with compensation, older adults attempt to maximize the abilities that are important to them and do not seek opportunities to expand the abilities that are not of interest or relevance. Many older adults turn to the pragmatics of intelligence, or the practical use of knowledge, and away from the mechanics of intelligence, or the skills typically measured on tests of ability. The quality of wisdom in later life develops as individuals become more interested in developing their abilities in the pragmatics of life.

8

Personality

In everyday language, people use the term "personality" to describe a person's characteristic way of feeling or behaving. For example, someone does you a favor because that person is "nice," "generous," or "friendly." Although psychologists use a variety of ways to define personality, there is no one consistent meaning that all psychologists use. Instead, psychologists who study personality approach its definition from the vantage point of their particular theoretical preference.

PSYCHODYNAMIC PERSPECTIVE

Freud is credited with having "discovered" the unconscious mind. This claim may be an exaggeration, but Freud did play an important role in drawing attention to the unobservable parts of personality that became the hallmark of his theory. Many current theories of adult development and personality are based on the psychodynamic perspective, even if they do not explicitly consider the role of unconscious forces in behavior.

Having left a rich body of work that later theorists would subsequently revise and reshape, Freud's legacy in the area of adult development and aging was to make the unfounded claim that personality does not change after early childhood. According to Freud, the major work of personality development is completed by the age of 5 when the child works through early sexual attachments to the parents. By the time the individual reaches adolescence, according to Freud, there are few substantive changes. As a result, therapy is of little value to individuals over the age of 50, who he believed had personalities so rigidly set that they could not be radically altered.

Fortunately, contemporary followers of Freud do not take such a pessimistic view of the potential for personality change in adulthood and have instead proposed ways in which traditional Freudian therapy can be adapted to people in their middle years and beyond. We have summarized the branches of psychodynamic theory in Figure 8.1.

One reason that Freud was so convinced that older adults could not change is that he believed that personality is virtually completely formed in early childhood. The part of personality most important to behavior, Freud theorized, was hidden in the unconscious, with the conscious mind being simply the small tip of a much larger iceberg. In order for a person to change, those hidden regions would need to be altered, and with increasing age he proposed that they become less and less amenable to alteration.

Freud used the term "id" to refer to the deepest part of the unconscious mind. The id is the part of personality that seeks fulfillment of desires that would lead people to commit unacceptable acts such as rape, murder, and incest. The id is kept in check by the ego, the structure in personality most accessible to conscious awareness, which performs the rational, executive functions of the mind. To protect the individual from knowledge of the id's unacceptable impulses, the ego uses a set of **defense mechanisms** that keep them out of conscious awareness. As we will see shortly, contemporary studies of psychodynamic psychology in adulthood focus heavily on changes in defense mechanisms.

The ultimate goal of development, according to Freud, is the ability to "love and work"; in other words, to be able to live from day to day without experiencing undue conflict. Freud maintained that defense mechanisms were necessary to allow the individual to function with a minimum of anxiety. Maturity and healthy use of defense mechanisms, according to Freud's view of the world, are less likely to be found in people who fail to resolve their childhood conflicts. They may spend a large proportion of their adult years

FIGURE 8.1

Branches of Psychodynamic Theory

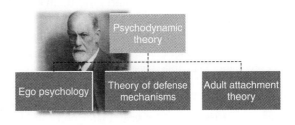

167

involved in unsuccessful efforts to rid themselves of inappropriate sexual attachments to parents or parent figures. Similarly, people who are unable to regulate their aggressive urges may find themselves plagued with guilt or anxiety about the harm that they have caused or might cause to others.

Ego Psychology

For many current psychologists who operate from a psychodynamic position, the most interesting and important component of personality is the ego. Freud regarded the ego as not having an independent role in personality but merely as serving the desires of the id. However, other theorists believe that the ego is equivalent to the conscious mind, performing the functions of integration, analysis, and synthesis of thought. The term **ego psychology** refers to the view that the ego plays a central role in actively directing behavior.

The main concern in studying development from the perspective of ego psychology is to learn how aging influences the ego's ability to adapt to the conditions and constraints of the outside world while managing to achieve expression of the individual's personal needs, desires, and wishes. Often, the ego is equated with the self, as in Erikson's use of the term "ego identity" to indicate the individual's self-attribution of personal characteristics.

Erikson's Psychosocial Theory. In Chapter 2, we reviewed the major principles of Erikson's theory of psychosocial development. To recapitulate briefly, the theory proposes that there are eight crisis stages in the maturation of the ego. Each stage represents a point of maximum vulnerability to biological, psychological, and social forces operating on the individual at that particular point in the life span. The outcome of each crisis stage may either be favorable (as in the attainment of identity) or unfavorable (as in the failure to achieve a coherent identity). The resolution of earlier stages forms the basis for resolution of later stages, according to Erikson, and the epigenetic principle lays out the ground plan for the unfolding of psychosocial crises throughout life. Although certain ages are associated with certain stages, earlier issues may arise at a later point in life, and the later stages may move to the forefront in earlier periods if conditions develop that stimulate the individual to confront those issues.

FIGURE 8.2

Rochester Adult Longitudinal Study

- Two cohorts:
  - 1946 first tested in 1966–67, n = 349
  - 1957 first tested in 1977–78, n = 299
- Four follow-ups 11 years apart, latest follow-up, 2000–02, (n's =182 and 136)
- Inventory of Psychosocial Development (IPD): 80-item questionnaire measuring each of the eight Eriksonian issues
- Family–work history questionnaire administered at each follow-up

Source: Adapted from Whitbourne, S. K., Sneed, J. R., & Sayer, A. (2009). Psychosocial development from college through midlife: A 34-year sequential study. *Developmental Psychology, 45,* 1328–1340.

The most extensive study based specifically on Erikson's theory is one conducted by the first author and her colleagues in the Rochester Adult Longitudinal Study (RALS), a sample of undergraduates and alumni from the University of Rochester (Figure 8.2). As we discussed in Chapter 3, this study began in 1966 when Constantinople (1969) administered a questionnaire measure of psychosocial development to a sample of more than 350 students in the classes of 1965–1968. The original sample was followed up 11 years later in 1977, at which time a new sample of 300 undergraduates was added to make it possible to conduct sequential analyses (Whitbourne & Waterman, 1979). In the second follow-up in 1988–1989, yet another undergraduate sample was added, allowing for sequential comparisons to be made among three cohorts of college students and two cohorts of adults in their early 30s. Longitudinal follow-up analyses were also made of adults from college up to age 43. Additional data were also collected on other measures of identity and life events at each of the follow-up testings (Van Manen & Whitbourne, 1997; Whitbourne et al., 1992).

The heart of the findings from the RALS regarding psychosocial development was the consistency of age changes across two cohorts in the two stages theorized to change the most in college and early adulthood: identity versus identity diffusion and intimacy versus isolation. Analysis of data from another measure given in 1988 to respondents from all three cohorts specifically intended to assess identity development showed convergent support for the notion of continued growth on this dimension during adulthood (Whitbourne & van Manen, 1996).

Most recently, in the 2000–02 testing of the RALS participants, the two oldest cohorts were compared in the patterns of changes they showed from college through the ages of 54 and 43, respectively (Whitbourne, Sneed, & Sayer, 2009). Statistical procedures involving growth curve modeling made it possible to examine why some people changed over time and why others did not. In general, the oldest group continued to show gains in such areas as identity and intimacy, but these gains occurred at a slower rate than was true during their earlier years.

Developmental advances were, however, observed in the scores of some participants who had lagged behind during their early adult years, showing that it was still possible to "catch up" for earlier deficits even in the midlife years. Some of the participants who started out in their adult years at a relative disadvantage in terms of having lower prestige jobs, less education, and fewer close relationships eventually reached or exceeded the psychosocial development of their more advantaged peers. This finding was especially impressive in the area of parenting; people who were "late bloomers" in terms of having children showed large gains in generativity during their 30s that exceeded those who became parents at earlier ages. These findings show that continued personality development is not only possible but predictable. Even the psychosocial stages associated with childhood showed continued gains for many of the RALS members during adulthood.

In addition to analyzing the quantitative results from the RALS, the first author investigated in depth the life history data from the oldest participants in the sample by looking for patterns in the events that had transpired in their 30s, 40s, and 50s. From that analysis, five patterns emerged that captured the trajectories of their lives (Whitbourne, 2010). (See Table 8.1.)

The five patterns or "pathways" were developed by analyzing the current well-being and psychosocial development scores of the participants and then tracing back through their lives their earlier scores and the major life choices they had made and experiences they encountered. In brief, the five pathways are described here.

TABLE 8.1
Five Pathways Through Adulthood

Pathway	Description
Authentic road	Achieves solid identity commitments through exploration and change
Triumphant trail	Overcomes challenges Is resilient
Straight and narrow way	Maintains consistent life pattern Is defensive about change
Meandering way	Fails to settle on a course in life Constantly searches for identity
Downward slope	Shows self-defeating behavior Makes poor decisions

Source: Adapted from Whitbourne, S. K. (2010). *The search for fulfillment*. New York: Ballantine.

The Meandering Way includes people who lack a clear identity and have not arrived at a consistent set of life choices. The Straight and Narrow Way includes, by contrast, those people who have followed the route of stability but feel constrained and trapped in their choices. People on the Downward Slope have made poor decisions that have come to haunt them in midlife and now regret the way that their lives have unfolded. The Triumphant Trail includes people who proved to be resilient and able to cope with personal adversity. Finally, the Authentic Road is the pathway that people follow when they remain open to change in order to reach maximum fulfillment.

The largest percentage of people studied both in the RALS and in subsequent studies using a pilot instrument called the "Pathways Questionnaire" seem to be on the Authentic Road. But for those who are not, it is possible to make the necessary changes to find that pathway. To do so may require taking risks such as giving up an unsatisfying job or following up on new interests, hobbies, or pursuits.

The five pathways have a connection to the identity processes we described in Chapter 2 and to which we will return later in this chapter. In identity assimilation, individuals attempt to maintain a consistent view of themselves over time. Like those on the Straight and Narrow Way, the people who use identity assimilation also fear change and prefer to think of themselves as stable even when situations might require that they change. Identity accommodation is similar to the Meandering Way because this identity process involves excessively changing in response to experiences when it would be preferable to maintain some consistency. Identity balance is very much like the Authentic Road; people who use identity balance are able to change flexibly in response to experiences but still maintain consistency of their sense of self over time.

A second longitudinal study of college students, this one focusing on women, began in the 1950s to 1960s by Ravenna Helson and her colleagues at Mills College, a private school in California. Although not originally intended as a study of Eriksonian development, a number of the findings were interpreted in terms of his theory. The study's founders originally intended to study leadership and creativity among college women (Helson, 1967) but, like the RALS, the study's scope continued to expand

FIGURE 8.3

Stages in Loevinger's (1976) Theory

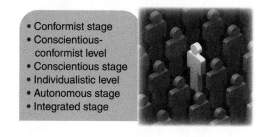

- Conformist stage
- Conscientious-conformist level
- Conscientious stage
- Individualistic level
- Autonomous stage
- Integrated stage

and it has now included five follow-ups of the sample, who are now about 70 years old.

Although the findings reported by Helson and her team in the early years presented evidence for considerable personality stability, there were several notable exceptions. The Mills women increased in the qualities of assurance, independence, and self-control, and decreased on a scale measuring their perceived femininity. There was also evidence of substantial individual differences in personality change patterns, which the investigators linked to variations in the level of ego development and identity. For example, women higher in identity at age 43 were more likely to have achieved higher levels of generativity at age 48 (Vandewater, Ostrove, & Stewart, 1997). Similar findings were obtained in a later analysis in which the identity of a woman at age 43 served to predict her well-being at the age of 60 (Helson & Srivastava, 2001). Social roles also influenced the development of women in this sample through late midlife in such qualities as dominance, masculinity/femininity, flexibility, and achievement (Helson & Soto, 2005).

Loevinger's Ego Development Theory. Closely related to Erikson's notion of psychosocial development is Jane Loevinger's (1976) view of the ego, which incorporates how people think as well as the structure of personality (see Figure 8.3). Loevinger defined the ego as the structure within personality that attempts to synthesize, master, and interpret experiences. She regarded the ego as involved in the ability to regulate impulses, relate to others, achieve self-understanding, and think about experiences. The development of the ego proceeds in a series of stages that move from lower to higher levels in these characteristics.

Individuals in the first, or Conformist, stage have only a very basic understanding of themselves, other people, and the reasons for following society's rules. They have simple views of right and wrong, and it is hard for them to understand why others think and feel the way they do. Loevinger believed that most adults fall into the second stage, known as the **Conscientious-Conformist stage**. Developmentally, this is the stage when people first have an internalized sense of right and wrong and are able to be aware of their own motives as well as those of other people. Next is the Conscientious stage, when people develop a true conscience, one that is an internalized understanding of society's rules and the reasons for those rules. People in the Conscientious stage are also able to have insight into their own emotions as well as the emotional needs of others.

The final three stages involve an increasing sense of individuality and self-determination. In the Individualistic stage, an appreciation and respect for individuality emerges. Next, people in the Autonomous stage, have even more clearly articulated inner standards. They recognize and appreciate the complexities of their own behavior and that of others. People in the Autonomous stages are also better able to live with uncertainty (somewhat like those in the postformal stage, which we described in Chapter 7). Finally, the Integrated stage, which Loevinger proposed would be reached by relatively few people, is one in which the individual has a clear sense of self, is able to recognize inner conflicts,

and highly values individuality. In this stage, the individual is able to achieve the expression of the true "inner self."

Loevinger's theory combines ego psychology with moral development, and in that sense is not a "typical" psychodynamically based theory. In fact, scores on Loevinger's measure of ego development have a strong cognitive component. Researchers conducting a large scale analysis of studies on more than 5,600 participants found that there were strong correlations between ego level and intellectual abilities. However, ego level is not completely synonymous with intelligence. People at higher levels of ego development according to Loevinger's theory, are also more likely to have high scores on personality variables such as assertiveness, conformity, and fearfulness (Cohn & Westenberg, 2004).

Vaillant's Theory of Defense Mechanisms

The psychodynamic theory proposed by George Vaillant (2000) emphasizes the development of defense mechanisms over the course of adulthood (see Table 8.2). As we mentioned earlier, intended to help protect the conscious mind from knowing about unconscious desires, defense mechanisms are strategies that people use almost automatically as protection against morally unacceptable urges and desires.

Unlike Freud, who proposed that personality is invariant after childhood, Vaillant regards the

TABLE 8.2
Categories of Defense Mechanisms Identified by Vaillant

Category	Examples
Psychotic	*Delusional projection*—attributing one's own bizarre ideas and feelings to others *Denial*—disclaiming the existence of a feeling, action, or event *Distortion*—significantly exaggerating and altering the reality of feelings and events
Immature	*Projection*—attributing unacceptable ideas and feelings to others *Hypochondriasis*—expressing psychological conflict as exaggerated physical complaints *Acting out*—engaging in destructive behavior that expresses inner conflicts
Neurotic	*Displacement*—transferring unacceptable feelings from the true to a safer object *Repression*—forgetting about a troubling feeling or event *Reaction formation*—expressing the opposite of one's true feelings
Mature	*Altruism*—turning unacceptable feelings into behavior that is helpful to others *Sublimation*—expressing unacceptable feelings in productive activity *Humor*—being able to laugh at an unpleasant or disturbing feeling or situation

ego defense mechanisms as becoming increasingly adaptive in adulthood, helping people cope with life's challenges ranging from stress at work to discrimination to marital unhappiness. Over time, Vaillant proposed, people use increasingly mature and adaptive defenses and fewer immature and maladaptive ways of minimizing anxiety. Immature defense mechanisms include acting out and denial.

You can understand these differences by considering these two scenarios. In acting out (an immature defense), you react when you are angry by throwing something, slamming a door, or hitting your fist against a wall. These actions may temporarily relieve your anger but they can also cause you (or your possessions) harm. You also will look quite ridiculous to your friends if you throw such a fit of rage in front of them. Using a more mature defense mechanism, such as humor in the face of anger, would help you feel better and avoid the social and practical costs of rash action.

The use of immature defense mechanisms becomes rarer with age, as Vaillant discovered in his Study of Adult Development (1993). In this study, Vaillant and his research team investigated the use of defense mechanisms in three diverse samples of individuals. The first consisted of men in what was known as the Harvard Grant Study. Begun in 1938, this study was intended to characterize the physical and psychological functioning of Harvard undergraduates on a wide variety of measures. Over the course of the subsequent decades, it continued to follow the men as they made their way through the early and middle years of life. Men in the second group, called the Core City sample, were a socioeconomically and racially diverse group chosen as a comparison to the Harvard men. In order to extend the findings beyond men, Vaillant eventually recruited a sample of women from a study originally focused on gifted children. The women in this sample were interviewed again for the purpose of the defense mechanism study when they were in their late 70s.

The initial set of findings provided evidence within each of the three samples for a positive relationship between maturity of defenses and various outcome measures. For instance, Core City men who used immature defenses (such as acting out) were more likely to experience alcohol problems,

unstable marriages, and antisocial behavior (Soldz & Vaillant, 1998).

Other longitudinal investigations support these findings. Cramer (2003) conducted a 24-year longitudinal study in which she followed more than 150 men and women from early to middle adulthood. As in the Vaillant studies, age was associated with the use of more mature defenses. In the subsequent 20 years from middle to later adulthood, Cramer and her colleagues found that the maladaptive defense mechanisms used by people with a narcissistic personality (whose gratification depends on the admiration of others) became less psychologically healthy (Cramer & Jones, 2008). Consistently, these studies show that older adults are able to manage their emotions through the use of mature defense mechanisms that involve the control of negative emotions or trying to put the situation into perspective (Diehl, Coyle, & Labouvie-Vief, 1996; Labouvie-Vief & Medler, 2002).

The general pattern that emerges is that older adults cope with anxiety, stress, or frustration by reacting in less self-destructive or emotional ways than they would have when they were younger. Rather than getting frustrated and giving up on a solution, older adults are more apt to try and understand the situation and figure out a way around it. They can suppress their negative feelings or channel those feelings into productive activities. By contrast, younger people (including adolescents and young adults) are more likely to react to psychologically demanding situations by acting out against others, projecting their anger onto others, or regressing to more primitive forms of behavior.

Consistent gender differences have also emerged in studies of defense mechanisms and coping (Diehl et al., 1996; Labouvie-Vief & Medler, 2002). Regardless of age, women are more likely to avoid unpleasant or stressful situations, to blame themselves when things go wrong, and to seek the support of others. Men are more likely to externalize their feelings and to use reaction formation, a defense mechanism in which people act in a way that is opposite to their unconscious feelings.

Adult Attachment Theory

The third branch of psychodynamic theory, known as attachment theory, examines the lifelong impact of the earliest relationships that children have with their parents (or caregivers). British psychoanalyst John Bowlby (1969) developed this theory after observing the developmental problems suffered by children growing up in orphanages during World War II. Though children raised in these group homes were given sufficient nourishment, their development was abnormal because, Bowlby theorized, they were not given sufficient human contact.

From these observations emerged a theory that eventually proposed a much broader role of attachment in the development of the self. Mothers who bond with their children help them develop a more secure sense of self. Caregivers who are unresponsive or hurtful to the child plant the seeds for the growth later in life of a negative self-concept and feelings of insecurity (Bowlby, 1973).

Attachment style is the term used to describe the way that people relate to their primary attachment figure. In adulthood, this figure shifts from mothers (or other caregivers) to romantic partners. Psychologist Mary Ainsworth tested Bowlby's ideas by developing an experimental procedure in which toddlers' reactions were measured when their mothers first left and then reentered a laboratory playroom (Ainsworth, Blehar, Waters, & Wall, 1978).

Children with a secure attachment style do not become angry or anxious by the mother's temporary departure. When the mother returns, they seek contact with her in a positive and enthusiastic manner. Children with avoidant attachment styles actually resist contact with the mother upon her return, and the child with the anxious attachment style appears to want to make contact with the mother but rejects her. Because of the mixed behavior of this last group of children, the anxious attachment style is also referred to as the anxious-ambivalent attachment style. The majority of children fall into the secure attachment style, and the remaining two types, together considered "insecure," are in the minority.

Researchers believe that attachment style has its effect on a person's sense of self through what they call the "internal working model." The child has a mental representation of relations with the mother and this sets the stage for how the child will later come to view relations with others, including romantic partners.

There is very little research on adult attachment style in samples past college age, in part because it is

People who are insecurely attached may continue to experience relationship difficulties in adulthood.

seen as a theory about how people choose and relate to romantic partners relatively earlier in adulthood. The few studies that exist suggest that insecure attachment is less prevalent in older adult samples. As is true of defense mechanisms, older adults (or at least those who survive until old age) are better able to manage situations involving close relationships with others.

Older adults also appear less likely to experience anxious types of attachment in comparison with younger adults (Segal, Needham, & Coolidge, 2009). Moreover, older adults who reported secure attachment with their parents state that they are currently happier on a daily basis than those who reported less secure attachment (Consedine & Magai, 2003). Although attachment style might seem to be a stable feature of personality, there is evidence that it can change even in as short a period as a few years (Zhang & Labouvie-Vief, 2004).

Older adults may also be more resilient in some ways to the effect of harsh early parenting. A cross-sectional investigation of the recollections of parenting practices by younger and older adults showed that older adults appeared less negatively affected by the punitive experiences recalled from their childhood (Magai, Consedine, Gillespie, O'Neal, & Vilker, 2004).

TRAIT APPROACHES

The second major theoretical approach to personality and aging proposes that personality is made up of **traits,** which are stable, enduring dispositions that persist over time. It is easy for most people to relate to trait theory because it fits so closely with the use of the term *personality* in everyday life. When you think about how to describe the personality of a friend, relative, or coworker, you most likely begin by listing a set of a characteristics or qualities that seem to fit the person's observable behavior. These characteristics typically take the form of adjectives such as "generous," or "outgoing," or perhaps, "quiet" and "unfriendly." Trait theories of personality propose that adjectives such as these capture the essence of the individual's psychological makeup. The fact that people use these adjectives in everyday life to describe themselves and others agrees with the basic principle of trait theory—namely, that personality is equivalent to a set of stable characteristic attributes.

Trait theories of personality are based on the assumption that the organization of these personal dispositions guides the individual's behavior. Trait theory is also increasingly viewed in terms of genetic theories of personality, which suggest that the enduring nature of personality traits over time reflect the fact that they are at least partially inherited (Bouchard, 2004).

The Five Factor Model

The predominant trait theory in the field of adult development and aging is based on Costa and McCrae's proposal that there are five major dimensions to personality (Figure 8.4). The **Five Factor Model** (also called the **"Big Five"**) is a theory intended to capture all the essential characteristics of personality in a set of five broad dispositions. Each disposition has six facets, which leads to a total of 30 personality components.

The Five Factor Model includes the personality traits of neuroticism, extraversion, openness to experience, agreeableness, and conscientiousness (you can remember these as spelling "OCEAN" or "CANOE"). A complete characterization of an individual on the five factors involves providing scores or ratings on each of the facets using the **NEO-PI-R**. According to trait theory, the shape of people's lives is strongly influenced by the nature of their personalities. Cynical people may be more likely to experience betrayal because they themselves are less trusting in the first place. Adventurous people are more likely to place themselves in injury-prone situations because they are more open to engaging in

FIGURE 8.4

Five Factor Model of Personality

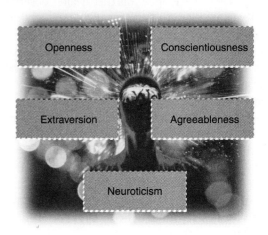

risk-taking behavior. In other words, people choose situations as a function of their personalities but rarely, according to this theory, do people change their personalities as a result of the life events they experience.

Research on Aging and the Five Factor Model

Studies based on the scales of the Five Factor Model and aging show a high degree of consistency over time in the scores of individuals throughout adulthood with correlations ranging from .70 to .75 (Roberts & DelVecchio, 2000). Although there are individual differences in the patterns of change over time, Costa, McCrae, and their associates contend that people maintain their relative positions in comparison to their age peers; the "highs" stay high and the "lows" stay low. If you had high neuroticism scores as a young adult, you would continue your high levels of worry, anxiety, and general malaise throughout your midlife years and beyond.

In the past decade, however, the Five Factor Model researchers have begun to revise their ideas about personality stability. This is in part because they have access to larger data sets, more sophisticated research methods, and more refined ways of looking at the Five Factor Scores. Rather than using only conscientiousness scores, for example, they look at all six facets of this trait and examine its changes over time using individual growth curve modeling. Studies employing this method show that, longitudinally, the self-discipline facet of conscientiousness declines in later life, meaning that older adults are less willing to engage in activities that they do not find personally stimulating or enjoyable. Conversely, the deliberation facet increases, meaning that as people get older they are less likely to act impulsively (Terracciano, McCrae, Brant, & Costa, 2005).

As you can see in Figure 8.5, which summarizes the current state of the art in the modeling of Five Factor Model scores over time, there are substantial overall trends even when examining scores at the trait rather than the facet level. Consequently, statements that personality is "set in plaster" by age 30 (to quote the famous psychologist William James), are now being rewritten to allow for the possibility that personality can continue to grow and mature throughout life.

Health and Personality Traits

The idea that personality traits could be related to significant health problems and health-related behaviors originated when researchers discovered what became known as the **Type A behavior pattern**, a collection of traits thought to increase a person's risk

of developing cardiovascular disease (Friedman & Rosenman, 1974). People with Type A personalities are competitive, impatient, feel a strong sense of time urgency, and are highly achievement oriented. Although a high-achievement orientation is not particularly damaging to health, when combined with hostility, the results can be deadly (see Figure 8.6).

The Type A–cardiovascular disease connection was for many years considered a case of correlation not equaling causation. It was only when researchers obtained longitudinal data that they were able to overcome the limitations of correlational approaches to the problem. In one important study, Duke University investigators followed male participants over a 10-year period, measuring their levels of hostility, depression, and anger, as well as levels of proteins (C3 and C4) considered to be strong indicators of heart disease or the risk of heart disease (Boyle, Jackson, & Suarez, 2007). Men who had high levels of personality risk also showed greater increases over the course of the study in both C3 and C4.

High levels of anxiety may also serve as risk factors for cardiovascular disease. In comparing the personality factors of anxiety, general levels of distress, and anger, researchers investigating predictors of cardiovascular heart disease over a 14-year period found that, in particular, people high in the trait of anxiety also were more likely to develop subsequent illness, even taking into account

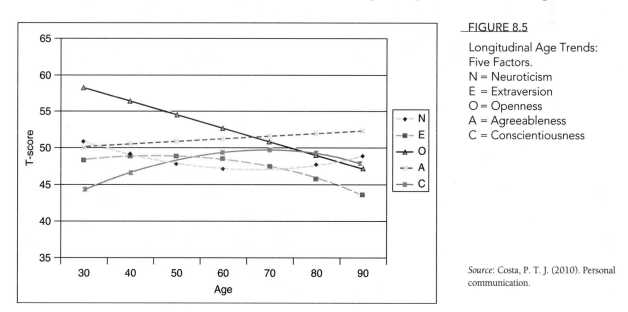

FIGURE 8.5

Longitudinal Age Trends: Five Factors.
N = Neuroticism
E = Extraversion
O = Openness
A = Agreeableness
C = Conscientiousness

Source: Costa, P. T. J. (2010). Personal communication.

their other risk factors such as smoking, cholesterol, BMI, and blood pressure (Kubzansky, Cole, Kawachi, Vokonas, & Sparrow, 2006).

The relationship between personality and health may go back as far as childhood. Researchers have observed relationships between low scores in childhood on the trait of conscientiousness and higher death rates in adulthood (Friedman et al., 1995). Being low in conscientiousness might lead people to be more careless about many aspects of life including control over diet and exercise patterns, leading them to develop higher BMIs. In turn, they are more likely to gain weight during adolescence and early adulthood (Pulkki-Raback, Elovainio, Kivimaki, Raitakari, & Keltikangas-Jarvinen, 2005).

The trait of conscientiousness continues to relate to greater weight gains during adulthood, particularly in women, placing them at risk for weight-related diseases. One 14-year longitudinal study showed a relationship between women's scores on neuroticism and weight gains (Brummett et al., 2006). Low scores on conscientiousness and high scores on neuroticism also relate to the likelihood of cigarette smoking (Terracciano & Costa, 2004). High neuroticism scores, particularly on the facet of vulnerability, relate to high rates of heroin and cocaine use among adults. Marijuana users, particularly young adults, score high on openness to experience and low on agreeableness and conscientiousness (Terracciano, Löckenhoff, Crum, Bienvenu, & Costa, 2008).

Conscientiousness continues to play a role in mortality in later adulthood as well. Among a sample of more than 1,000 Medicare recipients ranging from 65 to 100 years of age followed over a 3- to 5-year period, conscientiousness, particularly self-discipline (a facet of conscientiousness), predicted lower mortality risk over a 3-year period. As the study's authors point out, it is possible that high levels of self-discipline relate to a greater tendency to be proactive in engaging in behaviors that are protective of health and to avoid those behaviors that are damaging to health (Weiss & Costa, 2005). Reinforcing these findings, research from a large sample of Italian adults found that lower levels of conscientiousness (including impulsivity) were associated with lower levels of high-density lipoprotein (the "good" cholesterol) (Sutin et al., 2010) and interleukin-6, a protein important to bolstering immune function (Sutin et al., 2009).

Lower mortality is also related to other personality traits. In a sample of more than 2,300 individuals followed since 1958 in the Baltimore Longitudinal Study of Aging, longevity was associated with high scores on conscientiousness, low scores on neuroticism, and high scores on the activity facet of extraversion (Terracciano, Löckenhoff, Zonderman, Ferrucci, & Costa, 2008). High levels of openness, particularly emotional awareness and curiosity, also seem related to lower mortality rates, even after controlling for educational levels (Jonassaint et al., 2007). Insight into these findings came from a study examining personality traits and medical care utilization. Among older adults, rates of admission to hospital emergency departments were higher for individuals who were less agreeable and more extraverted (Chapman et al., 2009).

Openness to experience also relates to early life occurrences. In one study, young adults high in openness reported a higher number of stressful life events in childhood. However, individuals with high openness scores showed less physiological reactivity to a laboratory stressor in which they were asked to discuss a recent highly stressful event. Unlike their low openness peers, those high in openness even showed a slight boost in positive affect while experiencing the stressor (Williams, Rau, Cribbet, & Gunn, 2009).

Personality traits may also be related to risk of developing cognitive disorders, including development of Alzheimer's disease. An investigation of nearly 1,000 Catholic nuns and priests indicated that high conscientiousness while alive correlated with lower rates of Alzheimer's disease. Even among those whose brains showed a high degree of pathology upon

FIGURE 8.6

Relationship Between Personality and Health

- Cardiovascular risk factors related to Type A behavior and anxiety
- Lower BMI related to higher levels of conscientiousness
- Drug use and smoking related to lower levels of conscientious
- Lower mortality related to higher levels of openness
- Higher risk of Alzheimer's disease related to low conscientiousness and high neuroticism

autopsy, high levels of conscientiousness seemed to serve as a protective factor against the experience of cognitive symptoms associated with the disease (Wilson, Schneider, Arnold, Bienias, & Bennett, 2007). High levels of neuroticism in midlife also appear to be predictive of an earlier onset of the disease but only in women (Archer et al., 2009).

High levels of hostility in early adulthood may pose a risk factor for the development of depression during the ensuing years. Alumni of the University of North Carolina tested in college were followed up at the age of 47. College students with high hostility scores who remained high in hostility were at a significantly greater risk for developing depression in midlife. They also were more likely to experience negative changes in family life. Higher hostility in college was also associated with riskier health-related behaviors, including smoking and drinking. Changes in hostility over the study period also predicted obesity, failure to exercise, high-fat diets, social isolation, poor health, and, for women, lower income (Siegler et al., 2003).

Clearly, personality factors are integral aspects of the biopsychosocial model of development in adulthood and old age. Traits and behavior patterns that have their origins in inherited predispositions or through early life experiences influence the health of the individual through a variety of direct and indirect pathways. However, although personality traits may be an inherent part of "who" you are, they can modulate and change over adulthood (Staudinger & Kunzmann, 2005) even as they influence some of the most basic components of your ability to remain healthy.

SOCIAL COGNITIVE APPROACHES

As we have just seen, a significant focus of personality psychology is on how personality changes through life. There is also growing interest in the factors that cause people to feel emotions such as happiness or sadness. Researchers also investigate the "why's" of behavior, or motivation. Traditionally, emotion and motivation have long captured the attention of psychologists, and the area of social cognition and aging is no exception.

Some of the growing interest in emotions stems from a desire to help people feel better about themselves and their experiences, and some is based on a resurgence of a topic that has always been within

FIGURE 8.7

Socioemotional Selectivity Theory

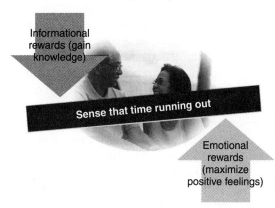

the domain of psychology. In looking at aging and emotions in particular, researchers are also gaining an increased appreciation for the ways that older adults are able to focus their attention on the positive, rather than negative, aspects of their daily lives. Research on motivation and aging helps provide insight into people's goals, desires, and needs and how they change through life.

According to one viewpoint in adult development and aging, emotions and motivation are intimately linked. **Socioemotional selectivity theory** proposes that throughout adulthood, people structure the nature and range of their relationships to maximize gains and minimize risks (see Figure 8.7) (Charles & Carstensen, 2010). According to this theory, people look for different rewards from their interactions with others as they approach the later years of their lives.

Essentially, this theory proposes that there are two types of functions served by interpersonal relationships. One is an informational function. Relationships that serve this function provide you with important knowledge that you would not otherwise have. For instance, when you moved into your college dormitory, you probably sought out the people who seemed to know the most about where to buy the items needed for your new life such as textbooks, school supplies, and the cheapest and best cup of coffee. The second role of relations with others is emotional. Relationships that serve this function contribute to your sense of well-being. Whether you are feeling good or bad on a given day often depends on whether the people close to you are pleased or displeased with you.

Socioemotional selectivity theory proposes that as people grow older, they become more focused on the emotional functions of relationships and less interested in the informational function. This shift, according to the theory, occurs as people become increasingly sensitive to the inevitable ending of their lives and recognize that they are "running out of time."

It is not aging so much as this recognition of less time left to live that triggers the shift in what people want out of their interactions. Young adults, when placed either under artificial time constraints through experimental manipulations or under real time constraints show similar preferences toward the emotional functions of social interactions as do older adults (Carstensen, Isaacowitz, & Charles, 1999). Endings of any kind bring out strong emotions and cause you to want to spend time with the people who have been closest to you. Think of times when significant life events have come to an end, such as when you graduated from high school or said goodbye to a friend who moved across the country. Knowing that you did not have much time left to spend with these people, you wanted to make the most out of the time you did have before it came to an end. The desire to maximize emotional rewards leads adults increasingly to prefer spending time with people who are familiar to them rather than seeking out new friends and acquaintances. Family and long-time friends are the people who will serve the positive emotional functions of self-validation and affect regulation. Older adults are less interested in meeting new people and broadening their social horizons because they prefer to maximize the emotional and minimize the information functions of their relationships (Lang & Carstensen, 2002).

As you think about this theory, it may be helpful to reflect on your own friendship patterns. You may be at a point in your life right now where spending time with friends and acquaintances is more important than spending time with your family. Your number of Facebook friends may well be over 500, full of people you have not spoken with for months, even years. As you navigate your way through your postgraduate years, you will most likely find that the number of people in your social network dwindles, and you are left with a much smaller network of close friends and family. As part of this transition, you will go through a "weeding out" process where you focus on

According to socioemotional selectivity theory, older adults prefer to spend time with the people close to them in their lives.

maintaining the positive relationships and removing (or "unfriending") the negative ones.

One intriguing approach to testing socioemotional selectivity is taken by Isaacowitz and his colleagues, who use eye-tracking instruments to examine the way in which older and younger adults approach stimuli varying in their positive emotional value. In one investigation (Isaacowitz, Wadlinger, Goren, & Wilson, 2006), older and younger adults were compared in their eye movements when viewing faces conveying happy, sad, and neutral emotional expressions. Older adults were less likely than younger adults to look at parts of the face conveying anger and sadness, and more likely to look at the parts conveying happiness. This study's findings imply that older adults would prefer, literally, to "accentuate the positive" when it comes to reading other people's facial expressions. Subsequent research has shown that older adults with higher levels of cognitive functioning were more likely to focus on positive images in an experimental manipulation that put them in a bad mood (Isaacowitz, Toner, & Neupert, 2009).

The findings on socioemotional selectivity are not consistent, however, in supporting the idea of a positivity bias among older adults. In a meta-analysis of a large number of studies comparing younger and older adults, Murphy and Isaacowitz (2008) observed that both older and younger adults showed a preference for positive emotional stimuli. Consistent with the theory, though, older adults were more likely to avoid negative emotional stimuli. There may also be cultural factors involved in the relationship between age and a positivity bias. Among a Chinese sample, older adults looked away from, not toward, happy faces (Fung et al., 2008).

Note that the theory does not imply that older people are less capable of showing or feeling emotions or that they are not interested in forming new relationships. The intensity of emotion experienced by an individual does not change over adulthood (Carstensen & Turk-Charles, 1994). Older adults can experience strong emotions when prompted with relevant stimuli. In one investigation of age differences in emotional reactivity, older adults were compared with younger adults in their reactions to movies with specific, age-relevant themes intended to provoke sadness (Kunzmann & Gruhn, 2005). Older adults felt appropriate levels of sadness as acutely as did young adults to the depiction of situations appropriate for their age group, such as loss associated with bereavement and chronic illness.

Nevertheless, it seems that older adults have an advantage in that they seem to react more slowly in emotionally provoking situations (Wieser, Muhlberger, Kenntner-Mabiala, & Pauli, 2006). Rather than fly into a fit of rage when irked, an older adult may be more likely to think twice and maintain emotional control (Charles & Carstensen, 2010). This may be because older adults are better able to regulate their emotions after exposure to negative stimuli more quickly than are younger adults (Larcom & Isaacowitz, 2009). They may also be less likely to report negative affect, as suggested by a longitudinal study of more than 2,800 adults studied from 1971 to 1994 (Charles, Reynolds, & Gatz, 2001).

Being less perturbed by emotional stimuli may also help older adults maintain their cognitive focus (Samanez-Larkin, Robertson, Mikels, Carstensen, & Gotlib, 2009). If you are better able to think logically and maintain your "cool," you will be less likely to forget something or slip up and make a mistake. Perhaps older adults have learned through the years that there is value in stepping back and not becoming highly aroused when something upsetting happens (Magai, Consedine, Krivoshekova, Kudadjie-Gyamfi, & McPherson, 2006).

As is true for identity assimilation, a process that causes people to minimize negative information, the desire to focus on the positive implied in socioemotional selectivity theory can have undesirable consequences. There are times when it is necessary to focus on the possibility of negative outcomes, particularly in the area of health. If you just refuse to think about the need to change your health habits when your medical provider tells you to do so, you are likely to run into problems. It does appear, however, that older adults can switch their focus to make health-related decision as needed to avoid negative outcomes (Luckenhoff & Carstensen, 2007).

COGNITIVE PERSPECTIVE

The cognitive perspective views people as driven by the desire to predict and control their experiences. Emerging from this perspective are **cognitive self theories**, which propose that people regard events in their lives from the standpoint of how relevant these are to their own sense of self. Cognitive perspective theories also place emphasis on coping, the mechanisms that people use to manage stress (see Figure 8.8).

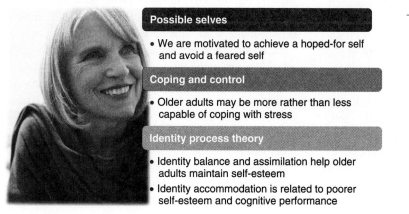

<u>FIGURE 8.8</u>

Theories Within the Cognitive Perspective

Possible selves
- We are motivated to achieve a hoped-for self and avoid a feared self

Coping and control
- Older adults may be more rather than less capable of coping with stress

Identity process theory
- Identity balance and assimilation help older adults maintain self-esteem
- Identity accommodation is related to poorer self-esteem and cognitive performance

Specific theories about aging and personality based on the cognitive perspective place importance on the ways that people interpret their experiences and understand themselves over time. An important principle of the cognitive perspective is the idea that people do not always view themselves realistically. In part, this is because people strive to maintain a sense of themselves as consistent (Baumeister, 1996; 1997). In other words, most people prefer to see themselves as stable and predictable (even if they are not). Another basic tendency is for people to view their abilities and personal qualities in a positive light (Baumeister, Bratslavsky, Finkenauer, & Vohs, 2001). These ideas are important to keep in mind as you read about the views about aging represented by the cognitive perspective.

Possible Selves Theory

The **possible selves** model (Markus & Nurius, 1986) proposes that the individual's view of the self, or self-schema, guides the choice and pursuit of future endeavors. The possible self means literally just that: what are you now, and what *could* you be in the future? These thoughts about the self can motivate you to act in certain ways so that you achieve your "hoped-for" possible self, or the person you would like to be. These self-conceptions about the person you will be in the future continue to shift as you develop throughout adulthood. People can remain hopeful of change until well into their later years (Smith & Freund, 2002). Increasingly important as you get older is your health-related possible self, meaning your hope that you will remain in good shape and free of disease (Frazier, Johnson, Gonzalez, & Kafka, 2002; Hooker & Kaus, 1994). A dreaded possible self is the opposite of the hoped-for possible self. With regard to health, most people would rather not become ill and so they will take action to avoid that outcome.

According to possible selves theory, people are motivated to strive for a hoped-for possible self and will attempt to avoid a dreaded or feared possible self. To the extent that they are successful in this process, positive feelings of life satisfaction are theorized to emerge. People think of themselves in a negative light and view their lives negatively when they are unable to realize a hoped-for possible self or to avoid the

dreaded possible self. For instance, you probably feel better when your grades confirm your possible self as a good student and study harder to avoid the dreaded self of a person who fails out of college.

However, people have ways to protect themselves from these negative self-evaluations. One tactic is to revise the possible self to avoid future disappointment and frustration if experiences suggest that the possible self may not be achievable. You may realize that you will not be a straight A student if your grades include enough A's, B's, or lower and so you revise your possible self accordingly. You will probably feel better about yourself in the long run if you do so even though you may continue to strive for good grades. A similar process seems to be at play for older adults. In one study, those older adults who underestimated their future selves (in both the physical and social domains) had higher well-being a year later than those who overestimated their future selves (Cheng, Fung, & Chan, 2009). By lowering their expectations, they evaluated more positively the outcomes they did achieve.

Coping and Control

Adult development researchers are interested in the field of aging and sense of personal control based, in part, on a popular belief that adults undergo a loss of the feeling that they control what happens to them as they age. The MacArthur Study of Adult Development, a large national survey of almost 3,500 adults, showed that contrary to the popular myth, older adults retain the feeling of being in control of their lives despite being aware of the constraints they may encounter. They do so by viewing their resources and potential positively rather than focusing on losses (Plaut, Markus, & Lachman, 2003).

Coping, a related process, refers to the way people attempt to manage stress. When you cope successfully with a stressful situation, your mood improves and you have a higher sense of well-being (Lachman, Rosnick, Röcke, Bosworth, & Hertzog, 2009). The process seems to be reciprocal—people who feel better also cope more successfully. One longitudinal investigation of coping in midlife adults followed over a 10-year period found that people who are less depressed are more likely to resolve problematic situations successfully. Being in good health and having extensive social networks also contribute to successful coping (Brennan, Schutte, & Moos, 2006). Having resolved a situation successfully, the older individual is then more resilient to some of the deleterious psychological consequences of being in poor health (Jonker, Comijs, Knipscheer, & Deeg, 2009).

Being resilient, or having a personality that allows you to "bounce back" readily from stressful life experiences seems, then, to be a positive attribute that can facilitate the coping process. This point was further demonstrated among a sample of older adult widows and widowers followed intensively over a 6-week period while they rated their daily experiences of stressful events and emotional reactions (Ong, Bergeman, Bisconti, & Wallace, 2006). The measure of resilience used in this study tapped such qualities as the respondent's ability to overcome negative emotions and adapt to new situations. The more resilient individuals were able to maintain a positive mood even on days when they experienced high degrees of stress.

Although some discussions of coping in later life regard older adults as passive rather than active copers, it is not necessarily a given that as people get older they adopt a fatalistic approach to managing their fortunes or that they become ineffective copers. A study of the victims of the 2005 Hurricane Katrina that devastated New Orleans showed that older and younger adults were equally effective in engaging in coping strategies to manage their responses to the disaster (Cherry, Silva, & Galea, 2009).

Thus, older adults can show initiative in managing their situations and making efforts to alter the course of events in their lives. People who show this type of initiative strongly wish to maintain a feeling of independence, even if they have been forced to relinquish some of their actual independence due to functional changes in their abilities (Duner & Nordstrom, 2005). The ability to take charge of potentially stressful situations, before they become problems, was found in one study of community-dwelling, active, older adults to be related to fewer health-related stressful situations (Fiksenbaum, Greenglass, & Eaton, 2006).

That aging may bring with it more effective ways of coping with stress was illustrated in one intriguing study comparing learning under stress between older and younger rats. The stress in this experiment consisted of being kept in restraint for a period of 21 days. The younger rats were more impaired while stressed in their ability to learn and remember than were the older animals (Bowman, 2005). Along similar lines, researchers comparing the cardiovascular reactivity of older and younger humans during a stressful laboratory task found that older adults actually increased their blood pressure more in response to stress than did their younger counterparts. However, the older adults managed to keep their negative emotions in check, even when it was apparent that their bodies were registering heightened levels of stress (Uchino, Berg, Smith, Pearce, & Skinner, 2006).

Researchers in this area regard it as a given that social support is an important resource for people of any age to have when faced with stressful experiences. Everyone knows how important it is to be able to talk to someone who can, if not help, at least hear you out when you have had something bad happen to you. Loss of functional abilities is certainly one important stressful area for older adults. In investigating responses of anxiety, depression, and self-esteem to loss of abilities in married older adults, one set of researchers found that a high level of marital closeness was a protective factor for psychological problems. Older adults with functional losses were able to maintain positive mood and self-regard if they were in marital relationships characterized by such factors as feeling loved, understood, and able to communicate (Mancini & Bonanno, 2006).

Identity Process Theory

According to identity process theory, the goal of development is optimal adaptation to the environment through establishing a balance between maintaining consistency of the self (identity assimilation) and changing in response to experiences (identity accommodation). The actions people take upon the environment reflect attempts to express their sense of self by engaging in the activities they regard as important and worthwhile. Through identity assimilation, people interpret events in a way that is consistent with their present identity. If an event occurs that is so discrepant a person cannot interpret it in terms

AGING IN THE NEWS

www.wiley.com/college/whitbourne   OLDER ADULTS WHO MADE THE HEADLINES   -VOL. 4, CHAPTER 8-

MS. SENIOR AMERICA CROWNED

Flanked by her "court," Gail King (center) at 60 years old was crowned in October 2009. A 20-year cancer survivor, King taught high school English for 35 years. An avid fund raiser and model for the Carol Baldwin Breast Cancer Research Foundation, her accomplishments range in areas from mentoring to volunteer animal rescue work, and acting in TV commercials. The Ms. Senior America pageant, held every October, seeks to honor the outstanding women who exemplify the dignity, maturity, and inner beauty of all senior Americans. Each contestant is put through rigors that rival those faced by their "junior" Ms. America Pageant contestants.

of identity at the moment, identity accommodation comes into play.

Most people have fairly positive views of themselves, but as they get older, more and more experiences occur that can potentially erode self-esteem. However, research on identity processes shows that adults increasingly rely on identity assimilation, and this is how older people are able to maintain positive self-esteem. The edge that assimilation has over accommodation is theorized to be just enough to maintain this positive view without leading individuals into self-views that are so off base as to be completely out of sync with experiences.

The multiple threshold model, described in Chapter 2, predicts that individuals react to specific age-related changes in their physical and psychological functioning in terms of the identity processes. This model was tested out in a study of nearly 250 adults ranging in age from 40 to 95 years (Whitbourne & Collins, 1998). Individuals who used identity assimilation with regard to these specific changes (i.e., they did not think about these changes or integrate them into their identities) had higher self-esteem than people who used identity accommodation (i.e., became preoccupied with these changes). A certain amount of denial, or at least minimization, seems to be important with regard to changes in the body and identity.

Later studies have examined the relationship between identity and self-esteem more generally and found self-esteem to be higher in people who use both identity balance and identity assimilation (Sneed & Whitbourne, 2003). Identity accommodation, by contrast, is related to lower levels of self-esteem throughout adulthood. However, men and women differ in their use of identity processes in that women use identity accommodation more than do men (Skultety & Whitbourne, 2004). In addition, some women who use identity assimilation may claim that they use identity balance to appear as though they are flexible and open to negative feedback when in reality, they prefer not to look inward and perhaps confront their flaws (Whitbourne et al., 2002).

That there may be an advantage to identity assimilation in terms of health and mortality was suggested by a fascinating analysis of self-perceptions of aging and longevity (Levy, Slade, Kunkel, & Kasl, 2002). Older adults who managed to avoid adopting negative views of aging (which may be seen as a form of identity assimilation) lived 7.5 years longer than those individuals who did not develop a similar resistance to accommodating society's negative views about aging into their identities. The advantage of denial against negative self-evaluations associated with aging (a form of identity assimilation) also was demonstrated in a long-term longitudinal investigation in which people who used denial had better psychological health (Cramer & Jones, 2007). Conversely, relying primarily on identity accommodation is associated with the experience of depressive symptoms (Weinberger & Whitbourne, 2010).

The tendency to use identity assimilation when thinking back on your life and how you have changed is a general bias that pervades the way people recall their previous experiences, a phenomenon known as the life story (Whitbourne, 1985). This tendency was demonstrated in one study investigating retrospective reports of personality change in a sample of nearly 260 men and women in their early 60s. Men, in particular, were likely to see themselves as having gained in such attributes as "confident power" between their 20s and 60s (Miner-Rubino, Winter, & Stewart, 2004).

Identity assimilation may also serve a protective function in other contexts in which older adults are faced with potentially negative information about their abilities. One group of researchers used a novel opportunity to study this process among older drivers referred to driver education classes due to a history of auto accidents. Those older drivers who overestimated their driving abilities became less depressed after receiving feedback about their actual driving abilities than older drivers who took a more pessimistic view of whether their driving abilities had changed (De Raedt & Ponjaert-Kristoffersen, 2006).

Throughout the book, as we have presented findings relevant to the identity process model, we have shown its relevance to a variety of topics pertaining to the ways in which adults perceive themselves as they develop through adulthood. This model attempts to highlight the importance both of individual differences in developmental processes and the need to take into account the ways in which individuals interpret their experiences as they get older. As personality research, with its focus on individual differences, continues to be integrated into studies within the field on topics as diverse as health, cognition, reactions to life events, and physical changes, greater understanding will be gained about how people vary in their reactions to the aging process. Such work will help further the development of the field in terms of biopsychosocial processes, leading both to a richer theoretical understanding of aging and practical implications for intervention.

MIDLIFE CRISIS THEORIES AND FINDINGS

The notion of the **midlife crisis**, derived from an age-stage approach to personality in adulthood, is a topic rooted in psychodynamic theory. Erikson's theory and, to a certain extent, Vaillant's, attempt to divide the years of adulthood into segments based on broad psychosocial issues. The midlife crisis approach emerged from this framework but took it much further by attempting to pinpoint specific psychological events occurring at specific ages; the most well known of these events is the midlife crisis.

Theory of the Midlife Crisis

It is safe to say that most people in contemporary American society are familiar with the term "midlife crisis." The topic of the midlife crisis has become a permanent fixture in popular psychology. A recent search of a popular commercial Web site revealed more than 100 books on the topic, and there is no sign of diminishing interest in the foreseeable future. The midlife crisis is commonly referred to in everyday speech and in the media, with books, magazine articles, and movies portraying the phenomenon, along with tips on how to survive it. It may therefore surprise you to learn that the concept is largely discounted in academic psychology. Despite the lack of supporting evidence, given the impact on the popular psyche, it is worth exploring the thinking and research that went into the original conceptualization of the midlife crisis.

The term midlife crisis originated in the early 1970s as a description of the radical changes in personality that supposedly accompanied entry into the midpoint of life (age 40 to 45). At this age, it was theorized, the individual is involved in extensive and intensive questioning of goals, priorities, and accomplishments. The prompt for this self-scrutiny, according to theory, was the individual's heightened awareness of the inevitability of death (Jaques, 1965).

The concept of the midlife crisis was first aired in the media when journalist Gail Sheehy (1974) published a best-selling paperback book called *Passages: Predictable Crises of Adult Life*. This book, which was based on a study being conducted at the time by Yale psychologist Daniel Levinson, described the supposed changes that occurred at each decade marker of adulthood. The years of the early 40s, according to this view, were marked by inner turmoil and outer acts of rebellion against the placid, middle-aged lifestyle into which the individual was destined to enter by the 50s.

Shortly after the publication of *Passages*, Levinson published his own best-seller called *The Seasons of a Man's Life*, which was a collaborative effort of a team of Yale psychologists, psychiatrists, and sociologists (Levinson, Darrow, Klein, Levinson, & McKee, 1978). This book focused exclusively on the experience of men in midlife through analysis of the interviews of 40 men ranging in age from the mid-30s to mid-40s. The men in the sample were intended to represent men from diverse backgrounds, with 10 from each of the following occupations: business executive, academic biologist, blue-collar worker, and novelist. In addition to these interviews, the authors included informal analyses of the biographies of famous men and the stories of men portrayed in literature.

The core of Levinson's theory of adult development is the **life structure**, defined as "the basic pattern or design of a person's life at a given time" (Levinson et al., 1978, p. 41). To analyze the individual's life structure, it is necessary to look at the sociocultural world, conscious and unconscious self, and participation in the world. Both central and peripheral themes can be identified in the life structure. These include family, work, friendship, religion, ethnicity, and leisure. According to Levinson and his colleagues, the life structure evolves through an orderly series of universal stages in adulthood. These stages alternate between periods of tranquility and periods of transition, and each stage has a specific focus. The stages and their associated ages are shown in Figure 8.9.

During periods of stability, the man builds his life structure around the decisions he made in the previous stage. If he chose to pursue a certain career

FIGURE 8.9

Stages of Adult Development According to Levinson

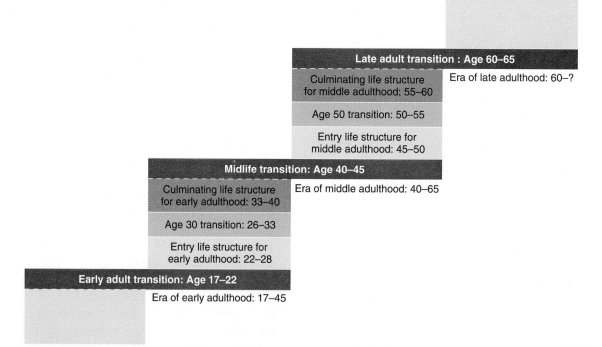

Levinson proposed that there are three important transitions in adulthood, with the midlife transition serving as the basis for the "midlife crisis."
Source: Levinson, D. J., Darrow, C. N., Klein, E. B., Levinson, M. H., & McKee, B. (1978). *The seasons of a man's life.* New York: Alfred A. Knopf.

path, he continues in that path throughout the period of stability. However, as the period reaches its close, the man becomes driven by both internal and external factors to question his previous set of commitments. For the next 4 or 5 years, during the transitional period that ensues, he explores different alternatives and seeks a new life structure or a modification of the existing one. Levinson believed that these transitional periods are inevitable. Choices are always imperfect, and as the outcome of one set of choices plays itself out, the individual begins to experience regrets and a desire for change. As stated by Levinson (p. 200), "no life structure can permit the living out of all aspects of the self."

The period called the midlife transition has a special quality compared to other transitional periods because it involves the most significant shift, from early to middle adulthood. As shown in Figure 8.9, the period of the midlife transition ("crisis") is targeted as 40 to 45. However, its beginning can occur anywhere between 38 and 43, and its ending can occur anywhere between the years of 44 to 47. This extends the period of the midlife crisis potentially to 9 years. This large time span allotted for the midlife crisis is but one of many problems with the theory, as it encompasses nearly the whole of the 40s. Nevertheless, returning to the substance of the midlife crisis, according to Levinson and colleagues, it is oriented around several themes.

The first theme of the midlife crisis is overcoming disillusionment due to failure to achieve the dreams of youth that inevitably cannot be fully realized. A new set of aspirations, more realistic ones, must be established. The second theme of the midlife crisis involves making decisions about how to pursue the life structure during middle adulthood. During this time, the man questions his marriage, comes to grips with the maturing of adolescent children, handles promotions or demotions at work, and reflects on the state of the nation and the world. He may begin to establish mentoring relationships with younger persons so that he may pass along the torch of what was handed to him during his early adulthood. Finally, the man must resolve the polarities of his personality involving masculinity and femininity, feelings about life and death, and the needs for both autonomy and dependence on others.

Although Levinson's theory predicts that the stage sequences are universal, it does allow for variations in progress through the late 30s that would affect the specific nature of the midlife crisis. In the most frequently observed pattern reported in the sample, a man advances steadily through a stable life structure but then encounters some form of failure. Usually, this need not be a catastrophic loss, such as getting fired or facing divorce, but it may be simply a perceived failure to achieve some particular desired goal by a certain age. For instance, he may not have won an award or distinction for which he was striving, such as the biologist who knows he will never win a Nobel Prize. Most people would not be distraught over such a "failure," particularly if they were generally well regarded in their profession or community. However, if this goal was part of an individual's "dream," it can lead to serious disappointment and self-questioning. Some men in the sample did in fact realize their dreams, others failed completely, and still others decided to change their life structures entirely out of boredom.

The characteristics of the midlife crisis are by now well known through their representation in contemporary literature, theater, movies, and song. For many people, they seem almost synonymous with the particular characteristics of the Baby Boomers, whom current society regards as being obsessed with aging, determined to stay young, and selfishly concerned with their own pleasure. However, as we mentioned before, Levinson regarded the midlife crisis to be a virtually universal process that has characterized human existence for at least 10,000 years.

In his subsequent publication on women, which was greeted with far less fanfare, Levinson claimed that similar alternations between change and stability characterize adult women (Levinson & Levinson, 1996). Other theories also emerged at about the same time as Levinson's, such as Gould's theory of transformations (Gould, 1978). Vaillant (1977) also temporarily espoused the midlife crisis concept but then renounced this view: "I believe transitions are merely by-products of development ... development creates transitions; transitions do not create development" (p. 163). Although Vaillant's view of adult development does depict the growth of the ego as occurring in stages, the midlife crisis is not one of them.

Critiques and Research on the Midlife Crisis

Apart from the original investigation by Levinson and colleagues, little empirical support has been presented for the existence of the midlife crisis as a universal phenomenon (Lachman, 2004). Even before the data were available, however, psychologists in the adult development field expressed considerable skepticism about the concept of the midlife crisis based on what at the time appeared to be extrapolation far beyond the available evidence (Brim, 1976; Whitbourne, 1986).

One of the most significant criticisms of the midlife crisis was the heavy reliance of Levinson's framework on age as a marker of development. On the one hand, Levinson and the other midlife crisis theorists were somewhat vague about exactly when the midlife crisis was supposed to occur. Was it 40 to 45, 38 to 47, or, as some had argued, at exactly age 43? The vagueness and fluidity of the age range is one type of weakness. People with any problems in their late 30s to almost 50 can claim that they are having a midlife crisis when things are not going their way in life. On the other hand, specificity of age 43 as the time of the event is another type of weakness because

This cartoon depiction of a middle-aged businessman illustrates the variety of issues supposedly confronting men as they go through the midlife crisis.

adults simply do not have such regularly timed events coinciding with a particular birthday.

In some ways, the Levinson (and Sheehy) approaches are like horoscopes, predicting that the calendar determines personality. People like reading their horoscopes because it gives them some ways to be able to impose seeming regularity onto the uncertain nature of life. However, the basis for these predictions is highly flawed. If horoscopes were valid, everyone with the same birth date (day, month, or year) would be the same, and clearly, this is not the case.

The Levinson study had other logical and theoretical problems. One was the nature of the original sample. Of the 40 men whose interviews formed the basis for the sample, one half represented the highly educated and intellectually oriented strata of society. Another one quarter of the sample consisted of successful business executives. The biased nature of this sample would not have been a problem if Levinson had not tried to generalize to the entire population (now and for all time). However, Levinson did make such extreme claims based on this highly educated, introspective, and financially privileged group of men. Their concerns, such as running companies, publishing novels, and competing for Nobel Prizes, are hardly those of the average man or woman.

A second theoretical problem has to do with the inspiration for the study and its source in the personal life of the investigator. Levinson was very clear in stating his own motivations for beginning the study: "The choice of topic also reflected a personal concern: at 46, I wanted to study the transition into middle age in order to understand what I had been through myself" (p. x). He speculated that perhaps the study's results reflected the "unconscious fantasies and anxieties" (p. 26) of himself and his middle-aged male colleagues. A third problem with the basis for the study was perhaps more technical. The process of rating the life stages was never clearly explicated. The usual standard procedures of establishing agreement among judges for rating interview material were not described. Furthermore, the interview questions were not published, so that the interviews themselves as well as the ratings were likely biased in the direction of proving the researchers' hypotheses. Given the many weaknesses in the study, it is understandable that other researchers subsequently were unable to replicate Levinson's findings.

One of the first empirical challenges to the midlife crisis concept came from the laboratories of McCrae and Costa, who used their extensive database on personality in adulthood to test predictions based on Levinson's theory (McCrae & Costa, 2003). They wanted to test specifically the possibility that a midlife crisis would be revealed with access to larger data sets and more comprehensive measures. When they plotted scores on the NEO scales by year across the supposed midlife crisis peak years, though, the scores were essentially flat; in fact, neuroticism was lower by a very small amount in the 43-year-olds.

Having explored this indirect approach, McCrae and Costa created a Midlife Crisis Scale and administered it to 350 men ages 30 to 60 years. Items on this scale concerned emotions thought to be related to the midlife crisis such as feelings of meaninglessness, turmoil, and confusion, job and family dissatisfaction, and fear of aging and death. If any questions had detected a midlife crisis, these surely would have. Yet they did not, either on the initial sample or in a different group of 300 men tested with a slightly shorter version (Costa & McCrae, 1978). The most telling data of all, however, emerged in this second study on the Midlife Crisis Scale. The data were from men participating in the Department of Veterans Affairs Normative Aging Study, one of the longitudinal personality investigations that eventually became part of the basis for the Five Factor Model. Men who had received higher scores on the neuroticism factor 10 years earlier were the ones who received higher scores on the Midlife Crisis Scale. This finding suggests that those with chronic psychological problems are more likely to experience a phenomenon such as the midlife crisis, not the average person.

So far, all the data contradicting the existence of the midlife crisis are from the laboratories of McCrae and Costa. There is ample documentation, however, from many other sources. One was a study conducted by the first author on nearly 100 adult men and women between the ages of 24 and 61 (Whitbourne, 1986). Extensive interview data were collected on identity and life histories. None of the participants, even those in their 40s, fit the criteria for a midlife crisis even when they were asked specifically about the impact of aging on their identities. A second study at around that time was conducted by another investigator on a sample of more than

FIGURE 8.10

Results of MIDUS Survey on the Midlife Crisis

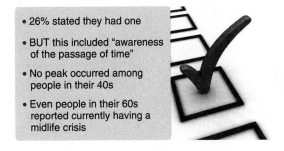

- 26% stated they had one
- BUT this included "awareness of the passage of time"
- No peak occurred among people in their 40s
- Even people in their 60s reported currently having a midlife crisis

300 men ranging from age 38 to 48, who completed survey questionnaires and semi-structured interviews in the years 1971–1974 (Farrell & Rosenberg, 1981). A smaller group of 20 men participated in a more intensive study involving further questionnaires, interviews, and even family interviews. Once again, however, the midlife crisis failed to appear either in the surveys or the interviews.

Looking broadly at data spanning early to late adulthood on trait-based personality measures, including those administered in the Mills study, the midlife crisis once again failed to be detected (Caspi & Roberts, 2001). Interestingly, in one of the Mills studies on women in midlife, the usual sort of factors that might be expected to trigger a midlife crisis among women did not have any effects on personality. Such potential triggers included menopause, having to care for parents, and being concerned about the children leaving the home. Having experienced these events did not lead to negative changes in personality as would be predicted from the midlife crisis theory (Helson & Wink, 1992).

More recently, the National Survey of Midlife Development in the United States (MIDUS) added another nail in the coffin to the midlife crisis concept (Wethington, Kessler, Pixley, Brim, & Ryff, 2004) (see Figure 8.10). The overall percentage of those who stated they had experienced a midlife crisis was 26%, more than the 10% previously reported in studies carried out in the 1980s (Wethington, 2000). However, the reason for this large percentage was the broad scope that respondents used to characterize the phenomenon. Respondents attributed to the midlife crisis such general phenomena as awareness of the passing of time. Even so, when categorized by age, there was no particular peak in the mid-40s, as would be expected. Some of the women in the sample even declared that the age of their midlife crisis was over 60, hardly considered "midlife" in the sense of being at the middle of life.

As a scientific concept, the midlife crisis simply fails to withstand multiple tests. By now you must surely be wondering why a concept so thoroughly debunked by the data continues to remain alive. Some argue that the idea of a midlife crisis makes a "good story" (Rosenberg, Rosenberg, & Farrell, 1999). People in their middle years, settled into stable patterns of both personality and social roles, find it exciting to think about getting that proverbial red sports car or leaving their jobs behind them and moving to some exotic new place. Sensational events such as hurricanes, tornadoes, and other disasters capture the attention of millions of television viewers. Similarly, the idea that personality is subject to major upheavals in the middle years may lead to the persistence of this phenomenon in the public mind far longer than warranted by the data. There also continue to be television and movie portrayals that capture the imagination of the midlife adult; one of the more recent examples was the short-lived 2010 television show "Men of a Certain Age" in which a group of three 50-something men acted out their midlife angst about their failed family, work, and emotional lives (the series only lasted for 10 episodes).

In summary, personality is characterized in multiple ways in psychology. Studying how personality develops over adulthood may lead to the realization that you need not become hardened into a rigid pattern of set dispositions. Change is possible throughout your life, if not in predictable stages, at least in ways that allow you to feel better about yourself as you grow older. As researchers explore relationships between health and personality, they will continue to provide greater understanding of how to maximize the chances of maintaining physical functioning as well.

SUMMARY

1. Studies of personality in adulthood are based on theories that attempt to define the nature and structure of personality. Within psychodynamic theory, ego psychology focuses on the role of the ego, the structure in personality that is theorized to perform the executive functions of personality. Ego psychologists include Erikson, Loevinger, and Vaillant. Several major longitudinal studies have provided tests of ego psychology theories. Psychosocial development from college to midlife was the focus of the Rochester Adult Longitudinal study, which also examined the relationship of life experiences to personality among men and women. In the Mills study, college women were followed using measures testing Erikson's and Loevinger's theories, as well as the interaction of personality and social context. The Vaillant study examined the use of ego defense mechanisms in three samples of adults. Coping and defense mechanisms have also been examined in several large national samples. Together the findings from this research suggest that through middle age and beyond, individuals become more accepting of themselves and better able to regulate their negative feelings. Social context also affects the course of development, and personality in turn affects the way individuals select and react to their experiences.

2. Attachment theory proposes that the earliest interactions with caregivers relate to adult personality and relationships. Studies on adult age differences in attachment style show that older adults are less likely to be anxiously attached and more likely to be dismissive compared with younger adults. However, the majority of adults are securely attached.

3. Socioemotional selectivity theory proposes that, over the course of adulthood, individuals select social interactions that will maximize the emotional rewards of relationships. Older adults appear better able than their younger counterparts to regulate negative affect.

4. Within the trait perspective, the Five Factor Model has stimulated a large body of longitudinal and cross-sectional studies on personality in men and women throughout the adult age range. There are also important individual differences in changes in personality over time, many of them related to health and behavioral risk patterns, such as the Type A behavior pattern.

5. Cognitive self theories propose that individuals view the events in their lives from the standpoint of the relevance of these events to the self. Identity process theory and the possible selves model fit into this category of theories.

6. According to the midlife crisis theory, there is a period in middle adulthood during which the individual experiences a radical alteration in personality, well-being, and goals. Midlife crisis theory was developed by Levinson and colleagues through an interview study of 40 adult males and has gained strong support in popular culture. However, subsequent researchers using a variety of empirical methods have failed to provide support for this theory, and it is generally disregarded within the field of adult development.

9

Relationships

Relationships with others are essential to one's existence throughout life. From intimate partners to family, friends, and the broader community, your social connections are a crucial part of who you are and how you feel on a day-to-day basis. It is difficult to capture the essential qualities and complexities of these many relationships, and it is perhaps even more challenging to study the way these relationships interact with developmental processes within the individual over time. Yet researchers must be able to translate that intuitive sense of the importance of relationships into quantifiable terms that can demonstrate the nature and impact of social processes in adulthood.

Changes in the broader society of the country and world heavily impact the nature of individual relationships. You can see from even brief glances at news stories in the media that patterns of marriage and family life change significantly with each passing year. In the United States at least, fewer people marry, and those who do are waiting longer than previous generations. Family composition changes as people leave and re-enter new long-term relationships, often involving children and extended families as well.

In this chapter, we examine these changing family patterns and try to provide an understanding of what theorists say about the qualities of close relationships and how they interact with the development of the individual.

MARRIAGE AND INTIMATE RELATIONSHIPS

The marital relationship has come under intense scrutiny in today's world. The union between two adults is thought to serve as the foundation of the entire family hierarchy that is passed along from generation to generation. You hear about the death of marriage as an institution, yet interest in marriage itself never seems to wane in the popular imagination, the media, and professional literature. The decision to marry involves a legal, social, and, some might say, moral commitment in which two people promise to spend the rest of their lives together. Furthermore, as the states in the United States arrive at positions on the legality of gay marriage, it seems clear that marriage is still a very relevant social institution.

Even as the definition of marriage continues to evolve, the statistics on its success rate prove to be as discouraging as ever for those who contemplate legalizing their own relationship with a partner. Given the current divorce statistics, you know that many people are not able to maintain the hopeful promises they make to each other in their wedding vows. What factors contribute to a successful marital relationship, and what might lead to its demise? Social scientists are nowhere near answers to these questions, but there are a plethora of theories as we shall see shortly.

Marriage

In the year 2009, 121.7 million adults were married and living with their spouse, a number that represents 50% of the population age 18 and older (see Table 9.1). Among the entire population 18 and older, the percent of those who have ever been married is far higher—approximately 74% of the population (U.S. Bureau of the Census, 2010d). The median age of marriage, 25.9 for women and 28.1 for men (U.S. Bureau of the Census, 2010e),

TABLE 9.1

Some Facts about Marriage

What is the...?	Fact
Percent in U.S. population currently married	50%
Percent married at least once by age 55	74%
Median age of marriage	Men = 28.1 Women = 25.9
Effect of marriage on mortality	9–15% reduction
Rates of marriage by race/ethnicity	Lowest (34%) Blacks Highest (62%) Asians

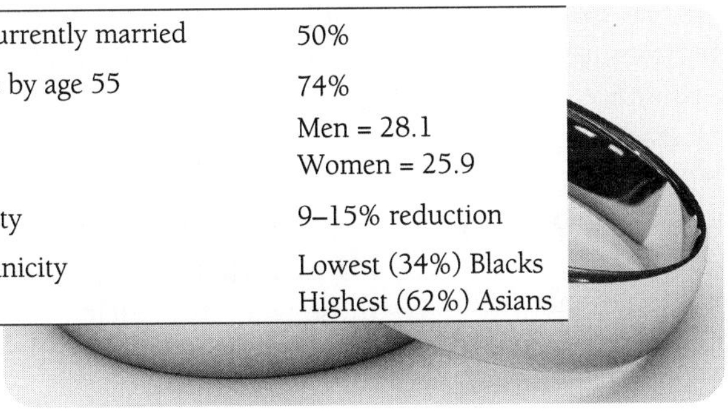

The wedding day is a momentous occasion celebrated by couples as the beginning of their new life together.

has steadily risen over the past decades as has the proportion of unmarried and never married adults (Goodwin, McGill, & Chandra, 2009). Among all adults 18 and older, over half of Whites (56%) are married. Asian-Americans (62%) are most likely to be currently married and living with a spouse, and Blacks (34%) the least (U.S. Bureau of the Census, 2010d).

As a social institution, **marriage** is defined as a legally sanctioned union between a man and a woman (in most U.S. states). People who are married often pay joint income tax returns and are given virtually automatic privileges to share the rest of their finances, as well as other necessities such as health care benefits and housing. They often share a last name, usually the husband's, although many wives never change their names. In the 1970s, couples began the practice of creating a new hyphenated last name, a trend that now appears to have decreased in popularity. Generally, marital partners are entitled to retirement, death, and health insurance benefits, as well as the entire portion of the estate when one partner dies. Although marriages need not legally conform to the statutes of a particular religion, they are often performed in a religious context.

Having explained the legal definition of marriage, you can clearly see what and who are excluded. People who are not legally married are not automatically entitled to the benefits available to those who are. Individuals living within a committed and long-term relationship not sanctioned by the law must seek exceptions to virtually all of the conditions that are set forth for married people. If these individuals are of the same sex and living within a committed homosexual relationship, they face additional barriers to the benefits granted to married persons.

Obviously, the legal definition of marriage includes no mention of the partners' emotional relationship with each other. People can be legally married and live apart, both literally and figuratively. Most social scientists distinguish between an intimate and a marital relationship because the two need not exist within the same couple. The legal commitment of marriage adds a dimension to an intimate relationship not present in a nonmarital close relationship in that ending a marital relationship is technically more difficult than ending a nonmarital one. Furthermore, many people view marriage as a moral and spiritual commitment that they cannot or will not violate.

Definitional concerns aside, there is a body of evidence on marriage in adulthood suggesting that married adults have many advantages compared with those who are unmarried. Researchers analyzing the findings of over 50 studies, including those based on more than 250,000 older adults from a variety of countries, showed a 9 to 15% reduction in mortality risk for married men and women (Manzoli, Villari, Pirone, & Boccia, 2007). This protective effect of marriage was greater in countries from Europe and North America compared to Israel and countries from Asia. Marriage also confers with it greater happiness and a variety of other benefits to the quality of life, a fact that came into question (particularly for women) in the 1980s, but now is accepted as well established (Wood, Goesling, & Avellar, 2007).

Among people 65 and older in the United States, there is a higher percentage of men (72%) than women (42%) married and living with a spouse (see Figure 9.1). Consequently, women over the age of 65 are about twice as likely (39%) as men (19%) to be living alone (Administration on Aging, 2009). Therefore, older women are at greater risk for some of the disadvantages that come with single status,

including fewer financial resources, less access to care, and lower social support.

Cohabitation

Living in a stable relationship prior to or instead of marrying is referred to as cohabitation. Since the 1960s, there has been a steady increase in the number of couples who choose this lifestyle. In 1960 an estimated 439,000 individuals in the United States reported that they were cohabitating with a person of the opposite sex. By 2009 this number was estimated at about 6.7 million (U.S. Bureau of the Census, 2010f). From 50 to 60% of all marriages are now preceded by cohabitation (Stanley, Amato, Johnson, & Markman, 2006); looking at the data on couples who cohabitate, approximately 28% of women 44 and under who cohabitate eventually marry their partner (National Center for Health Statistics, 2010).

FIGURE 9.1

Percent Married with Spouse Present

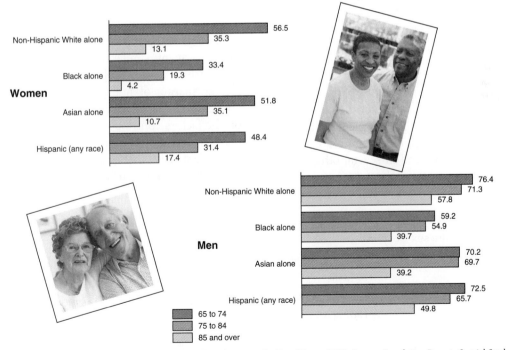

Source: He, W., Sangupta, M., Velkoff, V. A., & DeBarros, K. A. (2005). *65+ in the United States: 2005*. Current Population Reports Special Studies. U.S. Census Bureau, Current Population Reports, P23-209. Washington DC: U.S. Government Printing Office.

Though the commonsense wisdom is that the experience of living together contributes positively to the success of a marriage, the opposite seems to be true, at least in part. Data on divorce patterns show that there is a greater risk of marital breakup among people who cohabited before they became engaged. The greater likelihood of divorce among couples who cohabitate before they become engaged is referred to as the **cohabitation effect** (Cohan & Kleinbaum, 2002). One explanation for the cohabitation effect is that couples who would not have gotten married "slide" into marriage through inertia; in other words, the fact that they were already living together becomes the basis for entering into marriage even if the fit between the two partners is not all that good. Eventually they divorce due to the fact that they were not well matched at the outset. Not only are they more likely to divorce, but the people with this relationship history experience greater unhappiness during the period in which they remain under the same roof after their marriage (Rhoades, Stanley, & Markman, 2009).

Along with a rise in the overall number of couples who cohabitate is a parallel increase in the number of cohabitating adults with children under the age of 15. In 1960 this number amounted to 197,000, but by 2009 it was estimated to have increased greatly to the present estimated level of 2.6 million (U.S. Bureau of the Census, 2010d).

Same-Sex Couples

Gay marriage was first legalized in the United States by the Commonwealth of Massachusetts in 2004, and has since been legalized in several other states, including (at the current time) Vermont, Connecticut, the District of Columbia, Iowa, New Hampshire, and in the jurisdictions of several additional states. California, having legalized gay marriage through a state Supreme Court ruling in 2008, subsequently rejected its legality in a contentious 2008 ballot known as Proposition 8. Other U.S. states are considering similar legislation. Around the world, gay marriage is considered legal in seven countries, including Canada, Belgium, Norway, Spain, the Netherlands, Sweden, and South Africa. Clearly, based on the extent of debate about this issue in the United States and other countries, it is a topic that will remain on political agendas for the coming years (see Table 9.2).

As of 2009, 485,000 adults in the United States lived with a same-sex partner (Kreider, 2010); there are no data on same-sex married couples. The largest percentage (1.6%) of same-sex partners involves people of two or more races. San Francisco, Seattle, and Portland, Oregon, are the cities with the highest numbers of same-sex partnerships. It is estimated that 34% of lesbian couples and 22% of gay male couples who live together have children (Simmons & O'Connell, 2003).

In a comprehensive review of the characteristics of same-sex couples, Peplau and Fingerhut (2007) concluded that, compared with heterosexual couples, there are many similarities in the dynamics of the relationship. One notable exception, however, is a greater sharing of household tasks among lesbian and gay couples. Although there is little research on the factors contributing to the longevity of these relationships and partner satisfaction, the available evidence suggests that because most of the individuals living in these relationships are not legally bound to

TABLE 9.2
Some Facts about Same-sex Couples

What is the...?	Factual Information
Estimated number	594,000
Race/ethnicity	Most are people of two races
Percent with children	Lesbian = 34% Gay = 22%
Nature of relationship dynamics	Similar to heterosexual

FIGURE 9.2

Psychological Aspects of Divorce

FIGURE 9.2

Psychological Aspects of Divorce

- Practical consequences
- Child custody
- Lower psychological health
- Poorer health
- Problems with substance abuse
- More negative life events

each other, they are more likely to dissolve when the partnership is not working out. However, the majority of same-sex couples would prefer to legalize their relationship.

Divorce and Remarriage

Approximately 10% of the adult population in the United States is divorced (U.S. Bureau of the Census, 2010d). Taking into account all marriages that end in divorce, the average length of first marriage prior to divorce is about 8 years (Kreider, 2005). Divorce statistics also show important variations by race. Black women between the ages of 25 and 44 have higher divorce rates than White or Hispanic women (National Center for Health Statistics, 2010). Research on children of divorced parents suggests that for women, but not men, parental divorce is a stronger indicator of a lack of commitment and confidence in the marriage (Whitton, Rhoades, Stanley, & Markman, 2008).

Divorce rates have been declining since reaching a peak in 1980. Many factors are thought to account for this decreasing divorce rate. One is that people are marrying at later ages; the older a woman at marriage, the lower the probability that she will become divorced (Bramlett & Mosher, 2002). Second, the previously skyrocketing divorce rates increased consciousness in society about the need for prevention. Suggesting that such efforts can pay off, a study of over 2,200 households in the Midwest of the United States showed that couples who participated in premarital education had higher levels of marital satisfaction, lower levels of conflict, and reduced odds of divorce (Stanley et al., 2006). Research on second marriages suggests that couples are less likely to engage in premarital education compared with couples entering into first marriages; a trend linked to decreased marital happiness and increased rates of divorce (Doss, Rhoades, Stanley, Markman, & Johnson, 2009).

The dissolution of a marriage is ordinarily perceived by those involved as a disappointment and a sad if not tragic event (see Figure 9.2). One or both of the partners may be relieved to see the end of an unsuccessful relationship, but they are nevertheless affected in many ways by the inevitable consequences of the divorce on their daily lives, the lives of children, and the lives of extended family members. A range of practical issues must be resolved, such as changes in housing and financial affairs, but the greatest toll is the emotional one. For many couples, child custody arrangements present the most significant challenge caused by their altered status as a family.

Earlier we discussed the advantages of marriage in terms of benefits to health, financial security, well-being, and lifestyle. Studies on divorced (compared with married) individuals show that they have lower levels of psychological well-being, poorer health, higher mortality rates, more problems with substance abuse and depression, less satisfying sex lives, and more negative life events (Amato, 2000). The negative consequences of divorce are more severe for individuals who have young children, especially women (Williams & Dunne-Bryant, 2006). These effects may persist for many years, particularly for individuals who remain psychologically attached to their ex-partner, experience conflict in coparenting, or who have unusual difficulty in living on their own (Sweeper & Halford, 2006). Divorced or widowed adults who do not remarry are in poorer health (including chronic conditions and depressive symptoms) than those who remarry (Hughes & Waite, 2009). Divorce in older adults has negative effects on health in that newly divorced older adults experience more physical limitations in their daily lives (Bennett, 2006).

Although technically divorce rates in the population as a whole have declined, the media frequently cite the disturbing statistic that one out of every two marriages will end in divorce. However, the divorce statistics are much more complicated than this simple formula would imply. Those who divorce in a given year are generally not the same people as those who have gotten married, so the number of divorces cannot simply be compared with the number of marriages to determine the odds of divorcing. Furthermore, the divorce rate in any given year includes those people who are divorcing for a second or third time, people who tend to have a higher divorce rate than those who are getting a first divorce. Including these individuals in the divorce statistics artificially inflates the divorce rate for all marriages. Another factor influencing the divorce rate is the number of people in the population of marriageable age, which itself is influenced by birth and death rates. In the United States, approximately 18% of all marriages are second marriages, and 4% are third marriages. The average duration of a second marriage that ends in divorce is slightly longer than that of a first marriage—8 years for men and 9 years for women (Kreider, 2005). The probability of a second marriage ending in divorce after 10 years is .39, slightly higher than that of the ending of a first marriage, which is .33 (Bramlett & Mosher, 2002).

People who are more likely to contemplate divorce when their marriage is in trouble are said to be high on **divorce proneness.** These individuals are also more likely to have an extramarital affair (Previti & Amato, 2004). Those high in divorce proneness may have a long history of difficulties in the area of intimacy. Data from the first author's investigation described in Chapter 8 (the RALS) showed that women who in college had low intimacy scores were more likely to have divorced by their late 50s; the same was not true for men (Weinberger, Hofstein, & Whitbourne, 2008).

Approximately 1 million new children each year are affected by divorce, a figure that has remained constant since 1980 (U.S. Bureau of the Census, 1998). As difficult as it is for children to be caught in between parents who are divorced, it may be just as hard, if not harder, to be caught in between parents who are in a high-conflict marriage. In one longitudinal study of marriage, children 19 years of age and older were asked to state whether they felt they had been caught in between parental arguments. The children of parents whose marriages were characterized by a high degree of conflict felt most likely to be caught in the middle. Not surprisingly, these feelings were related to lower subjective well-being and poorer relationships with their parents. Thus, in some ways, the children were better off when their parents divorced than if they had remained together in an unhappy marriage (Amato & Afifi, 2006).

Among divorced couples, mediation is increasingly being seen as an effective means of reducing conflict and hence improving children's adjustment. Mediation is based on a model of cooperative dispute settlement rather than the more adversarial approach that occurs when lawyers become part of the scene. In one 12-year longitudinal study, divorced couples were randomly assigned to either mediation or legal assistance. Conflict significantly declined, particularly in the first year after divorce, among couples who participated in mediation (Sbarra & Emery, 2008).

Widowhood

When a marriage ends in the death of a partner, the survivor is faced with enormous readjustments in every aspect of life. Even when there is time to prepare, adjustment to widowhood is a difficult and painful process.

In the United States, currently there are approximately 14.3 million widowed adults ages 18 and older; 77% of these are 65 and older. The majority (81%) of the over-65 widowed adults are women. By the age of 85 and older, the majority of women are widows (76%), about double the rate for men (38%) (U.S. Bureau of the Census, 2010d). The highest rate of widowhood is among Black women 85 and older, among whom the large majority (87.5%) have lost their spouses (He, Sangupta, Velkoff, & DeBarros, 2005).

Adaptation to widowhood is influenced by the individual's previous psychological well-being. Those who adapt more readily are more likely to have higher well-being prior to the death of the spouse but in general, men seem particularly vulnerable to depression after the death of their wives (Bennett, Smith, & Hughes, 2005). Without remarriage, their levels of well-being may not return to preexisting levels even for as long as 8 years after the spouse has died (Lucas, Clark, Georgellis, & Diener, 2003). Among both men and women, anniversary reactions may continue for 35 years or longer following the spouse's death (Carnelley, Wortman, Bolger, & Burke, 2006).

In what is called the **widowhood effect**, there is a greater probability of death in those who have become widowed compared to those who are married (Manzoli et al., 2007), an effect that is stronger for men (Lee, DeMaris, Bavin, & Sullivan, 2001) (see Figure 9.3). People who become widows in later life also have a higher risk of suffering weight loss, a trend that is greater in Blacks (Umberson, Liu, & Powers, 2009). However, in neighborhoods with a high concentration of widows, the widowhood effect is reduced because, presumably, there are more opportunities for social interaction among clusters of widowed individuals (Subramanian, Elwert, & Christakis, 2008). Widows who receive positive support from their children 6 months after the death of their spouse report fewer depressive symptoms 18 months later (Ha, 2009).

Widows engage in behaviors that are potentially harmful to their health, particularly after recently becoming widowed. Some of these riskier behaviors include eating fewer fruits and vegetables, and more foods high in fat, and engaging in less physical activity. Longer-term widows are more likely to smoke (Wilcox et al., 2003). Women who remarry after becoming widows are favored in a number of ways over women who remain widows. The remarried have fewer depressive symptoms, worry less about money, and have higher incomes than women who remain widowed (Moorman, Booth, & Fingerman, 2006).

We will discuss more about widowhood from the perspective of bereavement in Chapter 13, focusing specifically on patterns of grief and adjustment over the transition from marriage to widowhood.

Psychological Perspectives on Long-Term Relationships

Throughout the vicissitudes of marriage, divorce, remarriage, and widowhood, most adults actively strive to maintain gratifying interactions with others on a day-to-day basis. Furthermore, for many adults,

FIGURE 9.3

The Widowhood Effect

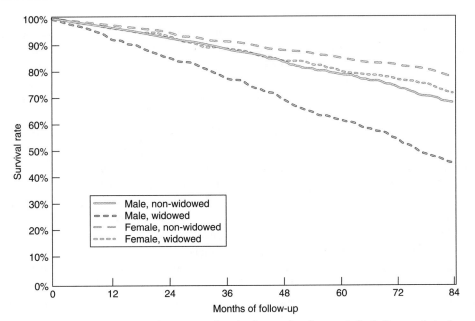

Age-adjusted survival rate for Mexican American men and women in widowed and non-widowed status; similar findings are obtained across racial and ethnic groups.

Source: Stimpson, J. P., Kuo, Y. F., Ray, L. A., Raji, M. A., & Peek, M. K. (2007). Risk of mortality related to widowhood in older Mexican Americans. *Annals of Epidemiology, 17,* 313–319.

TABLE 9.3
Perspectives on Long-term Relationships

Perspective	How Applied to Relationships
Socioemotional selectivity theory	Older couples experience more positive affect with each other
Social exchange theory	Relationships are evaluated according to costs and benefits
Equity theory	Balance is sought between what each contributes to the relationship
Marital similarity	Couples who are similar are happier
Need complementarity	Couples who are different are happier

the feeling of being part of a close relationship or network of relationships is the most salient aspect of identity (Whitbourne, 1986). Whether this relationship is called "marriage," "family," "friendship," or "partnership" is not as important as the feeling that one is valued by others and has something to offer to improve the life of other people.

Poets, philosophers, playwrights, and novelists, among others, have attempted for centuries to identify the elusive qualities of "love" (see Table 9.3). Although they have not been around for as long, psychologists and sociologists have also contributed their share of theories to account for why people develop close, loving, relationships and what factors account for their maintenance or dissolution over time.

The earliest sociological explanations of relationship satisfaction across the years of marriage attempted to relate the quality of marital interactions to the presence of children in the home and their ages. As relationships in the real world have seemed to become more complicated, however, so have the theories, and there is now greater recognition of the multiple variations that are possible when adults form close relationships. The emotional factors involved in long-term relationships are also gaining greater attention, as it is realized that some characteristics of human interactions transcend specific age- or gender-based boundaries.

Socioemotional selectivity theory, described in Chapter 8, implies that older adults would prefer to spend time with their marital partner (and other family members) rather than invest their energies in meeting new people. They should regard the long-term marital relationship as offering perhaps the most potential to serve emotional functions because their experience together over the years has allowed them

to understand and respond to each other's needs. Indeed, research suggests that older adults are more likely to keep sight of the positive aspects of their relationships even when they have disagreements (Story et al., 2007). In addition, if older adults are better able to control their emotions, particularly the negative ones, they should get along better with their partner because each is less likely to irritate the other one. Finally, because older adults do experience strong feelings, their affection for one another should not fade.

Attempts by sociologists and social psychologists to understand the dynamics of long-term relationships go back to the 1930s, when interest in marriage and the family had its formal beginnings as a field of inquiry. Some of the questions that researchers working in this tradition ask include the age-old puzzles involved in explaining why some relationships "work" and others do not. Early theories tended to focus on what now seem like simplistic notions such as whether "opposites attract" or whether, instead, "like attracts like" (later we will discuss these theories as they pertain to the quality of long-term relationships). Sociologists typically seek answers in examining factors such as socioeconomic status or geographic residence. Social psychologists are more likely to explore people's perceptions of themselves and others, as well as their ability to read interpersonal signals in relationships.

Social exchange theory attempts to predict the stability and dissolution of social relationships in terms of rewards and costs of an interaction. According to this theory, people continue in relationships when they perceive that the rewards of remaining in the relationship outweigh the rewards associated with its alternatives (Previti & Amato, 2003). The rewards of marriage include love, friendship, and feelings of commitment. If they believe the rewards outweigh the alternative of not being in that relationship, they will stay together. When considering a breakup, partners weigh the benefits of staying together against the barriers presented by legal, financial, social, and religious constraints. They might also take into account the presence of children. When the balance shifts so that rewards no longer outweigh the costs, one or both partners will initiate a breakup. Over time, exchange theory predicts that the intrinsic rewards of being in the relationship if not dependency on the partner increase to the point that the attractiveness of alternatives tends to fade.

In support of the notion of social exchange as a factor in relationship formation, researchers find that the earning potential of young women is becoming more important in determining their desirability as mates. With women making strides in the labor market, their income is now being seen by husbands as an important asset in their own movement up the occupational career ladder (Sweeney & Cancian, 2004).

It is not always obvious, though, what factors will be seen as assets when contemplating involvement with a new partner. Although women may cite earning potential and men state physical attractiveness as characteristics of an ideal mate, a study assessing speed dating and subsequent meetings found that these characteristics were not enough to predict romantic interest (Eastwick & Finkel, 2008).

However, there are still some very traditional determinants of what makes men happy, at least in the early years of marriage. In a 3-year longitudinal study of characteristics important in a mate, men were found to place higher value on good looks, a pleasing disposition, and a dependable character over time rather than financial prospect or favorable social status (Shackelford, Schmitt, & Buss, 2005).

For cohabiting couples, at least, sexuality seems to follow the principles of social exchange theory. In one study, comparisons of relationship dissolution among cohabiting and married couples showed that cohabitators were more likely to end relationships characterized by low frequency of sexual intercourse. Presumably, those who are cohabiting perceive fewer barriers to ending a relationship if the sexual dimension of the relationship no longer proves to be satisfactory (Yabiku & Gager, 2009).

Another theory with economic overtones is **equity theory**, in which the cost–benefit analysis in the relationship occurs specifically when evaluating the benefits that each partner brings to the relationship (Walster, Walster, & Berscheid, 1978). Do I benefit more than you do or is the opposite the case? According to equity theory, people become increasingly dissatisfied when the partners perceive that

AGING IN THE NEWS

www.wiley.com/college/whitbourne   **OLDER ADULTS WHO MADE THE HEADLINES**   -VOL. 4, CHAPTER 9-

GRANNY DJ ROCKS PARIS NIGHTCLUB

DJ Ruth Flowers is a 69-year-old disk jockey who spins at the most prestigious nightclubs in Paris. From Bristol, Flowers began playing at the age of 65, after wandering into her grandson's birthday party. She enjoyed seeing the kids have fun and decided that she could do that herself. Flowers, a trained singer, said it took her four years to learn to use the machines. French producer Aurelien Simon, who taught her how to spin, said: "I explained the basics of electro music, and then she created her own style." Flowers' sets mix techno and dance peppered with rock by the likes of Queen and the Rolling Stones. She is currently working on her first single and has no plans to retire.

there is some form of imbalance in how much each brings to the relationship. As their feelings of inequity grow, commitment to the relationship also decreases (Sprecher, 1988). Eventually a dwindling relationship commitment leads to a greater likelihood of ending it (Floyd & Wasner, 1994). Equity theory seems to apply particularly well to people in the early stages of a relationship when couples are deciding whether or not to build further ties with each other (Hatfield, Rapson, & Aumer-Ryan, 2008).

The **behavioral approach to marital interactions** emphasizes the actual behaviors that partners engage in with each other during marital interactions as an influence on marital stability and quality (Karney & Bradbury, 1997). According to this perspective, people will be more satisfied in a long-term relationship when their partners engage in positive or rewarding behaviors (such as expressing affection). Punishing or negative behaviors (such as criticism or abuse) decrease satisfaction (Gottman, Coan, Carrere, & Swanson, 1998). Not surprisingly, high levels of hostility expressed by partners also contribute to unhappy relationships (Matthews, Wickrama, & Conger, 1996). Couples may also be mismatched in their conflict styles. When one partner's style is avoidant and the other's is highly reactive or volatile, for example, it is unlikely that their interactions during disagreements will be satisfactory to either person (Busby & Holman, 2009).

One of the most interesting and important studies of relationship satisfaction was carried out by Gottman and his colleagues over a 14-year period. The researchers attempted to determine who would stay together and who would divorce, and when. You might liken this study to a very long but systematically carried out reality series in which behavioral ratings were made of couples over the course of the study. Couples whose marriages were described as "passionless" (that is, they showed neither positive nor negative affect) ultimately stayed married longer than couples who were more volatile emotionally during the early married years, who tended to divorce earlier. However, an emotionally bland relationship was a high risk factor for the relationship's ending. Emotional volatility is not necessarily desirable, but neither is a complete lack of positive affect (Gottman & Levenson, 2000; Gottman & Levenson, 2002).

Looking into the dynamics of a couple's behavioral interactions, Gottman and his colleagues found that the building blocks of intimacy lie in what they called "bids" for connection with the partner. Conflict increases when a partner either turns away from or turns against a partner who is trying to make an emotional connection. Women seemed particularly sensitive to the effect of their bids for connection because the husband's response to his wife played a stronger role in escalating or deescalating conflict than did her response to him (Gottman & Driver, 2005).

Conflict is detrimental not only to the relationship but also to the health of each partner. Higher physiological levels of stress, measured in terms of cortisol levels, are associated with the "wife demand husband withdraw" pattern of communication in resolving conflicts (Heffner et al., 2006). You might expect that couples habituate to these high levels of stress. However, researchers investigating the impact of marital discord on various measures of well-being found that even for individuals in their later years, couples who were constantly in conflict with each other suffered higher levels of depression and anxiety, and lower levels of self-esteem and life satisfaction (Whisman, Uebelacker, Tolejko, Chatav, & McKelvie, 2006).

Earlier we alluded to sociological theories that examine whether "like attracts like" or whether it is truer that "opposites attract" when it comes to who pairs up with whom. Here we will take a look at what these theories say about long-term relationships. According to the **need complementarity hypothesis**, people seek and are more satisfied with marital partners who are the opposite of themselves (Winch, 1958). Despite the anecdotal evidence you may have about this viewpoint from observing your extraverted cousin happily engaged to a shy introvert, the evidence seems to favor the opposite point of view.

The **similarity hypothesis** proposes that similarity of personality and values predicts both initial interpersonal attraction and satisfaction within long-term relationships (Gaunt, 2006). Sometimes the similarity may be more apparent than real, however. In one 13-year longitudinal study of marital relationships, researchers found that couples who perceived each other as higher in agreeableness than they actually were in reality were more in love during the early stages of marriage and more likely to remain in love over time (Miller, Niehuis, & Huston, 2006). Partner perceptions also play a role in marital satisfaction, particularly for wives; if they perceive their husband as being supportive, they rate their satisfaction with their marriage as higher (Priem, Solomon, & Steuber, 2009).

FAMILIES

The transformation of a marriage into a "family" traditionally is thought to occur when a child enters the couple's life on a permanent basis. Most of the psychological literature on children and families focuses not on the parents but on the children and their adjustment to the various arrangements for living worked out by their parents (Hetherington & Kelly, 2002). Here, we will examine areas of research specific to studies of adult development and aging.

Family Living Situations

Despite population trends toward more single-parent and cohabiting families, the large majority of households in the United States (77%) consist of people living together as a family. In the United States, the average household size is 2.57 people. Households with married couples constitute 53.6% of all households (U.S. Bureau of the Census, 2010d).

Changes in the family living situation in recent decades are often discussed in terms of **blended families**, also known as reconstituted families. Within these family situations, at least one adult is living with a child who is not a biological child of that adult. Often these family situations develop after a divorce and remarriage (or cohabitation) in which two adults establish a household together. The dynamics within these relationships, though the subject of many fictional accounts, are only beginning to receive empirical attention in the literature. Some evidence suggests that these relationships are more stressful in the case of mothers and stepchildren than between fathers and stepchildren (Ward, Spitze, & Deane, 2009).

The Transition to Parenthood

Much of the family literature focuses on the period in which a first child is born, the so-called **transition to parenthood**. From a biopsychosocial perspective, this event involves biological changes (when the mother bears the child) as her body adapts to rapid hormonal and other physiological alterations. Psychological changes include the emotional highs and lows associated with first-time parenthood for both parents. In addition, the individual's identity begins to incorporate the concept of being a parent during this crucial phase. Social changes involve the new role that adults acquire when they become parents, altering their status with other family members and the community. At the sociocultural level, there are also changing social expectations for parents, expectations that typically reflect social norms for men and women as fathers and mothers. Clearly, once the transition occurs, parenthood continues to make a multifaceted impact on the individual. Although biological factors recede in importance, psychological effects and social changes continue, in effect, for the rest of the individual's life.

Approximately 4.3 million women in the United States give birth each year. In the United States in 2006, 75% of all children were born to mothers between the ages of 20 and 34 years old (National Vital Statistics System, 2010). In 2008, the number and rate of births fell from its high point reached in 2007, reflecting the downturn in the economy. The exception to this overall trend was among women in their 40s who may have felt that despite the poor economic times, they could not wait longer to have a child (Hamilton, Martin, & Ventura, 2010).

Much of the literature on parenthood and its effects on adults is based on studies of the transition to parenthood within traditional two-parent families. The logic behind such research is that the most significant changes take place during this crucial time as the couple adjusts to its newest member of the family.

The original impetus for studies on the transition to parenthood was provided by the consistent finding based mainly on cross-sectional studies showing that marital satisfaction dips during the child-rearing years, a drop-off particularly marked for women. To a certain extent, the overall data still support this trend, including a recent longitudinal study of couples with and without children studied over an 8-year period prior to the time that the eventual parents first knew they were expecting. Following the birth of the child, new parents displayed steeper rates of relationship decline compared with couples without children (Doss, Rhoades, Stanley, & Markman, 2009).

However, it has long been known that although it is a stressful time, not all couples experience a decrease in relationship satisfaction, with the birth of the first child (Bradbury, Fincham, & Beach, 2000) (see Figure 9.4). There can be compensating factors as well from the pleasure derived in coparenting, particularly when the prebirth marital relationship was high (Van Egeren, 2004). When wives do become less satisfied with their marriage, it is largely because the birth of the child carries with it changes in the allocation of household tasks.

<u>FIGURE 9.4</u>

Predictors of Women's Satisfaction During the Transition to Parenthood

- "Doing gender"
- Attachment style
- Self-efficacy toward being a parent
- Expectations and feelings of competence

Typically, the division of labor in the home becomes more traditional after children are born. Working women without children already perform more household duties than men do, but after becoming mothers, the situation is exacerbated (Coltrane, 2000). Mothers assume more of the stereotypically female roles of performing household duties such as laundry, cooking, and cleaning, in addition to providing the bulk of the child care. Men increase their involvement in paid employment outside the home after the child enters the family (Christiansen & Palkovitz, 2001). In part, these changes reflect policies in the workplace as well as the beliefs that couples have about how family responsibilities should be equitably divided (Singley & Hynes, 2005).

In some cases, marital satisfaction is affected by the process referred to as **doing gender**. When the woman earns more money than her husband, this sets up a dynamic that violates normative expectations (Bittman, England, Sayer, Folbre, & Matheson, 2003). Rather than doing 50% or less of the housework, the wife actually takes on the majority of household duties, in the process enacting traditional gender expectations for women. If the woman perceives the share of the labor as unfair, the stage is set for both she and her husband to become psychologically more distressed (Grote, Clark, & Moore, 2004).

Women who are more likely to ease into their new roles as mothers tend to have other psychological characteristics. They will be happier during the transition if they enjoy performing family work, are oriented toward family in terms of their overall life goals, feel that they are particularly good in their new role, and do not view the unequal division of labor as unfair (Grote, Naylor, & Clark, 2002; Salmela-Aro, Nurmi, Saisto, & Halmesmaeki, 2001).

What about the situation in same-sex couples? Do they also change in their perception and enactment of household roles? In one short-term longitudinal study of lesbian women becoming first-time parents (Goldberg & Sayer, 2006), researchers observed similar patterns. Feelings of love tend to decrease and the amount of conflict tends to increase across the parenthood transition. As is also true with heterosexual couples, lesbian couples report that they have less time to spend with each other and are stressed by the new roles they have taken on as parents.

Attachment style may also play a role in influencing the adjustment that a woman makes to parenthood. Among a sample of 106 couples becoming first-time parents, women with ambivalent attachment styles became less satisfied with their marriages if they believed that their husbands no longer supported them emotionally. Their perceptions of support from husbands decreased further over time if they entered motherhood already having felt that their husbands were not providing them with the support they needed (Simpson & Rholes, 2002).

Early experiences with their own parents, or at least the recall of these experiences, may also influence adjustment through the transition to parenthood. In one study, interviews with couples becoming first-time parents revealed that if they recalled the marriages of their own parents as unhappy, their evaluation of their own marital quality was also more negative (Perren, Von Wyl, Bürgin, Simoni, & Von Klitzing, 2005). In a related investigation, couples who recalled their parents as having gotten along well were better able to maintain positive patterns of communication over the transition period (Curran, Hazen, Jacobvitz, & Sasaki, 2006).

Studying married couples over the 24 months following the birth of a child, another group of researchers found that fathers with insecure attachment styles had more negative interactions when the couple had experienced a high number of negatively escalating arguments. Unhealthy family alliances, in which one parent joined forces with a child against another parent, were more likely to occur in negatively escalating arguments when one parent was insecurely attached (Paley et al., 2005).

What are some of the factors that can lead to positive outcomes? In one investigation of pregnant women who were followed through motherhood, women who had high self-efficacy and were optimistic about their parenting role tended to weather the transition more favorably. After becoming mothers they experienced fewer depressive symptoms than women with lower expectations and feelings of competence about their role. In fact, for the majority of women in the study, the bonding with their infant and enjoyment of their new role allowed them to feel good about the experience of becoming a mother, effects that persisted for at least 4 months into the postpartum period (Harwood, McLean, & Durkin, 2007).

Fatherhood is increasingly being studied as an aspect of identity in adulthood reflecting, in part, the increasing role of fathers in the raising of their children (Marsiglio, Amato, Day, & Lamb, 2002). Becoming a first-time father can significantly influence a man's patterns of interaction outside the home. A 7-year longitudinal study of nearly 3,100 fathers of children under the age of 18 described the "transformative" process that occurs as new fathers become more involved with their own parents, grandparents, and other relatives. Fathers also become more involved with service-oriented groups and church. These effects occur along with the birth of each child, but are particularly pronounced at the time of the first child's birth (Knoester & Eggebeen, 2006).

The extent to which a single father is able to adjust to the role of solo parent is affected by the characteristics of the children, including their age and gender, and his own characteristics, including his age and educational level. The father's adjustment to this role is also affected by his ability to juggle the demands of parent and worker and maintain a relationship with his ex-wife or partner, as well as by his original desire to have custody (Greif, 1995). Overall, however, single fathers spend less time caring for their children than do single mothers, but more than do married fathers (Hook & Chalasani, 2008).

The Empty Nest

We have examined the factors that influence the transition of a couple that occurs when their first child is born. Now we will take a look at what happens during the reverse process, when the couple's children depart the home, a phenomenon referred to as the **empty nest**.

With the children gone from the home, couples potentially have the opportunity to enjoy more leisure-time activities together, a change that should bring them closer together (Gagnon, Hersen, Kabacoff, & Van Hasselt, 1999). For many years, though, the common belief was that the empty nest would be an unwelcome change, particularly for women. Although in fact women are not more likely to experience depressive symptoms when their last child moves out of the home, there are cultural variations in reactions to the empty nest (Mitchell & Lovegreen, 2009).

The positive feelings that parents experience with the departure of their youngest child include a sense of personal growth, more leisure time, improved marital relations, and feelings of mastery. These feelings may contribute to some of the reports of improved sexual relations in later life. An intensive study of a small sample of Canadian women married after the age of 50 found a shift away from an emphasis on sexual intercourse to greater valuing of other expressions of intimacy, such as cuddling, companionship, and affection. These women still felt that they had strong sexual chemistry with their husbands, even though the expression of that chemistry had changed from the passion of youth (Hurd Clarke, 2006).

Perhaps for these reasons, the empty nest may have some advantages in helping keep a couple's sexual relationship alive. When children do return home for whatever reason, the quality of a couple's sexual relationship may decline at least in terms of frequency of sexual activities (Dennerstein, Dudley, & Guthrie, 2002). In fact, a survey of more than 15,000 midlife Canadian women showed that the predictors of sexual activity within the past 12 months included age, marital status, race, income, alcohol use, smoking, and empty nest status (Fraser, Maticka-Tyndale, & Smylie, 2004). Women whose children were still living in the home were less likely to have intercourse than women who were empty nesters.

As these studies indicate, older individuals are able to maintain enjoyable sexual relations well into their later years (see Figure 9.5). Although physiological factors clearly play a role, as described in Chapter 4, the individual's interest in sexuality and

FIGURE 9.5

Percent of Older Men and Women Who Had Intercourse in the Previous Year

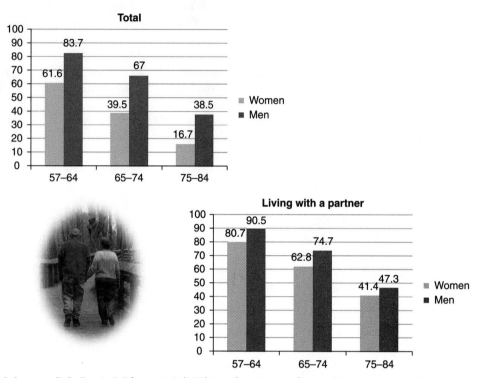

Source: Waite, L. J., Laumann, E. O., Das, A., & Schumm, L. P. (2009). Sexuality: Measures of partnerships, practices, attitudes, and problems in the National Social Life, Health, and Aging Study. *Journals of Gerontology Series B: Psychological Sciences and Social Sciences, 64* Supplement 1, 156–166.

availability of partners are more significant factors in keeping the sexual flames alive well after they have become grandparents (DeLamater & Sill, 2005).

Adult Parent–Child Relationships

When children move through the years of adulthood, there are many facets of relationships with their own parents that undergo change. For example, as children have their own families, they begin to gain greater insight into the role of being a parent. On the one hand, the children may now appreciate what their parents did for them, but on the other hand, they may resent their parents for not having done more. Another changing feature of the relationship stems from the child's increasing concern that parents will require help and support as they grow older. Adult children and their parents may also find that they do not agree on various aspects of life, from an overall philosophy and set of values (such as in the area of politics) to specific habits and behaviors (such

as methods of food preparation). Whether parents and their adult children live in the same geographic vicinity and actually see each other on a frequent basis must also be added into the equation.

Parent–child relationships maintain their importance throughout life (Allen, Blieszner, & Roberto, 2000) (see Table 9.4). The majority of adult children (56%) state that they feel close to their parents. Another large group (38%) see their relationships as ambivalent. Fortunately only a small minority (6%) see them as problematic (Fingerman, Hay, & Birditt, 2004).

For older adults, adult parent–child relationships can play a vital role in well-being, particularly with regard to the development of generativity, and particularly for women (An & Cooney, 2006). Aging parents who have good relationships with their adult children are less likely to feel lonely or depressed (Koropeckyj-Cox, 2002). At the same time, adult children who retain strong attachment ties to their parents also experience psychological benefits (Perrig-Chiello & Höpflinger, 2005).

Although the empty nest is viewed as the norm when discussing adult children and their parents, there are a growing number of adult sons and daughters living with their parents (ages 25 to 34 years old), a situation referred to by the slang term "boomerang" children in the United States and "Kids in Parents' Pockets Eroding Retirement Savings" (KIPPERS) or "kidults" in the United Kingdom. In part, the return of children back into the empty nest is associated with the economic downturn of the late 2000s (Palmer, 2009).

Movies such as "Failure to Launch" parody the dynamics of adult children living with their parents, but there is surprisingly little research on the topic. One Canadian survey reported cultural differences in the tendency of parents and young adult children to live together, with Asian and Latin American born parents most likely to host their 20- to 24-year-old children (Turcotte, 2006). Although parents with live-in children were more likely than parents whose children did not live at home to experience feelings of frustration over the time spent taking care of their adult children, the percentage of these negative feelings was very low (8% with live-in children versus 4% whose children did not live at home). The parents of children living at home also reported more conflict about money, the children themselves, and the distribution of labor in household responsibilities.

The situation seems more negative with boomerang children compared with children who had never left the home, particularly as mothers are likely to resent the fact that they are losing some of the freedom they gained when their children initially left the home. These parents are less likely to say that their children made them happier (57%) than the parents of non-boomerang children (68%). On the other hand, a larger percentage of parents of children living at home (64%) say they are satisfied with the amount of time spent with their offspring than are parents whose children had moved out (49%).

In some unfortunate instances, the lines of communication break down considerably and the result is an emotional gap known as a **developmental schism** (Fingerman, 2001), applying usually to mothers and daughters. One manifestation of the developmental schism is the mother's tendency to regard her daughter as more important than the daughter does the mother and for the daughter to regard the mother as more intrusive than the mother does the daughter. Mothers are also more likely to regard their daughters as confidants than daughters do their mothers. Another contributor to the developmental schism occurs when the daughter still seeks the approval of the mother and feels guilty when she feels that she is not living up to her mother's expectations for her. Because parents have more stake in the relationship than do children, when conflicts occur, parents are more likely than are their children to try to resolve conflicts using constructive strategies in which they attempt to maintain and build a positive relationship (Birditt, Rott, & Fingerman, 2009).

The term **role reversal** is occasionally encountered in the professional as well as the popular literature on the parents of adult children. According to this view, which is discredited among gerontologists, parents and their adult children switch responsibilities. The child becomes the parent when the parent undergoes physical, cognitive, and social changes. The concept is no longer considered valid because there is a great deal of data showing that most adult children and their parents have reciprocal relationships and that the flow of help goes in two directions (Blieszner, 2006). Unfortunately, however, the idea

TABLE 9.4
Concepts in Adult Parent–Child Relationships

Concept	Meaning
Developmental schism	Emotional gap between parents and children
Role reversal	Discredited view that parents and children switch roles
Filial maturity	Developmental changes in children
Filial anxiety	Worry about being forced to take on care of parents
Filial obligation (piety)	Feeling of commitment that the child should care for the parent

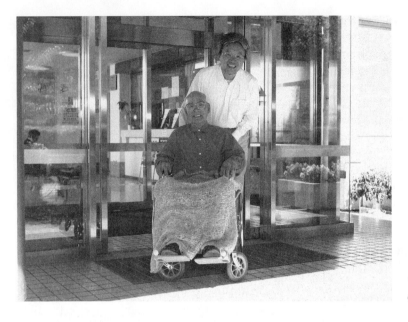

This son assisting his father may be expressing a sense of filial obligation.

that parents become their children's children is still prevalent in societal views of aging.

Children do undergo developmental changes that alter their relationships with parents, a concept referred to as **filial maturity** (Blenkner, 1963). During early adulthood, but particularly in the 30s, children begin to relate to their parents in a different way than they did when they were younger. By taking on the responsibilities and status of an adult (employment, parenthood, involvement in the community), the adult child begins to identify with the parent. Over time, the relationship may change as a consequence of this process, and parents and children relate to each other more like equals (Fingerman, 1996).

The prospect of being forced to take on the role of parent to the parent, even though it may never come to pass, creates a certain amount of concern and worry in the adult child. This fear of having to take care of the parent is referred to as **filial anxiety** (Cicirelli, 1988). People living in the United States and other Western industrialized nations are most likely to experience filial anxiety because prevailing social values stress independence and the nuclear family. In other cultures, notably Hispanic, Asian, and Black American, children have an attitude of **filial obligation** or **filial piety**, meaning that they feel committed to taking care of their parents should this become necessary. There are long-established traditions within Black (Wilson, 1986) and Hispanic (Keefe, Padilla, & Carlos, 1979)

families to define the extended family rather than the nuclear family as the basic family unit. Similarly, the norm in Asian cultures is for parents to live with their children (Velkoff & Lawson, 1998), although modernization, at least in China, may be eroding this cultural norm (Cheung & Kwan, 2009).

The potential difficulties between adult children and their parents, particularly for women, are thought to rise to the point of crisis when there is the need to provide **caregiving** to the parent. Caregiving, which we discussed in Chapter 5, consists of providing assistance in carrying out the tasks of everyday life to an infirm older adult. A large body of evidence has accumulated on this topic since the early 1980s, most of it cross-sectional. Based on this research, it was considered a foregone conclusion that the caregiving role was a traumatic one for the adult child. The daughters in this situation, referred to as "women in the middle" or the **sandwich generation** (sandwiched between their aging mothers and their teenaged children), were thought to be victims of extreme stress due to their caregiver burden. However, it appears that this label only applies to one third of later midlife women (ages 55–69) (Grundy & Henretta, 2006).

One factor that appears to play a role in reducing caregiving burden is that, consistent with exchange theory, monetary rewards in the form of an expected inheritance can balance out feelings of resentment toward aging parents (Caputo, 2002). The extent to which parents provided children with financial support when the children were younger also has an effect on the later social support provided by children of their aging parents (Silverstein, Conroy, Wang, Giarrusso, & Bengtson, 2002). Here again, though, countering the notion of role reversal, the likelihood is far greater that parents provide financial support to their adult children than vice versa (Van Gaalen & Dykstra, 2006). Even when daughters are in the caregiving role for their parents, their feelings of obligation often are tempered by gratitude for the help that the parents provided when the daughter's own children were young (Keefe & Fancey, 2002).

Among siblings there is a tendency to try to equalize the sense of shared responsibility, if not in reality then in the way that the situation is perceived (Ingersoll-Dayton, Neal, Ha, & Hammer, 2003). Caregiving stress can also be reduced by the provision of help by others in the family. Despite the belief that one child (the daughter) has sole responsibility for caregiving, spouses tend to share caregiving roles even when in dual-earner situations (Henz, 2010).

When parents do experience declines in health, it seems that the norms of filial responsibility lead to mutual adaptations between children and parents (Silverstein, Gans, & Yang, 2006). One in-depth study of a small group of adult children highlighted the concern that children had for respecting the

autonomy of their parents within the context of filial responsibility (Funk, 2010). In other words, children wanted to take care of their parents but not impinge on their independence either.

Rather than being a universally negative experience, then, caregiving may not present as traumatic a situation for middle-aged daughters as is often portrayed in the media. Although women in this age group face many demands on their time, they are also likely to be able to draw on other sources of help and emotional support.

A model incorporating the various dimensions present in the adult child–parent relations is the **intergenerational solidarity model** (Bengtson & Schrader, 1982; Silverstein & Bengtson, 1997). According to this model (see Figure 9.6), six dimensions characterize the cohesiveness of family relationships: distance apart, frequency of interaction, feelings of emotional closeness, agreement in areas such as values and lifestyles, exchanges of help, and feelings of obligation.

In research based on this model, the frequency of parent–child relationships was found to vary considerably according to the gender of the parent. Five types of relationships were identified: sociable, tight-knit, obligatory, detached, and intimate but distant. The most common type of mother–child relationship was tight-knit, and the most common

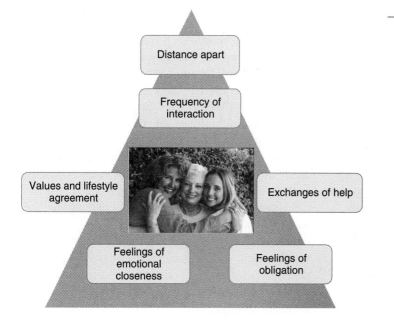

FIGURE 9.6

The Six Dimensions of the Intergenerational Solidarity Model

Distance apart

Frequency of interaction

Values and lifestyle agreement

Exchanges of help

Feelings of emotional closeness

Feelings of obligation

father–child relationship was detached. Thus, there appears to be greater intergenerational solidarity between mothers and adult children than between fathers and their children.

An extension of the intergenerational solidarity model to a German sample of adult daughters revealed further insights into adult parent–child relationships. Women who felt that they gave more to their mothers than they received felt less closely connected to them both in terms of intimacy and in terms of their admiration for them. In other words, daughters seemed to expect and desire more of a balanced relationship between their mothers and themselves. When the balance was off-kilter, the relationship suffered. In general, the model had greater applicability to daughter–mother relationships than to daughter–father relationships (Schwarz, Trommsdorff, Albert, & Mayer, 2005).

The intergenerational solidarity model was initially based on ratings of relationship quality by individuals within different generations of the same family. Researchers in the Netherlands decided to approach their study of intergenerational families with a set of more behavioral criteria. They rated how often parents and children saw each other, how much help was exchanged, and whether conflict was experienced over material and personal issues. On the basis of these behavioral indicators, the researchers identified five types of parent–child relationships: harmonious, ambivalent, obligatory, affective, and detached. The largest percentage (40%) consisted of harmonious relationships, but the second largest group consisted of ambivalent parent–child ties (29%). Relationships with mothers were more likely to be harmonious than relationships with fathers, and relationships with daughters more likely to be ambivalent than those with sons. Sons and fathers were more likely to have obligatory ties than were mothers and daughters (Van Gaalen & Dykstra, 2006).

Clearly, family relationships are multifaceted and complex, and the larger and more complex the family, the more complex the dynamics. Moreover, as most people know from their own experiences, family relationships rarely are simply "good" or "bad." The advantage of a multidimensional model is that it provides a way to try to establish order in viewing and understanding these relationships.

SIBLINGS

So far, we have looked at cross-generational relationships. The sibling relationship has many unique features within the constellation of family interactions (Van Volkom, 2006). Those who are siblings by birth share a genetic background, and those who have been raised together share many experiences dating to early childhood. By the time siblings reach later adulthood, it is quite possible that they are the only remaining members of their original family and that they have known each other longer than anyone else they have known in their entire lives. As is true for adult child–parent relationships, the sibling relationship is not one of choice, and, to be sure, many people allow their connections with brothers and sisters to fall by the wayside. However, even if they do not stay in frequent contact, they may still maintain the relationship and tend to value it in a positive manner (Bedford, Volling, & Avioli, 2000).

The potential exists for the sibling relationship to be the deepest and closest of an adult's life, and to bring with that closeness both shared joy and shared pain. For the most part, it appears that these relationships tend to be positive in middle and later adulthood (Gold, 1989). Nevertheless, siblings carry with them into midlife the perception that either they or their sibling was differentially favored by their parents and when this happens, they experience high levels of tension in their relationship (Suitor et al., 2009).

The sibling relationship is one that can, however, fluctuate throughout adulthood. Increased closeness between siblings is associated with a number of significant life events, such as marriage, the birth of children, divorce and widowhood, and the development of health problems or death of a family member (Connidis, 1992). The role of parental support in the sibling tie also appears to be a factor in maintaining relationships between siblings but perhaps in unexpected ways. In a test of the intergenerational solidarity model within the Netherlands samples, researchers found that the poorer the relationship with parents, the more support was exchanged between siblings. Thus, siblings may turn to each other to compensate for the failure to connect with parents (Voorpostel & Blieszner, 2008).

GRANDPARENTS

For many older adults, the rewards of family life begin to grow much richer when they reach the status of grandparents. At this point, they are in a position to be able to enjoy the benefits of expressing their generativity through interacting with the youngest generation. At the same time, grandparents can avoid the more arduous tasks of parenthood. One of the most challenging aspects of life for the older person is loss of a spouse. The opportunity to be a grandparent can offset some of this loss. Unfortunately not all grandparents are able to enjoy the benefits of their status, nor do all grandparents want to assume this role. Furthermore, increasingly grandparents are being asked to substitute for a parent who is not present in the home, or whose job has extensive time commitments.

Many people still think of grandparents as the warm, generous, older adults portrayed in the media as kindly relatives who have ample time to spend with their families and want to do so. However, variations in patterns of grandparenting, along with a rapidly increasing growth in the number of grandparents in the population, may require that this image be changed.

Grandparents Raising Grandchildren

Estimates are that there are approximately 56 million grandparents in the United States (Fields, O'Connell, & Downs, 2006); about 11% (6.2 million) live with their under-18-year-old grandchildren. Of grandparents living with grandchildren, 2.5 million are responsible entirely for their basic needs (U.S. Bureau of the Census, 2009b). This situation, referred to as a **skip generation family**, may occur for a variety of reasons, including substance abuse by parents, child abuse or neglect by parents, teenage pregnancy or failure of parents to handle children, and parental unemployment, divorce, AIDS, or incarceration.

Although only a small percentage (14%) of grandparents in skip generation households are over the age of 60 years, substantial percentages live in poverty (*Economist*, 2007). Many have a disability. However, on the positive side, the role of surrogate parent can contribute favorably to the grandparents' sense of identity, particularly for Black grandmothers (Pruchno & McKenney, 2002). Feeling that others are supportive can help ameliorate the negative effects of the stress and strain of caring for the grandchild (Musil, Warner, Zauszniewski, Wykle, & Standing, 2009).

With life expectancy increasing, great-grandparents are becoming more and more prevalent. Relationships across more than two generations are taking on increasing importance and will continue to do so into the foreseeable future (Bengston, 2001).

Patterns of Grandparenting

The classic study of grandparenting conducted by Neugarten and Weinstein (1964) identified five

This grandfather is enjoying his relationship with his grandchildren as they share storytelling time.

types of grandparents. The first type, the formal grandparent, follows what are believed to be the appropriate guidelines for the grandparenting role. Formal grandparents provide occasional services and maintain an interest in the grandchild, but do not become overly involved. By contrast, the fun seeker prefers the leisure aspects of the role and primarily provides entertainment for the grandchild. The surrogate parent is the third type and, as the name implies, takes over the caretaking role with the child. Fourth, the reservoir of family wisdom, which is usually a grandfather, is the head of the family who dispenses advice and resources but also controls the parent generation. Finally, the distant figure is the grandparent who has infrequent contact with the grandchildren, appearing only on holidays and special occasions.

Other attempts to characterize or delineate styles or categories of grandparenting have followed a similar pattern, with distinctions typically being made among the highly involved, friendly, and remote or formal types of grandparents (Mueller, Wilhelm, & Elder, 2002). The "remote-involved" dimension is one that seems to resonate in the attitudes that grandchildren have toward their grandparents as well (Roberto, 1990). The symbolic value of the grandparent in the family lineage, or the "family watchdog" (Troll, 1985), is another critical component identified in several classifications. There is evidence that the role of grandparent is more central in the lives of grandmothers than grandfathers (Pollet, Nelissen, & Nettle, 2009).

Although these variations may exist in patterns of grandparenting, it is safe to say that the role of grandparent is an important one for the older adult (Harwood, Sultzer, & Wheatley, 2000) and that grandparent identity is an important contributor to well-being (Reitzes & Mutran, 2004). Grandparents feel a strong sense of connection to the younger generation (Crosnoe & Elder, 2002) and may play a significant role in mediating relationships between parents and grandchildren during conflicts (Werner, Buchbinder, Lowenstein, & Livni, 2005).

Unfortunately for most grandparents, contact with their grandchildren declines steadily through the grandchild's early adulthood, particularly when they leave the home of their parents and start an independent life of their own (Geurts, Poortman, van

Tilburg, & Dykstra, 2009). Grandparents who are unable to maintain contact with their grandchildren due to parental divorce or disagreements within the family are likely to suffer a variety of ill consequences, including poor mental and physical health, depression, feelings of grief, and poorer quality of life (Drew & Smith, 2002).

FRIENDSHIPS

Of the areas of relationships examined in this chapter, friendship has probably received the least attention regarding its function, meaning, and changes over the course of adulthood. Yet oddly enough, everyone can attest to the importance of friends in their own life, and the many roles that friends play in providing many forms of support and boosting one's emotional well-being.

Theoretical Perspectives

From a life course perspective, the major dimension that underlies close friendships is reciprocity, or a sense of mutuality (Hartup & Stevens, 1997). The fundamental characteristic of reciprocity is that there is give and take within the relationship at a deep, emotional level involving intimacy, support, sharing, and companionship. At the behavioral level, reciprocity is expressed in such actions as exchanging favors, gifts, and advice.

Close friends in adulthood confide in each other, help each other in times of trouble, and attempt to enhance each other's sense of well-being. Although there may be developmental differences across the life span in the expression of reciprocity, the essence of all friendships remains this sense of deep mutuality. Another important function of friendships is socializing, or helping each other through life transitions in other spheres, such as changes in health, marital relationships, residence, and work.

Patterns of Friendships

When adults first enter long-term intimate relationships, they engage in "dyadic withdrawal," in which their individual friendships diminish and their joint friendships increasingly overlap (Kalmijn, 2003).

FIGURE 9.7

Characteristics of Friendships in Adulthood

- Follow a trajectory from formation to dissolution
- May be distinguished in terms of closeness
- Vary in terms of friendship styles
- Throughout adulthood are related to well-being and self-esteem

Overall this means a decline will occur in a person's total number of friends. One exception occurs among women who have become divorced, whose number of close friendships increases.

Friendship patterns at any age may be seen as following a developmental trajectory from formation to dissolution (see Figure 9.7) (Adams & Blieszner, 1994). You have probably experienced this trajectory with your own friends. The stage of friendship formation involves moving from being strangers to acquaintances to friends. The maintenance phase encompasses what is usually thought of as "friendship," during which friends sustain an active interest and involvement with each other. They may evaluate the quality of the friendship periodically during this phase, deciding to increase or decrease their level of involvement. In terms of Hartup's framework, it would be during the maintenance phase that reciprocity levels are highest. Friendships may remain in the maintenance phase for years, even decades, at varying levels of closeness. The end of a friendship, which occurs during the dissolution phase, may be hard to identify. A friendship may end gradually over a period of time as feelings of reciprocity dwindle and the relationship essentially falls by the wayside. Friendships may also end through a conscious decision based on insurmountable disagreements and conflict.

Friendships in adulthood may also be distinguished in terms of the closeness of the relationship, which may or may not change over time. People may maintain **peripheral ties**, which are not characterized by a high degree of closeness, for many years (Fingerman & Griffiths, 1999). Peripheral ties include people such as neighbors, coworkers, professional contacts, gym buddies, friends of friends, or the parents of one's children's friends. These relationships may be amicable and cordial but never progress beyond this level. Other peripheral ties may be those that are in the friendship formation stage and will later progress to close friendships. A third type of peripheral tie is one that was formerly a close friendship and has now moved to the dissolution/disinterest stage.

There may also be variations in friendship patterns in adulthood based on individual differences in approaches toward friends, called **friendship styles** (Matthews, 1986). Individuals who have an independent friendship style may enjoy friendly, satisfying, and cordial relationships with people but never form close or intimate friendships. The type known as discerning individuals are extremely selective in their choice of friends, retaining a small number of very close friends throughout their lives. Finally, people with an acquisitive friendship style are readily able to make and retain close friendships throughout their lives and therefore have a large social network.

People tend to choose as friends other people who are similar in gender, socioeconomic status, and ethnicity (Adams & Blieszner, 1994). Throughout adulthood, close social ties serve as a buffer against stress and are related to higher levels of well-being and self-esteem. Relationships with friends may even be more predictive of high levels of self-esteem than income or marital status (Siebert, Mutran, & Reitzes, 2002). For people who have no family members, friendships serve as an important substitute for keeping an individual socially active (Lang & Carstensen, 1994). Moreover, friendships play a particularly important role in the lives of older gay men and lesbians, who have considerably more elaborated conceptions of their friendship ties than do heterosexual individuals (De Vries & Megathlin, 2009).

As you have learned in this chapter, close social ties play an important role in development. Even as relationships respond to a changing social context, they continue to influence people's well-being and adaptation. There continue to be areas of research that need further work, however, particularly in the areas of grandparenting, siblings, and friendships.

From a biopsychosocial perspective, this research will provide greater understanding of the interactions among health, personality, and social context.

SUMMARY

1. Close relationships form an important component of adult life, and although these patterns are changing in the United States, development in adulthood and later life interacts in important ways with the ties that people have with others. The large majority of adults get married, and although marriage rates are decreasing and people are waiting longer to get married than in previous decades, the majority of adults are living in a marital relationship.

2. Cohabitation rates have been increasing in recent decades. According to the cohabitation effect, people living together before marriage are more likely to divorce. Approximately 10% of the adult population in the United States is divorced. The divorce rate is highest among men in their 50s, and taking into account all marriages that end in divorce, the average length of a first marriage prior to divorce is about 8 years. Divorce statistics also show important variations by race.

3. Birthrates have decreased over the past 20 years, and women are having children at later ages. Most women, however, have their first child before the age of 30. Women who have a child after they are 30 are more highly educated and have higher incomes, but they also have a higher risk of encountering medical complications. Men with higher education and occupation are more involved in raising their children but spend less time in providing care. The number of single fathers is increasing, but there are also more fathers who have no contact with the children.

4. Widowhood is a stressful event for men and women, but men are more likely to show the widowhood effect of increased mortality after becoming a widow. The effects of widowhood can persist for many years, and many people report various forms of attachment to their deceased spouse.

5. Studies of the transition to parenthood indicate that decreases in marital satisfaction are especially likely to occur when the division of labor assumes more traditional lines in the household. The study of adult child–parent relationships reveals a number of important phenomena related to changes in roles and their altered views of each other. Although caregiving is usually thought of in negative terms, there is some evidence of positive outcomes. The intergenerational solidarity model proposes six dimensions to characterize the cohesiveness of these relationships.

6. Siblings are another important family tie in adulthood, and closeness between siblings varies over the adult years along with other family and life events.

7. The majority of older adults are grandparents, a relationship that tends to be positive, but there is a trend toward grandparents raising grandchildren in a "skip generation" (no parents present) household. Theoretical explanations of grandparenting focus on the remote-involved dimension, and various categorization schemes are based on this concept.

8. Friendships are another source of important close relationships in adulthood, and even if individuals are not involved in tight-knit friendships, they may have many important peripheral ties.

10

Work, Retirement,

The majority of adults are involved in productive activities in some form of paid employment. For people who are fortunate enough to be in a job they enjoy, the experience of work is positive, fulfilling, and expressive of personal interests and abilities. Others view work as a means of supplying income that can be used toward fulfilling activities in the realms of leisure, recreation, or family. Yet others struggle to find employment, a recent concern for many Americans given the economic climate of the early part of this decade. Work provides the primary focus of life among most people from the 20s onward, until retirement or even their death. Factors influencing work, including the type of position, amount of income, and conditions in which it is conducted carry over to virtually every other area of life. Finally, many people define their identity in terms of their job title, prestige, security, and status.

Given the importance of work in adulthood, we will focus our later discussion on the impact of retirement of the individual as the older adult leaves the workforce. Researchers, theorists, and counselors have long been intrigued with this question, and as you will learn, there are no easy answers. Although the thought of retirement may seem very far away to the average college-aged student, planning for it is a lifelong process.

WORK PATTERNS IN ADULTHOOD

The **labor force** includes all civilians in the over-16 population who live outside of institutions (prisons, nursing homes, residential treatment centers) and have sought or are actively seeking employment. In 2010 the total civilian noninstitutionalized population over the age of 16 amounted to 236.8 million people, and of these, nearly two thirds (65%) were in the labor force. Reflecting the downturn in the U.S. economy beginning in late 2008, the percent employed in 2010 was 90%, down from 96% just three years earlier. This means that 58% of those in the labor force were occupying jobs.

Although Whites, Blacks, and Hispanics have similar labor force participation rates, the unemployment rates are higher for Blacks or African Americans (16.5%) and those of Hispanic or Latino ethnicity (12.6%) than for Whites (8.7%) and Asians (8.4%). Between 2009 and 2010, the number of people unemployed for 27 weeks and over rose from

214

and Leisure Patterns

2.7 million to 6.3. People with a college education are far more likely to be employed than people with a high school education or less (Bureau of Labor Statistics, 2010a). Employment rates rise after the early 20s from about 74% to a peak at about 83%; by the late 60s, the percent who are employed drops to about 30% (Bureau of Labor Statistics, 2010b). As depicted in Figure 10.1, projections are that by the year 2018, the size of the 55 and older workforce will rise from 18.1 at present to 23.9 (as a percent of the total workforce) (Bureau of Labor Statistics, 2010d). Age group is a

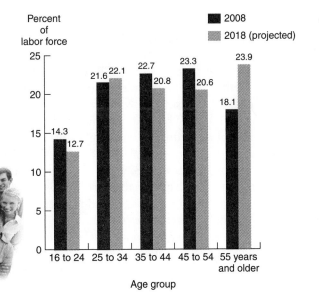

Percent of labor force

■ 2008
□ 2018 (projected)

16 to 24: 14.3, 12.7
25 to 34: 21.6, 22.1
35 to 44: 22.7, 20.8
45 to 54: 23.3, 20.6
55 years and older: 18.1, 23.9

Age group

<u>FIGURE 10.1</u>

Percent of Labor Force by Age Group, 2008 and 2018

Source: Bureau of Labor Statistics. (2010). Occupational outlook handbook, 2010–11 edition. Retrieved from http://www.bls.gov/oco/oco2003.htm#Labor%20Force.

FIGURE 10.2

Distribution of Full-time Wage and Salary Employment by Sex and Major Occupational Group, United States, 2008

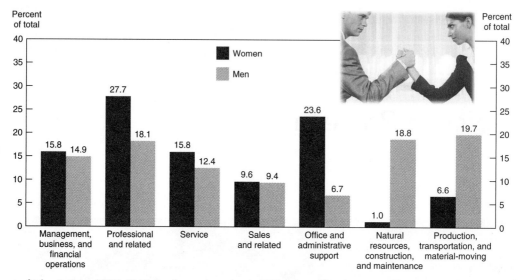

Source: Bureau of Labor Statistics. (2009). Highlights of women's earnings in 2008. Retrieved from http://www.bls.gov/cps/cpswom2008.pdf.

factor in income. The highest income is earned by men in the 45 to 64 age group; for women, the highest income was earned by those who were 55 to 64 (Bureau of Labor Statistics, 2010e).

Women comprise 46.5% of the labor force (U.S. Department of Labor, 2009). The labor force participation of women with young children rose steadily between 1984 and 2004 but has decreased both for married women and single women since 2004 (Hoffman, 2009).

Despite their increasing involvement in the labor force, women still earn less than men, a fact referred to as the **gender gap,** expressed as a proportion of women's to men's salaries. As of late 2009, full-time employed women earned 81.2% of the median for men. The gender gap is highest among Whites (79.9%) and lowest among Blacks (93.4%). The gender gap is particularly pronounced among women in the 55- to 64-year-old age group, who earn 78.7% of the income of men in the same age bracket. In the highest paid sector of the job market, management, professional, and related occupations, the discrepancy is greater with women earning only about 74% of the salaries of men. Interestingly, women outnumber men in this level of employment

by 52 to 48% (Bureau of Labor Statistics, 2010e) (see Figure 10.2).

Although students about to graduate from college often worry about whether they will get a job, a college degree is a benefit when it comes to occupational level and ultimately, lifetime earning potential. Statistically speaking, your income is likely to rise with each increase in your educational level (Bureau of Labor Statistics, 2010e). In the United States, those holding a college degree earned $1,121 per week compared to the $638 earned by high school graduates. Unfortunately, education alone does not account for earning potential. Even when controlling for education, Black and Hispanic workers typically have lower earnings than do Whites, a disparity particularly pronounced among men. For example, in 2009, among men with a bachelor's degree, college-educated and higher Black men earned 73% of the income of Whites, and Hispanic college graduates earned 82% of the income of White men. This disparity remains approximately the same even at the advanced graduate degree levels (Bureau of Labor Statistics, 2010e).

Educational levels within the United States vary considerably by age group. In general there has been an increasing trend over the past 40 years for older adults to have higher levels of education, with double the percentage in 2008 having received a college diploma (18.3%) than was true in 1985 (9.4%). This trend is certain to continue, as is evident from the fact that the 25- to 34-year-old age bracket now include the highest percentage of college graduates of all age groups of adults (23.5%) (U.S. Bureau of the Census, 2010f).

VOCATIONAL DEVELOPMENT

Development in the world of work is influenced in many ways by the social factors of education, race, gender, and age. However, a person's choice of an occupation, or **vocation**, reflects personal preferences and interests as well; preferably people are doing what they want to do rather than what is simply available. Of course with rising unemployment rates, more and more people are likely to make compromises. Nevertheless, vocational development theories are based on the premise that individual choice plays a large role in determining choice of career.

Your desire to enter a given field is what most likely has prompted your choice of a career path and hence your college major. You may be majoring in psychology, consumer studies, nursing, education, chemistry, or music. Assuming the process was not randomly made; it is more likely that your choice reflects your personality, skills, and experience. These are the factors that vocational development theories take into account when they attempt to explain the career choices that people make and determine people's levels of happiness and productivity once they have acted on those choices.

Holland's Vocational Development Theory

The most prominent theory in the vocational development literature is that of the late John Holland. According to **Holland's vocational development theory** (Holland, 1997), vocational aspirations and interests are the direct expression of the individual's personality. Holland proposed that there are six fundamental types (also called codes) that represent the universe of all possible vocational interests, competencies, and behaviors. Each of the six types is identified by its initial letter: Realistic (R), Investigative (I), Artistic (A), Social (S), Enterprising (E), and Conventional (C). Based on the letters that describe the six types, the theory is also referred to as the **RIASEC model** (see Figure 10.3).

Occupations can be described in terms of the same six RIASEC types as can vocational interests. According to Holland, occupations reflect particular patterns of job requirements and rewards that are characteristic of their environments. As such they serve as the settings that elicit, develop, and reward the specific interests, competencies, and behaviors associated with each of the types. The occupational types are the same as the interest types. For example, social occupations involve work with people, and realistic occupations involve work with one's hands.

In applying the RIASEC types, a combination of two or three of the initials are usually assigned rather than just one. The first letter reflects the primary type into which a person's interest or occupation falls ("S" for Social, for example). The second and third letters allow for a more accurate and differentiated picture of the individual or occupation. Both a construction worker and a corrections officer are

FIGURE 10.3

Holland's RIASEC Model

R code occupations, and both have the RE code designation. They differ in their third code, which is C for the construction worker and S for the corrections officer.

In addition to the theorized vocational and occupational descriptions, personality descriptions are thought to characterize each of the six types, based on correspondence between the Holland codes and scores on measures of the Five Factor Model. The translation of RIASEC codes into personality traits works particularly well when facets are used, rather than only the scores on the major trait domains (Armstrong & Anthoney, 2009). Putting the two together, researchers have suggested that there are three underlying dimensions: interest in people versus things, preference for abstract versus concrete ideas, and striving for personal growth versus striving for accomplishment. However, personality traits do not completely map onto vocational interests (Mount, Barrick, Scullen, & Rounds, 2005).

The six RIASEC types are organized theoretically to exist in a hexagonal structure. This structure implies that the types have a relationship to each other based on their distance from each other on the structure. Types that are most similar (such as R and C) are closest, and those that are the most dissimilar (such as C and A) are furthest away from each other.

The notion of the hexagon is an important one because it helps define the way that your interests correspond to your environments. You will be most satisfied in your jobs if you are in an environment that fits your personality type, a situation referred to as **congruence** or "fit." The hexagon can be thought of as two knobs, one on top of the other. Congruence is the situation where the two knobs are completely aligned.

Congruence also influences the ability to be effective on the job. According to vocational development theory, if you are happy, you will also be most productive. Unfortunately, as we mentioned earlier, people cannot always find jobs congruent with their interests, particularly in a tough economy. In these situations, the RIASEC model predicts that people will experience low job satisfaction and a high degree of instability until they can find fulfilling work environments. When they are unable to do so, their work productivity may suffer.

Supporting this idea, researchers have found that individuals with Artistic interests working in Realistic environments, for example, have lower work quality than people whose interests match their environments (Kieffer, Schinka, & Curtiss, 2004). Again, when jobs are scarce, people may have to take whatever work they can find and seek congruence elsewhere through leisure pursuits instead of through work. The Artistic type in the Realistic job may wait out the hours until the work day is over and then rush home to work on crafts, play a musical instrument, or go to a pottery studio.

The RIASEC theory is empirically derived from the responses of many thousands of individuals who have been tested over the years of its development. If you wanted to have your vocational interests assessed using this model, you could take one or both of the most common assessment instruments. The **Strong Vocational Interest Inventory (SVII)** (Harmon, Hansen, Borgen, & Hammer, 1994) consists of items in which respondents indicate their preferences for occupations, topics of study, activities, and types of people. The SVII is administered by a professional counselor and must be scored through a testing service. The second assessment method can be administered and scored on your own. The **Self-Directed Search (SDS)** (Holland, 1994) provides an assessment along the RIASEC dimensions, but also asks about your strengths, allowing you to determine the profile of your abilities as well as your interests (Gottfredson, 2002).

The RIASEC codes now have become fully integrated into **O*NET**, the **Occupational Information Network** (O*NET, 2010), an online interactive national database of occupations used by vocational placement agencies and state labor departments in the United States (see Figure 10.4). People who are trying to find a job that will fit their interests, training, and experience can be greatly aided by this system, even if they do not live in the United States.

O*NET provides a comprehensive and searchable database of occupations, along with important data such as salary and expected growth (in the United States) in the next 10 years. Occupations that have a high priority are flagged. The RIASEC model appears to be an appropriate fit for both men and women

FIGURE 10.4

The O*NET OnLine Web Site

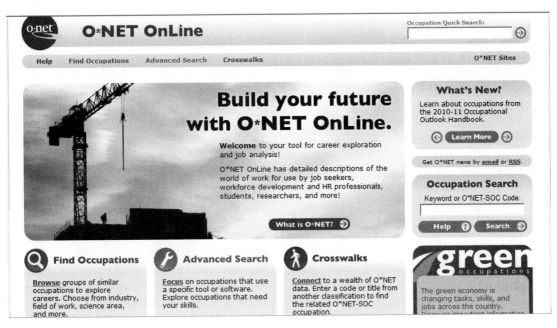

in the O*NET, meaning that gender adjustments do not have to be made in interpreting an individual's pattern of scores (Anthoney & Armstrong, 2010).

Because of its widespread incorporation into occupational interest inventories and classification schemes, the RIASEC model is likely to be prominent for some time to come. Vocational counselors have adopted the RIASEC model as an easily interpretable and user-friendly system. Assessment tools for both people and jobs are readily available and inexpensive, and there is adequate (if not perfect) empirical support for it from large-scale studies (Smith, Hanges, & Dickson, 2001). From the standpoint of vocational counseling for young adults, the codes seem to be relatively stable during the crucial career development years of the late teens and early 20s (Low, Yoon, Roberts, & Rounds, 2005). However, there are individual differences in patterns of stability, possibly corresponding to variations in personality. For example, people who are more open to new experiences may be more likely to change their career interests over time (Rottinghaus, Coon, Gaffey, & Zytowski, 2007).

Within the field of industrial-organizational (I/O) psychology, congruence is now a major focus when it comes to the business of matching people to jobs. At the same time, as anyone who has spent time in a workplace would attest to, it is also important to determine the fit or match among individuals working together as a team (Muchinsky, 1999). Does an RCE type get along better with another RCE, or would their similar styles lead to narrow thinking and lack of productivity among members of a work unit? Perhaps the RCE should be working alongside an SAI, whose "people" orientation will complement the "thing"-oriented approach of the Realistic individual.

The notion of congruence between people and jobs has received considerable empirical support, not only in terms of job ratings but also in terms of career change behavior. All other things being equal, people will tend to move out of incongruent jobs and into ones that are more suited to their interests (Donohue, 2006). Unfortunately, for many people, factors outside their control, such as race and ethnicity, limit these choices. For individuals whose vocational situations are affected by such constraints,

FIGURE 10.5

The Stages in Super's Self-concept Model

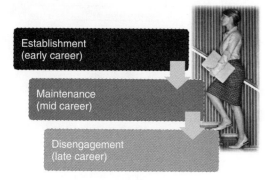

the role of identity and the possibility for realizing one's true vocational interests are far less significant than the reality of these sociocultural factors.

Super's Self-Concept Theory

The desire for adults to achieve full realization of their inner potential is at the heart of **Super's self-concept theory** (Super, 1957; Super, 1990). If you see yourself as an artist, then you will desire work in which you can express the view of yourself as an artist. In contrast to Holland's theory, which emphasizes vocational preferences (the fact that you prefer artistic work), Super's theory places the focus on the occupation that you see as most "true" to your inner self. Super's theory also takes into account that the constraints of the marketplace mean that people are not always able to achieve full realization of their self-concepts. In a society with relatively little demand for artists, the person with the artistic self-concept will need to seek self-expression in a job that allows for a certain degree of creativity but will also bring in a paycheck. Such an individual may seek a career in computer graphic design, for example, because that is a more viable occupation than that of an oil painter.

According to Super, the expression of self-concept through work occurs in a series of stages that span the years from adolescence to retirement (see Figure 10.5). In the exploration stage (teens to mid-20s), people explore career alternatives and select a vocation that they will find to be expressive of their self-concept. By the time they reach the establishment

stage (mid-20s to mid-40s), people are focused on achieving stability and attempt to remain within the same occupation. At the same time, people seek to move up the career ladder to managerial positions and higher. In the maintenance stage (mid-40s to mid-50s), people attempt to hold onto their positions rather than to seek further advancement. Finally, in the disengagement stage (mid-50s to mid-60s), workers begin to prepare for retirement, perhaps spending more time in their leisure pursuits.

Variations in Vocational Development

When Super first wrote about career development, the job market was much more stable than it is at the present time. In the 1950s, the business world tended to involve people employed by one company for their entire careers. Climbing up the career ladder was also seen as a fairly typical goal, particularly for workers in white-collar occupations, but also for blue-collar workers employed in such industries as steel or car manufacturing. This model began to change substantially in the 1980s when large corporations began programs of downsizing, particularly after the advent of computerized technology.

The modern workplace is likely to promote **recycling**, the process through which workers change their main field of career activity part way into occupational life. In recycling, middle-aged workers may find themselves once again in the establishment stage they thought they had left behind in their late 20s.

The second variation on the traditional stages described by Super occurs when workers remain indefinitely in a maintenance-like period. **Plateauing** (Ettington, 1998), as this process is referred to, means that although your salary may increase, your job level remains static. People may reach their plateau at a young age if they enter a so-called dead-end job, or if their moves within or between companies involve lateral changes rather than vertical advancement. At that point, the individual may decide that it is time to seek another job (Heilmann, Holt, & Rilovick, 2008). However, there are ways to combat plateauing; a study of more than 300 government employees showed that workers who reported that they were mentors were less likely to experience the negative effects of plateauing (Lentz & Allen, 2009).

Recent approaches within the vocational developmental literature increasingly concentrate on the **boundaryless career**, or a career that does not follow a set pathway. Many workers who, in the past, were restricted by the opportunities presented to them by their organization are now progressing through their careers at their own pace. People who have the boundaryless career mindset seek opportunities for development in their jobs and when they do not receive it, may feel less psychologically invested in the organization that employs them (Briscoe & Finkelstein, 2009).

The desire to determine your own career path is referred to as the **protean career**. A protean career attitude can help individuals gain insight into what is driving their career and ultimately to achieve career success (De Vos & Soens, 2008). Having the boundaryless mindset and protean career attitude appear to be particularly important for women seeking greater flexibility and self-direction in their career development (Cabrera, 2009). Looking at career paths in a more fluid and flexible manner is also becoming more important for those employed in knowledge-based occupations such as information technology because their career paths tend to be more fragmented than those of people in other professions (Donnelly, 2009).

Although the boundaryless and protean careers have some overlap, they are empirically distinct (Briscoe, Hall, & Frautschy DeMuth, 2006) and may provide an alternative to the traditional notion prevalent for so many years in the vocational literature of the "one life–one career" mentality. As changes continue to occur in the workplace and society leading to greater deviation from the standard organizational framework of the mid-20th century, vocational counselors will increasingly offer workers ideas about ways to manage their own careers around internal rather than external goals and employer-developed criteria (Raabe, Frese, & Beehr, 2007).

Even as the corporate culture becomes less stable, there is still a desire among many employers to reduce turnover rates because training new workers can be costly and inefficient. In some ways this desire to keep turnover to a minimum is made more difficult by changes in the mindset of employees, who look at such events in the world as corporate mergers and bankruptcies and worry about becoming too attached to their own companies. Vocational researchers have suggested, therefore, that the issue of job stability be examined in more depth.

The issue of worker loyalty is addressed by the model of organizational embeddedness shown in Table 10.1. Super's theory provides a framework for helping to maximize the sense of commitment among employees, particularly those who prefer to feel that they are in control of what happens to them in their careers (Ng & Butts, 2009). In the establishment stage, employees will feel more connected to their companies, and their professions in general, if they are given mentoring, adequate training, and favorable work hours. During the maintenance stage, having opportunities to develop leadership and managerial skills will help them to feel more loyal to their organization. Finally, when workers begin to look toward retirement in the disengagement stage, they will feel more tied to companies that can guarantee them pension funds and adequate insurance benefits. At this stage in their career, they may also expand

TABLE 10.1
Factors that Promote Occupational Commitment

Stage	Organizational (company)	Occupational (e.g. accountant)	Both
Establishment	Organizational socialization Organization-specific skills Work hours	Generalizable skills	Social ties Mentorship
Maintenance	Management & leadership responsibilities	Accumulation of career attainments	Career plateauing Reconciliation of goal discrepancy Family status
Disengagement	Pension funds & insurance benefits	Leadership role in profession	Risk aversion

their focus to the profession as a whole if they are in a field that promotes broader occupational commitments such as membership in a national organization (Ng & Feldman, 2007).

VOCATIONAL SATISFACTION

Given that work takes up anywhere from one quarter to one third of a person's waking life during the week, it is safe to assume that most people prefer to maximize their level of satisfaction. Although not everyone can achieve full self-realization through work, it is still possible to find sources of satisfaction either within the work itself or in the rewards it provides. On the other hand, a job may possess neither source of fulfillment but instead remain a daily grind that the person must endure to maintain self and family. Theories and research on **vocational satisfaction** deal with these questions of how people find enjoyment in the work that they do or, conversely, of what factors limit their ability to achieve an optimal vocational situation.

Vocational satisfaction refers, very simply, to the extent to which a worker has positive views of the job or aspects of a job (Dawis, 1996). In turn, the more that workers view the job as providing a sense of "fit" with their needs, the more satisfied they will be and ultimately the stronger their commitment will be to the job and the organization (Hoffman & Woehr, 2006).

Because of its presumed importance in determining both how productive and committed the worker is within the job, vocational satisfaction is one of the most heavily researched areas in vocational psychology. Although it may be relatively simple to define vocational satisfaction in general terms, it is surprisingly difficult to identify its components or, more importantly, determinants.

Intrinsic and Extrinsic Factors

A distinction universal to the various theories of vocational satisfaction is the difference between factors inherent in the work itself and those that are unrelated to the particular work involved in the job. The factors inherent in the work itself are referred to as **intrinsic factors** and include the physical and mental actions that the individual must perform in order to carry out the job. For example,

sculpting involves the intrinsic physical activities of molding clay or stone, and accounting involves the intrinsic mental activities of manipulating numbers. Obviously, sculpting involves mental work, as the artist plans the piece before and during its completion. Conversely, intrinsic to accounting is the physical manipulation of keys on the keyboard or the writing of numbers on the page with a pencil. However, these are secondary activities compared with the nature of the work itself. The central defining feature of an intrinsic factor is that it cannot be found in precisely the same fashion in a different type of job. Molding materials is intrinsic to sculpting, and computing numbers is intrinsic to accounting (see Figure 10.6).

Intrinsic factors can also be characterized as involving or engaging your sense of identity in that the work directly pertains to your feelings of competence, autonomy, and stimulation of personal growth. Highlighting this point, in one short-term longitudinal study of older workers, researchers found that identity as a worker related positively to changes in self-esteem (Reitzes & Mutran, 2006). Your ability to express autonomy and self-direction in the daily running of the job is also part of the intrinsic aspects of work because these factors are directly tied to your sense of self. Furthermore, the engagement of your intrinsic motivation in work that is cognitively challenging and self-directed maintains a constant stimulus for your cognitive activity and may serve to enhance your intellectual functioning over time (Schooler, Mulatu, & Oates, 1999).

The opposite of intrinsic factors in work are **extrinsic factors**, the features that accompany the

FIGURE 10.6

Intrinsic and Extrinsic Factors in Vocational Satisfaction

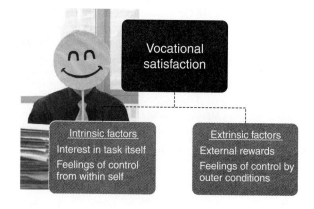

job but may also be found in other jobs with very different intrinsic characteristics. The easiest extrinsic factor to understand is salary. People may earn the same salary whether they work on a farm or provide care to preschool children. Paychecks are issued for work performed, and although some jobs earn more than others, the same amount of money can be earned in many alternative ways. A professional athlete may earn such a vast salary that it appears to be an inherent part of the job, but an oil magnate may earn the same six or seven figure paycheck for a very different set of job activities. Therefore, salary is not intrinsic to work. In the earlier example about accounting, using the pencil or keyboard is extrinsic because it is an activity that you can perform in a variety of jobs, from accounting to playwriting.

Other extrinsic factors are associated with the conditions of work such as the comfort of the environment, demands for travel, convenience of work hours, friendliness of coworkers, amount of status associated with the job, and adequacy of the company's supervision and employment policies. These aspects of work do not directly engage your sense of personal identity and competence. Although a high salary may certainly reinforce your sense of worth (particularly in Western society), as noted above, high salaries may be earned in many ways that are not necessarily tied to a person's true vocational passions. The racial climate is another condition of the workplace that may be particularly important for workers from racial and ethnic minority backgrounds. Supervisors may not always be aware of the importance of maintaining an environment that is nonracist and promotes respect (Lyons & O'Brien, 2006).

You may or may not have had a job yet in which you felt involvement at an intrinsic level. However, you can probably think of people you know whose work has intrinsic meaning to them. Perhaps you have encountered a sales or service person who seemed genuinely interested in helping you find a necessary item or solve a problem and was willing to work with you until you found the satisfactory solution. This may have been an employee who found the job to be intrinsically rewarding, feelings that were expressed in the apparent pride that he or she took in helping you with your situation.

Many vocational psychologists propose that intrinsic and extrinsic factors possess motivational properties. When workers are motivated for intrinsic reasons, they are thought to be doing so for the purpose of seeking their own personal expression, autonomy, and challenge. The control of their behaviors comes from within themselves rather than from an outside source such as a boss or the need to pay the rent. Conversely, extrinsic motivation is the desire to work to seek the benefits of pay, good job conditions, friendly coworkers, and an employer with fair and equitable policies. People motivated for extrinsic reasons are controlled by forces outside of themselves because someone or something outside of the job tasks themselves provides the rewards for their work. When considering these two forms of motivation, theorists have argued about which is more important or even whether the two are mutually exclusive.

One of the earliest theories about work motivation is the **two-factor theory** developed by Herzberg and colleagues in the late 1950s (Herzberg, Mausner, & Snyderman, 1959). According to this theory, intrinsic factors are motivators whose fulfillment allows the worker to achieve self-actualization. The extrinsic aspects of work are hygiene factors that either enhance or detract from an environment in which workers can realize their aspirations. The central hypothesis of the two-factor theory is that job motivators are more powerful than hygiene factors as causes of vocational satisfaction. Favorable hygiene factors could only prevent the development of job dissatisfaction, but they could not promote it. Growth, self-fulfillment, and feelings of achievement can only come from the fulfillment of job motivators, not from the hygiene factors (Herzberg, Mausner, & Bloch Snyderman, 2005).

Most recently, vocational researchers are using the propositions of **self-determination theory** that assumes that people are motivated in their occupations for complex reasons involving intrinsic and extrinsic factors (Deci & Ryan, 2008). According to this approach, the extrinsic rewards such as money actually reduce job satisfaction. This counter-intuitive suggestion is based on the idea that a focus on money causes employees to feel less in control of their work-related activities, leading their performance to suffer. The use of money as an incentive is a process called **motivational crowding out**—extrinsic rewards crowd out intrinsic satisfaction (James, 2005).

You may think that this theory leaves a lot to be desired because it is hard to imagine a job in which salary is unimportant. Obviously, everyone works for the extrinsic reward of money, and a theory that ignores this fact is bound to fall short of the mark (Bassett-Jones & Lloyd, 2005). The key to understanding this theory is to recognize its central proposal that to be maximally motivating, the work that you do must be an expression of your identity. If you can feel that your paid work gives you the opportunity to develop your innermost goals and desires, you will perform at higher levels of persistence and discipline.

Extrinsic motivation can be seen in self-determination theory as a dimension ranging from viewing rewards as completely outside your control to the view that your job is essential to your sense of identity (Gagne & Deci, 2005). The more that you see the job as a part of your identity, the greater your sense of internal control and hence the more intrinsic your work motivation.

Positive and Negative Moods

Job satisfaction can be affected not only by the motivation to work, but also by people's feelings about their jobs. You can have feelings *on* the job (such as being excited about the upcoming weekend) and feelings *about* the job (such as liking your job activities). According to **affective evaluation theory**,

positive and negative emotions at work are important influences on your satisfaction. Not surprisingly, if you experience positive events at work, such as being complimented by a supervisor, you will have a positive emotional experience and if you experience negative events, such as conflict with a coworker, your emotions will be negatively affected (Fisher, 2002).

Testing affective evaluation theory on one highly stressed group of employees, representatives who provide technical assistance at call service centers, researchers found that job satisfaction and positive emotions were correlated with such job characteristics as autonomy, participation in the organization, supervisory support, and concern by supervisors for employee welfare. Conversely, the stress of feeling overloaded was correlated with negative emotions (Wegge, von Dick, Fisher, West, & Dawson, 2006). Thus, on a day-to-day basis, the impact of negative events at work (such as when the copy machine breaks down) can be more potent than the personality of the employee (Niklas & Dormann, 2005).

Contrary to affective evaluation theory, approaches emphasizing **dispositional affectivity**, the general dimension of a person's affective responding, regard a person's overall outlook on life as relatively stable over time (Bowling, Banister, Sutton, Evans, & Windsor, 2002). A person may

AGING IN THE NEWS

www.wiley.com/college/whitbourne   OLDER ADULTS WHO MADE THE HEADLINES   -VOL. 4, CHAPTER 10-

OLDEST SUPREME COURT JUSTICE RETIRES AT 90

Justice John Paul Stevens announced his retirement 11 days before his 90th birthday. Appointed to the Supreme Court in 1975 by President Gerald Ford, Justice Stevens is the second-oldest justice member, and at the time of his retirement was the fourth longest serving justice. Stevens served as a lieutenant commander in the Navy during World War II, winning a Bronze Star. Perhaps best remembered for his dissent during Bush v. Gore in 2000 to halt the recount in Florida, he offered the following statement: "Although we may never know with complete certainty the identity of the winner of this year's presidential election, the identity of the loser is perfectly clear. It is the nation's confidence in the judge as the impartial guardian of the rule of law."

have the favorable trait of positive affectivity, meaning that he or she is upbeat and tends to look at the bright side of a situation. The converse, negative affectivity, refers to a state of being predisposed to experience negative moods.

Research on the dispositional affectivity dimension of personality has found a relationship between affectivity and satisfaction, commitment, and intention to leave one's job (Cropanzano, Rupp, & Byrne, 2003). People high in positive affectivity are more likely than those high on negative affectivity to be satisfied in their job, committed to it, and unlikely to leave when faced with problems or difficulties. On the other hand, people high in negative affectivity are more likely to feel unhappy and therefore be less satisfied.

Looking at the intrinsic–extrinsic dimension of vocational satisfaction, researchers have found that people with high neuroticism scores are less likely to feel that their jobs are intrinsically rewarding. Perhaps for this reason, neuroticism is negatively related to job satisfaction; by contrast, people high in the traits of conscientiousness and extraversion are more satisfied in their jobs (Furnham, Eracleous, & Chamorro-Premuzic, 2009; Judge, Heller, & Mount, 2002; Seibert & Kraimer, 2001).

The relationship between personality and job satisfaction works both ways. In one longitudinal study of adults in Australia, although personality changes predicted changes in work satisfaction, changes in personality were also found to result from higher job satisfaction. Over time, workers who were more satisfied with their jobs became more extraverted (Scollon & Diener, 2006).

People's affect can also have an impact on the extent to which they perceive that there is a good fit between their work-related needs and the characteristics of the job. People who tend to have a positive approach to life in general will approach their work in a more positive manner, which in turn will lead to a better person–environment fit (Yu, 2009).

Occupational Reinforcement Patterns

So far, we have looked at characteristics of the person, but one influential theory of vocational satisfaction focuses on a job's **occupational reinforcement patterns (ORPs)**, the work values and needs likely to be reinforced or satisfied by a particular occupation. According to the theory of work adjustment proposed by Dawis and Lofquist (1984), vocational satisfaction is directly related to the extent to which workers feel that the environment can fulfill their work-related needs. The ORPs include achievement, independence, recognition, relationships, support, and working conditions. For example, a job as a travel guide rates high on independence; in contrast, a job as a sales manager rates high in recognition.

Reflecting the importance of ORPs, O*NET incorporates ORPs into its job search system. Each occupation can be identified by a particular pattern of ORPs that it satisfies, making it possible for job-seekers to match their personal values with those likely to be met by the job.

Work Stress

Everyone knows what it is like to have a "bad day" at work. However, what if every day is a bad day? Work stress can be a major threat to people's feelings of well-being and eventually can come to take its toll on physical health as well.

In Chapter 5, we learned about metabolic syndrome, a physical condition that places people at greater risk for heart disease. The Whitehall II Study, a longitudinal investigation of health in more than 10,300 civil employees in Great Britain, provides compelling data to show the links between work-related stress and the risk of metabolic syndrome (Chandola, Brunner, & Marmot, 2006). Carried out over five phases from 1985 to 1997, the study included measurements of stress, social class, intake of fruits and vegetables, alcohol consumption, smoking, exercise, and obesity status at the start of the study. Holding all other factors constant and excluding participants who were initially obese, men under high levels of work stress over the course of the study had twice the risk of subsequently developing metabolic syndrome. Women with high levels of stress had over five times the risk of developing this condition.

More recent research suggests that Whitehall II men who reported higher justice at work (such as perceived job fairness) had a far lower risk of metabolic syndrome compared with men who experienced lower work justice (Gimeno et al.,

2010). For women, stress encountered at work independently predicted Type 2 diabetes, even after controlling for socioeconomic position and stressors unrelated to work (Heraclides, Chandola, Witte, & Brunner, 2009).

Physiological data obtained in the form of cortisol levels from Whitehall II also illustrates the impact on health of social position within the workplace (Kumari et al., 2010). Daily assessments of cortisol, the hormone involved in the response to stress and anxiety, were taken from an older Whitehall cohort six times throughout the day. Men in lower employment grades showed higher cortisol levels early in the morning, levels that remained higher throughout the day than was true for men in higher employment grades. These higher levels could be explained both by higher levels of stress during the day and by poorer quality of sleep at night.

Thus, maximizing workplace satisfaction, in addition to helping maintain worker productivity, also can make a key difference in promoting the health and long-term well-being of the individual (Olsson, Hemstrom, & Fritzell, 2009).

Conflict Between Work and Family

When people become adults, they divide their time, energy, and role involvement in many areas of life. The two that generally carry the most weight are occupation and family life. Both carry with them major obligations and responsibility, and both contribute heavily to the individual's sense of identity.

There are three basic models of work–family interrelations (see Figure 10.7). According to the **spillover model**, attitudes and behaviors associated with one domain have an effect on attitudes and behavior carried out in the other domain (Grzywacz & Marks, 2000). The negative spillover model proposes that unhappiness at work leads the individual to experience unhappiness at home, and vice versa. The positive variant of the spillover model proposes that there is role enhancement or enrichment between the domains of family and work (Greenhaus & Powell, 2006). The **role strain** model proposes that work and family involvement are inversely related, so that the higher the person's involvement in his or her work role, the lower the individual's involvement in the family. The workaholic, according to this view,

FIGURE 10.7

Models of Work–Family Relationships

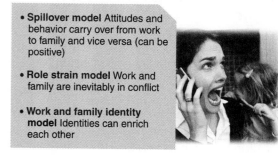

- **Spillover model** Attitudes and behavior carry over from work to family and vice versa (can be positive)
- **Role strain model** Work and family are inevitably in conflict
- **Work and family identity model** Identities can enrich each other

has little energy or time for family relationships. Conversely, high involvement with family should preclude total commitment to the job.

When work–family conflict does occur, it takes its toll on the individual's physical and mental health, causing emotional strain, fatigue, perception of overload, and stress (van Hooff et al., 2005). There are variations in the extent and impact of work–family conflict, however, and not all workers feel the same degree of conflict. Conflict is most likely to occur among mothers of young children, dual-career couples, and those who are highly involved with their jobs. Workers who devote a great deal of time to their jobs at the expense of their families ultimately pay the price in terms of experiencing a lower overall quality of life (Greenhaus, Collins, & Shaw, 2003). There are higher levels of work-family conflict among those employed in the private sector than those employed in the public sector (Dolcos & Daley, 2009).

Age also plays into the work–family conflict equation. Younger workers (under age 45) typically experience more conflict than older workers (46 and older); though when older workers experience conflict the effects seem to be stronger (Matthews, Bulger, & Barnes-Farrell, 2010). However, there are individual differences in personality that affect the work–family balance such as dispositional affectivity as well as variations on a day by day basis in levels of positive and negative affect the person experiences (Eby, Maher, & Butts, 2010).

Jobs with flexible hours help reduce conflict for perhaps some obvious reasons, such as by providing workers with the opportunity to meet more of their obligations at home within a broader time frame than the traditional work hours of 9 to 5 (Scandura & Lankau, 1997). Workers able to take advantage of a compressed work schedule (such as working four 10-hour days) or flextime (working desired hours) experience increases in the work and home relationship (McNall, Masuda, & Nicklin, 2010). There are tangible benefits to these situations. Accommodative work schedules may result in higher productivity and a reduction in turnover.

Social support from coworkers can also help to reduce the stress created by work–family conflict (Bhave, Kramer, & Glomb, 2010). Similarly, supportive supervisors, who recognize the inevitable commitments of family obligations and their possible impact on work performance, can also help ameliorate the experience of conflict (Schirmer & Lopez, 2001). In addition, if workers feel a strong sense of identification with their jobs, work can enrich family life. Conversely a strong family identity can promote feelings of satisfaction and commitment to the job (Wayne, Randel, & Stevens, 2006).

Age and Vocational Satisfaction

As people approach the end of their employment lives, do you think they are more or less satisfied with their work? On the one hand, it might make sense that people would eagerly await the release from the daily grind that comes with retirement. On the other hand, older workers might have eased themselves into a position that is more satisfactory because they have taken advantage of seniority and promotions. In fact, the evidence indicates that there is a tendency for workers at both ends of the age spectrum to feel satisfied with their jobs (Clark, Oswald, & Warr, 1996). People who reach a plateau in their career are likely to experience a drop in job satisfaction (Boudreau, Boswell, & Judge, 2001). Making this relationship a hard one to investigate is the fact that age is usually related to job tenure—the length of time a person has spent in the job. Gender, level of employment, and salary also interact with age differences in job satisfaction (Riordan, Griffith, & Weatherly, 2003).

Identity processes may come into play as a way of coping with plateauing or failing to reach previously aspired-to career goals. People who have reached their own peak, but perhaps not the one they hoped to reach when they were younger, begin to focus through identity assimilation on the positive aspects of their work accomplishments rather than their inability to meet earlier career goals. This process of identity assimilation may also increase the tendency to focus on family and nonwork commitments as sources of feelings of competence.

Identity assimilation with regard to work may also be part of a larger tendency to focus on positive aspects of life in general, a tendency reflected in higher life satisfaction scores among older adults (Warr, 1994). The reality is that most of these individuals will retire within the next 10 to 15 years, and they may be starting to make the mental shift toward the upcoming phase of their lives. Along these lines, researchers investigating job satisfaction in adulthood have begun to discuss core self-evaluations, which incorporate such constructs as self-esteem, self-efficacy, low neuroticism, and the belief that you control your fate.

Another factor that may affect the older worker's commitment and involvement in the job is exposure to age discrimination in the workplace. Although older workers are protected by federal law prohibiting discrimination (see below), as we saw in Chapter 1, negative stereotypes about the abilities and suitabilities of older persons in the workplace persist (Rupp et al., 2006). Older workers may begin to disengage mentally when they feel that they are subject to these age stereotypes, pressures to retire in the form of downsizing, and the message that their skills are becoming obsolete (Lease, 1998). These pressures can lead older workers to be less likely to engage in the career development activities that would enhance their ability to remain on the job or find a new one when their job is eliminated due to downsizing.

This general picture by no means applies to all workers. Gender may also play a major role in this process, particularly as women's roles in the workplace have shifted dramatically over the previous decades. Furthermore, discrimination may prohibit even the college-educated minority male from achieving his maximum employment potential, and therefore may keep him from reaching a point of perceived financial security in his late 40s and early 50s.

Level of occupation is yet another factor, as a person in a managerial position who is earning a high salary has the resources to invest time and energy in nonwork options. Of course, with a higher level of employment may go higher daily job demands, leading to less time for leisure pursuits. Individual differences in the extent to which an adult believes in the "work ethic" may also interact with the age–job satisfaction relationship. The work commitment of individuals with strong work ethic values may never taper off, even if their commitment does not translate into higher financial rewards.

Support from employers is a key factor in the relationship between age and job satisfaction. Older workers can also be more fully engaged in their job and hence achieve higher satisfaction if they feel that their employer values their contributions. Providing training and development programs specifically geared for older workers is a part of this process. Particularly important to keeping the older worker motivated and satisfied is providing job assignments to keep the work fresh and interesting (Armstrong-Stassen & Ursel, 2009).

Age-related changes in physical and cognitive functioning must also be taken into account. If these changes interfere with ability to perform the job satisfactorily, then the older worker will be unable to perform his or her duties or may only be able to do so with difficulty. If the aging process alters the degree of person–environment fit between the individual and the job, the worker will feel increasingly dissatisfied and unfulfilled. The role of the supervisor may be particularly important in this regard. A manager who is sensitive to, for example, an older worker's mobility problems may be able to lessen the demands for physical movement placed on the employee.

AGE AND VOCATIONAL PERFORMANCE

Are older workers more or less competent on the job than younger workers? When you think about this question, perhaps balance what could be the benefits of experience against the limitations of some potentially job-relevant skills. Younger cohorts are more highly educated and in better health than older workers. These and a host of other factors make the

overall relationship between age and job performance a complex one.

Significant individual differences both in abilities and attitudes toward work are important influences on job performance (see Figure 10.8). Some older workers focus on maintaining their current employment status and plan how to end their careers without jeopardizing this status. Others may have already experienced some disability and attempt to compensate for their losses while still maintaining their position at work. Many older workers, however, do not experience a loss in work functioning, and are able to maintain high levels of performance until they retire.

Initial interest in the quality of job performance among older workers can be traced to the early 1940s, when it appeared that population shifts were leading to a rising proportion of older (and possibly less productive) workers in the United States. Following World War II and the subsequent Baby Boom, these concerns were temporarily allayed, as the shifts then moved in the reverse direction toward a younger workforce. However, with the aging of the Baby Boomers, employers and policy makers are once again concerned about the characteristics and abilities of older workers and how their performance will affect the country's overall productivity. Society has moved in an increasingly technological direction since the

FIGURE 10.8

Characteristics of the Older Worker

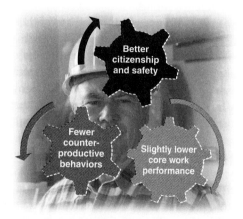

1940s; therefore, concerns about older workers have to do less with physical functioning than with their cognitive abilities. Will the aging Baby Boomers be able to keep up their productivity in an increasingly technological marketplace?

Research on cognitive functioning in later life provides important insights into the potential trade-off experienced by older persons between speed and capacity versus accumulated skill and experience (Warr, 1994). For example, jobs that require crystallized intelligence (which does not decrease until well past retirement) and depend on experience theoretically should show improved performance in later adulthood. Older workers in jobs with high crystallized components should be strongly motivated to put in the effort they need to perform well on the job because they realize that their efforts will most likely meet with success.

By contrast, if the job is highly dependent on strength, speed, or working memory, older workers will be less able to perform well and at the same time will be less motivated to put in effort that they believe may not pay off (Kanfer & Ackerman, 2004). Because of the variations that exist in job performance based on its particular demands, tailored assessments that take into account the job's characteristics are needed rather than generic evaluations about the job capabilities of older workers (Sluiter, 2006).

With this framework in mind, we can examine several areas of job performance studied with regard to age. One of these is shift work, in which the individual's work hours change from the daytime hours to evenings or nights. Although these schedules present a challenge for workers of all ages, they are particularly difficult for older workers (Bonnefond et al., 2006). Shift work jobs are a good example of occupations in which age effects are decidedly negative (sleep patterns), and there is no benefit of experience because a person cannot improve over time in a shift work job on this aspect of performance.

Absentee rates are another important factor in examining worker productivity and aging. Voluntary absences, which are those in which an employee decides not to report for work, are more frequent among younger workers by a factor of two to three. With regard to involuntary absenteeism, you might assume that older workers have higher rates of involuntary absenteeism due to illness; however, this is not the case. In fact, when all rates of absenteeism are combined, older workers still have lower rates compared with younger workers (Warr, 1994).

Injuries are a second area of investigation in understanding the relationship between age and job performance. Overall, workers over the age of 55 are nearly half as likely to suffer a nonfatal injury as those who are 35 years and younger, and about half as likely to suffer death due to a work-related injury. However, when older workers (55–64) must miss work due to injury or illness, they spend twice as many days away from work (12) per year than do younger workers (25–34) (Bureau of Labor Statistics, 2010c). Driving-related accidents in the transportation industry have the highest fatality rate of all U.S. industries, and it is in this job that older workers have the highest rate of dying as well (Pegula, Marsh, & Jackson, 2007).

With regard to overall physical fitness, decreases in strength and agility can certainly have a negative influence on job performance in some areas of employment, particularly when physical exertion is involved (Sluiter & Frings-Dresen, 2007). However, workers of any age can suffer from conditions that impair their performance, such as a cold or muscle ache. Furthermore, as pointed out by Warr (1994), every worker has restrictions in the kind of work that he or she can perform. The fact that older workers may have some limitations due to physical aging changes does not mean that they cannot achieve adequate performance on all types of jobs. People learn to cope with their limitations, and gravitate to jobs they are able to perform (Daly & Bound, 1996). If they become disabled enough, they will leave the job market altogether.

Passage of the **Age Discrimination in Employment Act (ADEA)** in 1967 made it illegal to fire or not employ workers on the basis of their age. This legislation was intended to provide protection for older workers (over 40) from discrimination by employers who would otherwise seek to replace them with younger, cheaper, and presumably more productive employees. In fact, the ADEA resulted in settlements amounting to approximately $72.1 million in the year 2009 alone. However, the ADEA does not protect workers in occupations in which age has a presumed effect on the performance of critical job tasks in these occupations. For example, the ADEA does not cover police officers and firefighters on the grounds that their occupations require that they be able to protect the public by engaging in highly demanding physical activity. Airline pilots are another group not protected by the ADEA, as they face mandatory retirement at age 65 (see Figure 10.9).

These findings on age and job performance, like those in the area of vocational satisfaction, point to the importance of applying knowledge about adult development and aging in general to specific questions relating to older workers. From a human resources perspective, managers need to attend to the varying capabilities of workers of different ages and also to take account of age dynamics as they play out in the workplace. Managers need to learn how to balance the complementary strengths of workers of younger and older ages (Brooke & Taylor, 2005).

Unfortunately, older workers must battle against ageist stereotypes, held both by employers and by workers themselves. Image norms, the view people have about how they "should" look in a particular occupation, may affect not only the way older workers are treated by their fellow workers but also the way they think of themselves (Giannantonio & Hurley-Hanson, 2006). As their self-image and abilities change, older workers can begin to doubt their self-efficacy; in terms of the identity model, they over-accommodate to the view that aging causes a loss of essential job skills. A self-fulfilling prophecy can develop, resulting in a decreased ability to keep up with new technologies.

According to Maurer (2001), there are a set of factors that contribute to feelings of self-efficacy in the job, including direct or vicarious (watching others) rewards, learning, persuasion, and changes in physiological functioning and health. Self-efficacy, in turn, influences attitudes toward training and development activities. Intervention at the point of raising self-efficacy may give the older workers the confidence needed to engage in these important development activities so they can retain their job skills.

RETIREMENT

Retirement may be the furthest thing from your mind, if you are a college student in your late teens or early 20s. You are most likely concentrating on finding a job rather than retiring from one. Ideally, you will find a job that you enjoy and that will also give you a solid basis for being able to spend 10 or 20 years (or more) enjoying your retirement years.

Traditionally, **retirement** is the end of an individual's work career. Many people think of retirement as an event that is marked by a ceremony such as the proverbial "gold watch" given to the retiree as thanks for years of loyal service. This traditional image of retirement is rapidly vanishing, though. In fact, even though it is a popular view, it may have ever applied in the past only to a minority of workers—men in the middle and upper middle social classes with organized or regular careers. Furthermore, compared with other celebratory rituals in adulthood, such as college graduation, marriage, and the birth of children, retirement is more likely to carry with it ambivalent associations.

Just as labor force participation affects and is affected by the health of the economy, the opportunities for financial security available to retirees are heavily dependent on economic factors such as interest rates, tax policies, inflation, and the overall growth of the economy. The fate of the millions of retired persons in the United States will depend on how these forces play out in the coming decades. You might feel as though you are years away from retirement and therefore are not affected by these debates, but if you take a close look at your paycheck at the section

FIGURE 10.9

Areas of Protection Under the Age Discrimination in Employment Act

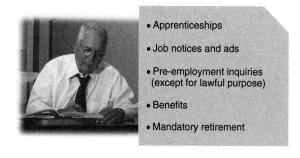

- Apprenticeships
- Job notices and ads
- Pre-employment inquiries (except for lawful purpose)
- Benefits
- Mandatory retirement

labeled Social Security taxes (called "FICA"), you will see that the topic is closer to you than you may think.

Definitions of Retirement

Retirement is defined simply as the withdrawal of an individual in later life from the labor force (Moen, 1996). As straightforward as this sounds, it is actually not all that easy a process to define. Most people do not just step off the job merry-go-round and onto the ground when they hit retirement.

There are five phases in the retirement process (see Figure 10.10) (Sterns & Gray, 1999): an anticipatory period that may last for decades, the decision to retire, the act of retirement, continual adjustment following the actual event, and making further decisions regarding the structuring of the individual's life and activity patterns. Because retirement is not simply an event with a defined start and end point, it is best conceptualized in terms of an adjustment process (Wang & Shultz, 2010).

Few retirees show a "crisp" pattern of leaving the workplace in a single, unreversed, clear-cut exit. Most experience a "blurred" exit in which they exit and reenter the workplace several times. They may have retired from a long-term job to accept bridge employment, such as an insurance agent who retires from the insurance business but works as a crossing guard or server at a fast-food restaurant. Other workers may retire from one job in a company and accept another job performing another role in the same company.

Workers who have a long, continuous history of employment in private sector jobs tend not to seek **bridge employment** because they typically have sufficient financial resources (Davis, 2003). In general, involvement in bridge employment is strongly related to financial need. Ultimately, the criteria for retirement are met when an individual in later life with a cohesive past work pattern has not worked for a sustained period of time and is not psychologically invested any longer in work (Beehr, Glazer, Nielson, & Farmer, 2000).

Facts About Retirement

Even though they may arrive there in phases, by the age of 65, the large majority of Americans are no

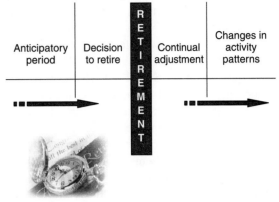

FIGURE 10.10

Phases of Retirement

longer in the labor force. At present, about 17% of the 65 and older population are still considered to be in the labor force, meaning that they are either working or actively seeking employment. Virtually all of those 75 years and older (93%) have ended their full-time participation in the nation's workforce (Bureau of Labor Statistics, 2010b). However, many remain employed on a part-time basis; nearly half of all men and 61% of all women 70 years and older engage in some paid work (He et al., 2005).

Approximately 10.5 million Americans receive pension benefits other than Social Security, and as of 2008, 35.5 million over the age of 65 were receiving Social Security benefits. The average monthly Social Security benefit for a retired worker through 2008 was $1,164 (Social Security Administration, 2009b). As of the end of 2007, 36% of the income of Americans 65 and older came from Social Security. The remaining percents of income come from earnings (29%), assets such as interest income (16%), and either private (9%) or government pensions (8%) or other sources (3%) (Social Security Administration, 2009a).

Retirement is in many ways a 20th-century phenomenon (Sterns & Gray, 1999). Throughout the 1700s and mid-1800s very few people retired, a trend that continued into the 1900s; in 1900 about 70% of all men over 65 years were still in the labor force. The jobs held by older workers often held high status and prestige. The wisdom and experience of older workers were valued, and it was considered a benefit to society to have them continuing to contribute to the workplace. However, pressures on the economy in combination with the growth of unions led, by the early 1930s, to the first instance in the United States of compulsory retirement (in the railroad industry). Because older workers were forced to retire but did not receive retirement benefits, they lived in poverty.

The passage of the **Social Security Act** in 1935 provided much-needed financial relief for the older population. By 1940, the percentage of older workers in the labor force had dropped to slightly over 40%, and the numbers have continued to decrease.

Attitudes toward retirement were largely negative in the United States until the mid-1960s because lack of employment was associated with poverty. People did not want to retire because their financial security would be placed at risk. However, with increases in earnings and Social Security benefits, retirement began to gain more acceptance. Changes in federal policy toward older workers were also occurring. As mentioned above, the passage of the ADEA in 1967 meant that workers in the 40 to 65 year age range were protected from age discrimination. An amendment to the ADEA in 1978 eliminated mandatory retirement before the age of 70, and in 1986 mandatory retirement was eliminated from most occupations. With these changes in retirement laws, it has also become easier for workers to continue in the jobs they have held throughout their lives or to find new employment even while they earn retirement benefits from their previous occupations. These changes in age discrimination and retirement laws have eased the potential stress of the transition, so that retired individuals no longer necessarily experience the poor health, low income, and loss of status that was associated with exit from the labor force earlier in the 1900s.

Furthermore, workers in the industrialized nations in Europe are increasingly looking favorably on retirement. The trend over the previous three decades is toward earlier retirement ages. Although this situation helps to give retirement a more positive image, it creates another problem by placing greater strain on pension plans (Disney & Johnson, 2001).

The future of Social Security is not bright; as you will learn in the next chapter, along with Medicare (the U.S. government's health insurance and entitlement plan for older adults), the funds available for both programs are at risk of being depleted within several decades. In the year 2009, $548 billion were paid out in benefits to retired workers (Social Security Administration, 2010). Social Security is almost entirely a pay-as-you-go program, meaning that today's workers pay into the system that pays today's retirees, although there is a Social Security Trust Fund that contains significant assets.

Most of the funding (83%) of Social Security comes from payroll taxes on current workers, and 76% of these revenues go out directly in retirement benefits (Social Security Administration, 2009a). In the future, to reduce this pressure on retirement benefits it may be necessary to entice older workers to remain in the labor force rather than retire. Given that current Baby Boomers are less likely to save for retirement (Devaney & Chiremba, 2005), there may be more financial incentives for them to remain in the labor market so that those enticements will not be necessary.

The Effects of Retirement on the Individual

Among sociological theories on the effect of aging on social roles, questions about the impact of retirement have consistently taken center stage. Does loss of the work role cause changes in mental and physical health? Do age-related losses in functioning precede retirement? Or is there not a clear-cut relationship between changes in work patterns and health in later life? The answers to these questions have implications for both the health and well-being of millions of older Americans, as well as potential importance for employers and retirement counselors.

There are three major theoretical perspectives on the effect of retirement on the individual (see Table 10.2). The predominant view of retirement for many years was based on **role theory**. According to this perspective, the individual's roles, or normative expectations for behavior, provide a major source of fulfillment because they integrate the individual with society. The more roles the individual fills (worker, family member, friend, community member), the higher the individual's physical and psychological well-being.

Among all the roles that adults may hold, the work role is one of the most important because it defines

TABLE 10.2
Theories of Retirement and the Individual

Theory	Proposed Effects of Retirement
Role theory	Roles provide source of fulfillment Loss of work role is harmful
Continuity theory	Retirees maintain previous sense of identity Retirement is not a crisis
Life course perspective	Normative timing of events Retirement stressful only when unexpected

the individual's daily activities, status, and social group. Role theory predicts that as older workers lose their social roles, they lose their integration with society. Loss of the work role through retirement in particular leads a person to experience financial hardship, which in turn leads to increased mortality risk (Tucker-Seeley, Li, Subramanian, & Sorensen, 2009). Feelings of isolation and depression would in turn further increase the risk of poor health and mortality. Thus, individuals who have had a strong psychological investment in their jobs are particularly likely to suffer after loss of their work role through retirement, according to this view.

Countering the role theory is the **continuity theory of retirement** (Atchley, 1989), which proposes that retirement does not lead to serious disruptions in the individual's sense of identity, social connections, or feelings of productivity. According to the continuity theory, changes in work patterns associated with retirement do not lead to a significant loss of self-definition. Retirees maintain their previous goals, patterns of activities, and relationships, even though they are no longer reporting for work on a daily basis. Older adults view retirement as another stage of their careers, one that they have planned for and positively anticipated. The fact that many individuals maintain some form of employment after they have officially retired is further evidence in favor of continuity theory, suggesting that people can move into and out of the labor force with relative ease. What determines whether older adults are satisfied depends on whether the role is desirable, be it worker, retiree, or part-time worker (Warr, Butcher, Robertson, & Callinan, 2004).

The life course perspective views retirement as a normative stage of vocational development. Changes that are associated with this period of life are seen as logical outgrowths of earlier life events. The factors that shaped the individual's prior vocational development will have a persisting influence throughout retirement. For example, women's work lives are shaped by different factors than those of men, and these factors will continue to play out in the way that they experience retirement (Kim & Moen, 2001). The life course perspective also emphasizes the normative timing of events. According to this view, retirement will be stressful and create difficulties when its timing is unexpected.

Retirement and Health

Implied in the role theory of retirement is the belief that loss of the work role leads to a general deterioration of the individual's well-being, both physical and mental. For many years, retirement researchers were convinced that lack of focus and sense of importance in life was the direct cause of poorer health, with an associated higher risk of death. In other words, the retiree, without a purpose in life, soon became ill and died. In the extreme version of this scenario, the retiree commits suicide due to a general sense of uselessness and irrelevance. However, many researchers now believe that the relationship between retirement and poor health most likely exists due to the fact that poor health causes early retirement (Brockmann, Muller, & Helmert, 2009). Furthermore, retirement may lead to improvements in health if the individual is retiring from a job being carried out in an unhealthy environment (Topa, Moriano, Depolo, Alcover, & Morales, 2009).

Thus, the reasons for retiring seem particularly important to consider in determining whether retirement has positive or negative effects on health. Findings from the Whitehall II study examining the longitudinal associations between retirement and physical functioning further reinforce this point. Retirement at age 60 caused by factors other than poor health was associated with improved mental health and physical functioning. Alternatively, retirement due to poor health was associated with decreased mental and physical health (Jokela et al., 2010).

In terms of psychological health, there is evidence that retirement does not have deleterious effects on self-esteem or depression and may actually have a positive impact on feelings of well-being, lowering stress levels, and reducing anxiety (Drentea, 2002). Having high levels of social support, being able to enjoy vacations, having a strong marriage, and participating in a set of enjoyable hobbies seems to be related to high retirement satisfaction (Vaillant, DiRago, & Mukamal, 2006).

Factors That Influence Adjustment to Retirement

Figure 10.11 shows adjustment to retirement as a biopsychosocial process. In general, having a diverse

FIGURE 10.11

Biopsychosocial Model of Retirement

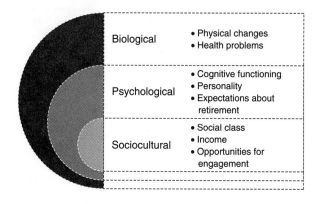

set of physical, psychological, and social resources seems to ease the transition to retirement, even among individuals who initially experience poor adjustment. According to the **resource model** of retirement, adaptation, even to difficult retirement transitions, can be facilitated by being able to draw from a range of strengths and opportunities in a variety of life domains (Wang, 2007). Financial resources (Pinquart & Schindler, 2007) and expectations about retirement both have important roles in influencing retirement adjustment, particularly adjustment during the early retirement period (Taylor, Goldberg, Shore, & Lipka, 2008).

The timing of retirement is considered by researchers to be a major influence on the older individual's feelings of well-being. From a life course perspective, the exiting of the work role in an "off-time" or premature fashion is seen as more stressful or disruptive than going through the transition in an "on-time" or expectable fashion (Gill et al., 2006). Related to the timing of retirement is control over the retirement decision. When early retirement suddenly becomes mandatory because of company downsizing, individuals lose control over the timing of their retirement and suffer negative consequences in terms of well-being (Armstrong-Stassen, 2001; Kalimo, Taris, & Schaufeli, 2003). A large multinational study in Europe of the retirement experience found, furthermore, that early retirement is predicted by poor work quality and low levels of life satisfaction (von Bonsdorff, Huuhtanen, Tuomi, & Seitsamo, 2010). Maintaining better working conditions could help stave off an early retirement decision and maintain the individual's quality of life for a longer period both during and after retirement (Siegrist, Wahrendorf, von dem Knesebeck, Jurges, & Borsch-Supan, 2007).

The amount of time allowed for retiring is another related factor. A minimum of 2 years planning prior to a person's retirement is related to a positive experience compared with a decision made 6 months or less prior to retirement (Hardy & Quadagno, 1995). As important as length of time, however, is the quality of retirement planning, which should include not only financial planning but also adequate discussion with the spouse (Noone, Stephens, & Alpass, 2009).

Socioeconomic level has a complex relationship to retirement satisfaction. People at higher socioeconomic levels are less likely to retire, and they retire at later ages. Intrinsic satisfaction associated with work is more likely to be found in individuals in the higher occupational levels of professionals, executives, and managers, causing them to be less likely to engage in retirement planning (Kosloski, Ekerdt, & DeViney, 2001). However, higher socioeconomic status makes it possible for the individual to take advantage of the opportunities that retirement offers for productive and enjoyable leisure activities, such as involvement in retirement learning communities and the chance to travel. Individuals with higher levels of education and previous experience in managerial or professional positions may be better able to find part-time employment after retirement if so desired. Past experience in community organizations and activities may also make it easier for such individuals to find rewarding opportunities for unpaid volunteer work and participation in clubs, organizations, and informal networks.

The continuity of an individual's work career is thought to be a further influence on the impact of retirement, at least for men. Those in **orderly careers** spend the majority of their employed years in related occupations. The higher the extent of orderliness in people's careers, the higher their attachments to their communities, friends, and social activities. The social integration these individuals maintain during their careers eases their retirement transition and means that they are likely to be in better physical and psychological health. Individuals with more continuous work histories also have higher socioeconomic status and income than those in disorderly careers, and

these are factors generally related to greater satisfaction with retirement. However, on the negative side, workers with orderly careers may be more attached to their jobs and therefore less satisfied with retirement (Gee & Baillie, 1999).

There has been somewhat of a debate in the literature concerning the effect of retirement on a married couple's relationship. One school of thought describes the "spouse underfoot syndrome," which traditionally applied to the husband, and meant that partners were more likely to experience conflict now that they were in each other's presence for most of the daytime as well as nighttime hours. However, there is a contrasting view of retirement as a second honeymoon, in which couples are now free to enjoy each other's company on a full-time basis without the constraints presented by the need to leave home for 8 or more hours a day. As with much of the data on retirement, there is no simple answer. The transition itself from work to retirement seems to take its toll on marital satisfaction when partners have high levels of conflict. The greatest conflict is observed when one partner is working while the other has retired. Eventually, however, these problems seem to subside, and after about 2 years of retirement for both partners, levels of marital satisfaction once again rise (Moen, Kim, & Hofmeister, 2001).

As we can see, work and retirement are broad and fascinating areas of study in the field of adult development and aging. Research from a developmental perspective has been somewhat slow to get off the ground. However, increasing information on the topics of vocational satisfaction and performance-retirement adjustment as these interact with personality and social structural factors are providing greater clarification regarding this significant component of adult life.

LEISURE PURSUITS IN LATER ADULTHOOD

Throughout adulthood, people express themselves not only in their work lives, but also in their hobbies and interests. Occupational psychologists and academics studying the relationship between job characteristics and satisfaction often neglect the fact that, for many adults, it is the off-duty hours rather than the on-duty hours that contribute the most to identity and personal satisfaction. In contrast, marketers recognize the value of developing promotional campaigns that appeal to the aging Baby Boomers who potentially have resources to spend on leisure pursuits (Ferguson & Brohaugh, 2010).

As people move through adulthood and into retirement, it becomes more crucial for them to develop leisure interests so that they will have activities to engage in during the day to provide focus and meaning to life. In addition, leisure pursuits can serve important functions in helping older adults maintain their health through physical activity and their cognitive functioning through intellectual stimulation. The social functions of leisure are also of potential significance, particularly for people who have become widowed or have had to relocate due to finances, a desire for more comfortable climates, or poor health.

Researchers who study leisure-time activities in later adulthood find strong evidence linking leisure participation to improvement in feelings of well-being, particularly among older adults who are trying to overcome deficits in physical functioning or social networks (Silverstein & Parker, 2002). Furthermore, cognitively challenging leisure activities can be at least if not more beneficial than physical exercise in helping individuals maintain their intellectual functioning, including lowering the risk for vascular dementia (Verghese, Wang, Katz, Sanders, & Lipton, 2009).

The effects of leisure on physical health can also be striking. In one particularly impressive study, a sample of 799 men ages 39 to 86 was divided into groups on the basis of whether or not they were bereaved. Involvement in social activities was found to moderate the negative effects of stress on the physical functioning of the bereaved men (Luoh & Herzog, 2002).

Regular leisure time physical activity can have important health consequences. A longitudinal study in Sweden followed men over five time points (Byberg et al., 2009). Participants were asked about their level of physical activity with questions such as "Do you often go walking or cycling for pleasure?" Increased engagement in physical activity was linked over time with significant reductions in mortality over the 35-year period of the study (see Figure 10.12).

As we discussed in Chapter 5, older adults are less likely than younger people to engage in physical activities as leisure time pursuits. There is evidence that, at least for men, public health efforts to increase the physical activity of older adults are having a moderately positive impact. In one large longitudinal study of health, over the two decades from the late 1970s to the late 1990s, there was only a slight drop in the proportion of sedentary men. Given that the sample was recruited from a long-term study that tended to be heavily biased toward health-conscious individuals, this finding signifies that there are gaps between the efforts to educate the public to adopt more healthy lifestyle leisure choices and the actual behavior of older adults (Talbot, Fleg, & Metter, 2003).

It is one thing to be able to document the favorable effects of leisure activities on health and well-being and another to be able to help people select appropriate activities in which to participate. Although involvement in highly social activities may be beneficial, for example, not everyone seeks out these types of experiences. Similarly, not everyone will engage in leisure activities that involve a high degree of cognitive stimulation. Based on this reasoning, researchers have found that the Holland RIASEC model can be applied to leisure activities in older adults (Kerby & Ragan, 2002). Just as people

FIGURE 10.12

Prediction of Mortality from Amount of Leisure-time Physical Activity

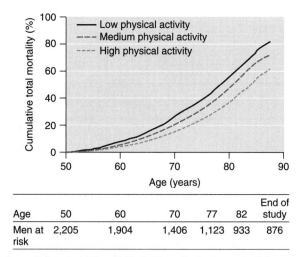

Age	50	60	70	77	82	End of study
Men at risk	2,205	1,904	1,406	1,123	933	876

Source: Byberg, L., Melhus, H. K., Gedeborg, R., Sundstrom, J., Ahlbom, A., Zethelius, B., & Michaelsson, K. (2009). Total mortality after changes in leisure time physical activity in 50 year old men: 35 year follow-up of population based cohort. *BMJ: British Medical Journal, 338.*

can be counseled to seek a person–environment fit for vocations, they might also be advised to find the leisure pursuit that will keep them motivated and, hence, active in a pursuit that will ultimately have value in maximizing their functional abilities.

In conclusion, changes in the labor force, the meaning of work, and the economic realities of an aging population all affect the nature of work and the workplace. As you contemplate your future career, thinking about what you will find to be most fulfilling should be your top priority. However, all workers will need to plan for these changes in the social context that will affect their adaptation to and satisfaction in the workplace.

SUMMARY

1. Work is a major focus of adult life from the 20s until retirement and beyond. Labor force age dynamics have shifted with movement of the Baby Boom generation and the aging of the labor force. There are disparities by race and gender in income levels, even controlling for educational attainment.

2. Contemporary vocational psychology is oriented primarily around Holland's RIASEC theory of vocational development, which is the basis for O*NET, a comprehensive catalog of occupations. The highest level of worker satisfaction and productivity is theorized to occur when there is congruence between persons and their environments. Super's self-concept theory proposes that individuals move through several stages of career development in which they attempt to maximize the expression of their self-concept in their work. Rather than proceed straight through these stages, however, individuals may plateau at the maintenance stage or recycle through earlier stages after a career change. The boundaryless career captures the concept that individuals direct their own career progression.

3. Theories and research on vocational satisfaction attempt to determine the relative influence of intrinsic and extrinsic factors on worker's happiness and productivity in a job. Occupational reinforcement patterns are the work values and needs that are likely to be satisfied in a job, and if these are present, the individual will be more satisfied. Self-determination theory proposes that in the highest form of extrinsic motivation people's jobs become the basis for their identities. Conflict between work and family is a source of potential vocational dissatisfaction. Researchers have not established whether age is related to vocational satisfaction because the influence of job tenure must also be taken into account.

4. The question of whether older workers are as productive as younger workers is another focus of occupational research. Older workers are relatively advantaged in jobs that rely on experience and perform more poorly in jobs that demand speed. Older workers have fewer fatalities on the job as well as lower absentee rates. Passage of the ADEA in 1967 offered protection to workers over 40 from discrimination by employers, although several occupations are excluded from this legislation.

5. Retirement is defined as the individual's withdrawal from the labor force in later life. Rather than being a discrete event, however, for most people it spans a process that may last for years. Most retired people do not suffer a loss of health, either mental or physical, but some do experience the transition as stressful. The resource model of retirement proposes that people will be most satisfied in retirement if they can draw on physical, psychological, and social sources of support.

6. Leisure activities can serve a variety of important functions for adults throughout their working lives, but particularly in later adulthood after retirement. Researchers have identified positive effects of leisure involvement on physical functioning, well-being, and ultimately, mortality.

11

Mental Health Issues

Up until this point, we have focused primarily on people who fit the definition of "normal" as they navigate the adult years. We will now turn our focus to psychological disorders, which touch the lives of many people. By some accounts, over half of the entire adult population struggle with the symptoms of one or another disorder or has had a family member experience symptoms. In this chapter, we focus our discussion on the most common disorders affecting people in adulthood and later life, but it is important to keep in mind that abnormal behavior rests on a continuum.

Furthermore, psychological disorders reflect developmental processes that continue throughout life. Whether psychological symptoms emerge in later adulthood reflects the balance of risk and protective factors as they evolve earlier in life (Whitbourne & Meeks, 2010).

PSYCHOLOGICAL DISORDERS IN ADULTHOOD

The criteria used to judge behavior as "abnormal" include feeling personal or subjective distress, being impaired in everyday life, causing a risk to the self or other people, and engaging in behavior that is socially or culturally unacceptable (Halgin & Whitbourne, 2008). The category of **psychological disorders** includes the range of behaviors and experiences that fall outside of social norms, create adaptational difficulty for the individual on a daily basis, and put the individual or others at risk of harm. People who have a hobby of collecting coins would not be considered abnormal, for example, because they are engaging in a behavior that does not hurt them or others and is culturally acceptable. By contrast, consider people known as "hoarders" who collect old newspapers, magazines, and cereal boxes until their homes are virtually unlivable because they are so squalid and overcrowded. These individuals might very well be considered to have a psychological disorder because they are not only engaging in behavior that is outside the norm but also may be putting themselves at risk for fire and other harm due to the dirt and debris that have accumulated in their home.

Specific sets of behaviors that meet the conditions of abnormality are given a diagnosis according to the criteria set forth in the psychiatric manual known as the **Diagnostic and Statistical Manual**, the most

and Treatment

recent version of which is the **Fourth Edition-Text Revision** known as the **DSM-IV-TR** (American Psychiatric Association, 2000). Unfortunately, for our purposes, the DSM-IV-TR was not developed with consideration of how the diagnostic categories for psychological disorders might change over the adult years. Given some of the distinctive characteristics of these disorders in later life, this creates problems in applying diagnoses to older adults. However, there is no alternative to this system, and therefore we must use it here to provide the framework for the chapter. The fifth edition is expected for publication in May 2013, and gerontologists hope that it will better address issues of diagnosis for use with older adults.

The DSM-IV-TR is organized into five axes or dimensions that are intended to characterize completely an individual seeking psychological help. Axis I includes all the major clinical syndromes: collections of symptoms that together form a recognizable pattern of disturbance comparable to an illness in medical terms. The major syndrome categories include mood disorders, dementia, anxiety disorders, substance-related disorders, **schizophrenia**, sexual disorders, eating disorders, sleep disorders, and disorders of childhood and adolescence.

Axis II includes disturbances that are of a more chronic or long-standing nature, what are known as **personality disorders.** One way to think of personality disorders is that they are exaggerations of personality traits found in everyone that, for some people, create significant problems in daily life. Mental retardation and disorders in the individual's ability to carry out the tasks of daily living are also included on Axis II.

The ratings on Axis III are used to characterize medical conditions that, although not a primary focus of treatment, have a bearing on the client's psychological condition. These are particularly important in diagnosing psychological disorders in older adults, for whom medical conditions may present a particular challenge. You have already learned in previous chapters that certain medical diagnoses are associated with anxiety or depressive symptoms. For older adults in particular, ratings on Axis III provide valuable diagnostic information.

Axis IV is used to rate psychosocial stressors and environmental problems. Again, these can be important influences on a middle-aged or older adult's psychiatric diagnosis, particularly for people

This man, an example of a hoarder, shows the thousands of possessions he has collected over many decades of never throwing anything away.

with low incomes, those who live alone, or and bereaved individuals suffering from recent losses.

Axis V is used to characterize the individual's overall level of functioning, ranging from suicidal (ratings of 1–20) to superior (91–100). By rating a person on Axis V, it is possible for the mental health worker to get a sense of how well the individual is coping, and gain information that can be useful in planning interventions.

Major Axis I Disorders in Adulthood

As stated in the previous section, Axis I is used to provide a diagnosis of which major disorder or disorders whose symptoms are shown by the individual seeking treatment. These conditions may persist for many years, and even if the symptoms dissipate over time, the individual may be on more or less constant alert for a renewed outbreak. Fortunately, a minority of adults experience these disorders, but those who do face struggles in their family relationships, work lives, and ability to live independently in the community. Table 11.1 lists the major Axis I disorders we focus on in this chapter, with a description of how the symptoms are manifest in adults over the age of 65.

Each Axis I diagnosis includes a set of specific criteria that must be met in order for the diagnosis to be correctly applied. Here we list their major features in abbreviated fashion, but in a real-world setting, whoever is providing the diagnosis must go carefully through each of the criteria to ensure that the individual actually should receive the diagnosis. In general, these criteria involve a fairly high degree of severity and persistence of symptoms over a period of time usually no less than two weeks. In other words, just because a person may seem to be depressed or anxious does not mean that the person should be diagnosed with the disorder on the spot.

Mood Disorders. Abnormalities in the individual's experience of emotion are known as **mood disorders**. There are essentially two categories of mood disorders. The first includes **depressive disorders**, characterized by periods of **dysphoria** (sad mood) lasting varying amounts of time and involving varying degrees of severity. In **major depressive disorder,** the major symptom is an extremely sad mood (lasting at least 2 weeks). Other symptoms include appetite and sleep disturbances, feelings of guilt, and a low sense of self-worth. The second category of mood disorders includes **bipolar disorder** (formerly known as manic depression). People with bipolar disorder experience what is known as a **manic episode**, a period typically lasting at least 1 week, in which they feel unusually "high," meaning that they are elated, grandiose, expansive, and highly energetic.

Over the course of adulthood, about 18% of adults are estimated to meet the diagnostic criteria for major depressive disorder. This figure represents the lifetime prevalence, meaning that it includes anyone who has ever received this diagnosis. At any given time, however, about 1 to 5% of adults in the United States have major depression or its milder and more chronic form, known as dysthymia. The rates of major depressive disorder and dysthymia in women are about double the rates for men (Kessler et al., 2005). Contrary to what you might think about older people and depression, people over 65 are actually less likely to experience a depressive disorder than are people under the age of 65 (Kessler et al., 2003).

Though the prevalence of a diagnosable mood disorder is lower in older than in younger adults, many older adults report symptoms of depressive disorders. As many as 15 to 30% of older adults living in the community experience depressive symptoms with higher rates among those seen in medical settings such as inpatient hospitals or clinics (Whitbourne & Meeks, 2010). Moreover, although women are more likely to experience the diagnosable condition of major depressive disorder, depressive symptoms are higher in men between the ages of 60 and 80. By that point, the rates of depressive symptoms in men

and women are roughly equal (Barefoot, Mortensen, Helms, Avlund, & Schroll, 2001).

However, there are age differences in the symptoms of depression, and what appears as a depressive symptom for a younger adult may not appear as one in an older adult. The traditionally recognized "psychological" symptoms of depression such as dysphoria, guilt, low self-esteem, and suicidal thoughts are less likely to be acknowledged by older adults. Rather than seeking treatment for these psychological symptoms, older people are more likely to seek treatment for physical symptoms such as pain and abdominal disturbances (Amore, Tagariello, Laterza, & Savoia, 2007).

Health care professionals are not well trained in recognizing the signs of depression in their older clients (Charney et al., 2003). In part this is because older adults do not necessarily report their symptoms in a manner that allows for accurate diagnosis. In addition, health care providers are not attuned to diagnosing psychological disorders in their older clients. Complicating the situation further, physicians spend less time per visit with an older patient than they do a younger patient.

TABLE 11.1
Selected Axis I Disorders of the DSM-IV-TR as Observed in Older Adults

Category	Description	Examples of Specific Disorders	Important Considerations for Older Adults
Mood disorders	Disturbance in mood	Major depressive disorder, bipolar disorder	Depression may appear as cognitive impairment or physical symptoms.
Anxiety disorders	Intense anxiety, worry, or apprehension	Generalized anxiety disorder, panic disorder, specific phobia, social phobia, obsessive-compulsive disorder, post-traumatic stress disorder	Symptoms of anxiety disorders may present or coexist with medical symptoms.
Schizophrenia	Psychotic symptoms such as distortion of reality and serious impairment in thinking, behavior, affect, and motivation	Schizophrenia, schizoaffective disorder, delusional disorder	Likelihood of complete remission is 20–25%; the 10% who continue to experience symptoms have higher suicide rates than other older adults.
Delirium, dementia, and amnestic disorders	Significant loss of cognitive functioning as result of neurological dysfunction or medical illness	Delirium, Alzheimer's disease, amnesia	Delirium may be misdiagnosed as dementia.
Substance related disorder	Use or abuse of psychoactive substances	Substance dependence, substance abuse, substance intoxication	Older adults are more at risk than is often thought.

Many insurance companies reimburse for mental health diagnosis and intervention at a lower rate than for physical disorders, adding to the likelihood that an older adult will not seek treatment for psychologically-based symptoms. The situation has improved for Medicare recipients with recent changes in Medicare reimbursement. In 2008, the U.S. Congress approved a revision to Medicare providing parity for mental health treatment meaning that the insured pay the same out-of-pocket expense that they would for medical care (Medicare Improvement for Patients and Providers Act, H.R. 6331).

Other deterrents to appropriate diagnosis of depressive disorders in older adults relate to attitudes toward depression among mental health professionals. Some may assume that depression is a natural consequence of aging and therefore pay less attention to its symptoms. Alternatively, a psychologist or physician may wish to avoid stigmatizing older clients by diagnosing them with a psychological disorder (Duberstein & Conwell, 2000). Misdiagnosis may also occur because the symptoms of mood disorders occur in conjunction with a medical condition, leading to the physician's failure to detect the mood disorder or to misattribute the symptoms to a physical cause (Delano-Wood & Abeles, 2005). Careful diagnosis with attention to possible underlying medical conditions or dementia is therefore vital (Small, 2009).

When trying to determine the cause of an older adult's depression, it is important for health care workers to look for possible psychosocial factors other than those that are more affective in nature. These additional factor include functional limitations (Okura et al., 2010), sensory impairments (Dillon, Gu, Hoffman, & Ko, 2010), the inability to provide basic self-care tasks (Yong, 2006), and pain (McCarthy, Bigal, Katz, Derby, & Lipton, 2009). Institutionalization presents another risk factor, as do changes in cognition and personality, particularly among the oldest-old (Margrett et al., 2010). Psychosocial issues such as bereavement, loneliness, and stressful life events can also serve as risk factors for depressive disorders in both middle (Kendler, Myers, & Zisook, 2008) and later adulthood (Holley & Mast, 2007).

An inability to employ successful coping strategies to deal with late-life stressors can also increase the individual's risk of developing depression. In one study covering a 10-year period, older adults who used ineffective coping methods, such as avoidance, were more likely to develop symptoms of depression compared with their age peers who attempted to handle their problems through direct, problem-focused coping methods (Holahan, Moos, Holahan, Brennan, & Schutte, 2005).

Medical disorders also present significant risk factors for depression (Sneed, Kasen, & Cohen, 2007); specifically, arthritis-related activity limitations (Shih, Hootman, Kruger, & Helmick, 2006), hip fracture (Lenze et al., 2007), diabetes (Campayo et al., 2010), metabolic syndrome (Almeida, Calver, Jamrozik, Hankey, & Flicker, 2009), stroke (Santos et al., 2009), and hypertension (Garcia-Fabela et al., 2009). Apart from these major medical conditions, there are some less obvious but still noteworthy contributors to late-life depression involving physical health. As we pointed out in Chapter 4, tooth loss is a condition that affects a substantial number of older adults. Perhaps not surprisingly, researchers have found that depressed older adults are more likely to have experienced tooth loss (Hugo, Hilgert, de Sousa Mda, & Cury, 2009). Another potentially overlooked risk factor is lack of sufficient vitamin D, which may also present a risk factor for cognitive impairment (Barnard & Colon-Emeric, 2010). Interventions that help to address these conditions could potentially spare many older adults unnecessary emotional suffering.

Not only do physical conditions increase the risk of major depressive disorder, but older adults become more likely to suffer further impairments in physical and cognitive functioning when their psychological symptoms are untreated (Boyle, Porsteinsson, Cui, King, & Lyness, 2010). Depressive symptoms predict mortality in older adults (St John & Montgomery, 2009), perhaps through the immune system. Depression may activate cytokines that eventually increase the risk of cardiovascular disease, osteoporosis, arthritis, Type 2 diabetes, cancers, periodontal disease, frailty, and functional decline (Kiecolt-Glaser & Glaser, 2002).

Researchers know considerably less about bipolar disorder in later adulthood than they do about major depressive disorder. Rates of bipolar disorder are lower in older adults (0.1%) than in the younger population (1.4%) (Depp & Jeste, 2004). There may be neurological contributions as suggested by the fact that bipolar disorder in older adults is related to a higher risk for cerebrovascular disease (Subramaniam, Dennis, & Byrne, 2007) and white matter hyperintensities (Zanetti, Cordeiro, & Busatto, 2007).

Bipolar disorder exacts a high psychosocial cost on those who have experienced its symptoms throughout their lives. For example, older adults with a lifetime history of "rapid cycling," in which their symptoms alternate frequently between depression and mania, feel that their life goals were significantly interfered with if not entirely derailed (Sajatovic et al., 2008).

Anxiety Disorders. Excessive anxiety is the major symptom of anxiety disorders; anxiety in relation to these disorders is defined as a state in which an individual is more tense, apprehensive, and uneasy about the future than would be warranted by the person's objective circumstances. As an example, if you lived in a neighborhood with a high rate of crime, worrying about someone breaking into your house would not be atypical. However, if you were living in a neighborhood with a low crime rate, an excessive preoccupation with being victimized might signify that your anxiety is symptomatic of a disorder.

Approximately 12% of adults are diagnosed with an anxiety disorder per year (Kessler et al., 2005). As is true with depressive disorders, older adults are less likely (7%) than young adults (21%) and middle-aged adults (19%) to be diagnosed with an anxiety disorder. Older women are nearly 5 times more likely than men to be diagnosed with an anxiety disorder (Gum, King-Kallimanis, & Kohn, 2009).

It is possible that the lower diagnosis of anxiety disorders in general among older adults reflects their greater resilience. It is also possible that, as with major depressive disorder, health care professionals are not well-trained in recognizing and diagnosing anxiety disorder symptoms in their older clients (Scogin, Floyd, & Forde, 2000). Similar to mood disorders, the symptoms of an anxiety disorder may present or coexist with medical symptoms (Mehta et al., 2007), particularly for some forms of anxiety disorders including post-traumatic stress disorder, panic attacks, and **agoraphobia** (which we discuss below) (Sareen, Cox, Clara, & Asmundson, 2005). As we also have seen, health practitioners may not

be attuned to diagnosing psychological symptoms in an older individual with physical health problems. As a result, the practitioners may miss the diagnosis of an anxiety disorder along with an opportunity for intervention. The implications of failing to diagnose anxiety disorders can be serious, as the presence of anxiety symptoms has been linked to mortality risk, particularly in African American older adults (Brenes et al., 2007).

Anxiety disorders fall into six general categories. **Generalized anxiety disorder** is associated with an overall sense of uneasiness and concern without specific focus. People who experience this disorder are very prone to worrying, especially over minor problems. They may also have additional symptoms such as feeling restless and tense, having trouble concentrating, being irritable, and having difficulty sleeping. About 2 to 5% of adults are reported to have symptoms of generalized anxiety disorder over a 1-year period; medical patients have higher rates (8%) (Wittchen, 2002). Among older adults, the 6-month prevalence (those who reported symptoms in the past 6 months) is 2%, and the lifetime prevalence is estimated to be 3.6%, with a median age of onset of 31 (Kessler et al., 2005). However the prevalence rates are higher among certain minority groups; older Latina/o immigrants to the United States seem to be particularly at risk (Jimenez, Alegria, Chen, Chan, & Laderman, 2010).

The form of anxiety disorder known as **panic disorder** involves the experience of panic attacks in which people have the physical sensation that they are about to die (e.g., shortness of breath, pounding heart, sweating palms, and so on). People who suffer from panic disorder may have these episodes at unpredictable times. Eventually they may also develop agoraphobia, the fear of being trapped or stranded during a panic attack. Their fear of having a panic attack leads them to avoid places such as elevators, shopping malls, or public transportation, where escape during an attack would be difficult.

Estimates are that approximately 4.7% of adults have a diagnosis of panic disorder, with a higher percent in early and mid-adulthood (Kessler et al., 2005). The prevalence of agoraphobia is estimated to be much lower than panic disorder, affecting up to 1.4% of the adult United States population (Kessler et al., 2006). Agoraphobia is also less common among

AGING IN THE NEWS

MARIJUANA USE BY SENIORS RISES AS BOOMERS AGE

Perry Parks, 67, grinds up marijuana to smoke at his home in Rockingham, N.C., Wednesday, February 17, 2010. The retired Army pilot suffered crippling pain from degenerative disc disease and arthritis before turning to marijuana, which he first had tried in college, and was amazed how well it worked for the pain.

older adults than among adults in their 30s to 60s (Kessler et al., 2005). Unlike younger adults, who may develop agoraphobia following a panic attack, it is more likely that this condition in older adults is related to fear of harm or embarrassment (Scogin, Floyd, & Forde, 2000).

People with a **specific phobia** have an irrational fear of a particular object or situation. This disorder is the most commonly observed form of anxiety disorder in older adults. Among all adults, the lifetime prevalence rate is estimated at 12.5% and among adults 60 and older the prevalence is also fairly high with estimates at 7.5% (Kessler et al., 2005). People can fear almost any specific object or situation, but the most common are fear of snakes, enclosed places, and seeing blood.

Social phobia involves anxiety in situations in which a person must perform some action in front of others. The term is somewhat misleading in that it is not literally a fear of other people but a fear of being publicly embarrassed or made to look foolish. In some cases, the individual becomes anxious at the thought of eating in the presence of other people. Severe symptoms of social phobia are present in about 12% of adults, with a peak in prevalence rate among adults in their 30s. Women are more likely to suffer from this disorder than are men (Kessler et al., 2005).

Obsessive-compulsive disorder is a form of anxiety disorder in which people suffer from obsessions, or repetitive thoughts (such as the belief that one's child will be harmed) and compulsions, which are repetitive behaviors (such as handwashing). The obsessions and compulsions are unrelenting, irrational, and distracting. There is also a condition on Axis II known as obsessive-compulsive personality disorder, in which an individual has the personality traits of being excessively rigid and perfectionistic. People with obsessive-compulsive anxiety disorder have persistent feelings of anxiety that are partially relieved only by performing compulsive rituals or thinking certain thoughts.

The lifetime prevalence of obsessive-compulsive disorder is about 1.6% of the adult population (Kessler et al., 2005). The lifetime prevalence among older adults is estimated at 0.7%, making this a relatively rare disorder in this age group. The condition known as hoarding, referred to at the beginning of the chapter, is a variant of obsessive-compulsive disorder. It is a progressive and chronic condition that researchers believe has its origin early in life (Ayers, Saxena, Golshan, & Wetherell, 2010).

In **post-traumatic stress disorder (PTSD)**, an individual suffers prolonged effects of exposure to a traumatic experience such as an earthquake, fire, physical assault, and war. Although many people who are exposed to these types of experiences suffer from an acute stress disorder that relents after several months, some develop symptoms that persist beyond that point, lasting for years if not decades. The symptoms of PTSD include flashbacks or reminders of the event, intrusions of thoughts about the disaster, hypersensitivity to events similar to the trauma, and attempt to avoid these disturbing images and reminders. The individual with PTSD may also become detached from other people and the ordinary events of daily life. In one study of Israeli veterans of the 1982 Lebanon War, symptoms such as recurrent images, hypervigilance, and difficulties in sleep and memory persisted for 20 years or more following combat. The likelihood of experiencing PTSD symptoms was particularly elevated in veterans who had experienced a stress reaction during their combat exposure (Solomon & Mikulincer, 2006).

Some clinicians expect that the incidence of PTSD among the older adult population will grow in future years due to the aging of Vietnam veterans. Estimates are that at the age of 19, the prevalence of PTSD among Vietnam soldiers was 15%. Since PTSD can arise many years after exposure to trauma, these numbers may well continue to increase (Department of Health and Human Services, 1999). Exposure to the terrorist attacks in the United States on September 11, 2001 led to greater likelihood of PTSD among older adults (DiGrande et al., 2008). Furthermore, as younger and middle-aged adults serving in the Iraq and Afghanistan Wars grow older, the incidence of PTSD will likely increase substantially in coming decades (Chan, Cheadle, Reiber, Unutzer, & Chaney, 2009).

Severe health problems such as heart disease can also increase the individual's risk of developing PTSD after exposure to combat (Spindler & Pedersen, 2005). PTSD, in turn, can also increase the individual's risk of developing heart disease. A longitudinal study of nearly 2,000 veterans in the Normative Aging Study revealed that, even after controlling for a number of risk factors, men who had experienced higher levels of PTSD were more likely to have heart attacks or develop coronary heart disease (Kubzansky, Koenen, Spiro, Vokonas, & Sparrow, 2007).

Late-onset stress symptomatology (LOSS) refers to a phenomenon observed in aging veterans who were exposed to stressful combat situations in young adulthood. Symptoms related to the combat experiences (such as an increase in memories about the trauma) begin to emerge in later life, perhaps as a function of exposure to stresses associated with aging, such as retirement and increased health problems (Davison et al., 2006). Symptoms of LOSS are similar to those of PTSD, but the progression is distinct in that it develops later in life. Researchers at the VA Boston Healthcare System have developed a survey designed to identify LOSS among older veterans, thereby allowing mental health professionals to help treat the symptoms and offer the needed support (King, King, Vickers, Davison, & Spiro, 2007).

Anxiety may occur in conjunction with depression, a condition now known as comorbid anxiety depression. This disorder is more likely to be observed in older women than older men (Schoevers, Beekman, Deeg, Jonker, & van Tilburg, 2003).

Schizophrenia and Other Psychotic Disorders. The psychological disorder known as schizophrenia is perhaps the one that most mystifies students of psychopathology because its symptoms seem so puzzling and extreme. A person with schizophrenia has a wide range of unusual symptoms, including hallucinations (false perceptions) and delusions (false beliefs), both of which are known as positive symptoms. However, many people with schizophrenia also experience the so-called negative symptoms of apathy, withdrawal, and lack of emotional expression. In addition to these symptoms, people with schizophrenia may suffer from disturbances in speech and motor behavior. There are several types of schizophrenia, but all share the common feature of involving a severe disturbance in the person's ability to remain in touch with reality.

Epidemiologists estimate that 1% of the population has schizophrenia at some point in their lives, with higher rates for adults 30 to 44 (1.5%) than people older than 65 (0.2%) (Keith, Regier, & Rae, 1991). The 1-year prevalence is estimated at .5% in the United States (Wu, Shi, Birnbaum, Hudson, & Kessler, 2006). In part the apparent decrease in older age groups reflects the fact that people with this disorder do not survive until old age. The nature of this disturbance and its association with other illnesses and substance abuse mean that a person with schizophrenia experiences feelings of isolation and an identity as being "different" (Quin, Clare, Ryan, & Jackson, 2009). Perhaps as a consequence, older adults with schizophrenia have higher suicide rates than older adults in the community without this diagnosis (Cohen, Abdallah, & Diwan, 2010). On the positive side, older adults who have suffered from schizophrenia for many years develop a wide range of coping skills (Solano & Whitbourne, 2001). Those naturally developing mechanisms can be augmented with clinical interventions that focus on methods to cope with everyday life problems.

The first systematic definition of schizophrenia as "premature dementia" (dementia praecox) was developed by the German psychiatrist Emil Kraepelin, and for many years it was thought of as a permanently disabling condition. However, it is now known that the long-term outcome of the disorder is highly variable. Approximately 20 to 25% of people who develop the disorder improve to the point of complete remission, and at the other end of the spectrum, 10% remain chronically impaired. Among the remaining 50 to 70%, the disorder shows a varying course with gradual improvements in social functioning and a reduction of psychotic symptoms (Meeks, 2000). Some individuals can achieve very significant recovery after many years of being chronically impaired, including being able to work, drive a car, and live independently in their own homes (Palmer et al., 2002).

For years, clinicians referred to a condition known as **late-onset schizophrenia**, a form of the disorder that was thought to originate in adults over the age of 45 years (Jeste et al., 1997). However, this condition is now thought not to be schizophrenia but rather some other phenotype of psychotic disorder, the risk factors for which may include sensory deficits, comorbid dementia and delirium, social isolation, and substance abuse (Whitbourne & Meeks, 2010).

Delirium, Dementia, and Amnestic Disorders. Disorders involving significant loss of cognitive functioning as the result of neurological dysfunction or medical illness form the category in DSM-IV-TR known as **delirium, dementia, and amnestic disorders**. In previous versions of the DSM these disorders were referred to as "organic" or "cognitive", indicating that they have different causes and characteristics than the other psychological disorders included in the diagnostic system. Although you might hear these

terms used, they were considered too imprecise to be useful and were dropped from official parlance.

The term dementia is used to apply to a change in cognitive functioning that occurs progressively over time. Its symptoms include loss of memory and of the ability to use language (aphasia), to carry out coordinated bodily movements (apraxia), to recognize familiar objects, and to make rational judgments. As we discussed in Chapter 5, Alzheimer's disease is one cause of dementia, but there can be others, such as long-term substance abuse, vascular disease, and Parkinson's disease, to name a few.

In contrast to the long-term changes that occur in dementia, the condition known as delirium, which we first discussed in Chapter 5, is an acute state in which the individual experiences a disturbance in consciousness and attention, as well as memory loss, disorientation, and an inability to use language. Delirium has many causes including substance use, intake of medications, head injury, high fever, and vitamin deficiency. Most cases of delirium subside within days, but the condition may persist as long as a month. Although relatively frequent in acute care medical settings, occurring in up to nearly 40% of hospitalized older adults (Boustani et al., 2010), the condition is uncommon within community-residing populations. Therefore, when an older person shows signs of delirium, treatment should be given right away (Andrew, Freter, & Rockwood, 2006). Unfortunately, the individual with delirium may be misdiagnosed with dementia, and an opportunity for intervention will have been lost or at least made more complicated.

People who suffer from **amnesia** have as their main symptom profound memory loss. Their amnesia may involve an inability to learn or remember information encountered after the damage (**anterograde**—into the future) or the inability to recall information learned prior to the damage (**retrograde**—going back into the past). Amnesia can be caused by chronic substance use, medications, exposure to environmental toxins, head trauma, loss of oxygen supply to the brain, or the sexually transmitted disease of herpes simplex.

Substance-Related Disorders. In 2008, illicit drugs were used by an estimated 20.1 million persons 12 years and older in the United States, representing 8% of the population (Substance Abuse and Mental

Health Services Administration, 2009b). The majority of adults who abuse or are dependent on alcohol or illicit drugs are in their late teens and early 20s, but the overall numbers and percents of older adults are on the rise with the aging of the Baby Boom generation.

As of 2008, an estimated 4.3 million adults aged 50 and older (4.7%) had used an illicit drug within the past year. Older adults are particularly at risk for abuse of prescription drugs, as 36% of the medications used in the United States are taken by adults over the age of 65 years. Nonmedical use of prescription drugs is the most common form of illicit drug abuse among people 65 and older with an estimated prevalence of .8% (double the percent who abuse marijuana) (Substance Abuse and Mental Health Services Administration, 2009a).

Attention has only recently been drawn to the problems of older drinkers. In part, this is because people who use alcohol to excess tend not to live past their 60s and 70s. By the time they reach the age of 70, they have either become abstinent or died from excessive alcohol use or from related high-risk behaviors such as smoking (Vaillant, 2003).

Nevertheless, a sizable number of older adults abuse substances with estimates ranging from 2 to 5% of men and 1% of women (Abeles et al., 1997) and another 1 to 2% of men and 0.3% of women over 65 who abuse alcohol (Grant et al., 1995) (see Figure 11.1). In contrast to the under-65 population, prevalence rates of alcohol abuse are higher for African Americans in the over-65 age group. Hispanic females over 65 have the lowest rates of alcohol abuse. Estimates are that, as is true for drug abuse, the problem of older drinkers and substance abusers is likely to grow with the aging of the current cohort of Baby Boomers (Department of Health and Human Services, 1999).

Symptoms of alcohol dependence are thought to be present in as many as 14% of older adults who receive medical attention in hospitals and emergency rooms. Alcohol use is also thought to be relatively prevalent in settings in which only older adults live, such as nursing homes and retirement communities. The risks of alcohol abuse among this population are considerable, ranging from cirrhosis of the liver (a terminal condition) to heightened rate of injury through hip fractures and motor vehicle accidents. Alcohol may also interact with the effects

FIGURE 11.1

Past Illicit Drug Use Among Adults 50 or Older

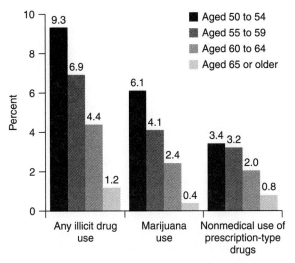

Source: Substance Abuse and Mental Health Services Administration. (2009, December 29). Illicit drug use among older adults. Findings from the SAMHSA 2006 to 2008 National Surveys on Drug Use and Health (NSDUHs). Retrieved from http://www.oas.samhsa.gov/2k9/168/168OlderAdultsHTML.pdf.

of prescription medications. Even without a change in drinking patterns, an older person may experience difficulties associated with physiological changes in the kidneys that affect tolerance. Long-term alcohol use may also lead to changes in the frontal lobes and cerebellum, exacerbating the effects of normal aging on cognitive and motor functioning (National Institute on Alcohol Abuse and Alcoholism, 1998). In severe and prolonged alcohol abuse, dementia can develop, leading to permanent memory loss and early death (as we discussed earlier and in Chapter 5).

There are treatment approaches that can be effective in reducing alcohol consumption among those older adults who continue to struggle with abuse and dependence. Participation in Alcoholics Anonymous, receiving support from family and friends, and using adaptive coping mechanisms can be effective methods of reducing an older adult's reliance on alcohol. As is true for younger people, the context of drinking is important. One of the most effective treatments may be finding a new network of friends who do not engage in or approve of drinking (Moos, Schutte, Brennan, & Moos, 2004).

Axis II Disorders in Adulthood

As you learned earlier, a personality disorder is a condition diagnosed on Axis II of the DSM-IV-TR to apply to long-standing and maladaptive dispositions. Personality disorders are estimated to be found among 9% of the general population (Samuels et al., 2002), an overall rate that is fairly steady across adulthood (Abrams & Horowitz, 1999).

The DSM-IV-TR diagnosis of antisocial personality disorder is characterized by **psychopathy**, a set of traits that are thought to lie at the disorder's very core. The traits associated with psychopathy fall into two dimensions. Factor 1 is a cluster of traits that represent disturbances in the capacity to experience emotions such as empathy, guilt, and remorse. This cluster also includes manipulativeness, egocentricity, and callousness. Factor 2 incorporates the unstable and impulsive behaviors that contribute to the socially deviant lifestyle of the individual with this disorder.

Studies of the relationship between age and antisocial personality disorder provide support for the notion that the maladaptive personality traits that constitute the essence of this personality disorder are extremely stable over time (Harpur, Hart, & Hare, 2002). One large-scale study of psychopathy, conducted on nearly 900 male prisoners between the ages of 18 and 89, showed that there were no age differences on Factor 1, which represents the "personality" contribution to the disorder. By contrast, scores on the items that reflect socially deviant and impulsive behaviors decrease dramatically across age groups. This characterization corresponds closely to data on the numbers of prisoners by age reported by the U.S. Department of Justice. The rate of imprisonment drastically decreases after the age of 45 (Harrison & Beck, 2005).

Changes over adulthood in the impulsive and antisocial element of psychopathy may reflect a number of factors other than changes in the personality disorder itself, however. Once again we return to an explanation involving survivor or attrition effects. The apparent decrease in antisocial behavior may reflect the fact that people who were high on Factor 2 (impulsivity) of psychopathy are no longer alive. In addition to having been killed in violent crime or as the result of drug or alcohol abuse, such individuals also have a higher than expected mortality rate due to poor health habits (Laub & Vaillant, 2000).

Other personality disorders also change in prevalence over adulthood (Segal, Coolidge, & Rosowsky, 2000). Histrionic and borderline personality disorders are less likely to be observed in older adults. By contrast, the prevalence is higher for obsessive-compulsive and schizoid personality disorders as well as dependent personality disorder. These rates fit the pattern suggested by the **maturation hypothesis**, which proposes that the "immature" personality types (borderline, histrionic, narcissistic, and antisocial) improve or at least become more treatable in older adults (see Figure 11.2). By contrast, the "mature" types (obsessive-compulsive, schizoid,

FIGURE 11.2

Maturation Hypothesis of Personality Disorders in Later Adulthood

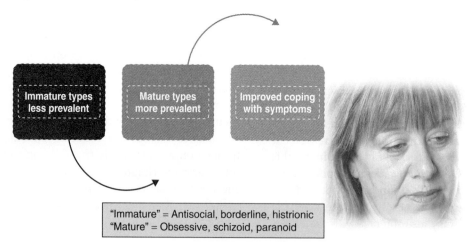

Immature types less prevalent → Mature types more prevalent → Improved coping with symptoms

"Immature" = Antisocial, borderline, histrionic
"Mature" = Obsessive, schizoid, paranoid

TABLE 11.2
Results of National Survey on Elder Abuse

Type of Abuse	Prevalence % (since age 60)	Past Year Prevalence %
Emotional mistreatment	13.5	4.6
Physical mistreatment	1.8	1.6
Sexual mistreatment	0.3	0.6
Potential neglect	No data	5.1
Financial mistreatment	No data	5.2

Source: Acierno, R., Hernandez, M. A., Amstadter, A. B., Resnick, H. S., Steve, K., Muzzy, W., . . . Kilpatrick, D. G., (2010). Prevalence and correlates of emotional, physical, sexual, and financial abuse and potential neglect in the United States: The National Elder Mistreatment Study. *American Journal of Public Health, 100,* 292–297.

and paranoid) become more symptomatic over time (Engels, Duijsens, Haringsma, & van Putten, 2003). There are many possible explanations for the maturation hypothesis, including brain injury, disease, and life stresses. It is also possible that older adults with longstanding personality disorders become better at coping with their symptoms (Segal, Hook, & Coolidge, 2001).

ELDER ABUSE

A condition that may become one of serious clinical concern is the abuse of an older adult through the actions taken by another person, or through self-neglect that leads to significant loss of functioning. The term **elder abuse** is used to refer to a large category of actions taken directly against older adults that inflict physical or psychological harm. To protect vulnerable adults, Adult Protective Services (APS) were mandated by Title XX of the Social Security Act in 1975. Although a federal program, there is little or no funding attached to it. This means that the states are responsible for enforcing the regulations and as a result, there is considerable variation in the definitions and reporting mechanisms for abuse.

Elder abuse is a notoriously difficult behavior to document because it is one surrounded by guilt, shame, fear, and the risk of criminal prosecution. Victims are afraid to report abuse because they are afraid of being punished by their abusers, and the perpetrators obviously do not wish to reveal that they are engaging in this socially unacceptable if not criminal activity. Estimates of the prevalence of elder abuse first became available in the 1980s when the issue received national attention after it was brought before the U.S. Select Committee on Aging in 1981. At that time, it was suggested that 4% of the 65 and older population are victims of moderate to severe abuse. The most recently conducted comprehensive survey, based on data from nearly 5,800 respondents across the United States, yielded estimates of prevalence within the last year for people 60 and older of 4.6% for emotional abuse, 1.6% for physical abuse, and 5.2% for financial abuse. Up to 10% of all respondents surveyed indicated that they had been abused or neglected within the past year (see Table 11.2) (Acierno et al., 2010).

The problem of elder abuse is a serious social and mental health issue. The victims are vulnerable to psychological distress (Yan & So-kum, 2001) and have higher mortality rates (Dong et al., 2009). Although many individuals throughout life are potentially victims of abuse or neglect, it is the older adults in poor health who are at particularly high risk. Targeting their caregivers, and providing them with better coping skills as well as adequate reimbursement and social support, are important preventative strategies to reduce the incidence of this very tragic situation (Nadien, 2006).

- Close to 90% have a diagnosable psychiatric disorder
- Age-adjusted suicide rate is highest for white males 85 and older
- Risk factors = depressive disorder, certain personality disorders, physical disease
- From 43 to 76% of suicide victims had seen a health care provider within a month of death

FIGURE 11.3

Facts about Suicide in Older Adults

SUICIDE

Although suicide is not a diagnosis in the DSM-IV-TR, suicide is a condition that is closely related to the issue of psychological disorders in later adulthood (see Figure 11.3). Approximately 90% of adults who complete suicide have a diagnosable psychiatric disorder. The most frequent diagnoses of suicidal individuals are major depressive disorder, alcohol abuse or dependence, and schizophrenia. Among suicidal adults of all ages, the rates of psychiatric disorders are very high, ranging from 71% to over 90%.

Each year, approximately 33,000 people in the U.S. population as a whole die of suicide. The majority are ages 25 to 54 (Xu et al., 2010). The age-adjusted suicide rate in the United States of all age, race, and sex groups is highest for all demographic categories among White males aged 85 and older at about 48 suicide deaths per 100,000 in the population (Centers for Disease Control and Prevention, 2010f). The actual number is approximately 800, but the rate is high because this is a small segment of the population as a whole. Nevertheless, the issue of suicide in older adults is one of concern for older adult White male widowers, particularly those who suffer from cancer and cardiovascular disease (Conwell, Duberstein, & Caine, 2002).

Depressive symptoms and major depressive disorder are strongly related to suicidal feelings in older adults (Barnow, Linden, & Freyberger, 2004). However, the older adult contemplating suicide may not appear even to a trained clinician to be severely depressed but instead may seem to show only mild to moderate symptoms of depression. As a result, suicides are much more difficult for health care workers to detect (Duberstein & Conwell, 2000). Other subclinical symptoms that older adults may have include hostility, sleep difficulties, anxiety, and depression (Liu & Chiu, 2009).

Given the difficulty of diagnosing depression among older adults, it would seem particularly important for health care providers to be aware of suicide risk factors when working with older adults. Sadly, it is estimated that from 43 to 76% of all suicide victims had seen a health care provider within a month of their death (Duberstein & Conwell, 2000). Greater sensitivity to symptoms of mood disorders in conjunction with more thorough evaluation of the additional psychological and medical risk factors could potentially increase the chances that these health care providers would have been able to intervene (Heisel, 2006).

TREATMENT ISSUES IN MENTAL HEALTH CARE

With the aging of the Baby Boom generation, mental health researchers are turning their attention with great concern toward the need for more research and training in providing services to older adults. Clearly, more training will be needed both for practitioners currently in the field and those who will be entering the ranks of therapists and other mental health care workers (Qualls, Segal, Norman, Niederehe, & Gallagher-Thompson, 2002). Publication of the APA Guidelines for Psychological Practice with Older Adults (American Psychological Association, 2004) led to the development of training models in the emerging field of **professional geropsychology** (Knight, Karel, Hinrichsen, Qualls, & Duffy, 2009), the application of gerontology to the psychological treatment of older adults (see Figure 11.4).

The psychological disorders we have discussed in this chapter involve a variety of potential causes and, therefore, may be treatable by a variety of approaches. Clinicians who work with adult populations recognize the need to differentiate the approaches they take to young and middle-aged adults from the approaches they take to older adults (Zarit & Zarit, 1998).

In addition to potentially different etiologies for disorders at different points in adulthood, clinicians must take into account the potential effects of chronic medical conditions as well as normal age-related changes in physical, cognitive, and social functioning (Hinrichsen & Dick-Siskin, 2000). Variations by ethnic and minority status must also be recognized by clinicians. It is essential that clinicians become competent in assessing and treating individuals from a range of backgrounds (Ferraro, 2002; Lau & Gallagher-Thompson, 2002).

Assessment

Clinicians begin their treatment of a client's psychological disorder by conducting a multi-faceted clinical assessment. The **assessment** procedure involves

FIGURE 11.4

The APA Guidelines

Selected items from the APA Geropsychology Guidelines

- Attitudes: Be aware of attitudes and beliefs about aging
- General knowledge: Gain expertise in aging
- Clinical issues: Understand psychopathology in older adults
- Assessment: Learn to use and interpret appropriate tools
- Service provision: Know about efficacy of interventions
- Education: Gain continuing education in geropsychology

Source: Adapted from American Psychological Association. (2004). Guidelines for psychological practice with older adults. *American Psychologist, 59,* 236–260.

evaluation of the psychological, physiological, and social factors that potentially affect the individual's current state of functioning. Psychological assessments provide a diagnosis (according to the DSM-IV-TR) and lay the groundwork for a treatment plan. In some cases, assessments may be used for special purposes, such as when the clinician is making legal determinations of mental competence or evaluating an individual's appropriateness for a particular occupation. When used in the context of treatment, psychological assessments focus on providing the most accurate reading possible of a client's specific disorder to provide the basis for treatment.

All clinical assessment involves differential diagnosis: the process of ruling out alternative diagnoses. In the case of older adults, differential diagnosis requires establishing whether the symptoms that appear to be due to psychological disorder could be better accounted for by a medical condition (Bartels & Mueser, 1999) or current and past substance abuse.

A key area of differential diagnosis is distinguishing between dementia and other psychological disorders, particularly depression. As we have seen, depression can cause pseudodementia, which is memory loss and difficulties in concentration leading to symptoms that closely resemble dementia. However, there are important differences in the symptom pattern of individuals with these disorders (Small, 2009). In depression, the symptoms of dysphoria are more severe, and the individual is likely to exaggerate the extent to which he or she is experiencing memory loss. People who have dementia tend, in contrast, to be overconfident about their cognitive abilities. They may show very wide variations in performance from one test to another, but older adults with dementia show a progressive loss of cognitive abilities that tends to affect them across the board. The timing of symptoms is another diagnostic key, because older adults with depression experience cognitive symptoms prior to depressive symptoms. If the cognitive symptoms persist after the depression has been treated, then the dementia is more likely the cause (Wilkins, Mathews, & Sheline, 2009). Differences between depression and dementia are important for clinicians to note in their assessment of older adults because, as we pointed out in Chapter 5, if the depression is caught in time there is a good chance of successful treatment.

Assessment should also be tailored to the physical and cognitive needs of older individuals. First, they should be made to feel comfortable and relaxed, and should be given sufficient time to ask questions about the procedure, which may be unfamiliar and hence stressful. There are also practical concerns that psychologists should address such as making sure that the people they are testing have the correct eyeglasses and hearing aids if necessary. An older adult who has difficulty writing due to arthritis, for instance, will be unable to complete paper-and-pencil measures. Rest periods may be necessary during a lengthy testing session, or the session may have to be divided into shorter segments. The clinician should also be aware of the changes in sensory abilities, motor functions, and cognitive processes that may hamper the older client's understanding of problems or questions given during the assessment process. For example, materials should be presented in large print to clients who are visually impaired. Even seemingly insignificant distractions, such as the hum of a computer, may compromise an older adult's performance (Edelstein, Martin, & McKee, 2000). It is also important to be sensitive to cultural or language differences between clinician and client, regardless of the age of the client (Diaz et al., 2009).

Clinical Interview. In a **clinical interview**, the clinician asks questions of the client to establish insight into the client's psychological processes. The clinician can also use the opportunity to interact face-to-face with the client to observe the client's behavior. There are several standardized instruments used to provide DSM-IV-TR diagnoses in as objective a fashion as possible. However, these are not typically adapted for use with older adults. An unstructured interview can also be beneficial in assessing older adults with cognitive difficulties who find it difficult to concentrate or need help in maintaining their focus (Edelstein, Martin, & McKee, 2000). However, to be most useful, the clinical interview should also be combined with more structured instruments (Blazer, 2004) such as those we describe below.

Mini-Mental State Exam. An assessment instrument used extensively in the diagnostic process for older adults is the mental status examination. The most well known is the Mini-Mental State Exam (MMSE) (Folstein, Folstein, & McHugh, 1975). Figure 11.5 contains sample items from the MMSE.

Although the MMSE is quick, relatively easy to administer and is useful for charting changes in

TIME ORIENTATION

Ask:

What is the year _____ (1), season _____ (1),
month of the year _____ (1), date _____ (1),
day of the week _____ (1)?

DRAWING

Say: Please copy this design.

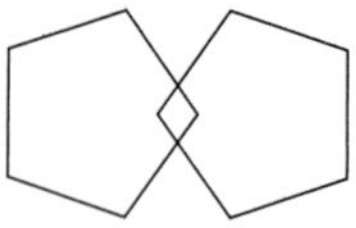

REGISTRATION OF THREE WORDS

Say: Listen carefully. I am going to say three words. You say them back after I stop.
Ready? Here they are. PONY (wait 1 second), QUARTER (wait 1 second), ORANGE
(wait 1 second). What were those words?

_____ (1)
_____ (1)
_____ (1)

Give 1 point for each correct answer, then repeat them until the patient learns all three.

FIGURE 11.5

Sample Items from the
Mini-Mental State Exam (MMSE)

dementing symptoms over time, it is not particularly specific to dementia and does not allow for precise measurement of cognitive functioning. Newer methods using computerized testing are more sensitive particularly to early signs of cognitive deficits (Saxton et al., 2009). Another problem with the MMSE is that it is a less effective tool for African Americans (Mast, Fitzgerald, Steinberg, MacNeill, & Lichtenberg, 2001) and Mexican Americans (Espino, Lichtenstein, Palmer, & Hazuda, 2004). Given these and other limitations of the MMSE, geropsychologists are increasingly turning to more sophisticated cognitive and neuropsychological testing methods that examine a broader range of abilities (Mast, MacNeill, & Lichtenberg, 2002).

Interview Measures for Specific Disorders.   Several interview-based measures exist for the assessment of specific symptoms in older adults. The Geriatric Depression Scale (GDS) includes a true–false set of questions about depressive symptoms that excludes somatic disturbances likely to be endorsed by older adults regardless of their level of depression (such as changes in energy level or sleep). Its validity is well established with older adult populations (Nyunt, Fones, Niti, & Ng, 2009).

The Anxiety Disorders Interview Schedule (ADIS-R) (DiNardo & Barlow, 1988) is useful in assessing older adults, as it has been found to provide ratings in agreement with clinical diagnoses of social phobia, general anxiety disorder, simple phobia, and panic disorder (Scogin, Floyd, & Forde, 2000). The Hamilton Rating Scale of Depression (Hamilton, 1967) and the Hamilton Anxiety Rating Scale (Hamilton, 1959) have also been tested with older adults and are useful in evaluating both the severity and number of the individual's symptoms. These instruments remain the most widely adopted by clinicians, although newer and more sensitive methods are being developed (Navarro et al., 2010).

Self-Report Clinical Inventories.   Easier to administer, but with a higher cost of placing greater burden on the test-taker, are self-report clinical inventories in which the client answers a set of questions concerning the experience of particular symptoms related to a diagnostic category. Many of these tests were developed for young or middle-aged adults, and therefore their applicability to older adults is either unknown or low. Unlike interviews, these measures cannot be adapted to the needs or background of the client. Older adults and people from diverse cultural backgrounds may not interpret the questions as the authors of the test had intended, leading to results that do not provide a valid indication of the client's psychological status.

Treatment

The strategies available to clinicians for treating psychological disorders in older adults fall into two categories: medically based treatments involving pharmacological or other bodily treatments and psychologically based treatments involving, primarily, psychotherapy.

Medically Based Treatments.   By far, the most common method of medically based treatments for psychological disorders involves **psychotherapeutic medications**, substances that by their chemical nature target the central nervous system (see Table 11.3). In prescribing these medications to older adults, clinicians must take precautions to avoid adverse drug reactions. As we have previously mentioned, medications take longer to clear the excretory system of the kidneys, so unless prescribed in lower doses, older adults are at risk of accumulating toxic levels in the blood.

Another risk in prescribing psychotherapeutic medications to older adults is that of polypharmacy, a condition we discussed in Chapter 5 in which people receive multiple prescription medications. In addition to having potent effects of their own, psychotherapeutic medications can also interact in harmful ways with other prescription medications. Because older adults typically see multiple health professionals, they are great risk for these unintended consequences. A physician might prescribe a sleep medication to an older adult patient who is already taking an antianxiety or cardiac medication. The sleep medication can have the undesirable outcome of causing the older person to become suicidal.

In the case of major depressive disorder, despite their potential drawbacks and side effects, psychotherapeutic medications are highly effective (50 to 70%) for older adults. The most commonly

TABLE 11.3
Forms of Medically Based Treatments

Type of Treatment	Benefits	Problems
Antidepressants Lithium carbonate Antianxiety Neuroleptics	Effectiveness in reducing symptoms (50–70% in the case of antidepressants)	Side effects Polypharmacy Interaction with medical conditions Failure to use psychosocial interventions
Electroconvulsive therapy (ECT)	Useful as a last resort	Can cause memory loss

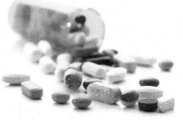

prescribed antidepressants include selective serotonin reuptake inhibitors (SSRIs), which are particularly useful for older adults (Klysner et al., 2002; Mottram, Wilson, Ashworth, & Abou-Saleh, 2002). Unfortunately, clinicians often fail to diagnose depression correctly in older adults, which may lead to either undertreatment of depressive symptoms or treatment with the wrong medication, such as antianxiety medications rather than antidepressants (Sonnenberg, Beekman, Deeg, & Van Tilburg, 2003).

Lithium carbonate is an effective medication for the treatment of bipolar disorder. To prevent recurrence of manic episodes, the individual must take lithium on a continuous basis. For older adults, it is particularly important to monitor lithium levels because, perhaps more so than other psychotherapeutic medications, it is not cleared through the kidneys as quickly as it is by the kidneys of younger adults (Howland, 2009).

In cases of severe depression in which medications do not produce results, individuals may undergo **electroconvulsive therapy (ECT)**. In this treatment, an electric current is applied through electrodes attached across the head. The individual suffers seizure-like symptoms (which can be controlled through muscle relaxants), but the main effect of the treatment is thought to result from the passage of electrical current through the brain. Despite the risks associated with this procedure, ECT is considered a method of last resort. It is an effective alternative for individuals over the age of 60 who have not responded to other forms of treatment (O'Connor et al., 2010).

A number of psychotherapeutic medications are used to treat anxiety disorders. Benzodiazepines are the most frequently prescribed antianxiety medications, and although effective, are highly addictive. They require higher and higher doses to obtain their intended outcome, and when discontinued, they are likely to lead to significant withdrawal symptoms. Older adults are particularly vulnerable to these effects and, furthermore, may experience a number of additional potentially dangerous side effects such as unsteadiness, daytime sleepiness, impaired cognitive functioning, and slowed reaction time resulting in increased risk of falling (Woolcott et al., 2009). The medication buspirone has fewer of these side effects, but it is not necessarily as effective in treating generalized anxiety disorder (Flint, 2005). There are also circumstances in which it is not appropriate to prescribe buspirone, such as when the individual also suffers from symptoms of depression (Flint, 2005).

Other medications useful in treating anxiety in older adults are beta-blockers, which reduce anxiety by lowering sympathetic nervous system activity. Older adults with certain chronic diseases such as cardiovascular disease cannot use this medication, however. SSRIs are another category of medications used in treating older adults with anxiety disorders although their effectiveness versus placebo in people with anxiety disorders is not well established (Lenze et al., 2009).

Medications for the treatment of schizophrenia include the antipsychotic medications known as **neuroleptics**. These medications alter dopamine activity and are effective in reducing delusions and other forms of thought disorder as well as lowering the chance of an individual's experiencing a relapse. People with early-onset schizophrenia are often maintained on these medications for many years, allowing them to live independently in the community. Older adults who develop late-life schizophrenia also seem to respond to neuroleptics. However, there are potent side effects, including confusion and agitation, dizziness, and motor disturbances. Some of these motor disturbances can resemble those of Parkinson's disease.

The most serious side effect of neuroleptic medication is tardive dyskinesia, which involves involuntary, repetitive movements, particularly in the muscles of the face. These movements include chewing, moving the jaw from side to side, and rolling the tongue. Older adults are more likely than younger adults to experience tardive dyskinesia, even after they stop taking these medications. In fact, these medications are the second most common cause of Parkinsonian symptoms in older adults (Thanvi & Treadwell, 2009). Medications that alter serotonin functioning used for treatment of schizophrenia (clozapine and resperidone) do not produce these effects on motor functioning. However, clozapine can have fatal side effects and must be carefully monitored, particularly in older adults (Kelly et al., 2010).

Exercise and Meditation. Building on the finding that physical fitness is inversely related to mental health (Galper, Trivedi, Barlow, Dunn, & Kampert, 2006), researchers have begun to use exercise as a therapeutic tool in the treatment of psychological disorders in later adulthood to supplant or replace medications (Blake, Mo, Malik, & Thomas, 2009). Meditation is another alternative approach that builds on the known association between pain and depressive symptoms in older adults. In one innovative investigation, both mindfulness meditation and education served to reduce pain and improve psychological functioning that was maintained for at least 4 months post treatment (Morone, Rollman, Moore, Li, & Weiner, 2009).

Psychologically Based Treatments. A wide range of treatment models have been shown to be effective for reducing symptoms of the major disorders experienced by older adults (Fiske, Wetherell, & Gatz, 2009). Research on the outcome of these treatments shows that psychotherapy in addition to, or instead of, pharmacological interventions can be highly efficacious (Schulberg et al., 2007).

Figure 11.6 illustrates the major forms of psychotherapy. Behavioral treatment focusing on increasing the number of positive reinforcements in the individual's life was shown a number of years ago to have beneficial effects in reducing depressive symptoms in older adults (Teri, 1994). Such an approach is based on the notion that older adults may be experiencing depressive symptoms owing to decreases in pleasant events in their lives associated with physical changes, loss of friends, and loss of rewarding social roles.

In **cognitive-behavioral treatment**, the clinician encourages the client to develop new behaviors and constructive ways of thinking about the self. This approach appears to have considerable relevance to work with older depressed clients, particularly for those who have a tendency to focus excessively on age-related changes in physical functioning, memory, and health. The elements of cognitive-behavioral treatment for older adults with depression include instructing clients to keep track of their pleasant and unpleasant events, helping them understand the relationship between their mood and these behaviors, looking for changes that can be made in daily life, increasing their social skills, and teaching them to be alert to and try to change their negative thoughts about the self (Satre, Knight, & David, 2006). Even

FIGURE 11.6

Models of Psychotherapy with Older Adults

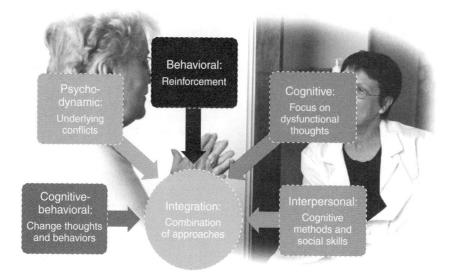

as few as seven sessions can produce positive results (Serfaty et al., 2009).

Social skills can also be taught through cognitive-behavioral methods to older adults suffering from schizophrenia, allowing them to have more satisfactory interactions with others in their environment (Patterson et al., 2002). One advantage of cognitive-behavioral therapy for treating older adults is that it can be adapted to a variety of settings, including physician's offices and even the telephone (Arean & Ayalon, 2005).

Increasingly, cognitive-behavioral therapy is being seen as an effective alternative to antianxiety medications in treating anxiety disorders in older adults (Mohlman & Price, 2006) although not for certain subgroups such as older individuals high in neuroticism and self-perceived health problems (Schuurmans et al., 2009). It can also be targeted to specific issues that impair quality of life in older adults, such as activity restrictions due to fear of falling (Zijlstra et al., 2009). Cognitive-behavior therapy can also be useful in reducing symptoms of insomnia and pain from osteoarthritis (Vitiello, Rybarczyk, Von Korff, & Stepanski, 2009). Relaxation training, a component of cognitive-behavioral therapy, can also be an effective intervention for

older adults with generalized anxiety disorder (Ayers, Sorrell, Thorp, & Wetherell, 2007).

There are also treatment methods geared specifically to older adults. In a variant of traditional psychodynamic therapy, which typically focuses on unresolved issues from early life, **life review therapy** (Butler, 1974) involves helping the older adult rework past experiences, both pleasant and unpleasant, with the goal of gaining greater acceptance of the past. This process facilitates the natural reminiscence process that accompanies resolution of the ego integrity versus despair psychosocial issue, as described by Erikson (see Chapter 8). In a variant of life review therapy called "creative reminiscence" clinicians were able to alleviate depressive symptoms in older adults with a lifelong history of severe disorder (Willemse, Depla, & Bohlmeijer, 2009).

Interpersonal therapy (IPT) integrates cognitive methods with a focus on social factors that contribute to psychological disturbance. Interpersonal therapy involves a combination of methods, but its main focus is on training in social skills, interpersonal relationships, and methods of conflict resolution. IPT is an effective treatment method either as an adjunct to or replacement of pharmacological interventions (Schulberg et al., 2007).

There are, then, encouraging results from studies investigating psychotherapy effectiveness in later life. However, psychotherapy with older individuals presents a number of challenges. These involve factors that alter both the nature of psychological difficulties experienced by older adults and the nature of the therapeutic process (Hinrichsen & Dick-Siskin, 2000).

Older adults, particularly those over the age of 75, have a greater probability of physical health impairments that can compromise the effectiveness of therapy because these conditions represent a significant threat to quality of life (Licht-Strunk, van der Windt, van Marwijk, de Haan, & Beekman, 2007). Changes in identity associated with these impairments can themselves stimulate the need for psychotherapy. However, by boosting the older adult's sense of mastery, even physical limitations can be overcome, and the older person's depressive symptoms can be alleviated (Steunenberg, Beekman, Deeg, Bremmer, & Kerkhof, 2007). Reducing symptoms of depression through psychotherapy can in turn lead to improvements in perceptions of disability (Karp et al., 2009) and health-related perceived quality of life (Chan et al., 2009).

Psychosocial issues involving relationships with family may also confront an older adult and should be taken into account by clinicians providing psychotherapy. These issues include death of family and friends, changes in relationships with children and spouses, and the need to provide care to a spouse or parent. Finally, the social context can play an important role in influencing the outcome of treatment. Just as there are relationships between mental health and SES, there is a link between the effectiveness of antidepressant treatment and social class. In one study older adults from lower social classes were found to be less likely to respond over the course of a 20-week period to a combination of psychotherapy and medication than individuals in middle and high income brackets (Cohen et al., 2006).

Family issues may, however, be alleviated through the provision of therapy for older adults experiencing symptoms of depression. Researchers investigating the impact of interventions including both medication and interpersonal therapy observed favorable effects on perceived burden among caregivers of the patients whose symptoms responded to treatment (Martire et al., 2010).

Generational differences between current cohorts of older adults and the middle-aged individuals more commonly seen in psychotherapy must be taken into account by clinicians as well. Older adults may be skeptical about the therapy process, having been less socialized than younger cohorts to accept the need for psychological interventions. Part of therapy may involve educating older adult clients to feel less embarrassed or stigmatized by the process. This seems particularly important in the case of older Black adults, who are less likely than older adult Whites to use psychotherapy when it is offered (Joo, Morales, de Vries, & Gallo, 2010). Both older and younger men attribute a greater stigma to psychotherapy than do women (Pepin, Segal, & Coolidge, 2009). Conversely, the therapist may bring to the situation negative attitudes and stereotypes about aging that complicate the therapeutic relationship with the older adult client.

Models other than the traditional provision of psychotherapy are clearly becoming seen as viable alternatives for work with older adults. Care managers can be used to coordinate services to individual clients, offering services through primary care physicians to ensure that the clients maintain their involvement in treatment. One study investigating this type of comprehensive model showed significant reductions in suicidal thinking and depressive symptoms in a sample of over 9,000 individuals 60 and older maintained over a 2-year period (Alexopoulos et al., 2009).

Although therapy can have many beneficial effects, equally important as treatment is prevention. Targeting specific older adults at risk, such as those who have become bereaved and have experienced illness or disability, can help to reduce not only the need for treatment but also to maximize the psychological functioning of older adults who might otherwise develop disorders such as depression (Schoevers et al., 2006).

SERIOUS PSYCHOLOGICAL DISTRESS

Though we have focused in this chapter on psychological disorders in older adults, it is important to remember that despite the presence of chronic

FIGURE 11.7

Percentage of Adults by Age Group with Serious Psychological Distress

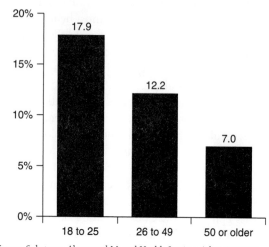

Source: Substance Abuse and Mental Health Services Administration. (2009). Results from the 2008 national survey on drug use and health: national findings. Retrieved from http://www.oas.samhsa.gov/ NSDUH/2k8NSDUH/2k8results.cfm#Ch2.

physical health conditions, the majority of older adults do not experience significant distress. This fact is borne out by the National Health Interview Survey, which tracks the incidence of serious psychological distress. Survey after survey in this series consistently reports lower rates of serious distress within the past year for adults 65 and older (2.3 in 65 and older versus 2.8 in those 18 to 24) (Pratt, Dey, & Cohen, 2007) (see Figure 11.7). These results are not limited to the United States. A large-scale investigation of nearly 7,500 adults in Australia ages 20 to 64 showed lower rates of anxiety and psychological distress among the older age groups (Jorm et al., 2005).

Clearly, although older adults are at higher risk in an objective sense for experiencing psychological disorders, a combination of selective survival, enhanced use of coping mechanisms, and an ability to maintain an optimistic attitude toward adversity seem to offer significant protective factors against psychological problems in later adulthood. Increasingly, new methods of treatment are becoming available to provide services to those older adults who need assistance in these adaptive processes.

In summary, when we think of the aging process, we are likely to anticipate a number of negative changes that would have adverse mental health effects. By contrast, the facts reveal that older adults are highly resilient to the physical, psychological, and social changes involved in the aging process. It is nevertheless true that there will be an increasing need for mental health workers in the coming decades trained in diagnosis, assessment and treatment, and there will also be an increased need for research on effective treatment methods for aging individuals in need of intervention.

SUMMARY

1. Psychological disorders are those behaviors that significantly alter the individual's adaptation. The DSM-IV-TR contains descriptions of the disorders that can affect children and adults; unfortunately it was not specifically written with the concerns of older adults in mind. In many cases, there are differences between the over-65 and under-65 populations of adults in the way that these disorders are manifested in behavior. Axis I disorders include clinical syndromes (organized patterns of disturbances), and Axis II includes personality disorders and mental retardation.

2. Epidemiological surveys place the prevalence of psychological disorders at between one third to one half of the adult population. There is a lower prevalence of all disorders among adults over the age of 65 years. Depressive symptoms are more likely to be found in the over-65 population than in the under-65 population. Older adults are more likely to experience physical symptoms of depression and are less likely to express emotional disturbances such as guilt or suicidality. Health care professionals may not be attuned to diagnosing depressive symptoms in older adults. Anxiety is also a relatively common disorder in the older adult population, and like mood disorders, estimates of anxiety symptoms are higher than estimates of the prevalence of anxiety disorders. It is thought that PTSD prevalence in the over-65 population will increase as Vietnam veterans become older. The majority of cases of schizophrenia emerge before the age of 40; cases that originate late in adulthood are referred to as late-onset schizophrenia. Delirium, dementia, and

cognitive disorders form another category of Axis I disorders. Substance-related disorders are more likely to occur in younger adults. However, alcohol abuse and dependence are becoming an area of concern for the over-65 population, as are disorders related to the use of prescription medications.

3. Personality disorders are found in Axis II of the DSM-IV-TR. According to the maturation hypothesis, adults with personality disorders in the immature category experience fewer symptoms in later life. This hypothesis is consistent with data on a reduction in the traits and behaviors associated with psychopathy (antisocial personality disorder) among older adults.

4. Two additional topics of concern in the area of mental health and aging are elder abuse and suicide. According to nationwide surveys, the incidence of elder abuse is as high as 5% of older adults; unfortunately, the large majority of cases normally escape detection. Adult children are most likely to be perpetrators of abuse. White men over the age of 85 have the highest risk of suicide in the population of the United States. The problem of suicide in older adults is exacerbated by the fact that older persons who are experiencing suicidal thoughts are unlikely to communicate these thoughts to health care practitioners.

5. The field of clinical geropsychology involves the provision of psychological services to older adults. Treatment begins with thorough assessment. A number of tools are available that can be applied specifically to persons in later life. These tools range from clinical interviews to structured self-report inventories. Assessment of people within this age group requires that the clinician adapt the test materials and the testing situation to the specific needs and cognitive or sensory limitations of the older adult. Therapy methods range from somatic treatments such as ECT and medications to psychotherapy. Cognitive and interpersonal therapy methods appear to hold considerable promise for treatment of older adults.

6. Despite the many threats to positive mental health, the majority of older adults do not report elevated levels of subjective distress.

12

Long-Term

Have you ever lived in an institution? Your first response may be to answer "no," unless you have been hospitalized for a physical or psychological disorder. However, think about the question in a slightly different way. An institutional facility is any residential setting in which nonfamily members are cared for under one roof. A dormitory is, according to this definition, an "institution." People living in dormitories, just as those who live in a hospital type of facility, must deal with problems inherent in communal living, such as being unable to control the levels of noise and temperature, needing to answer to people in charge, being served poor food, or suffering from the messy or rude behavior of roommates. Now imagine what it would be like adapting to these problems if you were infirmed and limited in your freedom to come and go as you please.

For the purposes of this chapter, an institutional facility provides individuals with medical or psychiatric care along with programs intended to restore their lost functioning. Hospitals are short-term institutional facilities to which people are admitted with the understanding that they will be discharged when they no longer need round-the-clock treatment. At the other end of the spectrum are residential facilities into which an individual moves permanently after losing the ability to live independently.

Closely related to the issue of treatment is the funding for health care, another topic covered in this chapter. Individuals in later life hospitalized for physical and psychological problems increasingly are confronting the rising cost of health care as a barrier to effective resolution of their difficulties. In addition to the problems that result from failure to receive proper treatment, this situation creates considerable stress and anguish for the older individual.

Although you may not spend much time thinking about the health care coverage available to you in your later years, you are surely aware of the hotly debated discussions surrounding the future of health care in the coming decades. From offering public options for health insurance to making prescription medications more affordable for older adults, the topic of health care is one of the most crucial issues facing the United States, as well as many other countries. We will examine the implications that recent policy changes to the structure and funding of health care may have on older adults.

Care

INSTITUTIONAL FACILITIES FOR LONG-TERM CARE

People with chronic disabilities, cognitive disorders, or physical infirmities that keep them from living independently may receive treatment in one of a variety of institutional long-term care settings. These institutions range from hospital-like facilities to living situations more like independent residences, providing minimal food and services (see Figure 12.1).

Nursing Homes

For individuals whose illness or disability requires daily nursing care as well as other support services, nursing homes provide comprehensive care in a single setting. A **nursing home** is a type of medical institution that provides a room, meals, skilled nursing and rehabilitative care, medical services, and protective supervision. The care provided in nursing homes includes treatment for problems that residents have in many basic areas of life including cognition, communication, hearing, vision, physical functioning, continence, psychosocial functioning, mood and behavior, nutrition, and dental care. To manage these problems, residents typically need to take medications on a regular basis. Residents of nursing homes may also receive training in basic care as well as assistance with feeding and mobility, rehabilitative activities, and social services.

Typically, nursing homes are thought of as permanent residences for the older adults who enter them, but about 30% of residents are discharged and able to move back into the community after

FIGURE 12.1

Types of Institutional Facilities for Older Adults

261

being treated for the condition that required their admission. About one quarter of people admitted to nursing homes die there, and another 36% move to another facility (Sahyoun, Pratt, Lentzner, Dey, & Robinson, 2001).

Nursing homes are certified by state and federal government agencies to provide services at one or more levels of care. **Skilled nursing facilities** provide the most intensive nursing care available outside of a hospital. Nurses and other health care workers in these settings apply dressings or bandages, help residents with daily self-care tasks, and may provide oxygen therapy. They are also responsible for taking vital signs including temperature, pulse, respiration, and blood pressure. In an **intermediate care facility**, health-related services are provided to individuals who do not require hospital or skilled nursing facility care but do require some type of institutional care beside food and a place to live.

Nursing home services have become big business in the United States. In the year 2008, nursing home expenditures were estimated to be $138.4 billion, or about 5% of the total health care expenditures in the United States (Center for Medicare and Medicaid Services, 2010c). The cost of nursing home care is rising faster than the cost of other medical care goods and services, with the yearly average private-pay facility costing slightly over $60,000 (in 2004 prices) (Stewart, Grabowski, & Lakdawalla, 2009). The percent of older adults in nursing homes has declined in the 20 years between 1985 and 2004 (see Figure 12.2), reflecting increases in home health

services and generally better health of the over-65 population. As of 2008, there were approximately 15,700 nursing homes in the Unites States with a total of over 1.7 million beds, 83% of which were occupied (National Center for Health Statistics, 2009).

Residential Care Facilities

An alternative to a nursing home is a **residential care facility**, which provides 24-hour supportive care services and supervision to individuals who do not require skilled nursing care. They provide meals, housekeeping, and assistance with personal care such as bathing and grooming. Some residential care facilities may provide other services such as management of medications and social and recreational activities.

Board and Care Homes. Board and care homes are group living arrangements designed to meet the needs of people who cannot live on their own in the community but who also need some nursing services. Typically, these homes provide help with activities of daily living such as bathing, dressing, and toileting. Although the name may imply that these homes provide a "home-like" setting, research refutes this idea. A survey conducted by the Institute of Medicine determined that board and care homes do not adjust the care they provide to the specific needs of the residents. They are typically understaffed, and the staff who work in these settings are not required to receive training (Wunderlich, Kohler, & Committee on Improving Quality in Long-Term Care, 2001).

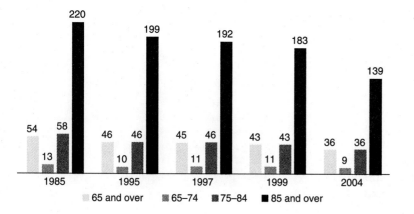

FIGURE 12.2

Rate of Nursing Home Residence among People 65 and Older (per 1,000 population)

Source: http://www.cdc.gov/nchs/data/nnhsd/ Estimates/nnhs/Estimates_Demographics_Tables .pdf#Table02.

Group Homes. Group homes provide independent, private living in a house shared by several older individuals. Residents split the cost of rent, housekeeping services, utilities, and meals.

Assisted Living Facilities. Housing complexes in which older persons live independently in their own apartments are known as **assisted living facilities**. The residents pay a regular monthly rent that usually includes meal service in communal dining rooms, transportation for shopping and appointments, social activities, and housekeeping service. Some facilities have health services available on location. These facilities are professionally managed and licensed and may represent one of several levels of care provided within the same housing community. The cost for living in an assisted living facility may range from hundreds to thousands of dollars a month. In some states, funds may be available for those who cannot afford to live in these facilities on their own through government support programs. However, most residents pay the rental and other fees out of their own funds.

The philosophy of assisted living is to combine private, residentially oriented buildings with high levels of service allowing residents to continue living in the same facility even if changes in health or physical and cognitive functioning occur. However, many facilities do not achieve these goals. Moreover, they are often too expensive for the moderate- and low-income older adults, and those that are affordable do not offer high levels of service or privacy (Wunderlich et al., 2001).

Adult Foster Care. An older adult may receive adult foster care, in which a family provides care in their home. The services provided in foster care include meals, housekeeping, and help with dressing, eating, bathing, and other personal care. These settings offer some advantages because of their home-like feeling, but because they are small and rely on a live-in caregiver for help with personal care, cooking, housekeeping, and activities, that caregiver's resources may be spread thin. If one resident becomes ill and requires more nursing care, other residents may suffer from lack of attention. Another problem in adult foster care is lack of privacy compared to a residential care setting (Wunderlich et al., 2001).

COMMUNITY-BASED FACILITIES

There are a variety of support services designed to allow older adults, even those with some form of disability, to live on their own in the community. Some of these services are offered by volunteer groups at no cost to the individual. Others are fee based and of these services, some may be paid for by Medicare.

Home Health Services

An increasing number of older adults who are ill or disabled are able to maintain an independent life in the community by utilizing **home health services**. A variety of services, some of them free, are available within this broad category of care. These include "Meals on Wheels," the provision of a hot meal once a day; so-called "friendly visiting," in which a volunteer comes to the home for a social visit; and assistance with shopping. Other home-based services include laundry, cooking, and cleaning.

Researchers have found that home health care that simulates the types of restorative services provided in nursing homes such as physical therapy, speech therapy, occupational therapy, rehabilitation, and interventions targeted at particular areas of functional decline can help to maintain the older person in the home longer, staving off institutionalization or emergency room care (Tinetti et al., 2002). Moreover, teaching older adults who are receiving home health care a variety of strategies to maintain their functional ability, such as fall prevention, muscle strength training, and home safety, can help maximize mobility and reduce costs associated with institutionalization (Gitlin et al., 2009). According to the most recent figures based on the 2004 National Nursing Home and Hospice Care Survey, nearly 1 million persons 65 years of age and over are home health care patients (Centers for Disease Control and Prevention, 2004). In the year 2008, $64.7 billion was spent in the United States on home health care; 79% of these costs were publicly funded (Center for Medicare and Medicaid Services, 2010b).

Geriatric Partial Hospital

In a **geriatric partial hospital**, daily outpatient therapy is provided with intensive, structured multidisciplinary services to older persons who have recently been discharged from a psychiatric facility. The partial hospital may also serve as an alternative to hospitalization. Therapists in this setting focus on medication management and compliance, social functioning, discharge planning, and relapse prevention. A less intense program than the geriatric partial hospital program is **geriatric continuing day treatment**, in which clients attend a day treatment program 3 days a week but are encouraged to live independently during the remaining days of the week. **Day care centers** are another form of community treatment in which individuals receive supervised meals and activities on a daily basis.

Accessory Dwelling Units

An older adult may maintain considerable autonomy but still have support nearby by living in a separate apartment in a relative's home. An accessory dwelling unit, also known as an "in-law apartment," is a second living space in the home that allows the older adult to have independent living quarters, cooking space, and a bathroom.

Subsidized Housing

Other alternatives in community care involve the provision of housing in addition to specialized services that can maintain the person in an independent living situation. **Subsidized senior housing** is provided for individuals with low to moderate incomes. People using subsidized housing live in low-rent apartment complexes and have access to help with routine tasks such as housekeeping, shopping, and laundry.

Continuing Care Retirement Community (CCRC)

A more comprehensive community living setting is a **continuing care retirement community (CCRC)**, which is a housing community that provides different levels of care based on the residents' needs. Within the same CCRC, there may be individual homes or apartments in which residents can live independently, an assisted living facility, and a nursing home. Residents move from one setting to another based on their needs, but they continue to remain part of their CCRC community. CCRCs typically are on the expensive side. Many require a large down payment prior to admission and also charge monthly fees. Some communities, however, allow residents to rent rather than buy into the facility.

Residents moving into CCRCs typically sign a contract that specifies the conditions under which they will receive long-term care. One option provides unlimited nursing care for a small increase in monthly payments. A second type of contract includes a predetermined amount of long-term nursing care; beyond this the resident is responsible for additional

AGING IN THE NEWS

www.wiley.com/college/whitbourne   OLDER ADULTS WHO MADE THE HEADLINES   -VOL. 4, CHAPTER 12-

WORLD'S OLDEST AND LONGEST RUNNING MAYOR

Hazel McCallion is certainly one amazing woman. At the age of 88, she has been mayor for Mississauga, the 6th largest city in Canada, for 31 years running. Mississauga boasts the distinction of being one of the few cities to be debt-free in Canada and has a $700 million (Canadian) reserve. It is not surprising that her approval rating is 92%. In her spare time she enjoys playing the Canadian national pastime, hockey, as well as hitting strikes and spares on the bowling lane.

Clearly it seems she's doing something right.

Nursing and assisted living are often provided within the same institution as in this Masonic facility.

payments. In the third option, the resident pays fees for service, which means full daily rates for all long-term nursing care.

If the older adult can afford this type of housing, there are definite advantages to living in CCRCs. In addition to the relative ease of moving from one level of care to another, the CCRCs provide social activities, access to community facilities, transportation services, companionship, access to health care, housekeeping, and maintenance. Residents may travel, take vacations, and become involved in activities outside the community itself.

CCRCs are accredited by a commission sponsored by the American Association of Homes and Services for the Aging. To be accredited, a CCRC must pass a 2 1/2 day test that evaluates the facility's governance and administration, resident services, finance, and health care.

THE FINANCING OF LONG-TERM CARE

It is impossible to open the newspaper or turn on the television without reading or hearing a discussion of the urgent need in the United States to address the economic issues involved in health care, particularly as the Baby Boomers grow older. These discussions often occur in the context of other issues affecting adults using a wide range of health care services, from outpatient medical care to private psychotherapy. Changes in health maintenance organizations (HMOs) have created havoc in many sectors of the health care industry, causing great anxiety among

the public, politicians, and health care professionals. In many ways, the health care financing crisis is a function of the huge expenses associated with the long-term care of older adults. Insecurity over the financing of health care can constitute a crisis for adults of any age, but particularly so for older persons with limited financial resources. The ability to receive proper treatment for chronic conditions is therefore a pressing social and an individual issue.

Long-term health care financing has a history dating back to the early 1900s and the first attempts in the United States to devise government health insurance programs. In the ensuing century, as these programs became established, their benefits structure and financing grew increasingly complex and diversified. Throughout this process, the developers of these plans, which involve state and federal agencies along with private insurance companies, have attempted to respond to the rapidly changing needs of the population and the even more rapidly changing nature of the nation's economy. Other countries, particularly Canada and many European nations, have worked out different solutions than those existing in the United States and are also encountering challenges to their economy as their populations age.

As you will see shortly, nursing homes and other facilities in which older adults receive treatment are subject to strict federal and state requirements to ensure that they comply with the standards set forth in the legislation that created the funding programs. The intimate connection between financing and regulation of these long-term care facilities has provided the incentive for nursing homes to raise their level of care so that they can qualify for this support.

Medicare

Title XVIII of the U.S. Social Security Act, passed and signed into law by President Lyndon B. Johnson in 1965, created the federal funding agency known as **Medicare** (designated "Health Insurance for the Aged and Disabled") (see Figure 12.3). At the time of its passage, the "pay as you go system" that formed the funding basis for Medicare seemed sound. Medicare's funding comes from payroll taxes, premiums, general revenue from income taxes, and some payments from the states. In the mid-1960s, there were far more employed workers than people 65 and older needing health care, and it appeared

FIGURE 12.3

Structure of Medicare

- Part A: Hospital insurance
- Part B: Medical insurance
- Part C: Medicare advantage plans
- Part D: Prescription drug coverage

that by taxing the employed workers to pay for those requiring care, the system would maintain itself indefinitely. There was apparently little reason at that time to be concerned about what would ultimately become a perfect storm of a rapid increase in life expectancy combined with an even more rapid increase in costs associated with health care.

Medicare has grown enormously since its inception. In 1966 Medicare covered 19.1 million people at a cost of $1.8 billion. By 2008 more than 37.6 million Americans 65 and older were covered, two thirds of whom are enrolled in Medicare drug plans (Center for Medicare and Medicaid Services, 2010a). Nursing homes received $25.7 billion from Medicare. The total benefits paid out by Medicare in 2008 totaled over $469 billion in 2009 or 3.2% of the gross domestic product. By 2083 Medicare is expected to reach 11.4% of the gross domestic product (Social Security Administration, 2010).

It is now projected that by the year 2018, there will be a deficit in the total Medicare budget due to the fact that expenditures will be greater than revenues. The gap between expenditures and revenue will continue to increase steadily through at least the year 2081. The situation was considered grave enough so that in its annual report of 2007, the Social Security Trustees issued their first-ever warning that the program is on its way to becoming unsustainable. This impending crisis became the immediate impetus for the Patient Protection and Affordable Care Act (PPACA) (P.L. 111–148), legislation signed into law by President Barack Obama in the spring of 2010.

Even since it first became law, however, Medicare has been subject to numerous legislative and administrative changes designed to improve health care services to older adults, the disabled, and the poor. In 1973 the program was expanded to broaden eligibility to citizens already receiving Social Security benefits, people over 65 who qualify for Social Security benefits, and individuals with end-stage renal

disease requiring continuous dialysis or kidney transplant. The Department of Health and Human Services (DHHS) has the overall responsibility for administration of the Medicare program, with the assistance of the Social Security Administration (SSA).

In 1977, the Health Care Financing Administration (HCFA) was established under the DHHS to administer Medicare and Medicaid; it was replaced in July 2001 by the Centers for Medicare & Medicaid Services (CMS) as part of a large-scale reform of services to beneficiaries. CMS is now the agency with responsibility for formulation of policy and guidelines, oversight and operation of contracts, maintenance and review of records, and general financing. State agencies also play a role in the regulation and administration of the Medicare program in consultation with CMS.

Medicare Part A (Hospital Insurance or HI) coverage includes the cost of a semiprivate hospital room, meals, regular nursing services, operating and recovery room, intensive care, inpatient prescription drugs, laboratory tests, X-rays, psychiatric hospital, and inpatient rehabilitation. All other medically necessary services and supplies provided in the hospital are also completely covered. Luxury items, cosmetic surgery, vision care, private nursing, private rooms (unless necessary for medical reasons), and rentals of television and telephone are not included in coverage.

Coverage in a skilled nursing facility is included in Part A only if it occurs within 30 days of a hospitalization of 3 days or more and is certified as medically necessary. It includes rehabilitation services and appliances (walkers, wheelchairs) in addition to those services normally covered for inpatient hospitalization. Patients must pay a copayment for days 21–100 of their care in this setting. Home health services are also included in Part A of Medicare for the first 100 visits following a 3-day hospital stay. Respite periods are also covered for hospice care to allow a break for the patient's caregiver. In 2009, opponents to health care reform stated that the changes would include "death panels" to decide who would receive palliative care; however, within existing Medicare legislation, hospice care was already fully insured, covering pain relief, supportive medical and social services, physical therapy, nursing services, and symptom management.

Medicare Part B provides benefits available to individuals age 65 and over with payment of a monthly premium that, starting in 2007, varies according to the individual's income. Included in Part B services are preventive treatments, including glaucoma and diabetes screenings as well as bone scans, mammograms, and colonoscopies. Other covered services include laboratory tests, chiropractor visits, eye exams, dialysis, mental health care, occupational therapy, outpatient treatment, flu shots, and home health services. A one-time physical examination is also included in Part B.

Part C of Medicare, also called Medicare Advantage, involves coverage through private health plans. Individuals who have both Part A and Part B can choose to get their benefits through a variety of risk-based plans including HMOs, Preferred Provider Organizations (PPOs), private fee-for-service plans, and a health insurance policy administered by the federal government. Established by the Balanced Budget Act of 1997 (Public Law 105-33), Part C first became available in 1998. Beginning in 2006, PPOs began to serve beneficiaries on a regional basis. The Department of Health and Human Services identified 26 regions across the nation in which PPO plans compete to provide services. The DHHS established these regions to ensure that all Medicare beneficiaries, including those in small states and

rural areas, would have the opportunity to enroll in a PPO, as well as to encourage private plans to participate. In 2006, 16% of beneficiaries were enrolled in Medicare Advantage plans, and by 2009, this number increased to 24%, reflecting the growth in the popularity of these programs.

Part D of Medicare, first available in 2006 provides prescription drug benefits (see Figure 12.4). Though providing welcome relief for Medicare recipients, as originally passed, its effectiveness was severely limited by what turned out to be a huge catch. As of 2010, Medicare pays 75% of drug costs between a deductible of $310 and $2,830. At this point, participants in the plan encounter a gap in coverage that became known as the "donut hole." It is called the donut hole because there is no coverage provided at all between prescription drug spending costs of $2,830 and $6,440 per year. It is only when drug costs exceed $6,400 (the starting point for catastrophic coverage) per year that Medicare pays almost the full amount (95%).

You might think that recipients could supplement Part D with private coverage to avoid the donut hole, but once you sign up for Part D you are no longer eligible to receive prescription benefits through private insurance companies. Skyrocketing prescription

FIGURE 12.4

Standard Medicare Prescription Drug Benefit in 2010

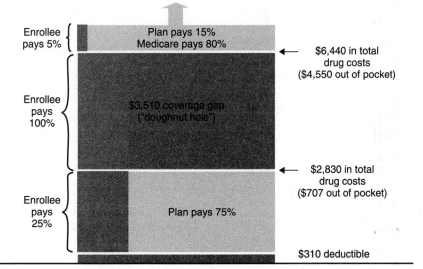

Source: Adapted from Neuman, P., & Cubanski, J. (2009). Medicare Part D update—lessons learned and unfinished business. *New England Journal of Medicine, 361,* 406–414.

drug costs exacerbate the problem. Of the 50 drugs most commonly used by older adults, the average annual cost per prescription is $2,810 (Families USA, 2010). Hence Part D's prescription privileges leave many older adults with significant out-of-pocket expenses for medications required to maintain them in good health. As a result, after Part D enrollees enter the donut hole, rates of medication adherence decline, as beneficiaries attempt to save money (Zhang, Donohue, Newhouse, & Lave, 2009). The PPACA of 2010 gave older adults entering the donut hole a $250 prescription drug rebate in 2010. Starting in 2011, qualified beneficiaries will pay 50% less on prescription drugs and by 2020 the donut hole will be closed completely.

Medicaid

Title XIX of the Social Security Act of 1965, known as **Medicaid**, is a federal and state matching entitlement program that provides medical assistance for certain individuals and families with low incomes and resources. Initially, Medicaid was formulated as a medical care extension of federally funded programs providing income assistance for the poor, with an emphasis on dependent children and their mothers, the disabled, and the over-65. Eligibility for Medicaid has expanded, however, and now is available to a larger number of low-income pregnant women, poor children, and some Medicare beneficiaries who are not eligible for any cash assistance program. Changes in legislation have also focused on increased access, better quality of care, specific benefits, enhanced outreach programs, and fewer limits on services. Another change is the addition of managed care as an alternative means of providing health services.

Medicaid provides assistance for a wide range of medical services for those considered in need by their state of residence. For older adults these services include inpatient and outpatient hospital services, physician services, nursing facility services, home health care for persons eligible for skilled nursing services, laboratory testing, X-ray services, prescribed drugs and prosthetic devices, optometrist services and eyeglasses, rehabilitation and physical therapy services, and home- and community-based care to cover certain chronic impairments.

Individuals covered by Medicare who are not otherwise "poor" may nevertheless require Medicaid when their benefits have run out and they cannot afford to pay their medical expenses. Many states have a "medically needy" program for such individuals, who have too much income to qualify as categorically needy. This program allows them to "spend down" their assets to the point of being eligible for Medicaid by paying medical expenses to offset their excess income. Medicaid then pays the remaining portion of their medical bills by providing services and supplies that are available under their state's Medicaid program. Services that are covered by both programs are paid first by Medicare. The difference is then paid by Medicaid, up to the state's payment limit. Medicaid also covers additional services such as skilled nursing facility care beyond the 100-day limit covered by Medicare, prescription drugs, eyeglasses, and hearing aids.

Medicaid is the largest source of funding for medical and health-related services for those in need of assistance. In 2008 it provided health care assistance amounting to $344.3 billion. Nursing homes received $56.3 billion from Medicaid in 2008. Together Medicare and Medicaid (federal and state) financed $813.5 billion in health care services in 2008, which was 34% of the nation's total health care bill of $2.3 trillion (private and public funding combined) and 82% of all federal spending on health (Center for Medicare and Medicaid Services, 2010b). As shown in Figure 12.5, there is considerable variation by state in the amount spent on long-term care; Louisiana has the highest percent in the United States at 26.6% (Kaiser Family Foundation, 2010b).

LEGISLATIVE ISSUES IN CARE OF OLDER ADULTS

The regulation of nursing homes and community-based services for older adults and the disabled is a major focus of health policy and legislation in the United States. As we mentioned earlier, this is because funding of these services is provided by federal and state agencies.

1987 Omnibus Budget Reconciliation Act of 1987 (OBRA 1987)

The current U.S. laws governing the operation of institutional facilities have their origins in a report completed by the prestigious Institute of Medicine in 1986 called "Improving the Quality of Care in Nursing Homes." This report recommended to Congress

FIGURE 12.5

Medicaid Spending on Long-term Care by State

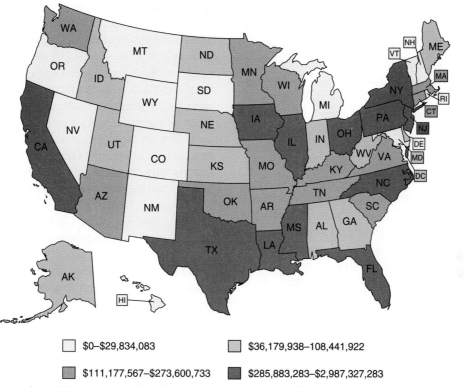

☐ $0–$29,834,083   ▨ $36,179,938–108,441,922

▨ $111,177,567–$273,600,733   ■ $285,883,283–$2,987,327,283

Source: Kaiser Family Foundation. (2010). State health facts. Retrieved from http://www.statehealthfacts.org/savemap.jsp?typ=4&ind=180&cat=4&sub=47.

major changes in the quality and nature of services provided to nursing home residents. The result of the report was the Omnibus Budget Reconciliation Act of 1987 (OBRA 1987) that included the **Nursing Home Reform Act (NHRA)**. OBRA 1987 mandated that facilities must meet physical standards, provide adequate professional staffing and services, and maintain policies governing their administrative and medical procedures. A significant component of this legislation was the provision of safeguards to assure quality of care and protection of residents' rights. The bottom line is that each resident must be provided with services and activities to attain or maintain the highest practicable physical, mental, and psychosocial well-being. Facilities are required to care for residents in a manner and an environment that promotes, maintains, or enhances quality of life.

The conditions of the Nursing Home Reform Act specify that nursing homes must be licensed in accordance with state and local laws, including all applicable laws pertaining to staff, licensing, and registration, fire, safety, and communicable diseases. They must have a governing body legally responsible for policies and the appointment of a qualified administrator. One or more physicians must be on call at all times to cover an emergency, and there must be 24-hour nursing care services, including at least one full-time registered nurse. The facility must admit eligible patients regardless of race, color, or national origin.

The specific services that are required in addition to availability of physicians and nurses are specialized rehabilitation, social services, pharmaceutical services, dietary services, dental services, and an ongoing activities program. As designated by the Health Care Reform Act, the goal of the activities program should be to encourage self-care and the individual's return to normal life in the community through social, religious, recreational activities, and visits with relatives and friends. Nursing homes are required to maintain confidential records, employ appropriate methods for obtaining and dispensing medications, and have arrangements in place for obtaining required clinical, laboratory, X-ray, and other diagnostic services.

The series of resident rights developed as part of the Nursing Home Reform Act include choice of physician and treatment, freedom from physical and mental abuse, the right to privacy and treatment with respect and dignity, the right to confidential records, and the right to have needs and preferences met. In addition, residents have the right to refuse medications and treatments, voice their grievances, and transfer or leave the facility when appropriate. They are also required to be informed in writing about services and fees before entering the nursing home, to have the right to manage their own money (or choose someone to do so), and be able to keep personal belongings and property to the extent that these do not interfere with the rights, health, or safety of others.

The legislation also established procedures to ensure that all conditions are met for maintaining compliance with the law. These procedures include monitoring of the performance of facilities by outside survey agencies to determine whether they comply with the federal conditions of participation.

1997 Balanced Budget Act

Changes to the nursing home rates for post-hospital care through Medicare were incorporated into the Balanced Budget Act of 1997 and implemented in March 2000. These changes involved moving to a prospective payment system in which rates paid to **skilled nursing facilities** cover the costs of furnishing most covered nursing home services, excluding payment for physicians and certain other practitioner services. Under the prospective payment system, each facility receives a fixed amount for treating patients diagnosed with a given illness, regardless of the length of stay or type of care received. Prior to the Balanced Budget Act changes, nursing homes filed bills to Medicare based on fee for service. The intention of the change in payments was to curb the rapidly rising costs of Medicare as well as to adjust the payments to the specific needs of the patient. By paying more for the patients whose medical expenses are legitimately higher than those who have less expensive medical needs, nursing homes could therefore provide better health care, adjusted for the needs of the individual resident.

1998 Nursing Home Initiative

Ten years after NHRA was put into place, a series of investigations and Senate hearings were conducted that called attention to serious weaknesses in federal and state survey and enforcement activities stipulated by that law. In 1997, the U.S. Senate Committee on Aging received reports that documented inadequate care in California nursing homes that caused widespread death and suffering of residents. These reports triggered a hearing in 1998 by the Committee on California nursing homes. At this hearing, a Government Accountability Office (GAO) report revealed that nationwide there was weak enforcement of the NHRA, putting many residents at risk of inadequate care. Fully 98% of nursing homes were found to have more than minimal (35%), substandard (33%), or serious (30%) deficiencies. Particularly troubling was the fact that even when serious problems were identified, there was no enforcement of actions that would ensure that the deficiencies were corrected and did not recur.

These shocking reports about nursing home abuse made it clear that NHRA enforcement procedures were not working. In response to these findings, President Bill Clinton's administration announced the 1998 Nursing Home Initiative. This initiative proposed a series of steps designed to improve enforcement of nursing home quality standards that were then adopted by HCFA. These included altering the timing of nursing home inspections to include both weekends and evenings as well as weekdays, providing more frequent inspections of previous violators, imposing immediate sanctions on nursing homes found guilty of a second offense involving violations that harm residents, allowing states to impose monetary penalties on violators, and not lifting sanctions against offenders until an onsite visit verified compliance with federal regulations.

Congressional Hearings on Nursing Home Abuse

In September 2000, a Senate Committee on Aging held a hearing on the outcomes of the Nursing Home Initiative. This hearing revealed that the initiative had resulted in improvements to state survey and federal oversight procedures, including increases in the number of surveyors, improved tracking of complaints, new methods to detect serious deficiencies, and improved organization of nursing home oversight activities.

However, additional hearings on nursing home quality held by the Senate Committee on Aging in 1999 and 2000 revealed that nursing home abuse was still rampant. Nationwide, 27% of nursing homes were cited with violations causing actual harm to residents or placing them at risk of death or serious injury; another 43% were cited for violations that created a potential for more than minimal harm.

The Senate hearings also revealed flaws in the surveys; significant problems were often missed, such as pressure sores, malnutrition, and dehydration. In some cases, nursing homes were cited because a member of the nursing staff committed acts of abuse against residents such as beatings, sexual abuse, and verbal abuse. Formal complaints made by residents or families were uninvestigated for weeks or months.

Making the problem worse was the fact that the filing of complaints was discouraged by state governmental agencies. Even if serious deficiencies were found, there was inadequate enforcement so that the nursing homes involved did not correct the problems. The Senate Committee also found that the majority (54%) of nursing homes were understaffed, putting residents at increased risk of hospitalization for avoidable causes, pressure sores, and significant weight loss (Minority Staff Special Investigations Division Committee on Government Reform U.S. House of Representatives, 2001).

2002 Nursing Home Quality Initiative

In November 2002, the federal government initiated the National Nursing Home Quality Initiative, a program intended to help consumers find the highest quality nursing homes. The 2002 Initiative combined new information for consumers about the quality of care provided in individual nursing homes with resources available to nursing homes to improve the quality of care in their facilities. Quality Improvement Organizations (QIOs), government contractors, were hired to offer assistance to skilled nursing facilities to help them improve their services. The 2002 Initiative also included a provision to train volunteers to serve as ombudspersons. The role of the ombudspersons is to help families and residents on a daily basis find nursing homes that provide the highest possible quality of care and give consumers tools they need to make an informed, educated decision on selecting a nursing home.

2007 GAO Report

The 2002 Initiative should have done a considerable amount to improve the quality of care in nursing homes, but like its predecessors, it too was ineffective

Family members hold personal pictures of their loved ones on January 17, 2009, who were allegedly abused in a nursing home in Albert Lea, Minnesota.

in achieving its goals. In 2007, the GAO issued a major report analyzing the effectiveness of the online reporting system based on data from 63 nursing homes in California, Michigan, Pennsylvania, and Texas, institutions that had a history of serious compliance problems (see Figure 12.6). From this analysis the GAO concluded that efforts to strengthen federal enforcement of sanctions had not been effective.

For example, nursing homes that were cited for harming or abusing residents can be sanctioned through fines, the assignment of monitors, temporary management, or even termination from their sources of federal and state financing. However, the report showed that when violations were reported, the institutions charged with the violations were often given some type of leeway, either in terms of the amount they were penalized or the length of time they were granted before being required to pay the penalty. Many homes showed a "yo-yo" pattern in which they made changes in order to comply with regulations only to slide back down until they were sanctioned. Residents continued to suffer abusive treatment because the fundamental problems were not corrected (Government Accountability Office, 2008).

As you will learn shortly, deficiencies in nursing homes remain a significant problem, limiting severely the quality of care that many residents receive. Continued reporting of these deficiencies, monitoring by government agencies, and involvement of family members advocating for residents are important safeguards. If you have a relative in a nursing home, it is important for you to be aware of these problems and vigilant for ways to prevent them from affecting your relatives.

CHARACTERISTICS AND NEEDS OF NURSING HOMES AND THEIR RESIDENTS

Although there is a relatively small percentage overall of people 65 and older living in nursing homes, the percentage of older adults who are institutionalized increases dramatically with age. As of 2004 (the most recent date available), the percentages rise from 0.9% for persons 65 to 74 years to 3.6% for persons 75 to 84 years and 13.9% for persons 85+ (Federal Interagency Forum on Age-Related Statistics, 2009). The average size of a nursing facility across the United

FIGURE 12.6

2007 GAO Report on Nursing Home Abuse

States is 108 beds, up slightly from 2003 (Harrington, Carrillo, & Blank, 2009).

Nearly two thirds (67%) of nursing homes in the United States fall into the category of "for-profit" facilities, meaning that they seek to have their revenue exceed their expenses. Nonprofit facilities, which includes primarily those run by religious organizations, constitute the second largest group (26.5%), and government-owned facilities, primarily those run by the Veterans Administration, compose the remainder (6%). Therefore, most nursing homes are run like a business with the goal of making a profit. Perhaps because they are less oriented toward the "bottom line," not-for-profit nursing homes have higher quality ratings than their for-profit counterparts (Comondore et al., 2009). Related to this issue is the payment mode of residents. When nursing homes have more private pay patients, they are able to provide better care because the rates for these patients are higher than the reimbursement rates that facilities receive from governmental subsidies.

Information about nursing homes and nursing home residents comes from the On-line Survey, Certification, and Reporting system (OSCAR). The

OSCAR system has information from the state surveys of all certified nursing facilities in the United States, which are entered into a uniform database. Surveyors assess both the process and the outcomes of nursing home care in 15 major areas. Each of these areas has specific regulations, which state surveyors review to determine whether facilities have met the standards. When a facility fails to meet a standard, a deficiency or citation is given. The deficiencies are given for problems that can result in a negative impact on the health and safety of residents.

Home health agencies are required to submit data on their effectiveness using the Outcomes Assessment and Information Set (OASIS), mandated for use by Medicare-certified home health agencies.

Characteristics of Residents

The most common primary diagnosis of nursing home residents when admitted to a nursing home is cardiovascular disease, and the strongest predictors of admission to a nursing home are inability to carry out basic activities of daily living, cognitive impairment, and prior nursing home admission (Gaugler, Duval, Anderson, & Kane, 2007). The greatest form of disability is loss of cognitive skills associated with Alzheimer's disease (Schultz, et al., 2002). Given that Alzheimer's disease is found in nearly half of all nursing home residents (45% in 2008), this means that difficulties in carrying out daily living skills are a significant problem among nursing home residents. In fact, 56.8% of nursing home residents are chairbound, meaning that they are restricted to a wheelchair. Despite the large number of residents with Alzheimer's disease, only 5% of nursing homes have special care units devoted specifically to their care (Harrington, Carrillo, & Blank, 2009).

Mood and anxiety disorders are present in nearly 20% of all older adults living in these settings (Sahyoun et al., 2001). Nearly two thirds (65.2%) of residents receive psychotropic medications, including antidepressants, antianxiety drugs, sedatives and hypnotics, and antipsychotics (Harrington et al., 2009). Though having more functional limitations than older adults living in their own homes, nursing home residents have more depressive symptoms and lower self-rated quality of life (Karakaya, Bilgin, Ekici, Kose, & Otman, 2009).

As of 2008, about two thirds (64%) of residents have their nursing home expenses paid for by Medicaid, slightly over one fifth (22%) pay for nursing homes themselves through their own funds or other forms of insurance, and the remainder (14%) have their nursing home expenses paid for by Medicare (Harrington, Carrillo, & Blank, 2009). Although quality control is intended to provide comparable care to all residents, those who are paying for their own nursing homes are afforded a greater range of facilities, better accommodations, and higher staff-to-patient ratios compared to those who are funded through Medicaid (Donoghue, 2006).

Nursing Home Deficiencies

As the U.S. government attempts to improve the quality of care provided by nursing homes, monitoring continues on a yearly basis through the listing of deficiencies as reported to OSCAR (see Figure 12.7). In the years between 2003 and 2008, there was a 7.5% average increase in the number of deficiencies from 8.6 to 9.25, showing that quality of care within nursing homes is on a steady decline. In 2008, 26% of the nation's nursing homes received deficiencies for poor quality of care. However, the average number of deficiencies varied substantially across the states. In 2008, the state with the highest number of deficiencies was Delaware, at 8% (Harrington, Carrillo, & Blank, 2009).

Deficiencies that cause harm or immediate jeopardy to residents are considered the most serious of all. In 2008, lack of accident prevention was the number one deficiency, occurring in 44% of all nursing homes in the United States. Delaware, Washington State, and Indiana all had percentages of 40% or greater (Kaiser Family Foundation, 2010a).

Some other areas of concern also deserve mention. For instance, continence (control over elimination of urine and feces) is a highly sensitive and personal area of life. Though training programs exist that are designed to help residents gain and maintain continence through use of diet, fluids, and regular schedules, these are rarely used; as of 2008 these were available to only 6.4% of residents despite the fact that 65.5% were reported to have urinary incontinence. Bowel incontinence occurs in 43.3% of all residents, but bowel training is available only to 3.7%. Clearly, when continence training is a need

FIGURE 12.7

Top Ten Deficiencies in Nursing Homes, 2008 (by percent)

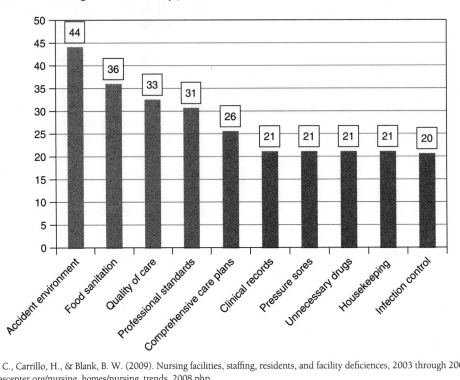

Source: Harrington, C., Carrillo, H., & Blank, B. W. (2009). Nursing facilities, staffing, residents, and facility deficiences, 2003 through 2008. Retrieved from http://www.pascenter.org/nursing_homes/nursing_trends_2008.php.

that is unmet, this can detract from the quality of an individual's life as well as the quality of the life of the staff. Worsening continence is one of the top reasons that older residents of nursing homes become socially disengaged (Dubeau, Simon, & Morris, 2006). Continuing education that addresses knowledge, beliefs, and attitudes may help ultimately in encouraging nursing staff to work on restoring continence in their patients (Saxer, de Bie, Dassen, & Halfens, 2009).

The use of physical and chemical (drug) restraints to keep residents from being aggressive is another key area of adjustment. Overall in 2008 about 4% of nursing homes employ physical restraints, a percent that is down overall by almost half from 2003 (Harrington, Carrillo, & Blank, 2009). However, in one New York State study, researchers found that Black elders living in nursing homes with a high percentage of White residents were more likely to be placed in restraints than Black residents living in homes that consisted largely of Blacks (Miller, Papandonatos, Fennell, & Mor, 2006).

PSYCHOLOGICAL ISSUES IN LONG-TERM CARE

Just as you wish to control certain aspects of your environment, residents of nursing homes also have the need to perceive that they can control what goes on around them. Even though residents may not have actual control, the perception that they do can help to ease the stress of adjusting to the institutional environment. Residents who feel that they can have mastery over at least some aspects of life in the institution feel less anxious and depressed, experiencing less of the stress that so often accompanies moving from their own homes to the institution. Their adaptation can further be facilitated if they feel that they have support in this adaptation process (Keister, 2006).

The psychosocial needs of residents and strategies that can be implemented to enhance the quality of life in nursing homes became a focus of OBRA 1987. Unfortunately, change is slow to come about. Researchers still believe that nursing homes in the

United States had not, at least as of the late 1990s, made significant changes in the freedom of choice afforded to residents on a day-to-day basis (Kane et al., 2007). In terms of the rhythm of life in the average nursing home, although deficiencies in activities exist in less than 10% of nursing homes, there still remains a good deal of room for improvement. A study of the daily life of residents conducted in 2002 revealed that, as was the case in the 1960s, residents spend almost two thirds of the time in their room, doing nothing at all (Ice, 2002). Thus, for many residents, there are simply not enough activities in the average nursing home (Martin et al., 2002). At the same time, training of specialists to work with the nursing home population is lagging; social workers are not given sufficient educational preparation to work in these challenging and often stressful settings (Allen, Nelson, & Netting, 2007).

Models of Adaptation

Theoretical models attempting to provide insight into the adaptation of the individual to the institutional environment of a long-term care facility began to develop in the 1970s with the increasing attention in gerontology given to ecological approaches to the aging process. In part, this interest developed in response to practical concerns about the best ways to minimize behavioral disturbances and maximize adaptation of older adult residents to institutional settings. Many researchers studying institutionalization believed that it was important to find ways to maximize the resident's ability to maintain independence even while having to adjust to an environment that inevitably fostered dependence (Gottesman & Bourestom, 1974).

Maximizing an older individual's adaptation to the environment is also tied in with the challenges that large institutions (such as college dorms) face in attempting to find ways to satisfy the needs of the so-called "average" resident. The average resident, like the "average" college student is a hypothetical construct. When trying to satisfy the needs of everyone, administrators of institutions will inevitably satisfy very few.

To put this issue in very concrete terms, consider the issue of temperature. For some people, a room temperature of 68 degrees is just right, but for others, 76 is the ideal place to set the thermostat. Most institutions must regulate the temperature of the entire building, however, because they do not have individual room thermostats. In attempting to please the average resident, the administrator would need to adjust the temperature to the mean of these two numbers, which would be 72. Neither group of residents will find this temperature to be a comfortable one, yet on the "average" it is the correct level.

Complications also arise from the fact that, in predicting adaptation to the institution, the actual qualities of the environment are only part of the equation. Researchers are interested in learning how residents perceive the institution's physical qualities and relating these perceptions to their adaptation (Sloane et al., 2002).

As important as the physical environment is to adaptation, the psychosocial needs of the residents also play a crucial role. These needs may have more to do with the amount of control people feel they have over their environments than with the physical characteristics of the institution. Feeling that you can control the temperature in your room if you desire may be even more important to your satisfaction than the actual temperature. This possibility was tested in an interview study of nursing home residents in Victoria, British Columbia. Scenarios were presented as vignettes in which residents were asked to make decisions such as what time to go to bed, what medicines to take, whether to move to a different room, and what type of end-of-life care to receive. Not everyone wished to have control over these decisions, though. Older adults with more years of education and a greater number of chronic illnesses were likely to state that they wished to be able to make these choices rather than have the decisions made for them by nursing home staff (Funk, 2004). Thus, resident characteristics are important to factor into the equation when evaluating the impact of the environment on adaptation to the institution.

Empirical interest in the institutionalization process has dwindled somewhat from the 1970s, when several teams of researchers were actively investigating environmental models and aging (Nehrke et al., 1981). However, one of these models offers some useful concepts for predicting how well people will adapt to an institutional setting. This model, the **competence-press model** (Lawton & Nahemow,

1973), predicts an optimal level of adjustment that institutionalized persons will experience on the basis of their levels of competence (physical and psychological) compared with the demands or "press" of the environment, or the demands it places upon individuals.

As shown in Figure 12.8, competence and press jointly influence adaptation. In the optimal situation, there is a match between an individual's abilities and the environment's demands. A small degree of discrepancy is acceptable, but when the mismatch goes outside this range, the individual will experience negative affect and maladaptive behaviors. For example, the intellectually competent older resident (high competence) will do well in a setting in which autonomous decisions are expected (high press), but a person with a significant cognitive impairment will adapt maximally when the environment is very structured (low press).

By considering the interaction between the individual and the environment of the institution, the competence–press model makes it possible to provide specific recommendations to institutions about how best to serve the residents. The model is essentially a biopsychosocial one, allowing room for multiple dimensions of competence and press to be considered when evaluating older adults (Lichtenburg, MacNeill, Lysack, Adam & Neufeld, 2003). Competence may be defined in terms of biological and psychological characteristics such as mobility and cognitive resources. The social factors in this model are incorporated into the level of press in the environment which include the expectations of staff and amount of stimulation provided by other the residents.

Suggestions for Improving Institutional Care

Clearly the environment plays an important role in affecting the individual's health, both inside and outside an institutional environment. Within the institutional setting, the implications of the competence–press model are that the needs of individuals should be met to the greatest extent possible. Innovations in nursing home care are being developed with the goal of maximizing the fit between the person and environment. For example, bathing, a situation that can be distressing when conducted in a way that embarrasses or exposes the

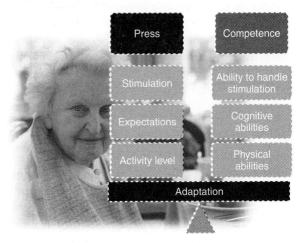

FIGURE 12.8

Competence–press Model of Adaptation

resident, can be treated in a more individualized manner, making it a less aversive experience (Camp, Cohen-Mansfield, & Capezuti, 2002). Even a change as simple as switching from individually plated to "family style" meals can have a beneficial effect on resident adjustment as measured by perceived quality of life, physical performance, and increases in body weight (Nijs, de Graaf, Kok, & van Staveren, 2006).

Nurses aides, who increasingly are managing many of the daily living activities of residents (Seblega et al., 2010), can be taught to use behavioral methods to help residents maintain self-care and, hence, independence (Burgio et al., 2002). Such interventions can also benefit staff–resident relationships. Since satisfaction with treatment by staff is such a significant component of satisfaction with the institution (Chou, Boldy, & Lee, 2002), any intervention that maximizes positive interactions between staff and residents is bound to have a favorable impact on the sense of well-being experienced by residents. Such training, even with patients who have severe dementia, can help reduce dependence on psychotropic medications (Fossey et al., 2006).

New models for nursing home design attempt to break up monotony to create more of a feeling of a community or neighborhood. Nursing stations are removed from view, allowing residents and staff to share lounges. Hallways have alcoves that can store medicine carts and nursing stations. Small group living clusters, improved interior design, and access to gardens can help maintain independence in residents whose autonomy would otherwise be threatened (Regnier & Denton, 2009).

Other models of change stress new ways of allocating staff to meet the care needs of residents. In one such model, rather than basing staff assignments on the completion of specific tasks for all residents (bathing, changing dressings, administering medications), staff are assigned to meet all the needs of a particular group of residents. Although such a system increases the staffing requirements, overall the institutions reduce their expenses in the areas of restraints and antipsychotic medications. Hospitalization rates, staff turnover, and success in rehabilitation also improve as does the satisfaction that residents express about their care. Another improvement involves the use of a team approach to providing mental health services. When staff work as a multidisciplinary team, residents receive better services; at the same time, staff are more informed and perform more effectively in their jobs (Bartels, Moak, & Dums, 2002).

The Green House model offers an alternative to the traditional nursing homes by offering older adults individual homes within a small community of 6 to10 residents and skilled nursing staff. The Green House residence is designed to feel like a home; medical equipment is stored away from sight, the rooms are sunny and bright, and the outdoor environment is easily accessible. Self-reports of quality of life among Green House residents are higher in comparison to traditional nursing homes (Kane, Lum, Cutler, Degenholtz, & Yu, 2007). Additionally, research comparing the Green House model to traditional nursing programs suggests that family members are more satisfied with the care provided by the Green House model (Lum, Kane, Cutler, & Yu, 2008).

These reforms in institutions can bring about much needed changes in the care of older adults. However, the broadest proposal for sweeping changes in the health care system in the United States goes beyond changes in institutional models. The Institute of Medicine (2008), issued a mandate for retooling the health care workforce to take into account the growth of older adults needing services at all levels. As shown in Figure 12.9, there is an increasing gap between the number of filled positions in geriatric psychiatry and the number of available positions.

The Institute of Medicine report focuses on three key areas: enhancing competence in geriatric care, increasing recruitment and retention, and improving models of care. Supporting these ideas, a large-scale meta-analysis of more than 2,700 published articles identified 15 new models of care ranging from acute care in patient homes, nurse–physician teams for nursing home residents, and models of comprehensive care in hospitals (Boult et al., 2009). Clearly, new ideas are needed to revamp the current health care system for the aging Baby Boomers, whose numbers, lifestyles, and values will almost invariably

The Leonard Florence Center for Living in Chelsea, Massachusetts, is based on the Green House model. Composed of ten homes, each containing ten private bedrooms and baths, the Center serves 100 residents within a six-story condominium-style complex.

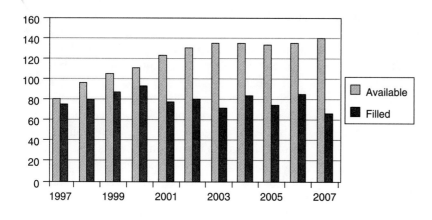

FIGURE 12.9

Discrepancy between Available and Filled Positions in Geriatric Psychiatry

Source: Institute of Medicine. (2008). Retooling for an aging America: Buildling the healthcare workforce. Retrieved from http://www.iom.edu/Reports/2008/Retooling-for-an-Aging-America-Building-the-Health-Care-Workforce.aspx.

lead to challenges of the status quo of care now being offered. These aging Baby Boomers may want to hear Rolling Stones music playing in the corridors of their care facilities rather than the quiet and soothing sounds of a string orchestra.

In conclusion, the concerns of institutionalized older adults are of great importance to individuals and to their families, many of whom are involved in helping to make long-term care decisions for their older relatives. The dignity and self-respect of the resident, which is fortunately now being regulated by state and federal certification standards, can best be addressed by multidimensional approaches that take into account personal and contextual factors. Interventions based on these approaches will ultimately lead to a higher quality of life for those who must spend their last days or months in the care of others.

SUMMARY

1. A wide range of treatment sites is available specifically designed for older adults such as nursing homes and residential care facilities. The percentage of older adults in these treatment sites with cognitive deficits is relatively high. Increasing attention is being given to home health care. Other residential sites include special housing that is designed for older adults.

2. Medicare is designed to provide hospital insurance and supplemental medical insurance. Other forms of insurance attached to Medicare are becoming increasingly available to older adults. Medicaid is intended to reduce the burden of health care costs among those who are in need of help in payment for medical services, but individuals receiving this assistance must "spend down" to eliminate their assets. The cost of Medicare is expected to skyrocket over the coming decades, and will lead to bankruptcy of the Social Security Trust fund unless preventive measures are taken.

3. The rights of nursing home residents became protected with passage of the Nursing Home Reform Act in 1987. Since passage of this legislation, complaints about nursing home care have decreased. However, problems in areas such as food sanitation remain a concern as does the use of restraint as a means of controlling resident behavior. Care in nursing homes is an area needing continued monitoring, as was evident by the findings obtained in the 2002 General Accountability Office report on nursing home abuse and more recently by the 2007 General Accountability Office's review of the enforcement of violations in nursing home standards.

4. Psychological issues in long-term care focus on the provision of an adequate environment that will maximally meet the needs of residents. The competence–press model proposes an ideal relationship between how demanding an environment is and the abilities of the resident to meet those demands. The environment of neighborhoods in which older adults live is also becoming a concern of researchers who are attempting to understand the relationship between well-being and feelings of safety and security in the residents of these neighborhoods.

13

Death and

For many people, the concept of death is as fascinating as it is frightening. By definition, death remains the great unknown; even individuals who have had so-called near-death experiences cannot claim with certainty that what happened to them is an accurate prediction of what is to come in the future.

If you are in good health, you may not give your own death much thought. However, those who live until the years of later adulthood may find themselves prone to consider the ending of their lives on a more frequent basis. Even if they do not give attention to the existential questions of their own mortality, they are faced with the need to make practical arrangements such as planning the funeral or finalizing the will. Perhaps what most people wish for is to live as long as possible in as healthy a state as possible and to experience a death that will be quick and relatively painless. Another theme relating to death is the desire to leave something behind to be remembered by and to have made an impact on other people's lives.

As you shall see many times throughout this chapter, death has a social meaning as well as a personal meaning to the individual. For example, after a person's death, the circumstances of that death recast that person's life in a different light in the minds

of those who knew that person. When a person dies at a young age, for example, the person may be thought of in terms of that early death. The meaning that death gives to the life that was lived is another dimension to what is already a very complicated and multifaceted process.

TECHNICAL PERSPECTIVES ON DEATH

From a medical and legal perspective, **death** is said to occur when there is irreversible cessation of circulatory and respiratory functions, or when all structures of the brain have ceased to function (President's Commission for the Study of Ethical Problems in Medicine and Biomedical and Behavioral Research, 1981). The term **dying** refers to the period during which the organism loses its vitality. At one time the demarcation between life and death was relatively clear. Determination of the point of death has become more complicated over the course of the past three decades, however, since the advent of life-prolonging machines. It is possible to keep a person alive almost indefinitely on life support systems such

Dying

as artificial respirators and heart pumps. It remains a debatable point to determine whether an individual, under these circumstances, is considered "alive."

Medical Aspects of Death

Although the death experience varies from person to person, there are some commonalities in the physical changes shown by a person whose functions are deteriorating to the point that death will occur within a few hours or days. In a dying person, the symptoms that death is imminent include being asleep most of the time, being disoriented, breathing irregularly, having visual and auditory hallucinations, being less able to see, producing less urine, and having mottled skin, cool hands and feet, an overly warm trunk, and excessive secretions of bodily fluids (Gavrin & Chapman, 1995). An older adult who is close to death is likely to be unable to walk or eat, recognize family members, in constant pain, and finds breathing to be difficult. A common syndrome observed at the end of life is the **anorexia-cachexia syndrome**, in which the individual loses appetite (anorexia) and muscle mass (cachexia). The majority of cancer patients experience cachexia, a condition also found commonly in patients who have AIDS and dementia. In addition to the symptoms already mentioned, patients who are dying are likely to experience nausea, difficulty swallowing, bowel problems, dry mouth, and edema, or the accumulation of liquid in the abdomen and extremities that leads to bloating. Anxiety, depression, confusion, and dementia are also common psychological symptoms experienced at the end of life (Field, Colditz, Willett, Longcope, & McKinlay, 1994).

Obviously the symptoms experienced by dying individuals involve pain and suffering, not only for the patients themselves but also indirectly for their family members. However, those who work with the dying observe that against this backdrop, the final period of life can also involve emotional and spiritual growth (Field, Cassel, & Committee on Care at the End of Life, 1997). As we will see later, the notion of "acceptance" as the final stage of dying implies an ability to transcend these painful physical symptoms.

Mortality Facts and Figures

Although based on statistics derived from death, **mortality data** provide a fascinating picture of the factors that influence the course of human life. In some ways, mortality can be regarded as the ultimate dependent variable in the study of physical and behavioral aspects of health because unlike rating scales of health, there is no question about its validity in that it is clear that a person is no longer alive. In the majority of cases, death statistics provide valid numbers that indicate the outcomes of particular environmental conditions or disease processes. However, mortality data are not always 100% clear. There may be some question about the validity of cause of death information as well as debate about the point at which death occurs, as in the case of people who have been on life support machines for prolonged periods.

The cause of an individual's death must be verified by a coroner or medical examiner, who must code the cause or causes of death, either through external examination or an autopsy. The cause of death information must then be recorded on a death certificate. The coding system in use throughout the world is the World Health Organization International Classification of Diseases, Tenth Revision (ICD-10), which went into effect in 1999.

In many cases, the cause of death may be established on the basis of the individual's symptoms prior to death, particularly if the death occurred while the individual was under medical supervision. However, in other cases, the cause of death can only be performed by autopsy, a medical procedure in which the body is opened and the internal organs and structures are examined. The coroner may then decide to perform laboratory tests to determine the conditions present in the body prior to death. A research autopsy may be performed in order to contribute knowledge to the scientific literature relating symptoms present in life with biological changes in the body. Such autopsies can be very useful as, for example, has occurred in the study of aging nuns (Iacono et al., 2009), an investigation in which autopsy permission was obtained prior to death. As we discussed earlier in the book, the findings from this study have revealed a number of intriguing relationships between actual brain physiology and behavioral symptoms.

Though they may not be 100% accurate in terms of recording cause of death, mortality data nevertheless provide a useful index of a population's health.

Ideally, deaths occur in the oldest sectors of the population, meaning that more people are alive until they reach the age at which death would "normally" occur; that is, there are fewer cases of child death or deaths in young and middle adulthood (see Figure 13.1).

Consider the following facts. In 2006, there were 2,423,712 deaths in the United States (Xu, Kochanek, Murphy, & Tejeda-Vera, 2010). This translated to an overall death rate, per 100,000, in the population of 803.6, meaning that 803.6 people died for every 100,000 in the population. However, this number does not tell the whole story. Deaths are more likely to occur in older age groups. The death rate among people ages 65–74 is 2,011, meaning that of 100,000 people ages 65–74, about 2,000 died. The death rate skyrockets to 12,946 among people 85 years and older. These numbers represent the **age-specific death rate**, which is the number of deaths per 100,000 of a particular age group.

Therefore, the overall number of 803.6 deaths per 100,000 in the United States is misleading because it does not control for the fact that more deaths occur in a smaller proportion of the population. A statistical correction must be applied to the overall death rate in order to take this into account. Applying this correction leads to the **age-adjusted death rate**, a weighted sum based on each age group's death rate and size within the population. Using this formula, the age-adjusted death rate in the United States becomes 760.2. The age-adjusted death rate of 760.2 in 2007 was substantially less than the prior year's rate, which was 776.5. Having these numbers allows

FIGURE 13.1

Age-specific and Age-adjusted Death Rate

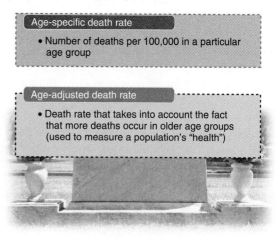

Age-specific death rate
- Number of deaths per 100,000 in a particular age group

Age-adjusted death rate
- Death rate that takes into account the fact that more deaths occur in older age groups (used to measure a population's "health")

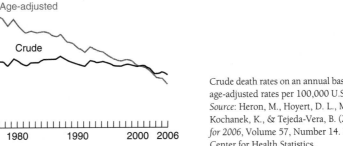

FIGURE 13.2

Crude and Age-adjusted Death Rates, U.S., 1960–2006

Crude death rates on an annual basis per 100,000 population; age-adjusted rates per 100,000 U.S. standard population. *Source*: Heron, M., Hoyert, D. L., Murphy, S. L., Xu, J., Kochanek, K., & Tejeda-Vera, B. (2009). *Deaths: Final data for 2006*, Volume 57, Number 14. Hyattsville MD: National Center for Health Statistics.

public health experts to conclude that the United States became "healthier" in 2007 compared to 2006 (see Figure 13.2).

With this number in hand, researchers can then move on to determine why the death rates in the United States continue to decline. The main contributors to this decline were decreases in the age-adjusted death rates for most chronic diseases, including diseases of the heart, cancer, cerebrovascular disease, and COPD. Health measures to improve these conditions seem, then, to be effectively lowering the death rate. What did not change and in fact what has risen in the past few years is the death rates from accidents, which rose steadily from 35.3 in 1999 to the current rate of 41.0 as of 2007.

The age-adjusted death rate provides a number that controls for the age distribution of a population and so makes it possible to compare the relative health of nations. Based on estimates from the World Health Organization, the unhealthiest countries are located in sub-Saharan Africa (World Health Organization, 2009). As shown in Figure 13.3, these countries also have the highest crude death rates. The majority of deaths in these African countries are due to infectious or parasitic diseases, with the highest rates occurring in Zimbabwe due to HIV/AIDS. Cardiovascular disease, in contrast, has the highest age-adjusted death rates in Kazakhstan, Ukraine, and Afghanistan, all of whose rates are far higher (600 to 700) than any state in the United

FIGURE 13.3

Crude Death Rates around the World, 2006

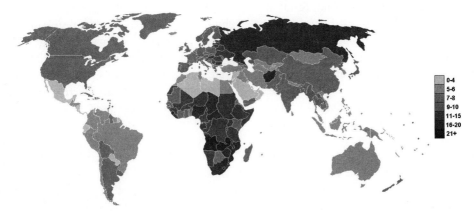

There are large variations around the world in death rates as can be seen from this figure. Death rates are given per 1,000 in the population.
Source: Central Intelligence Agency. (2010). The World Factbook. Retrieved from https://www.cia.gov/library/publications/the-world-factbook/rankorder/2066rank.html.

States, including those with highest cardiovascular death rates.

Improvements in health-related behaviors contributing to lower mortality rates from the major causes of death relate to what health experts call **compression of morbidity**, a reduction in disability prior to death (Manton, 2008). This concept means the same thing as the wish that some people express that they want to "die with my boots on."

In fact, people with healthy lifestyles are more likely to die with their boots on, so to speak. In one longitudinal study, people who were considered free of risk factors (they did not smoke, were active physically, and were of normal weight) had practically no disability scores for 10 years or more prior to their deaths. People with two or more unhealthy factors were more disabled over the study, particularly in the year and a half before their death. The period of disability was reduced to only 3 months prior to death among people with moderate risk. To achieve your own compression of morbidity, you need to minimize your own risky behaviors.

Unfortunately, although health care improvements seem to be contributing to compression of morbidity in the United States as a whole, increases in obesity may offset this trend (Manton, 2008). There are, however, large disparities within segments of the population in age-specific mortality rates. According to 2007 statistics (Xu et al., 2010), White females have the lowest age-adjusted mortality rate (647.7); non-Hispanic Black men have the highest (1210.9) followed by non-Hispanic White men (906.8). As shown in Figure 13.4, these discrepancies seem to follow regional variations (Kindig, Seplaki, & Libby, 2002). Looking at the top half of this figure, we see what resembles remarkably the maps we showed in Chapter 5 of the "stroke belt." It appears that these regional inequities in death rates are largely accounted for by variations due to race, because when race and Hispanic status are factored into the calculations (shown in the bottom half of the figure), the death rates in the Southeast actually become reduced to levels lower than in some Northeast states; the Midwest "advantage" remains, as does the high death rate in Nevada.

Marital status and education are two significant predictors of mortality. The age-adjusted death rate for those who never married is substantially higher than for those who were ever married, even taking into account the higher mortality of those who are widowed and divorced. The advantage holds for both men and women across all age groups of adults ages 15 and older (Xu et al., 2010). Educational status is also related to mortality rate. In all age groups, those with a college education or better have lower mortality rates.

These findings on education relate to the well-established relationship between social status and mortality (Adler et al., 1994). Since the mid-19th century, men in laboring and trade occupations are known to have higher death rates than those of the professional class (Macintyre, 1997). Data from the Whitehall II Study show why. Men in lower employment grades have a higher risk of coronary heart disease compared with men in higher employment grades (Marmot, Shipley, Hemingway, Head, & Brunner, 2008). Men and women from Whitehall II in lower socioeconomic positions had a 1.60 times higher risk of death compared with those in higher socioeconomic positions (Marmot et al., 2008). People in lower socioeconomic classes are also more likely to suffer from communicable diseases, exposure to lead, and work-related injuries (Pamuk, Makuc, Heck, Reuben, & Lochner, 1998). These results also apply to women from lower socioeconomic classes (Langford & Johnson, 2009).

Not only the level of occupation, but also the pattern of jobs people hold throughout adulthood, are related to mortality rates. The risk of mortality is lower in men who move up from manual to professional or managerial-level occupations (House, Kessler, Herzog, & Mero, 1990; Moore & Hayward, 1990). Men who hold a string of unrelated jobs have higher rates of early mortality than those with stable career progressions (Pavalko, Elder, & Clipp, 1993).

Although at one time the disparity in death rates was considered to be due to poorer sanitation, nutrition, and housing, current explanations focus on psychosocial factors as well. Stress is an important part of this equation. Researchers in the United States have established that people who report higher levels of subjective distress have higher mortality rates (Pratt, 2009). On-the-job stress is a major contributor to overall distress, particularly job stress in the form of lack of control over work conditions (Magnusson Hanson, Theorell, Oxenstierna, Hyde, & Westerlund, 2008). Workers in jobs who lack control over the pace and direction of what they do with their time (as is

Mortality rate adjusted by age and sex composition

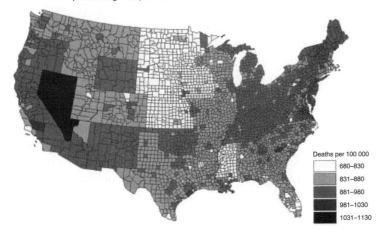

FIGURE 13.4

Mortality Rates within the United States

Deaths per 100 000
680–830
831–880
881–980
981–1030
1031–1130

Mortality rate adjusted by age and sex composition, percentage black, percentage hispanic, and socioeconomic composition

Deaths per 100 000
680–830
831–880
881–980
981–1030
1031–1130

true in an assembly-line or migrant farming job) are at higher risk of dying from cardiovascular disease. In a 25-year follow-up study of more than 12,500 male workers (aged 25 to 74), exposure to even 5 years of assembly-line work increased the risk of dying from heart disease. Assembly-line workers had an 83% higher mortality risk than would be expected on the basis of their age (Johnson, Stewart, Hall, Fredlund, & Theorell, 1996).

These findings were replicated in a variety of countries, including Spain (Muntaner et al., 2009), Sweden (Tiikkaja, Hemstrom, & Vagero, 2009), Portugal (Harding, Teyhan, Rosato, & Santana, 2008), Norway (Skalicka & Kunst, 2008), Russia (Perlman & Bobak, 2009), and Finland, where lower social class was related to higher suicide risk among

women (Maki & Martikainen, 2009). In part, some of these findings are due to income disparities. Across all countries studied by the World Health Organization, the poor are over four times as likely to die between the ages of 15 and 59 as are the nonpoor (World Health Organization, 2009). People with incomes below the poverty level are exposed to other risk factors as well. For example, low-income men are almost twice as likely to smoke as are men in the highest income groups (Schoenborn, Vickerie, & Barnes, 2003).

However, differences between income groups in a health risk behavior such as smoking are not sufficient to explain differences in mortality rates. Researchers suggest that lifelong exposure to social inequality is a key element of the income–mortality link. Such inequality incorporates a host of factors, including exposure to environmental health hazards, inequalities in health care, lack of social support, loss of a sense of mastery and control, chronic exposure to discrimination, and an impoverished childhood. Rather than focus on changing behaviors at the level of the individual, these findings suggest that more widespread changes are necessary to reduce inequities in the social structure (Williams & Jackson, 2005).

CULTURAL PERSPECTIVES

From the biological and medical perspectives, death is an event that can be defined entirely by a set of physical changes within the body's cells. By contrast, from a sociocultural perspective, death derives its meaning from the way that a society or culture interprets the processes through which life ends. Awareness of the end of life is a uniquely (so we think) human characteristic, as is the ability to endow this event with meaning. That meaning, in turn, is seen as a social creation that reflects the prevailing philosophy, economics, and family structure of a culture.

Beliefs About Death

According to the sociocultural perspective, people learn the social meaning of death from the language, arts, and death-related rituals of their cultures. A culture's **death ethos**, or prevailing philosophy of death, can be inferred from funeral rituals, treatment of those who are dying, belief in the presence of ghosts, belief in an afterlife, the extent to which death topics are taboo, the language people use to describe death (through euphemisms such as "passed away"), and the representation of death in the arts. Death may be viewed as sacred or profane, as an unwanted extinction of life or a welcome release from worldly existence (Atchley, 2000).

Throughout the course of Western history, cultural meanings and rituals attached to the process of death and to the disposition of dead bodies have gone through remarkable alterations. Perhaps the most well known of all death rituals were those practiced by the ancient Egyptians. They believed that a new, eternal life awaited the dead and that the body had to be

preserved through mummification in order to make it the permanent home for the spirit of the deceased. The mummies were buried in elaborate tombs, where they were decorated and surrounded by valued possessions. Family members would visit the tombs to bring offers of food to sustain the dead in the afterlife.

It was once thought that only Egyptian pharaohs and wealthy nobles were mummified, but it is now known that even ordinary people preserved their dead, though in a humbler manner than was true of nobility. Furthermore, although the Egyptian mummies are the most well known, they were by no means the only ones to exist, as was found in the investigation of the mummies in the Andean mountains of Peru conducted in the late 1990s.

Cultural views within Western society toward death and the dead have undergone many shifts from ancient times to the present (see Figure 13.5) (Aries, 1974; Aries, 1981). For many centuries until the early Middle Ages, death was considered "tame," accepted as a natural part of life, and neither to be avoided nor exalted. Beginning in the late Middle Ages the view of death as a time of final reckoning with God began to evolve, and people attached significance to personal tombs and epitaphs. The rise of scientific thinking and models led, in the 1700s, to a view of death as remote—a punishment or break with life. By the 1800s, with the rise of romanticism, death became glorified, and it was considered noble to die for a

FIGURE 13.5

Shifts in Death Ethos from Ancient Times to the Present

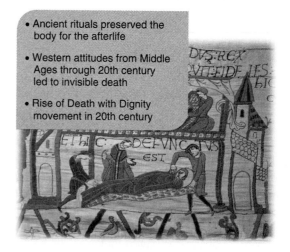

- Ancient rituals preserved the body for the afterlife
- Western attitudes from Middle Ages through 20th century led to invisible death
- Rise of Death with Dignity movement in 20th century

Following the January 2010 Haitian earthquake, an estimated 230,000 people died and countless more were missing and wounded.

cause (the "beautiful death"), as many people had in the revolutions in America and Europe. However, entry into the 20th century brought in the period known as "invisible death," involving the denial of death and medicalization of the dying process. People put their faith in science, which in turn took control over the dying individual. Rather than being a shared experience with others, death and mourning became private. In the large scheme of the universe of scientific discoveries, the death of an individual began to be seen as inconsequential.

Contemporary American attitudes toward death reflect this history but are also shaped by and reflect a complex mixture of contemporary media images, religious and cultural traditions, and health care practices. The media treatment of death is often sensationalistic, as shown in cases when many people die at once in a bombing, mass murder, plane crash, or earthquake. News stories involving massive loss of life, as occurred with the deaths due to the terrorist attacks on the World Trade Center on September 11, 2001, the Southeast Asia tsunami of December 2004, and the 2010 earthquake in Haiti, attempt to bring the losses to human proportions. Conversely, the death of one famous person may preoccupy the American or European media for weeks, as was the case in the deaths of Princess Diana in 1997 and John F. Kennedy, Jr., 2 years later, and Michael Jackson in 2009.

Horror stories may also be presented in the media coverage of people with terminal illness such as the case of Terry Schiavo, the Florida woman who existed on life support machines for 15 years before, in 2005, her husband was able to order that all interventions be stopped. Other less-publicized stories tell of people whose terminal care brings a family to the brink of poverty because their health insurance does not cover hospital costs. Death may also be presented in sentimentalized ways as when a loving wife and mother is depicted as being torn from her husband and children or when two young lovers are parted in an untimely way such as in Shakespeare's *Romeo and Juliet*. All of these contemporary images represent the worst fears that people have about their own death—that it will come tragically and prematurely or that it will follow a long, agonizing, painful, and expensive process. Because the age of dying has increased from 1900 to the present, death has increasingly become associated with the later decades of life. The dying process became institutionalized when it moved from the home to the hospital. People no longer are witnesses to the physical death of another, and therefore it is not as much a part of daily life as in years past (DeSpelder & Strickland, 1999). As death has become removed from the everyday world, it has acquired more fear and mystery. Furthermore, instead of developing our own personal meanings, we are at the mercy of whatever images of death we see in the media.

The development of increasingly sophisticated medical technology has in many ways complicated these already complex issues. Physicians can now keep people alive under far less tenable circumstances than they could in the past, and they can restore life to a person who has, temporarily, ceased to breathe or sustain a heartbeat. Issues of organ and tissue transplants further cloud the boundary between life and death. Related trends in attitudes toward death emphasize the quality of the death experience and the fear of enduring a prolonged period of terminal decline.

Death with dignity, the idea that death should not involve extreme physical dependency or loss of control of bodily functions, emerged from the desire of patients and their families to avoid a lengthy and protracted dying process (Humphrey, 1991). The next seemingly logical step to follow, initiated by Dr. Jack Kevorkian (1991), was to make it possible for a terminally ill patient to complete suicide. Social movements that advocated these measures were instrumental in stimulating the medical community to establish guidelines and practices for the care of the terminally ill at the end of life (see below). However, in terms of cultural attitudes, they reflect the dread that many in our society feel about losing the ability to control this most important aspect of life.

Fear of death and dying within contemporary Western society is thought to be linked not only to changes in the timing and location of death but also to fear of aging and growing old. The desire to stop or slow the aging process is evident throughout advertisements of everything from wrinkle creams to exercise machines, and America is often thought of as a youth-oriented culture, despite the aging of the Baby Boomers. Cultural depictions of death seem inextricably linked to fear of loss of capacity, attractiveness, and social relevance. Both reflect an unwillingness, which is perhaps part of the American tradition, to accept the limits imposed by the biological facts of aging and death (Field et al., 1997). People also fear the process of **social death**, through which the dying become treated as nonpersons by family or health care workers as they are left to spend their final months or years in the hospital or nursing home.

Another perspective on fear of death is based on **Terror Management Theory** (Solomon, Greenberg, & Pyszczynski, 1991). According to this social-psychological perspective, people regard with panic and dread the thought of the finitude of their lives. They engage in defensive mechanisms to protect themselves from the anxiety and threats to self-esteem that this awareness produces. The existential questions aroused by awareness of mortality may lead some with fundamental religious beliefs to turn to their faith as support and may explain why they turn to prayer rather than medical interventions when confronted with terminal illness (Vess, Arndt, Cox, Routledge, & Goldenberg, 2009).

The Role of Religion

Religious background provides comfort to the dying and bereaved through teachings that emphasize the existence of an afterlife and the belief that human events occur because of some higher purpose. The loss of a loved one, particularly when it occurs "prematurely" (i.e., before old age), may be seen as a test of one's faith. Grieving families and friends comfort themselves with the knowledge that they will be reunited in heaven with the deceased, where they will spend eternity together. Bereaved individuals may also seek solace in the belief or perception that they can sense the presence of departed loved ones. Another belief in which people may find comfort is that death is a blessed relief from a world of trouble and pain. As the bereaved or terminally ill attempt to come to grips with the ending of a life, they rely on these beliefs to make sense out of the death or achieve some kind of understanding of its meaning.

Strong religious beliefs may also lead the dying to be more likely to seek aggressive end-of-life care. A national study of nearly 350 patients with advanced cancer showed that those who used religion as a way to cope with their illness had a much higher rate of choosing mechanical ventilation to prolong their life (Phelps et al., 2009). In general, religious involvement may serve as a protective factor in mortality. Findings from a meta-analysis conducted in 2000 on 42 studies examining the relationship between religion and mortality concluded that higher involvement with religious activities was related to lower mortality (McCullough, Hoyt, Larson, Koenig, & Thoresen, 2000). Recent research from the Terman Life Cycle Study of Children with High Ability, a longitudinal study beginning in 1940 with numerous follow-ups, suggests that this relationship may be particularly true for women (McCullough, Friedman, Enders, & Martin, 2009). Women in the Terman sample who were identified as the least religious had a higher risk of dying compared with the more religious women. Religious involvement in the last year of life supports the notion that increased involvement may also be related to higher quality of life, including better reports of self-rated health and fewer depressive symptoms (Idler, McLaughlin, & Kasl, 2009). Reasons for such findings could in part be a reflection of the social support often involved within a religious community.

THE DYING PROCESS

Death is an event that marks the end of the process of dying, the period during which an organism loses its viability. The period of dying can last from a few days to several months. Most discussions of dying refer to individuals whose deaths are expected to occur within a period of days to months, although individuals with life-threatening illnesses would also be considered in a sense as "dying" (Field et al., 1997).

There are many variations in the dying process, a concept captured by the term **dying trajectory**, or the rate of decline in functioning prior to death (Glaser & Strauss, 1968). There are two major features of a dying trajectory—duration and shape. Those who die suddenly function normally and then show a precipitous descent. These would be people with no prior knowledge of illness, as in a victim of sudden cardiac failure, or people who die in accidents. The second and third trajectories include individuals who have advance warning of a terminal illness and who experience a lingering period of loss of function. A steady downward trajectory applies to people whose disease causes them to undergo a steady and predictable decline, a process that characterizes many people who die of cancer (see Figure 13.6). The third trajectory characterizes people who go through a generally downward course that is marked by a series of sharp drops. Eventually their death occurs during a crisis related to their illness or due to another fatal cause during which their functional abilities suddenly decrease (Teno, Weitzen, Fennell, & Mor, 2001).

Apart from the three dying trajectories, there are other patterns shown by people near the end of life. Some individuals are statistically at increased risk of dying, though technically they do not have a terminal disease. One set consists of individuals in their 80s or older who are in good health but have limited physical reserves. They may die from complications associated with an acute condition such as influenza or a broken hip due to a fall. In other cases, people whose organ systems are gradually deteriorating may slowly lose the ability to care for themselves while at the same time developing an illness such as renal failure or pneumonia that eventually causes them to die. This pattern may characterize individuals in the later stages of Alzheimer's disease. The immediate cause of death may be the illness, but it has occurred against a backdrop of general loss of function.

FIGURE 13.6

Dying Trajectories

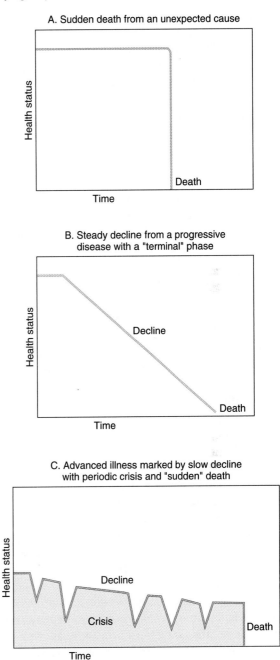

A. Sudden death from an unexpected cause

B. Steady decline from a progressive disease with a "terminal" phase

C. Advanced illness marked by slow decline with periodic crisis and "sudden" death

Source: Field, M. J., Cassel, C. K., & Committee on Care at the End of Life. (1997). *Approaching death: Improving care at the end of life*, Institute of Medicine, Division of Health Care Services. Washington, DC: National Academy Press.

Stages of Dying

Amid the growing institutionalization of death and the attempts by the medical establishment to prolong life, a small book published in 1969 was to alter permanently Western attitudes toward and treatment of the dying. This book, by Elisabeth Kübler-Ross (1969), called *On Death and Dying*, described five **stages of dying** considered to occur universally among terminally ill patients. These stages of dying have since become part of the cultural mystique surrounding the dying process, even as professionals challenge both the specific stages and the idea that stages occur at all.

The first stage in the Kübler-Ross framework is denial, a stage that includes the patient's immediate reaction to having been informed that he or she has a terminal illness. The individual going through denial simply refuses to accept the diagnosis. The second stage, anger, is the reaction following denial when the reality of the terminal illness first sets in. The individual feels cheated or robbed of the opportunity to live and is furious with the powers that are causing this to happen. In bargaining, the third stage, the patient attempts to strike a deal with God or whatever force is seen as responsible for the disease. Examples of bargaining would be offering to attend religious services on a regular basis if given the chance to live longer, if not recover. People in this stage may "ask" to be allowed to live until an important upcoming event such as the marriage of a child. Fourth comes depression and sense of loss, as the inevitability of the disease's progress is acknowledged. Finally, the individual reaches the fifth stage of acceptance, during which the finality of the disease is no longer fought or regretted. As death approaches, it is regarded as a natural end state and perhaps even a release from pain and suffering.

The critical point that Kübler-Ross attempted to make in her writing is that to reach acceptance of a fatal illness, the dying person must be allowed to talk openly with family members and health care workers. Rather than hide the diagnosis or pretend that everything will be alright, those who interact with the dying individual need to give that person a chance to express the many emotions that surface, ranging from fury to dejection. Recall that this book was written at the height of the idea of death as an "invisible" period, during which it was just as likely as not that a physician would not share the diagnosis of cancer with a patient and family.

Unfortunately the original views of Kübler-Ross became distorted as the book's popularity grew. The five stages began to be interpreted as a series of steps that must be followed by each dying patient. If a patient refused to engage in "bargaining," for instance, then it must mean something was wrong with the way that person was handling the terminal illness.

Critics of the stage approach pointed out that there could be many variations in the dying process that the five-stage model ignored. For example, not everyone would either live long enough or have the psychological resources to reach acceptance. Furthermore, people could fluctuate in the order through which they progress through the stages. Another point is that Kübler-Ross was writing about relatively young patients, and denial may very well have been a natural reaction to the news of their impending death. For older individuals, denial may not be the first reaction, or it may not occur at all. The Kübler-Ross formulation also ignores other emotions that dying individuals may experience, such as curiosity, hope, relief, and apathy. As with many events that take place during life, the dying process is highly individualized and may take many different forms depending on the individual's personality, life history, cultural background, age, and specific nature of the illness.

Psychological Perspectives on the Dying Process

Rather than proposing that dying individuals go through specific stages as they prepare for their final moments, others have suggested that as the end of life approaches, people attempt to make sense out of the past patterns of their life. According to Marshall (1980), people engage in these processes after coming to a concrete understanding that life is finite. Another process is the **awareness of finitude**, which is reached when an individual passes the age when parents or, perhaps, siblings, have died. For example, if a man's father died at the age of 66, a kind of counting-down process begins when the son reaches that age. He anticipates the end of life and understands that life really will end.

Having passed the age of awareness of finitude, individuals then embark on a process called **legitimization of biography** in which they attempt to gain perspective on their past life events. They attempt to see what they have done as having meaning, and they prepare the "story" of their lives by which they will be remembered in the minds of others. Some individuals may put their memoirs in writing, and others achieve an internal reckoning in which they evaluate their contributions as well as their shortcomings.

Personality also plays a role in influencing feelings about death and dying. In a study of older adults ranging from 60 to 100 years of age, researchers found that it was those people who believed in fate, chance, or luck as determining what happens to them who had higher self-esteem. As predicted by Terror Management Theory, people with higher self-esteem, in turn, were less likely to fear death as an end to the self (Cicirelli, 1997).

The notion that the awareness of life's end triggers an intense period of self-evaluation is also an important component of Erikson's concept of ego integrity, as described in Chapter 8. Erikson emphasized that during this period of life, individuals deal with mortality and questions related to the ending of their existence by attempting to place their lives into perspective. Presumably, this process may occur at any age, as the dying individual attempts to achieve a peaceful resolution with past mistakes and events that can no longer be made up for or changed. As we pointed out in Chapter 11, life review therapy may be useful for older adults who might not spontaneously engage in this potentially important process.

ISSUES IN END-OF-LIFE CARE

Improvements in medical technology along with changes in attitudes toward death and dying have led, within the past two decades, to radical alterations in the approach to the terminally ill (Lorenz et al., 2008). On the one hand, clinicians have become far more sensitive to the emotional and physical needs of dying patients, leading professionals in the field to examine and rework some of the standard approaches to end-of-life care. On the other hand, legislation and social movements that advocate for the rights of dying patients have argued that they should have greater autonomy and decision making power. These efforts attempt to establish as part of medical treatment a role for patients to participate actively not only in the course of their care, but also its ending. Many of these issues involve legal and ethical considerations as well as those that are strictly medical.

Advance Directives and the Patient Self-Determination Act

The **Patient Self-Determination Act (PSDA)** of 1990 guarantees the right of all competent adults to write an **advance directive (AD)** to participate in and direct their own health care decisions, and to accept or refuse treatment. The PSDA guarantees that prior to becoming ill, an individual can put in writing his or her wishes regarding end-of-life treatment. Furthermore, the PSDA mandates that health care professionals receive education about ADs as well as provide information to patients as they are being admitted to the hospital. The existence of an AD must be documented in the medical record. Each state is permitted to establish and define its own legislation concerning advance directives, but the basic federal requirements must be met in all Medicare- and Medicaid-funded facilities in order for them to continue to receive funding.

ADs include "code status," which specifies the conditions under which dying patients wish to be treated. Full code means that there should be no limit on life-sustaining treatment; in other words, the patient requests to be intubated or ventilated and resuscitated with CPR after fatal cardiac or pulmonary arrest. A **Do Not Resuscitate (DNR)** order directs health care workers not to use resuscitation if cardiac or pulmonary arrest occurs. Comfort care specifies that the patient receives just that: no resuscitation, no extraordinary measures, and no new treatments. If no prior decision is made about code status, then every measure will be taken to maintain the individual's life. ADs are also called living wills. Another component of an AD is the health care proxy, in which individuals specify who they wish to have make decisions for them should they become incapable of doing so (see Table 13.1).

In preparing an AD, patients should discuss their desires with family, their physicians, and other health care providers. Having considered these issues,

TABLE 13.1
Example of Living Will Provided by Five Wishes

Wish	Example of How Wish is Honored
The person I want to make care decisions for me when I can't	List names of health care agents
My wish for the kind of medical treatment I want or don't want	Specifies situations in which life-support or resuscitation should be provided
My wish for how comfortable I want to be	How much and what kind of pain medication and treatment should be provided
My wish for how I want people to treat me	Whether to die at home and to have others present
My wish for what I want my loved ones to know	Wish to be buried or cremated, desire to be remembered in specific way

Source: Adapted from Agingwithdignity.org.

people can then make legally binding arrangements, which state that they shall not be sustained by artificial life support if they are no longer able to make that decision themselves. Protection against abuse of the process is provided by various safeguards such as requirements for witnesses and the requirement that more than one physician determine that a condition is terminal. In addition to documenting the patient's wishes, the PSDA was intended to ensure more active involvement in planning and treatment by patients and to uphold the principles of respect for their dignity and autonomy.

Research on the End of Life

The passage of the PSDA in 1990 created a unique opportunity for researchers to investigate the impact of ADs on the quality of care in medical settings for terminally ill patients because it occurred during the midst of a major national study on the experience of dying patients. This study, the Study to Understand Prognoses and Preferences for Outcomes and Risks of Treatments (SUPPORT), at the time was about halfway through its initial phase when the PSDA was passed. The timing of the PSDA's passage made it possible for the researchers to compare the experiences of dying patients before and after the requirement that ADs be obtained by hospitalized patients.

For two separate 2-year periods (1989–1991 and 1992–1994), SUPPORT enrolled all patients who were in the advanced stages of diseases such as cancer, acute respiratory failure, multiple organ system failure, chronic obstructive pulmonary disease, congestive heart failure, and cirrhosis of the liver. The research team expected that about half of the people who enrolled in the study would die within a 6-month period after entry (Lynn et al., 1997). Along with SUPPORT, another sample (Hospitalized Elderly Longitudinal Project or "HELP") was enrolled that included persons 80 years of age and older who were hospitalized in one of four of the nationwide centers. This sample was included to make it possible to study the experience of hospitalized persons at advanced ages.

The first set of findings from SUPPORT and HELP concerned the proportion of deaths that occurred in institutional settings and homes. The majority of patients in SUPPORT stated that they preferred to die at home; nonetheless, most of the deaths occurred in the hospital (Pritchard et al., 1998). Furthermore, the percentage of SUPPORT patients who died in the hospital varied by more than double across the five hospitals in the study (from 29 to 66%). The primary factor accounting for the probability of a patient dying in the hospital rather than at home was the availability of hospital beds. Later studies in countries such as Great Britain, Belgium, and the Netherlands have confirmed that place of death varies according to availability of hospital beds rather than any specific characteristics of patients or wishes of their families (Houttekier et al., 2010).

The second major finding of SUPPORT was documentation of the physical and psychological characteristics of dying persons obtained through interviews with family members. During the last 3 days of life, approximately 40% of patients who were conscious were reported to have been in severe pain. Yet, adequate pain medication was not provided to alleviate this suffering (Twomey, McDowell, & Corcoran, 2007). More than half of those who died from a serious illness had great difficulty breathing (dyspnea), and about one quarter were severely confused. Nearly 80% of all patients experienced fatigue. As you might imagine, these physical symptoms caused great discomfort, as was reported by almost three quarters of the family members of dying patients (Lynn et al., 1997). Even more distressing, however, was the fact that the patients suffering the most severe pain and psychological symptoms (confusion, depression, and anxiety) were most dissatisfied with the level of pain control provided to them (Desbiens et al., 1996).

Not only were dying patients found to experience discomfort, but their care did not match their preferences. Here the researchers made the distinction between aggressive measures taken to prolong life and **palliative care**. Services provided in palliative care include reduction of symptoms such as nausea, pain, and dyspnea, physical therapy, and occupational therapy. According to the World Health Organization, palliative care should neither hasten nor postpone the end of life (WHO, 2002).

The provision of aggressive care in cases where patients express a preference for comfort only is referred to in the end-of-life literature as **overtreatment** (Field et al., 1997). The majority of patients in SUPPORT preferred to receive palliative rather than aggressive care, but from 3 to 17% (depending on diagnosis) were given life-sustaining treatments regardless of their preferences. These life-sustaining treatments included resuscitation attempts, being placed on a ventilator, or having a feeding tube inserted into the stomach. Overall, over half of the patients had one of these life-sustaining treatments within the 3 days before they died (Lynn et al., 1997). Furthermore, in contrast to aggressive life-sustaining procedures, no clear guidelines were provided for those who received palliative care (Goodlin, Winzelberg, Teno, Whedon, & Lynn, 1998).

In the case of patients with colorectal cancer specifically (who tended to be in the most pain), it appeared in SUPPORT that physicians and patients had difficulty communicating with each other about prognosis and treatment preferences (Haidet et al., 1998). Related studies were conducted under the auspices of SUPPORT on patients hospitalized with complications due to severe heart failure. As in the

AGING IN THE NEWS

www.wiley.com/college/whitbourne   **OLDER ADULTS WHO MADE THE HEADLINES**   -VOL. 4, CHAPTER 13-

OLDEST SCUBA DIVER AT 93, ASHES BURIED AT SEA

January 8, 2008. Bert Killbride, the self-proclaimed "Last Pirate of the Caribbean," scuba-dove throughout the waters off the British Virgin Islands, where he spent 50 years actively scouring for treasure among the sunken ruins of pirate ships. In 2004, the Guinnes Book of Records proclaimed Bert the "Oldest Scuba Diver in the world." His oldest son arranged with Neptune Memorial Reef to have Bert's ashes placed at one of the gates in the waters 3 miles off Key Biscayne, Florida.

larger study, physicians in the majority of cases did not accurately perceive the preferences of their patients for resuscitation (Krumholz et al., 1998).

The most critical aspect of SUPPORT was investigation of the effectiveness of the PSDA, the legislation that created the requirement of ADs. As we mentioned earlier, the two periods of testing (1989–1991 and 1992–1994) coincided with the 2 years before and the 2 years immediately after implementation of PSDA. Of the 9,105 patients in the study, 4,301 were enrolled in the early period and 4,804 in the second period. The patients studied in the second period were divided into two groups: an intervention group (2,652 patients) and a control group (2,152 patients) (Teno et al., 1997). The intervention consisted of communication by nurses of detailed information on the prognoses and preferences of patients, which was intended to promote discussions about the course of their care. However, the intervention failed to lead to changes in the frequency of discussions about treatment preferences between physicians and patients. The intervention had no effects on other aspects of end-of-life care, including those identified as most important in the experience of dying patients, such as pain control and overtreatment.

Data from DNRs further reinforced the point that the PSDA was not being effectively implemented. Investigators conducted an analysis of patients' preferences for cardiopulmonary resuscitation, severity of illness, and time to the first DNR order. Although DNR orders were issued sooner for patients who had requested a DNR order, only about one half of the patients who preferred not to be resuscitated actually had DNR orders written for them and placed in their charts. Furthermore, DNR orders were more likely to be issued for patients with poorer prognoses.

Regardless of their prognosis, though, patients who were over the age of 75 years were more likely to have a DNR written for them (Hakim et al., 1996). In a subsequent investigation within SUPPORT, the methods of resuscitation examined were expanded to include withholding of ventilator support, surgery, and dialysis according to age, prognosis, and patient preferences. Again, age was associated with the decision to withhold life-sustaining treatment. In addition, physicians were more likely to underestimate the preferences for life-sustaining care among older patients (Hamel et al., 1996).

Misunderstandings about patient preferences are more likely to arise when the patients are older because physicians assume that they would prefer not to be revived. Physicians also are less willing to take measures to keep patients alive who have dementia, whether or not the patients have an AD (Richardson, Sullivan, Hill, & Yu, 2007). The presence of a health care proxy, however, someone who is able to monitor and speak for the patient, can increase the chances that the dying individual's wishes will be respected (Fins et al., 1999). However, this proxy must be carefully chosen as one who will in fact represent the patient's wishes accurately (Fowler, Coppola, & Teno, 1999; Tsevat et al., 1998).

Other researchers have identified racial disparities in the presence of DNRs and living wills, with African Americans and Hispanics less likely to have ADs in their medical files (Degenholtz, Arnold, Meisel, & Lave, 2002). Similar cultural barriers were identified in studies on HIV-infected adults; physicians were less likely to communicate with African American and Latino patients about end-of-life issues compared with White patients (Wenger et al., 2001). Along similar lines, patients who are White, have greater access to resources and better health care, and better education are more likely to die in their own homes than in nursing homes (Gruneir et al., 2007).

There may also be cross-cultural variations in the provision of care at the end of life. In one intensive study on the experience of dying patients in Spain, nearly half of families of patients dying from dementia and heart failure reported that the symptoms such as pain were not adequately controlled in the last day before death and less than one fifth received some form of spiritual support. However, unlike some of the data from American studies, there was a fairly high percentage (approximately two thirds) of families who felt satisfied with the information they received (Formiga et al., 2007).

The findings of SUPPORT continue to be confirmed in subsequent studies that document further the continued need to monitor the experience of dying patients. In addition, studies show that there remains lack of coordination among health care providers, poor communication with dying patients, and failure to alleviate pain in terminally ill individuals (Bakitas et al., 2008). ADs are still not provided, leading to the feelings among the bereaved family that overly aggressive care was provided (Teno, Gruneir, Schwartz, Nanda, & Wetle, 2007).

However, there are encouraging signs from a major study spanning the years from 2000 and 2006 showing that for those older adults who did prepare an AD, there was a greater chance that their end-of-life experience conformed to their preferences (Silveira, Kim, & Langa, 2010). Interestingly, the Terry Schiavo case of 2005 seemed to provide an impetus for hospital patients to make decisions about advance care planning (Sudore, Landefeld, Pantilat, Noyes, & Schillinger, 2008).

Coordinated patient care palliative services have been shown to improve perceived quality of life even when patients still experience significant pain (Bakitas et al., 2009). A controlled study in Australia evaluating the effectiveness of advance care planning showed significantly greater satisfaction and less stress, anxiety, and depression in the bereaved relatives (Detering, Hancock, Reade, & Silvester, 2010). Involving families in the process of planning palliative care can also reduce their emotional burden (Radwany et al., 2009). Experiencing the death of their relative as peaceful is another key component to recovery of caregivers during the bereavement period (Akiyama, Numata, & Mikami, 2010).

One team of investigators has developed the notion of "peaceful awareness," a state in which dying patients are aware that they have a terminal illness but are accepting of this knowledge. In a multisite study of dying patients, researchers identified 18% of patients who fit these criteria for peaceful awareness. In comparing them to patients who did not have peaceful awareness, ratings of the overall quality of their death made by caregivers were significantly higher than for patients who were neither aware nor at peace (Ray et al., 2006).

Physician-Assisted Suicide and Euthanasia

Requesting an order for DNR and writing a living will are steps patients take to avoid prolonging life in the event that their bodily functions spontaneously cease to operate. These measures are taken as protection against the likelihood that the individual loses the capacity to make a conscious decision about allowing

FIGURE 13.7

Difference between Physician-assisted Suicide and Euthanasia

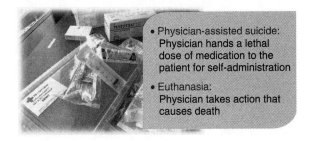

- Physician-assisted suicide: Physician hands a lethal dose of medication to the patient for self-administration
- Euthanasia: Physician takes action that causes death

life to end naturally. In **physician-assisted suicide (PAS)**, individuals make the conscious decision, while they are still able to do so, that they want their lives to end before dying becomes a protracted process. Similarly, in **euthanasia**, although the physician's action causes death, the intent is to prevent the suffering associated with a prolonged ending of life (Figure 13.7).

A strongly vocal proponent of physician-assisted suicide was Dr. Jack Kevorkian. In 1956 he was dubbed "Dr. Death," not because he assisted a patient's suicide, but because he published a journal article in which he discussed his efforts to photograph the eyes of dying patients. Throughout the 1980s he published numerous articles on euthanasia, and by 1989 he had built a "suicide machine" which he then used in 1990 on his first patient, a 54-year-old woman with Alzheimer's disease. Throughout the 1990s he conducted a series of over 100 assisted suicides. In a highly controversial televised segment on the program *60 Minutes*, aired in November 1998, Kevorkian ended the life of a 52-year old Michigan man suffering from a terminal neurological disease. In this case Kevorkian administered the lethal dose, so the death was technically euthanasia, not assisted suicide. Because this procedure was illegal (and was flagrantly performed in front of millions of TV viewers), Kevorkian was arrested and subsequently convicted on second-degree murder charges. In 2007, Kevorkian was released from prison after serving 8 years of a 10- to 25-year sentence. A new "Dr. Death" emerged in 2010 when Dr. Lawrence Egbert, of Georgia, was indicted for assisting in the suicide of a terminally ill patient with oral cancer.

Two states in the United States have legalized physician-assisted suicide. The Oregon Death with Dignity Act (OWDA), enacted in 1997, specifies that a physician may prescribe lethal medication to hasten death for competent, terminally ill persons who voluntarily request it. Patients must wait 15 days from the request, but the law does not require that the patient seek mental health interventions or notification of family. In January 2006, the Supreme Court upheld the Oregon law, which had been challenged by the administration of President George W. Bush, who had attempted to prosecute physicians for violating the Federal Substances Control Act. Two years later, Washington State passed the Washington Death with Dignity Act, Initiative 1000, which allows terminally ill adults seeking to end their life to request lethal doses of medication from medical and osteopathic physicians. These terminally ill patients must be Washington residents who have less than 6 months to live.

Directives specifying the withholding or withdrawal of life-extending medical treatment represent voluntary passive euthanasia. This procedure is legal in all states, whereas physician-assisted suicide is legal only in Oregon and Washington. Voluntary active euthanasia, which is a request for the physician to end the life of terminally ill patients, is legal in such European countries as Switzerland, the Netherlands, and Belgium.

Those who favor physician-assisted suicide (or active euthanasia) and who support measures such as the Oregon Death with Dignity Law regard as essential the individual's right to make the decision, the need to relieve suffering, and fears that life can be extended beyond the point when it has meaning. A study in the Netherlands found that taking into account the dying individual's wishes to die with dignity is perhaps the most important component of this process (Georges et al., 2007).

Those who oppose physician-assisted suicide regard as primary the physician's ethical code to "do no harm" and do not wish to present options to patients that they do not find morally acceptable (Curlin, Lawrence, Chin, & Lantos, 2007). Surveys conducted to determine the extent to which measures such as the Oregon DWDA are seen favorably show some variations in attitudes toward physician-assisted suicide. Several years after its passage, the large majority of Oregon psychologists were in favor of the DWDA, both in terms of supporting its enactment (78%) and in terms of stating that they would consider physician-assisted suicide for themselves (Fenn & Ganzini, 1999). Physicians (31%), however, were far less likely to support the enactment of such legislation (Cohen, Fihn, Boyko, Jonsen, & Wood, 1994). Although an important ethical question, practically speaking, there has been little in the way of change in Oregon in response to this law, because a relatively small number of terminally ill patients have chosen to end their lives in this manner (Hedberg, Hopkins, & Kohn, 2003).

One of the strongest arguments against physician-assisted suicide is based on evidence that the decision by the terminally ill individual to end life may be based on lack of appropriate care of dying individuals. Those dying patients who are suicidal may have treatable psychological symptoms that, when addressed properly, lead them to regain the will to live. There is tremendous variation even on a day-to-day basis in feelings about assisted suicide (Pacheco, Hershberger, Markert, & Kumar, 2003). People who make this decision may be suicidal because they are depressed, anxious, or in pain. However, the decision to hasten the end of life may evolve over the course of a person's terminal illness. Researchers in Canada who conducted intensive interviews with midlife and older adults diagnosed with terminal cancer found that although many patients initially thought of assisted suicide as an exit strategy, eventually they were ready to "let go" once they worked through a phase characterized by despair (Nissim, Gagliese, & Rodin, 2009).

Another argument against euthanasia and physician-assisted suicide is the one offered by opponents of health care reform in the United States during the year 2009, when talk of "death panels" was used as an argument against changes specifically to Medicare. According to this view, physicians and other health care providers would decide to end a patient's life prematurely as a cost-saving measure. However, a survey of physicians conducted in the United Kingdom suggests that costs are not the primary considerations in these situations. Instead, physicians regarded pain in the patient, no expectation for improvement, and expectation of further suffering in the patient as the main reasons to consider ending a patient's life (Seale, 2009).

There are ways that euthanasia and physician-assisted suicide can be humanely managed within a larger palliative approach. A study of nearly 1,700 patient deaths in Belgium, where euthanasia is legal, showed greater acceptance of these methods in settings that already provided palliative care. In fact, euthanasia and physician-assisted suicide were more likely to be performed in patients who received spiritual care compared to those who received no spiritual care at the end of life (Van den Block et al., 2009).

Suggestions for End-of-Life Care

Clearly, those who are dying wish to have their preferences respected with regard to the way they end their lives. Because there is no one scenario that best describes the type of ending that they envision, individuals must be given the opportunity to make the choice that best fits their values and desires (Vig, Davenport, & Pearlman, 2002). Unfortunately, this is generally not the case, in part because dying patients are often not able to express their wishes. This is why ADs and health care proxies are so important to ensure that the patients receive the care they desired.

Steps must be taken to avoid problems stemming from differences in cultural values between health care workers and patients. In one study, interviews with Chinese older adults living in Canada revealed a lack of acceptance of advance directives due to differences in values between Confucianist, Buddhist, and Taoist religions and those of Western medicine (Bowman & Singer, 2001). It is therefore necessary to understand the patient's cultural background when providing end-of-life care (Crawley, Marshall, Lo, & Koenig, 2002). Options should, if possible, be discussed with family members (Haley et al., 2002; Hickman, 2002).

There should also be coordination within long-term care facilities in the decision-making process used to initiate end-of-life care. Nursing home staff often have not developed procedures to communicate either among themselves or with patients to determine at what point in the resident's illness palliative care should begin (Travis et al., 2002). As with the provision of good nursing home care, an interdisciplinary approach can help to overcome the problems of lack of coordination and communication among health care workers (Connor, Egan, Kwilosz, Larson, & Reese, 2002).

Increasingly, the provision of end-of-life care designed to meet the needs of the individual patient is the domain of a facility known as a **hospice** (Ganzini et al., 2001). The term hospice is ordinarily used to refer to a site or program that provides medical and supportive services for dying patients and their families and friends. Within the hospice environment, the needs of dying patients are attended to with regard to their needs for physical comfort, psychological and social support, and the opportunity to express and have their spiritual needs met. The care is palliative, focusing on controlling pain and other symptoms, and it is likely to take place within the home, beginning when the patient no longer wishes active disease treatment. Physicians are involved, but there is no occupational or physical therapy, and spiritual and bereavement counselors are part of the patient care team. Hospice services fit closely with expressed patient needs of obtaining adequate pain control and symptom management, avoiding an extended period of dying, achieving a sense of personal control, relieving the burden they place on others, and strengthening ties with those who are close to them (Kelly et al., 2002) (see Figure 13.8).

Hospice care was introduced in the 1960s, with the goal of alleviating the pain, nausea, confusion, and sleep disturbances experienced by cancer patients within their last months of life. The first well-known hospice was St. Christopher's in London, which opened in 1967. The hospice movement spread to the United States in the 1970s. In 1982, hospice benefits were made available to persons on Medicare who had a life expectancy of less than 6 months.

FIGURE 13.8

Illness Timeline and Type of Care

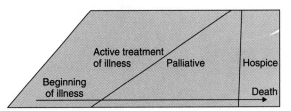

This figure shows the timeline of care provided to dying patients. As the illness progresses, active treatment is reduced and palliative care is increased. Toward the end of illness, hospice care replaces palliative care until death occurs.

In 1997, the American Medical Association approved a set of guidelines to establish quality care for individuals at the end of life (American Medical Association, 1997). These included providing patients with the opportunity to discuss and plan for end-of-life care, assurance that attempts will be made to provide comfort and respect the patient's end-of-life wishes, assurance of dignity, and attention to the individual's goals. These rights also include minimizing the burden to the family and assisting the bereaved through the stages of mourning and adjustment. There is some indication that efforts such as these are improving the quality of care provided to terminally ill patients. A 1996 survey of more than 1,000 physicians who had initially been studied 20 years earlier reported an increase in the willingness of these physicians to discuss issues related to end-of-life care (Dickinson, Tournier, & Still, 1999). Medical schools are increasingly incorporating palliative care into their curriculums (Dickinson, 2002).

Giving physicians, psychologists, and other health care workers education in end-of-life care should improve in the near future communication with dying patients and alleviation of their symptoms (Block & Billings, 2005). Programs in the United States, Canada, Sweden, and the United Kingdom are benefiting from knowledge about the dying trajectory, adjusting approaches to end-of-life care to the nature of the patient's needs, rhythms, and situations (Dy & Lynn, 2007) (see Table 13.2).

BEREAVEMENT

Bereavement is the process during which people cope with another person's loss through death. Bereavement may occur at any point in life. However, it is more likely to take place in later adulthood when people have an increased risk of losing spouses, siblings, friends, colleagues, and other peers.

The physical and psychological symptoms associated with bereavement are particularly severe in the first year following loss. The physical symptoms can include shortness of breath, frequent sighing, tightness in the chest, feelings of emptiness, loss of energy and strength, and digestive disturbances. In some cases, the individual may be vulnerable to physical illness due to the reduced effectiveness of the stress-sensitive immune system. The emotional reactions to bereavement include anger, depression, anxiety, sleep disturbances, and preoccupation with thoughts of the deceased. Other problems associated with bereavement include impairments in attention and memory, a desire to withdraw from social activities, and increased risk of accidents. The symptoms of bereavement, as difficult as they are, nevertheless appear to subside greatly in most people after a period of 1 year.

Death of a Spouse

The death of a spouse is regarded as one of the most stressful events of life, and for many older adults, widowhood involves the loss of a relationship that

TABLE 13.2
Getting Services for the Dying "Right"

	Trajectory		
	Rapid decline over a few weeks or months before death	**Chronic illness with intermittent exacerbations**	**Very poor function with long, slow decline**
Model of Care	Integration with hospice or palliative care	Disease management with education and rapid intervention	Long-term supportive care
Specific Care Needs	Maximize continuity Plan for rapid decline, changing needs, and death Manage patient's symptoms at home Provide support for caregiver	Provide education on self-care Attempt to avoid hospitalization when possible Assist in decision-making about interventions that might not work Plan for potential of sudden death	Plan for long-term care and future problems Avoid non-beneficial and harmful interventions Provide support and assistance for long-term caregivers Provide reliable institutional care when necessary

Source: Dy, S., & Lynn, J. (2007). Getting services right for those sick enough to die. BMJ: British Medical Journal, 334, 511–513.

This woman mourns the loss of her husband after his funeral. Adjustment to widowhood can be a long and difficult process.

may have lasted as long as 50 years or more. Consequently, associated with widowhood are a number of physical and psychological correlates ranging from higher mortality (the widowhood effect, which we discussed in Chapter 9) to symptoms of depression and anxiety. A number of factors affect the extent to which an individual experiences these adverse effects of widowhood (Stroebe, Schut, & Stroebe, 2007) including the circumstances surrounding the spouse's death (McNamara & Rosenwax, 2010).

Difficult emotional responses may follow the death of a spouse due to illnesses such as cancer and Alzheimer's disease that involved marked physical and mental deterioration and placed extensive burden on the caregivers (Ferrario, Cardillo, Vicario, Balzarini, & Zotti, 2004). Relief from the pressures of caregiving can lead to alleviation of symptoms of depression and stress present during the spouse's dying months or years (Bonanno, Wortman, & Nesse, 2004).

As we pointed out in Chapter 9, the widowhood effect is greater for men. Analyses of the impact of widowhood on health and mortality suggest a variety of reasons, including greater propensity to drink alcohol, poorer monitoring of health habits, and loss of a confidante (Stroebe et al., 2007). Having children seems to help buffer the effects of widowhood as was shown in a prospective study of Chinese widows;

interestingly, in this sample there was no differential effect of gender on widowhood impact (Li, Liang, Toler, & Gu, 2005).

There are varying responses to widowhood, however, even within similar demographic groups in the population. A major prospective study of more than 200 individuals who were tested before they became widowed, and followed for 18 months after, identified five patterns of bereavement: common grief, chronic grief, chronic depression, improvement during bereavement, and resilience (Bonanno et al., 2002). In common grief, a relatively infrequent occurrence, the individual experiences an initial increase in depression that diminishes over time. Resilient grief is far more common. In this pattern, the bereaved shows little or no distress following the loss. In chronic grief, the individual experiences high levels of both depression and grief within 6 months after the loss, and the grief does not subside over time. In chronic depression, the bereaved suffers from high levels of depression prior to and after the loss.

People with high levels of interpersonal dependency (including dependence on their spouses) are most likely to show the pattern of resilience, are most accepting of death, and are more likely to agree with the notion that the world is "just" (i.e., that people "get" what they "deserve"). Studies such as these underscore the notion that bereavement is not a unitary process and that there are multiple factors influencing reactions to the loss of a spouse.

Death of Other Family Members

The loss of an adult child is perhaps the most distressing and devastating of all forms of bereavement. The grief a parent experiences over a child's death is highly intense and is associated with increased risk of depression, guilt, and health complaints lasting for many years (Rogers, Floyd, Seltzer, Greenberg, & Hong, 2008). In addition, for older adults, loss of a child means the very practical loss of a central supportive figure in life (McKiernan, 1996). Loss of an adult child also violates the individual's normative expectations that a parent dies before the children. Although these feelings may never be completely overcome, bereaved parents eventually seem to be able to find a sense of meaning and purpose in life, particularly through making connections with other people and feeling connected with the deceased child

(Wheeler, 2001). Furthermore, parents may be able to compensate through providing specific forms of coping support to each other during the grieving process (Wijngaards-de Meij et al., 2008).

In the death of a grandchild, the emotional pain of the older individual is intensified by that shared with the child's parents. Feelings of guilt over being alive while one's grandchild is not may accompany the emotional devastation over the child's loss (Fry, 1997). The suffering of grandparents may be especially pronounced when they were involved in raising the child, as was documented for grandmothers of children killed in the Oklahoma City bombing of 1995. However, at least for these grandmothers, formation of a sense of community and use of each other for support fostered resilience even in the face of this profound loss (Allen, Whittlesey, Pfefferbaum, & Ondersma, 1999).

Compared with the death of a child or grandchild, the death of a parent is a far more normative event of adult life. Nevertheless, this experience can cause psychological distress and a deterioration of health status (Umberson & Chen, 1994). The death of a parent can also lead to increased marital conflict, particularly when the loss is of a father (Umberson, 1995). In general, daughters are more negatively affected by parental death than are sons who, in turn, tend to be more accepting of the loss (Moss, Resch, & Moss, 1997).

Although somewhat normative as well, the deaths of siblings and friends are also sources of distress in later adulthood. The death of a brother in particular may bring not only emotional pain but increased financial hardship (Hays, Gold, & Peiper, 1997). For those older adults who suffer the loss of friends,

in addition to feelings of grief there may be an increased incentive to develop new relationships, including closer relations with other friends and relatives (Roberto & Stanis, 1994).

Certain losses that occur in adulthood fall outside the category of family and friends but may be painful nevertheless. Individuals whose job places them in situations where they work with dying persons may experience severe anxiety symptoms that interfere with their daily lives and ability to perform their jobs. For example, not only survivors but also some recovery workers in a disaster site experience lingering effects of trauma. Those with a history of depression, generalized anxiety disorder, or post-traumatic stress disorder are particularly vulnerable to these effects (Evans, Patt, Giosan, Spielman, & Difede, 2009).

Theories of Bereavement

Until relatively recently, conventional and professional wisdom regarding bereavement was based on the assumption that the survivor must "work through" the death of the deceased (see Figure 13.9). According to this view, the individual must experience a period of mourning, but after that, it is time to move on and seek new relationships and attachments. In part, this view was based on the assumption within psychodynamic theory that to resolve grief normally, emotional bonds to the loved one must be broken (Bowlby, 1980).

An alternate view of bereavement emerged, however, in the last few decades. Researchers and theorists recognize that expressions of continuing attachment are potentially adaptive in providing the

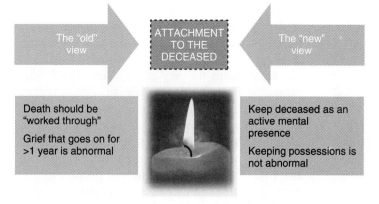

FIGURE 13.9

Theories of Bereavement

The "old" view

ATTACHMENT TO THE DECEASED

The "new" view

Death should be "worked through"

Grief that goes on for >1 year is abnormal

Keep deceased as an active mental presence

Keeping possessions is not abnormal

individual with a sense of continuity in the face of loss. This view, which is held within contemporary non-Western cultures such as the Japanese and Egyptian Muslim cultures, was also strongly maintained by 19th-century romanticists. Furthermore, though not necessarily advocated by the professional community, continued attachment to the deceased remains a part of the experience of bereaved individuals (Stroebe, Gergen, Gergen, & Stroebe, 1992).

Feelings of continued attachment to the deceased may be expressed in several of the behaviors noted earlier as "symptoms" of bereavement. For example, the sense of the spouse's presence helps maintain the feeling that the spouse is watching over or guiding the individual. Another form of attachment is to maintain the spouse's possessions because of their symbolic value. Comfort may also come from keeping alive the memories of the deceased spouse. Rather than abandoning all these forms of attachment to the spouse, part of successful adaptation seems to involve moving away from the concrete reminders of the deceased (possessions) to the more abstract ties that involve thoughts and memories (Field, Gal-Oz, & Bonanno, 2003). Such forms of coping may help the individual acknowledge and accept the death while making the transition to a new, single identity. Mastery over the loss may then occur, even as the deceased spouse remains an active mental presence. According to this view, the normal response to grief involves living with rather than "getting over it."

The **dual-process model of stress and coping** (Stroebe, Schut, & Boerner, 2010) proposes that there are two dimensions of stress associated with the loss of a partner. The first dimension is the sadness directly associated with the loss of the loved one as an attachment figure. The second includes the set of life changes that accompany the loss, including moving from an identity as being a part of a couple to the identity of being a single person. For example, becoming a "widow" can lead to social isolation when a woman's friends were all friends of the couple.

The dual-process model states that coping also falls into two dimensions. The "loss dimension" refers to coping with the direct emotional consequences of the death. The "restoration" dimension refers to coping with the life changes that accompany the loss.

Healthy adjustment, according to the dual-process model, is promoted by alternating between the two dimensions of coping. At times it is best to confront the emotional loss of the partner; at other times, it is most advantageous to avoid confronting these emotions and instead attempt to manage the secondary consequences of loss (Stroebe, Schut, & Stroebe, 2005). People seem to vary in their response to loss, according to this model, on the basis of their attachment style. Securely and insecurely attached individuals will show different patterns of mourning and require different types of help to be able to adapt to the loss (Stroebe, Schut, & Boerner, 2010).

Focusing specifically on personality factors as predictors of reactions to bereavement, Mancini and Bonanno (2009) propose that people who are best able to cope with loss are able to use flexible adaptation—the capacity to shape and adapt behavior to the demands of the stressful event. At other times, though, it is more beneficial to use "repressive coping," in which the painful event is expunged from conscious awareness. Other personal qualities that can help people cope with significant losses such as widowhood include optimism, the capacity for positive emotions, and ability to maintain a sense of continuity over time.

The idea that denial may be adaptive, at least for a time, fits well with identity process theory. It may be that as an initial reaction, identity assimilation has benefits with regard to widowhood. First, being able to avoid focusing on or ruminating over the loss, as in the healthy denial component of assimilation, may allow individuals to remain optimistic and feel a greater sense of personal control. Perhaps widows who wear their wedding rings and refer to themselves as "Mrs. X" for a time after their husband's death are displaying this type of adaptation. Continuing identification as a wife may help them retain this valued part of their sense of who they are within their families and communities. They are protecting themselves at least until the immediate pain of the loss passes over time, at which point they may be able to establish greater identity balance by gradually incorporating the notion of themselves as widows through identity accommodation.

There are lessons to be learned from the experience of people as they cope with death, dying, and bereavement. In particular, older adults have a remarkable ability to manage the fear of death that causes younger people to react with anxiety and efforts at denial. It may be the ability to move ahead without losing memory for the departed individuals in one's life that long-lived individuals possess and make it possible for them to survive repeated losses in later adulthood. These individuals have developed ways of integrating the pain of multiple losses into their lives and can take their lives in positive new directions. In the future, this process may be made that much less painful by the understanding among mental health professionals of the need that the bereaved have to retain rather than abandon the emotional ties of attachment.

SUMMARY

1. Death is defined as the point of irreversible loss of bodily functions, although this state may be difficult to determine as a result of the advent of life support systems that can keep people alive longer. At the end of life, individuals experience a number of physical changes, many of which are physically uncomfortable in addition to involving a great deal of pain.

2. Mortality data provide insight into the variations by age, sex, and race in the causes of death. Younger adults are more likely to die from accidents and older adults from heart disease. Variations exist, however, within age, race, and sex groups, reflecting sociocultural factors in lifestyles and risk factors. Mortality rates are decreasing around the world, primarily because of a decrease in infant mortality. However, mortality reductions vary according to the level of a country's economic development. The poor are disproportionately more likely to die in all countries around the world, particularly where there is inadequate health care.

3. A culture's death ethos is reflected in the traditions established by that culture in funeral rituals, belief in the afterlife, and the language used to describe death. Western attitudes toward death have undergone major shifts throughout history. Contemporary American attitudes regard death in a sensationalistic way, but there is a predominant tendency to institutionalize death and make it "invisible." The death with dignity movement has attempted to promote the idea that the individual should have control over the conditions of death. The dying process may occur through one of several dying trajectories, or rate of decline in functioning prior to death.

4. Issues in end-of-life care focus on the extent to which dying patients can exert control over their medical care. As a result of the Patient Self Determination Act, individuals can establish advance directives that indicate whether they wish to extend their lives through artificial means prior to needing to make this decision. The SUPPORT study on end-of-life care revealed a number of serious weaknesses in the medical care of dying patients in the United States. Many were in pain, felt their preference for palliative care was not respected, and did not believe that they had an adequate opportunity to discuss their preferences with their health care providers. Physician-assisted suicide is a controversial issue that is now legal in the states of Oregon and Washington. Hospices are settings that provide medical and supportive services for dying patients, allowing them to receive personal attention and maintain contact with family.

5. Bereavement is the process of mourning the loss of a close person. The death of a spouse is the most severe loss an individual can experience, but the death of other family members, especially children, causes extreme and long-lasting distress. In the past, theories of grief resolution focused on the need to "work through" a death. Current views are emphasizing an alternative in which the bereaved are more accepting of the sad feelings accompanying the loss.

14

Successful

Many people assume that the end of life is associated with precipitous drops in well-being and adjustment. However, as we have discussed throughout the book, survival into the later years of adulthood requires that individuals can negotiate the many threats presented to living a long life. These may include the threat of dying from accident, illness, and violent acts. Because older adults have managed to avoid these threats, there may be some special quality about increasingly older individuals that can account, in part, for their having reached advanced old age.

In this final chapter, we will explore the topics of psychological growth and creativity in the later adult years. Successful agers not only "survive" but they also achieve heightened levels of personal expression and happiness. These inspirational qualities can guide and sustain optimism and hope about your future adult years.

THEORETICAL PERSPECTIVES ON SUCCESSFUL AGING

Many factors contribute to the ability of the older individual to survive into the sixth and seventh decades of life and beyond. **Successful aging** involves the additional quality of enhancing the healthy spirit and sense of joy in life seen in older adults who seem to transcend whatever physical limitations they encounter. In many ways, successful aging is synonymous with "mental health" in that the qualities thought to be desirable for optimal adaptation, such as a positive outlook and greater self-understanding, are also part of the criteria for successful aging. The fact that these qualities are achieved in later adulthood, thought to be a time of loss and perhaps a diminution of energy, is regarded as placing this type of mental health into a special category of adaptive phenomena.

The most popular model of successful aging is based on a major research effort in the United States known as the MacArthur Foundation Study of Aging in America (Rowe & Kahn, 1998). There are three interactive components incorporated into this model. First is the absence of disease and the disability associated with disease. The second component of successful aging is maintaining high cognitive and physical function, which gives the individual the potential to be active and competent. The third component, called "engagement with life," means being involved in productive activity and maintaining

Aging

relationships with and concern for other people, preferably in ways that contribute to their well-being.

The successful aging model stands in stark contrast to the disengagement model of aging we discussed in Chapter 2, particularly in this third component of engagement with others. To clarify, the engagement discussed here can be psychological (caring about others) as well as physical (being an active participant in one's community).

Building on this three-fold model of successful aging, subsequent researchers continue to emphasize the point that although in order to age successfully you have to "not die" (as we continue to point out), there are additional elements involving multiple dimensions of functioning. These dimensions include adaptive processes that allow the older individual to compensate effectively for a variety of challenges to mental and physical health. Using criteria derived roughly from the Rowe and Kahn definition, it appears that over one third of older adults on average meet these criteria. Some studies have identified as many as 95% fitting the definition of successful agers (Depp & Jeste, 2006).

There is a social element to the idea of remaining engaged with life (Reichstadt, Depp, Palinkas, Folsom, & Jeste, 2007) including social support (Bowling et al., 2002), particularly support from family (Kissane & McLaren, 2006). The three components of successful aging also reinforce each other. People who feel that they are not contributing to the welfare of others—that is, who feel useless—suffer more cognitive deficits (Gruenewald, Karlamangla, Greendale, Singer, & Seeman, 2007) and ultimately may be more likely to die (Gruenewald, Karlamangla, Greendale, Singer, & Seeman, 2009).

Unfortunately, many younger people have a tendency to view the happy and productive older person as an anomaly. Cultural icons such as Jack LaLanne and Betty White are beloved by the young in part because they seem so atypical of their age group. Many people automatically assume that aging inevitably brings about depression and hopelessness, so when people do not show these qualities, they must be truly special. However, as we have seen elsewhere in this book, most older people do not become depressed, and personality development in middle and later adulthood appears to be in the positive direction of greater adaptiveness. Most older adults preserve their cognitive abilities to a very large degree. Studies of centenarians (Motta, Bennati, Ferlito, Malaguarnera, & Motta, 2005) and

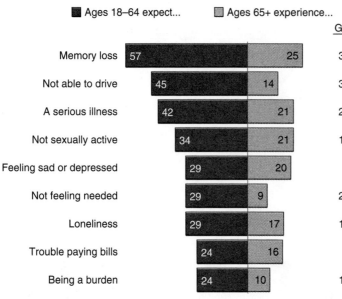

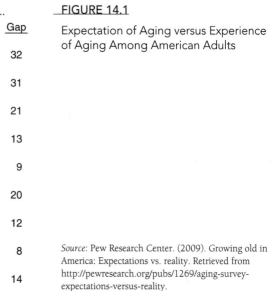

Source: Pew Research Center. (2009). Growing old in America: Expectations vs. reality. Retrieved from http://pewresearch.org/pubs/1269/aging-survey-expectations-versus-reality.

FIGURE 14.1

Expectation of Aging versus Experience of Aging Among American Adults

"super-centenarians" (those over 110) show that those who live to these advanced ages are sturdy both cognitively and physiologically (Schoenhofen et al., 2006).

One reason that the successful ager is thought of as the miraculous exception rather than the rule is that many theorists, researchers, and laypeople believe in the **social indicator model** (Mroczek & Kolarz, 1998). According to this model, demographic and social structural variables, such as age, gender, marital status, and income, account for individual differences in levels of well-being. Because by demographic standards older individuals are in a disadvantaged position on these indices they should therefore be less happy than the young. When an older adult is able to avoid becoming depressed by the potentially disturbing circumstances of poor health, widowhood, and low income, then that person seems deserving of some kind of special recognition.

Judged solely by the standards of being able to avoid the despair brought about by lower status on important social indicators, however, there would in fact be many successful agers. A national survey of almost 3,000 Americans showed that most older adults manage to enjoy relatively high subjective well-being on a variety of indices (Pew Research Center, 2009). Among respondents 75 and older, 81% said they were "very" or "pretty" happy and only 19% rated themselves as "not too happy." Interestingly, as

shown in Figure 14.1, most older adults rated their own experience of aging more favorably than younger adults would expect.

SUBJECTIVE WELL-BEING

The variable studied within the psychology of adult development and aging most closely related to the notion of successful aging is **subjective well-being**. In a general sense, subjective well-being refers to an individual's overall sense of happiness. For research purposes, however, the concept is divided into three components: positive affect, negative affect, and **life satisfaction**, or the cognitive evaluation of one's life circumstances (Diener, 1998).

Perhaps the most extensive recent investigation of the factors contributing to subjective well-being in middle adulthood was the Midlife in the United States Survey (MIDUS) carried out within the context of the MacArthur Study of Successful Midlife Development. The MIDUS sample was made up of more than 2,700 participants who were asked to complete mail and phone surveys focusing on issues of middle and later adulthood. The ages of the participants ranged from 25 to 74 years, with an average of 46, placing the sample squarely within midlife. The findings of MIDUS were consistent in many ways with earlier data in that the older adults in the sample emerged as successful agers, at least as judged in terms of their ratings of affect (Mroczek & Kolarz, 1998). However, personality also played a role. Extraverted men throughout adulthood in the MIDUS study had higher levels of well-being, a finding that points to the importance of considering individual variations in well-being throughout life.

The notion that well-being reflects personality traits such as extraversion is known as the **set point perspective** (see Table 14.1). According to the set point perspective, biologically determined temperament sets the boundaries for the levels of well-being people experience throughout life. Extraverts have an advantage over introverts according to this viewpoint, because people high on the trait of extraversion tend to view the world in a more positive light, regardless of their actual circumstances. Furthermore it is possible that extraverted people, because of their sunny natures, have more success in their dealings with others and, therefore, a stronger objective basis for their optimism. A large-scale longitudinal inves-

tigation of U.S. veterans supported this view, in that men high in extraversion tended to have consistently high life satisfaction throughout their adult years (Mroczek & Spiro, 2005). Additionally, having high self-esteem in childhood seems to play a protective role in that children high in self-esteem tend to have higher self-esteem throughout their lives (Robins & Trzesniewski, 2005). The idea that older adults maintain high subjective well-being despite facing challenges from their objective circumstances is a phenomenon referred to as the **paradox of well-being** (Mroczek & Kolarz, 1998). Even if they are living in less than ideal physical settings (Werngren-Elgstrolm, Carlsson, & Iwarsson, 2009) or experiencing negative life events (Gomez, Krings, Bangerter, & Grob, 2009), people in later life report that they feel good about themselves and their situations. Findings from countries around the world support this positive image of aging as a time of increased feelings of satisfaction (Diener, 1998).

TABLE 14.1
Concepts Relevant to the Relationship Between Age and Subjective Well-being

Viewpoint	Definition
Set point perspective	Biologically determined temperament sets boundaries for levels of well-being people experience throughout life
Paradox of well-being	Despite objectively poorer conditions, older adults maintain high levels of satisfaction
Adaptation	Older adults habituate to objectively negative circumstances
Social comparison	People compare themselves to others who are in poorer condition than they are
Life story	Older adults emphasize the positive in constructing a view of their lives

That being said, however, there are connections between objective social indicators and subjective well-being. Studies of older adults show positive associations between feelings of well-being and personal resources, including physical functioning and adequacy of financial support (Katz, 2009). Education level, in turn, predicts high levels of physical and cognitive functioning (two components of successful aging), which also predict high levels of subjective well-being (Jang, Choi, & Kim, 2009). As we have noted many times throughout the book, there are advantages to having higher educational levels and income in terms of health status—hence although money and status cannot guarantee happiness, they can help to resolve many of the adaptational problems associated with a lower standard of living (Deacon, 2008) (see Figure 14.2). Even after adjusting for medical conditions, lower socioeconomic status is related to depression and poorer health-related status (Rostad, Deeg, & Schei, 2009) and there is a strong positive linear relationship between income and life satisfaction (Deacon, 2008).

The varying findings concerning the relationship between objective circumstances and perceived well-being raise the question: What are the psychological mechanisms that people use to reach higher levels of well-being than their objective circumstances would warrant? Simple **adaptation** or habituation is one of these theorized psychological mechanisms that people may use to maintain high well-being in the face of objectively negative circumstances. Through adaptation, people learn to live at a certain level of health, income, or discomfort in their situations as they adjust their daily lives to fit the constraints presented to them (Easterlin, 2006). According to this view, even people living in poverty or in poorer health are able to achieve high well-being despite these life challenges. The extent to which people's experiences are consistent with their goals provides another basis for subjective well-being (Austin & Vancouver, 1996). If people are able to achieve or make progress toward reaching their goals, they will feel better about themselves and their experiences. They will be more satisfied with their objective situations in life if they see these as potentially contributing to the achievement of their goals (Diener & Fujita, 1995). For example, you might live in a cramped and uncomfortable dorm room or student apartment while in college but still have high levels of well-being if you see your circumstances helping to move you closer to your long-term educational goal of obtaining a degree in higher education.

There are life-span components to goal setting as well. Longitudinal data from a study of gifted individuals revealed that people who set high goals for themselves in midlife were the most likely to

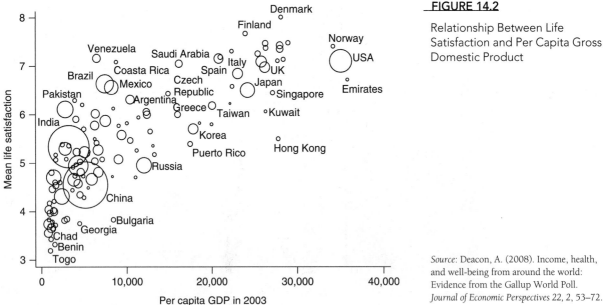

FIGURE 14.2

Relationship Between Life Satisfaction and Per Capita Gross Domestic Product

Source: Deacon, A. (2008). Income, health, and well-being from around the world: Evidence from the Gallup World Poll. *Journal of Economic Perspectives 22*, 2, 53–72.

have high goals in later adulthood, particularly if they valued having a rich cultural life and making contributions to the social good (Holahan & Chapman, 2002).

People may also alter their views of their life circumstances through problem-focused and emotion-focused coping strategies. Although the objective nature of people's life circumstances must be taken into account (Diener, Oishi, & Lucas, 2003), coping accounts for the way that people interpret these circumstances. For example, in one study, community-dwelling older adults in good physical condition with few depressive symptoms were better able to withstand stressful life events such as personal illness and death or illness of a friend or family member (Hardy, Concato, & Gill, 2004).

The type of coping people use may reflect their perceived sense of the ability to reduce stress. Older individuals with higher levels of self-efficacy are more likely to use problem-focused coping, but those who use emotion-focused coping are more likely to rate themselves high both in social support and perceived stress (Trouillet, Gana, Lourel, & Fort, 2009). Reducing stress is an important component of successful cognitive and emotional health for older adults (Depp, Vahia, & Jeste, 2010).

Religion also plays a role in adapting to difficult life circumstances, serving as another important coping resource for many older adults (Van Ness & Larson, 2002). Finally, cultures and nations vary in their norms or expectations for experiencing emotions. For example, people in China have the lowest frequency and intensity of both positive and negative emotions compared to people living in the United States, Australia, and Taiwan (Eid & Diener, 2001).

Another active adaptational process is **social comparison**, through which people look at the situations of others who are more unfortunate than they are, and comfort themselves with the thought that things could be worse (Michalos, 1985). In the face of threat, such as death from cancer, people manage to maintain a positive outlook by regarding themselves as having adjusted better than others with the disease (Helgeson & Taylor, 1993). Similarly, older individuals may use social comparison to help negotiate potentially stressful transitions, such as having to relocate their place of residence (Kwan, Love, Ryff, & Essex, 2003).

However, there is a flip side to the social comparison explanation—the phenomenon known as relative deprivation in which people compare themselves to others within their own social class and it is only when they perceive themselves to be disadvantaged compared to them that their well-being suffers. A national survey of midlife and older adults supported this phenomenon in part. People reported more stress-related diseases only if they felt that their social status was lower than those of others within their same self-defined grouping. In other words, your comparison group if you are middle-class is not upper-class individuals, but other middle-class people. If you think you are deprived relative to others in your own social class, you will suffer higher rates of stress-related disease. Wealthy people who think they are worse off than other wealthy people, similarly, will also experience more stress (Pham-Kanter, 2009).

Many adaptational processes seem to be at work in predicting the relationship between objective life circumstances and subjective well-being. In general, though, older people seem to be able to focus on the positive features of their lives. They can regulate their affect and also focus on the positive features of their relationships to maximize their feelings of happiness (Mroczek & Spiro, 2005).

It is not only the number of people in their social network, but also the quality of social support that can help older people feel more satisfied with their lives (Berg, Hassing, McClearn, & Johansson, 2006). Think of how this process applies in your own life; by having others regard you positively, it is likely that you will develop an enhanced sense of self-esteem, which in turn has positive effects on your subjective health, which in turn enhances your well-being, and so on. Interestingly, even physical performance factors, such as measures of gait (walking), may be improved by the social support that can make people feel better about themselves (Kim & Nesselroade, 2002). The specific aspect of self-esteem involved in these processes is the sense that you are valued by others (Bailis & Chipperfield, 2002). Conversely, feelings of loneliness present a risk factor for depression (Golden et al., 2009) and poorer health (high systolic blood pressure) (Hawkley, Thisted, Masi, & Cacioppo, 2010).

Thus, social support and relationships with others have an influence on feelings of well-being by

Members of the Red Hat Society at the Lord Mayor's parade in London on New Year's Day. The Red Hat Society is an organization of women 50 and older who get together for tea wearing red hats and purple dresses.

reinforcing the view that you are valued. At the same time, being concerned about family and having a sense of responsibility for children and other family members seems to have additional adaptive value. In one investigation of Australians ranging from 61 to 95 years of age, sense of belonging and concern about family predicted high scores on a measure assessing reasons for living (Kissane & McLaren, 2006). Sense of mastery, particularly for men, also seems to play a key role in influencing the relationship between social support and perceived stress (Gadalla, 2009).

Identity processes may provide a means of maintaining high levels of well-being in the face of less than satisfactory circumstances. Through identity assimilation, people may place a positive interpretation on what might otherwise cause them to feel that they are not accomplishing their desired objectives. The process of the **life story**, through which people develop a narrative view of the past that emphasizes the positive, is an example of identity assimilation as it alters the way that people interpret events that might otherwise detract from self-esteem (Whitbourne et al., 2002). For instance, older psychiatric patients minimized and in some cases denied the potentially distressing experience of having spent a significant part of their lives within a state mental hospital. Therefore, they were not distressed in thinking back on their lives and past experiences (Whitbourne & Sherry, 1991). People can maintain their sense of subjective well-being and can portray their identity in a positive light, even when their actual experiences would support less favorable interpretations.

PRODUCTIVITY AND CREATIVITY

As we have just seen, people use many strategies to enhance their well-being through an active process of interpreting and reinterpreting their experiences. People can also enhance their well-being by seeking out new experiences and encounters that will move them beyond their current levels of well-being and accomplishments. Successful aging involves more than maintaining a positive outlook on life, even as that life becomes potentially more stressful. The areas of productivity and creativity in adulthood provide this important perspective to the understanding of successful aging.

The Relationship Between Age and Creativity: Early Studies

Creativity is conventionally thought of as the ability to produce a notable or extraordinary piece of work. It is judged by a group of experts relative to a particular time period as having novelty, an impact on society, and an element of surprise. For almost two centuries, researchers and theorists have been interested in the question of whether aging is associated with changes in creativity as measured by the production of creative works. Examples of illustrious creative figures who continued to remain productive in old age, such as Michelangelo (1475–1564), challenge the stereotyped notion that youth is prime time for the expression of genius. The first empirical investigation of this question was conducted by Quetelet (1835/1968), who attempted to determine the quality of plays written by French playwrights over the course of the adult years.

The most extensive early investigation into the question of age and productivity was conducted by Lehman in his 1953 book *Age and Achievement* (Lehman, 1953). Lehman analyzed the production by age of creative works in all fields from the sciences to the arts. His analysis included both the number of works produced and their quality, but his main focus was on works that had significant impact in their fields. Lehman concluded that the peak of productivity in the adult years tends to occur prior to the age of 40, often between 30 and 35. However, he found that the age period corresponding to a creative peak, in terms of

quality and quantity, varied by discipline. Lehman concluded that earlier peaks are reached in the sciences and in fields in which success was dependent on intellectual imagination and physical ability. This phenomenon was later to be dubbed with the name the "Planck hypothesis" (Dietrich, 2004), after the brilliant German scientist Max Planck, and refers to the tendency of younger scientists to be at the peak of producing innovative ideas. As observed by Lehman, increasingly later peaks are reached in fields that rely on experience and diplomacy. The writing of "best books" falls in between these extremes, for an author's success involves imagination, discipline, and the philosophical perspectives gained from experience.

The next major investigation on age and creativity was conducted by Dennis (1966), who examined the total output, regardless of the quality of work, by contributors to seven domains within the arts and sciences. As seen in Figure 14.3, although there is a rather steep decline after the peak age in the arts, and somewhat less so in the sciences, productivity in terms of scholarship is maintained at a steady rate throughout later adulthood, with even a slight peak in the 60s. Dennis attempted to compensate for the differential ages that creators lived to be (which

AGING IN THE NEWS

www.wiley.com/college/whitbourne   OLDER ADULTS WHO MADE THE HEADLINES   -VOL. 4, CHAPTER 14-

BETTY WHITE HOSTS SNL AT THE AGE OF 88

After an intense Internet campaign that included a Facebook campaign by "Betty White to host SNL," the iconic TV sitcom star hosted the Mother's Day airing of the NBC live show on May 8, 2010.

Giving her impeccable performance, White exemplified the reasons why she has remained so well-loved by TV fans of all ages. It was no surprise that the episode was nominated for several Emmys and drew the highest ratings of SNL in 18 months.

FIGURE 14.3

Age and Productivity by Discipline as Judged by Dennis (1966)

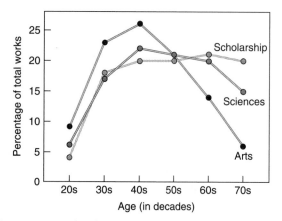

Source: Dennis, W. (1966). Creative productivity between the ages of 20 and 80 years. *Journal of Gerontology, 21,* 1–8.

would obviously cut down on productivity in the later years), by limiting his sample to people who lived to be at least 80 years old. Furthermore, unlike Lehman, who factored the impact of a work into his age curves, Dennis did not attempt to evaluate the quality of a contribution. Instead, Dennis relied entirely on counts of published or produced works.

The studies by Lehman and Dennis can be summarized as showing a rapid increase in creative output that reaches a career peak in the late 30s or early 40s, after which a steady decline begins. The peak and rate of decline vary by discipline, but the decline occurs nevertheless. Based on this research, one would have to argue that creative productivity is unlikely to be a component of successful aging.

Fortunately, the pessimistic interpretation of the early literature may not tell the whole story. Even Lehman (1953) observed that "older thinkers" and artists produced many great achievements. He noted that there was an upturn for painters in their 70s for producing "best" paintings but this apparent increase was in part a function of the fact that fewer individuals are alive at these ages. Those who are producing works of art represent a select portion of the population of artists who probably always were productive, a point that we will return to later. Although the tip of the peak is not as pronounced as in the earlier

years, it nevertheless represents the work of some exceptionally talented older artists.

Similar trends toward late-life upturns can also be found in other disciplines within Lehman's investigation, including mathematics, physics, astronomy, medicine, philosophy, music, and poetry. What might seem to be a striking omission is Ludwig van Beethoven, who produced some of his greatest work at the end of his life, including his renowned late string quartets. However, because he died at the age of 56, his late-career accomplishments would not technically fall into the category of late-life productivity (though 56 was "old" for that period of history). Similarly, the amazingly prolific Wolfgang Mozart died at the age of 35. These examples illustrate some of the problems of conducting research in which productive works are plotted simply by age because important figures who die at a younger age but who might have remained productive had they lived longer are not counted.

Simonton's Model of Age and Creative Productivity

The types of problems we just described in research on age and creative achievement led psychologist Dean Simonton to develop a model of late-life productivity that proves to be relatively insensitive to these methodological problems. Simonton (1997) devised a mathematical model in which he relates age to creative productivity, controlling for individual differences in creative potential, age, age of death, and the nature of an individual's field of endeavor. He developed this model through mathematical analyses of the previous data collected by Lehman, Dennis, and others.

Simonton's model of creative productivity is based on three elements (see Figure 14.4). The first is creative potential, which is a hypothetical count of the total number of works that someone would be able to produce in a life span with no upper limits. It can also be thought of as the number of original ideas that a given individual could ever theoretically produce. A person with a high creative potential might produce thousands of works of art during his or her career, but a person with low creative potential may produce ten, twenty, or perhaps just one (a "one-hit wonder"). The composer Mozart might be considered a person with high creative potential; in his short life of 35 years, he produced more than 600 works including symphonies, concertos, operas, sonatas, requiems, and songs. There is no evidence that he was slowing down even as he became ill within the last few months of his life.

The second element in predicting creative productivity is ideation, the process of producing the ideas themselves. It is one thing to have an idea, and another to translate it into something that you can see, hear, or ponder. The third element is elaboration—the laborious process of transforming ideas into actual products. For instance, as a young man, the photographer Ansel Adams was inspired by the majestic scenery of Yosemite and began to imagine taking photographs to capture its beauty (ideation). To convert those ideas into creative products (elaboration), Adams had to hike (in some cases) up the side of a mountain, take his photographs, develop the negatives, and print the negatives.

The productivity of an individual over a lifetime, then, is a function of these three elements: creative potential ("m"), ideation rate ("a"), and elaboration rate ("b"). To determine a person's creativity, all three factors must be considered.

A key aspect of Simonton's model is that the productivity of an individual is defined on the basis of **career age**, which is the age at which an individual begins to embark on his or her career. Prior researchers in this area based their theories on chronological age. As a result, they failed to take into account the fact that people begin their careers at different ages. In calculating peak age of productivity, the age at which a person embarks on a career must be accounted for to control for the fact that some people may be past their prime when others are just beginning theirs. Although Adams was relatively young when he began his career as a photographer, others were much older, including the artist Paul Gauguin, who began to paint at the age of 40.

Simonton modeled several variations in productivity according to age based on the three points in the career of a creative individual that seemed to matter the most. These are the first contribution, the "best" contribution (as judged by such factors as critical reviews), and the last contribution.

The age of first contribution corresponds to the age at which the first work of high quality is produced. This is the point that signifies the beginning of the individual's career. Consider the case of the long-lived artist Pablo Picasso (1881–1973), one of the most famous artists of all time. His first work was produced at the very young age of 10 years. The "best" contribution might be more subjective, but would represent the work that received the greatest acclaim. Many people regard Picasso's *Guernica* as his best work. The last work that Picasso completed was during the year of his death, 1973, so the end of his career corresponds to the end of his life. His last works still received critical acclaim, unlike some artists, whose last productions are regarded as derivative of their earlier work and therefore are seen as having very little noteworthy value. Think of some popular musicians you know whose later songs seem to be little more than reworkings of their first big hits.

On the average, according to Simonton's model, productivity in later life will be higher among people who begin their careers at a later age and so will the age of best work (see Table 14.2). However, people with high creative potential are more likely to have a high rate of productivity both early and late in their careers. There may be as long as a 20-year span between best and last work for highly creative people compared with the 10-year span for the less creative. Some individuals with very low creative potential may produce only one significant work, which is their first, best, and last contribution (the one-hit wonder, again).

FIGURE 14.4

Three Elements in Simonton's Model of Creative Productivity

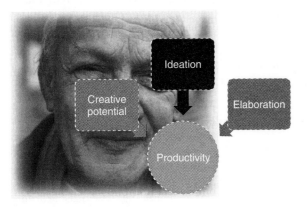

TABLE 14.2
Examples of High and Low Creative Potential and Career Onset

Creative potential	Career onset	Example
Low	Early	Laurie London ("He's Got the Whole World in His Hands" recorded at age 13)
Low	Late	Margaret Mitchell ("Gone With the Wind" at age 37)
High	Early	Pablo Picasso Wolfgang Mozart
High	Late	Grandma Moses Paul Gauguin

A person with high creative potential shows a rapid growth in productivity to the age of best contribution and maintains relatively high productivity until late in both career and actual ages. Such a person will peak later and continue to produce until a later actual age than those with an early onset. Individuals who begin early reach their peak early and achieve their last significant production at an earlier age than those who begin later.

Artists such as Picasso with higher creative potential remain more productive throughout their careers than those with lower potential, regardless of when they produce their first important work. Those with higher creative potential also achieve a significant production relatively earlier in their careers than those with lower potential. Those with higher creative potential also achieve their last important creative landmark at a later age than do those with lower potential.

The next question that might seem important is whether quality of creative productivity has any connection to quantity. According to the **equal odds rule**, there is a positive relationship between quality and quantity of work. Those who produce more output are more likely to score a "hit" or success than are those who produce fewer works (in sports this is referred to as the principle that "if you don't shoot you can't score"). An implication of the equal odds rule is the notion that people are most likely to produce their best work during their peak period of productivity on the basis of probability alone. Verdi composed his first operatic masterpiece at the age of 29 and his last at the age of 80. He had a relatively high probability of creating a masterwork during his late career because he continued to produce such a large number of pieces of music.

Even though later life may be associated with a drop from the time of peak productivity, Simonton's model allows for the existence of older individuals who retain high levels of productivity and creativity. Some of these individuals began their careers at relatively late ages. Anton Bruckner, for example, wrote his first symphony at the age of 42 and his first masterpiece at the age of 50.

The Neuroscience of Creativity

Having examined the statistics on age and creativity, we turn now to a completely different approach. Underlying the creative impulse are brain mechanisms responsible for generating new ideas. Learning and memory involve consolidating experiences, but coming up with new insights is a process that involves generating thoughts no one has had before. Researchers exploring the neurological basis of creativity have focused on the prefrontal cortex, the last structure of the brain to develop both in evolution and development, not reaching full maturity until the early 20s. Some scientists believe that the prefrontal cortex is the part of the brain responsible for generating new ideas.

Creativity is likely to be highest when the prefrontal cortex has sufficiently matured so that people are able to be flexible but at the same time have had sufficient training in their area of expertise so that they can put that flexibility to good use (Dietrich, 2004). Presumably, this happy coincidence occurs about 20 years into the career, when most people are in midlife (Feist, 2006). If not, people can also enhance their creativity by exercising these areas of the brain through mental activity; McFadden and Basting (2010, p. 154) point out that when it comes to creativity, "what's good for the person is usually good for the brain."

Working memory, attention, the ability to shift mental focus, necessary operations for creativity, are also associated with the anterior cingulate cortex. Based on the idea that the personality trait of openness to experience would be related to cognitive flexibility, researchers studied the correlation between brain activation and scores on this measure among older men and women tested 2 years apart. For men, higher openness scores were related to activation of the anterior cingulate cortex (involved in monitoring processes). Prefrontal activation (reflecting flexibility) was related to women's openness scores, and for both sexes openness was also related to frontal lobe activation (Sutin, Beason-Held, Resnick, & Costa, 2009). Thus, the brains of individuals who may be more creative dispositionally may differ in important ways.

Characteristics of Last Works

Until researchers know more about the neuroscience of aging and creativity, evidence about creativity and aging can be derived only by examining the creative products of older artists, composers, writers, and scientists. In the process of conducting such studies, researchers have found that creative works in late life possess special qualities not observed earlier in adulthood (see Figure 14.5).

One important quality seen in older creative adults is the ability to criticize their own creative products. An intensive study of Beethoven's letters and notes from conversations with others showed that as he aged, he was able to make more "accurate" assessments of the quality of his works, as judged by the frequency with which his works were subsequently performed and recorded (Kozbelt, 2007).

A second distinctive characteristic of last works is the **old age style** (Lindauer, 1998). The old age style is an approach to one's art that eliminates the fine details and instead presents the essence of the work's intended meaning. The work becomes less objective and focused on formal perfection and instead more subjective. In a painting, for example, the artist may simplify the image by eliminating details closely tied to accurate renditions of objects and people. A sculptor may concentrate more on the form and underlying emotion of the subject of the piece rather than on representing each and every detail such as each hair on the head or nail on the hand.

The emergence of an old age style can be seen in the works of many artists in addition to Michelangelo, including Rembrandt, Renoir, Matisse, Degas, Georgia O'Keeffe, and Picasso. Critics have noted that the older artist paints with a larger brushstroke, so that each packs a larger emotional

- **Swan song:** Last creative production
- **Old age style:** Simpler, more powerful
- **Integration and synthesis:** Later works provide perspective
- **Specific age interests:** Studies include aging

FIGURE 14.5

Characteristics of Last Works

Sculptor Daniel Chester French produced Lincoln's statue for the Lincoln Memorial in Washington, D.C., when he was 70.

punch. Instead of the painstakingly crafted renderings that a younger artist may produce, the older artist stands back and concentrates on form and meaning.

The artist Henri Matisse referred to this change in his style as a "distillation of form. I now keep only the sign which suffices, necessary for its existence in its own form, for the composition as I conceive it" (Brill, 1967). Another excellent example of the old age style is provided by the work of Michelangelo, whose two Pietas, produced in youth and old age, contrast sharply in their style and emotional tone. Some critics actually regard the late Pieta as more emotionally charged and hence effective than the earlier iconic one that resides in the Vatican (see photo).

The second characteristic is the choice of theme related to aging or death. It is not necessarily that the work has become morbid or depressing, but that it presents the reality of the artist's life and impending death in a manner that may have particular clarity and a strong impact on the viewer. These features of old age style are by no means universal, however. Some artists may continue to paint with the attention to detail and refinement they showed in their earlier work without making a transition to this more reflective and emotionally stronger approach.

The old age style may also be seen in a writer's novels, as they become more reflective, introspective, and subjective (Lubart & Sternberg, 1998). Characters in literature may be portrayed more realistically but also with greater empathy, and they come to take on greater complexity and a sense of timelessness (Adams-Price, 1998).

As a preface to the old age style, creativity may be expressed in midlife as "paring down life to the essentials." Midlife may bring with it not a crisis involving confrontation with mortality, but a heightened sense of urgency to create a lasting legacy. As an example, Strenger (2009) analyzed the productive works of a 20th-century educator in the business field, Charles Handy. At the age of 49, Handy left behind a prestigious position in industry because he felt he had lost touch with his sense of inner purpose. He started a new life as an author and having written 17 books between the ages of 50 and 75, sought and eventually found new meaning in life. The inspiration to create a lasting legacy expressed in Handy's life is reminiscent of the legacy observed among participants in the study conducted by the first author (Whitbourne, 2010) in which the truly fulfilled at midlife felt that they were making a difference in the world in a way that would outlive them after they were gone.

Related to old age style is the **swan song phenomenon**, a brief renewal of creativity that can stimulate the creation of new works and a new style of work (Simonton, 1989). Musical compositions that reflect the swan song phenomenon are characterized by shorter main themes and simpler melodies than the prior works of the composer. As a result, they are strong and evocative and tend to be easy to remember. Simonton considers the best example of the swan song to be "Lachrymosa," from Mozart's last work, the Requiem in D Minor. Although Mozart was not old when he died, he knew that his death was imminent and fittingly wrote a piece of music intended to honor the dead. Centuries later, this melody was to be the music played in the funeral scene of the movie, *Amadeus*, creating the emotionally compelling backdrop to the burial of Mozart's body in a pauper's grave.

As in Mozart's case, the resurgence of creativity that stimulates the swan song may come about with the composer's awareness of increased closeness to death. With the awareness of the proximity of their death, composers may strip away some of their professional and personal ties and focus with renewed vigor on composing a piece of music for the ages. These works often become some of the most successful that the composers produce, and thus in many ways may grant the composer a certain immortality. The swan song phenomenon is perhaps a special case of the old age style because it also implies a certain simplicity and paring away of distractions and details.

A third feature of the old age style is observed primarily among scientists and academicians. They shift their creative products away from innovation and discovery and instead become oriented toward integration and synthesis of existing knowledge. The aging scientist may become more involved in the writing of texts and integrative review articles rather than in conducting research to produce new scientific discoveries. In some cases, they may decide to focus their subject matter on studies of aging, as was true for B. F. Skinner toward the end of his life in his

Michelangelo's Pieta di Rondanini, one of his last sculptures, is thought to represent the essence of the old age style with its lack of detail and focus on raw emotions. It therefore contrasts dramatically with his early Pieta in the Sistine Chapel.

book, *Enjoy Old Age: A Practical Guide* (Skinner & Vaughan, 1983). This apparently was also the case for Sir John Floyer, who wrote the first geriatrics text in the early 1700s when he was 75 years old. A shift to age-related concerns may also be shown in a person's research or practical inventions, as was the case for Benjamin Franklin, who invented bifocals when he was 78 years old, actually well past the age when most people start to need them.

The old age style may be stimulated by proximity to death, a desire to leave behind a legacy, or perhaps age-related changes or health problems. Beethoven became deaf in his later years, and his musical style also changed. For example, in his late string quartets, he became more expressive and less bound by conventional forms. Blindness forced changes in the painting of a number of well-known older artists, including Georgia O'Keeffe, Mary Cassatt, Edgar Degas, and Claude Monet. Henri Matisse suffered from stomach cancer and was confined to a

wheelchair at the end of his life. Despite these severe limitations, these artists continued to produce great works until or nearly until their last years of life.

In the case of the artist Monet, whose work graces the front cover of our book, cataracts caused changes not only in the clarity of his vision but in his ability to see colors. When he developed cataracts, he was literally unable to see the colors on the canvas that he knew appeared in nature. Even special glasses (colored yellow) could not correct this defect, and it was not until he was successfully treated with cataract surgery at the age of 85 that his color vision was restored. His final work, an enormous series of water lilies, was installed in a Paris museum after his death. The colors in these final paintings were as vibrant as they had been in his earlier work. In 1908, he wrote, "These landscapes of water and reflections have become an obsession, it is beyond the strength of an old man, and yet I want to succeed in portraying what I feel. I have destroyed some, I have started all over again, and I hope that something will emerge from so much effort."

Similarly, unable to paint due to the discomfort of his illness, Matisse changed his medium to paper sculptures, which have since become some of the classic instances of this master's life contributions. Showing the same phenomenon but in another creative medium was the poet William Carlos Williams. He suffered a stroke in his 60s, after which he became severely depressed. Following treatment for depression, he went on to produce some of his greatest works, including the Pulitzer Prize-winning *Pictures From Bruegel*, published when he was 79.

The limitations caused by physical and sensory age-related changes suffered by some of these artists were not necessarily met with equanimity. Michelangelo, for example, attempted to destroy his last Pieta, and it was saved only through the efforts of his apprentices. Similarly, Monet destroyed many of the canvases he produced during the years he suffered from cataracts. Picasso's self-portrait *Facing Death* portrays the man who refuses to accept his own physical aging. Georgia O'Keeffe, who lived to the age of 98, was similarly frustrated with her inability to see in her last decade of life, and her need to change mediums from painting to sculpture and pottery because she could no longer see the canvas. Nevertheless, all of these individuals lived very long lives, and despite their personal frustrations, found ways to express their creative potential right up until the very end.

Sociocultural Variations

These models of successful aging and creativity are useful and inspiring, but one important shortcoming seen by some critics is that they fail to take sufficient account of sociocultural context. Socioeconomically and racially disadvantaged individuals have a much lower chance of ever reaching old age, much less "successful" old age, as traditionally defined within psychology or the arts. Certain sectors of the population, particularly minorities from low-income backgrounds, do not have the opportunity to achieve good health and full expression of their innate abilities. Everyone we have talked about up to now came from a relatively advantaged background or at least achieved material success. For many talented individuals who are not afforded the benefits of higher levels of education and income, the creative process faces more challenges. Education and income remain lower among Blacks in the United States, and even a college education does not protect a person from career discrimination, as we noted in Chapter 10.

A second critical fact in analyses of successful aging regards the definition of eminence as used in studies of aging and creativity. Women are far less likely than would be expected on the basis of chance to appear in lists of the creative and productive at any age. However, it is only within the area of children's literature that Lehman (1953) listed women as constituting anywhere near 50% of the notable contributors. A total of only 20 women were listed in the Lehman work as "worthy of mention" (p. 91).

Little, if any, mention in analysis of productivity is made of Blacks. Simonton (1998) explored the question of whether assessments of creative output among historical figures would show evidence of bias against members of minority cultures. Specifically, he examined whether African Americans who had achieved recognition within reference works focusing to Black scholarship would also be mentioned in reference works of the White majority culture. Although there was considerable convergence between the minority and majority reference works, one fifth of African Americans who had achieved eminence in the minority reference works were not mentioned in any of the majority indices of eminence. Furthermore, certain areas of accomplishment within Black culture were not recognized within the majority reference works, including law, education, religion, classical music, and the sciences. White reference works gave higher ratings to African Americans in the fields of athletics, and jazz and blues music, but African American sources gave greater recognition to those who achieved eminence in the civil rights movement.

These differential patterns of recognition point to differential opportunities that affect an individual's ability to achieve career recognition, if not personal fulfillment. Clearly differences in educational opportunities as well as cultural values play a role in determining the ultimate achievements of people from nonmajority backgrounds. Those who do manage to break through cultural barriers are likely to receive considerable recognition within their own as well as the majority culture. Some examples are Jackie Robinson, who was the first African American to play major league baseball; Booker T. Washington, first to receive an honorary degree from Harvard; and William Grant Still, first to conduct a major symphony orchestra and to have his own composition performed by a major American orchestra. These "famous firsts" seem particularly important within African American reference works of eminence because they attest to the ability of highly talented and persistent individuals to overcome the effects of discrimination. That their work has until recently been overlooked in studies of aging and creativity limits the generalizability of current models of successful aging.

SUCCESSFUL AGING: FINAL PERSPECTIVES

People in later life appear not only to manage to feel satisfied with their lives but also to be able to achieve new forms of creative expression. Many scientists, artists, writers, and political leaders have produced notable contributions in their later adult years. The accomplishments of these unusual individuals adds to the literature on subjective well-being to add support to the concept of successful aging. These outstanding examples of creativity and involvement in later life make them truly "Age Busters"—within their areas of accomplishment, they have managed to break through the expectations for older persons, and shown that the potential for significant accomplishments are possible at any age.

As we showed in the analysis of Simonton's model of creative productivity, people who begin their careers with a high degree of creative potential are likely to maintain higher creative output well into their 60s, 70s, and beyond. Where does this creative potential come from? In part, the level of talent needed to sustain such a long and productive career may have a neurological basis. Personality may also play a role. There is evidence from an unusual 45-year longitudinal study of men originally tested as graduate students that the personality qualities of openness and flexibility predict creativity and success in later adulthood. Those men with the highest numbers of awards and notable publications at age 72 were higher on scales of tolerance and psychological-mindedness at age 27 (Feist & Barron, 2003).

Analyzing the lives of a set of six highly creative older adults (including Grandma Moses), Antonini and colleagues (2008) identified a passionate commitment to the pursuit of their discipline as the common thread. These individuals also shared the trait of flexibility or plasticity and, rather than dwell on their accomplishments of the past, looked forward to new goals and new creative enterprises. They maintained their curiosity and, similar to the quality of openness to experience, were able to keep up with their times and adapt to changing circumstances.

Moving beyond the unusual contributions of highly creative individuals, we can see creativity as a process that can characterize ordinary people as well. There is creativity with a capital "C" and creativity with a little "c;" the latter characterizes the work by people who in their daily lives express themselves through cooking, crafts, gardening, or story-telling. Involvement in these activities can not only stimulate cognitive functioning and well-being but also illustrates the ability of older adults to engage creatively with life (McFadden & Basting, 2010).

Creativity can be also thought of as a process of personality development in which people develop a completely open mind to new experiences and are able to enjoy and appreciate the finer nuances of life. For the ordinary individual who does not achieve lasting fame, the process of successful aging may involve the creative process of constructing a personal narrative or life story (Luborsky, 1998). This narrative will involve a complex negotiation of cultural (Luborsky & McMullen, 1999) and personal forces (Whitbourne, 1985). Cultural forces shape the parameters that people use to evaluate their own contributions and those of others. Cultural forces also set the parameters for the opportunities that people have to achieve their goals.

Part of a "successful" life narrative may involve coming to grips with the recognition of how cultural constraints have affected your ability to realize the hopes and dreams of youth. Yet, people must also strive to transcend these constrictions and arrive at a personal sense of meaning in life that rises above the boundaries of culture and time. As you continue to develop and navigate through your adult years, we hope that you will find your personal sense of meaning to accompany a long and successful life.

SUMMARY

1. The process of successful aging involves being able to overcome the threats to physical and psychological well-being presented by the aging process. However, in addition to "survival," successful aging involves the ability to become engaged with life in terms of both relationships and productive activity. Subjective well-being, a component of successful aging, is higher in older adults, a phenomenon referred to as the paradox of well-being. There are several possible mechanisms through which higher subjective well-being is achieved, including adaptation, goal achievement, coping mechanisms, social comparison, and the use of identity assimilation in forming a life story.

2. Research on productivity and creativity has involved attempts to determine whether older individuals are more or less able to maintain the quality and quantity of works produced when younger. Variations by discipline were observed in early studies in which peak ages were reached earlier for areas in which imagination and physical ability are required. However, the findings of various authors indicated overall declines after peaks reached in young adulthood.

In some cases, upturns were noted in the productivity of individuals living until the 70s and beyond among exceptionally talented older persons. Many achievements have also been produced by people in advanced old age. This area of research is hampered by the fact that some individuals who may have maintained their productivity do not live until old age. Furthermore, average productivity rates do not take into account the individual variations shown in the quality and quantity of works. Simonton's model of creative productivity describes the relationship between age and production of creative works using a mathematical formula that incorporates creative potential, ideation, and elaboration based on the career age of an individual rather than chronological age. In this model, highly productive individuals begin early and maintain a high production rate long into their careers. Those who are more productive are also more likely to produce works of high quality.

3. The old age style characterizes the works of older artists and musicians. One component of the old age style is simplification of detail and increasing subjectivity. The swan song is a related phenomenon, referring to the tendency of composers to produce very simple themes in their last works. Among scientists and academicians, the old age style refers to a tendency to synthesize, producing works such as texts and reviews that integrate existing knowledge. The old age style may be a reaction to increasing proximity to death or to the presence of age-related changes or health problems. Age Busters also maintain their productivity throughout life.

4. For individuals who do not achieve lasting fame through their work, the expression of creativity may come about through the construction of a personal narrative. In this process, the individual comes to grips with the accomplishments and failures of his or her life and arrives at a personal sense of meaning.

GLOSSARY

Accommodation: process in Piagetian theory in which individuals change their existing mental structures to incorporate information from experiences.

Activity theory: proposal that it is harmful to the well-being of older adults to force them out of productive social roles.

Adaptation: psychological mechanisms that individuals may use to maintain high well-being in the face of objectively negative circumstances.

Adrenopause: age-related decline in dehydroepiandrosterone (DHEA).

Advance directive (AD): specification of the patient's desire to participate in and direct their own health care decisions, and to accept or refuse treatment.

Aerobic capacity: the maximum amount of oxygen that can be delivered through the blood.

Affective evaluation theory: theory proposing that positive and negative emotions at work should be considered as influences on our satisfaction.

Age-adjusted death rates: mortality statistic calculated by obtaining the weighted averages of the age-specific death rates, with the weights reflecting the proportion of individuals in that age group in the population.

Age-complexity hypothesis: proposal that due to slowing of central processes in the nervous system, age differences increase with increasing complexity of the task.

Age Discrimination in Employment Act (ADEA): federal law initially passed in 1967 to prohibit discrimination against workers on the basis of age; later expanded to prohibit mandatory retirement except in selected occupations.

Ageism: a set of beliefs, attitudes, social institutions, and acts that denigrate individuals or groups based on their chronological age.

Age-related macular degeneration (ARMD): progressive form of blindness in which there is a destruction of the photoreceptors located in the central region of the retina known as the macula.

Age-specific death rates: the number of deaths per 100,000 of the particular age group.

Agoraphobia: the fear of being trapped or stranded during a panic attack.

Alzheimer's disease: the most common form of dementia.

Amnesia: profound memory loss.

Amyloid: generic name for protein fragments that collect together in a specific way to form insoluble deposits.

Amyloid plaque: collection of dead and dying neurons surrounding a central core amyloid.

Amyloid precursor protein (APP): protein manufactured by neurons that plays a role in their growth and communication with each other, and perhaps contributes to the repair of injured brain cells.

Androgenetic alopecia: condition in which the hair follicles stop producing the long, thick, pigmented hair, leading ultimately to baldness.

Andropause: age-related decline in the male sex hormone testosterone.

Anorexia-cachexia syndrome: condition at the end of life that involves a loss of appetite (anorexia) and atrophy of muscle mass (cachexia).

Anterograde amnesia: inability to learn new information.

Anticholinesterase treatment: known as THA or tetrahydroaminoacridine, blocks the action of the enzyme cholinesterase, which destroys acetylcholine.

Anxiety disorders: psychological disorders in which the major symptom is excessive anxiety.

Apolipoprotein E (ApoE) gene: gene located on chromosome 19 that controls the production of ApoE, a protein that carries blood cholesterol throughout the body.

Apoptosis: the process of cell death.

APP gene: gene located on chromosome 21 that appears to control the production of the protein that generates beta-amyloid.

Archival research: a method of research in which investigators use existing resources that contain data relevant to a question about aging.

Arteriosclerosis: a general term for the thickening and hardening of arteries.

Assessment: evaluation of the psychological, physiological, and social factors that are potentially affecting the individual's current state of functioning.

Assimilation: process in Piagetian theory in which individuals interpret new experiences in terms of their existing mental structures.

Assisted living facility: professionally managed and licensed housing complex in which older persons live independently in their own apartments.

Atherosclerosis: a form of cardiovascular disease in which fat and other substances accumulate within the arteries at an abnormally high rate and substantially reduce the width of the arteries.

Attachment style: the way which people relate to their primary attachment figure.

Attention: ability to focus or concentrate on a portion of an experience while ignoring other features of the experience, to be able to shift that focus as demanded by the situation, and to be able to coordinate information from multiple sources.

Attentional resources: proposal that older adults have a limited amount of energy available for cognitive operations because of reductions in central nervous system capacity.

Autobiographical memory: recall of information from one's own past.

Awareness of finitude: point at which an individual passes the age when parents or, perhaps, siblings, have died.

Baby Boomers: generation of people who currently are between the ages of 45 and 65 years old, born between 1945 and 1965.

Balance theory of wisdom: view of wisdom as the ability to balance the various components of intelligence outlined in the theory and to apply them to problems involving the common good or welfare of others.

Behavioral approach to marital interactions: approach that emphasizes the actual behaviors that partners engage in with each other during marital interactions as an influence on marital stability and quality.

Bereavement: the process in which an individual attempts to overcome the death of another person with whom there was a relationship.

Biological age: the age of the individual based on the quality of functioning of the individual's organ systems.

Biopsychosocial perspective: a view of development as a complex interaction of biological, psychosocial, and social processes.

Bipolar disorder: Mood disorder characterized by the experience of manic episodes.

Blended families (also called reconstituted families): families in which the parents were not originally married to each other in which there are children and stepchildren of one or both parents.

Body Mass Index (BMI): an index of body fat, calculated as weight in kilograms divided by (height in meters) squared.

Boundaryless career: a career that does not follow a set pathway.

Bridge employment: employment in one job while officially retired from another job.

Brinley plot: graph in which reaction times of older adults are plotted against reaction times of younger adults.

Caloric restriction hypothesis: the view that restriction of caloric intake is the key to prolonging life.

Cardiac output: the amount of blood that the heart pumps per minute.

Career age: the age at which an individual begins to embark on his or her career.

Caregiver burden: the stress that these people experience in the daily management of their afflicted relative.

Caregivers: family members most likely to be the ones providing care for the patient; in particular, wives and daughters.

Caregiving: the provision of aid in daily living activities to an infirm older adult, often a relative.

Case report: a method of research in which an in-depth analysis of particular individuals is provided.

Caspase: enzyme that destroys neurons.

Cataract: clouding that has developed in the normally clear crystalline lens of the eye, resulting in blurred or distorted vision because the image cannot be focused clearly onto the retina.

Centenarians: people over the age of 100 years.

Cerebrovascular accident (also known as a stroke or brain attack): an acute condition in which an artery leading to the brain bursts or is clogged by a blood clot or other particle.

Chromosomes: distinct, physically separate units of coiled threads of deoxyribonucleic acid (DNA) and associated protein molecules.

Chronic obstructive pulmonary disease (COPD): respiratory disorder composed primarily of two related diseases, chronic emphysema and chronic bronchitis.

Circadian rhythm: daily variation in various bodily functions.

Climacteric: gradual winding down of reproductive ability.

Clinical geropsychology: specialty used primarily in applied settings such as hospitals, clinics, and long-term institutions.

Clinical interview: assessment method in which the clinician asks questions of the client to establish insight into the client's psychological processes.

Cognition: study of the abilities to learn, remember, solve problems, and become knowledgeable about the world.

Cognitive-behavioral treatment: form of psychotherapy in which the client is encouraged to develop new behaviors and constructive ways of thinking about the self.

Cognitive self theories: theories proposing that individuals view the events in their lives from the standpoint of the relevance of these events to the self.

Cohabitation effect: greater likelihood of divorce among couples who cohabitated before they become engaged.

Cohort: variable in developmental research used to signify the general era in which a person was born.

Collagen: substance found throughout the body, which makes up about one third of all bodily proteins.

Communication predicament model: model in which the use of patronizing speech (elderspeak) constrains the older person from being able to participate fully in conversations with others.

Competence-press model: proposal that there is an optimal level of adjustment that institutionalized persons will experience on the basis of their levels of competence compared to the demands or "press" of the environment.

Compression of morbidity: concept referring to the desirable state in which people live to be older before they die and also experience less disability prior to their death.

Congestive heart failure (or heart failure): a condition in which the heart is unable to pump enough blood to meet the needs of the body's other organs.

Congruence: "fit" between a person's RIASEC type and that of the occupation within Holland's vocational development theory.

Conscientious-Conformist stage: in Loevinger's theory, period when individuals begin to gain a "conscience," or internal set of rules of right and wrong, and start to gain self-awareness as well as understanding of the needs and thoughts of other people.

Context processing deficiency: proposal that aging affects the ability to take the context of information into account when making judgments in situations such as the sustained attention task.

Contextual influences on development: the effects of social processes on changes within the individual.

Continuing care retirement community (CCRC): a housing community that provides different levels of care based on the residents' needs.

Continuity theory: proposal that older adults will suffer a loss of well-being and negative effects of being excluded from social roles if this exclusion goes against their will.

Continuity theory of retirement: proposal that retirement does not lead to serious disruptions in the individual's sense of identity, social connections, or feelings of productivity.

Coping: the process used to manage stress.

Coronary artery disease (or coronary heart disease): a form of cardiovascular disease in which there is a lack of blood supply to the arteries that feed the heart muscle.

Correlational design: research design in which the relationship is observed between two or more variables.

Cross-sectional: developmental research design in which people of different ages are compared at the same point of measurement.

Crystallized intelligence (Gc): the acquisition of specific skills and information acquired through familiarity with the language, knowledge, and conventions of one's culture.

Day care center: form of community treatment in which individuals receive supervised meals and activities on a daily basis.

Death: the point when there is irreversible cessation of circulatory and respiratory functions, or when all structures of the brain have ceased to function.

Death ethos: a culture's prevailing philosophy of death.

Death with dignity: the idea that death should not involve extreme physical dependency or loss of control of bodily functions.

Debriefing: providing a research participant with information about the study's real purpose, after the participation has ended.

Defense mechanisms: in psychodynamic theory, unconscious strategies intended to protect the conscious mind from knowing the improper urges of the unconscious mind, which include a wide range of socially unacceptable behaviors.

Delirium: an acute state in which the individual experiences a disturbance in consciousness and attention; cognitive disorder characterized by temporary but acute confusion that can be caused by diseases of the heart and lung, infection, or malnutrition.

Delirium, dementia, and amnestic disorders: disorders involving significant loss of cognitive functioning as the result of neurological dysfunction or medical illness.

Dementia: clinical condition in which the individual experiences a loss of cognitive function severe enough to interfere with normal daily activities and social relationships.

Dependent variable: the variable on which people are observed to differ.

Depressive disorders: mood disorders characterized primarily by periods of intense sadness.

Developmental schism: an emotional gap created between parents and their children.

Developmental science: term replacing "developmental psychology" to reflect the need to take a broad, interdisciplinary approach to understanding patterns of change in life.

Diabetes: a disease caused by a defect in the process of metabolizing glucose.

Diagnostic and Statistical Manual-Fourth Edition-Text Revision or DSM-IV-TR: psychiatric manual published by the American Psychiatric Association.

Dialectical thinking: an interest in and appreciation for debate, arguments, and counterarguments.

Disengagement theory: proposal that there is an optimal relationship between the older individual and society—one in which the older person retreats from active involvement in social roles.

Dispositional affectivity: the general dimension of a person's affective responding.

Divided attention: task in which the individual is given information from two input sources (same as dual task).

Divorce proneness: characteristic of divorced people to be more likely to consider divorce as an option when their marriage is not going smoothly.

DNA (deoxyribonucleic acid): the basic unit of genetics that carries inherited information and that controls the functioning of the cell.

Doing gender: the process of enacting traditional gender roles.

Do not resuscitate (DNR) order: a document placed in a patient's hospital chart specifying the individual's desire not to be resuscitated if he or she should suffer a cardiac or respiratory arrest.

Dual-process model of stress and coping: a model of bereavement proposing that there are two processes involved in bereavement; the first with regard to loss of the attachment figure and the second with regard to loss of role and identity.

Dual task: task in which the individual is given information from two input sources (same as divided attention).

Dying: the period during which an organism loses its viability.

Dying trajectory: the rate of decline in functioning prior to death.

Dysphoria: sad mood.

Dysthermia: conditions in which the individual shows excessive raising of body temperature (hyperthermia) or excessive lowering of body temperature (hypothermia).

Early-onset familial Alzheimer's disease: form of Alzheimer's disease that begins in middle adulthood and shows an inherited pattern.

Ecological perspective: theoretical model emphasizing that changes occur throughout life in the relations between the individual and multiple levels of the environment.

Ego: in psychodynamic theory, structure in personality that, according to Freud's theory, is most accessible to conscious awareness, performs the rational, executive functions of mind, and organizes the individual's activities so that important goals can be attained. In Erikson's theory, the self.

Ego Integrity versus Despair: stage in Erikson's psychosocial development theory in which the individual attempts to establish a sense of acceptance and integration.

Ego psychology: framework of theorists whose conceptualizations of personality revolve around the role of the ego in actively directing behavior.

Elastase: enzyme that breaks down the elastin found in lung tissue.

Elder abuse: actions taken directly against an older adult through the inflicting of physical or psychological harm.

Elderspeak: a simplified speech pattern directed at older adults who presumably are unable to understand adult language.

Electroconvulsive therapy (ECT): somatic treatment in which an electric current is applied through electrodes attached across the head.

Empty nest: the departure of children from the home.

Epigenetic principle: the principle in Erikson's theory which states that each stage unfolds from the previous stage.

Episodic memory: memory for events ("episodes"), which can include the recall of material presented in a memory experiment such as a word list.

Equal odds rule: the fact that there is a positive relationship between quality and quantity of work.

Equilibrium: state in Piagetian theory through which individuals are able to interpret their experiences through a consistent framework but are able to change this framework when it no longer is helpful in organizing experiences.

Equity theory: proposal that relationships continue when the partners feel they are contributing equal benefits.

Erectile dysfunction: a condition in which a man is unable to achieve an erection sustainable for intercourse.

Ethnicity: the cultural background of an individual, reflecting the predominant values, attitudes, and expectations in which the individual has been raised.

Euthanasia: the direct killing of a patient by a physician who administers a lethal injection.

Experimental design: a research method in which an independent variable is manipulated and scores are then measured on the dependent variable. Involves random assignment of respondents to treatment and control groups.

Explicit memory: recall of information that the individual has consciously or deliberately attempted to recall.

Extrinsic factors: features that accompany a job that may also be found in other jobs.

Filial anxiety: the idea that one might be forced to take on the role of parent to the parent.

Filial maturity: the identification of the adult child with the parent.

Filial obligation (or filial piety): the feeling that one is obligated to take care of aging parents should this become necessary.

Five Factor Model (also called "Big Five"): theory intended to capture all the essential characteristics of personality described in other trait theories.

Fluid intelligence (Gf): the individual's innate abilities to carry out higher-level cognitive operations involving the integration, analysis, and synthesis of new information.

Focus group: a meeting of a group of respondents oriented around a particular topic of interest.

Formal operations: the ability of adolescents and adults to use logic and abstract symbols in arriving at solutions to complex problems.

Free radical: molecular fragment that seeks to bind to other molecules.

Friendship styles: friendship patterns in adulthood based on individual differences in approaches toward friends.

Frontotemporal dementia: dementia that attacks specifically the frontal lobes of the brain and is reflected in personality changes such as apathy, lack of inhibition, obsessiveness, and loss of judgment.

Functional age: a system of classifying individuals on the basis of their abilities rather than on chronological age.

Gender: the individual's identification as being male or female.

Gender gap: difference between the salaries of men and women.

Gene: a functional unit of a DNA molecule carrying a particular set of instructions for producing a specific protein or other molecules needed by the body's cells.

General slowing hypothesis: proposal that the age-related increase in reaction time reflects a general decline of information processing speed within the aging nervous system.

Generalized anxiety disorder: Anxiety disorder in which a person feels an overall sense of uneasiness and concern but without having a particular focus.

Generativity versus Stagnation: stage in Erikson's psychosocial development theory in which the individual focuses on the issues of procreation, productivity, and creativity.

Genome: the complete set of instructions for "building" all the cells that make up an organism.

Geriatric continuing day treatment: program in which clients attend a day treatment program three days a week but are encouraged to live independently during the remaining days of the week.

Geriatric partial hospital: treatment site in which daily outpatient therapy is provided with intensive, structured multidisciplinary services to older persons who have recently been discharged from a psychiatric hospital.

Gerontology: the scientific study of the aging process.

Geropsychology: applications of the field of gerontology to the psychological treatment of older adults.

Glaucoma: a group of conditions in which the optic nerve is damaged, causing loss of visual function.

Glucocorticoid cascade hypothesis: proposal that aging causes dangerous increases in cortisol levels affecting immune response, fat deposits, and cognition.

Gompertz equation: a function that expresses the relationship between age of the organism and age of death.

Hierarchical linear modeling: a method used for longitudinal studies in which individual patterns of change are investigated rather than simply comparing mean scores.

High-density lipoproteins (HDLs): the plasma lipid transport mechanism responsible for carrying lipids from the peripheral tissues to the liver where they are excreted or synthesized into bile acids.

Holland's vocational development theory: proposal by Holland that vocational aspirations and interests are the expression of an individual's personality.

Home health services: services provided to older adults who are ill or disabled but are able to maintain an independent life in the community.

Hormone: chemical messenger produced by the endocrine system.

Hormone replacement therapy (HRT): therapeutic administration of lower doses of estrogen than in ERT, along with progestin to reduce the cancer risk associated with ERT.

Hospice: a site or program that provides medical and supportive services for dying patients and their families and friends.

Hypertension: blood pressure that is chronically greater than or equal to the value of 140 mm Hg systolic pressure and 90 mm Hg diastolic pressure.

Identity: a composite of the individual's self-representations in biological, psychological, and social domains.

Identity accommodation: the process through which changes occur in the individual's view of the self.

Identity Achievement versus Identity Diffusion: stage in Erikson's psychosocial development theory in which the individual attempts to establish a sense of self.

Identity assimilation: the process through which individuals interpret new experiences relevant to the self in terms of their existing self-schemas or identities.

Identity process theory: theoretical perspective describing interactions between the individual and experiences.

Immune senescence: term used to refer to features of the aging immune system.

Impaired aging: processes that result from diseases that do not occur in all individuals.

Implicit memory: recall of information acquired unintentionally.

Independent variable: the variable that explains or "causes" the range of scores in the dependent variable.

Information processing: perspective in psychology in which cognitive functioning of humans is regarded as comparable to the functioning of a computer.

Informed consent: written agreement to participate in research based on knowing what that participation will involve.

Inhibitory deficit hypothesis: proposal that aging involves a reduction in the cognitive resources available for controlling or inhibiting attention.

Interactionist model: view that genetics and environments interact in complex ways and that the individual actively participates in his or her development through reciprocal relations with the environment.

Intergenerational solidarity model: model proposing six dimensions that characterize the cohesiveness of adult child–parent relationships.

Inter-individual differences: differences between individuals in developmental processes.

Intermediate care facility: treatment site in which health-related services are provided to individuals who do not require hospital or skilled nursing facility care but do require institutional care above the level of room and board.

Interpersonal therapy (IPT): form of psychotherapy integrating cognitive methods with a focus on social factors that contribute to psychological disturbance.

Intimacy versus Isolation: stage in Erikson's psychosocial development theory in which the individual attempts to establish an intimate relationship with another adult.

Intra-individual differences (also called multidirectionality of development): differences within individuals in developmental processes.

Intrinsic factors: aspects of a job inherent in the work itself.

Korsakoff syndrome: a form of dementia that occurs when there is a deficiency of vitamin B1 (thiamine).

Labor force: all civilians in the over-16 population who are living outside of institutions and who have or are actively seeking employment.

Laboratory study: a research method in which participants are tested in a systematic fashion using standardized procedures.

Late-onset familial Alzheimer's disease: inherited form of Alzheimer's disease that starts at the age of 60 or 65 years.

Late-onset schizophrenia: form of schizophrenia that can occur among adults over the age of 45 years.

Legitimization of biography: process in which older or dying individuals attempt to gain perspective on the events in their past lives.

Lewy bodies: tiny spherical structures consisting of deposits of protein found in dying nerve cells in damaged regions deep within the brains of people with Parkinson's disease.

Life course perspective: theoretical model in social gerontology that emphasizes the importance of age-based norms, roles, and attitudes as influences that shape events throughout development.

Life expectancy: the average number of years of life remaining to the people born within a similar period of time.

Life review: a time of taking stock through reminiscence or a mental reliving of events from the long-ago past.

Life review therapy: psychological intervention intended to help an older adult rework past experiences with the goal of gaining greater acceptance of previous life events.

Life satisfaction: the cognitive evaluation of one's life circumstances.

Life span: maximum length of life set by biological limits.

Life span perspective: the understanding of development as continuous from childhood through old age.

Life story: process through which individuals develop a narrative view of their lives that emphasizes the positive.

Life structure: basic pattern or design of an individual's life at a particular point in time.

Living will or advance directive (AD): written statement by an individual concerning preferred treatment should he or she require medical or surgical treatment to prolong life.

Logistic regression: method in which researchers test the likelihood of an individual receiving a score on a discrete yes–no variable.

Longitudinal: developmental research design in which the same people are compared at different ages.

Long-term memory: repository of information that is held for a period of time ranging from several minutes to a lifetime.

Major depressive disorder: mood disorder characterized by feelings of extreme sadness, appetite and sleep disturbances, feelings of guilt and a low sense of self-worth for at least 2 weeks.

Manic episode: period during which an individual feels unduly elated, grandiose, expansive, and energetic.

Marriage: legally sanctioned union between a man and a woman as traditionally defined.

Maturation hypothesis: proposal that the Cluster B or "immature" personality types (borderline, histrionic, narcissistic, and antisocial) improve or at least are more treatable in older adults.

Mechanics of intelligence: cognitive operations of speed, working memory, and fluid intelligence.

Mechanistic model: view in which "nurture" or the environment is regarded as the prime mover in development.

Medicaid: a federal and state matching entitlement program that pays for medical assistance for certain individuals and families with low incomes and resources.

Medicare: Title XVIII of the Social Security Act entitled Health Insurance for the Aged and Disabled.

Medicare Part A (Hospital Insurance or HI): coverage of inpatient hospitalization and related services.

Medicare Part B (Supplementary Medical Insurance (SMI)): medical benefits to individuals age 65 and over with payment of a monthly premium.

Medicare Part C (Medicare + Choice program): additional medical insurance available for purchase through Medicare.

Medicare Part D: subsidy for prescription drug privileges.

Memantine: Alzheimer's disease medication that operates on the glumatate system.

Memory controllability: beliefs about the effects of the aging process on memory.

Menopause: the point in a woman's life when menstruation stops permanently.

Metabolic syndrome: a clinical condition involving high levels of abdominal obesity, abnormal levels of blood cholesterol, hypertension, insulin resistance, high triglycerides, high levels of C-reactive proteins in the blood, and the presence of coronary plaques.

Midlife crisis: term that originated in the early 1970s as a description of the radical changes in personality that supposedly accompanied entry into the midpoint of life.

Mild cognitive impairment (MCI): a subtle loss of memory and learning abilities.

Modernization hypothesis: the view that ageism is associated with a society's increasing urbanization and industrialization.

Mood disorders: psychological disorders involving abnormalities in the individual's experience of emotion.

Mortality data: statistics derived from death.

Most Efficient Design: framework originated by Schaie to organize the collection of sequential data.

Motivational crowding out: the idea that extrinsic rewards crowd out intrinsic satisfaction.

Multidimensionality: the principle that there are multiple processes in development.

Multidirectionality of development: the principle that not all systems develop at the same rate within the person—some functions may show positive changes and others negative changes over time. Even within the same function, the same individual may show gains in one area, losses in another, and stability in yet a third domain.

Multi-infarct dementia or MID: most common form of vascular dementia, caused by transient ischemic attacks.

Multiple jeopardy hypothesis: the proposal that older adults who fit more than one discriminated-against category are affected by biases against each of these categorizations.

Multiple regression analysis: multivariate correlational research design in which a set of variables are used to predict scores on another variable.

Multiple threshold model: theoretical perspective proposing that personal recognition of aging occurs in a stepwise process across the years of adulthood.

Multivariate correlational design: research design that involves the analysis of relationships among multiple variables.

Mutations: alterations in genes that lead to changes in their functions.

Myocardial infarction: acute form of cardiovascular disease that occurs when the blood supply to part of the heart muscle (the myocardium) is severely reduced or blocked.

Need complementarity hypothesis: the proposal that people seek and are more satisfied with marital partners who are the opposite of themselves.

NEO Personality Inventory-Revised (NEO-PI-R): chief measure used to assess an individual's personality according to the Five Factor Model.

Neurofibrillary tangles: tangled fibers within neurons.

Neuroleptics: medications intended to reduce psychotic symptoms by altering dopamine activity.

Neuronal fallout model: view of the aging nervous system as involving progressive loss of brain tissue across the adult years that is noticeable by the age of 30.

Niche-picking: the notion that a child's genetically based abilities lead that child to select certain activities that further enhance the development of those abilities.

Nonnormative influences: random, chance factors that occur due to a combination of coincidence, the impact of earlier decisions on later events, and relationships with other people.

Normal aging: changes built into the hard wiring of the organism that occur more or less in all individuals (although at different rates) and are distinct from those changes associated with disease.

Normal pressure hydrocephalus: reversible form of dementia that can cause cognitive impairment, dementia, urinary incontinence, and difficulty in walking.

Normative age-graded influences: the influences on life that are linked to chronological age and associated with a society's expectations for people of a given age.

Normative history-graded influences: influences that transcend the individual's life and are associated with changes in a given culture or geopolitical unit as a whole.

Nursing home: a residence that provides a room, meals, skilled nursing and rehabilitative care, medical services, and protective supervision.

Nursing Home Reform Act (NHRA): U.S. federal legislation passed in 1987 which mandated that facilities must meet physical standards, provide adequate professional staffing and services, and maintain policies governing the administrative and medical procedures of the nursing facility.

Observational method: a research method in which conclusions are drawn about behavior through careful and systematic examination in particular settings.

Obsessive-compulsive disorder: a form of anxiety disorder in which individuals suffer from obsessions (repetitive thoughts) and compulsions (repetitive behaviors).

Occupational Information Network (O*NET): online interactive national database of occupations intended for purposes of job classification, training, and vocational counseling.

Occupational reinforcement patterns (ORPs): the work values and needs likely to be reinforced or satisfied by a particular occupation.

Old age style: an approach to one's art that eliminates the fine details and instead presents the essence of the work's intended meaning.

Old-old: portion of the over-65 population ages 75 to 84.

Oldest-old: portion of the over-65 population ages 85 and older.

Optimal aging (also called "successful aging"): avoidance of changes that would otherwise occur with age through preventative and compensatory strategies.

Orderly careers: occupations held by an individual that are logically connected.

Organismic model: view in which "nature" or genetics is regarded as the prime mover in development.

Osteoarthritis: a painful, degenerative joint disease that often involves the hips, knees, neck, lower back, or the small joints of the hands.

Osteoporosis: loss of bone mineral content of more than 2.5 standard deviations below the mean of young white, non-Hispanic women.

Overtreatment: the provision of aggressive care in cases where terminally ill patients express a preference for comfort only.

Palliative care: comfort care to dying individuals through measures such as pain control.

Panic disorder: anxiety disorder involving the experience of panic attacks.

Paradox of well-being: proposal that despite their objective difficulties, people in later life feel good about themselves and their situations.

Parkinson's disease: progressive neurological disorder causing motor disturbances, including tremors (shaking at rest), speech impediments, slowing of movement, muscular rigidity, shuffling gait, and postural instability or the inability to maintain balance.

Patient Self-Determination Act (PSDA): legislation affecting all organizations receiving Medicare or Medicaid guaranteeing the right of all competent adults to write a living will or advance directive (AD).

Perimenopause: three- to five-year span during which women gradually lose their reproductive ability.

Peripheral ties: friendships that persist but are not characterized by a high degree of closeness.

Persistent vegetative state: condition in which the subcortical areas of the brain remain intact and therefore are able to regulate basic bodily functions, including sleep–wake cycles, but the individual lacks conscious awareness.

Personal aging: changes occurring over time within the individual, also referred to as ontogenetic change.

Personality disorders: disorders thought to reflect a disturbance within the basic personality structure of the individual.

Perspective: a proposal that presents a position or set of ideas to account for a set of processes; less formal than a theory.

Photoaging: age changes caused by exposure to the sun's harmful radiation.

Physician-assisted suicide: situation in which a physician provides the means for a terminally ill patient to complete suicide.

Pick's disease: form of dementia that involves severe atrophy of the frontal and temporal lobes.

Plasticity: the proposal that the course of development may be altered depending on the nature of the specific interactions of the individual in the environment.

Plasticity model: view of the aging nervous system which proposes that although some neurons die, the remaining ones continue to develop.

Plateauing: the attainment of a point in one's career where further hierarchical advancement is unlikely.

Polypharmacy: condition in which the individual takes multiple drugs, sometimes without knowledge of the physician.

Possible selves: views of the self that guide the choice and pursuit of future endeavors.

Postformal operations: proposed stage following formal operations referring to the way that adults structure their thinking over and beyond that of the adolescent.

Post-traumatic stress disorder (PTSD): anxiety disorder in which an individual suffers prolonged effects of exposure to a traumatic experience.

Pragmatics of intelligence: application of a person's abilities to the solution of real-life problems.

Presbycusis: age-related hearing loss due to degenerative changes in the cochlea or auditory nerve leading from the cochlea to the brain.

Presbyopia: age-related change in the eye involving loss of accommodative power of the crystalline lens resulting in loss of the ability to focus on near objects.

Presenilin genes (PS1 and PS2): PS1 gene, a gene that is located on chromosome 14 and accounts for up to 50 to 80% of early-onset cases; PS2 gene, a gene that is located on chromosome 1 and accounts for a much smaller percentage of early-onset familial Alzheimer's disease.

Primary aging (also called normal aging): age-related changes that are universal, intrinsic, and progressive.

Primary mental abilities: factors in intelligence proposed by Thurstone incorporating verbal meaning, word fluency, number, spatial relations, memory, perceptual speed, and general reasoning.

Primary Mental Abilities (PMA) test: test of five primary mental abilities that is the basis for the Seattle Longitudinal Study data.

Procedural memory: knowledge of how to perform certain activities.

Prospective memory: recall of events to be performed in the future.

Protean career: a career in which the person has determination over his or her career path.

Proximal social relational level: level of interaction in the ecological perspective involving the individual's relationships with significant others, peers, and nuclear families.

Pseudodementia: cognitive symptoms of depression that appear to be dementia.

Psychological age: the age of the individual based on psychological measures such as intelligence, memory, and learning ability.

Psychological disorder: a condition that significantly alters the individual's adaptation.

Psychomotor speed: amount of time it takes a person to process a signal, prepare a response, and then execute that response.

Psychopathy: a set of traits thought to lie at the core of antisocial personality disorder.

Psychosocial: term used by Erikson to refer to developmental processes that involve a combination of psychological and social forces.

Psychotherapeutic medications: substances that by their chemical nature alter the individual's brain structure or function.

Quasi-experimental design: a research method in which groups are compared on predetermined characteristics.

Race: a biological term for classifications within species based on physical and structural characteristics.

Reaction time: time calculated for an individual to study a stimulus array and then respond when that stimulus array takes a certain form.

Reciprocal nature of development: the principle that people both influence and are influenced by the events in their lives.

Recycling: process in which workers change their main field of career activity part way into occupational life and reexperience the early career development stages.

Reliability: the consistency of a measurement procedure.

Religion: an individual's identification with an organized belief system.

Remote memory: recall of information from the distant past.

Replicative senescence: the loss of the ability to reproduce.

Reserve capacity: additional abilities possessed by older adults that are normally untapped.

Residential care facility: treatment site that provides 24-hour supportive care services and supervision to individuals not requiring skilled nursing care.

Resource model: proposal that adaptation even to difficult retirement transitions can be facilitated by having sufficient biological, psychological, and social resources.

Retirement: the withdrawal of an individual in later life from the labor force.

Retrograde amnesia: inability to remember events from the past.

Reversible dementias: loss of cognitive functioning due to the presence of a medical condition that affects but does not destroy brain tissue.

RIASEC model: Holland's vocational development theory, which proposes that there are six facets of vocational interests and environments: Realistic (R), Investigative (I), Artistic (A), Social (S), Enterprising (E), and Conventional (C).

Role reversal: discredited belief that parents and their adult children switch responsibilities.

Role strain: model proposing that work and family involvement are inversely related, so that the higher the person's involvement in his or her work role, the lower the individual's involvement in the family.

Role theory: proposal that normative expectations for behavior provide a major source of fulfillment because they integrate the individual with society.

Sandwich generation: popular term used to refer to women with aging parents needing help and teenage children living in the home.

Sarcopenia: progressive loss of muscle mass.

Schema: term used by Piaget to refer to the individual's existing mental structures.

Schizophrenia: severe form of psychopathology involving a wide range of unusual symptoms affecting thought, language, motivation, and the expression of emotion.

Secondary aging (also called impaired aging): changes in later life that are due to disease.

Secondary mental abilities: the broad constructs that underlie specific abilities.

Secretases: enzymes that snip proteins such as amyloid precursor protein.

Selective attrition: loss of respondents over time in a longitudinal study.

Selective optimization with compensation: the principle that adults attempt to preserve and maximize the abilities that are of central importance and put less effort into maintaining those that are not.

Self-determination theory: view that intrinsic motivation plays a central role in occupational satisfaction but that certain forms of extrinsic motivation can also have intrinsic components.

Self-Directed Search (SDS): self-administered and self-scored test based on Holland's vocational development theory.

Semantic memory: equivalent to "knowledge" and includes the words and definitions of words found in one's vocabulary or storehouse of historical facts.

Sequential designs: developmental research design in which the researcher conducts a sequence of cross-sectional or longitudinal studies.

Set point perspective: proposal that biologically determined temperament sets the boundaries for the levels of well-being an individual experiences throughout life.

Similarity hypothesis: the proposal that similarity and perceived similarity predict interpersonal attraction.

Skilled nursing facility: treatment site that provides the most intensive nursing care available outside of a hospital.

Skip generation family: family in which children are living with grandparents and no parents are present.

Sleep apnea: condition in which the individual experiences a particular form of snoring in which a partial obstruction in the back of the throat restricts airflow during inhalation.

Social age: the age of the individual based on occupying certain social roles, including within the family, work, and possibly the community.

Social aging: changes in people that occur along with or perhaps as the result of historical change.

Social clock: the normative expectations for the ages at which major life events should occur.

Social-cognitive: form of psychotherapy involving attempts to raise a client's sense of self-efficacy by enabling the client to have step-like increments in success at completing a previously unattainable goal.

Social comparison: process through which individuals look at the situations of others who are more unfortunate than they are and comfort themselves with the thought that things could be worse.

Social death: situation in which the dying are treated as nonpersons by family or health care workers as they are left to spend their final months or years in the hospital or nursing home.

Social exchange theory: proposal that relationships continue when partners perceive that the rewards of remaining in the relationship outweigh the rewards associated with alternatives.

Social indicator model: proposal that demographic and social structural variables account for individual differences in levels of well-being.

Social phobia: a form of anxiety disorder that applies to situations in which people must perform some action in front of others.

Social Security Act: law passed by Congress in 1935 that provided retirement income for older adults.

Sociocultural level: level of interaction in the ecological perspective involving relations with the larger social institutions of educational, public policy, governmental, and economic systems.

Socioeconomic status (or social class): an index of a person's position in society based on level of education and level of occupation.

Socioemotional selectivity theory: proposition that, throughout adulthood, individuals reduce the range of their relationships to maximize social and emotional gains and minimize risks.

Somatopause of aging: age-related decline in the somatotrophic axis (GH and IGF-1) of the endocrine system.

Source memory (source monitoring): recall of where information was heard or seen.

Specific phobia: an irrational fear of a particular object or situation.

Spillover model: proposal regarding work and family roles that attitudes and behaviors from one role carry over into the other.

Stages of dying: denial, anger, bargaining, depression, and acceptance.

Stereotype threat: our tendency to perform in ways consistent with negative stereotypes of the group to which we belong.

Strong Vocational Interest Inventory (SVII): test in which respondents indicate their preferences for occupations, topics of study, activities, and types of people.

Structural equation modeling: multivariate correlational research in which a set of relationships among variables are tested to determine whether the variables provide a good fit to the data.

Subdural hematoma: blood clot that creates pressure on brain tissue.

Subjective well-being: psychological state composed of positive affect, negative affect, and life satisfaction.

Subsidized senior housing: form of housing provided for individuals with low to moderate incomes.

Successful aging: term used to reflect the ability of an older person to adapt to the aging process.

Successful intelligence: the ability to achieve success in life according to one's personal standards and in the framework of one's sociocultural context.

Supercentenarians: people over the age of 110 years.

Super's self-concept theory: proposal that career development is a process driven by the individual's desire to achieve full realization of his or her self-concept in work that will allow the self-concept to be expressed.

Survey: a research method that involves asking people to provide answers to structured questions, with the intention of generalizing to larger populations.

Sustained attention: measure in which efficient performance depends on the ability to make a quick response even after a long delay of waiting for the target to appear.

Swan song phenomenon: a brief renewal of creativity that can stimulate the creation of new works and a new style of work.

Tau: protein that seems to play a role in maintaining the stability of the microtubules that form the internal support structure of the axons.

Telomere: the terminal region or tail of a chromosome that is made up of DNA but contains no genetic information.

Terror Management Theory: social-psychological perspective proposing that people regard the thought of the finitude of their lives with panic and dread.

Testing the limits: method developed by Baltes and his coworkers to determine how much the performance of older adults can be increased through training.

Theory of multiple intelligences: proposal that there are eight independent categories of intelligence, each of which can contribute to an individual's ability to adapt to the world.

Time of measurement: the year or period in which testing has occurred.

Tinnitus: condition in which the individual perceives sounds in the head or ear (such as a ringing noise) when there is no external source for it.

Trait: a stable, enduring attribute that characterizes one element of an individual's personality.

Transient ischemic attack (TIA) (also called a ministroke): a condition caused by the development of clots in the cerebral arteries.

Transition to parenthood: the period in which a first child is born to the parents.

Triarchic theory of intelligence: proposal that there are three aspects to intelligence: componential, experiential, and contextual.

Two-factor theory: theory of work motivation developed by Herzberg proposing that the intrinsic features of a job are motivators and the extrinsic features of a job are hygiene factors.

Type A behavior pattern: a collection of traits thought to increase a person's risk of developing cardiovascular disease.

Validity: the extent to which a test measures what it is supposed to measure.

Vascular dementia: progressive loss of cognitive functioning that occurs as the result of damage to the arteries supplying the brain.

Vertigo: a sense of movement when the body is actually at rest, usually the sense that one is spinning.

Vocation: pursuit of an occupation.

Vocational satisfaction: the extent to which the worker has positive views of the job or aspects of a job.

Wechsler Adult Intelligence Scale (WAIS): test of intelligence with Verbal and Performance scales.

Wernicke's disease: an acute condition involving delirium, eye movement disturbances, difficulties maintaining balance and movement, and deterioration of nerves to the hands and feet.

White matter hyperintensities: abnormalities in the brain thought to be made up of parts of deteriorating neurons.

Widowhood effect: the fact that there is a greater probability of death in those who have become widowed.

Wisdom: as defined by Baltes, a form of expert knowledge in the pragmatics of life.

Working memory: system that keeps information temporarily available and active while the information is being used in other cognitive tasks.

Young-old: portion of the over-65 population ages 65 to 74.

Aartsen, M. J., Smits, C. H., van Tilburg, T., Knipscheer, K. C., & Deeg, D. J. (2002). Activity in older adults: Cause or consequence of cognitive functioning? A longitudinal study on everyday activities and cognitive performance in older adults. *Journals of Gerontology Series B: Psychological Sciences and Social Sciences, 57*, P153–162.

Aartsen, M. J., Van Tilburg, T., Smits, C. H., Comijs, H. C., & Knipscheer, K. C. (2005). Does widowhood affect memory performance of older persons? *Psychological Medicine, 35*, 217–226.

Abeles, N., Cooley, S., Deitch, I., Harper, M. S., Hinrichsen, G., Lopez, M., et al. (1997). *What practitioners should know about working with older adults.* Washington DC: American Psychological Association.

Abrams, R. C., & Horowitz, S. V. (1999). Personality disorders after age 50: A meta-analytic review of the literature. In E. Rosowsky, R. C. Abrams, & R. A. Zweig (Eds.), *Personality disorders in older adults: Emerging issues in diagnosis and treatment* (pp. 55–68). Mahwah, NJ: Erlbaum.

Achem, S. R., & Devault, K. R. (2005). Dysphagia in aging. *Journal of Clinical Gastroenterology, 39*, 357–371.

Achenbaum, W. A. (1978). *Old age in the new land: The American experience since 1970.* Baltimore, MD: Johns Hopkins University Press.

Acierno, R., Hernandez, M. A., Amstadter, A. B., Resnick, H. S., Steve, K., Muzzy, W., . . . Kilpatrick, D. G. (2010). Prevalence and correlates of emotional, physical, sexual, and financial abuse and potential neglect in the United States: The National Elder Mistreatment Study. *American Journal of Public Health, 100*, 292–297.

Adams-Price, C. (1998). Aging, writing, and creativity. In C. Adams-Price (Ed.), *Creativity and successful aging: Theoretical and empirical approaches* (pp. 289–310). New York, NY: Springer.

Adams, R. G., & Blieszner, R. (1994). An integrative conceptual framework for friendship research. *Journal of Social and Personal Relationships, 11*, 163–184.

Adler, N. E., Boyce, T., Chesney, M. A., Cohen, S., Folkman, S., Kahn, R. L., . . . Syme, S. L. (1994). Socioeconomic status and health: The challenge of the gradient. *American Psychologist, 49*, 15–24.

Administration on Aging. (2009). A profile of older Americans: 2009. Retrieved from http://www.aoa.gov/AoARoot/Aging_Statistics/Profile/2009/8.aspx.

Aimoni, C., Bianchini, C., Borin, M., Ciorba, A., Fellin, R., Martini, A., . . . Volpato, S. (2010). Diabetes, cardiovascular risk factors and idiopathic sudden sensorineural hearing loss: A case-control study. *Audiology and Neurotology, 15*, 111–115.

Ainsworth, M., Blehar, M., Waters, E., & Wall, S. (1978). *Patterns of attachment: A psychological study of the strange situation.* Hillsdale, NJ: Erlbaum.

Akbaraly, T. N., Kivimaki, M., Shipley, M. J., Tabak, A. G., Jokela, M., Virtanen, M., . . . Singh-Manoux, A. (2010). Metabolic syndrome over 10 years and cognitive functioning in late midlife: The Whitehall II study. *Diabetes Care, 33*, 84–89.

Akbaraly, T. N., Singh-Manoux, A., Marmot, M. G., & Brunner, E. J. (2009). Education attenuates the association between dietary patterns and cognition. *Dementia and Geriatric Cognitive Disorders, 27*, 147–154.

Akiyama, A., Numata, K., & Mikami, H. (2010). Importance of end-of-life support to minimize caregiver's regret during bereavement of the elderly for better subsequent adaptation to bereavement. *Archives of Gerontology and Geriatrics, 50*, 175–178.

Alameel, T., Andrew, M. K., & Macknight, C. (2010). The association of fecal incontinence with institutionalization and mortality in older adults. *American Journal of Gastroenterology.* Retrieved from http://www.ncbi.nlm.nih.gov/entrez/query.fcgi?cmd=Retrieve&db=PubMed&dopt=Citation&list_uids=20216537 doi:ajg2010 77 [pii] 10.1038/ajg.2010.77.

Aldwin, C. M., & Gilmer, D. F. (1999). Health and optimal aging. In J. C. Cavanaugh & S. K. Whitbourne (Eds.), *Gerontology: Interdisciplinary perspectives* (pp. 123–154). New York, NY: Oxford University Press.

Alexandersen, P., Karsdal, M. A., & Christiansen, C. (2009). Long-term prevention with hormone-replacement therapy after the menopause: Which women should be targeted? *Womens Health (Lond Engl), 5*, 637–647.

Alexopoulos, G. S., Reynolds, C. F., III, Bruce, M. L., Katz, I. R., Raue, P. J., Mulsant, B. H., . . . Ten Have, T. (2009). Reducing suicidal ideation and depression in older primary care patients: 24-month outcomes of the PROSPECT study. *American Journal of Psychiatry, 166*, 882–890.

Allaire, J. C., & Marsiske, M. (2002). Well- and ill-defined measures of everyday cognition: Relationship to older adults' intellectual ability and functional status. *Psychology and Aging, 17,* 101–115.

Allegri, R. F., Glaser, F. B., Taragano, F. E., & Buschke, H. (2008). Mild cognitive impairment: Believe it or not? *International Review of Psychiatry, 20,* 357–363.

Allen, J. R., Whittlesey, S., Pfefferbaum, B., & Ondersma, M. L. (1999). Community and coping of mothers and grandmothers of children killed in a human-caused disaster. *Psychiatric Annals, 29,* 85–91.

Allen, K. R., Blieszner, R., & Roberto, K. A. (2000). Families in the middle and later years: A review and critique of research in the 1990s. *Journal of Marriage and Family, 62,* 911–926.

Allen, K. R., & Walker, A. J. (2000). Qualitative research. In C. Hendrick & S. S. Hendrick (Eds.), *Close relationships* (pp. 19–30). Thousand Oaks, CA: Sage.

Allen, P. D., Nelson, H. W., & Netting, F. E. (2007). Current practice and policy realities revisited: Undertrained nursing home social workers in the U.S. *Social Work Health Care, 45,* 1–22.

Almeida, O. P., Calver, J., Jamrozik, K., Hankey, G. J., & Flicker, L. (2009). Obesity and metabolic syndrome increase the risk of incident depression in older men: The health in men study. *American Journal of Geriatric Psychiatry, 17,* 889–898.

Alonso-Fernandez, P., Puerto, M., Mate, I., Ribera, J. M., & de la Fuente, M. (2008). Neutrophils of centenarians show function levels similar to those of young adults. *Journal of the American Geriatrics Society, 56,* 2244–2251.

Alsantali, A., & Shapiro, J. (2009). Androgens and hair loss. *Current Opinions in Endocrinology, Diabetes, and Obesity, 16,* 246–253.

Alzheimer's Association. (2010). 2010 Alzheimer's disease facts and figures. Retrieved from http://www.alz.org/national/documents/report_alzfactsfigures2009.pdf.

Amara, C. E., Marcinek, D. J., Shankland, E. G., Schenkman, K. A., Arakaki, L. S., & Conley, K. E. (2008). Mitochondrial function in vivo: Spectroscopy provides window on cellular energetics. *Methods, 46,* 312–318.

Amato, P. R. (2000). The consequences of divorce for adults and children. *Journal of Marriage and Family, 62,* 511–521.

Amato, P. R., & Afifi, T. D. (2006). Feeling caught between parents: Adult children's relations with parents and subjective well-being. *Journal of Marriage and Family, 68,* 222–235.

American Cancer Society. (2009). Estimated new cancer cases for selected cancer sites by state, US, 2009.

American Medical Association. (1997). Caring to the end: Conscientious end-of-life care can reduce concerns about care of the terminally ill. *American Medical News.*

American Psychiatric Association. (2000). *DSM-IV: Diagnostic and Statistical Manual of Mental Disorders Text Revision.* Washington, DC: American Psychiatric Association.

American Psychological Association. (2003). Ethical Principles of Psychologists and Code of Conduct. Retrieved from http://www.apa.org/ethics/code2002.html#8_02.

American Psychological Association. (2004). Guidelines for Psychological Practice with Older Adults. *American Psychologist, 59,* 336–265.

Amore, M., Tagariello, P., Laterza, C., & Savoia, E. M. (2007). Beyond nosography of depression in elderly. *Archives of Gerontology and Geriatrics, 44 Suppl 1,* 13–22.

An, J. S., & Cooney, T. M. (2006). Psychological well-being in mid to late life: The role of generativity development and parent-child relationships across the lifespan. *International Journal of Behavioral Development, 30,* 410–421.

Ancoli-Israel, S., & Cooke, J. R. (2005). Prevalence and comorbidity of insomnia and effect on functioning in elderly populations. *Journal of the American Geriatrics Society, 53,* S264–S271.

Andreoletti, C., Veratti, B. W., & Lachman, M. E. (2006). Age differences in the relationship between anxiety and recall. *Aging and Mental Health, 10,* 265–271.

Andrew, M. K., Freter, S. H., & Rockwood, K. (2006). Prevalence and outcomes of delirium in community and non-acute care settings in people without dementia: A report from the Canadian Study of Health and Aging. *BMC Medicine, 4,* 15.

Angelucci, L. (2000). The glucocorticoid hormone: From pedestal to dust and back. *European Journal of Pharmacology, 405,* 139–147.

Anger, J. T., Saigal, C. S., & Litwin, M. S. (2006). The prevalence of urinary incontinence among community dwelling adult women: Results from the National Health and Nutrition Examination Survey. *Journal of Urology, 175,* 601–604.

Anthoney, S. F., & Armstrong, P. I. (2010). Individuals and environments: Linking ability and skill ratings with interests. *Journal of Counseling Psychology, 57,* 36–51.

Antonini, F. M., Magnolfi, S. U., Petruzzi, E., Pinzani, P., Malentacchi, F., Petruzzi, I., . . . Masotti, G. (2008). Physical performance and creative activities of centenarians. *Archives of Gerontology and Geriatrics, 46,* 253–261.

Aoi, W. (2009). Exercise and food factors. *Forum in Nutrition, 61,* 147–155.

Archer, N., Brown, R. G., Reeves, S., Boothby, H., Lovestone, S., & Nicholas, H. (2009). Midlife neuroticism and the age of onset of Alzheimer's disease. *Psychological Medicine, 39,* 665–673.

Ardelt, M. (2004). Wisdom as expert knowledge system: A critical review of a contemporary operationalization of an ancient concept. *Human Development, 47,* 257–285.

Arean, P. A., & Ayalon, L. (2005). Assessment and treatment of depressed older adults in primary care. *Clinical Psychology: Science and Practice, 12,* 321–335.

Aries, P. (1974). *Western attitudes toward death: From the middle ages to the present.* Baltimore: Johns Hopkins University Press.

Aries, P. (1981). *The hour of our death.* New York, NY: Knopf.

Armstrong-Stassen, M. (2001). Reactions of older employees to organizational downsizing: The role of gender, job level, and time. *Journals of Gerontology Series B: Psychological Sciences and Social Sciences, 56*, P234–P243.

Armstrong-Stassen, M., & Ursel, N. D. (2009). Perceived organizational support, career satisfaction, and the retention of older workers. *Journal of Occupational and Organizational Psychology, 82*, 201–220.

Armstrong, P. I., & Anthoney, S. F. (2009). Personality facets and RIASEC interests: An integrated model. *Journal of Vocational Behavior, 75*, 346–359.

Arnett, J. J. (2000). Emerging adulthood: A theory of development from the late teens through the twenties. *American Psychologist, 55*, 469–480.

Arnold, J. T., Liu, X., Allen, J. D., Le, H., McFann, K. K., & Blackman, M. R. (2007). Androgen receptor or estrogen receptor-beta blockade alters DHEA-, DHT-, and E(2)-induced proliferation and PSA production in human prostate cancer cells. *Prostate, 67*, 1152–1162.

Artistico, D., Cervone, D., & Pezzuti, L. (2003). Perceived self-efficacy and everyday problem solving among young and older adults. *Psychology & Aging, 18*, 68–79.

Atchley, R. C. (1989). A continuity theory of normal aging. *Gerontologist, 29*, 183–190.

Atchley, R. C. (2000). *Social forces and aging* (9th ed.). Belmont, CA: Wadsworth/Thomson Learning.

Austin, J. T., & Vancouver, J. F. (1996). Goal constructs in psychology: Structure, process, and content. *Psychological Bulletin, 120*, 338–375.

Avagyan, H., Goldenson, B., Tse, E., Masoumi, A., Porter, V., Wiedau-Pazos, M., . . . Fiala, M. (2009). Immune blood biomarkers of Alzheimer disease patients. *Journal of Neuroimmunology, 210*, 67–72.

Ayers, C. R., Saxena, S., Golshan, S., & Wetherell, J. L. (2010). Age at onset and clinical features of late life compulsive hoarding. *International Journal of Geriatric Psychiatry, 25*, 142–149.

Ayers, C. R., Sorrell, J. T., Thorp, S. R., & Wetherell, J. L. (2007). Evidence-based psychological treatments for late-life anxiety. *Psychology and Aging, 22*, 8–17.

Baan, R., Grosse, Y., Straif, K., Secretan, B., El Ghissassi, F., Bouvard, V., . . . Cogliano, V. (2009). A review of human carcinogens—Part F: Chemical agents and related occupations. *Lancet Oncology, 10*, 1143–1144.

Baddeley, A. (2003). Working memory: Looking back and looking forward. *Nature Reviews Neuroscience, 4*, 829–839.

Bailis, D. S., & Chipperfield, J. G. (2002). Compensating for losses in perceived personal control over health: A role for collective self-esteem in healthy aging. *Journals of Gerontology Series B: Psychological Sciences and Social Sciences, 57*, P531–P539.

Bakitas, M., Ahles, T. A., Skalla, K., Brokaw, F. C., Byock, I., Hanscom, B., . . . Hegel, M. T. (2008). Proxy perspectives regarding end-of-life care for persons with cancer. *Cancer, 112*, 1854–1861.

Bakitas, M., Lyons, K. D., Hegel, M. T., Balan, S., Brokaw, F. C., Seville, J., . . . Ahles, T. A (2009). Effects of a palliative care intervention on clinical outcomes in patients with advanced cancer: The Project ENABLE II randomized controlled trial. *Journal of the American Medical Association, 302*, 741–749.

Baliunas, D. O., Taylor, B. J., Irving, H., Roerecke, M., Patra, J., Mohapatra, S., . . . Rehm, J. (2009). Alcohol as a risk factor for Type 2 diabetes: A systematic review and meta-analysis. *Diabetes Care, 32*, 2123–2132.

Ball, K., Berch, D. B., Helmers, K. F., Jobe, J. B., Leveck, M. D., Marsiske, M., . . . Willis, S. L. (2002). Effects of cognitive training interventions with older adults: A randomized controlled trial. *Journal of the American Medical Association, 288*, 2271–2281.

Baltes, P. B. (1979). Life-span developmental psychology: Some converging observations on history and theory. In P. B. Baltes & J. O. G. Brim (Eds.), *Life-span development and behavior* (Vol. 2, pp. 255–279). New York, NY: Academic Press.

Baltes, P. B., & Baltes, M. M. (1990). Psychological perspectives on successful aging: A model of selective optimization with compensation. In P. B. Baltes & M. M. Baltes (Eds.), *Successful aging: Perspectives from the behavioral sciences* (pp. 1–34). New York, NY: Cambridge University Press.

Baltes, P. B., & Graf, P. (1996). Psychological aspects of aging: Facts and frontiers. In D. Magnusson (Ed.), *The lifespan development of individuals: Behavioral, neurobiological, and psychosocial perspectives* (pp. 427–460). New York, NY: Cambridge University Press.

Baltes, P. B., & Kliegl, R. (1992). Further testing of limits of cognitive plasticity: Negative age differences in a mnemonic skill are robust. *Developmental Psychology, 28*, 121–125.

Baltes, P. B., & Schaie, K. W. (1976). On the plasticity of intelligence in adulthood and old age: Where Horn and Donaldson fail. *American Psychologist, 31*, 720–725.

Baltes, P. B., & Smith, J. (2008). The fascination of wisdom: Its nature, ontogeny, and function. *Perspectives on Psychological Science, 3*, 56–64.

Baltes, P. B., Staudinger, U. M., Maercker, A., & Smith, J. (1995). People nominated as wise: A comparative study of wisdom-related knowledge. *Psychology and Aging, 10*, 155–166.

Banks, J., Marmot, M., Oldfield, Z., & Smith, J. P. (2006). Disease and disadvantage in the United States and in England. *Journal of the American Medical Association, 295*, 2037–2045.

Baquer, N. Z., Taha, A., Kumar, P., McLean, P., Cowsik, S. M., Kale, R. K., . . . Sharma, D. (2009). A metabolic and functional overview of brain aging linked to neurological disorders. *Biogerontology, 10*, 377–413.

Barefoot, J. C., Mortensen, E. L., Helms, M. J., Avlund, K., & Schroll, M. (2001). A longitudinal study of gender differences in depressive symptoms from age 50 to 80. *Psychology and Aging, 16*, 342–345.

Barnard, K., & Colon-Emeric, C. (2010). Extraskeletal effects of vitamin D in older adults: Cardiovascular disease, mortality, mood, and cognition. *American Journal of Geriatric Pharmacotherapy, 8*, 4–33.

Barnow, S., Linden, M., & Freyberger, H. J. (2004). The relation between suicidal feelings and mental disorders in the elderly: Results from the Berlin Aging Study (BASE). *Psychological Medicine, 34*, 741–746.

Bartels, S. J., Moak, G. S., & Dums, A. R. (2002). Mental health services in nursing homes: Models of mental health services in nursing homes: A review of the literature. *Psychiatric Services, 53*, 1390–1396.

Bartels, S. J., & Mueser, K. T. (1999). Severe mental illness in older adults: Schizophrenia and other late-life psychoses. In M. A. Smyer & S. H. Qualls (Eds.), *Aging and mental health* (pp. 182–207). Malden, MA: Blackwell.

Bartzokis, G., Beckson, M., Lu, P. H., Nuechterlein, K. H., Edwards, N., & Mintz, J. (2001). Age-related changes in frontal and temporal lobe volumes in men: A magnetic resonance imaging study. *Archives of General Psychiatry, 58*, 461–465.

Basseches, M. (1984). *Dialectical thinking and adult development.* Norwood, NJ: Ablex.

Bassett-Jones, N., & Lloyd, G. C. (2005). Does Herzberg's motivation theory have staying power? *Journal of Management Development, 24*, 929–943.

Baumeister, R. F. (1996). Self-regulation and ego threat: Motivated cognition, self deception, and destructive goal setting. In P. M. Gollwitzer & J. A. Bargh (Eds.), *The psychology of action: Linking cognition and motivation to behavior* (pp. 27–47). New York, NY: Guilford Press.

Baumeister, R. F. (1997). Identity, self-concept, and self-esteem: The self lost and found. In R. Hogan, J. A. Johnson & S. R. Briggs (Eds.), *Handbook of personality psychology* (pp. 681–710). San Diego, CA: Academic Press.

Baumeister, R. F., Bratslavsky, E., Finkenauer, C., & Vohs, K. D. (2001). Bad is stronger than good. *Review of General Psychology, 54*, 323–370.

Bazzano, L. A. (2006). The high cost of not consuming fruits and vegetables. *Journal of the American Dietetic Association, 106*, 1364–1368.

Bechtold, M., Palmer, J., Valtos, J., Iasiello, C., & Sowers, J. (2006). Metabolic syndrome in the elderly. *Current Diabetes Reports, 6*, 64–71.

Bedford, V. H., Volling, B. L., & Avioli, P. S. (2000). Positive consequences of sibling conflict in childhood and adulthood. *International Journal of Aging & Human Development, 51*, 53–69.

Beehr, T. A., Glazer, S., Nielson, N. L., & Farmer, S. J. (2000). Work and nonwork predictors of employees' retirement ages. *Journal of Vocational Behavior, 57*, 206–225.

Beer, K. R. (2006). Comparative evaluation of the safety and efficacy of botulinum toxin type A and topical creams for treating moderate-to-severe glabellar rhytids. *Dermatologic Surgery, 32*, 184–197.

Beeri, M. S., Schmeidler, J., Sano, M., Wang, J., Lally, R., Grossman, H., . . . Silverman, J. M. (2006). Age, gender, and education norms on the CERAD neuropsychological battery in the oldest old. *Neurology, 67*, 1006–1010.

Beier, M. E., & Ackerman, P. L. (2001). Current-events knowledge in adults: An investigation of age, intelligence, and nonability determinants. *Psychology and Aging, 16*, 615–628.

Beier, M. E., & Ackerman, P. L. (2005). Age, ability, and the role of prior knowledge on the acquisition of new domain knowledge: Promising results in a real-world learning environment. *Psychology and Aging, 20*, 341–355.

Belleville, S., Gilbert, B., Fontaine, F., Gagnon, L., Ménard, É., & Gauthier, S. (2006). Improvement of episodic memory in persons with mild cognitive impairment and healthy older adults: Evidence from a cognitive intervention program. *Dementia and Geriatric Cognitive Disorders, 22*, 486–499.

Bellipanni, G., Bianchi, P., Pierpaoli, W., Bulian, D., & Ilyia, E. (2001). Effects of melatonin in perimenopausal and menopausal women: A randomized and placebo controlled study. *Experimental Gerontology, 36*, 297–310.

Ben-David, B. M., & Schneider, B. A. (2009). A sensory origin for color-word Stroop effects in aging: A meta-analysis. *Neuropsychology, Development, and Cognition. Section B, Aging Neuropsychology and Cognition, 16*, 505–534.

Bengston, V. L. (2001). Beyond the nuclear family: The increasing importance of multigenerational bonds. *Journal of Marriage and Family, 63*, 1–16.

Bengtson, V. L., & Schrader, S. S. (1982). Parent-child relations. In D. J. Mangen & W. A. Peterson (Eds.), *Research instruments in social gerontology, 2*, 115–185. Minneapolis, MN: University of Minnesota Press.

Benloucif, S., Orbeta, L., Ortiz, R., Janssen, I., Finkel, S. I., Bleiberg, J., . . . Zee, P. C. (2004). Morning or evening activity improves neuropsychological performance and subjective sleep quality in older adults. *Sleep, 27*, 1542–1551.

Bennett, D. A., Schneider, J. A., Tang, Y., Arnold, S. E., & Wilson, R. S. (2006). The effect of social networks on the relation between Alzheimer's disease pathology and level of cognitive function in old people: A longitudinal cohort study. *Lancet Neurology, 5*, 406–412.

Bennett, K. M. (2006). Does marital status and marital status change predict physical health in older adults? *Psychogical Medicine, 36*, 1313–1320.

Bennett, K. M., Smith, P. T., & Hughes, G. M. (2005). Coping, depressive feelings and gender differences in late life widowhood. *Aging and Mental Health, 9*, 348–353.

Benson, N., Hulac, D. M., & Kranzler, J. H. (2010). Independent examination of the Wechsler Adult Intelligence Scale-Fourth Edition (WAIS-IV): What does the WAIS-IV measure? *Psychological Assessment, 22*, 121–130.

Berg, A. I., Hassing, L. B., McClearn, G. E., & Johansson, B. (2006). What matters for life satisfaction in the oldest-old? *Aging and Mental Health, 10*, 257–264.

Betik, A. C., & Hepple, R. T. (2008). Determinants of VO2 max decline with aging: An integrated perspective. *Applied Physiology, Nutrition, and Metabolism, 33,* 130–140.

Bharucha, A. E., & Camilleri, M. (2001). Functional abdominal pain in the elderly. *Gastroenterology Clinics of North America, 30,* 517–529.

Bhave, D. P., Kramer, A., & Glomb, T. M. (2010). Work-family conflict in work groups: Social information processing, support, and demographic dissimilarity. *Journal of Applied Psychology, 95,* 145–158.

Bherer, L., Kramer, A. F., Peterson, M. S., Colcombe, S., Erickson, K., & Becic, E. (2008). Transfer effects in task-set cost and dual-task cost after dual-task training in older and younger adults: Further evidence for cognitive plasticity in attentional control in late adulthood. *Experimental Aging Research, 34,* 188–219.

Bieman-Copland, S., & Ryan, E. B. (2001). Social perceptions of failures in memory monitoring. *Psychology and Aging, 16,* 357–361.

Binkley, N. (2009). A perspective on male osteoporosis. *Best Practices in Research on Clinical Rheumatology, 23,* 755–768.

Birditt, K. S., Rott, L. M., & Fingerman, K. L. (2009). "If you can't say anything nice, don't say anything at all": Coping with interpersonal tensions in the parent-child relationship during adulthood. *Journal of Family Psychology, 23,* 769–778.

Bischoff-Ferrari, H. A., Kiel, D. P., Dawson-Hughes, B., Orav, J. E., Li, R., Spiegelman, D., . . . Willet, W. C. (2009). Dietary calcium and serum 25-hydroxyvitamin D status in relation to BMD among U.S. adults. *Journal of Bone and Mineral Research, 24,* 935–942.

Bittman, M., England, P., Sayer, L., Folbre, N., & Matheson, G. (2003). When does gender trump money? Bargaining and time in household work. *American Journal of Sociology, 109,* 186–214.

Blake, H., Mo, P., Malik, S., & Thomas, S. (2009). How effective are physical activity interventions for alleviating depressive symptoms in older people? A systematic review. *Clinical Rehabilitation, 23,* 873–887.

Blanchet, S., Belleville, S., & Peretz, I. (2006). Episodic encoding in normal aging: Attentional resources hypothesis extended to musical material. *Aging, Neuropsychology and Cognition, 13,* 490–502.

Blazer, D. G. (2004). The psychiatric interview of older adults. *Focus, 2,* 224–235.

Blenkner, M. (1963). Social work and family relations in later life with some thoughts on filial maturity. In E. Shanas & G. F. Streib (Eds.), *Social structure and the family: Generational relations* (pp. 46–59). Englewood Cliffs, NJ: Prentice-Hall.

Blieszner, R. (2006). A lifetime of caring: Dimensions and dynamics in late-life close relationships. *Personal Relationships, 13,* 1–18.

Block, S. D., & Billings, J. A. (2005). Learning from the dying. *New England Journal of Medicine, 353,* 1313–1315.

Bloom, H. G., Ahmed, I., Alessi, C. A., Ancoli-Israel, S., Buysse, D. J., Kryger, M. H., . . . Zee, P. C. (2009). Evidence-based recommendations for the assessment and management of sleep disorders in older persons. *Journal of the American Geriatrics Society, 57,* 761–789.

Boling, M. C., Bolgla, L. A., Mattacola, C. G., Uhl, T. L., & Hosey, R. G. (2006). Outcomes of a weight-bearing rehabilitation program for patients diagnosed with patellofemoral pain syndrome. *Archives of Physical Medicine and Rehabilitation, 87,* 1428–1435.

Bonanno, G. A., Wortman, C. B., Lehman, D. R., Tweed, R. G., Haring, M., Sonnega, J., . . . Nesse, R. M. (2002). Resilience to loss and chronic grief: A prospective study from preloss to 18-months postloss. *Journal of Personality & Social Psychology, 83,* 1150–1164.

Bonanno, G. A., Wortman, C. B., & Nesse, R. M. (2004). Prospective patterns of resilience and maladjustment during widowhood. *Psychology and Aging, 19,* 260–271.

Bonnefond, A., Härmä, M., Hakola, T., Sallinen, M., Kandolin, I., & Virkkala, J. (2006). Interaction of age with shift-related sleep-wakefulness, sleepiness, performance, and social life. *Experimental Aging Research, 32,* 185–208.

Borges, R., Temido, P., Sousa, L., Azinhais, P., Conceicao, P., Pereira, B., . . . Sobral, F. (2009). Metabolic syndrome and sexual (dys)function. *Journal of Sexual Medicine, 6,* 2958–2975.

Bortz, W. M. (2005). Biological basis of determinants of health. *American Journal of Public Health, 95,* 389–392.

Botwinick, J. (1977). Intellectual abilities. In J. E. Birren & K. W. Schaie (Eds.), *Handbook of the psychology of aging* (pp. 580–605). New York, NY: Van Nostrand Reinhold.

Bouchard, T. J. J. (2004). Genetic influence on human psychological traits: A survey. *Current Directions in Psychological Science, 13,* 148–151.

Boudreau, J. W., Boswell, W. R., & Judge, T. A. (2001). Effects of personality on executive career success in the United States and Europe. *Journal of Vocational Behavior, 58,* 53–81.

Boult, C., Green, A. F., Boult, L. B., Pacala, J. T., Snyder, C., & Leff, B. (2009). Successful models of comprehensive care for older adults with chronic conditions: Evidence for the Institute of Medicine's "retooling for an aging America" report. *Journal of the American Geriatrics Society, 57,* 2328–2337.

Boustani, M., Baker, M. S., Campbell, N., Munger, S., Hui, S. L., Castelluccio, P., . . . Callahan, C. (2010). Impact and recognition of cognitive impairment among hospitalized elders. *Journal of Hospital Medicine, 5,* 69–75.

Bowlby, J. (1969). *Attachment and loss: Attachment.* New York, NY: Basic Books.

Bowlby, J. (1973). *Attachment and loss: Separation, anxiety and anger.* New York, NY: Basic Books.

Bowlby, J. (1980). *Attachment and loss: Vol. 3. Loss: Sadness and depression.* London, England: Hogarth.

Bowling, A., Banister, D., Sutton, S., Evans, O., & Windsor, J. (2002). A multidimensional model of the quality of life in older age. *Aging and Mental Health, 6,* 355–371.

Bowman, K. W., & Singer, P. A. (2001). Chinese seniors' perspectives on end-of-life decisions. *Social Science and Medicine, 53*, 455–464.

Bowman, R. E. (2005). Stress-induced changes in spatial memory are sexually differentiated and vary across the lifespan. *Journal of Neuroendocrinology, 17*, 526–535.

Boylan, S., Welch, A., Pikhart, H., Malyutina, S., Pajak, A., Kubinova, R., ... Bobak, M. (2009). Dietary habits in three Central and Eastern European countries: The HAPIEE study. *BMC Public Health, 9*, 439.

Boyle, L. L., Porsteinsson, A. P., Cui, X., King, D. A., & Lyness, J. M. (2010). Depression predicts cognitive disorders in older primary care patients. *Journal of Clinical Psychiatry, 71*, 74–79.

Boyle, S. H., Jackson, W. G., & Suarez, E. C. (2007). Hostility, anger, and depression predict increases in C3 over a 10-year period. *Brain, Behavior, and Immunity, 21*, 816–823.

Bradbury, T. N., Fincham, F. D., & Beach, S. R. H. (2000). Research on the nature and determinants of marital satisfaction: A decade in review. *Journal of Marriage and Family, 62*, 964–980.

Braitman, K. A., Kirley, B. B., Chaudhary, N. K., & Ferguson, S. A. (2006). Factors leading to older drivers' intersection crashes. Retrieved from http://www.iihs.org/research/topics/pdf/older_drivers.pdf.

Bramlett, M. D., & Mosher, W. D. (2002). *Cohabitation, marriage, divorce, and remarriage in the United States*. National Center for Health Statistics. Vital and Health Statistics 23(22). Retrieved from http://www.cdc.nchs/data/series/sr_23/sr23_022.pdf.

Braver, T. S., & Barch, D. M. (2002). A theory of cognitive control, aging cognition, and neuromodulation. *Neuroscience and Biobehavioral Reviews, 26*, 809–817.

Brenes, G. A., Kritchevsky, S. B., Mehta, K. M., Yaffe, K., Simonsick, E. M., Ayonayon, H. N., ... Penninx, B. W. (2007). Scared to death: Results from the Health, Aging, and Body Composition Study. *American Journal of Geriatric Psychiatry, 15*, 262–265.

Brennan, P. L., Schutte, K. K., & Moos, R. H. (2006). Long-term patterns and predictors of successful stressor resolution in later life. *International Journal of Stress Management, 13*, 253–272.

Brickman, A. M., Zimmerman, M. E., Paul, R. H., Grieve, S. M., Tate, D. F., Cohen, R. A., ... Gordon, E. (2006). Regional white matter and neuropsychological functioning across the adult lifespan. *Biological Psychiatry, 60*, 444–453.

Brill, F. (1967). *Matisse*. London, England: Hamlyn.

Brim, O. G., Jr. (1976). Theories of the male mid-life crisis. *The Counseling Psychologist, 6*, 2–9.

Briones, T. L. (2006). Environment, physical activity, and neurogenesis: Implications for prevention and treatment of Alzheimer's disease. *Current Alzheimer Research, 3*, 49–54.

Briscoe, J. P., & Finkelstein, L. M. (2009). The "new career" and organizational commitment: Do boundaryless and protean attitudes make a difference? *Career Development International, 14*, 242–260.

Briscoe, J. P., Hall, D. T., & Frautschy DeMuth, R. L. (2006). Protean and boundaryless careers: An empirical exploration. *Journal of Vocational Behavior, 69*, 30–47.

Britto, R. R., Zampa, C. C., de Oliveira, T. A., Prado, L. F., & Parreira, V. F. (2009). Effects of the aging process on respiratory function. *Gerontology, 55*, 505–510.

Broach, K., Joseph, K. M., & Schroeder, D. J. (2003). Pilot age and accident reports 3: An analysis of professional air transport pilot accident rates by age. Retrieved from http://www.faa.gov/library/reports/medical/age60/media/age60_3.pdf

Brockmann, H., Muller, R., & Helmert, U. (2009). Time to retire—time to die? A prospective cohort study of the effects of early retirement on long-term survival. *Social Science and Medicine, 69*, 160–164.

Bronfenbrenner, U. (1995). Developmental ecology through space and time: A future perspective. In P. Moen, G. H. J. Elder & K. Luscher (Eds.), *Examining lives in context: Perspectives on the ecology of human development* (pp. 619–647). Washington, DC: American Psychological Association.

Bronfenbrenner, U., & Ceci, S. J. (1994). Nature-nurture reconceptualized in developmental perspective: A bioecological model. *Psychological Review, 101*, 568–586.

Brooke, L., & Taylor, P. (2005). Older workers and employment: Managing age relations. *Ageing and Society, 25*, 415–429.

Brookmeyer, R., Corrada, M. M., Curriero, F. C., & Kawas, C. (2002). Survival following a diagnosis of Alzheimer disease. *Archives of Neurology, 59*, 1764–1767.

Brown, S. C. (2004). Learning across the campus: How college facilitates the development of wisdom. *Journal of College Student Development, 45*, 134–148.

Brown, S. C., & Greene, J. A. (2006). The Wisdom Development Scale: Translating the conceptual to the concrete. *Journal of College Student Development, 47*, 1–19.

Brucker, A. J. (2009). Age-related macular degeneration. *Retina, 29*, S2–S4.

Brummett, B. H., Babyak, M. A., Williams, R. B., Barefoot, J. C., Costa, P. T., & Siegler, I. C. (2006). NEO personality domains and gender predict levels and trends in body mass index over 14 years during midlife. *Journal of Research in Personality, 40*, 222–236.

Brydon, L., Strike, P. C., Bhattacharyya, M. R., Whitehead, D. L., McEwan, J., Zachary, I., ... Steptoe, A. (2010). Hostility and physiological responses to laboratory stress in acute coronary syndrome patients. *Journal of Psychosomatic Research, 68*, 109–116.

Buford, T. W., & Willoughby, D. S. (2008). Impact of DHEA(S) and cortisol on immune function in aging: A brief review. *Applied Physiology, Nutrition, and Metabolism, 33*, 429–433.

Bugg, J. M., DeLosh, E. L., & Clegg, B. A. (2006). Physical activity moderates time-of-day differences in older adults' working memory performance. *Experimental Aging Research, 32*, 431–446.

Buja, A., Scafato, E., Sergi, G., Maggi, S., Suhad, M. A., Rausa, G., ... Perissinotto, E. (2009). Alcohol consumption and metabolic syndrome in the elderly: Results from the Italian longitudinal study on aging. *European Journal of Clinical Nutrition*, 64, 297–307.

Bureau of Labor Statistics. (2010a). Employment Situation Summary Table A. Household data, seasonally adjusted. Retrieved from http://www.bls.gov/news.release/empsit.a.htm.

Bureau of Labor Statistics. (2010b). Employment status of the civilian noninstitutional population by age, sex, and race. Retrieved from ftp://ftp.bls.gov/pub/special.requests/lf/aat3.txt.

Bureau of Labor Statistics. (2010c). Injuries, illnesses, and fatalities. Retrieved from http://www.bls.gov/iif/News.

Bureau of Labor Statistics. (2010d). Occupational outlook handbook, 2010-11 edition. Retrieved from http://www.bls.gov/oco/oco2003.htm#Labor%20Force.

Bureau of Labor Statistics. (2010e). Usual weekly earnings of wage and salary workers fourth quarter 2009. *News Releases*. Retrieved from http://www.bls.gov/news.release/pdf/wkyeng.pdf.

Burgio, K. L. (2009). Behavioral treatment of urinary incontinence, voiding dysfunction, and overactive bladder. *Obstetrics and Gynecology Clinics of North America*, 36, 475–491.

Burgio, L. D., Stevens, A., Burgio, K. L., Roth, D. L., Paul, P., & Gerstle, J. (2002). Teaching and maintaining behavior management skills in the nursing home. *Gerontologist*, 42, 487–496.

Burgmans, S., van Boxtel, M. P., Gronenschild, E. H., Vuurman, E. F., Hofman, P., Uylings, H. B., . . . Raz, N. (2010). Multiple indicators of age-related differences in cerebral white matter and the modifying effects of hypertension. *Neuroimage*, 49, 2083–2093.

Burke, D. M. (1997). Language, aging, and inhibitory deficits: Evaluation of a theory. *Journal of Gerontology Series B: Psychological Sciences and Social Sciences*, 52B, P254–P264.

Burke, K. E., & Wei, H. (2009). Synergistic damage by UVA radiation and pollutants. *Toxicology and Industrial Health*, 25, 219–224.

Burton, C. L., Strauss, E., Hultsch, D. F., & Hunter, M. A. (2006). Cognitive functioning and everyday problem solving in older adults. *Clinical Neuropsychology*, 20, 432–452.

Burton, C. L., Strauss, E., Hultsch, D. F., & Hunter, M. A. (2009). The relationship between everyday problem solving and inconsistency in reaction time in older adults. *Neuropsychology, Development, and Cognition. Section B, Aging, Neuropsychology and Cognition*, 16, 607–632.

Burton, C. L., Strauss, E., Hultsch, D. F., Moll, A., & Hunter, M. A. (2006). Intraindividual variability as a marker of neurological dysfunction: A comparison of Alzheimer's disease and Parkinson's disease. *Journal of Clinical and Experimental Neuropsychology*, 28, 67–83.

Busby, D. M., & Holman, T. B. (2009). Perceived match or mismatch on the Gottman conflict styles: Associations with relationship outcome variables. *Family Process*, 48, 531–545.

Butler, K. M., & Zacks, R. T. (2006). Age deficits in the control of prepotent responses: Evidence for an inhibitory decline. *Psychology and Aging*, 21, 638–643.

Butler, R. (1974). Successful aging and the role of life review. *Journal of the American Geriatrics Society*, 22, 529–535.

Byberg, L., Melhus, H. K., Gedeborg, R., Sundstrom, J., Ahlbom, A., Zethelius, B., . . . Michaelsson, K. (2009). Total mortality after changes in leisure time physical activity in 50 year old men: 35 year follow-up of population based cohort. *BMJ: British Medical Journal*, 338.

Byrne, C. M., Solomon, M. J., Young, J. M., Rex, J., & Merlino, C. L. (2007). Biofeedback for fecal incontinence: Short-term outcomes of 513 consecutive patients and predictors of successful treatment. *Diseases of the Colon and Rectum*, 50, 417–427.

Cabrera, E. F. (2009). Protean organizations: Reshaping work and careers to retain female talent. *Career Development International*, 14, 186–201.

Caggiano, D. M., Jiang, Y., & Parasuraman, R. (2006). Aging and repetition priming for targets and distracters in a working memory task. *Aging, Neuropsychology and Cognition*, 13, 552–573.

Callahan, C. M., Boustani, M. A., Unverzagt, F. W., Austrom, M. G., Damush, T. M., Perkins, A. J., . . . Hendrie, H. C. (2006). Effectiveness of collaborative care for older adults with Alzheimer disease in primary care: A randomized controlled trial. *Journal of the American Medical Association*, 295, 2148–2157.

Calle, E. E., Rodriguez, C., Walker-Thurmond, K., & Thun, M. J. (2003). Overweight, obesity, and mortality from cancer in prospectively studied cohort of U.S. adults. *New England Journal of Medicine*, 348, 1625–1638.

Camp, C. J., Cohen-Mansfield, J., & Capezuti, E. A. (2002). Use of nonpharmacologic interventions among nursing home residents with dementia. *Psychiatric Services*, 53, 1397–1404.

Campayo, A., de Jonge, P., Roy, J. F., Saz, P., de la Camara, C., Quintanilla, M. A., . . . Lobo, A. (2010). Depressive disorder and incident diabetes mellitus: The effect of characteristics of depression. *American Journal of Psychiatry*, 167, 580–588. doi:10.1176/appi.ajp.2009.09010038.

Cao, J. J., Wronski, T. J., Iwaniec, U., Phleger, L., Kurimoto, P., Boudignon, B., . . . Halloran, B. P. (2005). Aging increases stromal/osteoblastic cell-induced osteoclastogenesis and alters the osteoclast precursor pool in the mouse. *Journal of Bone and Mineral Research*, 20, 1659–1668.

Caputo, R. K. (2002). Adult daughters as parental caregivers: Rational actors versus rational agents. *Journal of Family & Economic Issues*, 23, 27–50.

Carnelley, K. B., Wortman, C. B., Bolger, N., & Burke, C. T. (2006). The time course of grief reactions to spousal loss: Evidence from a national probability sample. *Journal of Personality and Social Psychology*, 91, 476–492.

Carroll, C. C., Dickinson, J. M., Haus, J. M., Lee, G. A., Hollon, C. J., Aagaard, P., Trappe, T. A. (2008). Influence of aging on the in vivo properties of human patellar tendon. *Journal of Applied Physiology*, 105, 1907–1915.

Carstensen, L. L., Isaacowitz, D. M., & Charles, S. T. (1999). Taking time seriously: A theory of socioemotional selectivity. *American Psychologist*, 54, 165–181.

Carstensen, L. L., & Turk-Charles, S. (1994). The salience of emotion across the adult life span. *Psychology and Aging, 9,* 259–264.

Caruso, C., Candore, G., Colonna Romano, G., Lio, D., Bonafe, M., Valensin, S., . . . Franceschi, C. (2000). HLA, aging, and longevity: A critical reappraisal. *Human Immunology, 61,* 942–949.

Caspi, A., & Roberts, B. W. (2001). Target article: Personality development across the life course: The argument for change and continuity. *Psychological Inquiry, 12,* 49–66.

Cattell, R. B. (1963). Theory of fluid and crystallized intelligence: A critical experiment. *Journal of Educational Psychology, 54,* 1–22.

Cattell, R. B. (1971). *Abilities: Their structure, growth, and action.* Boston, MA: Houghton Mifflin.

Cauley, J. A., Lui, L. Y., Barnes, D., Ensrud, K. E., Zmuda, J. M., Hillier, T. A., . . . Black, D. M. (2009). Successful skeletal aging: A marker of low fracture risk and longevity. The Study of Osteoporotic Fractures (SOF). The *Journal of Bone Mineral Research, 24,* 134–143.

Cauley, J. A., Palermo, L., Vogt, M., Ensrud, K. E., Ewing, S., Hochberg, M., . . . Newman, A. B. (2008). Prevalent vertebral fractures in black women and white women. *Journal of Bone Mineral Research, 23,* 1458–1467.

Cavan, R. S., Burgess, E. W., Havighurst, R. J., & Goldhamer, H. (1949). *Personal adjustment in old age.* Chicago, IL: Science Research Associates.

Caycedo, A. M., Miller, B., Kramer, J., & Rascovsky, K. (2009). Early features in frontotemporal dementia. *Current Alzheimer Research, 6,* 337–340.

Center for Medicare and Medicaid Services. (2010a). Medicare enrollment: National trends. Retrieved from http://www.cms.hhs.gov/MedicareEnRpts/Downloads/HISMI08.pdf.

Center for Medicare and Medicaid Services. (2010b). National Health Expenditure Data. Retrieved from http://www.cms.hhs.gov/nationalhealthexpenddata/.

Center for Medicare and Medicaid Services. (2010c). National Health Expenditures 2008 Highlights. Retrieved from http://www.cms.hhs.gov/NationalHealthExpendData/downloads/highlights.pdf.

Centers for Disease Control and Prevention. (2004). National Nursing Home Survey. Retrieved from http://www.cdc.gov/nchs/data/series/sr_13/sr13_167.pdf.

Centers for Disease Control and Prevention. (2006). Heat-Related Deaths—United States, 1999–2003. *Morbidity and Mortality Weekly Reports, 55*(29), 796–798.

Centers for Disease Control and Prevention. (2010a). Defining overweight and obesity. Retrieved from http://www.cdc.gov/obesity/defining.html.

Centers for Disease Control and Prevention. (2010b). H1N1 and you. Retrieved from http://www.cdc.gov/H1N1flu/qa.htm.

Centers for Disease Control and Prevention. (2010c). Life expectancy. Retrieved from http://www.cdc.gov/nchs/fastats/lifexpec.htm.

Centers for Disease Control and Prevention. (2010d). National Diabetes Fact Sheet. Retrieved from http://www.cdc.gov/diabetes/pubs/estimates05.htm.

Centers for Disease Control and Prevention. (2010e). Teen drivers: Fact sheet. Retrieved from http://www.cdc.gov/MotorVehicleSafety/Teen_Drivers/teendrivers_factsheet.html.

Centers for Disease Control and Prevention, (2010f). Web-based Injury Statistics Query and Reporting System (WISQARS), Retrieved from www.cdc.gov/ncipc/wisqars.

Central Intelligence Agency. (2010). The World Factbook. Retrieved from https://www.cia.gov/library/publications/the-world-factbook/rankorder/2066rank.html.

Chan, D., Cheadle, A. D., Reiber, G., Unutzer, J., & Chaney, E. F. (2009). Health care utilization and its costs for depressed veterans with and without comorbid PTSD symptoms. *Psychiatric Services, 60,* 1612–1617.

Chan, S. W., Chiu, H. F., Chien, W. T., Goggins, W., Thompson, D., & Hong, B. (2009). Predictors of change in health-related quality of life among older people with depression: A longitudinal study. *International Psychogeriatrics, 21,* 1171–1179.

Chandola, T., Brunner, E., & Marmot, M. (2006). Chronic stress at work and the metabolic syndrome: Prospective study. *BMJ: British Medical Journal, 332,* 521–525.

Chang, Y. K., & Etnier, J. L. (2009). Exploring the dose-response relationship between resistance exercise intensity and cognitive function. *Journal of Sports Exercise Psychology, 31,* 640–656.

Chapman, B. P., Shah, M., Friedman, B., Drayer, R., Duberstein, P. R., & Lyness, J. M. (2009). Personality traits predict emergency department utilization over 3 years in older patients. *American Journal of Geriatric Psychiatry, 17,* 526–535.

Charles, S. T., & Carstensen, L. L. (2010). Social and emotional aging. *Annual Review of Psychology, 61,* 383–409.

Charles, S. T., Reynolds, C. A., & Gatz, M. (2001). Age-related differences and change in positive and negative affect over 23 years. *Journal of Personality & Social Psychology, 80,* 136–151.

Charlton, R. A., Barrick, T. R., Markus, H. S., & Morris, R. G. (2009). The relationship between episodic long-term memory and white matter integrity in normal aging. *Neuropsychologia, 48,* 114–122.

Charney, D. S., Reynolds, C. F., III, Lewis, L., Lebowitz, B. D., Sunderland, T., Alexopoulos, G. S., . . . Young, R. C. (2003). Depression and Bipolar Support Alliance consensus statement on the unmet needs in diagnosis and treatment of mood disorders in late life. *Archives of General Psychiatry, 60,* 664–672.

Chedraui, P., Perez-Lopez, F. R., Mendoza, M., Leimberg, M. L., Martinez, M. A., Vallarino, V., . . . Hidalgo, L. (2010). Factors related to increased daytime sleepiness during the menopausal transition as evaluated by the Epworth sleepiness scale. *Maturitas, 65,* 75–80.

Chen, J. C., Brunner, R. L., Ren, H., Wassertheil-Smoller, S., Larson, J. C., Levine, D. W., . . . Stefanick, M. L. (2008). Sleep duration and risk of ischemic stroke in postmenopausal women. *Stroke, 39,* 3185–3192.

Chen, L. Y., & Hardy, C. L. (2009). Alcohol consumption and health status in older adults: A longitudinal analysis. *Journal of Aging and Health, 21*, 824–847.

Cheng, S. T., Fung, H. H., & Chan, A. C. (2009). Self-perception and psychological well-being: The benefits of foreseeing a worse future. *Psychology and Aging, 24*, 623–633.

Cherkas, L. F., Aviv, A., Valdes, A. M., Hunkin, J. L., Gardner, J. P., Surdulescu, G. L., . . . Spector, T. D. (2006). The effects of social status on biological aging as measured by white-blood-cell telomere length. *Aging Cell, 5*, 361–365.

Cherkas, L. F., Hunkin, J. L., Kato, B. S., Richards, J. B., Gardner, J. P., Surdulescu, G. L., . . . Aviv, A. (2008). The association between physical activity in leisure time and leukocyte telomere length. *Archives of Internal Medicine, 168*, 154–158.

Cherry, K. E., Silva, J. L., & Galea, S. (2009). Natural disasters and the oldest-old: A psychological perspective on coping and health in late life. *Lifespan perspectives on natural disasters: Coping with Katrina, Rita, and other storms* (pp. 171–193). New York, NY: Springer Science + Business Media.

Cheung, C.-K., & Kwan, A. Y.-H. (2009). The erosion of filial piety by modernisation in Chinese cities. *Ageing and Society, 29*, 179–198.

Chitaley, K., Kupelian, V., Subak, L., & Wessells, H. (2009). Diabetes, obesity and erectile dysfunction: Field overview and research priorities. *Journal of Urology, 182*, S45–S50.

Chiu, C. J., Milton, R. C., Gensler, G., & Taylor, A. (2006). Dietary carbohydrate intake and glycemic index in relation to cortical and nuclear lens opacities in the Age-Related Eye Disease Study. *American Journal of Clinical Nutrition, 83*, 1177–1184.

Chodzko-Zajko, W. J., Proctor, D. N., Fiatarone Singh, M. A., Minson, C. T., Nigg, C. R., Salem, G. J., . . . Skinner, J. S. (2009). American College of Sports Medicine position stand. Exercise and physical activity for older adults. *Medicine and Science in Sports and Exercise, 41*, 1510–1530.

Chou, S.-C., Boldy, D. P., & Lee, A. H. (2002). Resident satisfaction and its components in residential aged care. *Gerontologist, 42*, 188–198.

Christiansen, S. L., & Palkovitz, R. (2001). Why the "good provider" role still matters: Providing as a form of paternal involvement. *Journal of Family Issues, 22*, 84–106.

Cicirelli, V. G. (1988). A measure of filial anxiety regarding anticipated care of elderly parents. *Gerontologist, 28*, 478–482.

Cicirelli, V. G. (1997). Relationship of psychosocial and background variables to older adults' end-of-life decisions. *Psychology and Aging, 12*, 72–83.

Clark, A., Oswald, A., & Warr, P. (1996). Is job satisfaction U-shaped in age? *Journal of Occupational and Organizational Psychology, 69*, 57–81.

Clarke, R., Emberson, J., Fletcher, A., Breeze, E., Marmot, M., & Shipley, M. J. (2009). Life expectancy in relation to cardiovascular risk factors: 38 year follow-up of 19,000 men in the Whitehall study. *BMJ: British Medical Journal, 339*, b3513.

Clerici, F., Vanacore, N., Elia, A., Spila-Alegiani, S., Pomati, S., Da Cas, R., . . . Mariani, C. (2009). Memantine in moderately-severe-to-severe Alzheimer's disease: A postmarketing surveillance study. *Drugs and Aging, 26*, 321–332.

Cluett, C., & Melzer, D. (2009). Human genetic variations: Beacons on the pathways to successful ageing. *Mechanisms of Ageing and Development, 130*, 553–563.

Coelho, S. G., Choi, W., Brenner, M., Miyamura, Y., Yamaguchi, Y., Wolber, R., . . . Hearing, V. J. (2009). Short- and long-term effects of UV radiation on the pigmentation of human skin. *Journal of Investigative Dermatology Symposium Proceedings, 14*, 32–35.

Cohan, C. L., & Kleinbaum, S. (2002). Toward a greater understanding of the cohabitation effect: Premarital cohabitation and marital communication. *Journal of Marriage and Family, 64*, 180–192.

Cohen, A., Houck, P. R., Szanto, K., Dew, M. A., Gilman, S. E., & Reynolds, C. F., III. (2006). Social inequalities in response to antidepressant treatment in older adults. *Archives of General Psychiatry, 63*, 50–56.

Cohen, C. I., Abdallah, C. G., & Diwan, S. (2010). Suicide attempts and associated factors in older adults with schizophrenia. *Schizophrenia Research, 119*(1–3), 253–257.

Cohen, J. S., Fihn, S. D., Boyko, E. J., Jonsen, A. R., & Wood, R. W. (1994). Attitudes toward assisted suicide and euthanasia among physicians in Washington State. *New England Journal of Medicine, 331*, 89–94.

Cohn, L. D., & Westenberg, P. M. (2004). Intelligence and maturity: Meta-analytic evidence for the incremental and discriminant validity of Loevinger's measure of ego development. *Journal of Personality and Social Psychology, 86*, 760–772.

Colcombe, S. J., Erickson, K. I., Scalf, P. E., Kim, J. S., Prakash, R., McAuley, E., . . . Kramer, A. F. (2006). Aerobic exercise training increases brain volume in aging humans. *Journal of Gerontology Series A: Biological Sciences and Medical Sciences, 61A*, 1166–1170.

Coleman, H. R., Chan, C. C., Ferris, F. L., III, & Chew, E. Y. (2008). Age-related macular degeneration. *Lancet, 372*, 1835–1845.

Coltrane, S. (2000). Research on household labor: Modeling and measuring the social embeddedness of routine family work. *Journal of Marriage & the Family, 62*, 1208–1233.

Comijs, H. C., Gerritsen, L., Penninx, B. W., Bremmer, M. A., Deeg, D. J., & Geerlings, M. I. (2010). The association between serum cortisol and cognitive decline in older persons. *American Journal of Geriatric Psychiatry, 18*, 42–50.

Commons, M., Richards, F., & Armon, C. (Eds.). (1984). *Beyond formal operations: Late adolescent and adult cognitive development.* New York, NY: Praeger.

Comondore, V. R., Devereaux, P. J., Zhou, Q., Stone, S. B., Busse, J. W., Ravindran, N. C., . . . Guyatt, G. H. (2009). Quality of care in for-profit and not-for-profit nursing homes: Systematic review and meta-analysis. *BMJ: British Medical Journal, 339*, b2732.

Congdon, N., Vingerling, J. R., Klein, B. E., West, S., Friedman, D. S., Kempen, J., . . . Taylor, H. R. (2004). Prevalence of cataract and pseudophakia/aphakia among adults in the United States. *Archives of Ophthalmology, 122,* 487–494.

Connidis, I. A. (1992). Life transitions and the adult sibling tie: A qualitative study. *Journal of Marriage and Family, 54,* 972–982.

Connor, S. R., Egan, K. A., Kwilosz, D. M., Larson, D. G., & Reese, D. J. (2002). Interdisciplinary approaches to assisting with end-of-life care and decision making. *American Behavioral Scientist, 46,* 340–356.

Consedine, N. S., & Magai, C. (2003). Attachment and emotion experience in later life: The view from emotions theory. *Attachment and Human Development, 5,* 165–187.

Constantinople, A. (1969). An Eriksonian measure of personality development in college students. *Developmental Psychology, 1,* 357–372.

Conwell, Y., Duberstein, P. R., & Caine, E. D. (2002). Risk factors for suicide in later life. *Biological Psychiatry, 52,* 193–204.

Cooney, M. T., Dudina, A., De Bacquer, D., Wilhelmsen, L., Sans, S., Menotti, A., . . . Graham, I. M. (2009). HDL cholesterol protects against cardiovascular disease in both genders, at all ages and at all levels of risk. *Atherosclerosis, 206,* 611–616.

Corona, G., & Maggi, M. (2010). The role of testosterone in erectile dysfunction. *Nature Review Urology, 7,* 46–56.

Costa, P. T. J., & McCrae, R. R. (1978). Objective personality assessment. In M. Storandt, I. C. Siegler, & M. F. Elias (Eds.), *The clinical psychology of aging* (pp. 119–143). New York, NY: Plenum.

Covinsky, K. E., Lindquist, K., Dunlop, D. D., & Yelin, E. (2009). Pain, functional limitations, and aging. *Journal of the American Geriatrics Society, 57,* 1556–1561.

Cowgill, D. O., & Holmes, L. D. (1972). *Aging and modernization.* New York, NY: Appleton-Century-Crofts.

Coyne, K. S., Margolis, M. K., Jumadilova, Z., Bavendam, T., Mueller, E., & Rogers, R. (2007). Overactive bladder and women's sexual health: What is the impact? *Journal of Sexual Medicine, 4,* 656–666.

Cramer, P. (2003). Personality change in later adulthood is predicted by defense mechanism use in early adulthood. *Journal of Research in Personality, 37,* 76–104.

Cramer, P., & Jones, C. J. (2007). Defense mechanisms predict differential lifespan change in self-control and self-acceptance. *Journal of Research in Personality, 41,* 841–855.

Cramer, P., & Jones, C. J. (2008). Narcissism, identification, and longitudinal change in psychological health: Dynamic predictions. *Journal of Research in Personality, 42,* 1148–1159.

Crawford, S., & Channon, S. (2002). Dissociation between performance on abstract tests of executive function and problem solving in real-life-type situations in normal aging. *Aging and Mental Health, 6,* 12–21.

Crawley, L. M., Marshall, P. A., Lo, B., & Koenig, B. A. (2002). Strategies for culturally effective end-of-life care. *Annals of Internal Medicine, 136,* 673–679.

Cropanzano, R., Rupp, D. E., & Byrne, Z. S. (2003). The relationship of emotional exhaustion to work attitudes, job performance, and organizational citizenship behaviors. *Journal of Applied Psychology, 88,* 160–169.

Crosnoe, R., & Elder, G. H., Jr. (2002). Life course transitions, the generational stake, and grandparent-grandchild relationships. *Journal of Marriage and Family, 64,* 1089–1096.

Cuddy, A. J. C., Norton, M. I., & Fiske, S. T. (2005). This old stereotype: The pervasiveness and persistence of the elderly stereotype. *Journal of Social Issues, 61,* 267–285.

Cumming, E., & Henry, W. E. (1961). *Growing old: The process of disengagement.* New York, NY: Basic Books.

Curlin, F. A., Lawrence, R. E., Chin, M. H., & Lantos, J. D. (2007). Religion, conscience, and controversial clinical practices. *New England Journal of Medicine, 356,* 593–600.

Curran, M., Hazen, N., Jacobvitz, D., & Sasaki, T. (2006). How representations of the parental marriage predict marital emotional attunement during the transition to parenthood. *Journal of Family Psychology, 20,* 477–484.

Cushman, M., Cantrell, R. A., McClure, L. A., Howard, G., Prineas, R. J., Moy, C. S., . . . Howard, V. J. (2008). Estimated 10-year stroke risk by region and race in the United States: Geographic and racial differences in stroke risk. *Annals of Neurology, 64,* 507–513.

da Silva Lara, L. A., Useche, B., Rosa, E. S. J. C., Ferriani, R. A., Reis, R. M., de Sa, M. F., . . . Silva, A. C. (2009). Sexuality during the climacteric period. *Maturitas, 62,* 127–133.

Daly, M. C., & Bound, J. (1996). Worker adaptation and employer accommodation following the onset of a health impairment. *Journal of Gerontology: Social Sciences, 51,* S53–S60.

Dangour, A. D., Allen, E., Elbourne, D., Fletcher, A., Richards, M., & Uauy, R. (2009). Fish consumption and cognitive function among older people in the UK: Baseline data from the OPAL study. *Journal of Nutrition, Health, and Aging, 13,* 198–202.

Davidson, D. J., Zacks, R. T., & Williams, C. C. (2003). Stroop interference, practice, and aging. *Neuropsychology, Development, and Cognition. Section B, Aging, Neuropsychology and Cognition, 10,* 85–98.

Davidson, P. S. R., Cook, S. P., & Glisky, E. L. (2006). Flashbulb memories for September 11th can be preserved in older adults. *Aging, Neuropsychology and Cognition, 13,* 196–206.

Davis, M. A. (2003). Factors related to bridge employment participation among private sector early retirees. *Journal of Vocational Behavior, 63,* 55–71.

Davison, E. H., Pless, A. P., Gugliucci, M. R., King, L. A., King, D. W., Salgado, D. M., . . . Bachrach, P. (2006). Late-life emergence of early-life trauma: The phenomenon of late-onset stress symptomatology among aging combat veterans. *Research on Aging, 28,* 84–114.

Dawis, R. V. (1996). Vocational psychology, vocational adjustment, and the workforce: Some familiar and unanticipated consequences. *Psychology, Public Policy, & Law, 2,* 229–248.

Dawis, R. V., & Lofquist, L. H. (1984). *A psychological theory of work adjustment.* Minneapolis, MN: University of Minnesota Press.

Dawson-Hughes, B., & Bischoff-Ferrari, H. A. (2007). Therapy of osteoporosis with calcium and vitamin D. *Journal of Bone and Mineral Research, 22* Suppl 2, V59–63.

de Jong, F. J., Masaki, K., Chen, H., Remaley, A. T., Breteler, M. M., Petrovitch, H., . . . Launer, L. J. (2009). Thyroid function, the risk of dementia and neuropathologic changes: The Honolulu-Asia aging study. *Neurobiology of Aging, 30,* 600–606.

de Jong, P. T. (2006). Age-related macular degeneration. *New England Journal of Medicine, 355,* 1474–1485.

De Raedt, R., & Ponjaert-Kristoffersen, I. (2006). Self-serving appraisal as a cognitive coping strategy to deal with age-related limitations: An empirical study with elderly adults in a real-life stressful situation. *Aging and Mental Health, 10,* 195–203.

De Vos, A., & Soens, N. (2008). Protean attitude and career success: The mediating role of self-management. *Journal of Vocational Behavior, 73,* 449–456.

De Vries, B., & Megathlin, D. (2009). The meaning of friendships for gay men and lesbians in the second half of life. *Journal of GLBT Family Studies, 5,* 82–98.

Deaton, A. (2008). Income, health, and well-being from around the world: Evidence from the Gallup World Poll. *Journal of Economic Perspectives, 22*(2), 53–72.

Deci, E. L., & Ryan, R. M. (2008). Self-determination theory: A macrotheory of human motivation, development, and health. *Canadian Psychology/Psychologie Canadienne, 49,* 182–185.

Degenholtz, H., Arnold, R., Meisel, A., & Lave, J. (2002). Persistence of racial disparities in advance care plan documents among nursing home residents. *Journal of American Geriatrics Society, 50,* 378–381.

DeLamater, J. D., & Sill, M. (2005). Sexual desire in later life. *Journal of Sex Research, 42,* 138–149.

Delano-Wood, L., & Abeles, N. (2005). Late-life depression: Detection, risk reduction, and somatic intervention. *Clinical Psychology: Science and Practice, 12,* 207–217.

Delgoulet, C., & Marquie, J. C. (2002). Age differences in learning maintenance skills: A field study. *Experimental Aging Research, 28,* 25–37.

Dellenbach, M., & Zimprich, D. (2008). Typical intellectual engagement and cognition in old age. *Neuropsychology, Development, and Cognition. Section B, Aging, Neuropsychology and Cognition, 15,* 208–231.

Deng, H., Miao, D., Liu, J., Meng, S., & Wu, Y. (2010). The regeneration of gingiva: Its potential value for the recession of healthy gingiva. *Medical Hypotheses, 74,* 76–77.

Dennerstein, L., Dudley, E., & Guthrie, J. (2002). Empty nest or revolving door? A prospective study of women's quality of life in midlife during the phase of children leaving and re-entering the home. *Psychological Medicine, 32,* 545–550.

Dennis, N. A., Daselaar, S., & Cabeza, R. (2007). Effects of aging on transient and sustained successful memory encoding activity. *Neurobiology of Aging, 28,* 1749–1758.

Dennis, W. (1966). Creative productivity between the ages of 20 and 80 years. *Journal of Gerontology, 21,* 1–8.

Department of Health and Human Services. (1999). *Mental health: A report of the Surgeon General.* Bethesda, MD: U.S. Public Health Service.

Depp, C., Vahia, I. V., & Jeste, D. (2010). Successful aging: Focus on cognitive and emotional health. *Annual Review of Clinical Psychology, 6,* 527–550.

Depp, C. A., & Jeste, D. V. (2004). Bipolar disorder in older adults: A critical review. *Bipolar Disorders, 6,* 343–367.

Depp, C. A., & Jeste, D. V. (2006). Definitions and predictors of successful aging: A comprehensive review of larger quantitative studies. *American Journal of Geriatric Psychiatry, 14,* 6–20.

Der, G., & Deary, I. J. (2006). Age and sex differences in reaction time in adulthood: Results from the United Kingdom Health and Lifestyle Survey. *Psychology and Aging, 21,* 62–73.

Desai, S., Upadhyay, M., & Nanda, R. (2009). Dynamic smile analysis: Changes with age. *American Journal of Orthodontic and Dentofacial Orthopathy, 136,* 310.e1–310.e10; discussion 310–311.

Desbiens, N. A., Wu, A. W., Broste, S. K., Wenger, N. S., Connors, A. F., Jr., Lynn, J., . . . Fulkerson, W. (1996). Pain and satisfaction with pain control in seriously ill hospitalized adults: Findings from the SUPPORT research investigations. For the SUPPORT investigators. Study to Understand Prognoses and Preferences for Outcomes and Risks of Treatment. *Critical Care Medicine, 24,* 1953–1961.

DeSpelder, L. A., & Strickland, A. L. (1999). *The last dance: Encountering death and dying* (5th ed.). Mountain View, CA: Mayfield.

Detering, K. M., Hancock, A. D., Reade, M. C., & Silvester, W. (2010). The impact of advance care planning on end of life care in elderly patients: Randomised controlled trial. *BMJ: British Medical Journal, 340,* c1345.

Devaney, S. A., & Chiremba, S. T. (2005). Comparing the retirement savings of the baby boomers and other cohorts. Retrieved from http://www.bls.gov/opub/cwc/cm20050114ar01p1.htm.

Devine, A., Dick, I. M., Islam, A. F., Dhaliwal, S. S., & Prince, R. L. (2005). Protein consumption is an important predictor of lower limb bone mass in elderly women. *American Journal of Clinical Nutrition, 81,* 1423–1428.

Devore, E. E., Stampfer, M. J., Breteler, M. M., Rosner, B., Hee Kang, J., Okereke, O., . . . Grodstein, F. (2009). Dietary fat intake and cognitive decline in women with type 2 diabetes. *Diabetes Care, 32,* 635–640.

Di Bonito, P., Di Fraia, L., Di Gennaro, L., Vitale, A., Lapenta, M., Scala, A., . . . Capaldo, B. (2007). Impact of impaired fasting glucose and other metabolic factors on cognitive function in elderly people. *Nutrition, Metabolism, and Cardiovascular Diseases, 17,* 203–208.

Diab, T., Condon, K. W., Burr, D. B., & Vashishth, D. (2006). Age-related change in the damage morphology of human cortical bone and its role in bone fragility. *Bone, 38,* 427–431.

Diaz, E., Miskemen, T., Vega, W. A., Gara, M., Wilson, D. R., Lesser, I., . . . Strakowski, S. (2009). Inconsistencies in diagnosis and symptoms among bilingual and English-speaking Latinos and Euro-Americans. *Psychiatric Services*, *60*, 1379–1382.

Dickin, D. C., Brown, L. A., & Doan, J. B. (2006). Age-dependent differences in the time course of postural control during sensory perturbations. *Aging: Clinical and Experimental Research*, *18*, 94–99.

Dickinson, G. E. (2002). A quarter century of end-of-life issues in U.S. medical schools. *Death Studies*, *26*, 635–646.

Dickinson, G. E., Tournier, R. E., & Still, B. J. (1999). Twenty years beyond medical school: Physicians' attitudes toward death and terminally ill patients. *Archives of Internal Medicine*, *159*, 1741–1744.

Diehl, M., Coyle, N., & Labouvie-Vief, G. (1996). Age and sex differences in coping and defense across the life span. *Psychology and Aging*, *11*, 127–139.

Diener, E. (1998). Subjective well-being: Three decades of progress. *Psychological Bulletin*, *125*, 276–302.

Diener, E., & Fujita, F. (1995). Resources, personal strivings, and subjective well-being: A nomothetic and idiographic approach. *Journal of Personality and Social Psychology*, *68*, 926–935.

Diener, E., Oishi, S., & Lucas, R. E. (2003). Personality, culture, and subjective well-being: Emotional and cognitive evaluations of life. *Annual Review of Psychology*, *54*, 403–425.

Dietrich, A. (2004). The cognitive neuroscience of creativity. *Psychonomic Bulletin & Review*, *11*, 1011–1026.

Diez, J. J., & Iglesias, P. (2004). Spontaneous subclinical hypothyroidism in patients older than 55 years: An analysis of natural course and risk factors for the development of overt thyroid failure. *Journal of Clinical Endocrinology and Metabolism*, *89*, 4890–4897.

DiGrande, L., Perrin, M. A., Thorpe, L. E., Thalji, L., Murphy, J., Wu, D., . . . Brackbill, R. M. (2008). Posttraumatic stress symptoms, PTSD, and risk factors among lower Manhattan residents 2–3 years after the September 11, 2001 terrorist attacks. *Journal of Trauma and Stress*, *21*, 264–273.

Dillon, C. F., Gu, Q., Hoffman, H. J., & Ko, C. W. (2010). Vision, hearing, balance, and sensory impairment in Americans aged 70 years and over: United States, 1999–2006. *NCHS Data Brief*, 1–8.

DiNardo, P. A., & Barlow, D. H. (1988). *Anxiety Disorders Interview Schedule-Revised (ADIS-R)*. Albany, NY: Graywind.

Ding, C., Cicuttini, F., Blizzard, L., Scott, F., & Jones, G. (2007). A longitudinal study of the effect of sex and age on rate of change in knee cartilage volume in adults. *Rheumatology (Oxford)*, *46*, 273–290.

Dionne, C. E., Dunn, K. M., & Croft, P. R. (2006). Does back pain prevalence really decrease with increasing age? A systematic review. *Age and Ageing*, *35*, 229–234.

Dishman, R. K., Berthoud, H. R., Booth, F. W., Cotman, C. W., Edgerton, V. R., Fleshner, M. R., . . . Zigmond, M. J. (2006). Neurobiology of exercise. *Scandinavian Journal of Medicine and Science in Sports*, *16*, 379–380.

Disney, R., & Johnson, P. (2001). *Pensions systems and retirement incomes from OECD countries*. Cheltenham, England: Elgar

Dixon, R. A., & Hultsch, D. F. (1999). Intelligence and cognitive potential in late life. In J. C. Cavanaugh & S. K. Whitbourne (Eds.), *Gerontology: Interdisciplinary perspectives* (pp. 213–237). New York, NY: Oxford University Press.

Djousse, L., Lee, I. M., Buring, J. E., & Gaziano, J. M. (2009). Alcohol consumption and risk of cardiovascular disease and death in women: Potential mediating mechanisms. *Circulation*, *120*, 237–244.

Dobbs, B. M. (2008). Aging baby boomers—a blessing or challenge for driver licensing authorities. *Traffic and Injury Prevention*, *9*, 379–386.

Dodson, C. S., Bawa, S., & Slotnick, S. D. (2007). Aging, source memory, and misrecollections. *Journal of Experimental Psychology: Learning, Memory, and Cognition*, *33*, 169–181.

Dolcos, S. M., & Daley, D. (2009). Work pressure, workplace social resources, and work-family conflict: The tale of two sectors. *International Journal of Stress Management*, *16*, 291–311.

Dong, X., Simon, M., Mendes de Leon, C., Fulmer, T., Beck, T., Hebert, L., . . . Evans, D. (2009). Elder self-neglect and abuse and mortality risk in a community-dwelling population. *Journal of the American Medical Association*, *302*, 517–526.

Donnelly, R. (2009). Career behavior in the knowledge economy: Experiences and perceptions of career mobility among management and It consultants in the UK and the USA. *Journal of Vocational Behavior*, *75*, 319–328.

Donoghue, C. (2006). The percentage of beds designated for Medicaid in American nursing homes and nurse staffing ratios. *Journal of Health and Social Policy*, *22*, 19–28.

Donohue, R. (2006). Person-environment congruence in relation to career change and career persistence. *Journal of Vocational Behavior*, *68*, 504–515.

Dorshkind, K., Montecino-Rodriguez, E., & Signer, R. A. (2009). The ageing immune system: Is it ever too old to become young again? *Nature Reviews Immunology*, *9*, 57–62.

Doss, B. D., Rhoades, G. K., Stanley, S. M., & Markman, H. J. (2009). The effect of the transition to parenthood on relationship quality: An 8-year prospective study. *Journal of Personality and Social Psychology*, *96*, 601–619.

Doss, B. D., Rhoades, G. K., Stanley, S. M., Markman, H. J., & Johnson, C. A. (2009). Differential use of premarital education in first and second marriages. *Journal of Family Psychology*, *23*, 268–273.

Drentea, P. (2002). Retirement and mental health. *Journal of Aging and Health*, *14*, 167–194.

Drew, L. M., & Smith, P. K. (2002). Implications for grandparents when they lose contact with their grandchildren: Divorce, family feud, and geographical separation. *Journal of Mental Health & Aging*, *8*, 95–119.

Drozdowski, L., & Thomson, A. B. (2006). Aging and the intestine. *World Journal of Gastroenterology*, *12*, 7578–7584.

Dubeau, C. E., Simon, S. E., & Morris, J. N. (2006). The effect of urinary incontinence on quality of life in older nursing home residents. *Journal of the American Geriatrics Society, 54*, 1325–1333.

Duberstein, P. R., & Conwell, Y. (2000). Suicide. In S. K. Whitbourne (Ed.), *Psychopathology in later life* (pp. 245–276). New York, NY: Wiley.

Dufour, A., & Candas, V. (2007). Ageing and thermal responses during passive heat exposure: Sweating and sensory aspects. *European Journal of Applied Physiology, 100*, 19–26.

Dufour, A. B., Broe, K. E., Nguyen, U. S., Gagnon, D. R., Hillstrom, H. J., Walker, A. H.,...Hannan, M. T. (2009). Foot pain: Is current or past shoewear a factor? *Arthritis & Rheumatism, 61*, 1352–1358.

Duner, A., & Nordstrom, M. (2005). Intentions and strategies among elderly people: Coping in everyday life. *Journal of Aging Studies, 19*, 437–451.

Dy, S., & Lynn, J. (2007). Getting services right for those sick enough to die. *BMJ: British Medical Journal, 334*, 511–513.

Easterlin, R. A. (2006). Life cycle happiness and its sources: Intersections of psychology, economics, and demography. *Journal of Economic Psychology, 27*, 463–482.

Eastwick, P. W., & Finkel, E. J. (2008). Sex differences in mate preferences revisited: Do people know what they initially desire in a romantic partner? *Journal of Personality and Social Psychology, 94*, 245–264.

Eby, L. T., Maher, C. P., & Butts, M. M. (2010). The intersection of work and family life: The role of affect. *Annual Review of Psychology, 61*, 599–622.

Economist. (2007). Grandparents raising grandchildren: Skipping a generation. *Economist, 383*. Retrieved from http://silk.library.umass.edu:2048/login?url=http://search.ebscohost.com/login.aspx?direct=true&db=qsh&AN=BSSI07124959&site=ehost-live&scope=site.

Edelstein, B., Martin, R. R., & McKee, D. R. (2000). Assessment of older adult psychopathology. In S. K. Whitbourne (Ed.), *Psychopathology in later life* (pp. 61–88). New York, NY: Wiley.

EDUCAUSE Center for Applied Research. (2008). The ECAR Study of Undergraduate Students and Information Technology, 2008. Retrieved from http://www.educause.edu/ers0808.

Eggermont, L. H., Milberg, W. P., Lipsitz, L. A., Scherder, E. J., & Leveille, S. G. (2009). Physical activity and executive function in aging: The MOBILIZE Boston Study. *Journal of the American Geriatrics Society, 57*, 1750–1756.

Eid, M., & Diener, E. (2001). Norms for experiencing emotions in different cultures: Inter- and intranational differences. *Journal of Personality & Social Psychology, 81*, 869–885.

Ekkekakis, P., Lind, E., & Vazou, S. (2009). Affective responses to increasing levels of exercise intensity in normal-weight, overweight, and obese middle-aged women. *Obesity (Silver Spring), 18*, 79–85.

El Ghissassi, F., Baan, R., Straif, K., Grosse, Y., Secretan, B., Bouvard, V.,...Cogliano, V. (2009). A review of human carcinogens—Part D: Radiation. *Lancet Oncology, 10*, 751–752.

Elder, G. H., Jr., Shanahan, M., & Clipp, E. C. (1994). When war comes to men's lives: Life course patterns in family, work, and health. *Psychology and Aging, 9*, 5–16.

Elias, M. F., Elias, P. K., D'Agostino, R. B., Silbershatz, H., & Wolf, P. A. (1997). Role of age, education, and gender on cognitive performance in the Framingham Heart Study: Community-based norms. *Experimental Aging Research, 23*, 201–235.

Eliasson, L., Birkhed, D., Osterberg, T., & Carlen, A. (2006). Minor salivary gland secretion rates and immunoglobulin A in adults and the elderly. *European Journal of Oral Sciences, 114*, 494–499.

Elliot, S. J., Karl, M., Berho, M., Xia, X., Pereria-Simon, S., Espinosa-Heidmann, D.,...Striker, G. E. (2006). Smoking induces glomerulosclerosis in aging estrogen-deficient mice through cross-talk between TGF-beta1 and IGF-I signaling pathways. *Journal of the Americal Society Nephrology, 17*, 3315–3324.

Elovainio, M., Kivimaki, M., Ferrie, J. E., Gimeno, D., De Vogli, R., Virtanen, M.,...Singh-Manoux, A. (2009). Physical and cognitive function in midlife: Reciprocal effects? A 5-year follow-up of the Whitehall II study. *Journal of Epidemiology and Community Health, 63*, 468–473.

Emaus, N., Berntsen, G. K., Joakimsen, R., & Fonnebo, V. (2006). Longitudinal changes in forearm bone mineral density in women and men aged 45–84 years: The Tromso Study, a population-based study. *American Journal of Epidemiology, 163*, 441–449.

Engels, G. I., Duijsens, I. J., Haringsma, R., & van Putten, C. M. (2003). Personality disorders in the elderly compared to four younger age groups: A cross-sectional study of community residents and mental health patients. *Journal of Personality Disorders, 17*, 447–459.

Enserink, M. (1998). First Alzheimer's disease confirmed. *Science, 279*, 2037.

Erickson, K. I., & Kramer, A. F. (2009). Aerobic exercise effects on cognitive and neural plasticity in older adults. *British Journal of Sports Medicine, 43*, 22–24.

Erickson, K. I., Prakash, R. S., Voss, M. W., Chaddock, L., Hu, L., Morris, K. S.,...Kramer, A. F. (2009). Aerobic fitness is associated with hippocampal volume in elderly humans. *Hippocampus, 19*, 1030–1039.

Erikson, E. H. (1963). *Childhood and society* (2nd ed.). New York, NY: Norton.

Erikson, E. H., Erikson, J. M., & Kivnick, H. Q. (1986). *Vital involvement in old age*. New York, NY: Norton.

Erqou, S., Kaptoge, S., Perry, P. L., Di Angelantonio, E., Thompson, A., White, I. R.,...Danesh, J. (2009). Lipoprotein(a) concentration and the risk of coronary heart disease, stroke, and nonvascular mortality. *Journal of the American Medical Association, 302*, 412–423.

Espay, A. J., Mandybur, G. T., & Revilla, F. J. (2006). Surgical treatment of movement disorders. *Clinics in Geriatric Medicine, 22*, 813–825.

Espino, D. V., Lichtenstein, M. J., Palmer, R. F., & Hazuda, H. P. (2004). Evaluation of the mini-mental state examination's internal consistency in a community-based sample of Mexican-American and European-American elders: Results from the San Antonio Longitudinal Study of Aging. *Journal of the American Geriatrics Society, 52,* 822–827.

Espiritu, J. R. (2008). Aging-related sleep changes. *Clinics in Geriatric Medicine, 24,* 1–14.

Ettington, D. R. (1998). Successful career plateauing. *Journal of Vocational Behavior, 52,* 72–88.

Evans, S., Patt, I., Giosan, C., Spielman, L., & Difede, J. (2009). Disability and posttraumatic stress disorder in disaster relief workers responding to September 11, 2001 World Trade Center disaster. *Journal of Clinical Psychology, 65,* 684–694.

Fallico, F., Siciliano, L., & Yip, F. (2005). Hypothermia-related deaths—United States, 2003–2004. *Morbidity and Mortality Weekly Report, 54,* 173–175.

Families USA (2010). Retrieved from http://www.familiesusa.org/.

Farrell, M. P., & Rosenberg, S. D. (1981). *Men at midlife.* Boston, MA: Auburn House.

Farrimond, S., Knight, R. G., & Titov, N. (2006). The effects of aging on remembering intentions: Performance on a simulated shopping task. *Applied Cognitive Psychology, 20,* 533–555.

Federal Interagency Forum on Age-Related Statistics. (2009). Older Americans 2008: Key indicators of well-being.

Feist, G. J. (2006). How development and personality influence scientific thought, interest, and achievement. *Review of General Psychology, 10,* 163–182.

Feist, G. J., & Barron, F. X. (2003). Predicting creativity from early to late adulthood: Intellect, potential, and personality. *Journal of Research in Personality, 37,* 62–88.

Feldman, H. A., Longcope, C., Derby, C. A., Johannes, C. B., Araujo, A. B., Coviello, A. D.,...McKinlay, J. B. (2002). Age trends in the level of serum testosterone and other hormones in middle-aged men: Longitudinal results from the Massachusetts male aging study. *Journal of Clinical Endocrinology and Metabolism, 87,* 589–598.

Felicissimo, M. F., Carneiro, M. M., Saleme, C. S., Pinto, R. Z., da Fonseca, A. M., & da Silva-Filho, A. L. (2010). Intensive supervised versus unsupervised pelvic floor muscle training for the treatment of stress urinary incontinence: A randomized comparative trial. *International Urogynecology: Journal of Pelvic Floor Dysfunction.* doi:10.1007/s00192-010-1125-1.

Fenn, D. S., & Ganzini, L. (1999). Attitudes of Oregon psychologists toward physician-assisted suicide and the Oregon Death With Dignity Act. *Professional Psychology: Research & Practice, 30,* 235–244.

Ferguson, R., & Brohaugh, B. (2010). The aging of Aquarius. *Journal of Consumer Marketing, 27,* 76–81.

Fernandes, M. A., Pacurar, A., Moscovitch, M., & Grady, C. (2006). Neural correlates of auditory recognition under full and divided attention in younger and older adults. *Neuropsychologia, 44,* 2452–2464.

Ferrari, S. L., & Rizzoli, R. (2005). Gene variants for osteoporosis and their pleiotropic effects in aging. *Molecular Aspects of Medicine, 26,* 145–167.

Ferrario, S. R., Cardillo, V., Vicario, F., Balzarini, E., & Zotti, A. M. (2004). Advanced cancer at home: Caregiving and bereavement. *Palliative Medicine, 18,* 129–136.

Ferraro, F. R. (2002). *Minority and cross-cultural aspects of neuropsychological assessment.* Bristol, PA: Swets and Zeitlinger.

Ferraro, K. F., & Farmer, M. M. (1996). Double jeopardy, aging as leveler, or persistent health inequality? A longitudinal analysis of white and black Americans. *Journal of Gerontology: Social Sciences, 51,* S319–S328.

Ferri, R., Gschliesser, V., Frauscher, B., Poewe, W., & Hogl, B. (2009). Periodic leg movements during sleep and periodic limb movement disorder in patients presenting with unexplained insomnia. *Clinics in Neurophysiology, 120,* 257–263.

Fetveit, A. (2009). Late-life insomnia: A review. *Geriatrics and Gerontology International, 9,* 220–234.

Field, A. E., Colditz, G. A., Willett, W. C., Longcope, C., & McKinlay, J. B. (1994). The relation of smoking, age, relative weight, and dietary intake to serum adrenal steroids, sex hormones, and sex hormone-binding globulin in middle-aged men. *Journal of Clinical Endocrinology and Metabolism, 79,* 1310–1316.

Field, M. J., Cassel, C. K., & Committee on Care at the End of Life. (1997). *Approaching death: Improving care at the end of life, Institute of Medicine, Division of Health Care Services.* Washington, DC: National Academy Press.

Field, N. P., Gal-Oz, E., & Bonanno, G. A. (2003). Continuing bonds and adjustment at 5 years after the death of a spouse. *Journal of Consulting & Clinical Psychology, 71,* 110–117.

Fields, J., O'Connell, M., & Downs, B. (2006). *Grandparents in the United States, 2001.* Paper presented at the annual meeting of the American Sociological Association, Montreal Convention Center, Montreal, Quebec, Canada, August 10, 2006.

Fiksenbaum, L. M., Greenglass, E. R., & Eaton, J. (2006). Perceived social support, hassles, and coping among the elderly. *Journal of Applied Gerontology, 25,* 17–30.

Fingerman, K. L. (1996). Sources of tension in the aging mother and adult daughter relationship. *Psychology and Aging, 11,* 591–606.

Fingerman, K. L. (2001). *Aging mothers and their adult daughters: A study in mixed emotions.* New York, NY: Springer.

Fingerman, K. L., & Griffiths, P. C. (1999). Seasons greetings: Adults' social contacts at the holiday season. *Psychology and Aging, 14,* 192–205.

Fingerman, K. L., Hay, E. L., & Birditt, K. S. (2004). The best of ties, the worst of ties: Close, problematic, and ambivalent social relationships. *Journal of Marriage and Family, 66,* 792–808.

Fins, J. J., Miller, F. G., Acres, C. A., Bacchetta, M. D., Huzzard, L. L., & Rapkin, B. D. (1999). End-of-life decision-making in the hospital: Current practice and future prospects. *Journal of Pain & Symptom Management, 17,* 6–15.

Fisher, C. D. (2002). Antecedents and consequences of real-time affective reactions at work. *Motivation and Emotion, 26,* 3–30.

Fiske, A., Wetherell, J. L., & Gatz, M. (2009). Depression in older adults. *Annual Review of Clinical Psychology, 5,* 363–389.

Fjell, A. M., Walhovd, K. B., Fennema-Notestine, C., McEvoy, L. K., Hagler, D. J., Holland, D.,...Dale, A. M. (2009). One-year brain atrophy evident in healthy aging. *Journal of Neuroscience, 29,* 15223–15231.

Flint, A. J. (2005). Generalised anxiety disorder in elderly patients: Epidemiology, diagnosis and treatment options. *Drugs and Aging, 22,* 101–114.

Floyd, F. J., & Wasner, G. H. (1994). Social exchange, equity, and commitment: Structural equation modeling of dating relationships. *Journal of Family Psychology, 8,* 55–73.

Foley, D. J., Vitiello, M. V., Bliwise, D. L., Ancoli-Israel, S., Monjan, A. A., & Walsh, J. K. (2007). Frequent napping is associated with excessive daytime sleepiness, depression, pain, and nocturia in older adults: Findings from the National Sleep Foundation "2003 Sleep in America" Poll. *American Journal of Geriatric Psychiatry, 15,* 344–350.

Folstein, M. F., Folstein, S. E., & McHugh, P. R. (1975). Mini-Mental State: A practical method for grading the cognitive state of patients for the clinician. *Journal of Psychiatric Research, 12,* 189–198.

Ford, D. H., & Lerner, R. M. (Eds.). (1992). *Developmental systems theory: An integrative approach.* Newbury Park, CA: Sage.

Formiga, F., Olmedo, C., Lopez-Soto, A., Navarro, M., Culla, A., & Pujol, R. (2007). Dying in hospital of terminal heart failure or severe dementia: The circumstances associated with death and the opinions of caregivers. [Article]. *Palliative Medicine, 21,* 35–40.

Forsmo, S., Langhammer, A., Forsen, L., & Schei, B. (2005). Forearm bone mineral density in an unselected population of 2,779 men and women—the HUNT Study, Norway. *Osteoporosis International, 16,* 562–567.

Fossey, J., Ballard, C., Juszczak, E., James, I., Alder, N., Jacoby, R.,...Howard, R. (2006). Effect of enhanced psychosocial care on antipsychotic use in nursing home residents with severe dementia: Cluster randomised trial. *BMJ: British Medical Journal, 332,* 756–761.

Fowler, F. J., Jr., Coppola, K. M., & Teno, J. M. (1999). Methodological challenges for measuring quality of care at the end of life. *Journal of Pain & Symptom Management, 17,* 114–119.

Fraser, J., Maticka-Tyndale, E., & Smylie, L. (2004). Sexuality of Canadian women at midlife. *Canadian Journal of Human Sexuality, 13,* 171–188.

Frazer, K. A., Ballinger, D. G., Cox, D. R., Hinds, D. A., Stuve, L. L., Gibbs, R. A.,...Stewart, J. (2007). A second generation human haplotype map of over 3.1 million SNPs. *Nature, 449,* 851–861.

Frazier, L. D., Johnson, P. M., Gonzalez, G. K., & Kafka, C. L. (2002). Psychosocial influences on possible selves: A comparison of three cohorts of older adults. *International Journal of Behavioral Development, 26,* 308–317.

Friedman, H. S., Tucker, J. S., Schwartz, J. E., Martin, L. R., Tomlinson-Keasey, C., Wingard, D. L.,...Criqui, M. H. (1995). Childhood conscientiousness and longevity: Health behaviors and cause of death. *Journal of Personality and Social Psychology, 68,* 696–703.

Friedman, M., & Rosenman, R. H. (1974). *Type A behavior and your heart.* New York, NY: Knopf.

Fry, P. S. (1997). Grandparent's reactions to the death of a grandchild: An exploratory factor analytic study. *Omega—Journal of Death & Dying, 35,* 119–140.

Fuiano, G., Sund, S., Mazza, G., Rosa, M., Caglioti, A., Gallo, G.,...Conte, G. (2001). Renal hemodynamic response to maximal vasodilating stimulus in healthy older subjects. *Kidney International, 59,* 1052–1058.

Fung, H. H., Lu, A. Y., Goren, D., Isaacowitz, D. M., Wadlinger, H. A., & Wilson, H. R. (2008). Age-related positivity enhancement is not universal: Older Chinese look away from positive stimuli. *Psychology and Aging, 23,* 440–446.

Funk, L. M. (2004). Who wants to be involved? Decision-making preferences among residents of long-term care facilities. *Canadian Journal of Aging, 23,* 47–58.

Funk, L. M. (2010). Prioritizing parental autonomy: Adult children's accounts of feeling responsible and supporting aging parents. *Journal of Aging Studies, 24,* 57–64.

Furnham, A., Eracleous, A., & Chamorro-Premuzic, T. (2009). Personality, motivation and job satisfaction: Hertzberg meets the Big Five. *Journal of Managerial Psychology, 24,* 765–779.

Gabay, O., Hall, D. J., Berenbaum, F., Henrotin, Y., & Sanchez, C. (2008). Osteoarthritis and obesity: Experimental models. *Joint Bone and Spine, 75,* 675–679.

Gabelle, A., & Dauvilliers, Y. (2010). Editorial: Sleep and dementia. *Journal of Nutrition Health and Aging, 14,* 201–202.

Gadalla, T. M. (2009). Sense of mastery, social support, and health in elderly Canadians. *Journal of Aging and Health, 21,* 581–595.

Gagne, M., & Deci, E. L. (2005). Self-determination theory and work motivation. *Journal of Organizational Behavior, 26,* 331–362.

Gagnon, M., Hersen, M., Kabacoff, R. L., & Van Hasselt, V. B. (1999). Interpersonal and psychological correlates of marital dissatisfaction in late life: A review. *Clinical Psychology Review, 19,* 359–378.

Galper, D. I., Trivedi, M. H., Barlow, C. E., Dunn, A. L., & Kampert, J. B. (2006). Inverse association between physical inactivity and mental health in men and women. *Medicine and Science in Sports and Exercise, 38,* 173–178.

Galvan, V., Gorostiza, O. F., Banwait, S., Ataie, M., Logvinova, A. V., Sitaraman, S.,...Bredesen, D. E. (2006). Reversal of Alzheimer's-like pathology and behavior in human APP transgenic mice by mutation of Asp664. *Proceedings of the National Academies of Sciences of the United States of America, 103,* 7130–7135.

Ganzini, L., Nelson, H. D., Lee, M. A., Kraemer, D. F., Schmidt, T. A., & Delorit, M. A. (2001). Oregon physicians' attitudes about and experiences with end-of-life care since passage of the Oregon

Death with Dignity Act. *Journal of the American Medical Association*, *285*, 2363–2369.

Garcia-Fabela, L., Melano-Carranza, E., Aguilar-Navarro, S., Garcia-Lara, J. M., Gutierrez-Robledo, L. M., & Avila-Funes, J. A. (2009). Hypertension as a risk factor for developing depressive symptoms among community-dwelling elders. *Revista de Investigacion Clinica 61*, 274–280.

Garden, S. E., Phillips, L. H., & MacPherson, S. E. (2001). Midlife aging, open-ended planning, and laboratory measures of executive function. *Neuropsychology*, *15*, 472–482.

Gardner, H. (1983). *Frames of mind: The theory of multiple intelligences*. New York, NY: Basic Books.

Gardner, H. (1993). *Multiple intelligences: The theory in practice*. New York, NY: Basic Books.

Gaugler, J. E., Duval, S., Anderson, K. A., & Kane, R. L. (2007). Predicting nursing home admission in the U.S: A meta-analysis. *BMC Geriatrics*, *7*, 13.

Gaunt, R. (2006). Couple similarity and marital satisfaction: Are similar spouses happier? *Journal of Personality*, *74*, 1401–1420.

Gauthier, S., & Scheltens, P. (2009). Can we do better in developing new drugs for Alzheimer's disease? *Alzheimers and Dementia*, *5*, 489–491.

Gavrin, J., & Chapman, C. R. (1995). Clinical management of dying patients. *Western Journal of Medicine*, *163*, 268–277.

Gazzaley, A., Clapp, W., Kelley, J., McEvoy, K., Knight, R. T., & D'Esposito, M. (2008). Age-related top-down suppression deficit in the early stages of cortical visual memory processing. *Proceedings of the National Academy of Sciences*, *105*, 13122–13126.

Geda, Y. E., Roberts, R. O., Knopman, D. S., Christianson, T. J., Pankratz, V. S., Ivnik, R. J.,...Rocca, W. A. (2010). Physical exercise, aging, and mild cognitive impairment: A population-based study. *Archives of Neurology*, *67*, 80–86.

Gee, S., & Baillie, J. (1999). Happily ever after? An exploration of retirement expectations. *Educational Gerontology*, *25*, 109–128.

Georges, J. J., Onwuteaka-Philipsen, B. D., Muller, M. T., Van Der Wal, G., Van Der Heide, A., & Van Der Maas, P. J. (2007). Relatives' perspective on the terminally ill patients who died after euthanasia or physician-assisted suicide: A retrospective cross-sectional interview study in the Netherlands. *Death Studies*, *31*, 1–15.

Geurts, T., Poortman, A.-R., van Tilburg, T., & Dykstra, P. A. (2009). Contact between grandchildren and their grandparents in early adulthood. *Journal of Family Issues*, *30*, 1698–1713.

Giannantonio, C. M., & Hurley-Hanson, A. E. (2006). Applying image norms across Super's career development stages. *The Career Development Quarterly*, *54*, 318–330.

Giannoulis, M. G., Sonksen, P. H., Umpleby, M., Breen, L., Pentecost, C., Whyte, M.,...Martin, F. C. (2006). The effects of growth hormone and/or testosterone in healthy elderly men: A randomized controlled trial. *Journal of Clinical Endocrinology and Metabolism*, *91*, 477–484.

Gilhooly, M. L., Gilhooly, K. J., Phillips, L. H., Harvey, D., Brady, A., & Hanlon, P. (2007). Real-world problem solving and quality of life in older people. *British Journal of Health Psychology*, *12*, 587–600.

Gill, S. C., Butterworth, P., Rodgers, B., Anstey, K. J., Villamil, E., & Melzer, D. (2006). Mental health and the timing of men's retirement. *Social Psychiatry and Psychiatric Epidemiology*, *41*, 933–954.

Gilstad, J. R., & Finucane, T. E. (2008). Results, rhetoric, and randomized trials: The case of donepezil. *Journal of the American Geriatrics Society*, *56*, 1556–1562.

Gimeno, D., Tabak, A. G., Ferrie, J. E., Shipley, M. J., De Vogli, R., Elovainio, M.,...Kivimaki, M. (2010). Justice at work and metabolic syndrome: The Whitehall II study. *Occupational and Environmental Medicine*, *67*, 256–262.

Gitlin, L. N., Hauck, W. W., Dennis, M. P., Winter, L., Hodgson, N., & Schinfeld, S. (2009). Long-term effect on mortality of a home intervention that reduces functional difficulties in older adults: Results from a randomized trial. *Journal of the American Geriatrics Society*, *57*, 476–481.

Glaser, B. G., & Strauss, A. L. (1968). *Time for dying*. Chicago, IL: Aldine.

Global Initiative for Chronic Obstructive Lung Disease (2009). *Global strategy for the diagnosis, management, and prevention of chronic obstructive pulmonary disease*. Medical Communications Resources.

Gluck, J., & Bluck, S. (2007). Looking back across the life span: A life story account of the reminiscence bump. *Memory and Cognition*, *35*, 1928–1939.

Goh, J. O., & Park, D. C. (2009). Neuroplasticity and cognitive aging: The scaffolding theory of aging and cognition. *Restorative Neurology and Neuroscience*, *27*, 391–403.

Gold, D. T. (1989). Sibling relationships in old age: A typology. *International Journal of Aging and Human Development*, *28*, 37–51.

Goldberg, A. E., & Sayer, A. (2006). Lesbian couples' relationship quality across the transition to parenthood. *Journal of Marriage and Family*, *68*, 87–100.

Golden, J., Conroy, R. M., Bruce, I., Denihan, A., Greene, E., Kirby, M.,...Lawlor, B. A. (2009). Loneliness, social support networks, mood and wellbeing in community-dwelling elderly. *International Journal of Geriatric Psychiatry*, *24*, 694–700.

Goldspink, D. F., George, K. P., Chantler, P. D., Clements, R. E., Sharp, L., Hodges, G.,...Cable, N. T. (2009). A study of presbycardia, with gender differences favoring ageing women. *International Journal of Cardiology*, *137*, 236–245.

Gomez, V., Krings, F., Bangerter, A., & Grob, A. (2009). The influence of personality and life events on subjective well-being from a life span perspective. *Journal of Research in Personality*, *43*, 345–354.

Goodlin, S. J., Winzelberg, G. S., Teno, J. M., Whedon, M., & Lynn, J. (1998). Death in the hospital. *Archives of Internal Medicine*, *158*, 1570–1572.

Goodwin, P., McGill, B., & Chandra, A. (2009). Who marries and when? Age at first marriage in the United States: 2002. *NCHS Data Brief, Number 19*, June.

Gottesman, L. E., & Bourestom, N. C. (1974). Why nursing homes do what they do. *Gerontologist, 14*, 501–506.

Gottfredson, G. D. (2002). Interests, aspirations, self-estimates, and the Self-Directed Search. *Journal of Career Assessment, 10*, 200–208.

Gottman, J., Coan, J., Carrere, S., & Swanson, C. (1998). Predicting marital happiness and stability from newlywed interactions. *Journal of Marriage and Family, 60*, 5–22.

Gottman, J. M., & Driver, J. L. (2005). Dysfunctional marital conflict and everyday marital interaction. *Journal of Divorce & Remarriage, 43*, 63–78.

Gottman, J. M., & Levenson, R. W. (2000). The timing of divorce: Predicting when a couple will divorce over a 14-year period. *Journal of Marriage and Family, 62*, 737–745.

Gottman, J. M., & Levenson, R. W. (2002). A two-factor model for predicting when a couple will divorce: Exploratory analyses using 14-year longitudinal data. *Family Process, 41*, 83–96.

Gouin, J. P., Hantsoo, L., & Kiecolt-Glaser, J. K. (2008). Immune dysregulation and chronic stress among older adults: A review. *Neuroimmunomodulation, 15*, 251–259.

Gould, R. L. (1978). *Transformations: Growth and change in adult life*. New York, NY: Simon & Schuster.

Government Accountability Office. (2008). Nursing homes: Federal monitoring surveys demonstrate continued understatement of serious care problems and CMS oversight weaknesses. Washington, DC: Government Accountability Office.

Gradinaru, V., Mogri, M., Thompson, K. R., Henderson, J. M., & Deisseroth, K. (2009). Optical deconstruction of Parkinsonian neural circuitry. *Science, 324*, 354–359.

Grant, B. S., Harford, T. C., Dawson, D. A., Chou, P., Dufour, M., & Pickering, R. (1995). Prevalence of DSM-IV alcohol abuse and dependence, United States, 1992. *Alcohol Health and Research World, 18*, 243–248.

Green, T. L., & Darity, W. A., Jr. (2010). Under the skin: Using theories from biology and the social sciences to explore the mechanisms behind the black-white health gap. *American Journal of Public Health, 100*, S36–S40.

Greene, J. A., & Brown, S. C. (2009). The wisdom development scale: Further validity investigations. *International Journal of Aging and Human Development, 68*, 289–320.

Greenhaus, J. H., Collins, K. M., & Shaw, J. D. (2003). The relation between work-family balance and quality of life. *Journal of Vocational Behavior, 63*, 510–531.

Greenhaus, J. H., & Powell, G. N. (2006). When work and family are allies: A theory of work-family enrichment. *Academy of Management Review, 31*, 72–92.

Greenwald, D. A. (2004). Aging, the gastrointestinal tract, and risk of acid-related disease. *American Journal of Medicine, 117 Suppl 5A*, 8S–13S.

Greif, G. L. (1995). Single fathers with custody following separation and divorce. *Marriage and Family Review, 20*, 213–231.

Groen, B. E., Smulders, E., de Kam, D., Duysens, J., & Weerdesteyn, V. (2010). Martial arts fall training to prevent hip fractures in the elderly. *Osteoporosis International, 21*, 215–221.

Grosse, Y., Baan, R., Straif, K., Secretan, B., El Ghissassi, F., Bouvard, V.,... Cogliano, V. (2009). A review of human carcinogens—Part A: Pharmaceuticals. *Lancet Oncology, 10*, 13–14.

Grote, N. K., Clark, M. S., & Moore, A. (2004). Perceptions of injustice in family work: The role of psychological distress. *Journal of Family Psychology, 18*, 480–492.

Grote, N. K., Naylor, K. E., & Clark, M. S. (2002). Perceiving the division of family work to be unfair: Do social comparisons, enjoyment, and competence matter? *Journal of Family Psychology, 16*, 510–522.

Grubeck-Loebenstein, B. (2010). Fading immune protection in old age: Vaccination in the elderly. *Journal of Comparative Physiology, 142*, S116–S119.

Gruenewald, T. L., Karlamangla, A. S., Greendale, G. A., Singer, B. H., & Seeman, T. E. (2007). Feelings of usefulness to others, disability, and mortality in older adults: The MacArthur Study of Successful Aging. *Journals of Gerontology Series B: Psychological Sciences and Social Sciences, 62*, P28–P37.

Gruenewald, T. L., Karlamangla, A. S., Greendale, G. A., Singer, B. H., & Seeman, T. E. (2009). Increased mortality risk in older adults with persistently low or declining feelings of usefulness to others. *Journal of Aging and Health, 21*, 398–425.

Grundy, E., & Henretta, J. C. (2006). Between elderly parents and adult children: A new look at the intergenerational care provided by the "sandwich generation". *Ageing and Society, 26*, 707–722.

Gruneir, A., Mor, V., Weitzen, S., Truchil, R., Teno, J., & Roy, J. (2007). Where people die: A multilevel approach to understanding influences on site of death in America. *Medical Care: Research and Review, 64*, 351–378.

Grzywacz, J. G., & Marks, N. F. (2000). Reconceptualizing the work-family interface: An ecological perspective on the correlates of positive and negative spillover between work and family. *Journal of Occupational Health Psychology, 5*, 111–126.

Guadalupe-Grau, A., Fuentes, T., Guerra, B., & Calbet, J. A. (2009). Exercise and bone mass in adults. *Sports Medicine, 39*, 439–468.

Gubin, D. G., Gubin, G. D., Waterhouse, J., & Weinert, D. (2006). The circadian body temperature rhythm in the elderly: Effect of single daily melatonin dosing. *Chronobiology International, 23*, 639–658.

Gum, A. M., King-Kallimanis, B., & Kohn, R. (2009). Prevalence of mood, anxiety, and substance-abuse disorders for older Americans in the National Comorbidity Survey-Replication. *American Journal of Geriatric Psychiatry, 17*, 782–792.

Ha, J. H. (2009). The effects of positive and negative support from children on widowed older adults' psychological adjustment: A longitudinal analysis. *Gerontologist, 50*, 471–481.

Hagestad, G. O., & Neugarten, B. L. (1985). Age and the life course. In R. H. Binstock & E. Shanas (Eds.), *Handbook of aging and the social sciences* (pp. 35–61). New York, NY: Van Nostrand Reinhold.

Haidet, P., Hamel, M. B., Davis, R. B., Wenger, N., Reding, D., Kussin, P. S.,...Phillips, R. S. (1998). Outcomes, preferences for resuscitation, and physician-patient communication among patients with metastatic colorectal cancer. SUPPORT Investigators. Study to Understand Prognoses and Preferences for Outcomes and Risks of Treatments. *American Journal of Medicine, 105*, 222–229.

Hakim, R. B., Teno, J. M., Harrell, F. E., Jr., Knaus, W. A., Wenger, N., Phillips, R. S.,...Lynn, J. (1996). Factors associated with do-not-resuscitate orders: Patients' preferences, prognoses, and physicians' judgments. SUPPORT Investigators. Study to Understand Prognoses and Preferences for Outcomes and Risks of Treatment. *Annals of Internal Medicine, 125*, 284–293.

Haley, W. E., Allen, R. S., Reynolds, S., Chen, H., Burton, A., & Gallagher-Thompson, D. (2002). Family issues in end-of-life decision making and end-of-life care. *American Behavioral Scientist, 46*, 284–298.

Halgin, R. P., & Whitbourne, S. K. (2008). *Abnormal psychology: Clinical perspectives on psychological disorders* (6th ed.). New York, NY: McGraw-Hill.

Hall, P. A., Dubin, J. A., Crossley, M., Holmqvist, M. E., & D'Arcy, C. (2009). Does executive function explain the IQ-mortality association? Evidence from the Canadian Study on Health and Aging. *Psychosomatic Medicine, 71*, 196–204.

Hamel, M. B., Phillips, R. S., Teno, J. M., Lynn, J., Galanos, A. N., Davis, R. B.,...Goldman, L. (1996). Seriously ill hospitalized adults: Do we spend less on older patients? Support Investigators. Study to Understand Prognoses and Preference for Outcomes and Risks of Treatments. *Journal of the American Geriatrics Society, 44*, 1043–1048.

Hamilton, B. E., Martin, J. A., & Ventura, S. J. (2010). Births: Preliminary data for 2008. *National Vital Statistics Reports, 58, No. 16.*

Hamilton, M. (1959). The assessment of anxiety states by rating. *British Journal of Medical Psychology, 32*, 50–55.

Hamilton, M. (1967). Development of a rating scale for primary depressive illness. *British Journal of Social and Clinical Psychology, 6*, 278–296.

Hanke, T. A., & Tiberio, D. (2006). Lateral rhythmic unipedal stepping in younger, middle-aged, and older adults. *Journal of Geriatric Physical Therapy, 29*, 22–27.

Harber, M. P., Konopka, A. R., Douglass, M. D., Minchev, K., Kaminsky, L. A., Trappe, T. A.,...Trappe, S. (2009). Aerobic exercise training improves whole muscle and single myofiber size and function in older women. *American Journal of Physiology: Regulative, Integrative, and Comparative Physiology, 297*, R1452–R1459.

Harding, S., Teyhan, A., Rosato, M., & Santana, P. (2008). All cause and cardiovascular mortality in African migrants living in Portugal: Evidence of large social inequalities. *European Journal of Cardiovascular and Preventive Rehabilitation, 15*, 670–676.

Hardy, M., & Quadagno, J. (1995). Satisfaction with the early retirement decision: Making choices in the auto industry. *Journal of Gerontology, 50*, S217–S228.

Hardy, S. E., Concato, J., & Gill, T. M. (2004). Resilience of community-dwelling older persons. *Journal of the American Geriatrics Society, 52*, 257–262.

Harmer, P. A., & Li, F. (2008). Tai Chi and falls prevention in older people. *Medicine and Science in Sports and Exercise, 52*, 124–134.

Harmon, L. W., Hansen, J. C., Borgen, F. H., & Hammer, A. L. (1994). *Strong Interest Inventory applications and technical guide.* Palo Alto, CA: Consulting Psychologists Press.

Harms, C. A. (2006). Does gender affect pulmonary function and exercise capacity? *Respiratory Physiology and Neurobiology, 151*, 124–131.

Harold, D., Abraham, R., Hollingworth, P., Sims, R., Gerrish, A., Hamshere, M. L.,...Williams, J. (2009). Genome-wide association study identifies variants at CLU and PICALM associated with Alzheimer's disease. *Nature Genetics, 41*, 1088–1093.

Harpur, T. J., Hart, S. D., & Hare, R. D. (2002). Personality of the psychopath. In P. T. J. Costa & T. A. Widiger (Eds.), *Personality disorders and the five-factor model of personality* (2nd ed., pp. 299–324). Washington, DC: American Psychological Association.

Harrington, C., Carrillo, H., & Blank, B. W. (2009). Nursing facilities, staffing, residents, and facility deficiences, 2003 through 2008. Retrieved from http://www.pascenter.org/nursing_homes/nursing_trends_2008.php.

Harrington, J., & Lee-Chiong, T. (2009). Obesity and aging. *Clinics in Chest Medicine, 30*, 609–614.

Harrison, P. M., & Beck, A. J. (2005). Prisoners in 2004. *Bureau of Justice Statistics Bulletin, NCJ 210677.*

Hartup, W. W., & Stevens, N. (1997). Friendships and adaptation in the life course. *Psychological Bulletin, 121*, 355–370.

Harwood, D. G., Sultzer, D. L., & Wheatley, M. V. (2000). Impaired insight in Alzheimer disease: Association with cognitive deficits, psychiatric symptoms, and behavioral disturbances. *Neuropsychiatry, Neuropsychology, and Behavioral Neurology, 13*, 83–88.

Harwood, K., McLean, N., & Durkin, K. (2007). First-time mothers' expectations of parenthood: What happens when optimistic expectations are not matched by later experiences? *Developmental Psychology, 43*, 1–12.

Haskell, W. L., Lee, I. M., Pate, R. R., Powell, K. E., Blair, S. N., Franklin, B. A.,...Bauman, A. (2007). Physical activity and public health: Updated recommendation for adults from the American College of Sports Medicine and the American Heart Association. *Medicine and Science in Sports and Exercise, 39*, 1423–1434.

Hastings, E. C., & West, R. L. (2009). The relative success of a self-help and a group-based memory training program for older adults. *Psychology and Aging, 24*, 586–594.

Hatfield, E., Rapson, R. L., & Aumer-Ryan, K. (2008). Social justice in love relationships: Recent developments. *Social Justice Research, 21*, 413–431.

Hawkley, L. C., Thisted, R. A., Masi, C. M., & Cacioppo, J. T. (2010). Loneliness predicts increased blood pressure: 5-year cross-lagged analyses in middle-aged and older adults. *Psychology and Aging, 25*, 132–141.

Hayflick, L. (1994). *How and why we age.* New York, NY: Ballantine Books.

Hays, J. C., Gold, D. T., & Peiper, C. F. (1997). Sibling bereavement in late life. *Omega—Journal of Death & Dying, 35*, 25–42.

He, W., Sangupta, M., Velkoff, V. A., & DeBarros, K. A. (2005). *65+ in the United States: 2005. Current Population Reports Special Studies. U.S. Census Bureau, Current Population Reports, P23-209.* Washington, DC: U.S. Government Printing Office.

Head, D., Kennedy, K. M., Rodrigue, K. M., & Raz, N. (2009). Age differences in perseveration: Cognitive and neuroanatomical mediators of performance on the Wisconsin Card Sorting Test. *Neuropsychologia, 47*, 1200–1203.

Heckman, G. A., & McKelvie, R. S. (2008). Cardiovascular aging and exercise in healthy older adults. *Clinical Journal of Sports Medicine, 18*, 479–485.

Hedberg, K., Hopkins, D., & Kohn, M. (2003). Five years of legal physician-assisted suicide in Oregon. *New England Journal of Medicine, 348*, 961–964.

Heffner, K. L., Loving, T. J., Kiecolt-Glaser, J. K., Himawan, L. K., Glaser, R., & Malarkey, W. B. (2006). Older spouses' cortisol responses to marital conflict: Associations with demand/withdraw communication patterns. *Journal of Behavioral Medicine, 29*, 317–325.

Heilmann, S. G., Holt, D. T., & Rilovick, C. Y. (2008). Effects of career plateauing on turnover: A test of a model. *Journal of Leadership & Organizational Studies, 15*, 59–68.

Heisel, M. J. (2006). Suicide and its prevention among older adults. *Canadian Journal of Psychiatry, 51*, 143–154.

Helfand, B. T., Evans, R. M., & McVary, K. T. (2010). A comparison of the frequencies of medical therapies for overactive bladder in men and women: Analysis of more than 7.2 million aging patients. *European Urologist, 57*(4), 586–591.

Helgeson, V. S., & Taylor, S. E. (1993). Social comparisons and adjustment among cardiac patients. *Journal of Applied Social Psychology, 23*, 1171–1195.

Helson, R. (1967). Personality characteristics and developmental history of creative college women. *Genetic Psychology Monographs, 76*, 205–256.

Helson, R., & Soto, C. J. (2005). Up and down in middle age: Monotonic and nonmonotonic changes in roles, status, and personality. *Journal of Personality and Social Psychology, 89*, 194–204.

Helson, R., & Srivastava, S. (2001). Three paths of adult development: Conservers, seekers, and achievers. *Journal of Personality and Social Psychology, 80*, 995–1010.

Helson, R., & Wink, P. (1992). Personality change in women from the early 40s to the early 50s. *Psychology and Aging, 7*, 46–55.

Henry, J. D., & Phillips, L. H. (2006). Covariates of production and perseveration on tests of phonemic, semantic and alternating fluency in normal aging. *Aging, Neuropsychology and Cognition, 13*, 529–551.

Henz, U. (2010). Parent care as unpaid family labor: How do spouses share? *Journal of Marriage and Family, 72*, 148–164.

Heraclides, A., Chandola, T., Witte, D. R., & Brunner, E. J. (2009). Psychosocial stress at work doubles the risk of type 2 diabetes in middle-aged women: Evidence from the Whitehall II study. *Diabetes Care, 32*, 2230–2235.

Hersch, E. C., & Merriam, G. R. (2008). Growth hormone (GH)-releasing hormone and GH secretagogues in normal aging: Fountain of Youth or Pool of Tantalus? *Clinical Interventions in Aging, 3*, 121–129.

Herzberg, F., Mausner, B., & Bloch Snyderman, B. (2005). *The motivation to work.* Piscataway, NJ: Transaction.

Herzberg, F., Mausner, B., & Snyderman, B. B. (1959). *The motivation to work.* New York, NY: Wiley.

Hess, T. M., Auman, C., Colcombe, S. J., & Rahhal, T. A. (2003). The impact of stereotype threat on age differences in memory performance. *Journals of Gerontology Series B: Psychological Sciences and Social Sciences, 58*, P3–P11.

Hess, T. M., & Hinson, J. T. (2006). Age-related variation in the influences of aging stereotypes on memory in adulthood. *Psychology and Aging, 21*, 621–625.

Hetherington, E. M., & Kelly, J. (2002). *For better or for worse: Divorce reconsidered.* New York, NY: Norton.

Hickman, S. E. (2002). Improving communication near the end of life. *American Behavioral Scientist, 46*, 252–267.

Hinrichsen, G. A., & Dick-Siskin, L. P. (2000). Psychotherapy with older adults. In S. K. Whitbourne (Ed.), *Psychopathology in later life.* New York, NY: Wiley.

Hintsa, T., Shipley, M., Gimeno, D., Elovainio, M., Chandola, T., Jokela, M., . . . Kivimaki, M. (2009). Do pre-employment influences explain the association between psychosocial factors at work and coronary heart disease? The Whitehall II study. *Journal of Occupational and Environmental Medicine.* doi:oem.2009.048470 [pii] 0.1136/oem.2009.048470.

Hoffman, B. J., & Woehr, D. J. (2006). A quantitative review of the relationship between person-organization fit and behavioral outcomes. *Journal of Vocational Behavior, 68*, 389–399.

Hoffman, S. D. (2009). The changing impact of marriage and children on women's labor force participation. *Monthly Labor Review, 132*(2), 3–14.

Hofland, B. F., Willis, S. L., & Baltes, P. B. (1980). Fluid performance in the elderly: Intraindividual variability and conditions of assessment. *Journal of Educational Psychology, 73*, 573–586.

Hogervorst, E., Huppert, F., Matthews, F. E., & Brayne, C. (2008). Thyroid function and cognitive decline in the MRC

Cognitive Function and Ageing Study. *Psychoneuroendocrinology*, *33*, 1013–1022.

Holahan, C. J., Moos, R. H., Holahan, C. K., Brennan, P. L., & Schutte, K. K. (2005). Stress generation, avoidance coping, and depressive symptoms: A 10-year model. *Journal of Consulting and Clinical Psychology*, *73*, 658–666.

Holahan, C. K., & Chapman, J. R. (2002). Longitudinal predictors of proactive goals and activity participation at age 80. *Journals of Gerontology Series B: Psychological Sciences and Social Sciences*, *57*, P418–P425.

Holland, J. L. (1994). *The Self-Directed Search*. Odessa, FL: Psychological Assessment Resources.

Holland, J. L. (1997). *Making vocational choices: A theory of vocational personalities and work environments* (3rd ed.). Odessa, FL: Psychological Assessment Resources.

Holley, C. K., & Mast, B. T. (2007). The effects of widowhood and vascular risk factors on late-life depression. *American Journal of Geriatric Psychiatry*, *15*, 690–698.

Hook, J. L., & Chalasani, S. (2008). Gendered expectations? Reconsidering single fathers' child-care time. *Journal of Marriage and Family*, *70*, 978–990.

Hooker, K., & Kaus, C. R. (1994). Health-related possible selves in young and middle adulthood. *Psychology and Aging*, *9*, 126–133.

Horn, J. L. (1970). Organization of data on life-span development of human abilities. In L. R. Goulet & P. B. Baltes (Eds.), *Life-span developmental psychology: Theory and research* (Vol. 1, pp. 211–256). New York, NY: Academic Press.

Horn, J. L., & Cattell, R. B. (1966). Refinement and test of the theory of fluid and crystallized intelligence. *Journal of Educational Psychology*, *57*, 253–270.

Hornsby, P. J. (2009). Senescence and life span. *Pflugers Archives*.

House, J. S., Kessler, R. C., Herzog, A. R., & Mero, R. P. (1990). Age, socioeconomic status, and health. *Milbank Quarterly*, *68*, 383–411.

Houston, D. K., Nicklas, B. J., & Zizza, C. A. (2009). Weighty concerns: The growing prevalence of obesity among older adults. *Journal of the American Dietetic Association*, *109*, 1886–1895.

Houttekier, D., Cohen, J., Bilsen, J., Addington-Hall, J., Onwuteaka-Philipsen, B. D., & Deliens, L. (2010). Place of death of older persons with dementia. A study in five European countries. *Journal of the American Geriatrics Society*, *58*, 751–756.

Howland, R. H. (2009). Effects of aging on pharmacokinetic and pharmacodynamic drug processes. *Journal of Psychosocial Nursing and Mental Health Services*, *47*, 15–16, 17–18.

Hoyle, R. H. (Ed.). (1995). *Structural equation modeling: Concepts, issues, and applications*. Thousand Oaks, CA: Sage.

Hoyte, K. J., Brownell, H., & Wingfield, A. (2009). Components of speech prosody and their use in detection of syntactic structure by older adults. *Experimental Aging Research*, *35*, 129–151.

Hsu, Y. H., Venners, S. A., Terwedow, H. A., Feng, Y., Niu, T., Li, Z., Laird, N., Brain, J. D., Cummings, S. R., Bouxsein, M. L., Rosen, C. J., Xu, X. (2006). Relation of body composition, fat mass, and serum lipids to osteoporotic fractures and bone mineral density in Chinese men and women. *American Journal of Clinical Nutrition*, *83*, 146–154.

Hughes, M. E., & Waite, L. J. (2009). Marital biography and health at mid-life. *Journal of Health and Social Behavior*, *50*, 344–358.

Hugo, F. N., Hilgert, J. B., de Sousa Mda, L., & Cury, J. A. (2009). Oral status and its association with general quality of life in older independent-living south-Brazilians. *Community Dentistry and Oral Epidemiology*, *37*, 231–240.

Humphrey, D. (1991). *Final exit: The practicalities of self-deliverance and assisted suicide for the dying*. Eugene, Oregon: Hemlock Society.

Hunter, D. J., & Eckstein, F. (2009). Exercise and osteoarthritis. *Journal of Anatomy*, *214*, 197–207.

Hurd Clarke, L. (2006). Older women and sexuality: Experiences in marital relationships across the life course. *Canadian Journal of Aging*, *25*, 129–140.

Hy, L. X., & Keller, D. M. (2000). Prevalence of AD among whites: A summary by levels of severity. *Neurology*, *55*, 198–204.

Iacono, D., Markesbery, W. R., Gross, M., Pletnikova, O., Rudow, G., Zandi, P., . . . Troncoso, J. C. (2009). The nun study: Clinically silent AD, neuronal hypertrophy, and linguistic skills in early life. *Neurology*, *73*, 665–673.

Ice, G. H. (2002). Daily life in a nursing home: Has it changed in 25 years? *Journal of Aging Studies*, *16*, 345–359.

Idler, E. L., McLaughlin, J., & Kasl, S. (2009). Religion and the quality of life in the last year of life. *Journals of Gerontology Series B: Psychological Sciences and Social Sciences*, *64*, 528–537.

Igwebuike, A., Irving, B. A., Bigelow, M. L., Short, K. R., McConnell, J. P., & Nair, K. S. (2008). Lack of dehydroepiandrosterone effect on a combined endurance and resistance exercise program in postmenopausal women. *Journal of Clinical Endocrinology and Metabolism*, *93*, 534–538.

Imai, K., Hamaguchi, M., Mori, K., Takeda, N., Fukui, M., Kato, T., . . . Kojima, T. (2010). Metabolic syndrome as a risk factor for high-ocular tension. *International Journal of Obesity*. doi:ijo201032[pii] 10.1038/ijo.2010.32.

Ingersoll-Dayton, B., Neal, M. B., Ha, J.-H., & Hammer, L. B. (2003). Redressing inequity in parent care among siblings. *Journal of Marriage and Family*, *65*, 201–212.

Institute of Medicine. (2008). Retooling for an aging America: Building the healthcare workforce. Retrieved from http://www.iom.edu/Reports/2008/Retooling-for-an-Aging-America-Building-the-Health-Care-Workforce.aspx.

Isaacowitz, D. M., Toner, K., & Neupert, S. D. (2009). Use of gaze for real-time mood regulation: Effects of age and attentional functioning. *Psychology and Aging*, *24*, 989–994.

Isaacowitz, D. M., Wadlinger, H. A., Goren, D., & Wilson, H. R. (2006). Selective preference in visual fixation away from negative images in old age? An eye-tracking study. *Psychology and Aging*, *21*, 40–48.

Ishigami, Y., & Klein, R. M. (2009). Is a hands-free phone safer than a handheld phone? *Journal of Safety Research*, *40*, 157–164.

Iyer Parameswaran, G., & Murphy, T. F. (2009). Chronic obstructive pulmonary disease: Role of bacteria and updated guide to antibacterial selection in the older patient. *Drugs and Aging, 26,* 985–995.

Jackson, R. A., Vittinghoff, E., Kanaya, A. M., Miles, T. P., Resnick, H. E., Kritchevsky, S. B., . . . Brown, J. S. (2004). Urinary incontinence in elderly women: Findings from the Health, Aging, and Body Composition Study. *Obstetrics and Gynecology, 104,* 301–307.

Jakes, R. W., Day, N. E., Patel, B., Khaw, K. T., Oakes, S., Luben, R., . . . Wareham, N. J. (2002). Physical inactivity is associated with lower forced expiratory volume in 1 second: European Prospective Investigation into Cancer—Norfolk Prospective Population Study. *American Journal of Epidemiology, 156,* 139–147.

James, H. S. J. (2005). Why did you do that? An economic examination of the effect of extrinsic compensation on intrinsic motivation and performance. *Journal of Economic Psychology, 26,* 549–566.

James, L. E., & MacKay, D. G. (2007). New age-linked asymmetries: Aging and the processing of familiar versus novel language on the input versus output side. *Psychology and Aging, 22,* 94–103.

Jang, S.-N., Choi, Y.-J., & Kim, D.-H. (2009). Association of socioeconomic status with successful ageing: Differences in the components of successful ageing. *Journal of Biosocial Science, 41,* 207–219.

Janowsky, J. S. (2006). The role of androgens in cognition and brain aging in men. *Neuroscience, 138,* 1015–1020.

Janse, E. (2009). Processing of fast speech by elderly listeners. *Journal of the Acoustical Society of America, 125,* 2361–2373.

Janson, C., Lindberg, E., Gislason, T., Elmasry, A., & Boman, G. (2001). Insomnia in men—A 10-year prospective population based study. *Sleep, 24,* 425–430.

Jaques, E. (1965). Death and the mid-life crisis. *International Journal of Psychoanalysis, 46,* 502–514.

Jaunin, J., Bochud, M., Marques-Vidal, P., Vollenweider, P., Waeber, G., Mooser, V., . . . Paccaud, F. (2009). Smoking offsets the metabolic benefits of parental longevity in women: The CoLaus study. *Preventive Medicine, 48,* 224–231.

Jeste, D. V., Symonds, L. L., Harris, M. J., Paulsen, J. S., Palmer, B. W., & Heaton, R. K. (1997). Nondementia nonpraecox dementia praecox? Late onset schizophrenia. *American Journal of Geriatric Psychiatry, 5,* 302–317.

Jimenez, D. E., Alegria, M., Chen, C. N., Chan, D., & Laderman, M. (2010). Prevalence of psychiatric illnesses in older ethnic minority adults. *Journal of the American Geriatrics Society, 58,* 256–264.

Johnson, J., Stewart, W., Hall, E., Fredlund, P., & Theorell, T. (1996). Long-term psychosocial work environment and cardio-vascular mortality among Swedish men. *American Journal of Public Health, 86,* 324–331.

Jokela, M., Ferrie, J. E., Gimeno, D., Chandola, T., Shipley, M. J., Head, J., . . . Kivimaki, M. (2010). From midlife to early old age: Health trajectories associated with retirement. *Epidemiology.* doi:10.1097/EDE.0b013e3181d61f53.

Jonassaint, C. R., Boyle, S. H., Williams, R. B., Mark, D. B., Siegler, I. C., & Barefoot, J. C. (2007). Facets of openness predict mortality in patients with cardiac disease. *Psychosomatic Medicine, 69,* 319–322.

Jones, K. M., Whitbourne, S. K., Whitbourne, S. B., & Skultety, K. M. (2009). Identity processes and memory controllability in middle and later adulthood. *Journal of Applied Gerontology, 28,* 582–599.

Jones, T. E., Stephenson, K. W., King, J. G., Knight, K. R., Marshall, T. L., & Scott, W. B. (2009). Sarcopenia—mechanisms and treatments. *Journal of Geriatric Physical Therapy, 32,* 39–45.

Jonker, A. l. A. G. C., Comijs, H. C., Knipscheer, K. C. P. M., & Deeg, D. J. H. (2009). The role of coping resources on change in well-being during persistent health decline. *Journal of Aging and Health, 21,* 1063–1082.

Joo, J. H., Morales, K. H., de Vries, H. F., & Gallo, J. J. (2010). Disparity in use of psychotherapy offered in primary care between older African-American and white adults: Results from a practice-based depression intervention trial. *Journal of the American Geriatrics Society, 58,* 154–160.

Jorm, A. F., Windsor, T. D., Dear, K. B., Anstey, K. J., Christensen, H., & Rodgers, B. (2005). Age group differences in psychological distress: The role of psychosocial risk factors that vary with age. *Psychological Medicine, 35,* 1253–1263.

Joseph, J. A., Shukitt-Hale, B., & Willis, L. M. (2009). Grape juice, berries, and walnuts affect brain aging and behavior. *Journal of Nutrition, 139,* 1813S–1817S.

Judge, T. A., Heller, D., & Mount, M. K. (2002). Five-factor model of personality and job satisfaction: A meta-analysis. *Journal of Applied Psychology, 87,* 530–541.

Kadar, T., Silbermann, M., Weissman, B. A., & Levy, A. (1990). Age-related changes in the cholinergic components within the central nervous system. II. Working memory impairment and its relation to hippocampal muscarinic receptors. *Mechanisms of Ageing and Development, 55,* 139–149.

Kaiser Family Foundation. (2010a). Percent of certified nursing facilities with top ten deficiences, 2008. Retrieved from http://www.statehealthfacts.org/comparebar.jsp?ind=421&cat=8&sub=97&yr=63&typ=2&rgnhl=1.

Kaiser Family Foundation. (2010b). State Health Facts. Retrieved from http://www.statehealthfacts.org/savemap.jsp?typ=4&ind=180&cat=4&sub=47.

Kalimo, R., Taris, T. W., & Schaufeli, W. B. (2003). The effects of past and anticipated future downsizing on survivor well-being: An equity perspective. *Journal of Occupational Health Psychology, 8,* 91–109.

Kalmijn, M. (2003). Shared friendship networks and the life course: An analysis of survey data on married and cohabiting couples. *Social Networks, 25,* 231–249.

Kamel, N. S., & Gammack, J. K. (2006). Insomnia in the elderly: Cause, approach, and treatment. *American Journal of Medicine, 119*, 463–469.

Kamimoto, L. A., Easton, A. N., Maurice, E., Husten, C. G., & Macera, C. A. (1999). Surveillance for five health risks among older adults—United States, 1993–1997. *Morbidity and Mortality Weekly Reports, 48*(SS08), 89–130.

Kane, R. A., Lum, T. Y., Cutler, L. J., Degenholtz, H. B., & Yu, T. C. (2007). Resident outcomes in small-house nursing homes: A longitudinal evaluation of the initial green house program. *Journal of the American Geriatrics Society, 55*, 832–839.

Kanfer, R., & Ackerman, P. L. (2004). Aging, adult development, and work motivation. *Academy of Management Review, 29*, 440–458.

Kannus, P., Uusi-Rasi, K., Palvanen, M., & Parkkari, J. (2005). Non-pharmacological means to prevent fractures among older adults. *Annals of Medicine, 37*, 303–310.

Karakaya, M. G., Bilgin, S. C., Ekici, G., Kose, N., & Otman, A. S. (2009). Functional mobility, depressive symptoms, level of independence, and quality of life of the elderly living at home and in the nursing home. *Journal of the American Medical Directors Association, 10*, 662–666.

Karavirta, L., Tulppo, M. P., Laaksonen, D. E., Nyman, K., Laukkanen, R. T., Kinnunen, H., . . . Hakkinen, K. (2009). Heart rate dynamics after combined endurance and strength training in older men. *Medicine and Science in Sports and Exercise, 41*, 1436–1443.

Karney, B., & Bradbury, T. (1997). Neuroticism, marital interaction, and the trajectory of marital satisfaction. *Journal of Personality and Social Psychology, 72*, 1075–1092.

Karp, J. F., Skidmore, E., Lotz, M., Lenze, E., Dew, M. A., & Reynolds, C. F., III (2009). Use of the late-life function and disability instrument to assess disability in major depression. *Journal of the American Geriatrics Society, 57*, 1612–1619.

Katz, R. (2009). Intergenerational family relations and subjective well-being in old age: A cross-national study. *European Journal of Ageing, 6*, 79–90.

Katzel, L. I., Sorkin, J. D., & Fleg, J. L. (2001). A comparison of longitudinal changes in aerobic fitness in older endurance athletes and sedentary men. *Journal of the American Geriatric Society, 49*, 1657–1664.

Kaufman, A. S., Kaufman, J. L., McLean, J. E., & Reynolds, C. R. (1991). Is the pattern of intellectual growth and decline across the adult life span different for men and women? *Journal of Clinical Psychology, 47*, 801–812.

Kawas, C., Gray, S., Brookmeyer, R., Fozard, J., & Zonderman, A. (2000). Age-specific incidence rates of Alzheimer's disease: The Baltimore Longitudinal Study of Aging. *Neurology, 54*, 2072–2077.

Keefe, J. M., & Fancey, P. J. (2002). Work and eldercare: Reciprocity between older mothers and their employed daughters. *Canadian Journal of Aging, 21*, 229–241.

Keefe, S. E., Padilla, A. M., & Carlos, M. L. (1979). The Mexican-American extended family as an emotional support system. *Human Organization, 38*, 144–152.

Keith, S. J., Regier, D. A., & Rae, D. S. (1991). Schizophrenic disorders. In L. N. Robins & D. A. Regier (Eds.), *Psychiatric disorders in America* (pp. 33–52). New York, NY: Free Press.

Keister, K. J. (2006). Predictors of self-assessed health, anxiety, and depressive symptoms in nursing home residents at week 1 postrelocation. *Journal of Aging and Health, 18*, 722–742.

Kelly, B., Burnett, P., Pelusi, D., Badger, S., Varghese, F., & Robertson, M. (2002). Terminally ill cancer patients' wish to hasten death. *Palliative Medicine, 16*, 339–345.

Kelly, D. L., McMahon, R. P., Liu, F., Love, R. C., Wehring, H. J., Shim, J. C., . . . Conley, R. R. (2010). Cardiovascular disease mortality in patients with chronic schizophrenia treated with clozapine: A retrospective cohort study. *Journal of Clinical Psychiatry, 71*, 304–311.

Kemper, S., Greiner, L. H., Marquis, J. G., Prenovost, K., & Mitzner, T. L. (2001). Language decline across the life span: Findings from the Nun Study. *Psychology and Aging, 16*, 227–239.

Kemper, S., Marquis, J., & Thompson, M. (2001). Longitudinal change in language production: Effects of aging and dementia on grammatical complexity and propositional content. *Psychology and Aging, 16*, 600–614.

Kendler, K. S., Myers, J., & Zisook, S. (2008). Does bereavement-related major depression differ from major depression associated with other stressful life events? *American Journal of Psychiatry, 165*, 1449–1455.

Kerby, D. S., & Ragan, K. M. (2002). Activity interests and Holland's RIASEC system in older adults. *International Journal of Aging & Human Development, 55*, 117–139.

Kessel, L., Jorgensen, T., Glumer, C., & Larsen, M. (2006). Early lens aging is accelerated in subjects with a high risk of ischemic heart disease: An epidemiologic study. *BMC Ophthalmology, 6*, 16.

Kessler, R. C., Berglund, P., Demler, O., Jin, R., Koretz, D., Merikangas, K. R., . . . Wang, P. S. (2003). The epidemiology of major depressive disorder: Results from the National Comorbidity Survey Replication (NCS-R). *Journal of the American Medical Association, 289*, 3095–3105.

Kessler, R. C., Berglund, P., Demler, O., Jin, R., Merikangas, K. R., & Walters, E. E. (2005). Lifetime prevalence and age-of-onset distributions of DSM-IV disorders in the National Comorbidity Survey Replication. *Archives of General Psychiatry, 62*, 593–602.

Kessler, R. C., Chiu, W. T., Jin, R., Ruscio, A. M., Shear, K., & Walters, E. E. (2006). The epidemiology of panic attacks, panic disorder, and agoraphobia in the National Comorbidity Survey Replication. *Archives of General Psychiatry, 63*, 415–424.

Kevorkian, J. (1991). *Prescription medicide: The goodness of planned death.* Buffalo, NY: Prometheus Books.

Kiecolt-Glaser, J. K., & Glaser, R. (2002). Depression and immune function: Central pathways to morbidity and mortality. *Journal of Psychosomatic Research, 53*, 873–876.

Kieffer, K. M., Schinka, J. A., & Curtiss, G. (2004). Person-environment congruence and personality domains in the prediction of job performance and work quality. *Journal of Counseling Psychology, 51,* 168–177.

Kim, H., Yoshida, H., & Suzuki, T. (2010). The effects of multidimensional exercise on functional decline, urinary incontinence, and fear of falling in community-dwelling elderly women with multiple symptoms of geriatric syndrome: A randomized controlled and 6-month follow-up trial. *Archives of Gerontology and Geriatrics.* doi:10.1097/EDE.0b013e3181d61f53.

Kim, J. E., & Moen, P. (2001). Is retirement good or bad for subjective well-being? *Current Directions in Psychological Science, 10,* 83–86.

Kim, J. E., & Nesselroade, J. R. (2002). Relationships among social support, self-concept, and wellbeing of older adults: A study of process using dynamic factor models. *International Journal of Behavioral Development, 27,* 49–63.

Kim, J. M., Stewart, R., Kim, S. W., Yang, S. J., Shin, I. S., & Yoon, J. S. (2009). Insomnia, depression, and physical disorders in late life: A 2-year longitudinal community study in Koreans. *Sleep, 32,* 1221–1228.

Kindig, D. A., Seplaki, C. L., & Libby, D. L. (2002). Death rate variation in US subpopulations. *Bulletin of the World Health Organization, 80,* 9–15.

King, A. C., Atienza, A., Castro, C., & Collins, R. (2002). Physiological and affective responses to family caregiving in the natural setting in wives versus daughters. *International Journal of Behavioral Medicine, 9,* 176–194.

King, L. A., King, D. W., Vickers, K., Davison, E. H., & Spiro, A., III. (2007). Assessing late-onset stress symptomatology among aging male combat veterans. *Aging and Mental Health, 11,* 175–191.

Kinsella, K., & He, W. (2009). An aging world 2008: International Population Reports P95/09-1. Retrieved from http://www.census.gov/prod/2009pubs/p95-09-1.pdf.

Kissane, M., & McLaren, S. (2006). Sense of belonging as a predictor of reasons for living in older adults. *Death Studies, 30,* 243–258.

Kite, M. E., & Wagner, L. S. (2002). Attitudes toward older adults. In T. D. Nelson (Ed.), *Ageism: Stereotyping and prejudice against older persons* (pp. 129–161). Cambridge, MA: The MIT Press.

Klass, M., Baudry, S., & Duchateau, J. (2007). Voluntary activation during maximal contraction with advancing age: A brief review. *European Journal of Applied Physiology, 100,* 543–551.

Klemmack, D. L., Roff, L. L., Parker, M. W., Koenig, H. G., Sawyer, P., & Allman, R. M. (2007). A cluster analysis typology of religiousness/spirituality among older adults. *Research on Aging, 29,* 163–183.

Klerman, E. B., Duffy, J. F., Dijk, D. J., & Czeisler, C. A. (2001). Circadian phase resetting in older people by ocular bright light exposure. *Journal of Investigative Medicine, 49,* 30–40.

Klysner, R., Bent-Hansen, J., Hansen, H. L., Lunde, M., Pleidrup, E., Poulsen, D. L., . . . Peterson, H. E. (2002). Efficacy of citalopram in the prevention of recurrent depression in elderly patients: Placebo-controlled study of maintenance therapy. *British Journal of Psychiatry, 181,* 29–35.

Knight, B. G., Karel, M. J., Hinrichsen, G. A., Qualls, S. H., & Duffy, M. (2009). Pikes Peak model for training in professional geropsychology. *American Psychologist, 64,* 205–214.

Knoester, C., & Eggebeen, D. J. (2006). The effects of the transition to parenthood and subsequent children on men's well-being and social participation. *Journal of Family Issues, 27,* 1532–1560.

Knopman, D. S. (2007). Cerebrovascular disease and dementia. *British Journal of Radiology, 80 Spec No 2,* S121–S127.

Koropeckyj-Cox, T. (2002). Beyond parental status: Psychological well-being in middle and old age. *Journal of Marriage and Family, 64,* 957–971.

Kosek, D. J., Kim, J.-s., Petrella, J. K., Cross, J. M., & Bamman, M. M. (2006). Efficacy of 3 days/wk resistance training on myofiber hypertrophy and myogenic mechanisms in young vs. older adults. *Journal of Applied Physiology, 101,* 531–544.

Kosloski, K., Ekerdt, D., & DeViney, S. (2001). The role of job-related rewards in retirement planning. *Journals of Gerontology Series B: Psychological Sciences and Social Sciences, 56,* P160–P169.

Kostka, T. (2005). Quadriceps maximal power and optimal shortening velocity in 335 men aged 23–88 years. *European Journal of Applied Physiology, 95,* 140–145.

Kozbelt, A. (2007). A quantitative analysis of Beethoven as self-critic: Implications for psychological theories of musical creativity. *Psychology of Music, 35,* 144–168.

Kramer, A. F., Boot, W. R., McCarley, J. S., Peterson, M. S., Colcombe, A., & Scialfa, C. T. (2006). Aging, memory and visual search. *Acta Psychologica (Amsterdam), 122,* 288–304.

Kramer, A. F., & Madden, D. J. (2008). Attention. In F. I. M. Craik & T. A. Salthouse (Eds.), *The handbook of aging and cognition* (3rd ed., pp. 189–249). New York, NY: Psychology Press.

Kreider, R. M. (2005). Number, timing, and duration of marriages: 2001 *Current Population Reports P70-97.* Washington, DC: U.S. Bureau of the Census.

Kreider, R.M. (2010). Increase in opposite sex cohabiting couples in ASEC to the CPS. Retrieved from http://www.census.gov/population/www/socdemo/Inc-Opp-sex-2009-to-2010.pdf.

Krumholz, H. M., Phillips, R. S., Hamel, M. B., Teno, J. M., Bellamy, P., Broste, S. K., . . . Goldman, L. (1998). Resuscitation preferences among patients with severe. *Circulation, 98,* 648–655.

Kryger, A. I., & Andersen, J. L. (2007). Resistance training in the oldest old: Consequences for muscle strength, fiber types, fiber size, and MHC isoforms. *Scandinavian Journal of Medicine and Science in Sports, 17,* 422–430.

Kübler-Ross, E. (1969). *On death and dying.* New York, NY: Macmillan.

Kubo, N., Kato, A., & Nakamura, K. (2006). Deterioration of planning ability with age in Japanese monkeys (Macaca fuscata). *Journal of Comparative Psychology, 120,* 449–455.

Kubzansky, L. D., Cole, S. R., Kawachi, I., Vokonas, P., & Sparrow, D. (2006). Shared and unique contributions of anger, anxiety, and depression to coronary heart disease: A prospective study in the Normative Aging Study. *Annals of Behavioral Medicine, 31,* 21–29.

Kubzansky, L. D., Koenen, K. C., Spiro, A., III, Vokonas, P. S., & Sparrow, D. (2007). Prospective study of posttraumatic stress disorder symptoms and coronary heart disease in the Normative Aging Study. *Archives of General Psychiatry, 64,* 109–116.

Kujala, U. M. (2009). Evidence on the effects of exercise therapy in the treatment of chronic disease. *British Journal of Sports Medicine, 43,* 550–555.

Kukat, A., & Trifunovic, A. (2009). Somatic mtDNA mutations and aging—facts and fancies. *Experimental Gerontology, 44,* 101–105.

Kumari, M., Badrick, E., Chandola, T., Adler, N. E., Epel, E., Seeman, T., . . . Marmot, M. G. (2010). Measures of social position and cortisol secretion in an aging population: Findings from the Whitehall II study. *Psychosomatic Medicine, 72,* 27–34.

Kung, H.-C., Hoyert, D. L., Xu, J., & Murphy, S. L. (2008). Deaths: Final data for 2005. *National Vital Statistics Reports, 56(10),* 1–120.

Kunzmann, U., & Gruhn, D. (2005). Age differences in emotional reactivity: The sample case of sadness. *Psychology and Aging, 20,* 47–59.

Kuzuya, M., Ando, F., Iguchi, A., & Shimokata, H. (2006). Effect of smoking habit on age-related changes in serum lipids: A cross-sectional and longitudinal analysis in a large Japanese cohort. *Atherosclerosis, 185,* 183–190.

Kwan, C. M., Love, G. D., Ryff, C. D., & Essex, M. J. (2003). The role of self-enhancing evaluations in a successful life transition. *Psychology and Aging, 18,* 3–12.

Labouvie-Vief, G., & Medler, M. (2002). Affect optimization and affect complexity: Modes and styles of regulation in adulthood. *Psychology and Aging, 17,* 571–588.

Lachman, M. E. (2004). Development in midlife. *Annual Review of Psychology, 55,* 305–331.

Lachman, M. E. (2006). Perceived control over aging-related declines. *Current Directions in Psychological Science, 15,* 282–286.

Lachman, M. E., & Andreoletti, C. (2006). Strategy use mediates the relationship between control beliefs and memory performance for middle-aged and older adults. *Journals of Gerontology Series B: Psychological Sciences and Social Sciences, 61,* P88–P94.

Lachman, M. E., Neupert, S. D., Bertrand, R., & Jette, A. M. (2006). The effects of strength training on memory in older adults. *Journal of Aging and Physical Activity, 14,* 59–73.

Lachman, M. E., Rosnick, C. B., Röcke, C., Bosworth, H. B., & Hertzog, C. (2009). The rise and fall of control beliefs and life satisfaction in adulthood: Trajectories of stability and change over ten years. *Aging and cognition: Research methodologies and empirical advances* (pp. 143–160). Washington, DC: American Psychological Association.

Lafreniere, D., & Mann, N. (2009). Anosmia: Loss of smell in the elderly. *Otolaryngology Clinics of North America, 42,* 123–131, x.

Lamina, S., Okoye, C. G., & Dagogo, T. T. (2009). Therapeutic effect of an interval exercise training program in the management of erectile dysfunction in hypertensive patients. *Journal of Clinical Hypertension, 11,* 125–129.

Lang, F. R., & Carstensen, L. L. (1994). Close emotional relationships in late life: Further support for proactive aging in the social domain. *Psychology and Aging, 9,* 315–324.

Lang, F. R., & Carstensen, L. L. (2002). Time counts: Future time perspective, goals, and social relationships. *Psychology and Aging, 17,* 125–139.

Lang, T., Streeper, T., Cawthon, P., Baldwin, K., Taaffe, D. R., & Harris, T. B. (2009). Sarcopenia: Etiology, clinical consequences, intervention, and assessment. *Osteoporosis International, 21(4),* 543–559.

Langford, A., & Johnson, B. (2009). Social inequalities in adult female mortality by the National Statistics Socio-economic Classification, England and Wales, 2001–03. *Health Statistics Quarterly, 42,* 6–21.

Lapointe, J., & Hekimi, S. (2010). When a theory of aging ages badly. *Cellular and Molecular Life Sciences, 67,* 1–8.

Larbi, A., Fulop, T., & Pawelec, G. (2008). Immune receptor signaling, aging and autoimmunity. *Advances in Experimental Medicine and Biology, 640,* 312–324.

Larcom, M. J., & Isaacowitz, D. M. (2009). Rapid emotion regulation after mood induction: Age and individual differences. *Journals of Gerontology Series B: Psychological Sciences and Social Sciences, 64,* 733–741.

Lau, A. W., & Gallagher-Thompson, D. (2002). Ethnic minority older adults in clinical and research programs: Issues and recommendations. *Behavior Therapist, 25,* 10–11.

Laub, J. H., & Vaillant, G. E. (2000). Delinquency and mortality: A 50-year follow-up study of 1,000 delinquent and nondelinquent boys. *American Journal of Psychiatry, 157,* 96–102.

Lavender, A. P., & Nosaka, K. (2007). Fluctuations of isometric force after eccentric exercise of the elbow flexors of young, middle-aged, and old men. *European Journal of Applied Physiology, 100,* 161–167.

Lawton, M. P., & Nahemow, L. (1973). Ecology and the aging process. In C. Eisdorfer & M. P. Lawton (Eds.), *The psychology of adult development and aging* (pp. 619–674). Washington, D.C.: American Psychological Association.

Lease, S. H. (1998). Annual review, 1993–1997: Work attitudes and outcomes. *Journal of Vocational Behavior, 53,* 154–183.

Leboeuf-Yde, C., Nielsen, J., Kyvik, K. O., Fejer, R., & Hartvigsen, J. (2009). Pain in the lumbar, thoracic or cervical regions: Do age and gender matter? A population-based study of 34,902 Danish twins 20–71 years of age. *BMC Musculoskeletal Disorders, 10,* 39.

Lee, G. R., DeMaris, A., Bavin, S., & Sullivan, R. (2001). Gender differences in the depressive effect of widowhood in later life. *Journals of Gerontology Series B: Psychological Sciences and Social Sciences, 56,* S56–S61.

Lefevre, M., Redman, L. M., Heilbronn, L. K., Smith, J. V., Martin, C. K., Rood, J. C., . . . Ravussin, E. (2009). Caloric restriction alone and with exercise improves CVD risk in healthy non-obese individuals. *Atherosclerosis, 203,* 206–213.

Lehman, H. C. (1953). *Age and achievement.* Princeton, NJ: Princeton University Press.

Lentz, E., & Allen, T. D. (2009). The role of mentoring others in the career plateauing phenomenon. *Group and Organization Management, 34,* 358–384.

Lenze, E. J., Munin, M. C., Skidmore, E. R., Dew, M. A., Rogers, J. C., Whyte, E. M.,...Reynolds, C. F., III. (2007). Onset of depression in elderly persons after hip fracture: Implications for prevention and early intervention of late-life depression. *Journal of the American Geriatrics Society, 55,* 81–86.

Lenze, E. J., Rollman, B. L., Shear, M. K., Dew, M. A., Pollock, B. G., Ciliberti, C.,...Reynolds, C. F., III. (2009). Escitalopram for older adults with generalized anxiety disorder: A randomized controlled trial. *Journal of the American Medical Association, 301,* 295–303.

Leonardelli, G. J., Hermann, A. D., Lynch, M. E., & Arkin, R. M. (2003). The shape of self-evaluation: Implicit theories of intelligence and judgments of intellectual ability. *Journal of Research in Personality, 37,* 141–168.

Lerma, E. V. (2009). Anatomic and physiologic changes of the aging kidney. *Clinics in Geriatric Medicine, 25,* 325–329.

Lerner, R. M. (1995). Developing individuals within changing contexts: Implications of developmental contextualism for human development, research, policy, and programs. In T. J. Kindermann & J. Valsiner (Eds.), *Development of person-context relations* (pp. 13–37). Hillsdale, NJ: Erlbaum.

Lerner, R. M. (1996). Relative plasticity, integration, temporality, and diversity in human development: A developmental contextual perspective about theory, process, and method. *Developmental Psychology, 32,* 781–786.

Letenneur, L., Proust-Lima, C., Le George, A., Dartigues, J. F., & Barberger-Gateau, P. (2007). Flavonoid intake and cognitive decline over a 10-year period. *American Journal of Epidemiology, 165,* 1364–1371.

Leveille, S. G. (2004). Musculoskeletal aging. *Current Opinions in Rheumatology, 16,* 114–118.

Levey, A., Lah, J., Goldstein, F., Steenland, K., & Bliwise, D. (2006). Mild cognitive impairment: An opportunity to identify patients at high risk for progression to Alzheimer's disease. *Clinical Therapeutics, 28,* 991–1001.

Levinson, D. J., Darrow, C. N., Klein, E. B., Levinson, M. H., & McKee, B. (1978). *The seasons of a man's life.* New York, NY: Knopf.

Levinson, D. J., & Levinson, J. D. (1996). *The seasons of a woman's life.* New York, NY: Knopf.

Levy, B. R., Slade, M. D., Kunkel, S. R., & Kasl, S. V. (2002). Longevity increased by positive self-perceptions of aging. *Journal of Personality and Social Psychology, 83,* 261–270.

Li, L., Liang, J., Toler, A., & Gu, S. (2005). Widowhood and depressive symptoms among older Chinese: Do gender and source of support make a difference? *Social Science and Medicine, 60,* 637–647.

Lichtenburg, P. A., MacNeill, S. E., Lysack, C. L. B., Adam, L., & Neufeld, S. W. (2003). Predicting discharge and long-term outcome patterns for frail elders. *Rehabilitation Psychology, 48,* 37–43.

Licht-Strunk, E., van der Windt, D. A., van Marwijk, H. W., de Haan, M., & Beekman, A. T. (2007). The prognosis of depression in older patients in general practice and the community. A systematic review. *Family Practice, 24,* 168–180.

Lindauer, M. S. (1998). Artists, art, and arts activities: What do they tell us about aging? In C. Adams-Price (Ed.), *Creativity and successful aging: Theoretical and empirical approaches* (pp. 237–250). New York, NY: Springer.

Lipton, S. A. (2006). Paradigm shift in neuroprotection by NMDA receptor blockade: Memantine and beyond. *Nature Reviews: Drug Discovery, 5,* 160–170.

Lister, J. P., & Barnes, C. A. (2009). Neurobiological changes in the hippocampus during normative aging. *Archives of Neurology, 66,* 829–833.

Liu-Ambrose, T., Nagamatsu, L. S., Graf, P., Beattie, B. L., Ashe, M. C., & Handy, T. C. (2010). Resistance training and executive functions: A 12-month randomized controlled trial. *Archives of Internal Medicine, 170,* 170–178.

Liu, C. Y., Zhou, H. D., Xu, Z. Q., Zhang, W. W., Li, X. Y., & Zhao, J. (2009). Metabolic syndrome and cognitive impairment amongst elderly people in Chinese population: A cross-sectional study. *European Journal of Neurology, 16,* 1022–1027.

Liu, H., Bravata, D. M., Olkin, I., Friedlander, A., Liu, V., Roberts, B.,...Hoffman, A. R. (2008). Systematic review: The effects of growth hormone on athletic performance. *Annals of Internal Medicine, 148,* 747–758.

Liu, I. C., & Chiu, C. H. (2009). Case-control study of suicide attempts in the elderly. *International Psychogeriatrics, 21,* 896–902.

Lloyd-Jones, D., Adams, R., Carnethon, M., De Simone, G., Ferguson, T. B., Flegal, K.,...Hong, Y. (2009). Heart disease and stroke statistics—2009 update: A report from the American Heart Association Statistics Committee and Stroke Statistics Subcommittee. *Circulation, 119,* e21–e181.

Lloyd-Jones, D., Adams, R. J., Brown, T. M., Carnethon, M., Dai, S., De Simone, G.,...Wylie-Rosett, J. (2010). Heart disease and stroke statistics—2010 update: A report from the American Heart Association. *Circulation, 121,* e24–e215.

Lobjois, R., & Cavallo, V. (2009). The effects of aging on street-crossing behavior: From estimation to actual crossing. *Accident Analysis and Prevention, 41,* 259–267.

Loevinger, J. (1976). *Ego development: Conceptions and theories.* San Francisco, CA: Jossey-Bass.

Lombardi, G., Tauchmanova, L., Di Somma, C., Musella, T., Rota, F., Savanelli, M. C.,...Colao, A. (2005). Somatopause: Dismetabolic and bone effects. *Journal of Endocrinological Investigation, 28,* 36–42.

Lopez-Miranda, J., Perez-Jimenez, F., Ros, E., De Caterina, R., Badimon, L., Covas, M. I., . . . Yiannakouris, N. (2010). Olive oil and health: Summary of the II international conference on olive oil and health consensus report, Jaén and Córdoba (Spain) 2008. *Nutrition, Metabolism, and Cardiovascular Diseases, 20,* 284–294.

Lorenz, K. A., Lynn, J., Dy, S. M., Shugarman, L. R., Wilkinson, A., Mularski, R. A., . . . Shekelle, P. G. (2008). Evidence for improving palliative care at the end of life: A systematic review. *Annals of Internal Medicine, 148,* 147–159.

Lovasi, G. S., Lemaitre, R. N., Siscovick, D. S., Dublin, S., Bis, J. C., Lumley, T., Heckbert, S. R., Smith, N. L., Psaty, B. M. (2007). Amount of leisure-time physical activity and risk of nonfatal myocardial infarction. *Annals of Epidemiology, 17,* 410–416.

Low, K. S. D., Yoon, M., Roberts, B. W., & Rounds, J. (2005). The stability of vocational interests from early adolescence to middle adulthood: A quantitative review of longitudinal studies. *Psychological Bulletin, 131,* 713–737.

Lubart, T. I., & Sternberg, R. J. (1998). Life span creativity: An investment theory approach. In C. Adams-Price (Ed.), *Creativity and successful aging: Theoretical and empirical approaches* (pp. 21–41). New York, NY: Springer.

Luber, G. E., & Sanchez, C. A. (2006). Heat-related deaths—United States, 1999–2003. *Morbidity and Mortality Weekly Report, 55,* 796–798.

Luborsky, M. R. (1998). Creative challenges and the construction of meaningful life narratives. In C. Adams-Price (Ed.), *Creativity and successful aging: Theoretical and empirical approaches* (pp. 311–337). New York, NY: Springer.

Luborsky, M. R., & McMullen, C. K. (1999). Culture and aging. In J. C. Cavanaugh & S. K. Whitbourne (Eds.), *Gerontology: Interdisciplinary perspectives* (pp. 65–90). New York, NY: Oxford University Press.

Lucas, R. E., Clark, A. E., Georgellis, Y., & Diener, E. (2003). Reexamining adaptation and the set point model of happiness: Reactions to changes in marital status. *Journal of Personality and Social Psychology, 84,* 527–539.

Luckenhoff, C. E., & Carstensen, L. L. (2007). Aging, emotion, and health-related decision strategies: Motivational manipulations can reduce age differences. *Psychology and Aging, 22,* 134–146.

Lum, T. Y., Kane, R. A., Cutler, L. J., & Yu, T. C. (2008). Effects of Green House nursing homes on residents' families. *Health Care Financing Review, 30,* 35–51.

Luoh, M.-C., & Herzog, A. R. (2002). Individual consequences of volunteer and paid work in old age: Health and mortality. *Journal of Health & Social Behavior, 43,* 490–509.

Lupien, S., Lecours, A. R., Schwartz, G., Sharma, S., Hauger, R. L., Meaney, M. J., . . . Nair, N. P. (1996). Longitudinal study of basal cortisol levels in healthy elderly subjects: Evidence for subgroups. *Neurobiology of Aging, 17,* 95–105.

Lupien, S. J., McEwen, B. S., Gunnar, M. R., & Heim, C. (2009). Effects of stress throughout the lifespan on the brain, behaviour and cognition. *Nature Reviews Neuroscience, 10,* 434–445.

Lynch, N. A., Ryan, A. S., Evans, J., Katzel, L. I., & Goldberg, A. P. (2007). Older elite football players have reduced cardiac and osteoporosis risk factors. *Medicine and Science in Sports and Exercise, 39,* 1124–1130.

Lynn, J., Teno, J. M., Phillips, R. S., Wu, A. W., Desbiens, N., Harrold, J., . . . Connors, A. F. Jr. (1997). Perceptions by family members of the dying experience of older and seriously ill patients. SUPPORT Investigators. Study to Understand Prognoses and Preferences for Outcomes and Risks of Treatments. *Annals of Internal Medicine, 126,* 97–106.

Lyons, H. Z., & O'Brien, K. M. (2006). The role of person-environment fit in the job satisfaction and tenure intentions of African American employees. *Journal of Counseling Psychology, 53,* 387–396.

Macintyre, S. (1997). The Black report and beyond: What are the issues? *Social Science and Medicine, 44,* 723–745.

Madden, D. J. (2001). Speed and timing of behavioural processes. In J. E. Birren & K. W. Schaie (Eds.), *Handbook of the psychology of aging* (5th ed.). San Diego, CA: Academic Press.

Magai, C., Consedine, N. S., Gillespie, M., O'Neal, C., & Vilker, R. (2004). The differential roles of early emotion socialization and adult attachment in adult emotional experience: Testing a mediator hypothesis. *Attachment and Human Development, 6,* 389–417.

Magai, C., Consedine, N. S., Krivoshekova, Y. S., Kudadjie-Gyamfi, E., & McPherson, R. (2006). Emotion experience and expression across the adult life span: Insights from a multimodal assessment study. *Psychology and Aging, 21,* 303–317.

Magnusson, D. (Ed.). (1996). *The lifespan development of individuals: Behavioral, neurobiological, and psychosocial perspectives: A synthesis.* New York, NY: Cambridge University Press.

Magnusson Hanson, L. L., Theorell, T., Oxenstierna, G., Hyde, M., & Westerlund, H. (2008). Demand, control and social climate as predictors of emotional exhaustion symptoms in working Swedish men and women. *Scandinavian Journal of Public Health, 36,* 737–743.

Mahlberg, R., Tilmann, A., Salewski, L., & Kunz, D. (2006). Normative data on the daily profile of urinary 6-sulfatoxymelatonin in healthy subjects between the ages of 20 and 84. *Psychoneuroendocrinology, 31,* 634–641.

Maki, N., & Martikainen, P. (2009). The role of socioeconomic indicators on non-alcohol and alcohol-associated suicide mortality among women in Finland. A register-based follow-up study of 12 million person-years. *Social Science and Medicine, 68,* 2161–2169.

Maltais, M. L., Desroches, J., & Dionne, I. J. (2009). Changes in muscle mass and strength after menopause. *Journal of Musculoskeletal and Neuronal Interactions, 9,* 186–197.

Mancini, A. D., & Bonanno, G. A. (2006). Marital closeness, functional disability, and adjustment in late life. *Psychology and Aging, 21,* 600–610.

Mancini, A. D., & Bonanno, G. A. (2009). Predictors and parameters of resilience to loss: Toward an individual differences model. *Journal of Personality, 77*, 1805–1832.

Manini, T. M., Everhart, J. E., Anton, S. D., Schoeller, D. A., Cummings, S. R., Mackey, D. C., . . . Harris, T. B. (2009). Activity energy expenditure and change in body composition in late life. *American Journal of Clinical Nutrition, 90*, 1336–1342.

Manton, K. G. (2008). Recent declines in chronic disability in the elderly U.S. population: Risk factors and future dynamics. *Annual Review of Clinical Psychology, 29*, 91–113.

Manzoli, L., Villari, P., M Pirone, G., & Boccia, A. (2007). Marital status and mortality in the elderly: A systematic review and meta-analysis. *Social Science & Medicine, 64*, 77–94.

Margrett, J., Martin, P., Woodard, J. L., Miller, L. S., MacDonald, M., Baenziger, J., . . . Arnold, J. (2010). Depression among centenarians and the oldest old: Contributions of cognition and personality. *Gerontology, 56*, 93–99.

Markland, A. D., Richter, H. E., Burgio, K. L., Bragg, C., Hernandez, A. L., & Subak, L. L. (2009). Fecal incontinence in obese women with urinary incontinence: Prevalence and role of dietary fiber intake. *American Journal of Obstetrics and Gynecology, 200*, 566.

Marks, B. L., Katz, L. M., & Smith, J. K. (2009). Exercise and the aging mind: Buffing the baby boomer's body and brain. *Physical Sportsmedicine, 37*, 119–125.

Markus, H., & Nurius, P. (1986). Possible selves. *American Psychologist, 41*, 954–969.

Marmot, M., & Brunner, E. (2005). Cohort Profile: The Whitehall II study. *International Journal of Epidemiology, 34*, 251–260.

Marmot, M. G., Shipley, M. J., Hemingway, H., Head, J., & Brunner, E. J. (2008). Biological and behavioural explanations of social inequalities in coronary heart disease: The Whitehall II study. *Diabetologia, 51*, 1980–1988.

Marshall, V. W. (1980). *Last chapters: A sociology of aging and dying*. Monterey, CA: Brooks-Cole.

Marsiglio, W., Amato, P., Day, R. D., & Lamb, M. E. (2002). Scholarship on fatherhood in the 1990s and beyond. *Journal of Marriage and Family, 62*, 1173–1191.

Marsiske, M., & Margrett, J. A. (2006). Everyday problem solving and decision making. In J. E. Birren & K. W. Schaire (Eds.), *Handbook of the psychology of aging* (6th ed., pp. 315–342). Philadelphia, PA: Elsevier.

Martens, A., Greenberg, J., Schimel, J., & Landau, M. J. (2004). Ageism and death: Effects of mortality salience and perceived similarity to elders on reactions to elderly people. *Personality and Social Psychology Bulletin, 30*, 1524–1536.

Martin, M. D., Hancock, G. A., Richardson, B., Simmons, P., Katona, C., Mullan, E., et al. (2002). An evaluation of needs in elderly continuing-care settings. *International Psychogeriatrics, 14*, 379–388.

Martire, L. M., Schulz, R., Reynolds, C. F., III, Karp, J. F., Gildengers, A. G., & Whyte, E. M. (2010). Treatment of late-life depression alleviates caregiver burden. *Journal of the American Geriatrics Society, 58*, 23–29.

Masayesva, B. G., Mambo, E., Taylor, R. J., Goloubeva, O. G., Zhou, S., Cohen, Y., . . . Califano, J. (2006). Mitochondrial DNA content increase in response to cigarette smoking. *Cancer Epidemiology Biomarkers and Prevention, 15*, 19–24.

Mast, B. T., Fitzgerald, J., Steinberg, J., MacNeill, S. E., & Lichtenberg, P. A. (2001). Effective screening for Alzheimer's disease among older African Americans. *Clinical Neuropsychologist, 15*, 196–202.

Mast, B. T., MacNeill, S. E., & Lichtenberg, P. A. (2002). A MIMIC model approach to research in geriatric neuropsychology: The case of vascular dementia. *Aging, Neuropsychology and Cognition, 9*, 21–37.

Masunaga, H., & Horn, J. (2001). Expertise and age-related changes in components of intelligence. *Psychology and Aging, 16*, 293–311.

Matthews, L., Wickrama, K., & Conger, R. (1996). Predicting marital instability from spouse and observer reports of marital interaction. *Journal of Marriage and Family, 58*, 641–655.

Matthews, R. A., Bulger, C. A., & Barnes-Farrell, J. L. (2010). Work social supports, role stressors, and work-family conflict: The moderating effect of age. *Journal of Vocational Behavior, 76*, 78–90.

Matthews, S. H. (1986). *Friendships through the life course*. Beverly Hills, CA: Sage.

Maurer, T. J. (2001). Career-relevant learning and development, worker age, and beliefs about self-efficacy for development. *Journal of Management, 27*, 123–140.

Mayhew, P. M., Thomas, C. D., Clement, J. G., Loveridge, N., Beck, T. J., Bonfield, W., . . . Reeve, J. (2005). Relation between age, femoral neck cortical stability, and hip fracture risk. *Lancet, 366*, 129–135.

McArdle, J. J., Ferrer-Caja, E., Hamagami, F., & Woodcock, R. W. (2002). Comparative longitudinal structural analyses of the growth and decline of multiple intellectual abilities over the life span. *Developmental Psychology, 38*, 115–142.

McArdle, J. J., & Hamagami, F. (2006). Longitudinal tests of dynamic hypotheses on intellectual abilities measured over sixty years. In C. S. Bergeman & S. M. Boker (Eds.), *Methodological issues in aging research* (pp. 43–98): Mahwah, NJ: Erlbaum.

McAuley, E., Marquez, D. X., Jerome, G. J., Blissmer, B., & Katula, J. (2002). Physical activity and physique anxiety in older adults: Fitness, and efficacy influences. *Aging and Mental Health, 6*, 222–230.

McCarthy, L. H., Bigal, M. E., Katz, M., Derby, C., & Lipton, R. B. (2009). Chronic pain and obesity in elderly people: Results from the Einstein aging study. *Journal of the American Geriatric Society, 57*, 115–119.

McCleane, G. (2007). Pharmacological pain management in the elderly patient. *Clinical Interventions in Aging, 2*, 637–643.

McCrae, R. R., & Costa, P. T. J. (2003). *Personality in adulthood, Personality in adulthood: A five-factor theory perspective* (2nd ed.). New York, NY: Guilford.

McCullough, M. E., Friedman, H. S., Enders, C. K., & Martin, L. R. (2009). Does devoutness delay death? Psychological investment in religion and its association with longevity in the Terman sample. *Journal of Personality and Social Psychology, 97,* 866–882.

McCullough, M. E., Hoyt, W. T., Larson, D. B., Koenig, H. G., & Thoresen, C. (2000). Religious involvement and mortality: A meta-analytic review. *Health Psychology, 19,* 211–222.

McDonald-Miszczak, L., Hertzog, C., & Hultsch, D. F. (1995). Stability and accuracy of metamemory in adulthood and aging: A longitudinal analysis. *Psychology and Aging, 10,* 553–564.

McFadden, S. H., & Basting, A. D. (2010). Healthy aging persons and their brains: Promoting resilience through creative engagement. *Clinics in Geriatric Medicine, 26,* 149–161.

McGue, M., & Christensen, K. (2002). The heritability of level and rate-of-change in cognitive functioning in Danish twins aged 70 years and older. *Experimental Aging Research, 28,* 435–451.

McKeith, I. G. (2006). Consensus guidelines for the clinical and pathologic diagnosis of dementia with Lewy bodies (DLB): Report of the Consortium on DLB International Workshop. *Journal of Alzheimers Disease, 9,* 417–423.

McKhann, G., Drachman, D., Folstein, M., Katzman, R., Price, D., & Stadlan, E. M. (1984). Clinical diagnosis of Alzheimer's Disease: Report of the NINCDS-ADRDA Work Group under the auspices of Department of Health and Human Services Task Force on Alzheimer's Disease. *Neurology, 34,* 939–944.

McKiernan, F. (1996). Bereavement and attitudes toward death. In R. T. Woods (Ed.), *Handbook of the clinical psychology of ageing* (pp. 159–182). Chichester, England: Wiley.

McLean, K. C. (2008). Stories of the young and the old: Personal continuity and narrative identity. *Developmental Psychology, 44,* 254–264.

McNall, L. A., Masuda, A. D., & Nicklin, J. M. (2010). Flexible work arrangements, job satisfaction, and turnover intentions: The mediating role of work-to-family enrichment. *Journal of Psychology, 144,* 61–81.

McNamara, B., & Rosenwax, L. (2010). Which carers of family members at the end of life need more support from health services and why? *Social Science and Medicine, 70,* 1035–1041.

Meeks, S. (2000). Schizophrenia and related disorders. In S. K. Whitbourne (Ed.), *Psychopathology in later life* (pp. 189–215). New York, NY: Wiley.

Mehta, K. M., Yaffe, K., Brenes, G. A., Newman, A. B., Shorr, R. I., Simonsick, E. M., . . . Covinsky, K. E. (2007). Anxiety symptoms and decline in physical function over 5 years in the health, aging and body composition study. *Journal of the American Geriatrics Society, 55,* 265–270.

Meunier, N., Beattie, J. H., Ciarapica, D., O'Connor, J. M., Andriollo-Sanchez, M., Taras, A., . . . Polito, A. (2005). Basal metabolic rate and thyroid hormones of late-middle-aged and older human subjects: The ZENITH study. *European Journal of Clinical Nutrition, 59,* S53–S57.

Meyer, B. J. F., Talbot, A. P., & Ranalli, C. (2007). Why older adults make more immediate treatment decisions about cancer than younger adults. *Psychology and Aging, 22,* 505–524.

Michalos, A. C. (1985). Multiple discrepancies theory (MDT). *Social Indicators Research, 16,* 347–413.

Miller, L. J., Myers, A., Prinzi, L., & Mittenberg, W. (2009). Changes in intellectual functioning associated with normal aging. *Archives of Clinical Neuropsychology, 24,* 681–688.

Miller, P. J. E., Niehuis, S., & Huston, T. L. (2006). Positive illusions in marital relationships: A 13-year longitudinal study. *Personality and Social Psychology Bulletin, 32,* 1579–1594.

Miller, S. C., Papandonatos, G., Fennell, M., & Mor, V. (2006). Facility and county effects on racial differences in nursing home quality indicators. *Social Science and Medicine, 63,* 3046–3059.

Miner-Rubino, K., Winter, D. G., & Stewart, A. J. (2004). Gender, social class, and the subjective experience of aging: Self-perceived personality change from early adulthood to late midlife. *Personality and Social Psychology Bulletin, 30,* 1599–1610.

Minority Staff Special Investigations Division Committee on Government Reform U.S. House of Representatives. (2001, July 30). Abuse of Residents Is a Major Problem in U.S. Nursing Homes Prepared for Rep. Henry A. Waxman. Retrieved from http://www.cbsnews.com/htdocs/pdf/waxman_nursing.pdf

Mireles, D. E., & Charness, N. (2002). Computational explorations of the influence of structured knowledge on age-related cognitive decline. *Psychology and Aging, 17,* 245–259.

Mitchell, B. A., & Lovegreen, L. D. (2009). The empty nest syndrome in midlife families: A multimethod exploration of parental gender differences and cultural dynamics. *Journal of Family Issues, 30,* 1651–1670.

Mitchell, S. L., Teno, J. M., Kiely, D. K., Shaffer, M. L., Jones, R. N., Prigerson, H. G., . . . Hamel, M. B. (2009). The clinical course of advanced dementia. *New England Journal of Medicine, 361,* 1529–1538.

Mitsumune, T., Senoh, E., Nishikawa, H., Adachi, M., & Kajii, E. (2009). The effect of obesity and smoking status on lung age in Japanese men. *Respirology, 14,* 757–760.

Mitty, E. (2009). Nursing care of the aging foot. *Geriatric Nursing, 30,* 350–354.

Mocchegiani, E., Malavolta, M., Muti, E., Costarelli, L., Cipriano, C., Piacenza, F., . . . Lattanzio, F. (2008). Zinc, metallothioneins and longevity: Interrelationships with niacin and selenium. *Current Pharmaceutical Design, 14,* 2719–2732.

Moen, P. (1996). A life course perspective on retirement, gender, and well-being. *Journal of Occupational Health Psychology, 1,* 131–144.

Moen, P., Kim, J. E., & Hofmeister, H. (2001). Couples' work/retirement transitions, gender, and marital quality. *Social Psychology Quarterly, 64,* 55–71.

Mohammadi, S., Mazhari, M. M., Mehrparvar, A. H., & Attarchi, M. S. (2009). Cigarette smoking and occupational noise-induced hearing loss. *European Journal of Public Health*. doi:ckp 167 [pii] 10.1093/eurpub/ckp167.

Mohlman, J., & Price, R. (2006). Recognizing and treating late-life generalized anxiety disorder: Distinguishing features and psychosocial treatment. *Expert Reviews in Neurotherapy*, 6, 1439–1445.

Moore, D. E., & Hayward, M. D. (1990). Occupational careers and mortality of elderly men. *Demography*, 27, 31–53.

Moorman, S. M., Booth, A., & Fingerman, K. L. (2006). Women's romantic relationships after widowhood. *Journal of Family Issues*, 27, 1281–1304.

Moos, R. H., Schutte, K., Brennan, P., & Moos, B. S. (2004). Ten-year patterns of alcohol consumption and drinking problems among older women and men. *Addiction*, 99, 829–838.

Morales, A. M., Mirone, V., Dean, J., & Costa, P. (2009). Vardenafil for the treatment of erectile dysfunction: An overview of the clinical evidence. *Clinical Interventions in Aging*, 4, 463–472.

Morone, N. E., Rollman, B. L., Moore, C. G., Li, Q., & Weiner, D. K. (2009). A mind-body program for older adults with chronic low back pain: Results of a pilot study. *Pain Medicine*, 10, 1395–1407.

Morris, M. C., Evans, D. A., Tangney, C. C., Bienias, J. L., & Wilson, R. S. (2005). Fish consumption and cognitive decline with age in a large community study. *Archives of Neurology*, 62, 1849–1853.

Morrow, D. G., Miller, L. M., Ridolfo, H. E., Magnor, C., Fischer, U. M., Kokayeff, N. K., . . . Stine-Morrow, E. A. (2009). Expertise and age differences in pilot decision making. *Neuropsychology, Development, and Cognition. Section B, Aging Neuropsychology and Cognition*, 16, 33–55.

Moss, M. S., Resch, N., & Moss, S. Z. (1997). The role of gender in middle-age children's responses to parent death. *Omega—Journal of Death & Dying*, 35, 43–65.

Motta, M., Bennati, E., Ferlito, L., Malaguarnera, M., & Motta, L. (2005). Successful aging in centenarians: Myths and reality. *Archives of Gerontology and Geriatrics*, 40, 241–251.

Mottram, P. G., Wilson, K. C., Ashworth, L., & Abou-Saleh, M. (2002). The clinical profile of older patients' response to antidepressants—an open trial of sertraline. *International Journal of Geriatric Psychiatry*, 17, 574–578.

Mount, M. K., Barrick, M. R., Scullen, S. M., & Rounds, J. (2005). Higher-order dimensions of the big five personality traits and the big six vocational interest types. *Personnel Psychology*, 58, 447–478.

Mroczek, D. K., & Kolarz, C. M. (1998). The effect of age on positive and negative affect: A developmental perspective on happiness. *Journal of Personality and Social Psychology*, 75, 1333–1349.

Mroczek, D. K., & Spiro, A., III. (2005). Change in life satisfaction during adulthood: Fndings from the Veterans Affairs Normative Aging Study. *Journal of Personality and Social Psychology*, 88, 189–202.

Muchinsky, P. (1999). Application of Holland's theory in industrial and organizational settings. *Journal of Vocational Behavior*, 55, 127–125.

Mueller, M. M., Wilhelm, B., & Elder, G. H., Jr. (2002). Variations in grandparenting. *Research on Aging*, 24, 360–388.

Muntaner, A., Borrell, C., Sola, J., Mari-Dell'olmo, M., Chung, H., Rodriguez-Sanz, M., . . . Noh, S. (2009). Capitalists, managers, professionals and mortality: Findings from the Barcelona social class and all cause mortality longitudinal study. *Scandinavian Journal of Public Health*, 37, 826–838.

Munzer, T., Harman, S. M., Sorkin, J. D., & Blackman, M. R. (2009). Growth hormone and sex steroid effects on serum glucose, insulin, and lipid concentrations in healthy older women and men. *Journal of Clinical Endocrinology and Metabolism*, 94, 3833–3841.

Murase, T., Haramizu, S., Ota, N., & Hase, T. (2009). Suppression of the aging-associated decline in physical performance by a combination of resveratrol intake and habitual exercise in senescence-accelerated mice. *Biogerontology*, 10, 423–434.

Murphy, D. R., Daneman, M., & Schneider, B. A. (2006). Why do older adults have difficulty following conversations? *Psychology and Aging*, 21, 49–61.

Murphy, N. A., & Isaacowitz, D. M. (2008). Preferences for emotional information in older and younger adults: A meta-analysis of memory and attention tasks. *Psychology and Aging*, 23, 263–286.

Musil, C., Warner, C., Zauszniewski, J., Wykle, M., & Standing, T. (2009). Grandmother caregiving, family stress and strain, and depressive symptoms. *Western Journal of Nursing Research*, 31, 389–408.

Nadien, M. B. (2006). Factors that influence abusive interactions between aging women and their caregivers. *Annals of the New York Academy of Sciences*, 1087, 158–169.

National Cancer Institute. (2010). Understanding cancer. Retrieved from http://www.cancer.gov/cancertopics/understandingcancer/.

National Center for Health Statistics. (2009). *Health United States*. Washington, DC: U.S. Department of Health and Human Services.

National Center for Health Statistics. (2010). Marriage and cohabitation in the United States: A statistical portrait based on Cycle 6 (2002) of the National Survey of Family Growth. Series 23, Number 28. Hyattsville, MD: Vital and Health Statistics.

National Health Interview Survey. (2009). Early release of selected estimates based on data From the January–March 2009 National Health Interview Survey.

National Institute of Aging. (2009). Caring for a person with Alzheimer's Disease. NIH Publication Number: 09-6173. Retrieved from http://www.nia.nih.gov/NR/rdonlyres/6A0E9F3C-E429-4F03-818E-D1B60235D5F8/0/100711_LoRes2.pdf.

National Institute on Alcohol Abuse and Alcoholism. (1998). *Alcohol and aging*. Rockville, MD.

National Library of Medicine. (2010). Melatonin. Retrieved from http://www.nlm.nih.gov/medlineplus/druginfo/natural/patient-melatonin.html.

National Vital Statistics System. (2010). Births 2006. Retrieved from http://205.207.175.93/VitalStats/TableViewer/tableView.aspx?ReportId=15095

Navarro, B., Andres, F., Parraga, I., Morena, S., Latorre, J. M., & Lopez-Torres, J. (2010). Approach to major depression in old people. *International Psychogeriatrics, 18*, 1–6.

Nehrke, M. F., Turner, R. R., Cohen, S. H., Whitbourne, S. K., Morganti, J. B., & Hulicka, I. M. (1981). Toward a model of person-environment congruence: Development of the EPPIS. *Experimental Aging Research, 7*, 363–379.

Neikrug, A. B., & Ancoli-Israel, S. (2009). Sleep disorders in the older adult: A mini-review. *Gerontology.* doi:000236900 [pii] 10.1159/000236900.

Nelson, E. A., & Dannefer, D. (1992). Aged heterogeneity: Fact or fiction? The fate of diversity in gerontological research. *Gerontologist, 32*, 17–23.

Neugarten, B. L., & Weinstein, K. K. (1964). The changing American grandparent. *Journal of Marriage and the Family, 26*, 199–204.

Neupert, S. D., Almeida, D. M., Mroczek, D. K., & Spiro, A. III. (2006). Daily stressors and memory failures in a naturalistic setting: Findings from the VA Normative Aging Study. *Psychology and Aging, 21*, 424–429.

Neupert, S. D., Lachman, M. E., & Whitbourne, S. B. (2009). Exercise self-efficacy and control beliefs: Effects on exercise behavior after an exercise intervention for older adults. *Journal of Aging and Physical Activity, 17*, 1–16.

Newson, R. S., & Kemps, E. B. (2006). Cardiorespiratory fitness as a predictor of successful cognitive ageing. *Journal of Clinical and Experimental Neuropsychology: Section A, Neuropsychology, Development, and Cognition, 28*, 949–967.

Ng, T. W. H., & Butts, M. M. (2009). Effectiveness of organizational efforts to lower turnover intentions: The moderating role of employee locus of control. *Human Resource Management, 48*, 289–310.

Ng, T. W. H., & Feldman, D. C. (2007). Organizational embeddedness and occupational embeddedness across career stages. *Journal of Vocational Behavior, 70*, 336–351.

Nijs, K. A., de Graaf, C., Kok, F. J., & van Staveren, W. A. (2006). Effect of family style mealtimes on quality of life, physical performance, and body weight of nursing home residents: Cluster randomised controlled trial. *BMJ: British Medical Journal, 332*, 1180–1184.

Nikitin, N. P., Loh, P. H., de Silva, R., Witte, K. K., Lukaschuk, E. I., Parker, A., . . . Cleland, J. G. (2006). Left ventricular morphology, global and longitudinal function in normal older individuals: A cardiac magnetic resonance study. *International Journal of Cardiology, 108*, 76–83.

Niklas, C. D., & Dormann, C. (2005). The impact of affect on job satisfaction. *European Journal of Work and Organizational Psychology, 14*, 367–388.

Nissim, R., Gagliese, L., & Rodin, G. (2009). The desire for hastened death in individuals with advanced cancer: A longitudinal qualitative study. *Social Science & Medicine, 69*, 165–171.

Noone, J. H., Stephens, C., & Alpass, F. M. (2009). Preretirement planning and well-being in later life: A prospective study. *Research on Aging, 31*, 295–317.

Nunes, A., & Kramer, A. F. (2009). Experience-based mitigation of age-related performance declines: Evidence from air traffic control. *Journal of Experimental Psychology: Applied, 15*, 12–24.

Nygaard, R. W., Echt, K. V., & Schuchard, R. A. (2008). Models of reading performance in older adults with normal age-related vision. *Journal of Rehabilitation Research and Development, 45*, 901–910.

Nyunt, M. S., Fones, C., Niti, M., & Ng, T. P. (2009). Criterion-based validity and reliability of the Geriatric Depression Screening Scale (GDS-15) in a large validation sample of community-living Asian older adults. *Aging and Mental Health, 13*, 376–382.

O'Brien, L. T., & Hummert, M. L. (2006). Memory performance of late middle-aged adults: Contrasting self-stereotyping and stereotype threat accounts of assimilation to age stereotypes. *Social Cognition, 24*, 338–358.

O'Connor, D. W., Gardner, B., Presnell, I., Singh, D., Tsanglis, M., & White, E. (2010). The effectiveness of continuation-maintenance ECT in reducing depressed older patients' hospital re-admissions. *Journal of Affective Disorders, 120*, 62–66.

O'Donovan, D., Hausken, T., Lei, Y., Russo, A., Keogh, J., Horowitz, M., . . . Jones, K. L. (2005). Effect of aging on transpyloric flow, gastric emptying, and intragastric distribution in healthy humans—impact on glycemia. *Digestive Diseases and Sciences, 50*, 671–676.

O'Hanlon, L., Kemper, S., & Wilcox, K. A. (2005). Aging, encoding, and word retrieval: Distinguishing phonological and memory processes. *Experimental Aging Research, 31*, 149–171.

O*NET. (2010). O*NET. http://www.onetcenter.org.

Ohtani, N., Mann, D. J., & Hara, E. (2009). Cellular senescence: Its role in tumor suppression and aging. *Cancer Science, 100*, 792–797.

Oken, B. S., Zajdel, D., Kishiyama, S., Flegal, K., Dehen, C., Haas, M., . . . Levya, J. (2006). Randomized, controlled, six-month trial of yoga in healthy seniors: Effects on cognition and quality of life. *Alternative Therapies in Health and Medicine, 12*, 40–47.

Okereke, O., Kang, J. H., Ma, J., Hankinson, S. E., Pollak, M. N., & Grodstein, F. (2007). Plasma IGF-I levels and cognitive performance in older women. *Neurobiology of Aging, 28*, 135–142.

Okonkwo, O. C., Crowe, M., Wadley, V. G., & Ball, K. (2008). Visual attention and self-regulation of driving among older adults. *International Psychogeriatrics, 20*, 162–173.

Okura, H., Takada, Y., Yamabe, A., Kubo, T., Asawa, K., Ozaki, T., . . . Yoshida, K. (2009). Age- and gender-specific changes in the left ventricular relaxation: A Doppler echocardiographic study in healthy individuals. *Circulation: Cardiovascular Imaging, 2*, 41–46.

Okura, T., Plassman, B. L., Steffens, D. C., Llewellyn, D. J., Potter, G. G., & Langa, K. M. (2010). Prevalence of neuropsychiatric symptoms and their association with functional limitations in older adults in the United States: The aging, demographics, and memory study. *Journal of the American Geriatrics Society, 58,* 330–337.

Old, S. R., & Naveh-Benjamin, M. (2008). Differential effects of age on item and associative measures of memory: A meta-analysis. *Psychology and Aging, 23,* 104–118.

Olsson, G., Hemstrom, O., & Fritzell, J. (2009). Identifying factors associated with good health and ill health: Not just opposite sides of the same coin. *International Journal of Behavioral Medicine, 16,* 323–330.

Oneill, C., Jamison, J., McCulloch, D., & Smith, D. (2001). Age-related macular degeneration: Cost-of-illness issues. *Drugs and Aging, 18,* 233–241.

Ong, A. D., Bergeman, C. S., Bisconti, T. L., & Wallace, K. A. (2006). Psychological resilience, positive emotions, and successful adaptation to stress in later life. *Journal of Personality and Social Psychology, 91,* 730–749.

Organisation for Economic Co-operation and Development (2007). Table 1321. Percentage of the Adult Population Considered to be Obese. Retrieved from http://www.oecd.org/document/62/0,2340,en_2649_34489_2345918_1_1_1_1,00.html.

Osorio, A., Ballesteros, S., Fay, S., & Pouthas, V. (2009). The effect of age on word-stem cued recall: A behavioral and electrophysiological study. *Brain Research, 1289,* 56–68.

Otsuki, T., Maeda, S., Kesen, Y., Yokoyama, N., Tanabe, T., Sugawara, J., . . . Matsuda, M. (2006). Age-related reduction of systemic arterial compliance induces excessive myocardial oxygen consumption during sub-maximal exercise. *Hypertension Research, 29,* 65–73.

Pacheco, J., Hershberger, P. J., Markert, R. J., & Kumar, G. (2003). A longitudinal study of attitudes toward physician-assisted suicide and euthanasia among patients with noncurable malignancy. *American Journal of Hospital Palliative Care, 20,* 99–104.

Packer, D. J., & Chasteen, A. L. (2006). Looking to the future: How possible aged selves influence prejudice toward older adults. *Social Cognition, 24,* 218–247.

Paley, B., Cox, M. J., Kanoy, K. W., Harter, K. S., Burchinal, M., & Margand, N. A. (2005). Adult attachment and marital interaction as predictors of whole family interactions during the transition to parenthood. *Journal of Family Psychology, 19,* 420–429.

Palmer, B. W., Heaton, R. K., Gladsjo, J. A., Evans, J. D., Patterson, T. L., Golshan, S., . . . Jeste, D. V. (2002). Heterogeneity in functional status among older outpatients with schizophrenia: Employment history, living situation, and driving. *Schizophrenia Research, 55,* 205–215.

Palmer, K. (2009, June 28). The new parent trap: more boomers help adult kids out financially. *U.S. News & World Report.*

Pamuk, E., Makuc, D., Heck, K., Reuben, C., & Lochner, K. (1998). *Socioeconomic status and health chartbook. Health, United States, 1998.* Hyattsville, MD: National Center for Health Statistics.

Park, D. C., & Reuter-Lorenz, P. (2009). The adaptive brain: Aging and neurocognitive scaffolding. *Annual Review of Psychology, 60,* 173–196.

Park, S. K., Tedesco, P. M., & Johnson, T. E. (2009). Oxidative stress and longevity in Caenorhabditis elegans as mediated by SKN-1. *Aging Cell, 8,* 258–269.

Patterson, T. L., McKibbin, C., Taylor, M., Goldman, S., Davila-Fraga, W., Bucardo, J., . . . Jeste, D. V. (2003). Functional Adaptation Skills Training (FAST): A pilot psychosocial intervention study in middle-aged and older patients with chronic psychotic disorders. *American Journal of Geriatric Psychiatry, 11,* 17–23.

Paulson, Q. X., Hong, J., Holcomb, V. B., & Nunez, N. P. (2010). Effects of body weight and alcohol consumption on insulin sensitivity. *Nutrition Journal, 9,* 14.

Pavalko, E. K., Elder, G. H., & Clipp, E. C. (1993). Work lives and longevity: Insights from a life course perspective. *Journal of Health and Social Behavior, 34,* 363–380.

Paxton, J. L., Barch, D. M., Storandt, M., & Braver, T. S. (2006). Effects of environmental support and strategy training on older adults' use of context. *Psychology and Aging, 21,* 499–509.

Pearson, K. J., Baur, J. A., Lewis, K. N., Peshkin, L., Price, N. L., Labinskyy, N., . . . de Cabo, R. (2008). Resveratrol delays age-related deterioration and mimics transcriptional aspects of dietary restriction without extending life span. *Cell Metabolism, 8,* 157–168.

Pedrera-Zamorano, J. D., Lavado-Garcia, J. M., Roncero-Martin, R., Calderon-Garcia, J. F., Rodriguez-Dominguez, T., & Canal-Macias, M. L. (2009). Effect of beer drinking on ultrasound bone mass in women. *Nutrition, 25,* 1057–1063.

Peelle, J. E., Troiani, V., Wingfield, A., & Grossman, M. (2010). Neural processing during older adults' comprehension of spoken sentences: Age differences in resource allocation and connectivity. *Cerebral Cortex, 20,* 773–782.

Pegula, S., Marsh, S. M., & Jackson, L. L. (2007). Fatal occupational injuries—United States, 2005. *Morbidity and Mortality Weekly Report, 56,* 13, 297–301.

Pelletier, A. L., Thomas, J., & Shaw, F. R. (2009). Vision loss in older persons. *American Family Physician, 79,* 963–970.

Pepin, R., Segal, D. L., & Coolidge, F. L. (2009). Intrinsic and extrinsic barriers to mental health care among community-dwelling younger and older adults. *Aging and Mental Health, 13,* 769–777.

Peplau, L. A., & Fingerhut, A. W. (2007). The close relationships of lesbians and gay men. *Annual Review of Psychology, 58,* 405–424.

Peppone, L. J., Hebl, S., Purnell, J. Q., Reid, M. E., Rosier, R. N., Mustian, K. M., . . . Morrow, G. R. (2009). The efficacy of calcitriol therapy in the management of bone loss and fractures: A qualitative review. *Osteoporosis International.* doi:10.1007/s00198-009-1136-2.

Perez-Lopez, F. R., Chedraui, P., Haya, J., & Cuadros, J. L. (2009). Effects of the Mediterranean diet on longevity and age-related morbid conditions. *Maturitas, 64,* 67–79.

Perez, V. I., Bokov, A., Remmen, H. V., Mele, J., Ran, Q., Ikeno, Y., . . . Richardson, A. (2009). Is the oxidative stress theory of aging dead? *Biochimica et Biophysica Acta, 1790,* 1005–1014.

Perlman, F., & Bobak, M. (2009). Assessing the contribution of unstable employment to mortality in posttransition Russia: Prospective individual-level analyses from the Russian longitudinal monitoring survey. *American Journal of Public Health, 99,* 1818–1825.

Perren, S., Von Wyl, A., Bürgin, D., Simoni, H., & Von Klitzing, K. (2005). Intergenerational transmission of marital quality across the transition to parenthood. *Family Process, 44,* 441–459.

Perrig-Chiello, P., & Höpflinger, F. (2005). Aging parents and their middle-aged children: Demographic and psychosocial challenges. *European Journal of Ageing, 2,* 183–191.

Perruccio, A. V., Badley, E. M., & Trope, G. E. (2007). Self-reported glaucoma in Canada: Findings from population-based surveys, 1994–2003. *Canadian Journal of Ophthalmology, 42,* 219–226.

Peters, R., Peters, J., Warner, J., Beckett, N., & Bulpitt, C. (2008). Alcohol, dementia and cognitive decline in the elderly: A systematic review. *Age and Ageing, 37,* 505–512.

Petrofsky, J. S., McLellan, K., Bains, G. S., Prowse, M., Ethiraju, G., Lee, S., . . . Schwab, E. (2009). The influence of ageing on the ability of the skin to dissipate heat. *Medical Science Monitor, 15,* CR261–268.

Pew Research Center. (2009). Growing old in America: Expectations vs. reality. Retrieved from http://pewresearch.org/pubs/1269/aging-survey-expectations-versus-reality.

Pfirrmann, C. W., Metzdorf, A., Elfering, A., Hodler, J., & Boos, N. (2006). Effect of aging and degeneration on disc volume and shape: A quantitative study in asymptomatic volunteers. *Journal of Orthopedics Research, 24,* 1086–1094.

Pfisterer, M. H., Griffiths, D. J., Schaefer, W., & Resnick, N. M. (2006). The effect of age on lower urinary tract function: A study in women. *Journal of the American Geriatrics Society, 54,* 405–412.

Pham-Kanter, G. (2009). Social comparisons and health: Can having richer friends and neighbors make you sick? *Social Science & Medicine, 69,* 335–344.

Phelps, A. C., Maciejewski, P. K., Nilsson, M., Balboni, T. A., Wright, A. A., Paulk, M. E., . . . Prigerson, H. G. (2009). Religious coping and use of intensive life-prolonging care near death in patients with advanced cancer. *Journal of the American Medical Association, 301,* 1140–1147.

Pietschmann, P., Rauner, M., Sipos, W., & Kerschan-Schindl, K. (2009). Osteoporosis: An age-related and gender-specific disease—a mini-review. *Gerontology, 55,* 3–12.

Pinilla, F. G. (2006). The impact of diet and exercise on brain plasticity and disease. *Nutrition and Health, 18,* 277–284.

Pinquart, M., & Schindler, I. (2007). Changes of life satisfaction in the transition to retirement: A latent-class approach. *Psychology and Aging, 22,* 442–455.

Piolino, P., Desgranges, B., Benali, K., & Eustache, F. (2002). Episodic and semantic remote autobiographical memory in ageing. *Memory, 10,* 239–257.

Plassman, B. L., Langa, K. M., Fisher, G. G., Heeringa, S. G., Weir, D. R., Ofstedal, M. B., . . . Wallace, R. B. (2007). Prevalence of dementia in the United States: The aging, demographics, and memory study. *Neuroepidemiology, 29,* 125–132.

Plaut, V. C., Markus, H. R., & Lachman, M. E. (2003). Place matters: Consensual features and regional variation in American well-being and self. *Journal of Personality & Social Psychology, 83,* 160–184.

Plemons, J. K., Willis, S. L., & Baltes, P. B. (1978). Modifiability of fluid intelligence in aging: A short-term longitudinal training approach. *Journal of Gerontology, 33,* 224–231.

Pollet, T. V., Nelissen, M., & Nettle, D. (2009). Lineage based differences in grandparental investment: Evidence from a large British cohort study. *Journal of Biosocial Science, 41,* 355–379.

Pongchaiyakul, C., Nguyen, T. V., Kosulwat, V., Rojroongwasinkul, N., Charoenkiatkul, S., & Rajatanavin, R. (2005). Effect of urbanization on bone mineral density: A Thai epidemiological study. *BMC Musculoskeletal Disorders, 6,* 5.

Portin, R., Saarijaervi, S., Joukamaa, M., & Salokangas, R. K. R. (1995). Education, gender and cognitive performance in a 62-year-old normal population: Results from the Turva Project. *Psychological Medicine, 25,* 1295–1298.

Pratt, L. A. (2009). Serious psychological distress, as measured by the K6, and mortality. *Annals of Epidemiology, 19,* 202–209.

Pratt, L. A., Dey, A. N., & Cohen, A. J. (2007). Characteristics of adults with serious psychological distress as measured by the K6 scale: United States, 2001–04. *Advance Data from Vital and Health Statistics, No. 382, March 30.*

President's Commission for the Study of Ethical Problems in Medicine and Biomedical and Behavioral Research. (1981). *Defining death.* Washington, DC: U.S. Government Printing Office.

Previti, D., & Amato, P. R. (2003). Why stay married? Rewards, barriers, and marital stability. *Journal of Marriage and Family, 65,* 561–573.

Previti, D., & Amato, P. R. (2004). Is infidelity a cause or a consequence of poor marital quality? *Journal of Social and Personal Relationships, 21,* 217–230.

Priem, J. S., Solomon, D. H., & Steuber, K. R. (2009). Accuracy and bias in perceptions of emotionally supportive communication in marriage. *Personal Relationships, 16,* 531–551.

Pritchard, R. S., Fisher, E. S., Teno, J. M., Sharp, S. M., Reding, D. J., Knaus, W. A., . . . Lynn, J. (1998). Influence of patient preferences and local health system characteristics on the place of death. SUPPORT Investigators. Study to Understand Prognoses and Preferences for Risks and Outcomes of Treatment. *Journal of the American Geriatrics Society, 46,* 1242–1250.

Pruchno, R. A., & McKenney, D. (2002). Psychological well-being of Black and White grandmothers raising grandchildren: Examination of a two-factor model. *Journals of Gerontology Series B: Psychological Sciences and Social Sciences, 57,* P444–P452.

Pulkki-Raback, L., Elovainio, M., Kivimaki, M., Raitakari, O. T., & Keltikangas-Jarvinen, L. (2005). Temperament in childhood predicts body mass in adulthood: The Cardiovascular Risk in Young Finns Study. *Health Psychology, 24,* 307–315.

Qualls, S. H., Segal, D. L., Norman, S., Niederehe, G., & Gallagher-Thompson, D. (2002). Psychologists in practice with older adults: Current patterns, sources of training, and need for continuing education. *Professional Psychology: Research & Practice, 33,* 435–442.

Quetelet, A. (1835/1968). *A treatise on man and the development of his faculties.* New York: Franklin.

Quin, R. C., Clare, L., Ryan, P., & Jackson, M. (2009). "Not of this world": The subjective experience of late-onset psychosis. *Aging and Mental Health, 13,* 779–787.

Raabe, B., Frese, M., & Beehr, T. A. (2007). Action regulation theory and career self-management. *Journal of Vocational Behavior, 70,* 297–311.

Radwany, S., Albanese, T., Clough, L., Sims, L., Mason, H., & Jahangiri, S. (2009). End-of-life decision making and emotional burden: Placing family meetings in context. *American Journal of Hospice and Palliative Care, 26,* 376–383.

Rahhal, T. A., Colcombe, S. J., & Hasher, L. (2001). Instructional manipulations and age differences in memory: Now you see them, now you don't. *Psychology and Aging, 16,* 697–706.

Raj, I. S., Bird, S. R., & Shield, A. J. (2010). Aging and the force-velocity relationship of muscles. *Experimental Gerontology, 45,* 81–90.

Ram, N., Rabbitt, P., Stollery, B., & Nesselroade, J. R. (2005). Cognitive performance inconsistency: Intraindividual change and variability. *Psychology and Aging, 20,* 623–633.

Raudenbush, S. W., & Bryk, A. S. (2002). *Hierarchical linear models: Applications and data analysis methods* (2nd ed.). Newbury Park, CA: Sage.

Rawson, N. E. (2006). Olfactory loss in aging. *Science of Aging Knowledge Environment, 2006,* pe6.

Ray, A., Block, S. D., Friedlander, R. J., Zhang, B., Maciejewski, P. K., & Prigerson, H. G. (2006). Peaceful awareness in patients with advanced cancer. *Journal of Palliative Medicine, 9,* 1359–1368.

Reardon, J. Z., Lareau, S. C., & ZuWallack, R. (2006). Functional status and quality of life in chronic obstructive pulmonary disease. *American Journal of Medicine, 119,* 32–37.

Reelick, M. F., van Iersel, M. B., Kessels, R. P., & Rikkert, M. G. (2009). The influence of fear of falling on gait and balance in older people. *Age and Ageing, 38,* 435–440.

Reeves, N. D., Narici, M. V., & Maganaris, C. N. (2006). Myotendinous plasticity to ageing and resistance exercise in humans. *Experimental Physiology, 91,* 483–498.

Regnier, V., & Denton, A. (2009). Ten new and emerging trends in residential group living environments. *NeuroRehabilitation, 25,* 169–188.

Reichstadt, J., Depp, C. A., Palinkas, L. A., Folsom, D. P., & Jeste, D. V. (2007). Building blocks of successful aging: A focus group study of older adults' perceived contributors to successful aging. *American Journal of Geriatric Psychiatry, 15,* 194–201.

Reitz, C., Honig, L., Vonsattel, J. P., Tang, M. X., & Mayeux, R. (2009). Memory performance is related to amyloid and tau pathology in the hippocampus. *Journal of Neurology Neurosurgery and Psychiatry, 80,* 715–721.

Reitzes, D. C., & Mutran, E. J. (2004). Grandparent identity, intergenerational family identity, and well-being. *Journals of Gerontology Series B: Psychological Sciences and Social Sciences, 59B,* S213–S219.

Reitzes, D. C., & Mutran, E. J. (2006). Self and health: Factors that encourage self-esteem and functional health. *Journals of Gerontology Series B: Psychological Sciences and Social Sciences, 61,* S44–S51.

Resnick, B., Shaughnessy, M., Galik, E., Scheve, A., Fitten, R., Morrison, T., . . . Agness, C. (2009). Pilot testing of the PRAISEDD intervention among African American and low-income older adults. *Journal of Cardiovascular Nursing, 24,* 352–361.

Reynolds, C. A., Finkel, D., Gatz, M., & Pedersen, N. L. (2002). Sources of influence on rate of cognitive change over time in Swedish twins: An application of latent growth models. *Experimental Aging Research, 28,* 407–433.

Reynolds, K., Lewis, L. B., Nolen, J. D. L., Kinney, G. L., Sathya, B., & He, J. (2003). Alcohol consumption and risk of stroke: A meta-analysis. *Journal of the American Medical Association, 289,* 579–588.

Rhoades, G. K., Stanley, S. M., & Markman, H. J. (2009). The pre-engagement cohabitation effect: A replication and extension of previous findings. *Journal of Family Psychology, 23,* 107–111.

Rhone, M., & Basu, A. (2008). Phytochemicals and age-related eye diseases. *Nutrition Reviews, 66,* 465–472.

Richards, J. B., Kavvoura, F. K., Rivadeneira, F., Styrkarsdottir, U., Estrada, K., Halldorsson, B. V., . . . Spector, T. D. (2009). Collaborative meta-analysis: Associations of 150 candidate genes with osteoporosis and osteoporotic fracture. *Annals of Internal Medicine, 151,* 528–537.

Richardson, E. D., & Marottoli, R. A. (2003). Visual attention and driving behaviors among community-living older persons. *Journals of Gerontology Series A: Biological Sciences and Medical Sciences, 58,* M832–M836.

Richardson, S. S., Sullivan, G., Hill, A., & Yu, W. (2007). Use of aggressive medical treatments near the end of life: Differences between patients with and without dementia. *Health Services Research, 42,* 183–200.

Riggs, K. M., Lachman, M. E., & Wingfield, A. (1997). Taking charge of remembering: Locus of control and older adults' memory for speech. *Experimental Aging Research, 23,* 237–256.

Riordan, C. M., Griffith, R. W., & Weatherly, E. W. (2003). Age and work-related outcomes: The moderating effects of status characteristics. *Journal of Applied Social Psychology, 33,* 37–57.

Roberson, E. D., & Mucke, L. (2006). 100 Years and Counting: Prospects for defeating Alzheimer's Disease. *Science, 314,* 781–784.

Roberto, K. A. (1990). Grandparent and grandchild relationships. In T. H. Brubaker (Ed.), *Family relationships in later life* (2nd ed., pp. 100–112). Newbury Park, CA: Sage.

Roberto, K. A., & Stanis, P. I. (1994). Reactions of older women to the death of their close friends. *Omega—Journal of Death & Dying, 29,* 17–27.

Roberts, B. W., & DelVecchio, W. F. (2000). The rank-order consistency of personality traits from childhood to old age: A quantitative review of longitudinal studies. *Psychological Bulletin, 126,* 3–25.

Robins, R. W., & Trzesniewski, K. H. (2005). Self-esteem development across the lifespan. *Current Directions in Psychological Science, 14,* 158–162.

Rogers, C. H., Floyd, F. J., Seltzer, M. M., Greenberg, J., & Hong, J. (2008). Long-term effects of the death of a child on parents' adjustment in midlife. *Journal of Family Psychology, 22,* 203–211.

Roig, M., Macintyre, D. L., Eng, J. J., Narici, M. V., Maganaris, C. N., & Reid, W. D. (2010). Preservation of eccentric strength in older adults: Evidence, mechanisms and implications for training and rehabilitation. *Experimental Gerontology, 45*(6), 400–409. doi:S0531-5565(10)00122-1 [pii] 10.1016/j.exger.2010.03.008

Ronnlund, M., & Nilsson, L.-G. (2006). Adult life-span patterns in WAIS-R Block Design performance: Cross-sectional versus longitudinal age gradients and relations to demographic factors. *Intelligence, 34,* 63–78.

Rosenberg, S. D., Rosenberg, H. J., & Farrell, M. P. (1999). The midlife crisis revisited. In J. D. Reid & S. L. Willis (Eds.), *Life in the middle: Psychological and social development in middle age* (pp. 25–45). San Diego, CA: Academic Press.

Rostad, B., Deeg, D. J. H., & Schei, B. (2009). Socioeconomic inequalities in health in older women. *European Journal of Ageing, 6,* 39–47.

Rottinghaus, P. J., Coon, K. L., Gaffey, A. R., & Zytowski, D. G. (2007). Thirty-year stability and predictive validity of vocational interests. *Journal of Career Assessment, 15,* 5–22.

Rowe, G., Hasher, L., & Turcotte, J. (2009). Age and synchrony effects in visuospatial working memory. *Quarterly Journal of Experimental Psychology, 62,* 1873–1880.

Rowe, J. W., & Kahn, R. L. (1998). *Successful aging.* New York, NY: Pantheon Books.

Rubin, D. C., Rahhal, T. A., & Poon, L. W. (1998). Things learned in early adulthood are remembered best. *Memory and Cognition, 26,* 3–19.

Rumawas, M. E., Meigs, J. B., Dwyer, J. T., McKeown, N. M., & Jacques, P. F. (2009). Mediterranean-style dietary pattern, reduced risk of metabolic syndrome traits, and incidence in the Framingham Offspring Cohort. *American Journal of Clinical Nutrition, 90,* 1608–1614.

Rupp, D. E., Vodanovich, S. J., & Crede, M. (2006). Age bias in the workplace: The impact of ageism and causal attributions. *Journal of Applied Social Psychology, 36,* 1337–1364.

Rush, B. K., Barch, D. M., & Braver, T. S. (2006). Accounting for cognitive aging: Context processing, inhibition or processing speed? *Aging, Neuropsychology and Cognition, 13,* 588–610.

Ryan, E. B., Hummert, M. L., & Boich, L. H. (1995). Communication predicaments of aging: Patronizing behavior toward older adults. *Journal of Language and Social Psychology, 14,* 144–166.

Ryder, K. M., Shorr, R. I., Bush, A. J., Kritchevsky, S. B., Harris, T., Stone, K., . . . Tylavsky, F. A. (2005). Magnesium intake from food and supplements is associated with bone mineral density in healthy older white subjects. *Journal of the American Geriatrics Society, 53,* 1875–1180.

Sabia, S., Kivimaki, M., Shipley, M. J., Marmot, M. G., & Singh-Manoux, A. (2009). Body mass index over the adult life course and cognition in late midlife: The Whitehall II Cohort Study. *American Journal of Clinical Nutrition, 89,* 601–607.

Sabia, S., Nabi, H., Kivimaki, M., Shipley, M. J., Marmot, M. G., & Singh-Manoux, A. (2009). Health behaviors from early to late midlife as predictors of cognitive function: The Whitehall II study. *American Journal of Epidemiology, 170,* 428–437.

Sacher, G. A. (1977). Life table modification and life prolongation. In C. E. Finch & L. Hayflick (Eds.), *Handbook of the biology of aging* (pp. 582–638). New York, NY: Van Nostrand Reinhold.

Saczynski, J. S., Sigurdsson, S., Jonsdottir, M. K., Eiriksdottir, G., Jonsson, P. V., Garcia, M. E., . . . Launer, L. J. (2009). Cerebral infarcts and cognitive performance: Importance of location and number of infarcts. *Stroke, 40,* 677–682.

Saczynski, J. S., Willis, S. L., & Schaie, K. W. (2002). Strategy use in reasoning training with older adults. *Aging, Neuropsychology and Cognition, 9,* 48–60.

Sahni, S., Hannan, M. T., Blumberg, J., Cupples, L. A., Kiel, D. P., & Tucker, K. L. (2009). Inverse association of carotenoid intakes with 4-y change in bone mineral density in elderly men and women: The Framingham Osteoporosis Study. *American Journal of Clinical Nutrition, 89,* 416–424.

Sahyoun, N. R., Pratt, L. A., Lentzner, H., Dey, A., & Robinson, K. N. (2001). *The changing profile of nursing home residents: 1985–1997. Aging Trends; No. 4.* Hyattsville, MD: National Center for Health Statistics.

Saito, M., & Marumo, K. (2010). Collagen cross-links as a determinant of bone quality: A possible explanation for bone fragility in aging, osteoporosis, and diabetes mellitus. *Osteoporos International 21,* 195–214.

Sajatovic, M., Jenkins, J. H., Safavi, R., West, J. A., Cassidy, K. A., Meyer, W. J., . . . Calabrese, J. R. (2008). Personal and societal construction of illness among individuals with rapid-cycling bipolar disorder: A life-trajectory perspective. *American Journal of Geriatric Psychiatry, 16,* 718–726.

Salari, S. M., & Rich, M. (2001). Social and environmental infantilization of aged persons: Observations in two adult day care centers. *International Journal of Aging and Human Development, 52,* 115–134.

Salloway, S. (2008). Taking the next steps in the treatment of Alzheimer's disease: Disease-modifying agents. *CNS Spectrum, 13,* 11–14.

Salmela-Aro, K., Nurmi, J.-E., Saisto, T., & Halmesmaeki, E. (2001). Goal reconstruction and depressive symptoms during the transition to motherhood: Evidence from two cross-lagged longitudinal studies. *Journal of Personality & Social Psychology, 81,* 1144–1159.

Salthouse, T. A. (1996). The processing-speed theory of adult age differences in cognition. *Psychological Review, 103,* 403–428.

Salthouse, T. A. (2001). Structural models of the relations between age and measures of cognitive functioning. *Intelligence, 29,* 93–115.

Salthouse, T. A., & Ferrer-Caja, E. (2003). What needs to be explained to account for age-related effects on multiple cognitive variables? *Psychology and Aging, 18,* 91–110.

Samanez-Larkin, G. R., Robertson, E. R., Mikels, J. A., Carstensen, L. L., & Gotlib, I. H. (2009). Selective attention to emotion in the aging brain. *Psychology and Aging, 24,* 519–529.

Samuels, J., Eaton, W. W., Bienvenu, O. J. I., Brown, C., Costa, P. T., Jr, & Nestadt, G. (2002). Prevalence and correlates of personality disorders in a community sample. *British Journal of Psychiatry, 180,* 536–542.

Santos, M., Kovari, E., Hof, P. R., Gold, G., Bouras, C., & Giannakopoulos, P. (2009). The impact of vascular burden on late-life depression. *Brain Research Reviews, 62,* 19–32.

Sareen, J., Cox, B. J., Clara, I., & Asmundson, G. J. (2005). The relationship between anxiety disorders and physical disorders in the U.S. National Comorbidity Survey. *Depression and Anxiety, 21,* 193–202.

Satre, D. D., Knight, B. G., & David, S. (2006). Cognitive-behavioral interventions with older adults: Integrating clinical and gerontological research. *Professional Psychology: Research and Practice, 37,* 489–498.

Saxer, S., de Bie, R. A., Dassen, T., & Halfens, R. J. (2009). Knowledge, beliefs, attitudes, and self-reported practice concerning urinary incontinence in nursing home care. *Journal of Wound Ostomy and Continence Nursing, 36,* 539–544.

Saxton, J., Morrow, L., Eschman, A., Archer, G., Luther, J., & Zuccolotto, A. (2009). Computer assessment of mild cognitive impairment. *Postgraduate Medical Journal, 121,* 177–185.

Sbarra, D. A., & Emery, R. E. (2008). Deeper into divorce: Using actor-partner analyses to explore systemic differences in coparenting conflict following custody dispute resolution. *Journal of Family Psychology, 22,* 144–152.

Scandura, T. A., & Lankau, M. J. (1997). Relationships of gender, family responsibility and flexible work hours to organizational commitment and job satisfaction. *Journal of Organizational Behavior, 18,* 377–391.

Scarr, S., & McCartney, K. (1983). How people make their own environments: A theory of genotype greater than environment effects. *Child Development, 54,* 424–435.

Schaie, K. W. (1965). A general model for the study of developmental change. *Psychological Bulletin, 64,* 92–107.

Schaie, K. W. (1994). The course of adult intellectual development. *American Psychologist, 49,* 304–313.

Schaie, K. W. (1996). Intellectual development in adulthood. In J. E. Birren, K. W. Schaie, R. P. Abeles, M. Gatz, & T. A. Salthouse (Eds.), *Handbook of the psychology of aging* (4th ed.) (pp. 266–286). San Diego, CA: Academic Press.

Schaie, K. W. (2005). *Developmental influences on adult intelligence: The Seattle Longitudinal Study.* New York, NY: Oxford University Press.

Schaie, K. W., Nguyen, H. T., Willis, S. L., Dutta, R., & Yue, G. A. (2001). Environmental factors as a conceptual framework for examining cognitive performance in Chinese adults. *International Journal of Behavioral Development, 25,* 193–202.

Schaie, K. W., Willis, S. L., & Caskie, G. I. (2004). The Seattle Longitudinal Study: Relationship between personality and cognition. *Aging, Neuropsychology and Cognition, 11,* 304–324.

Schaie, K. W., & Zanjani, F. A. K. (2006). Intellectual development across adulthood. In C. Hoare (Ed.), *Handbook of adult development and learning.* (pp. 99–122). New York, NY: Oxford University Press.

Schiffman, S. S. (2009). Effects of aging on the human taste system. *Annals of the New York Academy of Science, 1170,* 725–729.

Schirmer, L. L., & Lopez, F. G. (2001). Probing the social support and work strain relationship among adult workers: Contributions of adult attachment orientations. *Journal of Vocational Behavior, 59,* 17–33.

Schneider, C., Jick, S. S., & Meier, C. R. (2009). Risk of gynecological cancers in users of estradiol/dydrogesterone or other HRT preparations. *Climacteric, 12,* 514–524.

Schnitzspahn, K. M., & Kliegel, M. (2009). Age effects in prospective memory performance within older adults: The paradoxical impact of implementation intentions. *European Journal of Ageing, 6,* 147–155.

Schoenborn, C. A., & Heyman, K. M. (2009). Health characteristics of adults aged 55 years and over: United States 2004–2007 *National Health Statistics Reports: no. 16.* Hyattsville, MD: National Center for Health Statistics.

Schoenborn, C. A., Vickerie, J. L., & Barnes, P. M. (2003). Cigarette smoking behavior of adults: United States, 1997–98 *Advance Data from Vital and Health Statistics: no. 331.* Hyattsville, MD: National Center for Health Statistics.

Schoenhofen, E. A., Wyszynski, D. F., Andersen, S., Pennington, J., Young, R., Terry, D. F., . . . Perls, T. T. (2006). Characteristics of 32 supercentenarians. *Journal of the American Geriatrics Society, 54,* 1237–1240.

Schoevers, R. A., Beekman, A. T., Deeg, D. J., Jonker, C., & van Tilburg, W. (2003). Comorbidity and risk-patterns of depression, generalised anxiety disorder and mixed anxiety-depression in later life: Results from the AMSTEL study. *International Journal of Geriatric Psychiatry, 18,* 994–1001.

Schoevers, R. A., Smit, F., Deeg, D. J., Cuijpers, P., Dekker, J., van Tilburg, W., . . . Beekman, A. T. (2006). Prevention of late-life depression in primary care: Do we know where to begin? *American Journal of Psychiatry, 163,* 1611–1621.

Schooler, C., Mulatu, M. S., & Oates, G. (1999). The continuing effects of substantively complex work on the intellectual functioning of older workers. *Psychology and Aging, 14,* 483–506.

Schroeder, D. H., & Salthouse, T. A. (2004). Age-related effects on cognition between 20 and 50 years of age. *Personality and Individual Differences, 36*, 393–404.

Schulberg, H. C., Post, E. P., Raue, P. J., Have, T. T., Miller, M., & Bruce, M. L. (2007). Treating late-life depression with interpersonal psychotherapy in the primary care sector. *International Journal of Geriatric Psychiatry, 22*, 106–114.

Schultz, S. K., Ellingrod, V. L., Moser, D. J., Kutschner, E., Turvey, C., & Arndt, S. (2002). The influence of cognitive impairment and psychiatric symptoms on daily functioning in nursing facilities: A longitudinal study. *Annals of Clinical Psychiatry, 14*, 209–213.

Schuurmans, J., Comijs, H., Emmelkamp, P. M., Weijnen, I. J., van den Hout, M., & van Dyck, R. (2009). Long-term effectiveness and prediction of treatment outcome in cognitive behavioral therapy and sertraline for late-life anxiety disorders. *International Psychogeriatrics, 21*, 1148–1159.

Schwarz, B., Trommsdorff, G., Albert, I., & Mayer, B. (2005). Adult parent-child relationships: Relationship quality, support, and reciprocity. *Applied Psychology: An International Review, 54*, 396–417.

Scogin, F., Floyd, M., & Forde, J. (2000). Anxiety in older adults. In S. K. Whitbourne (Ed.), *Psychopathology in later life* (pp. 117–140). New York, NY: Wiley.

Scollon, C. N., & Diener, E. (2006). Love, work, and changes in extraversion and neuroticism over time. *Journal of Personality and Social Psychology, 91*, 1152–1165.

Seale, C. (2009). Hastening death in end-of-life care: A survey of doctors. *Social Science & Medicine, 69*, 1659–1666.

Seblega, B. K., Zhang, N. J., Unruh, L. Y., Breen, G. M., Seung Chun, P., & Wan, T. T. (2010). Changes in nursing home staffing levels, 1997 to 2007. *Medical Care: Research and Review, 67*, 232–246.

Secretan, B., Straif, K., Baan, R., Grosse, Y., El Ghissassi, F., Bouvard, V., . . . WHO International Agency for Research on Cancer Monograph Working Group. (2009). A review of human carcinogens—Part E: Tobacco, areca nut, alcohol, coal smoke, and salted fish. *Lancet Oncology, 10*, 1033–1034.

Segal, D. L., Coolidge, F. L., & Rosowsky, E. (2000). Personality disorders. In S. K. Whitbourne (Ed.), *Psychopathology in later life*. New York, NY: Wiley.

Segal, D. L., Hook, J. N., & Coolidge, F. L. (2001). Personality dysfunction, coping styles, and clinical symptoms in younger and older adults. *Journal of Clinical Geropsychology, 7*, 201–212.

Segal, D. L., Needham, T. N., & Coolidge, F. L. (2009). Age differences in attachment orientations among younger and older adults: Evidence from two self-report measures of attachment. *International Journal of Aging and Human Development, 69*, 119–132.

Seibert, S. E., & Kraimer, M. L. (2001). The five-factor model of personality and career success. *Journal of Vocational Behavior, 58*, 1–21.

Seidman, S. N. (2007). Androgens and the aging male. *Psychopharmacology Bulletin, 40*, 205–218.

Semba, R. D., Bandinelli, S., Sun, K., Guralnik, J. M., & Ferrucci, L. (2010). Relationship of an advanced glycation end product, plasma carboxymethyl-lysine, with slow walking speed in older adults: The InCHIANTI study. *European Journal of Applied Physiology, 108*, 191–195.

Senchina, D. S. (2009). Effects of regular exercise on the aging immune system: A review. *Clinical Journal of Sport Medicine, 19*, 439–440.

Serfaty, M. A., Haworth, D., Blanchard, M., Buszewicz, M., Murad, S., & King, M. (2009). Clinical effectiveness of individual cognitive behavioral therapy for depressed older people in primary care: A randomized controlled trial. *Archives of General Psychiatry, 66*, 1332–1340.

Serra-Majem, L., Roman, B., & Estruch, R. (2006). Scientific evidence of interventions using the Mediterranean diet: A systematic review. *Nutrition Reviews, 64*, S27–S47.

Serste, T., & Bourgeois, N. (2006). Ageing and the liver. *Acta Gastro-enterologica Belgium, 69*, 296–298.

Shackelford, T. K., Schmitt, D. P., & Buss, D. M. (2005). Mate preferences of married persons in the newlywed year and three years later. *Cognition and Emotion, 19*, 1262–1270.

Shafto, M. A., Burke, D. M., Stamatakis, E. A., Tam, P. P., & Tyler, L. K. (2007). On the tip-of-the-tongue: Neural correlates of increased word-finding failures in normal aging. *Journal of Cognitive Neuroscience, 19*, 2060–2070.

Shafto, M. A., Stamatakis, E. A., Tam, P. P., & Tyler, L. K. (2010). Word retrieval failures in old age: The relationship between structure and function. *Journal of Cognitive Neuroscience, 22*, 1530–1540.

Sharma, K. K., & Santhoshkumar, P. (2009). Lens aging: Effects of crystallins. *Biochimica et Biophysica Acta, 1790*, 1095–1108.

Sheehy, G. (1974). *Passages: Predictable passages of adult life*. New York, NY: Dutton.

Sheu, Y., Cauley, J. A., Wheeler, V. W., Patrick, A. L., Bunker, C. H., Kammerer, C. M., . . . Zmuda, J. M. (2009). Natural history and correlates of hip BMD loss with aging in men of African ancestry: The Tobago Bone Health Study. *Journal of Bone Mineral Research, 24*, 1290–1298.

Shih, M., Hootman, J. M., Kruger, J., & Helmick, C. G. (2006). Physical activity in men and women with arthritis: National Health Interview Survey, 2002. *American Journal of Preventive Medicine, 30*, 385–393.

Shin, J. S., Hong, A., Solomon, M. J., & Lee, C. S. (2006). The role of telomeres and telomerase in the pathology of human cancer and aging. *Pathology, 38*, 103–113.

Shu, C. H., Hummel, T., Lee, P. L., Chiu, C. H., Lin, S. H., & Yuan, B. C. (2009). The proportion of self-rated olfactory dysfunction does not change across the life span. *American Journal of Rhinology and Allergy, 23*, 413–416.

Shumway-Cook, A., Guralnik, J. M., Phillips, C. L., Coppin, A. K., Ciol, M. A., Bandinelli, S., . . . Ferrucci, L. (2007). Age-associated declines in complex walking task performance: The Walking

InCHIANTI toolkit. *Journal of the American Geriatrics Society, 55,* 58–65.

Siebert, D. C., Mutran, E. J., & Reitzes, D. C. (2002). Friendship and social support: The importance of role identity to aging adults. *Social Work, 44,* 522–533.

Siegler, I. C., Costa, P. T., Brummett, B. H., Helms, M. J., Barefoot, J. C., Williams, R. B., . . . Rimer, B. K. (2003). Patterns of change in hostility from college to midlife in the UNC Alumni Heart Study predict high-risk status. *Psychosomatic Medicine, 65,* 738–745.

Siegrist, J., Wahrendorf, M., von dem Knesebeck, O., Jurges, H., & Borsch-Supan, A. (2007). Quality of work, well-being, and intended early retirement of older employees: Baseline results from the SHARE Study. *European Journal of Public Health, 17,* 62–68.

Sigurdsson, G., Aspelund, T., Chang, M., Jonsdottir, B., Sigurdsson, S., Eiriksdottir, G., . . . Lang, T. G. (2006). Increasing sex difference in bone strength in old age: The Age, Gene/Environment Susceptibility-Reykjavik study (AGES-REYKJAVIK). *Bone, 39,* 644–651.

Silveira, M. J., Kim, S. Y., & Langa, K. M. (2010). Advance directives and outcomes of surrogate decision making before death. *New England Journal of Medicine, 362,* 1211–1218.

Silverstein, M., & Bengtson, V. L. (1997). Intergenerational solidarity and the structure of adult child-parent relationships in American families. *American Journal of Sociology, 103,* 429–460.

Silverstein, M., Conroy, S. J., Wang, H., Giarrusso, R., & Bengtson, V. L. (2002). Reciprocity in parent-child relations over the adult life course. *Journals of Gerontology Series B: Psychological Sciences and Social Sciences, 57,* S3–S13.

Silverstein, M., Gans, D., & Yang, F. M. (2006). Intergenerational support to aging parents: The role of norms and needs. *Journal of Family Issues, 27,* 1068–1084.

Silverstein, M., & Parker, M. G. (2002). Leisure activities and quality of life among the oldest old in Sweden. *Research on Aging, 24,* 528–547.

Simmons, T., & O'Connell, M. (2003). Married-couple and unmarried-partner households: 2000. Retrieved from http://www.census.gov/prod/2003pubs/censr-5.pdf.

Simonton, D. K. (1989). The swan-song phenomenon: Last-works effects for 172 classical composers. *Psychology and Aging, 4,* 42–47.

Simonton, D. K. (1997). Creative productivity: A predictive and explanatory model of career trajectories and landmarks. *Psychological Review, 104,* 66–89.

Simonton, D. K. (1998). Achieved eminence in minority and majority cultures: Convergence versus divergence in the assessments of 294 African Americans. *Journal of Personality and Social Psychology, 74,* 804–817.

Simpson, J. A., & Rholes, W. S. (2002). Attachment orientations, marriage, and the transition to parenthood. *Journal of Research in Personality, 36,* 622–628.

Singley, S., & Hynes, K. (2005). Transitions to parenthood: Work-family policies, gender, and the couple context. *Gender and Society, 19,* 376–397.

Sinnott, J. D. (1989). A model for solution of ill-structured problems: Implications for everyday and abstract problem-solving. In J. D. Sinnott (Ed.), *Everyday problem solving: Theory and applications* (pp. 72–99). New York, NY: Praeger.

Skalicka, V., & Kunst, A. E. (2008). Effects of spouses' socioeconomic characteristics on mortality among men and women in a Norwegian longitudinal study. *Social Science and Medicine, 66,* 2035–2047.

Skinner, B. F., & Vaughan, M. E. (1983). *Enjoy old age: A practical guide.* New York, NY: Norton.

Skultety, K. M., & Whitbourne, S. K. (2004). Gender differences in identity processes and self-esteem in middle and later adulthood. *Journal of Women and Aging, 16,* 175–188.

Sliwinski, M. J., & Hall, C. B. (1998). Constraints on general slowing: A meta-analysis using hierarchical linear models with random coefficients. *Psychology and Aging, 13,* 169.

Sliwinski, M. J., Stawski, R. S., Hall, C. B., Katz, M., Verghese, J., & Lipton, R. (2006). Distinguishing preterminal and terminal cognitive decline. *European Psychologist, 11,* 172–181.

Sloane, P. D., Mitchell, C. M., Weisman, G., Zimmerman, S., Foley, K. M., Lynn, M., . . . Montgomery, R. (2002). The Therapeutic Environment Screening Survey for Nursing Homes (TESS-NH): An observational instrument for assessing the physical environment of institutional settings for persons with dementia. *Journals of Gerontology Series B: Psychological Sciences and Social Sciences, 57,* S69–S78.

Sluiter, J. K. (2006). High-demand jobs: Age-related diversity in work ability? *Applied Ergonomics, 17,* 429–440.

Sluiter, J. K., & Frings-Dresen, M. H. (2007). What do we know about ageing at work? Evidence-based fitness for duty and health in fire fighters. *Ergonomics, 50,* 1897–1913.

Small, G. W. (2009). Differential diagnoses and assessment of depression in elderly patients. *Journal of Clinical Psychiatry, 70,* e47.

Smith, A. D., & Refsum, H. (2009). Vitamin B-12 and cognition in the elderly. *American Journal of Clinical Nutrition, 89,* 707S–711S.

Smith, C. D., Walton, A., Loveland, A. D., Umberger, G. H., Kryscio, R. J., & Gash, D. M. (2005). Memories that last in old age: Motor skill learning and memory preservation. *Neurobiology of Aging, 26,* 883–890.

Smith, D. B., Hanges, P. J., & Dickson, M. W. (2001). Personnel selection and the five-factor model: Reexamining the effects of appplicant's frame of reference. *Journal of Applied Physiology, 86,* 304–315.

Smith, J., & Freund, A. M. (2002). The dynamics of possible selves in old age. *Journals of Gerontology Series B: Psychological Sciences and Social Sciences, 57,* P492–P500.

Sneed, J. R., Kasen, S., & Cohen, P. (2007). Early-life risk factors for late-onset depression. *International Journal of Geriatric Psychiatry, 22,* 663–667.

Sneed, J. R., & Whitbourne, S. K. (2003). Identity processing and self-consciousness in middle and later adulthood. *Journals of*

Gerontology Series B: Psychological Sciences and Social Sciences, 58, P313–P319.

Snitz, B. E., O'Meara, E. S., Carlson, M. C., Arnold, A. M., Ives, D. G., Rapp, S. R., . . . DeKosky, S. T. (2009). Ginkgo biloba for preventing cognitive decline in older adults: A randomized trial. *Journal of the American Medical Association, 302,* 2663–2670.

Social Security Administration. (2009a). Fast facts and figures about Social Security, 2009. Retrieved from http://www.ssa.gov/policy/docs/chartbooks/fast_facts/2009/fast_facts09.pdf.

Social Security Administration. (2009b). Monthly statistical snapshot, December 2009. Retrieved from http://www.ssa.gov/policy/docs/quickfacts/stat_snapshot/.

Social Security Administration (2010). Status of the Social Security and Medicare Programs. Retrieved from http://www.ssa.gov/OACT/TRSUM/index.html.

American Cancer Society (2009). Estimated new cancer cases for selected cancer sites by state, US, 2009.

Sohal, R. S. (2002). Role of oxidative stress and protein oxidation in the aging process. *Free Radical Biology and Medicine, 33,* 37–44.

Solano, N. H., & Whitbourne, S. K. (2001). Coping with schizophrenia: Patterns in later adulthood. *International Journal of Aging and Human Development, 53,* 1–10.

Soldz, S., & Vaillant, G. E. (1998). A 50-year longitudinal study of defense use among inner city men: A validation of the DSM-IV defense axis. *Journal of Nervous and Mental Disease, 186,* 104–111.

Solfrizzi, V., Scafato, E., Capurso, C., D'Introno, A., Colacicco, A. M., Frisardi, V., . . . Panza, F. (2009). Metabolic syndrome and the risk of vascular dementia. The Italian Longitudinal Study on Aging. *Journal of Neurological and Neurosurgical Psychiatry.* doi:jnnp.2009.181743 [pii] 10.1136/jnnp.2009.181743.

Solomon, S., Greenberg, J. & Pyszczynski, T. (1991). A terror management theory of social behavior: The psychological functions of self-esteem and cultural worldviews. In M. P. Zanna (Ed.), *Advances in experimental social psychology* (Vol. 24, pp. 93–159). Orlando, FL: Academic Press.

Solomon, Z., & Mikulincer, M. (2006). Trajectories of PTSD: A 20-year longitudinal study. *American Journal of Psychiatry, 163,* 659–666.

Sonnenberg, C. M., Beekman, A. T., Deeg, D. J., & Van Tilburg, W. (2003). Drug treatment in depressed elderly in the Dutch community. *International Journal of Geriatric Psychiatry, 18,* 99–104.

Spearman, C. (1904). "General intelligence:" Objectively determined and measured. *American Journal of Psychology, 15,* 201–292.

Spearman, C. (1927). *The abilities of man.* New York, NY: Macmillan.

Spindler, H., & Pedersen, S. S. (2005). Posttraumatic stress disorder in the wake of heart disease: Prevalence, risk factors, and future research directions. *Psychosomatic Medicine, 67,* 715–723.

Spira, A. P., Stone, K., Beaudreau, S. A., Ancoli-Israel, S., & Yaffe, K. (2009). Anxiety symptoms and objectively measured sleep quality in older women. *American Journal of Geriatric Psychiatry, 17,* 136–143.

Sprecher, S. (1988). Investment model, equity, and social support determinants of relationship commitment. *Social Psychology Quarterly, 51,* 318–328.

Squire, L. R. (1989). On the course of forgetting in very long term memory. *Journal of Experimental Psychology: Learning, Memory, and Cognition, 15,* 241–245.

St. John, P. D., & Montgomery, P. R. (2009). Do depressive symptoms predict mortality in older people? *Aging and Mental Health, 13,* 674–681.

Stanley, S. M., Amato, P. R., Johnson, C. A., & Markman, H. J. (2006). Premarital education, marital quality, and marital stability: Findings from a large, random household survey. *Journal of Family Psychology, 20,* 117–126.

Starr, J. M., Deary, I. J., Fox, H. C., & Whalley, L. J. (2007). Smoking and cognitive change from age 11 to 66 years: A confirmatory investigation. *Addictive Behaviors, 32,* 63–68.

Staudinger, U. M., & Kunzmann, U. (2005). Positive adult personality development: Adjustment and/or growth? *European Psychologist, 10,* 320–329.

Staudinger, U. M., Marsiske, M., & Baltes, P. B. (1995). Resilience and reserve capacity in later adulthood: Potentials and limits of development across the life span. In D. Cicchetti & D. J. Cohen (Eds.), *Developmental psychopathology* (Vol. 2: Risk, disorder, and adaptation, pp. 801–847). New York, NY: Wiley.

Staudinger, U. M., Smith, J., & Baltes, P. B. (1993). Wisdom-related knowledge in a life review task: Age differences and role of professional specialization. *Psychology and Aging, 7,* 271–281.

Steele, C. M., Spencer, S. J., Aronson, J., & Zanna, M. P. (2002). Contending with group image: The psychology of stereotype and social identity threat. In *Advances in Experimental Social Psychology, Vol. 34* (pp. 379–440). San Diego, CA: Academic Press.

Stengel, B., Couchoud, C., Cenee, S., & Hemon, D. (2000). Age, blood pressure and smoking effects on chronic renal failure in primary glomerular nephropathies. *Kidney International, 57,* 2519–2526.

Sternberg, R. J. (1985). *Beyond IQ: A triarchic theory of human intelligence.* New York, NY: Cambridge University Press.

Sternberg, R. J. (1998). A balance theory of wisdom. *Review of General Psychology, 3,* 347–365.

Sternberg, R. J. (1999). The theory of successful intelligence. *Review of General Psychology, 3,* 292–316.

Sterns, H. L., & Gray, J. H. (1999). Work, leisure, and retirement. In J. C. Cavanaugh & S. K. Whitbourne (Eds.), *Gerontology: Interdisciplinary perspectives* (pp. 355–390). New York, NY: Oxford University Press.

Steunenberg, B., Beekman, A. T., Deeg, D. J., Bremmer, M. A., & Kerkhof, A. J. (2007). Mastery and neuroticism predict recovery of depression in later life. *American Journal of Geriatric Psychiatry, 15,* 234–242.

Stevens, J. A., Ryan, G., & Kresnow, M. (2006). Fatalities and injuries from falls among older adults—United States, 1993–2003 and 2001–2005. *Morbidity and Mortality Weekly Report, 55*, 45, 1221–1224.

Stewart, K. A., Grabowski, D. C., & Lakdawalla, D. N. (2009). Annual expenditures for nursing home care: Private and public payer price growth, 1977 to 2004. *Medical Care: Research and Review, 47*, 295–301.

Stewart, R., & Wingfield, A. (2009). Hearing loss and cognitive effort in older adults' report accuracy for verbal materials. *Journal of the American Academy of Audiology, 20*, 147–154.

Stine-Morrow, E. A., Milinder, L., Pullara, O., & Herman, B. (2001). Patterns of resource allocation are reliable among younger and older readers. *Psychology and Aging, 16*, 69–84.

Stine-Morrow, E. A. L., & Miller, L. M. S. (1999). Basic cognitive processes. In J. C. Cavanaugh & S. K. Whitbourne (Eds.), *Gerontology: Interdisciplinary perspectives* (pp. 186–212). New York, NY: Oxford University Press.

Stine-Morrow, E. A., Soederberg Miller, L. M., Gagne, D. D., & Hertzog, C. (2008). Self-regulated reading in adulthood. *Psychology and Aging, 23*, 131–153.

Story, T. N., Berg, C. A., Smith, T. W., Beveridge, R., Henry, N. J., & Pearce, G. (2007). Age, marital satisfaction, and optimism as predictors of positive sentiment override in middle-aged and older married couples. *Psychology and Aging, 22*, 719–727.

Straif, K., Benbrahim-Tallaa, L., Baan, R., Grosse, Y., Secretan, B., El Ghissassi, F., . . . Cogliano, V. (2009). A review of human carcinogens—part C: Metals, arsenic, dusts, and fibres. *Lancet Oncology, 10*, 453–454.

Strenger, C. (2009). Paring down life to the essentials: An epicurean psychodynamics of midlife changes. *Psychoanalytic Psychology, 26*, 246–258.

Stroebe, M., Gergen, M. M., Gergen, K. J., & Stroebe, W. (1992). Broken hearts or broken bonds: Love and death in historical perspective. *American Psychologist., 47*, 1205–1212.

Stroebe, M., Schut, H., & Boerner, K. (2010). Continuing bonds in adaptation to bereavement: Toward theoretical integration. *Clinical Psychology Review, 30*, 259–268.

Stroebe, M., Schut, H., & Stroebe, W. (2007). Health outcomes of bereavement. *Lancet, 370*, 1960–1973.

Stroebe, W., Schut, H., & Stroebe, M. S. (2005). Grief work, disclosure and counseling: Do they help the bereaved? *Clinical Psychology Review, 25*, 395–414.

Styczynska, M., Strosznajder, J. B., Religa, D., Chodakowska-Zebrowska, M., Pfeffer, A., Gabryelewicz, T., . . . Barcikowska, M. (2008). Association between genetic and environmental factors and the risk of Alzheimer's disease. *Folia Neuropathologica, 46*, 249–254.

Subramaniam, H., Dennis, M. S., & Byrne, E. J. (2007). The role of vascular risk factors in late onset bipolar disorder. *International Journal of Geriatric Psychiatry, 22*, 733–737.

Subramanian, S. V., Elwert, F., & Christakis, N. (2008). Widowhood and mortality among the elderly: The modifying role of neighborhood concentration of widowed individuals. *Social Science & Medicine, 66*, 873–884.

Substance Abuse and Mental Health Services Administration. (2009a). Illicit drug use among older adults. *Findings from the SAMHSA 2006 to 2008 National Surveys on Drug Use and Health (NSDUHs)*.

Substance Abuse and Mental Health Services Administration. (2009b). Results from the 2008 National Survey on Drug Use and Health: National Findings. Retrieved from http://www.oas.samhsa.gov/NSDUH/2k8NSDUH/2k8results.cfm#Ch2.

Sudore, R. L., Landefeld, C. S., Pantilat, S. Z., Noyes, K. M., & Schillinger, D. (2008). Reach and impact of a mass media event among vulnerable patients: The Terri Schiavo story. *Journal of General and Internal Medicine, 23*, 1854–1857.

Suitor, J. J., Sechrist, J., Plikuhn, M., Pardo, S. T., Gilligan, M., & Pillemer, K. (2009). The role of perceived maternal favoritism in sibling relations in midlife. *Journal of Marriage and Family, 71*, 1026–1038.

Sun, M. K., Hongpaisan, J., & Alkon, D. L. (2009). Postischemic PKC activation rescues retrograde and anterograde long-term memory. *Proceedings of the National Academies of Sciences of the United States of America, 106*, 14676–14680.

Sun, X., Chen, Y., Chen, X., Wang, J., Xi, C., Lin, S., & Liu, X. (2009). Change of glomerular filtration rate in healthy adults with aging. *Nephrology (Carlton), 14*, 506–513.

Super, D. E. (1957). *The psychology of careers.* New York, NY: Harper.

Super, D. E. (1990). A life span, life-space approach to career development. In D. Brown & L. Brooks (Eds.), *Career choice and development* (2nd ed.). San Francisco, CA: Jossey-Bass.

Sutin, A. R., Beason-Held, L. L., Resnick, S. M., & Costa, P. T. (2009). Sex differences in resting-state neural correlates of openness to experience among older adults. *Cerebral Cortex, 19*, 2797–2802.

Sutin, A. R., Terracciano, A., Deiana, B., Naitza, S., Ferrucci, L., Uda, M. et al. (2009). High neuroticism and low conscientiousness are associated with interleukin-6. *Psychological Medicine*, 1–9.

Sutin, A. R., Terracciano, A., Deiana, B., Uda, M., Schlessinger, D., Lakatta, E. G., . . . Costa, P. J., Jr. (2010). Cholesterol, triglycerides, and the five-factor model of personality. *Biological Psychology.* doi:S0301-0511(10)00017-7 [pii] 10.1016/j.biopsycho.2010.01.012.

Sweeney, M. M., & Cancian, M. (2004). The changing importance of White women's economic prospects for assortative mating. *Journal of Marriage and Family, 66*, 1015–1028.

Sweeper, S., & Halford, K. (2006). Assessing adult adjustment to relationship separation: The Psychological Adjustment to Separation Test (PAST). *Journal of Family Psychology, 20*, 632–640.

Sweet, M. G., Sweet, J. M., Jeremiah, M. P., & Galazka, S. S. (2009). Diagnosis and treatment of osteoporosis. *American Family Physician, 79*, 193–200.

Tadic, S. D., Zdaniuk, B., Griffiths, D., Rosenberg, L., Schafer, W., & Resnick, N. M. (2007). Effect of biofeedback on psychological burden and symptoms in older women with urge urinary incontinence. *Journal of the American Geriatrics Society*, *55*, 2010–2015.

Takahashi, K., Takahashi, H. E., Nakadaira, H., & Yamamoto, M. (2006). Different changes of quantity due to aging in the psoas major and quadriceps femoris muscles in women. *Journal of Musculoskeletal and Neuronal Interactions*, *6*, 201–205.

Talbot, L. A., Fleg, J. L., & Metter, E. J. (2003). Secular trends in leisure-time physical activity in men and women across four decades. *Preventive Medicine*, *37*, 52–60.

Tanaka, H., & Seals, D. R. (2003). Invited review: Dynamic exercise performance in Masters athletes: Insight into the effects of primary human aging on physiological functional capacity. *Journal of Applied Physiology*, *95*, 2152–2162.

Tang, H. Y., Harms, V., Speck, S. M., Vezeau, T., & Jesurum, J. T. (2009). Effects of audio relaxation programs for blood pressure reduction in older adults. *European Journal of Cardiovascular Nursing*, *8*, 329–336.

Tanzi, R. E., & Bertram, L. (2008). Alzheimer's disease: The latest suspect. *Nature*, *454*, 706–708.

Taylor, J. L., Kennedy, Q., Noda, A., & Yesavage, J. A. (2007). Pilot age and expertise predict flight simulator performance: A 3-year longitudinal study. *Neurology*, *68*, 648–654.

Taylor, M. A., Goldberg, C., Shore, L. M., & Lipka, P. (2008). The effects of retirement expectations and social support on post-retirement adjustment: A longitudinal analysis. *Journal of Managerial Psychology*, *23*, 458–470.

Teichtahl, A. J., Wluka, A. E., Wang, Y., Hanna, F., English, D. R., Giles, G. G., . . . Cicuttini, F. M. (2009). Obesity and adiposity are associated with the rate of patella cartilage volume loss over 2 years in adults without knee osteoarthritis. *Annals of the Rheumatic Diseases*, *68*, 909–913.

Tekcan, A. I., & Peynircioglu, Z. F. (2002). Effects of age on flashbulb memories. *Psychology and Aging*, *17*, 416–422.

Teno, J., Lynn, J., Connors, A. F., Jr., Wenger, N., Phillips, R. S., Alzola, C., . . . Knaus, W. A. (1997). The illusion of end-of-life resource savings with advance directives. SUPPORT Investigators. Study to Understand Prognoses and Preferences for Outcomes and Risks of Treatment. *Journal of the American Geriatrics Society*, *45*, 513–518.

Teno, J. M., Gruneir, A., Schwartz, Z., Nanda, A., & Wetle, T. (2007). Association between advance directives and quality of end-of-life care: A national study. *Journal of the American Geriatrics Society*, *55*, 189–194.

Teno, J. M., Weitzen, S., Fennell, M. L., & Mor, V. (2001). Dying trajectory in the last year of life: Does cancer trajectory fit other diseases? *Journal of Palliative Medicine*, *4*, 457–464.

Tentori, K., Osherson, D., Hasher, L., & May, C. (2001). Wisdom and aging: Irrational preferences in college students but not older adults. *Cognition*, *81*, B87–B96.

Teri, L. (1994). Behavioral treatment of depression in patients with dementia. *Alzheimer's Disease and Associated Disorders*, *8*, 66–74.

Terracciano, A., & Costa, P. T. J. (2004). Smoking and the five-factor model of personality. *Addiction*, *99*, 472–481.

Terracciano, A., Löckenhoff, C. E., Crum, R. M., Bienvenu, O. J., & Costa, P. T., Jr. (2008). Five-factor model personality profiles of drug users. *BMC Psychiatry*, *8*.

Terracciano, A., Löckenhoff, C. E., Zonderman, A. B., Ferrucci, L., & Costa, P. T., Jr. (2008). Personality predictors of longevity: Activity, emotional stability, and conscientiousness. *Psychosomatic Medicine*, *70*, 621–627.

Terracciano, A., McCrae, R. R., Brant, L. J., & Costa, P. T. J. (2005). Hierarchical linear modeling analyses of the NEO-PI-R Scales in the Baltimore Longitudinal Study of Aging. *Psychology and Aging*, *20*, 493–506.

Thanvi, B., & Treadwell, S. (2009). Drug induced Parkinsonism: A common cause of Parkinsonism in older people. *Postgraduate Medical Journal*, *85*, 322–326.

Theodoraki, A., & Bouloux, P. M. (2009). Testosterone therapy in men. *Menopause International*, *15*, 87–92.

Thomas, A. K., & Bulevich, J. B. (2006). Effective cue utilization reduces memory errors in older adults. *Psychology and Aging*, *21*, 379–389.

Thompson-Torgerson, C. S., Holowatz, L. A., & Kenney, W. L. (2008). Altered mechanisms of thermoregulatory vasoconstriction in aged human skin. *Exercise and Sport Sciences Review*, *36*, 122–127.

Thornton, W. J. L., & Dumke, H. A. (2005). Age differences in everyday problem-solving and decision-making effectiveness: A meta-analytic review. *Psychology and Aging*, *20*, 85–99.

Thurstone, L. L. (1938). *Primary mental abilities*. Chicago, IL: University of Chicago Press.

Tiikkaja, S., Hemstrom, O., & Vagero, D. (2009). Intergenerational class mobility and cardiovascular mortality among Swedish women: A population-based register study. *Social Science and Medicine*, *68*, 733–739.

Tinetti, M. E., Baker, D., Gallo, W. T., Nanda, A., Charpentier, P., & O'Leary, J. (2002). Evaluation of restorative care vs usual care for older adults receiving an acute episode of home care. *Journal of the American Medical Association*, *287*, 2098–2105.

Tinetti, M. E., & Kumar, C. (2010). The patient who falls: "It's always a trade-off." *Journal of the American Medical Association*, *303*, 258–266.

Titone, D. A., Koh, C. K., Kjelgaard, M. M., Bruce, S., Speer, S. R., & Wingfield, A. (2006). Age-related impairments in the revision of syntactic misanalyses: Effects of prosody. *Language and Speech*, *49*, 75–99.

Tolomio, S., Ermolao, A., Travain, G., & Zaccaria, M. (2008). Short-term adapted physical activity program improves bone quality in osteopenic/osteoporotic postmenopausal women. *Journal of Physical Activity and Health*, *5*, 844–853.

Topa, G., Moriano, J. A., Depolo, M., Alcover, C.-M. A., & Morales, J. F. (2009). Antecedents and consequences of retirement planning and decision-making: A meta-analysis and model. *Journal of Vocational Behavior*, *75*, 38–55.

Tostain, J. L., & Blanc, F. (2008). Testosterone deficiency: A common, unrecognized syndrome. *Nature Clinical Practice Urology, 5,* 388–396.

Tran, K., Levin, R. M., & Mousa, S. A. (2009). Behavioral intervention versus pharmacotherapy or their combinations in the management of overactive bladder dysfunction. *Advances in Urology,* 345324.

Travis, S. S., Bernard, M., Dixon, S., McAuley, W. J., Loving, G., & McClanahan, L. (2002). Obstacles to palliation and end-of-life care in a long-term care facility. *Gerontologist, 42,* 342–349.

Travison, T. G., Araujo, A. B., Beck, T. J., Williams, R. E., Clark, R. V., Leder, B. Z., . . . McKinlay, J. B. (2009). Relation between serum testosterone, serum estradiol, sex hormone-binding globulin, and geometrical measures of adult male proximal femur strength. *Journal of Clinical Endocrinology and Metabolism, 94,* 853–860.

Travison, T. G., O'Donnell, A. B., Araujo, A. B., Matsumoto, A. M., & McKinlay, J. B. (2007). Cortisol levels and measures of body composition in middle-aged and older men. *Clinical Endocrinology, 67,* 71–77.

Troll, L. E. (1985). The contingencies of grandparenting. In V. L. Bengston & J. F. Robertson (Eds.), *Grandparenthood* (pp. 135–149). Beverly Hills CA: Sage.

Trouillet, R. l., Gana, K., Lourel, M., & Fort, I. (2009). Predictive value of age for coping: The role of self-efficacy, social support satisfaction and perceived stress. *Aging and Mental Health, 13,* 357–366.

Trunk, D. L., & Abrams, L. (2009). Do younger and older adults' communicative goals influence off-topic speech in autobiographical narratives? *Psychology and Aging, 24,* 324–337.

Tsevat, J., Dawson, N. V., Wu, A. W., Lynn, J., Soukup, J. R., Cook, E. F., . . . Phillips, R. S. (1998). Health values of hospitalized patients 80 years or older. HELP Investigators. Hospitalized Elderly Longitudinal Project. *Journal of the American Medical Association, 279,* 371–375.

Tu, J. V., Nardi, L., Fang, J., Liu, J., Khalid, L., & Johansen, H. (2009). National trends in rates of death and hospital admissions related to acute myocardial infarction, heart failure and stroke, 1994–2004. *Canadian Medical Association Journal, 180,* E118–E125.

Tucker-Samaras, S., Zedayko, T., Cole, C., Miller, D., Wallo, W., & Leyden, J. J. (2009). A stabilized 0.1% retinol facial moisturizer improves the appearance of photodamaged skin in an eight-week, double-blind, vehicle-controlled study. *Journal of Drugs and Dermatology, 8,* 932–936.

Tucker-Seeley, R. D., Li, Y., Subramanian, S. V., & Sorensen, G. (2009). Financial hardship and mortality among older adults using the 1996–2004 Health and Retirement Study. *Annals of Epidemiology, 19,* 850–857.

Tucker, K. L. (2009). Osteoporosis prevention and nutrition. *Current Osteoporosis Reports, 7,* 111–117.

Turcotte, M. (2006). Parents with adult children living at home. *Canadian Social Trends, March 2006,* 11–14.

Twomey, F., McDowell, D. K., & Corcoran, G. D. (2007). End-of-life care for older patients dying in an acute general hospital—can we do better? *Age and Ageing, 36,* 462–464.

Tyler, L. K., Shafto, M. A., Randall, B., Wright, P., Marslen-Wilson, W. D., & Stamatakis, E. A. (2010). Preserving syntactic processing across the adult life span: The modulation of the frontotemporal language system in the context of age-related atrophy. *Cerebral Cortex, 20,* 352–364.

U.S. Bureau of the Census. (1998). Marital status and living arrangements, March 1998 (update) P20-514. Retrieved from http:// www.census.gov / prod / 99pubs / p20-514.pdf (summary)- also listed as Lugaila http://www.census.gov/prod/99pubs/p20-514u.pdf(tables).

U.S. Bureau of the Census. (2009a). Age and sex in the United States: 2008. Retrieved from http://www.census .gov/population/www/socdemo/age/age_sex_2008.html

U.S. Bureau of the Census. (2009b). Grandparents Day 2009: Sept. 13. Retrieved from http://www.census.gov/Press-Release/www/releases/archives/facts_for_features_special_editions/013971.html.

U.S. Bureau of the Census. (2010a). 2008 National Population Projections Tables and Charts. Retrieved from http://www .census.gov/population/www/projections/tablesandcharts.html.

U.S. Bureau of the Census. (2010b). International data base. Retrieved from http://www.census.gov/cgi-bin/broker.

U.S. Bureau of the Census. (2010c). U.S. Interim projections by age, sex, race, and hispanic origin: 2000-2050. Retrieved from http://www.census.gov/population/www/projections/usinter improj/.

U.S. Bureau of the Census. (2010d). America's families and living arrangements: 2009. Retrieved from http://www.census.gov/population/www/socdemo/hh-fam/cps2009.html.

U.S. Bureau of the Census. (2010e). U.S. Census Bureau News. Retrieved from http://www.census.gov/Press-Release/www/releases/archives/families_households/014540.html.

U.S. Bureau of the Census. (2010f). Statistical abstract of the United States. Retrieved from http://www.census.gov/compendia/statab/cats/education.html.

U.S. Department of Labor. (2009). Quick stats on women, 2008. Retrieved from http://www.dol.gov/wb/stats/main.htm.

Uchino, B. N., Berg, C. A., Smith, T. W., Pearce, G., & Skinner, M. (2006). Age-related differences in ambulatory blood pressure during daily stress: Evidence for greater blood pressure reactivity with age. *Psychology and Aging, 21,* 231–239.

Umberson, D. (1995). Marriage as support or strain: Marital quality following the death of a parent. *Journal of Marriage and the Family, 57,* 709–723.

Umberson, D., & Chen, M. D. (1994). Effects of a parent's death on adult children: Relationship salience and reaction to loss. *American Sociological Review, 59,* 152–168.

Umberson, D., Liu, H., & Powers, D. (2009). Marital status, marital transitions, and body weight. *Journal of Health and Social Behavior, 50*, 327–343.

Vaillant, G. E. (1977). *Adaptation to life*. Boston, MA: Little, Brown.

Vaillant, G. E. (1993). *The wisdom of the ego*. Cambridge, MA: Harvard University Press.

Vaillant, G. E. (2000). Adaptive mental mechanisms: Their role in a positive psychology. *American Psychologist, 55*, 89–98.

Vaillant, G. E. (2003). A 60-year follow-up of alcoholic men. *Addiction, 98*, 1043–1051.

Vaillant, G. E., DiRago, A. C., & Mukamal, K. (2006). Natural history of male psychological health, XV: Retirement satisfaction. *American Journal of Psychiatry, 163*, 682–688.

Valentijn, S. A. M., Hill, R. D., Van Hooren, S. A. H., Bosma, H., Van Boxtel, M. P. J., Jolles, J., . . . Ponds, R. W. H. M. (2006). Memory self-efficacy predicts memory performance: Results from a 6-year follow-up study. *Psychology and Aging, 21*, 165–172.

van den Berg, E., Dekker, J. M., Nijpels, G., Kessels, R. P., Kappelle, L. J., de Haan, E. H., . . . Biessels, G. J. (2008). Cognitive functioning in elderly persons with type 2 diabetes and metabolic syndrome: The Hoorn study. *Dementia and Geriatric Cognitive Disorders, 26*, 261–290.

Van den Block, L., Deschepper, R., Bilsen, J., Bossuyt, N., Van Casteren, V., & Deliens, L. (2009). Euthanasia and other end of life decisions and care provided in final three months of life: Nationwide retrospective study in Belgium. *BMJ: British Medical Journal, 339*.

van den Kommer, T. N., Dik, M. G., Comijs, H. C., Jonker, C., & Deeg, D. J. (2008). Homocysteine and inflammation: Predictors of cognitive decline in older persons? *Neurobiology of Aging*. doi:S0197-4580(08)00349-7 [pii]10.1016/j.neurobiolaging.2008.09.009.

Van Egeren, L. A. (2004). The development of the coparenting relationship over the transition to parenthood. *Infant Mental Health Journal, 25*, 453–477.

Van Gaalen, R. I., & Dykstra, P. A. (2006). Solidarity and conflict between adult children and parents: A latent class analysis. *Journal of Marriage and Family, 68*, 947–960.

van Hooff, M. L., Geurts, S. A., Taris, T. W., Kompier, M. A., Dikkers, J. S., Houtman, I. L., . . . van den Heuvel, F. M. (2005). Disentangling the causal relationships between work-home interference and employee health. *Scandinavian Journal of Work and Environmental Health, 31*, 15–29.

Van Manen, K.-J., & Whitbourne, S. K. (1997). Psychosocial development and life experiences in adulthood: A 22-year sequential study. *Psychology and Aging, 12*, 239–246.

Van Ness, P. H., & Larson, D. B. (2002). Religion, senescence, and mental health: The end of life is not the end of hope. *American Journal of Geriatric Psychiatry, 10*, 386–397.

Van Volkom, M. (2006). Sibling relationships in middle and older adulthood: A review of the literature. *Marriage and Family Review, 40*, 151–170.

Vandewater, E. A., Ostrove, J. M., & Stewart, A. J. (1997). Predicting women's well-being in midlife: The importance of personality development and social role involvements. *Journal of Personality and Social Psychology, 72*, 1147–1160.

Vannorsdall, T. D., Waldstein, S. R., Kraut, M., Pearlson, G. D., & Schretlen, D. J. (2009). White matter abnormalities and cognition in a community sample. *Archives of Clinical Neuropsychology, 24*, 209–217.

Velagaleti, R. S., & O'Donnell, C. J. (2010). Genomics of heart failure. *Heart Failure Clinics, 6*, 115–124.

Velkoff, V. A., & Lawson, V. A. (1998). Gender and aging: Caregiving. *International Brief* (December).

Verghese, J., Wang, C., Katz, M. J., Sanders, A., & Lipton, R. B. (2009). Leisure activities and risk of vascular cognitive impairment in older adults. *Journal of Geriatric Psychiatry and Neurology, 22*, 110–118.

Verweij, L. M., van Schoor, N. M., Deeg, D. J., Dekker, J., & Visser, M. (2009). Physical activity and incident clinical knee osteoarthritis in older adults. *Arthritis Rheumatology, 61*, 152–157.

Vess, M., Arndt, J., Cox, C. R., Routledge, C., & Goldenberg, J. L. (2009). Exploring the existential function of religion: The effect of religious fundamentalism and mortality salience on faith-based medical refusals. *Journal of Personality and Social Psychology, 97*, 334–350.

Vig, E. K., Davenport, N. A., & Pearlman, R. A. (2002). Good deaths, bad deaths, and preferences for the end of life: A qualitative study of geriatric outpatients. *Journal of the American Geriatrics Society, 50*, 1541–1548.

Vitale, S., Cotch, M. F., & Sperduto, R. D. (2006). Prevalence of visual impairment in the United States. *Journal of the American Medical Association, 295*, 2158–2163.

Vitiello, M. V., Rybarczyk, B., Von Korff, M., & Stepanski, E. J. (2009). Cognitive behavioral therapy for insomnia improves sleep and decreases pain in older adults with co-morbid insomnia and osteoarthritis. *Journal of Clinical Sleep Medicine, 5*, 355–362.

von Bonsdorff, M. E., Huuhtanen, P., Tuomi, K., & Seitsamo, J. (2010). Predictors of employees' early retirement intentions: An 11-year longitudinal study. *Occupational Medicine (London), 60*, 94–100.

von Muhlen, D., Laughlin, G. A., Kritz-Silverstein, D., & Barrett-Connor, E. (2007). The Dehydroepiandrosterone And WellNess (DAWN) study: Research design and methods. *Contemporary Clinical Trials, 28*, 153–168.

Voorpostel, M., & Blieszner, R. (2008). Intergenerational solidarity and support between adult siblings. *Journal of Marriage and Family, 70*, 157–167.

Wagg, A., Wyndaele, J. J., & Sieber, P. (2006). Efficacy and tolerability of solifenacin in elderly subjects with overactive bladder syndrome: A pooled analysis. *American Journal of Geriatric Pharmacotherapy, 4*, 14–24.

Waite, L. J., Laumann, E. O., Das, A., & Schumm, L. P. (2009). Sexuality: Measures of partnerships, practices, attitudes, and problems in the National Social Life, Health, and Aging Study.

Journals of Gerontology Series B: Psychological Sciences and Social Sciences, 64, P56–P66.

Waiter, G. D., Deary, I. J., Staff, R. T., Murray, A. D., Fox, H. C., Starr, J. M., . . . Whalley, L. J. (2010). Exploring possible neural mechanisms of intelligence differences using processing speed and working memory tasks: An fMRI study. *Intelligence, 37,* 199–206.

Walford, R. L., Mock, D., Verdery, R., & MacCallum, T. (2002). Calorie restriction in biosphere 2: Alterations in physiologic, hematologic, hormonal, and biochemical parameters in humans restricted for a 2-year period. *Journal of Gerontology Series A: Biological Sciences and Medical Sciences, 57,* B211–B224.

Walker, A. E., Eskurza, I., Pierce, G. L., Gates, P. E., & Seals, D. R. (2009). Modulation of vascular endothelial function by low-density lipoprotein cholesterol with aging: Influence of habitual exercise. *American Journal of Hypertension, 22,* 250–256.

Walster, E., Walster, G. W., & Berscheid, E. (1978). *Equity: Theory and research.* Boston, MA: Allyn & Bacon.

Walton, A., Scheib, J. L., McLean, S., Zhang, Z., & Grondin, R. (2008). Motor memory preservation in aged monkeys mirrors that of aged humans on a similar task. *Neurobiology of Aging, 29,* 1556–1562.

Wang, M. (2007). Profiling retirees in the retirement transition and adjustment process: Examining the longitudinal change patterns of retirees' psychological well-being. *Journal of Applied Psychology, 92,* 455–474.

Wang, M., & Shultz, K. S. (2010). Employee retirement: A review and recommendations for future investigation. *Journal of Management, 36,* 172–206.

Wang, S. Q., & Dusza, S. W. (2009). Assessment of sunscreen knowledge: A pilot survey. *British Journal of Dermatology, 161,* 28–32.

Ward, R. A., Spitze, G., & Deane, G. (2009). The more the merrier? Multiple parent-adult child relations. *Journal of Marriage and Family, 71,* 161–173.

Warr, P. (1994). Age and employment. In H. C. Triandis, M. D. Dunnette & L. M. Hough (Eds.), *Handbook of industrial and organizational psychology* (pp. 485–550). Palo Alto, CA: Consulting Psychologists Press.

Warr, P., Butcher, V., Robertson, I., & Callinan, M. (2004). Older people's well-being as a function of employment, retirement, environmental characteristics and role preference. *British Journal of Psychology, 95,* 297–324.

Wayne, J. H., Randel, A. E., & Stevens, J. (2006). The role of identity and work-family support in work-family enrichment and its work-related consequences. *Journal of Vocational Behavior, 69,* 445–461.

Weatherbee, S. R., & Allaire, J. C. (2008). Everyday cognition and mortality: Performance differences and predictive utility of the Everyday Cognition Battery. *Psychology and Aging, 23,* 216–221.

Wechsler, D. (2008). Wechsler Adult Intelligence Scales–IV. Retrieved from http://www.pearsonassessments.com/HAIWEB/Cultures/en-us/Productdetail.htm?Pid=015-8980-808.

Wedisinghe, L., & Perera, M. (2009). Diabetes and the menopause. *Maturitas, 63,* 200–203.

Wegge, J., von Dick, R., Fisher, G. K., West, M. A., & Dawson, J. F. (2006). A test of basic assumptions of Affective Events Theory (AET) in call centre work. *British Journal of Management, 17,* 237–254.

Weige, C. C., Allred, K. F., & Allred, C. D. (2009). Estradiol alters cell growth in nonmalignant colonocytes and reduces the formation of preneoplastic lesions in the colon. *Cancer Research, 69,* 9118–9124.

Weinberger, M. I., Hofstein, Y., & Whitbourne, S. K. (2008). Intimacy in young adulthood as a predictor of divorce in midlife. *Personal Relationships, 15,* 551–557.

Weinberger, M. I., & Whitbourne, S. K. (2010). Depressive symptoms, self-reported physical functioning, and identity in community-dwelling older adults. *Ageing International.* doi:10.1007/s12126-010-9053-4.

Weiner, D. K., Rudy, T. E., Morrow, L., Slaboda, J., & Lieber, S. (2006). The relationship between pain, neuropsychological performance, and physical function in community-dwelling older adults with chronic low back pain. *Pain Medicine, 7,* 60–70.

Weiss, A., & Costa, P. T., Jr. (2005). Domain and facet personality predictors of all-cause mortality among Medicare patients aged 65 to 100. *Psychosomatic Medicine, 67,* 724–733.

Welge-Lussen, A. (2009). Ageing, neurodegeneration, and olfactory and gustatory loss. *B-ENT, 5 Supplement 13,* 129–132.

Weltman, A., Weltman, J. Y., Roy, C. P., Wideman, L., Patrie, J., Evans, W. S., . . . Veldhuis, J. D. (2006). Growth hormone response to graded exercise intensities is attenuated and the gender difference abolished in older adults. *Journal of Applied Physiology, 100,* 1623–1629.

Wenger, N. S., Kanouse, D. E., Collins, R. L., Liu, H., Schuster, M. A., Gifford, A. L., . . . Shapiro, M. F. (2001). End-of-life discussions and preferences among persons with HIV. *Journal of the American Medical Association, 285,* 2880–2887.

Werner, P., Buchbinder, E., Lowenstein, A., & Livni, T. (2005). Mediation across generations: A tri-generational perspective. *Journal of Aging Studies, 19,* 489–502.

Werngren-Elgstrom, M., Carlsson, G., & Iwarsson, S. (2009). A 10-year follow-up study on subjective well-being and relationships to person-environment (P-E) fit and activity of daily living (ADL) dependence of older Swedish adults. *Archives of Gerontology and Geriatrics, 49,* e16–e22.

West, R., & Schwarb, H. (2006). The influence of aging and frontal function on the neural correlates of regulative and evaluative aspects of cognitive control. *Neuropsychology, 20,* 468–481.

West, R. L., Bagwell, D. K., & Dark-Freudeman, A. (2008). Self-efficacy and memory aging: The impact of a memory intervention based on self-efficacy. *Neuropsychology, Development, and Cognition. Section B, Aging Neuropsychology and Cognition, 15,* 302–329.

West, R. L., Thorn, R. M., & Bagwell, D. K. (2003). Memory performance and beliefs as a function of goal setting and aging. *Psychology and Aging, 18,* 111–125.

Westoby, C. J., Mallen, C. D., & Thomas, E. (2009). Cognitive complaints in a general population of older adults: Prevalence, association with pain and the influence of concurrent affective disorders. *European Journal of Pain, 13*, 970–976.

Wetherell, J. L., Reynolds, C. A., & Gatz, M. P., Nancy L. (2002). Anxiety, cognitive performance, and cognitive decline in normal aging. *Journals of Gerontology Series B: Psychological Sciences and Social Sciences, 57B*, P246–P255.

Wethington, E. (2000). Expecting stress: Americans and the "midlife crisis." *Motivation and Emotion, 24*, 85–103.

Wethington, E., Kessler, R. C., Pixley, J. E., Brim, O. G., & Ryff, C. D. (2004). Turning points in adulthood. In O. G. Brim, C. D. Ryff, & R. C. Kessler (Eds.), *How healthy are we?: A national study of well-being at midlife.* (pp. 586–613). Chicago, IL: University of Chicago Press.

Wheeler, I. (2001). Parental bereavement: The crisis of meaning. *Death Studies, 25*, 51–66.

Whisman, M. A., Uebelacker, L. A., Tolejko, N., Chatav, Y., & McKelvie, M. (2006). Marital discord and well-being in older adults: Is the association confounded by personality? *Psychology and Aging, 21*, 626–631.

Whitbourne, S. K. (1985). The life-span construct as a model of adaptation in adulthood. In J. E. Birren & K. W. Schaie (Eds.), *Handbook of the psychology of aging* (2nd ed., pp. 594–618). New York, NY: Van Nostrand Reinhold.

Whitbourne, S. K. (1986). *The me I know: A study of adult identity.* New York, NY: Springer-Verlag.

Whitbourne, S. K. (2010). *The search for fulfillment.* New York, NY: Ballantine.

Whitbourne, S. K., & Collins, K. C. (1998). Identity and physical changes in later adulthood: Theoretical and clinical implications. *Psychotherapy, 35*, 519–530.

Whitbourne, S. K., & Connolly, L. A. (1999). The developing self in midlife. In J. D. Reid & S. L. Willis (Eds.), *Life in the middle: Psychological and social development in middle age* (pp. 25–45). San Diego, CA: Academic Press.

Whitbourne, S. K., Culgin, S., & Cassidy, E. (1995). Evaluation of infantilizing intonation and content of speech directed at the aged. *International Journal of Aging and Human Development, 41*, 107–114.

Whitbourne, S. K., & Meeks, S. (2010). Psychopathology, bereavement, and aging. In K. W. Schaie & S. L. Willis (Eds.), *Handbook of the psychology of aging.* New York, NY: Cambridge University Press.

Whitbourne, S. K., & Sherry, M. S. (1991). Subjective perceptions of the life span in chronic mental patients. *International Journal of Aging and Human Development, 33*, 65–73.

Whitbourne, S. K., & Sneed, J. R. (2002). The paradox of well-being, identity processes, and stereotype threat: Ageism and its potential relationships to the self in later life. In T. D. Nelson (Ed.), *Ageism: Stereotyping and prejudice against older persons.* (pp. 247–273). Cambridge, MA: The MIT Press.

Whitbourne, S. K., Sneed, J. R., & Sayer, A. (2009). Psychosocial development from college through midlife: A 34-year sequential study. *Developmental Psychology, 45*, 1328–1340.

Whitbourne, S. K., Sneed, J. R., & Skultety, K. M. (2002). Identity processes in adulthood: Theoretical and methodological challenges. *Identity, 2*, 29–45.

Whitbourne, S. K., & van Manen, K.-J. (1996). Age differences and correlates of identity status in from college through middle adulthood. *Journal of Adult Development, 3*, 59–70.

Whitbourne, S. K., & Waterman, A. S. (1979). Psychosocial development during the adult years: Age and cohort comparisons. *Developmental Psychology, 15*, 373–378.

Whitbourne, S. K., & Wills, K.-J. (1993). Psychological issues in institutional care of the aged. In S. B. Goldsmith (Ed.), *Long-term care administration handbook* (pp. 19–32). Gaithersburg, MD: Aspen.

Whitbourne, S. K., & Willis, S. L. (Eds.). (2006). *The baby boomers grow up: Contemporary perspectives on midlife.* Mahwah, NJ: Erlbaum.

Whitbourne, S. K., Zuschlag, M. K., Elliot, L. B., & Waterman, A. S. (1992). Psychosocial development in adulthood: A 22-year sequential study. *Journal of Personality & Social Psychology, 63*, 260–271.

Whitfield, K. E., Allaire, J. C., & Wiggins, S. A. (2004). Relationships among health factors and everyday problem solving in african americans. *Health Psychology, 23*, 641–644.

Whitlock, G., Lewington, S., Sherliker, P., Clarke, R., Emberson, J., Halsey, J., . . . Peto, R. (2009). Body-mass index and cause-specific mortality in 900 000 adults: Collaborative analyses of 57 prospective studies. *Lancet, 373*, 1083–1096.

Whitmer, R. A., Gustafson, D. R., Barrett-Connor, E., Haan, M. N., Gunderson, E. P., & Yaffe, K. (2008). Central obesity and increased risk of dementia more than three decades later. *Neurology, 71*, 1057–1064.

Whitton, S. W., Rhoades, G. K., Stanley, S. M., & Markman, H. J. (2008). Effects of parental divorce on marital commitment and confidence. *Journal of Family Psychology, 22*, 789–793.

Wickremaratchi, M. M., & Llewelyn, J. G. (2006). Effects of ageing on touch. *Postgraduate Medical Journal, 82*, 301–304.

Wieser, M. J., Muhlberger, A., Kenntner-Mabiala, R., & Pauli, P. (2006). Is emotion processing affected by advancing age? An event-related brain potential study. *Brain Research, 1096*, 138–147.

Wiggs, C. L., Weisberg, J., & Martin, A. (2006). Repetition priming across the adult lifespan—the long and short of it. *Aging, Neuropsychology and Cognition, 13*, 308–325.

Wijngaards-de Meij, L., Stroebe, M., Schut, H., Stroebe, W., van den Bout, J., van der Heijden, P. G. M., . . . Dijkstra, I. (2008). Parents grieving the loss of their child: Interdependence in coping. *British Journal of Clinical Psychology, 47*, 31–42.

Wilcox, S., Evenson, K. R., Aragaki, A., Wassertheil-Smoller, S., Mouton, C. P., & Loevinger, B. L. (2003). The effects of widowhood on physical and mental health, health behaviors, and health outcomes: The Women's Health Initiative. *Health Psychology, 22,* 513–522.

Wilkins, C. H., Mathews, J., & Sheline, Y. I. (2009). Late life depression with cognitive impairment: Evaluation and treatment. *Clinical Interventions and Aging, 4,* 51–57.

Wilkins, C. H., Sheline, Y. I., Roe, C. M., Birge, S. J., & Morris, J. C. (2006). Vitamin D deficiency is associated with low mood and worse cognitive performance in older adults. *American Journal of Geriatric Psychiatry, 14,* 1032–1040.

Willemse, B. M., Depla, M. F., & Bohlmeijer, E. T. (2009). A creative reminiscence program for older adults with severe mental disorders: Results of a pilot evaluation. *Aging and Mental Health, 13,* 736–743.

Williams, D. R., & Jackson, P. B. (2005). Social sources of racial disparities in health. *Health Affairs, 24,* 325–334.

Williams, K., & Dunne-Bryant, A. (2006). Divorce and adult psychological well-being: Clarifying the role of gender and child age. *Journal of Marriage and Family, 68,* 1178–1196.

Williams, K. N., & Warren, C. A. (2009). Communication in assisted living. *Journal of Aging Studies, 23,* 24–36.

Williams, P. G., Rau, H. K., Cribbet, M. R., & Gunn, H. E. (2009). Openness to experience and stress regulation. *Journal of Research in Personality, 43,* 777–784.

Willis, S. L., Blieszner, R., & Baltes, P. B. (1981). Intellectual training research in aging: Modification of performance on the fluid ability of figural relations. *Journal of Educational Psychology, 73,* 41–50.

Willis, S. L., Schaie, K. W., Martin, M., Bengston, V. L., Gans, D., Pulney, N. M.,...Silverstein, M. (2009). Cognitive plasticity. In *Handbook of theories of aging* (2nd ed., pp. 295–322). New York, NY: Springer.

Willis, S. L., Tennstedt, S. L., Marsiske, M., Ball, K., Elias, J., Koepke, K. M.,...Wright, E. (2006). Long-term effects of cognitive training on everyday functional outcomes in older adults. *Journal of the American Medical Association, 296,* 2805–2814.

Wilsgaard, T., Emaus, N., Ahmed, L. A., Grimnes, G., Joakimsen, R. M., Omsland, T. K.,...Berntsen, G. R. (2009). Lifestyle impact on lifetime bone loss in women and men: The Tromso Study. *American Journal of Epidemiology, 169,* 877–886.

Wilson, M. N. (1986). The black extended family: An analytical consideration. *Developmental Psychology, 22,* 246–258.

Wilson, R. S., Arnold, S. E., Tang, Y., & Bennett, D. A. (2006). Odor identification and decline in different cognitive domains in old age. *Neuroepidemiology, 26,* 61–67.

Wilson, R. S., Schneider, J. A., Arnold, S. E., Bienias, J. L., & Bennett, D. A. (2007). Conscientiousness and the incidence of Alzheimer disease and mild cognitive impairment. *Archives of General Psychiatry, 64,* 1204–1212.

Winch, R. F. (1958). *Mate selection: A study of complementary needs.* New York, NY: Harper & Row.

Wittchen, H. U. (2002). Generalized anxiety disorder: Prevalence, burden, and cost to society. *Depression and Anxiety, 16,* 162–171.

Wolkove, N., Elkholy, O., Baltzan, M., & Palayew, M. (2007). Sleep and aging: 2. Management of sleep disorders in older people. *Canadian Medical Association Journal, 176,* 1449–1454.

Womack, C. J., Harris, D. L., Katzel, L. I., Hagberg, J. M., Bleecker, E. R., & Goldberg, A. P. (2000). Weight loss, not aerobic exercise, improves pulmonary function in older obese men. *Journal of Gerontology Series A: Biological Sciences and Medical Sciences, 55,* M453–M457.

Wong, P. C. M., Jin, J. X., Gunasekera, G. M., Abel, R., Lee, E. R., & Dhar, S. (2009). Aging and cortical mechanisms of speech perception in noise. *Neuropsychologia, 47,* 693–703.

Wood, R. G., Goesling, B., & Avellar, S. (2007). The effects of marriage on health. *ASPE Research Brief.*

Woods, J., Woods, C. A., & Fonn, D. (2009). Early symptomatic presbyopes—what correction modality works best? *Eye and Contact Lens, 35,* 221–226.

Woolcott, J. C., Richardson, K. J., Wiens, M. O., Patel, B., Marin, J., Khan, K. M.,...Marra, C. A. (2009). Meta-analysis of the impact of 9 medication classes on falls in elderly persons. *Archives of Internal Medicine, 169,* 1952–1960.

Woolf, S. H. (2010). The 2009 breast cancer screening recommendations of the US Preventive Services Task Force. *Journal of the American Medical Association, 303,* 162–163.

World Health Organization. (2001). The World Health Report 2001. Mental health: New understanding, new hope. Retrieved from http://www.who.int/whr2001/2001/main/en/index.htm.

World Health Organization. (2002). *National cancer control programmes: Policies and managerial guidelines.* Geneva, Switzerland: World Health Organization.

World Health Organization. (2009). Disease and injury country estimates. Retrieved from http://www.who.int/healthinfo/global_burden_disease/estimates_country/en/index.html.

World Health Organization. (2010). Diabetes. Retrieved from http://www.who.int/dietphysicalactivity/publications/facts/diabetes/en/.

Wu, E. Q., Shi, L., Birnbaum, H., Hudson, T., & Kessler, R. (2006). Annual prevalence of diagnosed schizophrenia in the USA: A claims data analysis approach. *Psychological Medicine, 36,* 1535–1540.

Wunderlich, G. S., Kohler, P. O., & Committee on Improving Quality in Long-Term Care, Division of Health Care Services, Institute of Medicine (Eds.). (2001). *Improving the quality of long-term care.* Washington, DC: National Academies Press.

Wyatt, C. M., Kim, M. C., & Winston, J. A. (2006). Therapy insight: How changes in renal function with increasing age affect cardiovascular drug prescribing. *Nature Clinical Practice: Cardiovascular Medicine, 3,* 102–109.

Xiong, K. L., Yang, Q. W., Gong, S. G., & Zhang, W. G. (2010). The role of positron emission tomography imaging of beta-amyloid in patients with Alzheimer's disease. *Nuclear Medicine Communications, 31,* 4–11.

Xu, Z., Kochanek, K. D., Murphy, S. L., & Tejeda-Vera, B. (2010). Deaths: Final data for 2007. *National Vital Statistics Reports (Volume 58, No. 19)*. Hyattsville, MD: National Center for Health Statistics.

Yabiku, S. T., & Gager, C. T. (2009). Sexual frequency and the stability of marital and cohabiting unions. *Journal of Marriage and Family, 71*, 983–1000.

Yamamoto, Y., Uede, K., Yonei, N., Kishioka, A., Ohtani, T., & Furukawa, F. (2006). Effects of alpha-hydroxy acids on the human skin of Japanese subjects: The rationale for chemical peeling. *Journal of Dermatology, 33*, 16–22.

Yan, E., & So-kum, T. C. (2001). Prevalence and psychological impact of Chinese elder abuse. *Journal of Interpersonal Violence, 16*, 1158–1174.

Yeung, S. E., Fischer, A. L., & Dixon, R. A. (2009). Exploring effects of type 2 diabetes on cognitive functioning in older adults. *Neuropsychology, 23*, 1–9.

Yong, H. H. (2006). Can attitudes of stoicism and cautiousness explain observed age-related variation in levels of self-rated pain, mood disturbance and functional interference in chronic pain patients? *European Journal of Pain, 10*, 399–407.

Yoshida, M., Takashima, Y., Inoue, M., Iwasaki, M., Otani, T., Sasaki, S., . . . Tsugane, S. (2007). Prospective study showing that dietary vitamin C reduced the risk of age-related cataracts in a middle-aged Japanese population. *European Journal of Nutrition, 46*, 118–124.

Ystad, M. A., Lundervold, A. J., Wehling, E., Espeseth, T., Rootwelt, H., Westlye, L. T., . . . Lundervold, A. (2009). Hippocampal volumes are important predictors for memory function in elderly women. *BMC Medical Imaging, 9*, 17.

Yu, K. Y. T. (2009). Affective influences in person-environment fit theory: Exploring the role of affect as both cause and outcome of P-E fit. *Journal of Applied Psychology, 94*, 1210–1226.

Yung, L. M., Laher, I., Yao, X., Chen, Z. Y., Huang, Y., & Leung, F. P. (2009). Exercise, vascular wall and cardiovascular diseases: An update (part 2). *Sports Medicine, 39*, 45–63.

Zamboni, M., Mazzali, G., Fantin, F., Rossi, A., & Di Francesco, V. (2008). Sarcopenic obesity: A new category of obesity in the elderly. *Nutrition, Metabolism, and Cardiovascular Diseases, 18*, 388–395.

Zanetti, M. V., Cordeiro, Q., & Busatto, G. F. (2007). Late onset bipolar disorder associated with white matter hyperintensities: A pathophysiological hypothesis. *Progress in Neuropsychopharmacology and Biological Psychiatry, 31*, 551–556.

Zanon-Moreno, V., Garcia-Medina, J. J., Zanon-Viguer, V., Moreno-Nadal, M. A., & Pinazo-Duran, M. D. (2009). Smoking, an additional risk factor in elder women with primary open-angle glaucoma. *Molecular Vision, 15*, 2953–2959.

Zarit, S. H., & Zarit, J. M. (1998). *Mental disorders in older adults: Fundamentals of assessment and treatment*. New York, NY: Guilford.

Zeleznik, J. (2003). Normative aging of the respiratory system. *Clinics in Geriatric Medicine, 19*, 1–18.

Zhang, C., Wu, B., Beglopoulos, V., Wines-Samuelson, M., Zhang, D., Dragatsis, I., . . . Shen, J. (2009). Presenilins are essential for regulating neurotransmitter release. *Nature, 460*, 632–636.

Zhang, F., & Labouvie-Vief, G. (2004). Stability and fluctuation in adult attachment style over a 6-year period. *Attachment and Human Development, 6*, 419–437.

Zhang, Y., Donohue, J. M., Newhouse, J. P., & Lave, J. R. (2009). The effects of the coverage gap on drug spending: A closer look at Medicare Part D. *Health Affairs, 28*, w317–w325.

Zhang, Y., Qiu, C., Lindberg, O., Bronge, L., Aspelin, P., Backman, L., . . . Wahlund, L. O. (2010). Acceleration of hippocampal atrophy in a non-demented elderly population: The SNAC-K study. *International Psychogeriatrics, 22*, 14–25.

Zhou, A., & Jia, J. (2009). Different cognitive profiles between mild cognitive impairment due to cerebral small vessel disease and mild cognitive impairment of Alzheimer's disease origin. *Journal of the International Neuropsychology Society, 15*, 898–905.

Zijlstra, G. A., van Haastregt, J. C., Ambergen, T., van Rossum, E., van Eijk, J. T., Tennstedt, S. L., . . . Kempen, G. I. (2009). Effects of a multicomponent cognitive behavioral group intervention on fear of falling and activity avoidance in community-dwelling older adults: Results of a randomized controlled trial. *Journal of the American Geriatrics Society, 57*, 2020–2028.

PHOTO CREDITS

Chapter 1

Page 3: Digital Vision/Getty Images, Inc. Page 4: Robert L. Zentmaier/Photo Researchers, Inc. Page 7 (top): Ty Allison/Getty Images, Inc. Page 7 (bottom): T. Grill/Corbis RF/Alamy. Page 9 (top): Sean Justice/Corbis/Jupiter Images Corp. Page 9 (center): Annabella Bluesky/Photo Researchers, Inc. Page 9 (bottom): Catherine Yeulet/iStockphoto. Page 11 (far left): B2M Productions/Getty Images, Inc. Page 11 (left): digitalskillet/iStockphoto. Page 11 (left of center): Huchen Lu/iStockphoto. Page 11 (center): Compassionate Eye Foundation/Chris Ryan/OJO Images Ltd/Photodisc/Getty Images, Inc. Page 11 (right): Mark Edward Atkinson/Getty Images, Inc. Page 12: Charlie Varley/SIPA Press/NewsCom. Page 13: Kristoffer Tripplaar/Sipa Press/NewsCom.

Chapter 2

Page 21: Alena Brozova/Shutterstock. Page 22: Age Fotostock/Superstock. Page 27: Stephanie Diani for the New York Times/Redux Pictures. Page 28: Courtesy The Equality Authority, Dublin. Page 29: Stephen Schildbach/Photodisc/Getty Images, Inc. Page 31: Chabruken/Taxi/Getty Images, Inc. Page 35: Jean Michel Foujols/Getty Images, Inc. Page 38 (left): Cindy Singleton/iStockphoto. Page 38 (right): Rick and Nora Bowers/Alamy.

Chapter 3

Page 48: Joseph Sohm/Visions of America, LLC/Alamy. Page 49: NewsCom. Page 51: Salih Dastan/iStockphoto. Page 52: Amanda Rohde/iStockphoto. Page 57: Evgeny Kuklev/iStockphoto. Page 59: Reena Rose Sibayan/The Jersey Journal/Landov LLC. Page 61: Michael Newman/PhotoEdit.

Chapter 4

Page 67: SHNS photo by Tom Sweeney/Minneapolis Star Tribune/NewsCom. Page 78: Catherine Yeulet/iStockphoto. Page 80: SOMOS/SuperStock. Page 82: WireImage/Getty Images, Inc. Page 87: From S.J. Colcombe, et al., Aerobic exercise training increases brain volume in aging humans. Journal of Gerontology Series A: Biological Sciences and Medical Sciences 61A, 1166–1170, 2006. Page 88: jonathansloane/iStockphoto. Page 90 (top): Purestock/Getty Images, Inc. Page 90 (bottom): MedicalRF.com/Alamy. Page 94: Hans Neleman/Getty Images, Inc.

Chapter 5

Page 101: Kevin Russ/iStockphoto. Page 103: Gerald Bernard/iStockphoto. Page 104: Salih Dastan/iStockphoto. Page 106: Vince Bucci/©AP/Wide World Photos. Page 108: Tomaz Levstek/iStockphoto. Page 110: Jordan Chesbrough/iStockphoto. Page 117: Tatiana Popova/iStockphoto. Page 118: Suprijono Suharjoto/iStockphoto. Page 119: Jupiter Images/Getty Images, Inc.

Chapter 6

Page 127: iStockphoto. Page 128: Willie B. Thomas/iStockphoto. Page 129: Theo Wargo/WireImage/Getty Images, Inc. Page 130: Courtesy Susan Krauss Whitbourne. Page 131: Blend Images/Alamy. Page 134: Cliff Parnell/iStockphoto. Page 135: image100/Age Fotostock America, Inc. Page 137: DNY59/iStockphoto. Page 139: Simone van den Berg/Alamy.

Chapter 7

Page 146: image100/Age Fotostock America, Inc. Page 147: Bob Collier/PA Wire/AP/Wide World Photos. Page 148: Jason Lindsey/Alamy. Page 151: Elena Eliseeva/iStockphoto. Page 153: Yuri Arcurs/Age Fotostock America, Inc.

Chapter 8

Page 167: Time & Life Pictures/Getty Images, Inc. Page 168: Photo courtesy of Rush Rhees Library, Rochester University. Page 169: Frances Twitty/iStockphoto. Page 170: Kyu Oh/iStockphoto. Page 173: Rafal Strzechowski/Age Fotostock America, Inc. Page 174: Ikon Images/Alamy. Page 176: John Slater/Photodisc/Getty Images, Inc. Page 177: Daniel Bendjy/iStockphoto. Page 178: Annett Vauteck/iStockphoto. Page 179: Ryan McVay/Getty Images, Inc. Page 182: Courtesy Senior America, Inc. Page 186: Ikon Images/SuperStock. Page 187: cogal/iStockphoto.

Chapter 9

Page 191 (center): Geckly/iStockphoto. Page 192: Digital Vision/Superstock. Page 193 (bottom left): iStockphoto. Page 193 (center right): Wave Royalty Free/Alamy. Page 194: Christine Gonsalves/iStockphoto. Page 195: iStockphoto. Page 199: PhotoPQR/Le Parisien/Delphine Goldsztejn/NewsCom. Page 202: Age Fotostock/SuperStock. Page 204: Jamie Wilson/iStockphoto. Page 206: Urikiri-Shashin-Kan/Alamy. Page 207: Dana Fry/iStockphoto. Page 209: Timur Nisametdinov/iStockphoto. Page 211: Nicholas Monu/iStockphoto.

Chapter 10

Page 215: iStockphoto. Page 216: Dimitry Shironosov/iStockphoto. Page 217: Lise Gagne/iStockphoto. Page 219: Department of Labor. Page 220: David Trood/Getty Images, Inc. Page 222: Blue Jean Images/Alamy. Page 224: Charles Dharapak/©AP/Wide World Photos. Page 226: Don Bayley/iStockphoto. Page 228: Golden Pixels LLC/Alamy. Page 230: iStockphoto. Page 231: Corbis Premium RF/Alamy. Page 233: Steve Cole/iStockphoto.

Chapter 11

Page 240: Roger Bamber/Alamy. Page 244: Chuck Burton/©AP/Wide World Photos. Page 248: iStockphoto. Page 249: Abel Mitja Varela/iStockphoto. Page 250: Sheryl Griffin/iStockphoto. Page 254: Stefan Klein/iStockphoto. Page 256: Furgolle/Age Fotostock America, Inc.

Chapter 12

Page 261: Directphoto.org/Alamy. Page 264: Xinhua/Landov LLC. Page 265: Steve Skjold/Alamy. Page 269: Distribution of Medicaid Spending on Long Term Care, FY2008: ICF-MR", statehealthfacts.org, The Henry J. Kaiser Family Foundation, 2010. Page 271: Brie Cohen/Albert Lea Tribune/©AP/Wide World Photos. Page 272: U.S. Government Accountability Office. Page 276: Stephen Pell/iStockphoto. Page 277: Courtesy Leonard Florence Center for Living, Chelsea, MA.

Chapter 13

Page 282: Steve Debenport/iStockphoto. Page 283: Central Intelligence Agency, 2010, #1430. Page 285: ©World Health Organization. Page 286: Gianni Dagli Orti/©Corbis. Page 287: Thony Belizaire/AFP/Getty Images, Inc. Page 293: Wilfredo Lee/©AP/Wide World Photos. Page 295: Etienne Ansotte/AFP/Getty Images, Inc. Page 299: Jeremiah Deasey/iStockphoto. Page 300: Jasmin Awad/iStockphoto.

Chapter 14

Page 307: Caro/Alamy. Page 310: David Crausby/Alamy. Page 311: Dana Edelson/NBCU Photo Bank/©AP/Wide World Photos. Page 313: Tomas Bercic/iStockphoto. Page 314: Imo/iStockphoto. Page 315: Adam Berent/iStockphoto. Page 317: Alinari/Art Resource.

NAME INDEX